ENCYCLOPEDIA
OF THE GREAT BLACK
MIGRATION

Greenwood Milestones in African American History

Encyclopedia of Antislavery and Abolition
Edited by Peter Hinks and John McKivigan

Encyclopedia of Slave Resistance and Rebellion
Edited by Junius P. Rodriguez

Encyclopedia of American Race Riots
Edited by Walter Rucker and James Nathaniel Upton

Encyclopedia of the Reconstruction Era
Edited by Richard Zuczek

ENCYCLOPEDIA OF THE GREAT BLACK MIGRATION

Volume 1: A–L

Edited by
Steven A. Reich

Greenwood Milestones in African American History

GREENWOOD PRESS
Westport, Connecticut • London

Library of Congress Cataloging-in-Publication Data

Encyclopedia of the great Black migration : Greenwood milestones in African American
history / edited by Steven A. Reich.
    p. cm.
    Includes bibliographical references and index.
    ISBN 0-313-32982-6 ((set) : alk. paper)—ISBN 0-313-32983-4 ((vol. 1) : alk. paper)—
ISBN 0-313-32984-2 ((vol. 2) : alk. paper)—ISBN 0-313-33739-X ((vol. 3) : alk.
paper) 1. African Americans—Migrations—History—20th century—Encyclopedias.
2. Migration, Internal—United States—History—20th century—Encyclopedias. 3. Rural-urban
migration—United States—History—20th century—Encyclopedias. I. Reich, Steven A. (Steven
Andrew), 1965-
E185.6.E54 2006
307.2'408996073075—dc22   2005033783

British Library Cataloguing in Publication Data is available.

This book is included in the African American Experiences database from Greenwood
Electronic Media. For more information, visit www.africanamericanexperience.com.

Library of Congress Catalog Card Number: 2005033783
ISBN: 0-313-32982-6 (set)
        0-313-32983-4 (vol. 1)
        0-313-32984-2 (vol. 2)
        0-313-33739-X (vol. 3)

First published in 2006

Greenwood Press, 88 Post Road West, Westport, CT 06881
An imprint of Greenwood Publishing Group, Inc.
www.greenwood.com

Printed in the United States of America

The paper used in this book complies with the
Permanent Paper Standard issued by the National
Information Standards Organization (Z39.48-1984).

10 9 8 7 6 5 4 3 2 1

Every reasonable effort has been made to trace the owners of copyright materials in this book,
but in some instances this has proven impossible. The editor and publisher will be glad to receive
information leading to more complete acknowledgments in subsequent printings of the book and
in the meantime extend their apologies for any omissions.

To my children,
Annaka and Riley

CONTENTS

ALPHABETICAL LIST OF ENCYCLOPEDIA ENTRIES

Abbott, Robert S. (1870-1940)
African Blood Brotherhood (ABB)
African Methodist Episcopal (AME)
  Church
Agricultural Adjustment
  Administration (AAA)
Alexander, Sadie Tanner Mossell
  (1898-1989)
Ali, Muhammad (1942-)
American Federation of Labor (AFL)
American Negro Exposition (1940)
Appalachia
Armstrong, Louis (1901-1971)
Asian Immigrants and Asian
  Americans, Relations with Black
  Migrants
Asian Immigration, Comparison
  with the Great Black Migration
Associated Negro Press (ANP)
Atlanta, Georgia
Attaway, William (1911-1986)
Attorneys
Automobile Workers
Automobility
Aviation Industry, Black
  Employment in
Baker, Ella Josephine (1903-1986)
Baldwin, James Arthur (1924-1980)

Baltimore, Maryland
Baltimore Afro-American
Banks and Bankers
Baptist Church
Baraka, Amiri (1934-)
Barbers
Basie, William "Count" (1904-1984)
Basketball
Bearden, Romare (1911-1988)
Beaumont, Texas, Race Riot of 1943
Beauty Culture
Bebop
Benson, Al (1910-1980)
Bethune, Mary McLeod (1875-1955)
Birmingham, Alabama
Black Appeal Radio
Black Arts Movement
Black Aviators
Black Consumer Market
Black Film
Black-Jewish Relations
Black Legislators
Black Mayors
Black Metropolis (Drake and
  Cayton)
Black Migration before World War I,
  Patterns of
Black Nationalism

LIST OF PRIMARY DOCUMENTS

GUIDE TO RELATED TOPICS

Business, the Professions, and Professionals

Abbott, Robert S. (1870–1940)
Associated Negro Press (ANP)
Attorneys
Baltimore Afro-American
Banks and Bankers
Barbers
Beauty Culture
Black Appeal Radio
Black Consumer Market
Black Press
Black Swan Records
California Eagle
Chicago Defender
Cleveland Gazette
Foster, Andrew "Rube" (1879–1930)
Greenlee, William Augustus "Gus" (1897–1952)
Hospitals
Houston Informer
Insurers and Insurance Companies
Johnson Publishing Company
Metropolitan Mutual Assurance Company (MMAC)
Negro Leagues

New York Age
Nurses
Physicians
Pittsburgh Courier
Posey, Cumberland (1890–1946)
Simmons, Roscoe Conkling (c. 1881–1951)
Supreme Liberty Life Insurance Company
Taxicab Operators
Undertakers
Walker, Madam C. J. (1867–1919)
Wright, Richard Robert, Sr. (1855–1947)

Cities and Regions

Appalachia
Atlanta, Georgia
Baltimore, Maryland
Birmingham, Alabama
Black Towns
Boston, Massachusetts
Buffalo, New York
Charlotte, North Carolina
Chicago, Illinois
Cincinnati, Ohio

Demography of the Great Migration

Government Programs and Policies

Urban Renewal
War Camp Community Service
(WCCS)
War Manpower Commission
(WMC)
War on Poverty
Welfare State
Works Progress Administration
(WPA)

Health Care

Childbirth
Folk Medicine and Folk Magic
Hospitals
Nurses
Physicians

Institutions and Organizations

American Negro Exposition (1940)
Fraternal Orders
Hospitals
Howard University
National Association of Colored
Women (NACW)
National Training School for
Women and Girls (NTSWG)
National Urban League (NUL)
Settlement Houses
State Clubs
Tuskegee Normal and Industrial
Institute
Young Men's Christian Association
(YMCA)
Young Women's Christian
Association (YWCA)

Jim Crow and Rural South

Black Migration before World War I,
Patterns of
Black Populism
Boll Weevil
Cotton Belt
Elaine, Arkansas, Massacre of 1919
Exodusters

Great Migration, Black
Opposition to
Great Migration, White
Opposition to
Gulf South
Involuntary Servitude
Jim Crow
Low Country South Carolina and
Georgia
Lynching
Mechanical Cotton Harvester
Migrants, Cultural Identity of
Nadir of Race Relations
Reverse Freedom Rides (1962)
Share Croppers Union (SCU)
Southern Tenant Farmers' Union
(STFU)
Wilmington, North Carolina, Race
Riot of 1898

Literature, Poetry, Drama, and Writers

Attaway, William (1911-1986)
Baldwin, James Arthur (1924-
1980)
Baraka, Amiri (1934-)
Bonner, Marita (1899-1971)
Brooks, Gwendolyn (1917-2000)
Brown, Sterling Allen (1901-1989)
Chicago Renaissance
Dunbar, Paul Laurence (1872-
1906)
Ellison, Ralph Waldo (1914-1994)
Fauset, Jessie Redmon (1882-1961)
Harlem Renaissance
Henderson, George Wylie (1904-
1965)
Himes, Chester (1909-1984)
Hughes, James Mercer Langston
(1902-1967)
Hurston, Zora Neale (1891-1960)
Johnson, James Weldon (1871-
1938)
Larsen, Nella (1891-1964)
Literature, the Great Migration in
Locke, Alain Leroy (1886-1954)

Swing
Tharpe, Sister Rosetta (1915-1973)
Youth Culture

Politics, Protest, and Resistance

African Blood Brotherhood (ABB)
Baker, Ella Josephine (1903-1986)
Black Legislators
Black Mayors
Black Nationalism
Black Panther Party
Black Populism
Black Power
Briggs, Cyril V. (1888-1966)
Brown, Willie L., Jr. (1934-)
Civil Rights Movement
Communists and the Communist
    Party
Community Organizing
Congress of Racial Equality (CORE)
Dawson, William Levi (1877-1969)
DePriest, Oscar (1871-1951)
Desegregation
"Don't Buy Where You Can't Work"
    Campaigns
Double V Campaign
Electoral Politics
Emigrationism
Exodusters
Farmer, James L., Jr. (1920-1999)
Garvey, Marcus Mosiah, Jr. (1887-
    1940)
Great Migration, Black
    Opposition to
Great Migration, White
    Opposition to
Harrison, Hubert Henry (1883-
    1927)
Hatcher, Richard Gordon (1933-)
Intraracial Class Conflict
Johnson, James Weldon (1871-
    1938)
King, Martin Luther, Jr. (1929-1968)
Malcolm X (1925-1965)
March on Washington Movement
    (MOWM)

Messenger
Mitchell, Arthur Wergs (1883-1968)
National Association for the
    Advancement of Colored People
    (NAACP)
National Association of Colored
    Women (NACW)
New Negro
Open Housing
Owen, Chandler (1889-1967)
Political Activism (1915-1945)
Political Realignment
Poor People's Campaign
Powell, Adam Clayton, Jr. (1908-
    1972)
Randolph, Asa Philip (1889-1979)
Reverse Freedom Rides (1962)
Simmons, Roscoe Conkling
    (c. 1881-1951)
Socialists and Socialism
Southern Tenant Farmers' Union
    (STFU)
Stokes, Carl B. (1927-1996)
Universal Negro Improvement
    Association (UNIA)
Uplift
Washington, Booker Taliaferro
    (1856-1915)
White, Walter Francis (1893-1955)
Young, Coleman Alexander (1918-
    1997)

Racial Discrimination

Blockbusting
Desegregation
Employment Discrimination
Ghettos
Great Migration, Black
    Opposition to
Great Migration, White
    Opposition to
Homelessness
Housing and Living Conditions
Hypersegregation
Involuntary Servitude
Jim Crow

Haynes, George Edmund (1880–1960)
Howard University
Johnson, Charles Spurgeon (1893–1956)
Johnson, James Weldon (1871–1938)
Moton, Robert Russa (1867–1940)
Reid, Ira De Augustine (1901–1968)
Schomburg, Arthur Alfonso (1874–1938)
Schoolteachers and Teaching
Scott, Emmett Jay (1873–1957)
Talbert, Mary B. (1866–1923)
Terrell, Mary Church (1863–1954)
Tuskegee Normal and Industrial Institute
Washington, Booker Taliaferro (1856–1915)
Weaver, Robert C. (1907–1997)
Wells-Barnett, Ida B. (1862–1931)
Wesley, Charles Harris (1891–1987)
White, Walter Francis (1893–1955)
Woodson, Carter Godwin (1875–1950)

Social and Living Conditions

Asian Immigrants and Asian Americans, Relations with Black Migrants
Black-Jewish Relations
Black Suburbanization
Childbirth
Crime and Criminals
European Immigrants, Relations with Black Migrants
Farm Security Administration (FSA)
Hispanic Immigrants and Hispanic Americans, Relations with Black Migrants
Homelessness
Home Ownership among Migrants
Housing and Living Conditions
Intraracial Class Conflict
Masculinity
Migrants, Cultural Identity of
Migrants, Settlement Patterns of

National Training School for Women and Girls (NTSWG)
National Urban League (NUL)
Passing
Public Housing
Settlement Houses
Uplift
Visiting
Women

Sport, Leisure, and Entertainment

Ali, Muhammad (1942–)
Automobility
Basketball
Benson, Al (1910–1980)
Black Appeal Radio
Black Aviators
Black Consumer Market
Black Film
Black Swan Records
Blaxploitation
Cooper, Jack L. (1888–1970)
Dance Halls and Nightclubs
Football
Foster, Andrew "Rube" (1879–1930)
Foster, William (1884–1940)
Gibson, Joshua (1911–1947)
Greenlee, William Augustus "Gus" (1897–1952)
Johnson, Jack (1878–1946)
Louis, Joe (1914–1981)
Micheaux, Oscar (1881–1951)
Negro Leagues
Owens, Jesse (1913–1980)
Paige, Leroy Robert "Satchel" (c. 1906–1982)
Policy Gambling
Posey, Cumberland (1890–1946)
Powell, William J. (1899–1943)
Prostitutes and Prostitution
Quilts
Red-Light Districts
Sport
Street Festivals and Parades
Young Men's Christian Association (YMCA)

PREFACE

The *Encyclopedia of the Great Black Migration* situates, within its broadest social, economic, cultural, and political context, the movement of southern African Americans to the urban North and Far West over the course of the twentieth century. The *Encyclopedia* was designed with different levels of students, teachers, and researchers in mind and was constructed in a way useful to each. First, the nearly 400 entries, written by over 200 scholars working in a dozen academic disciplines, provide students and researchers with information about the key people, places, organizations, and events that defined the era of the migration, from the late 1870s through the 1980s. Thus the *Encyclopedia* can serve as a useful guide to assist students working on school projects or college research papers. Each entry is accessible but authoritative and refers readers to additional sources for further research. Schoolteachers can use the *Encyclopedia* to broaden their teaching of the Great Migration, a topic that is often covered only briefly in high-school textbooks. The *Encyclopedia* suggests the breadth of the impact migration had on African American life, affecting everything from politics and labor to literature and the popular arts. The *Encyclopedia* also offers seventy-six primary sources that can serve both as a springboard for research and as a means for more in-depth classroom exploration of some of the topics introduced in the entries.

In addition to providing a starting point for information and research for students and teachers, the *Encyclopedia* will also be useful to graduate students and professional scholars. These volumes draw upon the expertise of leading scholars—many of whom contributed to this project—in a range of disciplines, including art history, anthropology, demography, economics, geography, history, journalism, literary criticism, music history, political science, and sociology. The entries thus not only introduce topics but also incorporate the interpretations and insights of recent scholarship. In this way, the *Encyclopedia* surveys the current state of the scholarly literature on the Great Migration. Graduate students working on seminar papers, preparing for comprehensive examinations, or searching for research topics should find much in the entries to help structure their studies and inspire ideas for further inquiry. By showcasing work on the Great Migration done by scholars from numerous disciplines, the *Encyclopedia* can help promote dialogue among professional academics across disciplinary boundaries. As the *Encyclopedia* makes clear, devoted scholars in many disciplines have investigated the Great Migration, thus creating rich opportunities for other enterprising scholars to find ways to combine these fields and thereby further our understanding of the history of black migration in the United States.

Arranged in alphabetical order, the entries not only cover the cities and regions affected by black migration but evaluate the impact of black migration on politics, employment, religion, social and living conditions, and racial discrimination and violence. Entries also assess how migration informed African American visual arts, music, literature, and popular culture. The "Guide to Related Topics" subdivides the entries into twenty-one broad categories to assist readers in locating information about a particular topic. The introduction explains the Great Migration, surveys how scholarly approaches to its study have changed over the last 100 years, and describes the logic of the selection of entries in the *Encyclopedia*. Readers should also note that this is an encyclopedia of the Great Migration rather than of twentieth-century African American history in general. Thus each entry, instead of offering general information easily accessible in other fine reference works, situates its topic within the context of black migration and articulates connections between the entry topic and the history of black migration. The entry on the *Chicago Defender*, for example, does not offer a brief history of that black newspaper but instead focuses on how the paper reported on and editorialized about the Great Migration. Many entries are illustrated by photographs.

Each entry contains extensive cross-referencing to help readers draw connections across topics. Related entries mentioned within the text of each entry are highlighted in boldfaced type. A brief section at the end of each entry refers readers to related entries within the *Encyclopedia* that are not mentioned in the text. Entries conclude with a list of further readings that contains the sources, both primary and secondary, on which the contributor based the entry. The entry bibliography also identifies other important sources for further reading on the subject. Some entries also refer readers to Internet sites, microfilm, and archival resources especially relevant to the study of that topic's relationship to the Great Migration. In addition, readers should consult the selected bibliography, which lists monographs, journal articles, and dissertations grouped into twenty-seven categories. The Selected Bibliography also identifies Internet sites and microfilm resources relevant to the study of the Great Migration.

Many of the entries also refer readers to related primary sources contained in Volume 3. Each of the seventy-six primary sources is numbered (a complete list of the primary sources follows the alphabetical list of entries), and a line at the end of the entry cross-references refers readers to related primary sources by number. Primary sources include a range of materials, such as oral histories, letters, excerpts from autobiographies, and other testimonies of black migrants. Other sources offer contemporary social commentary and investigations of migration excerpted from newspapers, magazines, and government reports, as well as examples of how the migration was captured in song and poetry. Each primary source contains an introductory headnote that situates the source in its historical context. The headnote also sometimes contains cross-references to other related primary sources in Volume 3 as well as to related entries in the *Encyclopedia*.

The *Encyclopedia* provides more than just an introduction to the history of the Great Black Migration. Its entries, primary sources, and bibliographic references will inspire further reading, research, and understanding of the importance of the Great Migration to twentieth-century African American and U.S. history. In so doing, I hope that it contributes to continuing the excitement, vitality, and creativity found in the study of the black migration experience.

ACKNOWLEDGMENTS

As the sole editor of a collaborative, scholarly endeavor of this magnitude, I have accumulated enormous debts in the thirty months that I have spent putting this project together. I especially wish to thank Eric Arnesen, who first recommended to Greenwood Press that I edit the project that became the *Encyclopedia of the Great Black Migration*. Eric has provided enormous encouragement, advice, and support over the years, and I hope that this final product reflects his confidence in my abilities.

These volumes would not have been possible without the hard work, expertise, and dedication to excellence in scholarship of the 213 authors who contributed to this reference work. When I first began to develop the entry list for this encyclopedia, I combed countless journals, monographs, recent dissertations, and databases of scholarly literature, looking not only for topics that needed to be included but for authors who would have the expertise to contribute to this project. When I started to contact these scholars, many of whom I did not know personally, but whose scholarship I had gotten to know quite well, I was overwhelmed by their unanimously positive reaction. Many—from veterans of the profession to outstanding graduate students embarking on promising careers—not only graciously accepted my invitation to contribute but did so with enthusiasm, support, critical advice, and encouragement. Over the course of our collaboration, they responded to my charge with energy, cheerfully (in most cases) kept to deadlines, and willingly made the revisions that I requested. Our collaborations stimulated many fruitful exchanges, and each of these contributors taught me a great deal. Short biographies of all the contributors appear in the section titled "About the Editor and Contributors," and I encourage readers to learn about these individuals and read their scholarship.

Many individuals provided special assistance. Charles Hardy, Todd Michney, Nina Mjagkij, and Dorothy Salem all did extra work in providing me with illustrations or primary documents for inclusion in Volume 3. I am especially thankful to Charles Hardy, who made available to me transcripts of his extensive interviews with black migrants to Philadelphia, two of which are excerpted in Volume 3. Todd Michney retrieved excellent archival materials on black migrants in Cleveland, two of which also appear in the volume of primary documents. My colleagues at James Madison University, particularly Kevin Borg and Michael Galgano, patiently listened to my endless brainstorming about the project. Each read portions of the manuscript. I especially wish to thank Michael, head of the Department of History, not only for the consistent wisdom of his advice but for establishing a supportive academic environment in which to work. Eric Arnesen, Wallace D. Best, and William D. Carrigan also read portions of the manuscript and offered crucial advice. At Greenwood Press, I would like to thank Kevin Ohe, Managing editor, print & electronic, for suggesting the volume initially and for securing approval of the proposal. Acquisitions Editor Mike Herman, who oversaw the project at Greenwood, offered excellent advice early on, making the wise suggestion to expand the scope of the encyclopedia beyond the World War I–era migration to cover the history of black migration throughout the twentieth century. John Wagner, senior development editor, did a marvelous job coordinating this project, keeping all the material that I submitted to him well organized, and meticulously preparing the manuscript for timely transmission to production. His efforts were essential to the success of the encyclopedia. I received important help at a critical stage from Nick Fite, a student of mine at JMU, who organized the entries that had been submitted and who initiated the search for appropriate illustrations. The staff at Interlibrary Loan at JMU's Carrier Library, especially Susan Johnson, did a brilliant job obtaining for me numerous sources. Their efforts saved me countless hours of travel.

Finally, I wish to thank my family, which has had to endure this project from its inception on a daily basis. My father, George Reich, endorsed this endeavor from the beginning, and his frequent calls for progress reports prodded me along. In ways too numerous to count, Lori helped to fit this enterprise into the ever-complicated and chaotic schedule of our household. She and our children, Annaka and Riley, were wonderfully supportive throughout and patient with my long absences from home when deadlines loomed. It is their love and companionship that inspire and sustain me.

INTRODUCTION

Although African Americans had been leaving the South since the days of slavery, it was not until the twentieth century that they migrated on a massive scale to begin new lives in the urban North. From about 1910 to 1970, millions of African American migrants embarked on millions of individual journeys that resulted in a dramatic redistribution of the African American population. This Great Black Migration, as it came to be called, occurred in two waves. In the first, between 1915 and 1930, some 1.25 million black southerners relocated to the North. These migrants, attracted by the industrial expansion of World War I and the subsequent economic development in the 1920s, predominantly settled in a few industrial cities such as Chicago, Detroit, Cleveland, Pittsburgh, Philadelphia, and New York. Out-migration from the South slowed during the Great Depression of the 1930s, but World War II spawned a Second Great Migration of a magnitude far greater than that of the first. From 1940 to 1970 some 4.5 million black southerners left the South. Although the industrial North and Midwest remained the destination of many, larger numbers relocated to the cities of the West Coast, drawn by employment opportunities in the nation's defense industries. Over the course of the twentieth century, black migration shifted the center of African American social, economic, political, and cultural life from the rural South to the urban North and West. The expansion of urban, black communities made possible black political mobilization and realignment; the growth of black business and capital; the emergence of new trends in black art, literature, and culture; and the fostering of a new mentality and outlook among African Americans that ultimately proved instrumental in the grassroots assault on Jim Crow later in the twentieth century.

As early as 1917, contemporaries—black and white—recognized the profound demographic transformation that was unfolding, deploying metaphors of exodus and the search for promised lands to describe the Great Migration.

The sudden influx of black southerners into the urban North captured the imagination of journalists, activists, and social workers, who struggled to comprehend the population changes before them. Even as black activists promoted migration with sensational tales about the "promised land" and some white commentators saw the social benefits of this population movement, there was a palpable uneasiness among other white journalists who wondered whether southern cotton pickers would long survive the rigors of northern cities.[1]

This combination of hope and fear about the changes being wrought by black migration inspired federal and municipal government agencies, churches, and private social welfare organizations to sponsor a number of studies, under the direction of black and white university-trained sociologists, to investigate the social, cultural, and economic impact of black migration to the North. Despite the diversity of this research, it tended to have three central concerns: to determine the immediate causes of black migration, to evaluate migrants' adjustment to northern, urban life, and to assess the impact of black migration on race relations and racial conflict. These sociologists compiled mountains of data and statistics, collected ethnographies of migrants, and conducted surveys of the housing and living conditions, settlement patterns, family relationships, educational facilities, recreational habits, and employment histories of black newcomers. Many of these writers, such as Charles S. Johnson, George E. Haynes, and Emmett J. Scott, combined scholarly inquiry with an activist's dedication to social change. They saw migration's potential for bringing political empowerment and economic betterment to African Americans at the same time that they addressed the obstacles confronting migrants. By documenting the social ills associated with in-migration—crime, prostitution, juvenile delinquency, alcoholism, unemployment, and racial violence—they sought to advocate solutions and policy recommendations for state and municipal governments.[2]

Social commentary on black migration tapered off in the late 1920s as the influx of black southerners lost its novelty and seemed less newsworthy and as migration slowed with the onset of the Great Depression. Scholarly interest in the fate of black migrants received a boost in the mid-1930s when the Federal Writers' Project (FWP), a division of the New Deal's Works Progress Administration (WPA), commissioned a number of research projects that concentrated on the study of black urban life. Although these researchers focused their investigations less centrally on migration, they developed important studies of the communities and institutions that black migrants built in such places as Chicago, Pittsburgh, San Francisco, and Washington, D.C. Together, these sociologists and anthropologists created sophisticated studies and compiled impressive evidence that would inform the work of later generations of historians. Their work remains an essential source for the study of the Great Migration.[3]

It was not until the 1960s and early 1970s that historians took interest in the Great Migration. This generation of historians drew upon the earlier sociological studies in an effort to locate the historical roots of nearly all-black ghettos that by the 1960s had become havens of poverty, unemployment, decaying housing stock, heroin addiction, juvenile delinquency, high homicide rates, police brutality, and riots. Black migration, these scholars contended, was a key factor in the process of ghetto formation. They argued that patterns of black residential segregation in northern cities predated World War I and that the high rates of black in-migration after 1915 intensified the concentration of black residents into these distinct and increasingly overcrowded neighborhoods. These studies made important differentiations between the urban experiences of European immigrants and those of black migrants. Unlike ethnic enclaves, which were seldom the domain of a single nationality, black segregation in the urban ghetto was complete, compulsory, and permanent. Emphasizing the impact of racially restrictive covenants, neighborhood property owners' associations, blockbusting, and violence on patterns of housing discrimination, these studies drew important attention to the extent to which white racism circumscribed the development of urban black communities. The ghetto-formation framework, however, tended to regard black migrants merely as victims of a hostile world. Focusing on what they saw as the social disorder and pathology of black urban life, they described the ghetto as a tragic, enduring, perpetual, and hopeless place from which there was little escape.[4]

In the 1980s Joe William Trotter questioned the ghetto synthesis by challenging historians to think about urban blacks not as ghetto dwellers but as industrial workers. Inspired by the research agenda of the new labor history, Trotter and others shifted their concerns away from ghetto formation and toward questions of working-class formation. Movement north for black migrants meant entry into the northern industrial working class. But as Trotter emphasizes, this process did not put blacks on the same path of downward social mobility and loss of autonomy over craft skill that it did for white workers. Wage work in northern factories, however tenuous, was an incremental but significant step up for southern black rural sharecroppers and nonfactory common laborers. Factory wages made for an expanding economic base in black, working-class communities that allowed a precarious but vibrant black bourgeoisie to emerge and provided community resources to combat and challenge the structural constraints of the expanding ghetto. Black workers developed a class as well as a racial consciousness that complicated and strained their relations with the expanding black middle class. By regarding migration as the making of a black working class, Trotter focused attention away from ghettos as timeless tragedies and toward thinking about them as dynamic places that underwent economic, social, and political change.[5]

In the last fifteen years a wealth of new scholarship has challenged both the ghetto-formation and working-class-formation theses. In a number of ways, historians questioned the narrow focus on migrants as male, working-class, urban dwellers who were acted upon by the structural forces that defined the ghetto. New studies have reexamined the Great Migration by asking how migration looks different when scholars consider migrants as southerners, as women, as family members rooted in complex networks of kith and kin, as Christians, as consumers, or as political activists who not only adjusted to city life but also acted in a variety of ways to transform the urban environments in which they settled. These scholars have employed a much wider variety of sources—census records; vital statistics and records of various state and federal agencies; municipal vice records; oral history; folklore; records of black churches, schools, businesses, and civic groups; photographs; archival material on black film, theater, and music; popular culture; and literature—to create a richer, more complex portrait of black migrants and their world. These scholars, many of whom have contributed entries to this encyclopedia, have so expanded our understanding of black migration that the field looks nothing like it did fifteen years ago.

A rich sociological literature, drawing upon newly available census data, has been able to identify with much greater precision who the migrants were, where they came from, and why they left the South. Carole Marks, for example, found in her study that migrants before 1930 were more likely to have been artisans and nonagricultural laborers who came from southern cities and towns than sharecroppers coming directly from the countryside. Subsequent scholarship has tended to confirm Marks's conclusions. Scholars have mined the Public Use Microdata Samples (PUMS) and have made inventive use of marriage records and World War I selective service registration cards to confirm a profile of the migrants as urban and educated. These scholars have also demonstrated that in the early years of the Great Migration, migrants overwhelmingly came from border states such as Virginia and Kentucky, and it was only later that the Deep South became the key sending area. Scholars have submitted common generalizations about why migrants left the South—boll weevil infestation, lynching, mechanization of agriculture—to rigorous scrutiny, calling into question causal links between these phenomena and out-migration. Although much work remains to be done and scholars are still experimenting with what can be learned from the PUMS files, this work certainly underscores that scholars can no longer uncritically accept the assumption that the typical black migrant was only "one step removed from slavery," steeped in rural habits, and ignorant of urban life. Migrants were a diverse group who left for a variety of reasons under a range of circumstances.[6]

New interpretations of the Great Migration also emerged from studies that are tightly focused on the migrants. James R. Grossman's important book on black migration to Chicago, published in 1989, reexamined the Great Migration "from the perspective of its participants." Since the participants were southerners, he argued for placing migration within the context of southern, not just urban, history. Grossman portrayed migration as a grassroots social movement and emphasized the way ordinary blacks orchestrated movement north through elaborate networks of communication—letter writing, visiting, migration clubs—in which prospective migrants acquired critical information about life in Chicago. Grossman thus reminds us that migration was a conscious decision, made within the context of family and community, rather than the product of historical imperatives. For black migrants, the Chicago environment promised freedom from the southern obsession with racial control by providing legal protection, political rights, and access to the paths of security and mobility. But southern experience had also taught blacks to distrust whites. Many newcomers looked forward to freedom from whites and evinced little desire to integrate. Whenever possible, migrants relished the fellowship provided by black institutions. Thus for Grossman, understanding the cultural baggage that black southerners brought with them holds the key to understanding how they reacted and adjusted to their new homes.[7]

Several recent works not only focus on migrants as historical actors but place migrant women at the center of historical analysis. As Victoria Wolcott remarks in her recent study of interwar Detroit, "a narrow focus on male industrial workers...has hidden the complexity of this city's African American community." These works both explore the lives of migrant women and bring gender analysis to the history of black urban communities. Shifting the focus from the shop floor to the neighborhood, Wolcott uncovers a wide range of female migrant experiences, including social workers and women's club leaders as well as domestic servants, gamblers, prostitutes, and dance-hall performers. By examining the interaction of these women, she uncovers intraracial conflicts over the meaning of racial uplift and respectability that were central to the culture of Detroit's black community between the world wars. The southern black women who migrated to Washington, D.C., to work as domestic servants, argues Elizabeth Clark-Lewis, transformed their working relationships from one of master and servant to a more favorable employer-employee relationship. Drawing upon her extensive oral interviews with former migrants, Gretchen Lemke-Santangelo stresses a similar activism among migrant women in building their new communities in Oakland, California, during the 1940s and 1950s. Female migrants to the East Bay encountered formidable obstacles, but they drew upon a set of values and ethics rooted in their struggles against Jim Crow in the South—self-determination, helping networks, economic independence, and institution building—to create and sustain migrant communities. In her study of black migration to Cleveland, Kimberley Phillips recovers the role of women as "the vanguard of community-based militancy."[8]

Female migrants were particularly active in urban churches, and scholars of religious history have broadened our understanding of migration by exploring the critical relationship between the Great Migration and the creation of modern African American churches, a subject much slighted in the ghetto-formation and working-class-formation frameworks. Recent studies have examined the role of churches in promoting migration, their response to the influx of migrants, and the emerging conflicts within congregations between older residents and black southerners over worship style and religious practice. Many migrants created their own, less pretentious storefront churches that combined elements of southern folk sensibilities, "down-home" ways, and worship patterns with the realities of modern urban life. Migrant churches were also arenas for women's social and political activism because they constituted nearly 70 percent of the membership. Others have traced the distinctively migrant origins of the Nation of Islam, linking its rise in the 1930s and 1940s to its particular appeal to black migrants confronting the limitations of the urban North. New studies of other religious sects, such as Baptists and Pentecostals, within the migration context further add to our understanding of connections between migration and modern African American religious life.[9]

As urban preachers well understood, churches competed with the expanding secular attractions of the city. Scholars have broadened our understanding of migration-era black culture beyond the Harlem Renaissance to investigate a diverse world of popular arts, athletics, black film, and urban spectacles. Sports such as sandlot baseball leagues, basketball clubs, and boxing offered migrants the opportunity for self-organization and expression, fostered neighborhood identity, and were an arena, removed from the despair and supervision of factory work, in which blacks could compete and display their prowess and competence. Migrants flocked to night spots in cities where black patrons jitterbuggd, slow-dragged, and did the lindy hop. These clubs, as Shirley Moore has explained in her study of black migration to Richmond, California, were social centers that helped orient newcomers to the city, functioning in much the same way that the saloon did in the nineteenth century for male, European immigrants in the cities of the Northeast and Midwest. Nightclubs were also sites of social activism. Not only did the lyrics of the music convey the frustrations and aspirations of patrons, but the clubs became places where activists planned collective campaigns to better their lives. Union drives sometimes had their start in such places. Patronage of the clubs was always mixed sex, and the places were free of the gender constraints that were found elsewhere in the city and were especially present in the South. Women visited, performed, and even owned clubs, which were important places of female entrepreneurial activity. In such refuges from racial hostility, migrants gathered to hear music that affirmed black value and dignity and life experience, which was not often found in the steel mills, shipyards, and stockyards.[10]

Moore's study of Richmond is one among a number of recent works that expand the history of the Great Migration by shifting the story away from the Northeast and Midwest. In recent years several new studies have explored black migration to the West Coast, with books on black migration to San Francisco, Seattle, Oakland, and Los Angeles. As Josh Sides has argued, the story from the West challenges predominant features of the Great Migration narrative. Migration westward expands the temporal boundaries of the story beyond the era of World War I. Black migration to the West began in earnest with World War II when southern migrants flocked to western cities, seeking the prospect of steady, high-paying work in the expanding defense industries. Black migrants to the West were overwhelmingly urban, coming directly from southern cities such as Houston, Texas. Migrants to the West, then, were already part of a black, working-class population that had experienced its formation in the South. Unlike black migrants to the North, African American newcomers in the West encountered a world populated by other nonwhites and competed with Asians and Hispanics in a labor market of complicated racial and ethnic hierarchies. Finally, black migrants to the West were neither culturally dislocated nor lacking in political sophistication. They brought a spirit of activism with them to create what Sides in his study of Los Angeles called "migrant-infused civil rights movements."[11]

Several recent works have made explicit connections between black migration and the development of a new, urban political activism. World War I, movement north, and urbanization raised expectations among African

Americans that full citizenship rights were due. Some migrants, along with longer-term northern black residents and West Indian immigrants, challenged the servile politics of what A. Philip Randolph called the Old Crowd of black leaders in the North. Migrant activism gave birth to a host of political campaigns dedicated to fulfilling those expectations, including the New Negro movement and Universal Negro Improvement Association of the 1920s, "Don't Buy Where You Can't Work" campaigns of the 1930s, and the March on Washington Movement and Double V campaign of the 1940s. Many of these studies also make explicit the connections between migration, labor activism, and grassroots political mobilization. Migrants also reshaped electoral politics, and recent studies have investigated black migrants' use of the franchise in the North and West. The increasing concentration of black population in northern and western cities allowed blacks to influence local politics and eventually, through the election of representatives in Congress, national politics. Key shifts in racial demographics made this political change possible, but it was grassroots activism in urban neighborhoods through voter registration drives and community organizing behind local candidates that fulfilled the political possibilities created by migration.[12]

With this emphasis on self-determination, activism, and vitality in black migrant communities, scholars have long abandoned the misguided but seemingly enduring image of the typical migrant as an unsophisticated, culturally dislocated rural sharecropper. Black migrants were neither tragic ghetto dwellers nor destitute sharecroppers who left behind forever their rural past to join the ranks of the proletariat of the American industrial revolution. Migration no longer appears as a process of rupture, maladjustment, and tragic sameness but instead as one of fusion, of intertwining old and new worlds in which migrants redefined the social, cultural, and political contours of their receiving cities as much as the cities redefined the identity of migrants. Migrants in these studies constantly negotiated the tensions between migration's possibilities and its limits, promises, and failures. They inhabited worlds that were at once southern and northern, rural and urban, old and new, traditional and modern, sacred and secular.

Even as scholars emphasize the creative energy of black urban communities overlooked in the ghetto synthesis, they are not indifferent to the original concerns of that scholarship. They hold no illusion about the severe obstacles that migrants confronted in northern and western cities. Residential segregation, a fragile entry into the industrial workforce, deep intraracial class conflicts, and periodic, if not systemic, racial violence circumscribed migrants' lives and remain key to these narratives. But if migrants were able to adapt to and fight against these conditions to create communities in which they could survive and at times thrive, they encountered new obstacles in the aftermath of World War II that threatened the viability of their communities and their institutions. Deindustrialization, the loss of manufacturing jobs, urban renewal, and white flight in the 1950s and 1960s emerge as the key factors that marginalized those urban communities that migrants had struggled so hard to build. The collapse of the economic base of migrant neighborhoods—rather than the tragic sameness of the ghetto—exacerbated problems of underfunded education, insufficient public services, unemployment, crime, and police brutality. Frustrations reached a boiling point in the 1960s when black residents—often young, unemployed, black males—rebelled in urban riots in places such as Watts, Detroit, and Newark. Massive economic restructuring of the industrial economy—what historian Thomas Sugrue described as deproletarianization—had a devastating impact on those places that African Americans had once hoped would be a promised land.[13]

The proliferation of new directions in migration studies makes an encyclopedia devoted to the Great Black Migration all the more important. Despite the significance of this exciting literature to our understanding of black migration, scholarship on the Great Migration continues to run the risk of segmentation. Most historians, for example, still regard the Great Migration as an event associated with World War I. The scholarship on the World War I–era migration is thus extensive, whereas studies of black migration from 1940 to 1970 still remain few. Scholars have written far more on the black experience in the urban North than on that in the urban West; community studies of black migrants' experiences in a single city far outnumber those that adopt a comparative framework; scholarship has tended to focus more on black, male industrial workers than on the migration experiences of black women; and although historians have taught us much about the experiences of black migrants in their new location, we remain less knowledgeable about the Great Migration's impact on the lives of blacks who remained in the South. This reference work brings together all of these aspects of the nearly 100-year history of the Great Black Migration.

Selection of Included Entries and Documents

In conceptualizing the entry list and the primary sources to be included, I have taken an expansive view of migration. It covers the history of the subject from the Exodusters of the late nineteenth century to the return migrants of the late twentieth century. The wide selection of entries testifies not only to the range of topics that the study of black migration now encompasses but also to the various disciplines of scholarly inquiry active in the field. The primary sources try to offer examples of the range of sources that scholars studying migration use. Although the *Encyclopedia* includes nearly 400 entries, they fall into some broader categories.

The migration of black southerners to the North that began during World War I was part of a much larger and longer process by which southern blacks had long migrated within the South in search of social, economic, and political justice. Many of the entries in the *Encyclopedia* explore this history of migration within the South. Entries evaluate pre–World War I migration patterns, as well as exploring early migrants such as the Exodusters and the emigrationists of the late nineteenth century. Entries on southern cities examine how black migration contributed to southern urbanization; others consider the impact of out-migration on subregions of the South such as the Mississippi Delta, the Gulf Coast, the Low Country, and Appalachia. Other entries are devoted to life in the South and the conditions that constrained black aspirations and were contributing causes to migration northward and westward later in the twentieth century. Thus the reader will find articles on Jim Crow, lynching, the boll weevil, and involuntary servitude, to name a few.

Another category of entries covers the many destinations that attracted black migrants. There are entries on all the major cities of the North and West. Other entries situate black migration into a wider, regional context—western states, midwestern states, and northeastern states. Contributors not only examine regionwide black migration patterns but also consider migrants who settled outside the region's metropolises. Related to the entries on destinations is the series of entries that consider the demography of black migration. These entries explain the broader patterns of migration, including key shifts in the number of migrants, as well as changes in the rates and causes of migration. Other entries provide demographic profiles of the migrants, with articles on migrants' expectations, their economic and social characteristics, and settlement patterns.

Since much black migration was a search for better employment opportunities, many of the entries cover work and labor. Entries examine male and female employment patterns, occupational mobility, and employment discrimination. Other entries provide information on the key industries in which black migrants found employment. Related to these are the entries that consider how federal government agencies both responded to black migration and facilitated African Americans' search for work. Several of these are related to the larger process of mobilization during the two world wars—the Division of Negro Economics, the National War Labor Board, the War Manpower Commission, and the Fair Employment Practices Committee, for example—whereas others explore the impact of New Deal agencies on migrants' search for economic empowerment.

Another category of entries focuses on the building of the black "metropolises" of the North and West. Some explore the key institutions that blacks created and that in turn served migrant communities, including settlement houses, YMCAs and YWCAs, women's clubs, and the National Urban League. Other entries examine migrant participation in the development of black businesses and the professions. Contributors consider the growth of black media—newspapers, radio, film, and record companies—instrumental to sustaining a sense of cohesion in migrant enclaves. Others cover the importance of sport, leisure, and recreation to the making of the black metropolis. The impact of the Great Migration on religion receives coverage in entries dedicated to various denominations, such as African Methodism, Pentecostalism, and the Nation of Islam. Entries on black migrant encounters with other immigrants—Asians, Europeans, Hispanics, and Jews—complicate the story of the color line in the urban North and West. The grimmer realities of black urban life, such as unemployment, homelessness, juvenile delinquency, prostitution, and crime also receive considerable space. Biographical entries profile the lives of ministers, sport figures, and entrepreneurs.

Several entries explore the Great Migration in the visual arts, music, and literature. Art historians relate in a number of entries how different painters such as Walter Ellison, Archibald Motley, Aaron Douglas, and Jacob Lawrence interpreted the migration through the images they created. Entries devoted to music explore how a migration context influenced the development of various genres, including jazz, blues, swing, and bebop. Entries also investigate individual musicians—Ma Rainey, Louis Armstrong, and John Coltrane, to name just a few—many of them migrants themselves, and not only how their music was influenced by migration and migrant audiences but also how they offered probing commentary on the Great Migration in their sounds and lyrics. The *Encyclopedia* also reflects the recent interest among literary critics in the migration narrative in African American literature.[14] Several biographical entries on novelists and poets not only examine these writers' own personal migrations but explore how they engaged with black migration in the literature they wrote.

For African Americans, migration north and west was never a route of escape from discrimination and racial violence. Several entries document the profound limitations of life outside the South. The *Encyclopedia* considers discrimination in housing that contributed to residential segregation and substandard living conditions, as well as racism in employment that restricted migrants' access to industrial employment and skilled labor and limited their occupational mobility. Despite the distinct advantages that white urban residents and newcomers had over blacks, they still considered black migrants a threat to their job security and access to housing and other scarce resources of the city. Racial tensions flared during the era of the Great Migration, especially during the two world wars, and exploded into a series of race riots. Several entries probe these connections between black migration and antiblack violence.

If African Americans were victims of race riots and intense discrimination, they also mobilized politically to advance their interests. Several entries explore the relationship between migration and the various expressions of black politics. Entries on socialists and Communists evaluate the appeal of radical politics to black migrants; others consider how black migration stimulated a politics of racial separatism, energizing the black nationalism of Marcus Garvey's Universal Negro Improvement Association. Other entries describe how the limitations of migration in the context of World War II heightened the contradictions between racism in the United States and war against fascism abroad, breeding an activist political consciousness among African Americans. Biographical entries explore the lives of black legislators and mayors, community activists, and labor organizers.

A final category of entries situates post–World War II developments within a migration context. Several entries consider the impact of deindustrialization, white flight, urban renewal, and desegregation on black ghettos. In the midst of the deepening urban crisis, black residents did not remain passive. As several entries reveal, many responded through community organizing, tried to take advantage of War on Poverty programs, campaigned for black politicians, agitated for open housing, participated in the Poor People's Campaign, or joined more radical groups such as the Black Panther Party. Other migrants, concluding that cities were no longer a promised land, if they ever had been, returned to the South in a search for a more hopeful racial climate and a more promising future in the wake of the civil rights movement.

In editing this *Encyclopedia*, I have tried to showcase the remarkable achievements in the scholarship on black migration in the last twenty years, as well as the wealth of information about the subject that is now available. My hope is that it satisfies three related goals. First, it offers beginning researchers and students of African American history an introduction to the key people, places, organizations, and events that defined the era of the migration and directs them to the best, most reliable scholarship in the field. Second, I hope that as the first reference work devoted to the Great Black Migration in its entirety, it helps integrate the various histories of black migration. It should suggest to scholars the connections between the northern and the western story of migration, between the migrations of World War I and those of World War II, and between the migrant worlds of work and those of neighborhood and culture. Finally, by assembling leading scholars in history, economics, demography, sociology, anthropology, journalism, geography, literature, art history, and music history as contributors, the *Encyclopedia* promotes interdisciplinary collaboration in future studies of black migration.

Notes

1. For examples of the range of white opinion, see Helen B. Pendleton, "Cotton Pickers in Northern Cities," *Survey* 37 (February 17, 1917): 569-71; Rollin Lynde Hartt, "When the Negro Comes North," *World's Work* 48 (May 1924): 83-89 and (June 1924): 184-90; Blanton Fortson, "Northward to Extinction," *Forum* 72 (November 1924): 593-600; and S. J. Holmes, "Will the Negro Survive in the North?" *Scientific Monthly* 27 (December 1928): 557-61.

2. U.S. Department of Labor, Division of Negro Economics, *Negro Migration in 1916-17* (1919; reprint, New York: Arno Press, 1969); George Edmund Haynes, *Negro Newcomers in Detroit, Michigan* (1918; reprint, New York: Arno Press, 1969); Emmett J. Scott, *Negro Migration during the War* (1920; reprint, New York: Arno Press, 1969); Chicago Commission on Race Relations, *The Negro in Chicago: A Study of Race Relations and a Race Riot in 1919* (1922; reprint, New York: Arno Press, 1968); T. J. Woofter, ed., *Negro Problems in Cities* (1928; reprint, New York: Negro Universities Press, 1969); Louise V. Kennedy, *The Negro Peasant Turns Cityward: Effects of Recent Migrations in Northern Cities* (New York: Columbia University Press, 1930); and Clyde Vernon Kiser, *Sea Island to City: A Study of St. Helena Islanders in Harlem and Other Urban Centers* (New York: Columbia University Press, 1932). The periodical literature—in both the black and white press—on black migration published between 1915 and the late 1920s is voluminous. For an extensive listing of articles published between 1915 and 1918, see Scott, *Negro Migration*, 175-84.

3. St. Clair Drake and Horace R. Cayton, *Black Metropolis: A Study of Negro Life in a Northern City*, 2 vols., rev. ed. (Chicago: University of Chicago Press, 1993); Sterling Brown, *The Negro in Washington* (1937; reprint, New York: Arno Press, 1969); Laurence A Glasco, ed., *The WPA History of the Negro in Pittsburgh* (Pittsburgh: University of Pittsburgh Press, 2004); and Charles S. Johnson, *The Negro War Worker in San Francisco* (San Francisco: YWCA, 1944).

4. Gilbert Osofsky, *Harlem: The Making of a Ghetto; Negro New York, 1890-1930* (1964; rev. ed., New York: Harper Torchbooks, 1971); Gilbert Osofsky, "The Enduring Ghetto," *Journal of American History* 55, no. 2 (September 1968): 243-55; Allan H. Spear, *Black Chicago: The Making of a Negro Ghetto, 1890-1920* (Chicago:

University of Chicago Press, 1967); David M. Katzman, *Before the Ghetto: Black Detroit in the Nineteenth Century* (Urbana: University of Illinois Press, 1973); Kenneth L. Kusmer, *A Ghetto Takes Shape: Black Cleveland, 1870–1930* (Urbana: University of Illinois Press, 1976); and Thomas Philpott, *The Slum and the Ghetto* (New York: Oxford University Press, 1978).

5. Joe William Trotter, Jr., *Black Milwaukee: The Making of an Industrial Proletariat, 1915–45* (Urbana: University of Illinois Press, 1985); Joe William Trotter, Jr., *Coal, Class, and Color: Blacks in Southern West Virginia, 1915–32* (Urbana: University of Illinois Press, 1990); and Dennis C. Dickerson, *Out of the Crucible: Black Steelworkers in Western Pennsylvania, 1875–1980* (New York: State University of New York Press, 1986). The exhibit on the Great Migration at the National Museum of American History at the Smithsonian Institution that first went on display in the 1980s titled Field to Factory: Afro-American Migration, 1915–1940 adopts the working-class-formation framework espoused by Trotter. Joe William Trotter has offered detailed critiques of the scholarly literature on black migration written before 1990; see Trotter, *Black Milwaukee*, 264–82; and "Black Migration in Historical Perspective: A Review of the Literature," in *The Great Migration in Historical Perspective: New Dimensions of Race, Class, and Gender*, edited by Joe William Trotter, Jr. (Bloomington: Indiana University Press, 1991), 1–21.

6. Carole Marks, *Farewell—We're Good and Gone: The Great Black Migration* (Bloomington: Indiana University Press, 1989); J. Trent Alexander, "The Great Migration in Comparative Perspective," *Social Science History* 22 (1998): 349–76; Craig Heinicke, "African-American Migration and Urban Labor Skills: 1950 and 1960," *Agricultural History* 68, no. 2 (1994): 185–98; Stewart E. Tolnay, "Educational Selection in the Migration of Southern Blacks, 1880–1990," *Social Forces* 77 (1998): 487–514; Arvarh Strickland, "The Strange Affair of the Boll Weevil: The Pest as Liberator," *Agricultural History* 68 (Spring 1994): 157–68; Stewart E. Tolnay, "Racial Violence and Black Migration in the American South, 1910–1930," *American Sociological Review* 57 (February 1992): 103–16; and Craig Heinicke, "African-American Migration and Mechanized Cotton Harvesting, 1950–1960," *Explorations in Economic History* 31, no. 4 (1994): 501–20. For an excellent review of this literature, see Stewart E. Tolnay, "The African American 'Great Migration' and Beyond," *Annual Review of Sociology* 29 (2003): 209–32. On how historians can make use of the PUMS, see James N. Gregory, "The Southern Diaspora and the Urban Dispossessed: Demonstrating the Public Use Microdata Samples," *Journal of American History* 82, no. 1 (1995): 111–34.

7. James R. Grossman, *Land of Hope: Chicago, Black Southerners, and the Great Migration* (Chicago: University of Chicago Press, 1989). The quotation is from page 4. Another outstanding study that examines the southern origins of black migrants to industrial Pittsburgh is Peter Gottlieb, *Making Their Own Way: Southern Blacks' Migration to Pittsburgh, 1916–30* (Urbana: University of Illinois Press, 1987).

8. Victoria W. Wolcott, *Remaking Respectability: African American Women in Interwar Detroit* (Chapel Hill: University of North Carolina Press, 2001), 2; Elizabeth Clark-Lewis, *Living In, Living Out: African American Domestics in Washington, D.C., 1910–1940* (Washington, DC: Smithsonian Institution Press, 1994); Gretchen Lemke-Santangelo, *Abiding Courage: African American Migrant Women and the East Bay Community* (Chapel Hill: University of North Carolina Press, 1996); and Kimberley L. Phillips, *AlabamaNorth: African-American Migrants, Community, and Working-Class Activism in Cleveland, 1915–45* (Urbana: University of Illinois Press, 1999). For a similar analysis in a southern city, see Georgina Hickey, *Hope and Danger in the New South City: Working-Class Women and Urban Development in Atlanta, 1890–1940* (Athens: University of Georgia Press, 2003).

9. Robert Gregg, *Sparks from the Anvil of Oppression: Philadelphia's African Methodists and Southern Migrants, 1890-1940* (Philadelphia: Temple University Press, 1993); Milton Sernett, *Bound for the Promised Land: African American Religion and the Great Migration* (Durham, NC: Duke University Press, 1997); Wallace Best, *Passionately Human, No Less Divine: Religion and Culture in Black Chicago, 1915-1952* (Princeton, NJ: Princeton University Press, 2005); Claude Andrew Clegg III, *An Original Man: The Life and Times of Elijah Muhammad* (New York: St. Martin's Press, 1997); Shalanda Denise Dexter, "Sojourners in a Strange Land: The Impact of Northern Urbanization on Black Pentecostal Identity and Culture in Chicago from 1940 to 1980" (Ph.D. diss., Princeton University, 2001); and Julia Robinson-Harmon, "Reverend Robert L. Bradby: Establishing the Kingdom of God among Migrants, Women and Workers, 1910-1946" (Ph.D. diss., Michigan State University, 2002).

10. Rob Ruck, *Sandlot Seasons: Sport in Black Pittsburgh* (Urbana: University of Illinois Press, 1987); Neil Lanctot, *Negro League Baseball: The Rise and Ruin of a Black Institution* (Philadelphia: University of Pennsylvania Press, 2004); Shirley Ann Wilson Moore, *To Place Our Deeds: The African American Community in Richmond, California, 1910-1963* (Berkeley: University of California Press, 2001). See also Burton W. Peretti, *The Creation of Jazz: Music, Race, and Culture in Urban America* (Urbana: University of Illinois Press, 1992); Lewis Erenberg, *Swingin' the Dream: Big Band Jazz and the Rebirth of American Culture* (Chicago: University of Chicago Press, 1998); Joel Dinerstein, *Swinging the Machine: Modernity, Technology, and African American Culture between the World Wars* (Amherst: University of Massachusetts Press, 2003); Jacqueline Najuma Stewart, *Migrating to the Movies: Cinema and Black Urban Modernity* (Berkeley: University of California Press, 2005); and Davarian L. Baldwin, "Chicago's New Negroes: Race, Class, and Respectability in the Midwestern Black Metropolis, 1915-1935" (Ph.D. diss., New York University, 2002).

11. Josh Sides, "Rethinking Black Migration: A Perspective from the West," in *Moving Stories: Migration and the American West, 1850-2000*, edited by Scott E. Casper and Lucinda M. Long (Reno: Nevada Humanities Committee, 2001), 203. Important recent books on the Great Migration to the West include Albert Broussard, *Black San Francisco: The Struggle for Racial Equality in the West, 1900-1954* (Lawrence: University Press of Kansas, 1993); Marilynn S. Johnson, *The Second Gold Rush: Oakland and the East Bay in World War II* (Berkeley: University of California Press, 1993); Quintard Taylor, *The Forging of a Black Community: Seattle's Central District, from 1870 through the Civil Rights Era* (Seattle: University of Washington Press, 1994); Lemke-Santangelo, *Abiding Courage*; Quintard Taylor, *In Search of the Racial Frontier: African Americans in the American West, 1528-1990* (New York: W. W. Norton, 1998); Moore, *To Place Our Deeds*; Josh Sides, *L.A. City Limits: African American Los Angeles from the Great Depression to the Present* (Berkeley: University of California Press, 2003); and Robert O. Self, *American Babylon: Race and the Struggle for Postwar Oakland* (Princeton, NJ: Princeton University Press, 2003).

12. Eric Arnesen, ed., *Black Protest and the Great Migration: A Brief History with Documents* (Boston: Bedford, 2003); Beth Tompkins Bates, *Pullman Porters and the Rise of Protest Politics in Black America, 1925-1945* (Chapel Hill: University of North Carolina Press, 2001); Sides, *L.A. City Limits*; Steven A. Reich, "Soldiers of Democracy: Black Texans and the Fight for Citizenship, 1917-1921," *Journal of American History* 82 (March 1996): 1478-504, and "The Great War, Black Workers, and the Rise and Fall of the NAACP in the South," in *The Black Worker: Race, Labor, and Civil Rights since Emancipation*, edited by Eric Arnesen (Urbana: University of Illinois Press, 2006); and Cheryl Greenberg, *"Or Does It Explode?" Black Harlem in the Great Depression* (New York: Oxford University Press, 1991). On labor activism, see, for example, Rick

Halpern, *Down on the Killing Floor: Black and White Workers in Chicago's Packinghouses, 1904-54* (Urbana: University of Illinois Press, 1997); Roger Horowitz, *"Negro and White, Unite and Fight": A Social History of Industrial Unionism in Meatpacking, 1930-90* (Urbana: University of Illinois Press, 1997); and Eric Arnesen, *Brotherhoods of Color: Black Railroad Workers and the Struggle for Equality* (Cambridge, MA: Harvard University Press, 2001). On electoral politics, see, for example, David R. Colburn and Jeffrey S. Adler, eds., *African-American Mayors: Race, Politics, and the American City* (Urbana: University of Illinois Press, 2001); Leonard N. Moore, *Carl B. Stokes and the Rise of Black Political Power* (Urbana: University of Illinois Press, 2002); Wilbur C. Rich, *Coleman Young and Detroit Politics* (Detroit: Wayne State University Press, 1989); William J. Grimshaw, *Bitter Fruit: Black Politics and the Chicago Machine, 1931-1991* (Chicago: University of Chicago Press, 1992); Lisa Gail Materson, "Respectable Partisans: African American Women in Electoral Politics, 1877 to 1936" (Ph.D. diss., University of California at Los Angeles, 2001); and Christopher Manning, "The Ties That Bind: William L. Dawson and the Limits of Electoral Politics, 1942-1970" (Ph.D. diss., Northwestern University, 2003).

13. Thomas J. Sugrue, *The Origins of the Urban Crisis: Race and Inequality in Postwar Detroit* (Princeton, NJ: Princeton University Press, 1996).

14. Farah Jasmine Griffin, *"Who Set You Flowin'?" The African-American Migration Narrative* (New York: Oxford University Press, 1995); and Lawrence R. Rodgers, *Canaan Bound: The African-American Great Migration Novel* (Urbana: University of Illinois Press, 1997).

A

AAA *See* Agricultural Adjustment Administration (AAA)

ABB *See* African Blood Brotherhood (ABB)

Abbott, Robert S. (1870–1940)

From the day Robert S. Abbott published the first issue of the American American newspaper the ***Chicago Defender*** to the day he died, he was subjected to almost constant public scrutiny. Some saw him as a prophet leading southern blacks to the northern "promised land." Others, like black nationalist leader **Marcus Garvey**, pronounced him a lying traitor responsible for dragging black America through the muck. Both camps, however, recognized that he had the power to influence millions.

Interestingly, however, nothing about Abbott's early childhood suggested that he would become one of the most influential blacks in American history. He was raised on the outskirts of Savannah, Georgia, by his mother and stepfather. By 1887, at the age of seventeen, Abbott began his college career at Claflin College in Orangeburg, South Carolina, and two years later he matriculated at Hampton Institute to study printing.

After graduation Abbott, now twenty-six, headed for **Chicago** in search of the American Dream. After a few encounters with racial discrimination in the workforce, Abbott made the watershed decision to start his own newspaper in Chicago and become self-sufficient.

The first issue of the *Defender* appeared on May 5, 1905. Three hundred copies were printed at a cost of $13.75. These early issues were handbill size and consisted of only four pages. Abbott was the sole writer, editor, investigative journalist, and newsboy. For the first four years of the *Defender*'s publication, it remained a relatively unknown and struggling paper. In 1909, however, things began to change.

First, Abbott tapped into what the masses wanted to read—muckraking crusades. Then, with the new growth in readership, Abbott began investing profits back into the paper. He hired additional writers, expanded distribution, increased advertising, and reorganized and restructured the form and content of his paper. By 1919 the *Defender* was selling 230,000 copies a week to more than 1,452 towns and cities across America—far and away the most read black newspaper in the nation.

Abbott's contribution to the development, popularity, and distribution of the **black press** in America, however, was not his only salient accomplishment during this period. Equally noteworthy was his contribution to America's first Great Black Migration. For almost three years, from 1917 through the summer of 1919, Abbott and his paper fervently called for discontented blacks to leave their oppressive South and come to the "Land of Hope" in the North. Commenting on the impact that Abbott's paper had on this mass expansion, Carl Sandburg observed that the *Defender*, more than any other agency or institution, precipitated the black exodus from the South. White newspaper editors throughout the South, worried about the loss of cheap black labor in the region, repeatedly denounced the *Defender* as a disturbing source of outside agitation and social unrest. Even the U.S. Department of Labor credited Abbott's newspaper for being more effective in carrying off southern black workers than all the **labor agents** put together.

The **Chicago race riot of 1919**, fueled by returning soldiers anxious to reaffirm the prewar, premigration caste system, became the coup de grâce of Abbott's campaign. It was clear to him that many of the same problems that existed in the South were also present in the North. Consequently, Abbott, in good conscience, could no longer portray Chicago as the "promised land." It simply became another place where the black American Dream was deferred. Until his death in 1940, Robert S. Abbott continued to fight for the rights of working black Americans and remained an active leader in the black Chicago community he helped create. *See also* Associated Negro Press (ANP); Simmons, Roscoe Conkling; Primary Documents 7, 11, 65.

Further Reading

DeSantis, Alan D. "A Forgotten Leader: Robert S. Abbott and the *Chicago Defender* from 1910-1920." *Journalism History* 23, no. 2 (1997): 63–71.

Grossman, James R. *Land of Hope: Chicago, Black Southerners, and the Great Migration*. Chicago: University of Chicago Press, 1989.

Ottley, Roi. *The Lonely Warrior: The Life and Times of Robert S. Abbott*. Chicago: Henry Regnery Co., 1955.

Ross, Felicia G. Jones, and Joseph P. McKerns. "Depression in 'The Promised Land': The *Chicago Defender* Discourages Migration, 1929-1940." *American Journalism* 21, no. 1 (2004): 55–73.

Alan D. DeSantis

AFL *See* American Federation of Labor (AFL)

African Blood Brotherhood (ABB)

The African Blood Brotherhood, or ABB, as it is sometimes called, was the first independent **socialist/Communist** organization composed exclusively of persons of African descent in the United States. Very little is known about the ABB, yet it was an unusual Afro-Marxist organization established in **New York City**'s Harlem within a sociopolitical climate influenced by the Great Black Migration, World War I, dissension within the white socialist movement, a rift between Harlem's African American and West Indian socialists, a renaissance among Harlem's African American intellectuals, and the popular **Universal Negro Improvement Association** led by **Marcus Garvey**. The migration of southern African Americans to the urban, industrial cities of the North and Midwest, along with the first wave of West Indian immigration, not only brought a shift in population but significantly altered African American social, political, and cultural consciousness and transformed African Americans into what **Howard University** professor **Alain Locke** described as the "**New Negro**."

Within this milieu, **Cyril V. Briggs**, a West Indian immigrant and publisher of the *Crusader* magazine, organized the African Blood Brotherhood. It is unclear exactly when the organization was initiated, but the date is somewhere between 1917 and 1919. Briggs established the ABB as a revolutionary secret organization along the lines of a **fraternal order** specifically for men and women of African descent. But the organization came to public attention as a result of its interaction with Marcus Garvey's Universal Negro Improvement Association and its implication in the **Tulsa, Oklahoma**, race riot of 1921.

The purpose and program of the ABB was the liberation of Africa and people of African descent and the redemption of the African race. The program espoused racial pride, **black nationalism**, pan-Africanism, and the economic nature of the African American struggle, which it linked to colonialism and imperialism.

In addition to these precepts, the ABB's program advocated the organization of African American unions, opposition to the **Ku Klux Klan**, industrial development, higher wages, shorter work hours, better living conditions, education, cooperation with other darker peoples and revolutionary class-conscious white workers, and a united African American front. The ABB also put forward the idea of a secret protective military cell for defensive purposes.

Although the ABB began as an independent organization, by 1921 it had established close ties with the Communist Party. Several of the ABB members later joined the Communist Party. By 1925, as one-time ABB member Harry Haywood recalled, "the Brotherhood had ceased to exist as an autonomous organized expression of the national revolutionary trend" (Haywood, 126).

What set the African Blood Brotherhood apart from other political organizations of the time was its combination of revolutionary black nationalism with Marxism and Communism. The ABB was also an extension of the radical black nationalist tradition and a precursor of the revolutionary black nationalism of the mid-1960s and early 1970s, which saw such organizations as the **Black Panther Party**, the Black Liberation Army, the Symbionese Liberation Army, the Revolutionary Action Movement, and the Republic of New Africa adopt many of the program elements of the ABB. *See also* Caribbean Migration; Harlem Renaissance; Harrison, Hubert Henry; *Messenger*; Owen, Chandler; Political Activism (1915–1945); Randolph, Asa Philip.

Further Reading

Cruse, Harold. *The Crisis of the Negro Intellectual.* New York: Morrow, 1967.
Haywood, Harry. *Black Bolshevik: Autobiography of an Afro-American Communist.* Chicago: Liberator Press, 1978.
Kuykendall, Ronald A. "African Blood Brotherhood, Independent Marxist during the Harlem Renaissance." *Western Journal of Black Studies* 26 (2002): 16–21.
Vincent, Theodore G. *Black Power and the Garvey Movement.* San Francisco: Ramparts Press, 1971.
———. "The *Crusader* Monthly's Black Nationalist Support for the Jazz Age." *Afro-Americans in New York Life and History* 15 (1991): 63–76.

Ronald A. Kuykendall

African Methodist Episcopal (AME) Church

The African Methodist Episcopal (AME) Church is the oldest black independent church in the United States. Founded by free people of color in **Philadelphia** in the aftermath of the American Revolution, the church blossomed in the nineteenth century into the premier African American institution in the nation, with more than half a million members, spread across every American state and mission fields as far afield as Haiti and South Africa. Yet in the first decades of the twentieth century the church lost much of its primacy, largely because of its inability to adapt to the new circumstances created by the Great Migration.

The AME Church's origins reach back to 1792, when black Methodists in Philadelphia walked out of the city's St. George's Methodist Church in protest against an attempt to segregate them in a newly constructed gallery. Word of the Philadelphians' action quickly spread, sparking similar walkouts in other cities. In 1816 leaders of several black Methodist congregations in Pennsylvania, Maryland, Delaware, and New Jersey formally seceded from the white Methodist Episcopal Church and chartered a denomination of their own, the AME Church.

African Methodism grew steadily in the antebellum years, attracting adherents from all along the eastern seaboard, as well as from the scattered free black communities in the Midwest. The AME Church also boasted a short-lived congregation in Charleston, South Carolina, but it was closed by authorities in 1822 after the abortive Denmark Vesey slave uprising. The religious culture that developed within the church reflected the convictions and priorities of these embattled free people of color. Church leaders stressed the importance of education and of the classical Methodist virtues of self-discipline, temperance, and industry, qualities vital to the survival of a despised, impoverished population. They also placed great emphasis on respectability and on maintaining order and decorum in worship in order to demonstrate to skeptical whites the capacity of black people to manage their own affairs soberly and responsibly.

The coming of the Civil War presented the AME Church with new opportunities and new challenges. As the Union army pushed southward, AME
missionaries followed in its wake, organizing congregations and schools, dis-
pensing the sacraments, and solemnizing the marriages of formerly enslaved
men and women. For the freedpeople, the opportunity to worship in churches of their own, free from white supervision, was a crucial dimension of
freedom, and they flocked to the new church. In the space of just thirty years,
total church membership increased tenfold to more than 500,000. Georgia
alone was host to more than 100,000 African Methodists.

The church's spread across the South had a profound effect on the social
and religious lives of the freedpeople, as well as on the institutional face of
African Methodism. Former slaves, many of whom were accustomed to wor-
shiping in small, secret cells, entered a structured, hierarchical institution
whose traditions of educated leadership, respectability, and decorous worship
were alien to their own experiences and sensibilities. Northern church leaders, in turn, were distinctly uneasy with the enthusiastic worship styles that
prevailed among the freedpeople, with their shouting, dancing, and "weird
singing." Tensions between northerners and southerners remained a signature
feature of the AME Church, flaring anew during the Great Migration.

The Great Migration wrought profound changes in African American
Christianity in general and in the AME Church in particular. The influx of new
migrants, many with no experience of urban life, strained the resources of
existing churches and opened new gulfs of class, education, and experience
within northern congregations. The migration also coincided with and contributed to an ongoing process of secularization, which challenged the
church's primacy in black life. New forms of association and recreation, from
political machines to music halls, competed with the church for African
Americans' patronage and scarce resources. The challenge was especially
acute for the AME Church, which saw its southern heartland depopulated. In
South Carolina alone, more than 100 AME congregations were abandoned in
the years between 1916 and 1926. In all, the church lost nearly half its
southern adherents to migration.

AME Church leaders were slow to respond to these new circumstances.
Even as southern **ministers** reported declines in church membership of 80
percent and more, the AME House of Bishops urged black southerners to
remain where they were. "We beg to advise you who are still in the South to
remain on the farms, and buy small or large tracts of land while you can, and
practice honesty, industry, and frugality," advised Bishop Benjamin F. Lee in
1916 (Campbell, 297). In **Chicago** a group of AME ministers signed a letter
warning would-be migrants of the rigors of northern life, including the cold
weather. Such advice reflected abiding American concerns about the perils
of urban life for simple rural folk, but it also revealed a distinct note of ambivalence about southern migrants among black northerners, who feared that
the influx of rural migrants would inflame white prejudice and endanger their
own social positions.

While most church leaders viewed the migration with unease, a few saw
in it the seeds of a better future for African Americans, as well as of new
opportunities for ministry for the church. Probably the most conspicuous

example was **Reverdy Ransom**, a maverick minister and pioneer of the black Social Gospel. In the early twentieth century Ransom had braved the opposition of local and national AME leaders to found Chicago's Institutional AME Church, a church and social service agency designed to serve the needs of new urban migrants. In addition to a 2,000-seat tabernacle, Institutional Church boasted an employment bureau, a day-care center, and a **settlement house**, modeled on Jane Addams's nearby Hull House. The migration presented "obligations and opportunities which can neither be avoided or ignored," Ransom told fellow African Methodists. "The church must create new forms of service and new lines of activity to meet the instant demands of a new situation" (Gregg, 197).

The debate among AME leaders was recapitulated at the local level, with individual ministers and congregations reacting in different ways to the migration. Some churches strove to make the new arrivals feel welcome, offering housing and employment assistance and adapting music and preaching styles to appeal to southern sensibilities. Other churches, however, refused to adapt, maintaining existing modes of worship and treating new migrants with indifference, even disdain. Not surprisingly, many migrants responded by taking refuge in other churches—in **Baptist** churches or any of the multiplying number of so-called **storefront churches** sprouting in the burgeoning black **ghettos** of northern cities. In such institutions, southern migrants found the kind of warmth and spirited music and preaching to which they were accustomed. While these defections did not endanger the church's survival, they did lead, in the words of a recent historian, to "declining numbers . . . and a palpable loss of social prestige" (Best, 121). *See also* Great Migration, Black Opposition to; Turner, Henry McNeal; Wright, Richard Robert, Jr.

Further Reading

Best, Wallace. *Passionately Human, No Less Divine: Religion and Culture in Black Chicago, 1915–1952.* Princeton, NJ: Princeton University Press, 2005.

Campbell, James T. *Songs of Zion: The African Methodist Episcopal Church in the United States and South Africa.* New York: Oxford University Press, 1995.

Gregg, Robert. *Sparks from the Anvil of Oppression: Philadelphia's African Methodists and Southern Migrants, 1890–1940.* Philadelphia: Temple University Press, 1993.

Walker, Clarence. *A Rock in a Weary Land: The African Methodist Episcopal Church during the Civil War and Reconstruction.* Baton Rouge: Louisiana State University Press, 1982.

James T. Campbell

Agricultural Adjustment Administration (AAA)

During the first 100 days of his administration in 1933, President Franklin D. Roosevelt signed into law the Agricultural Adjustment Act, a measure designed to revitalize American agriculture. Housed within the Department of Agriculture and administered by Secretary of Agriculture Henry Wallace, the Agricultural Adjustment Administration (AAA) was a federal crop-reduction

program that paid farmers to voluntarily reduce the acreage that they cultivated in order to raise the price of agricultural produce. In the South, particularly in the **Mississippi Delta**, planters manipulated the program at the local
level and controlled its benefits at the expense of their sharecroppers and
tenant farmers. The AAA thus strengthened agribusiness interests in the South,
further displaced sharecroppers, and hastened the mechanization of agriculture. Evicted from their land in the midst of the Great Depression, sharecroppers and tenant farmers, particularly African Americans, were reduced to
migrant, agricultural day laborers.

Under the AAA, Congress paid farmers in an attempt to equalize their
purchasing power. These payments were "parity" or subsidy checks. Under
the provisions of the legislation, parity checks were issued to farmers to balance the supply and demand of certain agricultural crops like corn, wheat,
peanuts, cotton, tobacco, and milk. Congress encouraged farmers to limit
the acreage used for these staple crops by also giving them money to diversify.

In 1936, under the Soil Conservation and Domestic Allotment Act, Congress
encouraged conservation of resources by paying benefits for planting soil-
building crops. Thus, by diversifying crops and rewarding farmers for doing
so, the administration was able to generate income for farmers. The program
paid nearly $1.5 billion in benefits to farmers by the end of 1936. However,
in the Supreme Court decision *United States v. Butler* (1936), this practice of
"parity" was deemed unconstitutional because one group was taxed to pay
another group. Thus a revised form of the AAA funded by general taxation was
enacted in 1938.

The most important revision to the AAA was the ability of Congress to make
loans to farmers on staple crops in years of high yields. They could store the
surplus produce and release it in years of low harvests. The Soil Conservation
Act was still actively participated in, and farmers could even have a say in
establishing quotas of certain staple crops. Even critics of the New Deal
programs acknowledge that the Agricultural Adjustment Administration gave
farmers hope in a time of despair. Farmers all across the country were struggling to make ends meet, and the AAA gave them an opportunity to live with a
sense of dignity.

Despite the intended goals and these accomplishments, New Deal agricultural policies favored agribusiness over the interests of small-scale farmers and
especially tenants and sharecroppers. Administration of the AAA was left to
local committees composed of extension service agents, planters, and county
officials. Localized control empowered planters to withhold parity payments
from their tenants and sharecroppers. Under the provisions of the act, planters were required to share federal payments with their renters, giving half the
payments to sharecroppers and three-fourths of the payments to tenants.
Planters resorted to myriad tactics to deceive and intimidate illiterate tenants
into signing over their subsidy payments to landlords. In many cases, landowners simply plowed under all the land rented to a sharecropper, evicted
the cropper, kept the full subsidy payment, and then hired the tenants back
as wage workers with whom they would not have to share subsidy payments.

The results were devastating to the sharecroppers of the Delta. In Arkansas, Mississippi, and the bootheel region of Missouri, the displacement of tenant farmers was dramatic. Some estimates put the decline of tenant sharecropping in the Mississippi Delta during the 1930s at 40 percent. During the same time the Delta's wealthiest landowners enriched themselves on federal parity payments. According to a U.S. Senate committee in 1936, planters in Arkansas received $2.1 million in subsidy payments between 1933 and 1936, and planters in Mississippi received $2.5 million.

Sharecroppers and tenant farmers in the region did not accept these changes without a fight. In 1934 white and black tenant farmers organized the **Southern Tenant Farmers' Union**. The union demanded that federal parity payments be made directly to sharecroppers and tenants rather than to landowners, and it proposed a series of reforms to grant greater security and protection from eviction to sharecroppers and tenants in farm rental contracts. Sharecroppers in Missouri staged a vigorous protest in 1939. In January the Reverend Owen Whitfield organized approximately 2,000 black and white sharecroppers along Missouri Highways 60 and 61 to raise awareness of their dismal situation. The protest captured national attention. Even First Lady Eleanor Roosevelt wrote about the plight of the sharecroppers in her column, "My Day." Eventually Whitfield was able to establish a farming cooperative at Cropperville, and ten others followed under the **Farm Security Administration**. These farming co-ops closed after World War II when African Americans continued to migrate to the urban North and West.

But the tenant farmers had few allies and were unable to influence meaningful change in federal agricultural policy. New Deal farm programs, followed by the mechanization of agriculture during World War II, unleashed a reorganization of farm operations that ultimately displaced millions of small-scale farmers, tenants, sharecroppers, and wage hands. Many of these refugees from southern agriculture eventually joined the Great Migration, heading for destinations north and west. *See also* Cotton Belt; Demographic Patterns of the Great Black Migration (1915–1940); Demographic Patterns of the Great Black Migration (1940–1970); Mechanical Cotton Harvester.

Further Reading

Daniel, Pete. *Breaking the Land: The Transformation of Cotton, Tobacco, and Rice Cultures since 1880.* Urbana: University of Illinois Press, 1985.

Fite, Gilbert. *Cotton Fields No More: Southern Agriculture, 1865–1980.* Lexington: University Press of Kentucky, 1984.

Kirby, Jack Temple. *Rural Worlds Lost: The American South, 1920–1960.* Baton Rouge: Louisiana State University Press, 1987.

Oh Freedom after While: The Missouri Sharecropper Protest of 1939. Directed by Steven John Ross. Produced by Lynn Rubright and Candace O'Connor. Narrated by Julian Bond. 56 minutes. California Newsreel, 1999. Videocassette.

Saloutos, Theodore. *The American Farmer and the New Deal.* Ames: Iowa State University Press, 1982.

Delia C. Gillis

Alexander, Sadie Tanner Mossell (1898–1989)

Sadie Tanner Mossell Alexander was born in **Philadelphia, Pennsylvania**, on January 2, 1898, into a prominent African American family. She was raised in **Washington, D.C.**, where she attended the M Street Public School. Aaron Mossell, her father, was the first African American to receive a law degree from the University of Pennsylvania. Benjamin Tucker Tanner, her grandfather, was a bishop in the **African Methodist Episcopal Church** and edited the *African Methodist Episcopal Review*. Painter **Henry Ossawa Tanner** was her uncle. In 1916, as black southerners first migrated north to her birthplace in Philadelphia, Alexander entered the University of Pennsylvania, to study education. She completed her undergraduate degree in 1918. Before the next wave of migrants to her city in 1922–1924, she obtained an M.A. and a Ph.D. in economics in 1919 and 1921, respectively. In 1927 she took a law degree as a member of the *University of Pennsylvania Law Review*. Although Alexander held the elitist view that southern migrants would set back the progress of Philadelphia's African American community, her life as a scholar, practicing lawyer, and civic leader helped make their lives better.

Alexander's concern about the acculturation of southern black migrants emerged with her 1921 doctoral work "The Standard of Living among One Hundred Negro Migrant Families in Philadelphia," published in the *Annals of the American Academy of Political and Social Science* (1921). Modeled on **W.E.B. DuBois**'s *The Philadelphia Negro* (1899), Alexander's investigation analyzed data collected from postwar migrants in Philadelphia about their **housing**, employment, earnings, and household expenditures to assess their material needs and formulate strategies for their acculturation. Continuing her scholarly interest in the living conditions of southern migrants, Alexander investigated their health care and in 1923 published her *Study of the Negro Tuberculosis Problem in Philadelphia*. In 1935, with her husband, Raymond Pace Alexander, with whom she practiced law and who would in 1951 become Philadelphia's first African American trial judge, Alexander challenged the "Colored Only" sections of Philadelphia's movie theaters. They also aided in drafting the Pennsylvania state public accommodation law.

Actively practicing law in Philadelphia during the migration after World War II, in 1946 Alexander accepted President Harry Truman's appointment to the Commission to Study the Civil Rights of All Races and Faiths. Here her earlier interest in the living conditions of southern migrants took shape in a national concern with the social, economic, and educational aspects of civil rights. The commission's report, *To Secure These Rights* (1948), recommended **desegregation** of the armed services. For Philadelphia's black migrant community through the 1960s, housing discrimination remained a serious concern. Public hearings about the growth of Philadelphia's nonwhite households anticipated the emergence of a city with a predominantly African American population. From 1950 to 1967, no doubt concerned with keeping African Americans in the mainstream of American society, Alexander served as a member of the Philadelphia Commission on Human Relations and for a period was the commission's chair. Alexander practiced law until she was eighty-five years old. She died on November 6, 1989, in Philadelphia. *See also* Attorneys; Civil Rights Movement; Women.

Further Reading

Mossell, Sadie Tanner. "The Standard of Living among One Hundred Negro Migrant Families in Philadelphia." *Annals of the American Academy of Political and Social Science* 98 (November 1921): 173–218.

————. *A Study of the Negro Tuberculosis Problem in Philadelphia*. Philadelphia: Henry Phipps Institute, 1923.

Trotter, Joe William, Jr., and Eric Ledell Smith, eds. *African Americans in Pennsylvania: Shifting Historical Perspectives*. Harrisburg: Pennsylvania Historical and Museum Commission; University Park: Pennsylvania State University Press, 1997.

Michael Benjamin

Ali, Muhammad (1942–)

The roots of Muhammad Ali's transformation from gifted boxer to racial protest figure were intertwined with the Great Migration. Ali's relocation during the late 1960s to **Chicago** from his hometown of **Louisville, Kentucky**, put into geographic terms the cultural changes that had been building within the fighter's life for several years. The most recognizable symbol of this conversion was the boxer's name change from Cassius Marcellus Clay, after the white, nineteenth-century Kentucky legislator and antislavery crusader, to Muhammad Ali.

For Muhammad Ali, the key factor in this alteration was the **Nation of Islam**, a religious sect that tailored Muslim theology to a black American context. Led by **Elijah Muhammad**, who had come to **Detroit** from Georgia in 1923 to seek employment, the Nation of Islam became a site for new southern migrants to make sense of northern cities they mistakenly had perceived as lands of opportunity. In particular, Muhammad's ascendancy to the head of the organization and subsequent relocation to Chicago in 1934 after the disappearance of founder W. D. Fard positioned it to become a receiving ground for wayward migrants who had arrived in that city in response to promises of work issued by the *Chicago Defender*.

During the 1950s and 1960s the Nation of Islam served as a northern alternative to the southern **civil rights movement**. Although nonviolent political protest was a standard of black resistance for some, others insisted that the ideas and tactics adopted by civil rights leaders were not appropriate to tackle the problems faced by black Americans who had moved north, particularly poverty and **unemployment**. However, there was also common ground between civil rights protesters and their urban counterparts, and Muhammad Ali's draft resistance during the Vietnam War helped strengthen such alignments. Like **Martin Luther King** and other southern **ministers**, Ali's opposition to the conflict was rooted in sacred tradition. Elijah Muhammad had spent four years in prison for his refusal to be drafted during World War II, and members of the Nation of Islam were taught to serve only in holy wars.

The management and promotion of Ali's boxing career also reflected a migration of sorts from southern to northern sensibilities. Following a gold-medal performance in the 1960 Olympics, Ali had been signed to a six-year contract by the Louisville Sponsoring Group, an all-white and old-moneyed syndicate of Kentucky millionaires. Although Ali's biographers have described the relationship as beneficial to Ali, the fighter blasted the arrangement in his 1975 autobiography, *The Greatest*. In 1966 Ali terminated his contract with the Louisville Sponsoring Group and formed Main Bout, a Nation of Islam–led corporation that sought to create a network that would position large numbers of blacks to share the revenues generated by Ali's championship matches. This move from white southern financing of his title bouts to an emphasis on black economic autonomy reflected a larger movement by African Americans during the late 1960s away from southern integrationist political protest strategies toward northern black nationalist economic initiatives. *See also* Johnson, Jack; Louis, Joe; Sport.

Further Reading

Ali, Muhammad, with Richard Durham. *The Greatest: My Own Story*. New York: Random House, 1975.

Evanzz, Karl. *The Messenger: The Rise and Fall of Elijah Muhammad*. New York: Pantheon Books, 1999.

Hauser, Thomas. *Muhammad Ali: His Life and Times*. New York: Touchstone, 1991.

Michael Ezra

AME *See* African Methodist Episcopal (AME) Church

American Federation of Labor (AFL)

The Great Migration transformed African Americans and, in the process, forced the American Federation of Labor (AFL) to evolve. Ultimately, the American labor movement became far more inclusive, thereby better representing the interests of not just African Americans but all workers. Although it is not well known, the African American struggle for equality within the labor movement is an integral component of the **civil rights movement**. The Great Migration was central in this battle, providing both numbers and passion.

In 1900 the AFL was a typical white institution: most members were racist, and the organization itself treated blacks as second-class. In theory, the AFL refused to tolerate affiliated unions that closed their doors to blacks. In practice, the AFL allowed unions to do so or practice "**Jim Crow** unionism," maintaining segregated locals, particularly in the South. Black workers grudgingly accepted this situation, but inevitably the practice reemphasized race consciousness over interracial working-class solidarity. However, some black workers, especially outside the South, refused to accept segregated unionism, forming independent black unions or refusing to join any. The most important exception was the United Mine Workers of America (UMWA), which counted many thousands of black members and gave them greater opportunities, if not equality, within the union. Yet despite the UMWA and open membership policies in the longshoremen's, cigar, and clothing unions, most AFL unions practiced exclusion. Although blacks were about 12 percent of the nation's population and overwhelmingly working class, they made up less than 3 percent of the AFL.

Amid the Great Migration, the AFL seriously considered black inclusion only when their numbers demanded it. AFL unionists generally acted with hostility and prejudice to the migration; as early as 1916, white unionists at the AFL national convention labeled black migrants a profound threat. Furthermore, most southern black migrants had no experience with unions and were desperate to find work. Their actions only confirmed preexisting prejudices, so that *black* and *scab* became synonyms to many white workers. Many of the era's antiblack race riots were sparked by job competition, among them the 1917 **East St. Louis race riot** that left at least thirty-nine blacks dead. To organize black workers in crafts where AFL unions excluded them, the AFL chartered "federal locals" that directly belonged to it rather than the constituent craft union. These locals had less power (namely, to demand the prevailing union wage, because the AFL rarely heeded black demands), but black unionists accepted this alternative as temporary and better than a nonunion shop.

A look at a few cases helps illuminate conflicts in the era. In 1919 a strike shook the **Chicago** stockyards and an even larger, national strike rocked the steel industry. In both instances northern blacks, with experience in industry and unionism, supported the strikes; however, southern migrants, following black middle-class leadership and suspicious of white workers, had few compunctions about scabbing. The well-known **Chicago race riot** in July 1919 was fueled, at least partially, by the former conflict. Similarly, in the 1920s there were perhaps a thousand black longshoremen in **New York**, the overwhelming majority of whom had arrived during the Great Migration. The International Longshoremen's Association (ILA) admitted some blacks, who held no power in the union and still struggled to find work. These blacks resoundingly supported unionization but attributed their admission to their white counterparts' fear of black strikebreakers, not the ILA's commitment to equality.

The best-known black union in the AFL was the **Brotherhood of Sleeping Car Porters** (BSCP), and its relationship was typically rocky. Blacks long had played an important role in **railroads**, but unions retained strict bars against admitting blacks. Founded in 1925 under the leadership of **A. Philip Randolph** and Milton Webster, the BSCP fought a viciously antiunion employer for more than a decade before securing its first contract. The Brotherhood also was prevented by craft unions from receiving an international charter, so the AFL created thirteen federal union locals. It was not until 1936 that the BSCP received independent standing.

The AFL underwent profound changes during the Great Depression. Led by the UMWA, the AFL tapped into the surging energy of the American working class to unionize mass-production industries. Soon many of these new unions broke with the AFL and formed the rival **Congress of Industrial Organizations** (CIO). Alas for the quest of black equality in the AFL, many of the unions most committed to black equality, along with most black unionists, left with the CIO. Crucially, as a craft, not an industrial, union, the BSCP remained in the AFL. Further, the ILA retained large numbers of blacks in its ranks. In fact, when CIO organizers tried to persuade black longshoremen in **New Orleans** to realign, the black dockers stuck with the ILA.

During the 1940s blacks inside and outside the AFL pressured the federal government for a fair share of jobs in the burgeoning defense industries. As the nation geared up for war, Randolph castigated the federal government for its failure to open up jobs, becoming the undeniable national leader of African Americans' economic interests. After Randolph threatened to bring many thousands of blacks to a march on Washington in 1941, President Franklin D. Roosevelt issued an executive order outlawing racial discrimination in all defense-related industrial work, a landmark. Blacks simultaneously found new doors open to them in the working world yet continued suffering from discrimination. Nevertheless, the gains far outweighed the problems, and blacks consistently sought to unionize whenever possible.

Not as well known among the public, African Americans, veterans and others, fully intended after World War II to push for full equality. Struggles were touched off over voting and workplace issues almost immediately, but the onset of the Cold War chilled the possibilities for social change for at least a decade. As part of this initial wave of rebellion, black longshoremen in New York challenged the openly racist ILA leadership, which predictably attempted to red-bait the protesters and pit Irish and Italian members against black ones. Black unionists were forced to wait yet again.

In 1955, after twenty years of bitter feuding, the AFL and CIO merged into the AFL-CIO. With unification, hundreds of thousands more blacks found themselves in the new alliance. Now there were African Americans from the **steelworkers'**, miners', and other unions. Crucially, the more conservative and less racially progressive AFL dominated the new organization. George Meany, an Irish American plumber from the Bronx, was the first AFL-CIO president. His administration was not sympathetic to the civil rights movement, despite its rhetoric.

Thus black activists formed caucuses within their unions in order to press for equal treatment. For instance, while blacks made up a large percentage of the steelworkers, they found themselves locked into jobs with lower pay, more risk, and fewer skilled positions, while they were trapped on segregated seniority lists. Blacks had suffered such inequities in the rural South, but now many of these migrants, inspired by the democratic rhetoric of World War II, stood up. However, when blacks sought to bring civil rights into the labor movement, they experienced "massive resistance" in northern, allegedly liberal communities. Randolph, the unrivaled leader of all black unionists, continued pressuring the organization but famously was taunted by Meany in 1959, "Who the hell appointed you as the guardian of all the Negroes in America?" Subsequently Randolph formed the Negro American Labor Council to caucus within the organization. Thanks to black activism and important white allies, the AFL-CIO endorsed the civil rights agenda of the 1960s and was instrumental in getting the Civil Rights Act of 1964, including Title VII, passed.

In the 1960s and beyond, African American unionists and migrants faced a cruel fate. Just as they achieved a greater measure of equality in their unions, thanks to decades of activism and increased numbers, America's manufacturing economy was beginning its long and now-familiar slide. Thus black unionists in steel, coal, meatpacking, railroads, and other fields found themselves competing for jobs in a shrinking market because of automation and economic restructuring. This situation was particularly dire in industrial cities where hundreds of thousands of African Americans had migrated in previous decades and continued to. Cities like **Detroit**, Chicago, Youngstown, **Gary**, and others that had lured blacks with the promise of higher-paying jobs and no Jim Crow were in the midst of collapse. Black workers remained committed to the AFL-CIO. It was just that by 1970 there was less to be committed to.

Nevertheless, African Americans had transformed the American labor movement and remained a higher percentage of the AFL-CIO's membership than their percentage of the general population. African Americans had struggled mightily within the AFL and later the AFL-CIO for an equal place. Though often left out of traditional narratives of the modern civil rights movement, black union struggles were central to the movement's larger goals. Indeed, as civil rights activists achieved their political goal of tearing down legal segregation, they increasingly realized that economic empowerment for the overwhelmingly working-class black community could be achieved only through unionism. Often that meant first fighting their white coworkers to get into the union or be treated fairly within it. The ongoing Great Migration provided the needed shock troops and much of the passion in this part of the freedom struggle. *See also* March on Washington Movement (MOWM); Organized Labor; Packinghouse Workers and Unions; Strikebreaking; Primary Document 38.

Further Reading

Arnesen, Eric. *Brotherhoods of Color: Black Railroad Workers and the Struggle for Equality*. Cambridge, MA: Harvard University Press, 2001.

Barrett, James R. *Work and Community in the Jungle: Chicago's Packinghouse Workers, 1894–1922*. Urbana: University of Illinois Press, 1987.

Bracey, John H., Jr., August Meier, and Elliott Rudwick, eds. *Black Workers and Organized Labor*. Belmont, CA: Wadsworth, 1971.

Foner, Philip S. *History of the Labor Movement in the United States*. Vol. 2, *From the Founding of the American Federation of Labor to the Emergence of American Imperialism*. 2nd ed. New York: International Publishers, 1975.

———. *Organized Labor and the Black Worker, 1619–1973*. New York: Praeger, 1974.

Grossman, James R. *Land of Hope: Chicago, Black Southerners, and the Great Migration*. Chicago: University of Chicago Press, 1989.

Halpern, Rick. *Down on the Killing Floor: Black and White Workers in Chicago's Packinghouses, 1904–54*. Urbana: University of Illinois Press, 1997.

Harris, William. *Keeping the Faith: A. Philip Randolph, Milton P. Webster, and the Brotherhood of Sleeping Car Porters, 1925–37*. Urbana: University of Illinois Press, 1977.

Nelson, Bruce. *Divided We Stand: American Workers and the Struggle for Black Equality*. Princeton, NJ: Princeton University Press, 2001.

Spero, Sterling D., and Abram L. Harris. *The Black Worker: The Negro and the Labor Movement*. 1931. Reprint, New York: Atheneum, 1968.

Peter Cole

American Negro Exposition (1940)

The American Negro Exposition (also known as the Afra-Merican Emancipation Exposition, the Diamond Jubilee Exposition, and the Negro World's Fair) was held in **Chicago, Illinois**, from July 4 to September 2, 1940. Over 200,000 people traveled to the Chicago Coliseum to celebrate the seventy-fifth anniversary of the Thirteenth Amendment to the U.S. Constitution. Exhibits included largely optimistic descriptions of African Americans' gradual economic and political progress since emancipation, as well as the **Henry Ossawa Tanner** Art Exhibit and a nightclub, Tropics after Dark, which staged nightly performances of theater pieces written by Arna Bontemps and **Langston Hughes**. New Deal agencies were the single most prominent institutions at the fair, but the main hall also included exhibits from African American newspapers, civic and business associations, and churches, as well as presentations by most states in the nation and Liberia. In addition, dioramas and murals memorialized African Americans' achievements in politics, art, the press, the military, and **sports**. Altogether, the exhibits provide an important view into sociologists', politicians', and artists' perspectives on African American migration.

The exposition reflected Chicago's cultural importance during what has been described as the **Chicago Renaissance**, a unique period when the Popular Front combination of labor and civil rights activism connected with black entrepreneurialism. The exposition brought together the main players in this renaissance: the federal government, social scientists, and numerous African American writers and artists.

The New Deal exhibits, the Social Science Exhibit, and the Tanner Art Exhibit offered three different sources for perspectives on black migration. Through the Department of Agriculture's display, Illinois representative **Arthur W. Mitchell**—the first African American elected to the House as a Democrat and the sponsor of the bill that allocated $75,000 in federal funds to the exposition—and Secretary of Agriculture Henry A. Wallace argued that African Americans ought to return to or remain in the South to take advantage of ostensible technological innovations and political reform in the region. On the other hand, sociologist **E. Franklin Frazier** constructed the Social Science Exhibit, which argued that life was better for migrants in the North, but that the migration itself created challenges that compounded slavery's destructive legacies. Reflecting his arguments in *The Negro Family in the United States* (1939), the exhibit pointed to the need for black families to rise above the damaging legacies of slavery and rural "backwardness" to reform the two-parent patriarchal family. Finally, the Tanner Art Exhibit included dozens of pieces that demonstrated the diversity of African Americans' experiences and achievements while at least indirectly contradicting the New Deal and sociological messages. Works such as Charles White's *There Were No Crops This Year* (1940) and Hale Woodruff's *By Parties Unknown* (1938), for example, dramatized the violence and poverty that made a back-to-the-farm movement untenable and caused many people to migrate. **Jacob Lawrence**'s series of paintings portraying the Haitian Revolution, *The Life* of *Toussaint L'Ouverture* (1938), suggested black peasants' revolutionary potential, contrary to sociological descriptions of backward rural African Americans. Elizabeth Catlett's prize-winning sculpture *Mother and Child* (1940) presented a remarkable alternative to the images of the black matriarchy as a source of social pathology. *See also* Black Consumer Market; Chicago School of Sociology (CSS); Visual Arts, the Great Migration in.

Further Reading

Bontemps, Arna, ed. *Cavalcade of the American Negro.* Chicago: Diamond Jubilee Exposition Authority, 1940.

"Cavalcade of the American Negro." The African American Mosaic. A Library of Congress Resource Guide for the Study of Black History and Culture. www.loc.gov/exhibits/african/afam013.html.

Frazier, E. Franklin. *The Negro Family in the United States.* 2nd ed. New York: Dryden Press, 1948.

Locke, Alain. *The Negro in Art.* 2nd ed. New York: Hacker Art Books, 1968.

Mullen, Bill V. *Popular Fronts: Chicago and African-American Cultural Politics, 1935–46.* Urbana: University of Illinois Press, 1999.

Jeffrey Helgeson

ANP *See* Associated Negro Press (ANP)

Appalachia

Between 1890 and 1930 significant numbers of southern blacks who participated in the Great Migration opted to migrate to the coal-mining regions of Appalachia, which consisted of eastern Kentucky, southwestern Virginia, and southern West Virginia. African Americans who settled in Appalachia during these years came predominantly from the agricultural Piedmont of Virginia and North Carolina and to a lesser extent from the coal district of northern Alabama. Like those who migrated to the cities of the industrial Northeast and Midwest, black migrants to Appalachia came in search of economic opportunity and an environment with greater social and political freedoms than in the South. These newcomers found steady employment at comparably higher wages and a relatively relaxed racial climate. Most black migrants who settled in Appalachia, however, did not regard their moves to the southern mountains as permanent. When the Great Depression and then the adoption of new mining technologies after World War II eroded employment opportunities, blacks left the region in droves, making Appalachia a sending rather than a receiving region for black migrants.

Coal mining attracted black migrants to Appalachia. Beginning in the 1880s, industrialists transformed Appalachia from a region of vast virgin forests dotted with mountain farms to one of **railroads**, coal mines, and company towns. Once coal operators cut the forests and constructed the railroad network necessary to move coal to market, they began to mine the mountains' rich deposits of bituminous coal. By 1930 the region mined nearly 80 percent of the nation's coal. The black population of Appalachia swelled with the

Coal mining attracted thousands of southern black migrants to Appalachia, such as these African American miners in Lorado, West Virginia, in 1918. Courtesy of the Library of Congress.

emergence of industrialization. Whereas only 14,360 African Americans lived in central Appalachia before industrialization, the region was home to 64,251 by 1910 and 108,872 by 1930. The black population of southern West Virginia, the state that attracted the most Appalachian-bound black migrants, grew from 4,794 in 1880 to 40,503 by 1910 and to 79,007 by 1930. The concentration of the black population in central Appalachia also shifted to the coal-producing counties of the region during these years. In 1870 only 36 percent of the black population in central Appalachia lived in the sixteen major coal-mining counties, but by 1920, 96 percent of the region's blacks did.

Black migrants came to Appalachia by a variety of routes. Because the coal region was remote and the local population slight, coal operators relied on **labor agents** to recruit their industrial labor force. Operators sent agents throughout the South who were, according to one contemporary observer, "skillfully selected for their persuasive eloquence and conscienceless disregard for the truth" (Lewis, 83). With "pockets full of money," labor agents offered blacks free rail transportation and many promises about the benefits of employment in Appalachia. One agent was reported to have recruited more than 5,000 southern blacks in one six-month period in 1916. Although many blacks undoubtedly came at the behest of recruiters working on behalf of coal operators, historians have found that most southern blacks who came to the region did so of their own accord. Like black migrants to the urban North in this period, they relied on networks of kith and kin to dispatch information about Appalachia and to spread news about social and economic conditions there. As one observer of African Americans leaving Alabama noted, only about 10 percent of the migrants returned, but those who did so came back to get friends and relatives. "It is the returned negroes," he remarked, "who carry the others off" (Trotter, 54–55). The **black press** in West Virginia also aided the flow of information. The editor of the *McDowell Times*, a small black weekly that circulated in the state and in western Virginia, regularly beckoned blacks to abandon the South and published extensive profiles of African Americans who had settled in the coal camps of the Mountain State.

Of the black migrants who came to Appalachia, most did not consider settling there permanently. Many of these migrants came from western Virginia and North Carolina, where they or their relatives owned farms. These farmers had long pursued off-season employment in forest industries, railroads, domestic service, and other nonagricultural sectors. Cash income from these endeavors allowed farmers to sustain their agricultural enterprises through difficult seasons or to expand their operations in flush times. Many considered employment in the coal mines of Appalachia an extension of this process and thought of coal as a cash crop that would enable them to retain their rural ways. These migrants were also no more than a day or two's travel time to their homeplaces; thus they could make frequent return visits. Farms in relatively close proximity also gave migrant miners a refuge during downturns in the business cycle when employment was less steady. Many of these black miners sustained their agricultural roots not only through frequent visits home but by raising livestock and cultivating extensive gardens in the coal camps, giving these places more the look of a rural village than an industrial town.

Close proximity to their homes allowed black migrants to transplant their institutional life to the mining towns of Appalachia. The semirural character of coal camps allowed black migrants to re-create rural family patterns. Most black migrant miners were married and lived in coal camps with their wives and children. Since **women** confronted few employment options in these communities, many wives and children tended the family gardens and livestock while their husbands labored underground in the mines. Not all black migrants to Appalachia were miners. Some professionals came to build small businesses, and skilled craftsmen came to ply their trades to serve the black migrant population of these growing coal towns. Black migrants also created their own churches. Most were **Baptists**. Some of the more spiritually inclined miners would preach to small congregations of migrants on Sundays, and these little clusters would become community churches led by clergy with little formal training. As the towns grew, other churches emerged that were led by educated clergy. Congregations of rural southerners resisted the encroachment of these professional **ministers** who looked down on their enthusiastic styles of worship and who lectured them on self-improvement and middle-class values. These church conflicts mirrored those in the urban North at this time between established houses of worship and the emergent congregations of southern migrants who gathered in places such as **storefront churches**. Much of the social life circulated around churches, which organized sporting events, picnics, reading groups, and other activities. Like other rural industrial towns, the coal camps of Appalachia were also populated with gamblers, pimps, and bootleggers. The *McDowell Times* frequently warned its readers to be wary of what it referred to as " 'Jonahs' and 'kid-glove dudes,' who moved into coal fields, exploited the miners, and, often, moved on" (Trotter, 61).

Black migrants who came to Appalachia not only sought employment but also anticipated a more relaxed racial environment. Certainly most black migrant miners came to West Virginia because it did not have the same history of racial violence as did the South, it offered better educational facilities, and it did not restrict the vote by race. Black migrants who came from the **Birmingham** coal district not only sought the higher wages paid in the West Virginia coalfields but also hoped to escape the onerous contract labor and convict lease system of employment practiced by Alabama operators. Black migrants, however, did not encounter a region free of racial discrimination or segregation. Although black migrants experienced relative equality on the job, they did find themselves largely restricted to the more dangerous and dirtier jobs of loader and laborer, and few blacks were promoted to supervisory positions. Because coal towns were the private property of coal operators, company policy rather than state law established the town's system of racial order. Many coal operators, out of an effort both to appease white workers and to foment racial divisions and distrust among workers, implemented racial segregation of towns and their facilities. Because towns were not incorporated, blacks had no access to political power to challenge segregated policies. Nevertheless, segregation in West Virginia tended to be more flexible than in the South, and coal operators' policy of equal pay for equal work eased racial tensions among workers.

African Americans continued to migrate to Appalachia as long as the coal industry thrived. The Great Depression, however, took its toll on the industry, ending the demand for workers. In the late 1930s coal operators began to introduce mechanical loaders and other technological innovations that eliminated many of the unskilled positions held by African American miners. Having lost their foothold in coal mining, the one thing that attracted them to Appalachia, African Americans abandoned the region. As the number of black workers in the industry fell from more than 30,000 to less than 4,000 between 1950 and 1970, so too did the black population of Appalachia. With few viable alternatives in the immediate region, blacks embarked for industrial areas in close proximity to Appalachia such as **Pittsburgh**, Youngstown, Akron, and **Cleveland**. The black exodus from Appalachia that began in the 1930s and accelerated after World War II surprised few. As sociologist James T. Laing observed in his 1933 survey of black miners in West Virginia, African Americans had only regarded Appalachia "as a stopping place devoid of sentiment" that was "to be endured but not loved" (Laing, 331). *See also* American Federation of Labor (AFL); Employment, Black Male Patterns of; Employment Discrimination; Great Migration, Causes of; Migrants, Expectations of; Organized Labor.

Further Reading

Burchett, Michael H. "Promise and Prejudice: Wise County, Virginia, and the Great Migration, 1910-1920." *Journal of Negro History* 82, no. 3 (Summer 1997): 312-27.

Laing, James T. "The Negro Miner in West Virginia." Ph.D. diss., Ohio State University, 1933.

Lewis, Ronald L. "From Peasant to Proletarian: The Migration of Southern Blacks to the Central Appalachian Coalfields." *Journal of Southern History* 55, no. 1 (1989): 77-102.

Trotter, Joe William, Jr. "Race, Class, and Industrial Change: Black Migration to Southern West Virginia, 1915–1932." In *The Great Migration in Historical Perspective: New Dimensions of Race, Class, and Gender*, edited by Joe William Trotter, Jr., 46–67. Bloomington: Indiana University Press, 1991.

Steven A. Reich

Armstrong, Louis (1901–1971)

Louis Armstrong was the first great **jazz** soloist. More than anyone else, Armstrong made jazz the anthem of the Great Black Migration.

Armstrong was born out of wedlock on August 4, 1901, in **New Orleans**'s slums. As a boy, Armstrong began taking part in the exciting black street-band scene. At age eleven he was sent by his mother to an orphanage, where he received lessons on the cornet. At this time the **blues**, **ragtime**, and brass-band music were being fused into New Orleans jazz, and older musicians tutored Armstrong in its ways. At seventeen he became a full-time musician, traveling the Mississippi on Streckfus riverboats as a member of Fate Marable's band. Marable's **St. Louis** musicians read from sheet music and rarely improvised, so Armstrong was an outsider in this group.

He was not an outsider in Joe "King" Oliver's Creole Jazz Band, one of New Orleans's finest ensembles. Oliver had tutored Armstrong on the cornet, and in 1922 he hired him to join the band in **Chicago**. Oliver's ambitious group played at Lincoln Gardens on the South Side, where the expanding African American community enjoyed relative prosperity and where black and white patronage created a vibrant entertainment district. In 1923 the band toured the Midwest and made the first important black jazz recordings; "Chimes Blues" featured Armstrong's first recorded solo. The portly young musician's adjustment to the North was epitomized by his marriage to his second wife, Lil Hardin, the Oliver band's talented pianist. Hardin encouraged Armstrong to raise his professional ambitions, and in 1924 he joined Fletcher Henderson's orchestra at the prestigious Roseland Ballroom in midtown Manhattan. The innovative Henderson had sought a "hot" improviser to complement his more urbane players (young black men who, like Henderson, had middle-class or northern backgrounds). Armstrong's yearlong stint made him well known in

Louis Armstrong in New York, 1946. Courtesy of Photofest.

New York City, but nevertheless he returned to Chicago. Now playing the trumpet, he fronted a series of historic "Hot Five" and "Hot Seven" recording sessions, which became perhaps the most celebrated 1920s "hot" jazz combo recordings. His exultant trumpet and "scat" singing solos (distilled from lengthy bandstand improvisations) made Armstrong the most influential stylist in jazz, a player who shaped the work of generations of trumpeters, vocalists, and others.

In 1929 he relocated to Manhattan, where he performed at Connie's Inn in Harlem and appeared in the Broadway revue *Hot Chocolates*. Beginning in 1932, he toured the nation and Europe as a star soloist. The able Joe Glaser became Armstrong's manager and arranged lucrative appearances and recording and film work, allowing the performer to weather dramatic changes in popular musical taste. In the 1940s Armstrong and his fourth wife, Lucille Wilson Armstrong, moved to Corona, Queens, a comfortable neighborhood that was home to many prosperous African American musicians. Between musical jobs Armstrong displayed a literary gift, writing drafts of various autobiographies and maintaining a voluminous correspondence. The Louis Armstrong All-Stars tours, beginning in 1947, cemented his reputation as the grand old man of jazz. State Department tours in the 1950s made him an international goodwill ambassador, although he publicly criticized segregation in the American South.

Armstrong was celebrated for his warm persona as well as for his artistry, but after 1950 militant African Americans increasingly criticized him for his alleged "Uncle Tomming" onstage. In the 1960s, though, Armstrong's renditions of "Hello, Dolly!" and "What a Wonderful World" brought him to the peak of his popularity as a vocalist and film star. He died of heart failure at his home in Corona on July 6, 1971. More than a century after his birth, Louis Armstrong continues to embody southern African American migrants' rise from poverty and their conquest of the nation's popular musical styles in the twentieth century. *See also* Dance Halls and Nightclubs; Harlem Renaissance; Recording Industry; Primary Document 1.

Further Reading

Brothers, Thomas, ed. *Louis Armstrong, in His Own Words: Selected Writings*. New York: Oxford University Press, 1999.

Collier, James Lincoln. *Louis Armstrong: An American Genius*. New York: Oxford University Press, 1983.

Burton W. Peretti

Asian Immigrants and Asian Americans, Relations with Black Migrants

The lives of Asian immigrants and Asian Americans intersected with those of black migrants at work, in the neighborhood, and during the struggle for civil rights and equality. Through their competitive and cooperative collaborations, activists and other citizens of Asian descent complicated, and at times strengthened, the binary white versus black categorization that shaped the social, economic, and political lives of all Americans. Despite the obvious importance of these two groups as they interacted, the dearth of historical studies on the issue makes it difficult to draw a historical portrait of this relationship. Nevertheless, one may look at interracial and interethnic relations during the period of the Great Migration as part of the larger encounter between Asian and black Americans. More than any "essential" characteristics arising from either the race or color of the two groups, the vicissitudes in the United States' industrial demand for labor, the legacy of segregation in the United States, and the racialized nature of U.S. wars in Asia were among the factors that facilitated such relations.

Just as a trickle of black southerners began to leave for northern and western cities, **Booker T. Washington** expressed his deep concern about the influx of foreign workers into the United States. He was aware that white owners of **railroad** companies, plantations, mines, and factories took little notice of black migrants because of the abundant pool of cheaply employable foreign workers from Asia and Europe arriving on American shores. In an 1895 speech in Atlanta, he warned his mostly white audience not to "look to the incoming of those of foreign birth and strange tongue and habits for the prosperity of the South," but instead to "cast down your bucket . . . among the eight million negroes whose habits you know." His admonition echoed a deep-rooted bias among black leaders against immigrants in general, who "elbowed out of employment" the black man, as Frederick Douglass stated in the mid-nineteenth century.

As the century turned, black animosity against Asian immigrants grew sharper. Stigmatization of Asian immigrants took some of the most extreme forms during the first three decades of the twentieth century. Washington argued that not only would immigrants take jobs from African Americans, but that Asians, in particular, "lacked moral standards" and thus "could never assimilate to occidental civilization." A 1928 article in the *Norfolk Journal and Guide* concurred, claiming that immigrants were "crude, illiterate, and hopelessly unsympathetic with American institutions and ideals" and were "used to press us further down the economic ladder." Such invectives served to strengthen racial hierarchies and the logic of white supremacy as constructed by white workers, racial scientists, and policy makers in the early twentieth century. They also legitimized the notion that the core of American identity was not only white, but also urban, industrial, and northern, thus relegating both black southern migrants and Asian immigrants and their descendants to a real or symbolic status as second-class citizens.

Black leaders' opposition to Asian workers stemmed from multiple sources. For one thing, white employers favored Asian workers, who were deemed cheap and disposable, over black Americans. After the implementation of the Chinese Exclusion Law of 1882—a federal statute vigorously defended by the African American press—industrialists, railroad companies, and mine owners, along with ranchers and vineyard and orchard holders, found among Japanese immigrants a convenient labor source to replace now-unavailable Chinese workers. After the 1907 Gentlemen's Agreement limiting the number of Japanese immigrants, white employers looked to Korean, Filipino, and Mexican workers. These practices infuriated the **black press** and leadership, who held, as *Washington Colored America* stated in 1902, that "Negro labor is native labor and should be preferred to that of the offscourings of Europe and Asia."

Another reason for employers' preference for Asian workers lay in what white America deemed the alien nature of Asians and the temporary status of their residence. These alleged characteristics of Asian laborers rendered them the most exploitable type of worker, comparable to Mexicans. The Pullman Company, for example, hired Filipinos as scabs partly in an attempt to undermine **A. Philip Randolph**'s efforts to organize black workers in the 1920s. The Great Depression dampened the job prospects of black men and **women**. A large proportion of these black workers were southern migrants, and they were the first to be laid off from the industrial jobs they had acquired during World War I and after. The strategic use of Asian laborers as scabs and scapegoats was nothing new, but this practice strengthened existing anti-immigrant feelings among both black leaders and the rank and file, who largely endorsed the restrictions that culminated in the federal laws of 1917, 1921, and 1924 that placed a total ban on Asian immigration.

Asian immigrants, for their part, learned quickly the existing racial order in the United States by which becoming white and becoming American were tightly interwoven. As a result, Asian workers and students—with the exception of those from India—while aware of their nonwhite, non-Caucasian status, sought to distance themselves from black Americans. Japanese were particularly concerned with where they and their U.S.-born children stood within the racial hierarchy of America. In 1925 a **Los Angeles**-based Japanese-language newspaper, *Hokubei Jiji*, stated that the greatest concern for *issei* parents was that their *nisei*, U.S.-born offspring, "might become the second blacks" who lacked full recognition of their citizenship in the U.S. polity and were denied equal treatment in American industrial democracy. These fears were realized in the bleakest way possible when the outbreak of the Pacific War led to President Franklin D. Roosevelt's decision to remove the entire Japanese community on the West Coast, including immigrants and U.S. citizens of Japanese descent alike, and incarcerate them in internment camps.

While black Americans and Asian immigrants and Asian Americans each held on to their separate interests and identities, with internal divisions along ethnic, national, and increasingly class lines, cross-racial identification and pan-ethnic solidarity grew among people who underwent similar experiences of racism. The internment of Japanese Americans provoked deep concern in the black community, for example. **National Association for the Advancement of Colored People** branch director Closter Current noted that black Americans throughout the country felt a sense of alarm familiar to all people living under oppression: "Today them, tomorrow us." In 1945 representatives from the African American community, together with their Filipino and Korean counterparts, met with federal, state, and local delegates in **San Francisco** to establish the Pacific Coast Fair Play Committee. They agreed that "any attempt to make capital for their own racial groups at the expense of the Japanese would be sawing off their limbs on which they themselves sat."

The postwar era fostered further cross-racial and cross-ethnic alliances among African American and Asian activists. **Martin Luther King, Jr.**, Vernon

Jordan, and Benjamin Hooks expressed a humanitarian point of view, strongly supporting admission into the United States of Indochinese refugees as "an embattled minority." Black leaders did not turn a blind eye to economic difficulties, a principal source of tension and competition between African Americans and refugees as they struggled to maintain employment, **housing**, and access to government and corporate services in Los Angeles, **Seattle**, and San Francisco. But a humanitarian perspective nurtured in the struggle for civil rights led black leaders to see their "struggle for economic and political freedom" as a "moral obligation" that was "inextricably linked to the struggle of Indochinese refugees."

The postwar militancy of African Americans was also important in creating a common ground from which Asian American students and grassroots activists, as well as Native Americans and Latinos, could articulate their grievances relating to discrimination at home and to the U.S. war in Vietnam and elsewhere in Asia. "We followed what blacks did," as one Asian American student put it.

This cosmopolitan perspective toward coalition building was not shared by all or even most of the women and men making up either group, however. Their interests were increasingly divided along class lines within and across the respective groups. Newcomers such as Vietnamese, Cambodians, Laotians, and, to a lesser extent, Hmongs competed with urban African Americans— many of whom had migrated from the South—for jobs, housing, **bank** loans, and public programs. Settled groups, including U.S. citizens of Chinese, Japanese, and Korean descent, followed paths closely resembling those of European origin. More recent arrivals from Hong Kong and university-educated Indian computer engineers, for their part, had and have little trouble building their institutions and networks with little or no funding from the U.S. government. The economic success of the latter two groups has strengthened the stereotype of Asians as the "model minority" while glossing over the difficulties faced by the first group. It also highlighted another racial stereotype, that of urban African Americans as a "**ghetto** minority."

Real and imagined antagonism between the two minorities came to a head during the 1992 Los Angeles riots. Immediately after an all-white jury acquitted four white L.A. police officers charged with the assault of Rodney King, a circle of anger and violence ignited in Los Angeles. Starting in South Central L.A. (one of the city's poorest neighborhoods), countless acts of destruction, ranging from looting and arson to injuring and even killing spread throughout the city. The nation was in the midst of a recession, the unemployment rates in African American and Latino neighborhoods had reached Depression-era levels, and many blacks purportedly resented the way Korean shop owners treated them, as their small businesses served and benefitted from largely black communities. (A number of Korean businesses were set on fire during the riots.) Although the exact causes and impact of ethnic tensions in the L.A. riots remain to be debated, the alleged problem of the black-Korean conflict in particular, and the black-Asian conflict in general, have become one of the most pressing concerns for the media and intellectuals alike. *See also* Asian Immigration, Comparison with the Great Black Migration; Black-Jewish Relations; European Immigrants, Relations with Black Migrants; Hispanic Immigrants and Hispanic Americans, Relations with Black Migrants; Primary Documents 3, 62.

Further Reading

Fuchs, Lawrence. "The Reactions of Black Americans to Immigration." In *Immigration Reconsidered: History, Sociology, and Politics*, edited by Virginia Yans-McLaughlin, 293–314. New York: Oxford University Press, 1990.

Lie, John. "The Black-Asian Conflict?" In *Not Just Black and White: Historical and Contemporary Perspectives on Immigration, Race, and Ethnicity in the United States*, edited by Nancy Foner and George M. Fredrickson, 301–14. New York: Russell Sage Foundation, 2004.

Lipsitz, George. " 'Frantic to Join . . . the Japanese Army': The Asia Pacific War in the Lives of African American Soldiers and Civilians." In *The Politics of Culture in the Shadow of Capitalism*, edited by Lisa Lowe and David Lloyd. Durham, NC: Duke University Press, 1997.

Yukari Takai

Asian Immigration, Comparison with the Great Black Migration

Immigration from Asia to the United States was undertaken by a population that was diverse in ethnic, national, and geographic origin and amounted to approximately 700,000 between 1820 and 1930. Massive labor migration from Asia to the United States began in the mid-nineteenth century with the arrival of Chinese indentured laborers in the then independent kingdom of Hawai'i, as well as fortune seekers who went to gold-rush-era California. Japanese, Koreans, Filipinos, and Indians came after them, first to Hawai'i and then the mainland United States, starting in the latter part of the nineteenth century and continuing into the twentieth century. Asian migration continues today, undertaken by **women** and men who hail largely, but not exclusively, from the Philippines, Vietnam, Cambodia, Laos, Thailand, Iran, India, Pakistan, and Bangladesh. The very heterogeneity of these people stands in sharp contrast to the Great Migration of African Americans from 1900 to 1970, largely defined, whose geographic origin and itineraries fell within the boundaries of the United States, and whose physical movement took place either by train or by foot.

Overemphasizing this distinction, however, glosses over the fundamental ways in which these two major migrations are comparable. These groups were, and indeed still are, faced with economic, political, and social dislocation in their respective homelands; they were affected by the powerful economic "pull" of American industrial development; and they both encountered varying levels of deception, prejudice, and hostility when they arrived at their destinations. Members of these migrating populations also demonstrated a willingness to create lives of their own and the capability to do so in a new land that had hitherto been predominantly white, Anglo-Saxon, and Protestant. The significance of these similarities notwithstanding, the fact remains that imperialism, citizenship, and legally sanctioned discrimination created important variations and contrasts between and within Asian and African American experiences of migration.

Although the industrial demand for labor—whether found in the northern and western cities and fields, Hawai'ian plantations, or the Rocky Mountains—ranked as an important factor for the movement of both African American and Asian migrants, differences between the political economies of the societies of departure led to different starting points for residents of the southern United States and immigrants leaving various parts of Asia. Whereas slavery, emancipation, and the **Jim Crow** system precipitated the departure of black southerners, Asian migration, with the exception of the Japanese, emerged against the backdrop of European, Asian, and U.S. imperialism in their homelands. South China, which was the departure point for most Chinese migrants, was the main contact point in Asia for the British government, which "opened" China to European and U.S. trade after the first Opium War (1839–1842). In addition, a long tradition of political rebellions such as the Taiping Rebellion (1850–1864) devastated the Pearl River Delta, making life precarious for the Cantonese men and women in the region. Emigration thus became not just a way to attain a better life, but a necessary means for survival.

Colonial rule also affected the lives of Koreans. Thousands left the peninsula in response to the recruiting efforts of Christian missionaries and the Hawai'ian Sugar Planters Association, which had difficulties with increasingly militant Japanese workers at the turn of the century. Emigration came to a sudden end in 1905 when Japanese representatives in Korea banned departures of Koreans in an attempt to protect Japanese laborers in Hawai'i. Korean nationalists, reacting to tightened control under Japanese colonial rule, either went underground or fled abroad. The Korean communities around the world—in Russia, Manchuria, and China; Europe; and Hawai'i and the continental United States—thus provided nationalists with shelters and financial support for their struggle against Japanese colonial rule.

Both Asian and African American migrants entered new lands where their limited economic resources and racial status sparked more hostility than support. Yet legally sanctioned discrimination on the basis of citizenship set the intolerance of exclusionary laws that affected Asian immigrants apart from the segregation imposed on African Americans. A series of immigration laws (the Chinese Exclusion Law of 1882, followed by the Acts of Immigration in 1917, 1921, and 1924—the last culminating in the total ban of Asian immigration) restricted the geographic mobility of Asian immigrants. Furthermore, alien land laws and court rulings on citizenship (*Takao Ozawa v. United States* in 1922 and *United States v. Bhagat Singh Thind* in 1923) limited their social mobility at the federal, state, and municipal levels. Because these statutes and decisions were hinged on the federal status of Asian immigrants, rather than arbitrary xenophobia, exclusionists deemed them fair and justifiable.

One result of these exclusionary laws was a skewed gender ratio among most Asian groups. Miscegenation laws forbidding marriage between white persons and "Negroes, mulattoes, and Mongolians" added to the difficulty for Asian men attempting to find marriage partners. The number of African American men far exceeded the number of women who migrated throughout the World War I period, but geographic proximity made it relatively easy for them to visit home or to bring a wife and child to where they worked and lived. Japanese men addressed these difficulties by relying on the so-called picture marriage, a transpacific version of marriage by proxy that was widely practiced at the time whereby a man in the United States wrote to his family, relatives, or acquaintances in Japan to find a wife for him and, after exchanging photographs with his prospective bride, sent for her to cross the ocean to join him. More than

20,000 Japanese women, mostly picture brides, landed on American shores between 1909 and 1921. Their arrival radically transformed the Japanese community in the United States, which had hitherto been a society of bachelor sojourners. The emergence of a more vibrant Japanese community that began to include both women and men, as well as U.S.-born children, who were consequently U.S. citizens, in turn evoked violent hostility that spread up the West Coast from **San Francisco** to Vancouver.

In the case of Indian men living in the United States, who were mostly Punjabis, more than half were married, but the 1911 report of the Immigration Commission makes clear that many had left their wives "abroad." As their stays in the United States lengthened, many ended up forming unions with Mexican American women, a practice that further complicated racial categories.

Filipinos presented another problem for the white American establishment because of their courtship of white women, which sometimes led to marriage. In 1933 Salvador Roldans won his petition at California's Court of Appeals to marry a white woman because Filipinos were considered Malay, not Mongolian. The state legislature quickly amended the legal loophole by modifying the antimiscegenation law to include Malays as well, and Oregon, Nevada, and Washington soon followed suit.

Asian migrants were confronted with a U.S. state apparatus that denied them the means to attain a livelihood and political power through the extended application of the logic of "separate but equal." But racial discrimination did not undermine the strength of the target groups. Rather, it created a culture of resistance and instigated a fight for the justice denied to them that can be seen as manifested at the O'ahu sugar plantations (1920) and in Salinas, California (1932). The internment of approximately 120,000 Japanese immigrants and U.S. citizens of Japanese origin during World War II was one of the most serious breaches of civil liberty in U.S. history. After the war the Japanese American community, led by the Japanese American Citizens League, struggled for redress and reparations in order to obtain apology and compensation from the U.S. government for its wrongdoing. In August 1988, over four decades after the relocation occurred, President Ronald Reagan signed the redress bill. *See also* Asian Immigrants and Asian Americans, Relations with Black Migrants; European Immigration, Comparison with the Great Black Migration; Hispanic Migration, Comparison with the Great Black Migration; Western States, Black Migration to; Primary Document 62.

Further Reading

Chan, Suchen. *Asian Americans: An Interpretive History*. New York: Twayne Publishers, 1991.

———. "European and Asian Immigration into the United States in Comparative Perspective, 1820s to 1920s." In *Immigration Reconsidered: History, Sociology, and Politics*, edited by Virginia Yans-McLaughlin, 37–75. New York: Oxford University Press, 1990.

Lewis, Carl. "Race." In *Encyclopedia of the United States in the Twentieth Century*. Vol. 1. New York: Charles Scribner's Sons, 1996.

Okihiro, Gary Y. *The Columbia Guide to Asian American History*. New York: Columbia University Press, 2001.

Trotter, Joe W. "The Great Migration, African Americans, and Immigrants in the Industrial City." In *Not Just Black and White: Historical and Contemporary Perspectives on Immigration, Race, and Ethnicity in the United States*, edited by Nancy Foner and George M. Fredrickson, 82–99. New York: Russell Sage Foundation, 2004.

Yukari Takai

Associated Negro Press (ANP)

Claude Albert Barnett was born on September 16, 1890, in Sanford, Florida, the son of William and Celena Anderson Barnett. He died in 1967 in **Chicago**, where he was a resident for all but nine months of his life. It was in the nation's second-largest city that he established in 1919 the Associated Negro Press (ANP), a national and international news service that was to be his life's work.

Like the national **black press** it served, the ANP in its origins was clearly a product of the forces set in motion by the Great Migration in the first half of the twentieth century of African Americans from the rural South to the urban North. In many ways it remained such a product throughout its existence. While the idea of a black cooperative national news service had first emerged in the immediate post–Civil War decades, it took the Great Migration to bring thought to fruition. Just as that migration with its concentration of black masses in urban locales where they would now count politically, economically, and culturally in new ways, begin to command new resources, and have new needs gave birth to the great national black weekly newspaper, so too in turn did the migration climate give birth to the fact of a national black news service that found its highest expression in the career and work of Claude Barnett.

The desire to establish a national news service was nurtured by a philosophy of service to his people and a business ethic that Barnett imbibed at the **Tuskegee Normal and Industrial Institute** of **Booker T. Washington**, from which he graduated in 1906. "No institution," ANP's director wrote, "has exerted so profound an influence on my life as Tuskegee Institute" (Hogan, 47). Of the many lessons taught at Tuskegee, none was stressed more than the value of business development for the advancement of African Americans. Washington predicated his solution to America's race problem on the ameliorative effect of blacks working in their own businesses. He put special value on cooperation within the ranks of business and between business-people and consumers as a way of alleviating the problems of limited resources. In pursuing business success, a black entrepreneur could realize economic gain in service to his people and earn the respect of white people who counted.

From its founding in 1919 through its demise in the early 1960s this business and people-service ethic motivated an Associated Negro Press that became the premier reporting and news-gathering and dissemination instrument for blacks and their newspapers in the United States and abroad. From the agency's beginning, its member papers could count on a twice-weekly news packet that by the 1930s contained enough news and feature material to make up a twenty-four-page newspaper. With correspondents and stringers reporting from across the country and abroad, the news agency gave African American newspapers a critical, comprehensive coverage of personalities, events, and institutions relevant to the lives of black Americans.

During its first four decades the ANP served a black press that reached for and secured mass circulations on the national, regional, state, and local levels. Among the most influential of these papers were **Robert Abbott**'s *Chicago Defender*, Robert Vann's *Pittsburgh Courier*, Carl Murphy's *Baltimore Afro-American*, and P. B. Young's *Norfolk Journal and Guide*. Measured by circulation, readership influence, quality and extent of coverage, and the national community these papers reported on and to, this period was arguably the golden age of America's greatest ethnic press. The story of the ANP and Claude Barnett offers a rich perspective from which to view twentieth-century African American journalism during years when self-made publishers were building newspapers with national circulations in black urban population centers throughout America.

While always maintaining for his ANP a primary focus on the black population throughout the United States, in the mid-1950s Claude Barnett began to put an increasing emphasis on a deeply held interest he shared with his wife, the noted entertainer Etta Moten Barnett, in the cultures, interests, and contemporary problems of black African peoples who were moving toward independence after long periods of colonial domination. In 1951 the news agency began to put out three releases per week. During the 1950s and into the 1960s these releases came to concentrate more and more on events and peoples from the African continent. By the end of the 1950s some seventy-five African papers were subscribing to the service. They could receive releases written in French as well as in English and prepared at an African desk in the agency's headquarters.

The coming of the modern **civil rights movement** and the onset of integration brought the decline of the great black national weekly of the 1930s, 1940s, and 1950s and, in turn, the diminished need for an independent black news service to serve the news needs of that press. Reporters and editors in the mainstream press began to look for the first time in a serious way for news from behind what **W.E.B. DuBois** called the "veil." Former ANP associate editor and longtime managing editor of the *Pittsburgh Courier* Percival Prattis commented on the significance of these changes in a column he wrote after Barnett had closed down the ANP. "In the early twenties when he and I worked together, neither of us could have foreseen that come a few years, something called integration was going to get the best of us. The dailies are beating us to the streets. If this news is good, they are out with it before our publication day comes around. That has been and is a problem for the Negro papers themselves. It was more of a problem for ANP" (Hogan, 249). The Associated Negro Press records, now archived at the Chicago Historical Society, are an unmatched historical resource for students seeking to probe from the inside the heart and mind of black Americans during the first half of the twentieth century. *See also* Black Consumer Market; *Cleveland Gazette*; Desegregation; *Houston Informer*; *New York Age*.

Further Reading

Bunie, Andrew. *Robert L. Vann of the "Pittsburgh Courier": Politics and Black Journalism*. Pittsburgh: University of Pittsburgh Press, 1974.

Hogan, Lawrence. *A Black National News Service: The Associated Negro Press and Claude Barnett*. Haworth, NJ: St. Johann Press, 2002.

Ottley, Roi. *The Lonely Warrior: The Life and Times of Robert S. Abbott*. Chicago: Henry Regnery Co., 1955.

Lawrence D. Hogan

Atlanta, Georgia

An embarkation point, a stopover, a destination: Atlanta fulfilled all these roles for the African American participants of twentieth-century migrations. The city's location at the nexus of several rail lines and its spectacular economic and physical growth in the post–Civil War era helped draw many blacks into, or at least through, the city. Atlanta hosted several premier educational institutions for African Americans, most notably Spelman and Morehouse colleges and Atlanta University, and helped produce a cohort of enormously successful entrepreneurs. Thriving black neighborhoods and business districts, such as Sweet Auburn, just east of downtown, and, later, West End, demonstrated the strength and size of the city's African American population. An independent **black press** and a wealth of social, spiritual, and service organizations grew with the city throughout the twentieth century, supporting a substantial, if conservative, elite leadership and contributing to the city's attraction for rural black southerners. The industrial growth of Atlanta, however, offered few openings to African Americans, leaving the population underemployed and largely confined to the service sector. These economic conditions, along with an increasingly entrenched system of **Jim Crow**, caused some blacks to flee the city when jobs opened in other regions.

The zenith of African American migration to the city came during the last third of the nineteenth century, when the arrival of blacks far exceeded that of whites. In the decades leading up to the turn of the century the city's population quadrupled, and African Americans accounted for well over 40 percent of the population during these years.

African American migration to the city continued in the twentieth century, but appeared

An African American neighborhood in Atlanta, Georgia, 1936. Courtesy of the Library of Congress.

much less dramatic as Atlanta attracted more and more whites. Blacks moving to **Detroit**, **Chicago**, and other industrial centers in the urban North during the 1910s and 1920s also slowed permanent migration to Atlanta. By 1920 blacks accounted for only 31.2 percent of the city's population, the lowest proportion since the start of the Civil War, and the percentage crept up only slightly, to 33.3 percent, by 1930. The percentage of blacks in the city's population did not jump again until 1970, when **white flight** from the declining urban center did more to account for this increase than the in-migration of African Americans.

World War I–era migration brought many rural southern blacks to Atlanta, but discussion in both the local white and African American press focused mainly on the movement of blacks out of the state. Atlanta's moderate whites and elite blacks called for better treatment of African Americans as a means of inducing blacks to stay in Georgia. The white perspective, represented by the *Atlanta Constitution*, recognized that the migration threatened to leave the South short of menial laborers and asked white readers to consider how bad schools, poor wages, and racial violence had all induced African Americans to seek their fortunes in the urban North. Local black leaders, such as Benjamin Davis, Sr., editor of the African American weekly newspaper the *Atlanta Independent*, saw an opportunity in these local white reactions. He picked up on the threat of a loss of black labor and used the migration to push for political inclusion and improved economic opportunities for blacks in the region. Population statistics reveal, however, that the issue of black out-migration was hardly a threat to the city of Atlanta. African Americans increased their numbers in the city by 43 percent during the 1920s.

World War II and postwar migration generated less comment from Atlantans, perhaps because it brought more new residents to the city than the wave that preceded it. The city's central location in the South and its continuing fine transportation connections via both **railroads** and, later, air continued to draw migrants through the city on their way north or west. Economic, political, and social developments did encourage many to make Atlanta their home, and the city's black population grew by 16 percent between 1940 and 1950. Defense and government work become available to blacks, although often not without the concerted efforts of African Americans themselves. The local chapter of the **National Urban League**, for example, fought hard to have training and work in the nearby Bell Aircraft plant opened to African Americans in 1942, and the **Congress of Industrial Organizations** successfully organized black workers at the plant a year later. The city's growth during and immediately after the war years also triggered significant expansion in traditional arenas of black employment in the service sector. The hiring of African American police officers in the late 1940s and black firemen in the early 1960s spoke well of the city's racial progress. A 1944 Supreme Court decision disallowing the all-white primaries that the Democratic Party had used to keep African Americans out of politics also held out the hope of political inclusion for blacks in Atlanta. Compared with western cities that were drawing migrants during the middle of the twentieth century, however, Atlanta's long-standing and well-established Jim Crow customs and laws and an entrenched conservative black elite limited the city's appeal for many

African Americans as anything more than a stopping point on the way out of the South.

In the 1960s and 1970s Atlanta began experiencing many of the same challenges as the urban North, and, just as in these other cities, African Americans experienced the worst of these changes in terms of **housing** and employment. While the city desegregated its public spaces relatively peacefully during the **civil rights movement** of the early 1960s, especially in comparison with its southern neighbors such as **Birmingham**, economic trends and extreme residential segregation decreased the attractiveness of Atlanta for many blacks. A shifting economic base moved new sectors of employment to the northern, racially whiter outskirts of the city, leaving many African Americans isolated in the city core. **Urban renewal** razed black neighborhoods in favor of convention centers and baseball stadiums while providing relatively little new housing. A major freeway project brought "the connector" (the merging of Interstates 75 and 85 in the center of Atlanta) through the heart of Auburn Avenue, cutting off what had been the center of black life in the city since the 1910s from downtown and speeding the movement of whites out of the city proper. By 1970 a complicated pattern of in-, out-, and through-migration of both blacks and whites had made Atlanta into a majority-black city.

Further Reading

Bayor, Ronald H. *Race and the Shaping of Twentieth-Century Atlanta*. Chapel Hill: University of North Carolina Press, 1996.

Dittmer, John. *Black Georgia in the Progressive Era*. Urbana: University of Illinois Press, 1977.

Ferguson, Karen. *Black Politics in New Deal Atlanta*. Chapel Hill: University of North Carolina Press, 2002.

Hunter, Tera. *To 'Joy My Freedom: Southern Black Women's Lives and Labors after the Civil War*. Cambridge, MA: Harvard University Press, 1997.

Kuhn, Clifford, Harlon E. Joye, and E. Bernard West. *Living Atlanta: An Oral History of the City, 1914–1948*. Atlanta: Atlanta Historical Society and University of Georgia Press, 1990.

Pomerantz, Gary. *Where Peachtree Meets Sweet Auburn: The Saga of Two Families and the Making of Atlanta*. New York: Scribner, 1996.

Spritzer, Lorraine Nelson, and Jean B. Bergmark. *Grace Towns Hamilton and the Politics of Southern Change*. Athens: University of Georgia Press, 1997.

Georgina Hickey

Attaway, William (1911–1986)

Novelist William Attaway was born in Greenwood, Mississippi, in 1911, and at the age of five he moved with his family to **Chicago** as part of the Great Black Migration. In the early 1930s a young Attaway joined countless other Great Depression migrants in wandering across the western United States, working odd jobs to support himself along the way. Attaway drew upon the latter experiences in his first novel, *Let Me Breathe Thunder* (1939), which describes the struggles of white migrant workers named Step and Ed, along with an orphaned Mexican child whom the pair nicknames Hi Boy.

Attaway's second novel, *Blood on the Forge*, looks back to the experiences of black migrants from the rural, agricultural South to the urban, industrial North during World War I. Specifically the novel follows the lives of brothers Melody, Chinatown, and Big Mat Moss from a life of sharecropping in Kentucky to a steel-mill town resembling World War I–era Homestead, Pennsylvania. To Attaway's credit, he captures broader patterns in the Great Black Migration experience by representing the Moss brothers' decision to move northward as stemming from both a push and a pull. The push comes mainly in the form of depleted land and, more urgently, the imminent threat to Big Mat's life for having struck a white man, while the pull is manifest in a recruiter's promises of big wages offered by the steel mills of western Pennsylvania.

Equally significant, *Blood on the Forge* offers a detailed account of migration itself. As did many World War I–era black migrants, the Moss brothers escape the South under cover of darkness—in this case, by means of a clandestine boxcar arranged by the steel company's recruiting agent. In the manner of a Middle Passage experience, this journey strips the migrants of nearly all their material possessions and brutally buffets the Moss brothers' bodies in a way that forecasts their later experiences with the harsh material environment of the northern steel mills.

Like many social realist novelists of his day, Attaway refuses to present migration as a solution to the problems of his protagonists. Rather, because they have been recruited along with other black migrants as strikebreakers to a community composed predominantly of Slavic immigrants, the Moss brothers soon confront a double bind of marginalization from white labor unions and exploitation by industrial capitalists, as well as the new dangers and rigorous demands of work in the steel mills. The novel's tragic conclusion finds Big Mat slain while working as a hired thug with the steel company's strikebreakers, Chinatown physically blinded and psychologically broken by an industrial accident, and the musically inclined Melody unable to play his guitar since his hand has been mangled in a separate workplace accident at the mill. As a young **Ralph Ellison** observed in a review at the time of the novel's publication, Attaway offered very little to suggest how thousands of black migrants successfully managed to build new lives for themselves in the urban North, but arguably Attaway remains the most astute literary chronicler of the challenges posed to male participants in the Great Black Migration. *See also* European Immigrants, Relations with Black Migrants; Literature, the Great Migration in; Steelworkers; Strikebreaking.

Further Reading

Margolies, Edward. *Native Sons: A Critical Study of Twentieth-Century Negro American Authors*. Philadelphia: J. B. Lippincott, 1968.

Morgan, Stacy I. "Migration, Material Culture, and Identity in William Attaway's *Blood on the Forge* and Harriette Arnow's *The Dollmaker*." *College English* 63 (July 2001): 712–40.

Yarborough, Richard. Afterword to *Blood on the Forge*, by William Attaway. New York: Monthly Review Press, 1987.

Stacy I. Morgan

Attorneys

In 1928 Charles Hamilton Houston, who would become vice-dean of the **Howard University** Law School, surveyed the South for actively practicing black lawyers. Answers to his letter sent to the clerks of southern county courts revealed a determined and often dramatic opposition to blacks engaged in the practice of law. Before World War I black lawyers who practiced in the North did so for the most part with a limited white clientele. However, from the northern migration prompted by and after that war, the earnings and presence of black citizens created new opportunities for black lawyers to practice law. In the North black lawyers were better trained, more research oriented, and thus more progressive than those engaged in southern practices.

Because the system of judicial administration was historically white, a black criminal defendant or civil claimant in need of legal services did not retain the services of a black lawyer. However, over the period of the Great Migration, as civil and criminal juries added larger percentages of black jurors and increasing numbers of black judges, black lawyers saw greater opportunities to practice before county courts. According to Raymond Pace Alexander, Harvard law graduate, **Philadelphia** lawyer, and trial judge in the 1930s, a successful black lawyer in a northern city could earn an annual income of $5,000. In some northern cities the expanded presence of African Americans also enhanced black lawyers' opportunities for commercial law practices. Many lawyers assumed civic, political, and governmental positions available in the northern cities to which black southerners migrated. With such earnings and opportunities black lawyers who followed the southern migration north regained some of the prestige lost to their status in the South.

From the beginning of the migration, the struggles of black lawyers to succeed in the cities were keen. Whites generally controlled the administration of the courts at all levels. They also controlled the local political leadership, which influenced judicial appointments. Moreover, white law firms, the downtown business district, and in some instances the bar associations were hostile to the handful of black lawyers who came to practice in the first decades of the Great Migration. Public accommodations for black lawyers in the city's business districts could not be taken for granted. Because of the racially restrictive social conditions of the bar and business environment in the 1920s and 1930s, black lawyers were limited to criminal law, minor real estate work, and domestic relations. In the trial courts black lawyers were not permitted to sit in seating reserved for members of the bar. According to Alexander, as late as the 1950s the experiences of black lawyers trying in the courts could be racially humiliating.

Yet in the 1920s and 1930s professional experiences among black lawyers tended to create closer bonds. For example, in Philadelphia, Pennsylvania, the

Census Bureau reported that in the 1930s there were a total of 2,251 lawyers. Of this total, 1,972 were native born and 249 were foreign born. Of this population, there were 30 black lawyers, all of them male. In the 1940s, of a total of 2,224 lawyers in Philadelphia, 21 were black, of whom 1 was female. In this period preceptors, or lawyers willing to supervise the training of new members to the bar, were required. With so few black lawyers, a single lawyer's availability to a new member often meant that lawyer's availability to succeeding members. For this reason the black lawyer preceptor often emerged as a bar group leader capable of fostering closely knit professional ties.

Black lawyers in **Detroit, Michigan**, used their city's postwar production to build practices. In the 1920s and 1930s there were no more than 100 black lawyers in Detroit. However, of this bar two law firms operated, with one principally engaged in business law. With the boom in automobile production after World War II, lawyers followed the migration of blacks to the city. The black bar in **Chicago, Illinois**, also grew with its black population's increase from the Great Migration. By one estimate in 1981 there were 820 black lawyers at the Chicago metropolitan bar.

In the North, as black lawyers came to the bar in increasing numbers, civil rights organizations emerged to bring lawsuits that required financial support. The growing cadre of black lawyers might have expected the recently formed **National Association for the Advancement of Colored People** (NAACP) to require their skills to bring its civil rights litigation. However, early on the leadership of the NAACP favored the skills and resources of prominent white attorneys to conduct its litigation. Through the 1950s the hostilities of the courts to civil rights litigation may have influenced if not dictated this representation and would be the greatest challenge black lawyers and those concerned with the civil rights of African Americans would face.

Black southerners entered the migration period with the Supreme Court ruling in *Plessy v. Ferguson* (1896). That ruling gave legal authority to the practice of "separate but equal" public accommodations for African Americans. In time, Charles Hamilton Houston, who would lead much of the NAACP's legal work, formulated its strategies for civil rights, including the groundbreaking decision in the middle of the Great Migration of *Brown v. The Board of Education of Topeka, Kansas* (1954). The Court's decision in *Brown* reversed its premigration ruling in *Plessy* and began to address the nation's inequalities that motivated many of the decisions that led to the Great Migration. *See also* Black Legislators.

Further Reading

Porter, Aaron C. "The Career of a Professional Institution: A Study of Norris, Schmidt, Green, Harris, Higginbotham, and Associates." Ph.D. diss., University of Pennsylvania, 1993.

Segal, Geraldine R. *Blacks in the Law: Philadelphia and the Nation*. Philadelphia: University of Pennsylvania Press, 1983.

Smith, J. Clay, Jr. *Emancipation: The Making of the Black Lawyer, 1844-1944*. Philadelphia: University of Pennsylvania Press, 1993.

Michael Benjamin

Automobile Workers

In the first half of the twentieth century, hundreds of thousands of black southerners moved to northern cities and found work inside automobile and auto parts factories in the industrial Midwest. Most black migrants employed in the auto industry worked in plants in **Detroit, Michigan**. Led by the Ford Motor Company, General Motors, and Chrysler, Detroit emerged as a global center of automobile production by World War I. Before World War I most automobile manufacturers refused to hire African Americans. White plant managers doubted that rural migrants could adjust to the discipline of industrial labor and feared that black employment would disrupt production by triggering a backlash among white workers. During World War I the United States experienced a labor shortage that forced auto companies to change their policy of racial exclusion and hire African Americans. In Detroit in 1910, automobile factories employed just over 100 black workers out of a black population of around 6,000. By 1920 the number of African Americans employed in the city's auto plants had increased to 8,000. Most of these newly employed black automobile workers were recent southern migrants, in some cases recruited by **labor agents** sent south by manufacturers. During the next two decades the percentage of black employees in automobile factories increased gradually to 4 percent. World War II triggered a renewed migration of black southerners to northern cities that increased the percentage of black automobile workers to 15 percent of the industry by the end of the war in 1945.

Black southern migrants who found work in automobile factories confronted an entrenched system of **employment discrimination**. Hiring discrimination led to an uneven distribution of black employees in the industry's factories. Most black Ford employees, for example, worked at the River Rouge plant in Dearborn, Michigan, while most black Chrysler employees worked at the Dodge Main plant in Hamtramck, Michigan. Black automobile workers faced inequality inside the factories, working in the least desirable jobs as low-paid, unskilled workers. Black men were concentrated in departments like foundry or spray-painting, and employers confined most of the few black **women** they hired to custodial jobs or cafeteria work.

Initially, black migrants in the automobile industry did not directly challenge racial discrimination or poor working conditions in the factories. The hiring policies and philanthropy in the black community of the Ford Motor Company helped generate a procompany outlook among many migrants in the 1920s and 1930s. Partly as an antiunion strategy, Henry Ford hired more black migrants than any of his competitors. By the late 1930s Ford employed between 10,000 and 12,000 black workers. Ford also tended to promote black workers to a broader range of unskilled and skilled jobs in the factories than other automobile companies. Ford, for example, employed seventy-five black tool and die makers by 1939. The relatively high wages of black Ford workers sustained the livelihood of the black professional class in cities such as Detroit, winning Ford the loyalty of influential **ministers**, doctors, **attorneys**, and business owners. Ford also strengthened his ties to black professionals through financial contributions to ministers and community leaders, whom he often empowered to supervise the labor recruitment of southern migrants.

In the late 1930s and early 1940s a growing number of black migrants challenged the control automobile companies and black professionals exerted over their working conditions. Black migrants in the automobile plants embraced direct action to improve their conditions by joining unions like the **United Automobile Workers** (UAW). By the spring of 1941 the UAW had unionized all of the Big Three automobile corporations, shattering the control black professionals had over the hiring of migrants in the automobile industry. During World War II the tens of thousands of new black migrants who entered the city's automobile factories increasingly looked toward the UAW to advance their interests. Black automobile workers also organized independent civil rights groups to get better jobs and to confront the **housing** shortage facing black southern migrants. In the postwar years the black migrants who had become automobile workers between 1916 and 1945 brought stability to their neighborhoods and leadership to an emerging **civil rights movement**. *See also* Automobility; Congress of Industrial Organizations (CIO); Organized Labor; Primary Document 5.

Further Reading

Meier, August, and Elliott Rudwick. *Black Detroit and the Rise of the UAW*. New York: Oxford University Press, 1979.

Thomas, Richard. *Life for Us Is What We Make It: Building Black Community in Detroit, 1915–1945*. Bloomington: Indiana University Press, 1992.

David Lewis-Colman

Automobility

Between 1915 and 1940 the United States became a nation of automobile owners, and automobility became one of the defining changes of the twentieth century. Although African Americans' access to automobile ownership was limited in this period, cars represented one of the keys to greater personal mobility and economic opportunity for the growing black middle class. For rural migrants and entrepreneurs, automobiles offered new avenues of work and business ownership. For black professionals, the automobile became a tool with which to circumvent the humiliation of **Jim Crow** segregation in public transportation, as well as a material expression of middle-class status and race progress.

The automobile industry provided a powerful magnet for migration north after mass production in 1913. For migrants to **Detroit**, work in Ford's River Rouge plant offered better pay than southern farm labor and a chance at skilled industrial work. Chauffeuring and, later, taxi services became a way for black mechanics and drivers to own their own businesses. In northern and western cities a small number of black inventors and entrepreneurs took advantage of their automotive skill to run driving schools for chauffeurs and start their own automotive companies. The **black press** recorded the contributions of African Americans to motoring as auto mechanics, inventors, entrepreneurs, and driving instructors as examples of progress.

Most important, for a professional class of African Americans who could afford their own cars, the automobile promised escape from Jim Crow

African American Auto Club, Tucson, Arizona. Courtesy of the Arizona Historical Society/ Tucson.

segregation on trains and streetcars. Between 1918 and 1939 automobility promised middle-class African Americans greater spatial and social equality as they sought full citizenship after World War I. In 1930 journalist George Schuyler observed that "all Negroes who can do so purchase an automobile as soon as possible in order to be free of discomfort, discrimination, segregation and insult" (Schuyler, 432).

Car ownership among African Americans grew slowly during the interwar period, limited by purchasing power and discriminatory practices of auto insurers. Yet automobile ownership became a material signifier of race progress. Taking stock of the increase in automobile ownership within the black middle class in the 1920s, the president of the **Tuskegee Normal and Industrial Institute**, **Robert R. Moton**, observed that motorcars were a mark of prosperity among the black middle class. More black Americans purchased automobiles after 1918 than did so before the war, as the resale market grew. Black publications, such as the *Crisis* and *Opportunity*, and black newspapers, such as the *California Eagle*, promoted car ownership as a form of independence and a key to middle-class life similar to **home ownership**.

Despite the promise of autonomy, African Americans understood that simply owning an automobile would not free them from segregation. Rather than welcoming black motorists, much of the new, national auto culture reinscribed older forms of racial discrimination. The growing numbers of white-owned hotels, resorts, and auto camps that grew up alongside the road often did not admit blacks. Sociologists in this period recorded the segregated landscape of automobility. In her study of a middle-class black community in Pennsylvania, Lillian Rhodes concluded that most service stations, hotels, and other tourist services were closed to black motorists (Rhodes, 76).

In response, black leaders used several strategies to ensure participation in the new motor culture. They produced images of black drivers as inventive and respectable, they legally challenged discrimination by auto insurance companies and hotels, and they created separate systems of travel that protected black motorists. With the help of the **National Association for the Advancement of Colored People** (NAACP), black motorists attempted to end the discriminatory policies of auto insurance companies and hotels. Black drivers had great difficulty acquiring automobile insurance because of the stereotype of black drivers as negligent. The NAACP initiated legal challenges to insurance companies covering automobile liability. The denial of liability insurance put an unnecessary burden on black drivers by forcing them to prove their financial security and pay higher premiums and sometimes by denying them a driver's license.

At the same time, African American business leaders created protective associations for black motorists. Black auto enthusiasts in Chicago formed the Afro-American Automobile Association in 1924. In 1936 Victor Green, a black travel agent in **New York City**, produced a national guidebook of hotels and other motor services that catered to black motorists. *The Negro Motorist Green Book* began as a local publication in 1936, but the desire for copies was so great that the booklet was sold nationally in 1937. The publication offered advice on automotive upkeep, but its primary duty was to provide accurate information on hotels that would accommodate black motorists. In this way the *Green Book* was a pioneering effort and helped create a safe, if separate, road for African American motorists. Despite these early efforts, hotel discrimination persisted throughout the 1930s; landmark legislation did not come until 1964, when the *Heart of Atlanta Motel v. United States* case made discrimination in the operation of public accommodations illegal under free-commerce laws.

Historians could know more about the role of transportation and, in particular, the automobile in the Great Black Migration. In 1991 historian Joe Trotter called for scholars to place the Great Migration in broader historical context and to pay attention to differences based on gender, class, and region. Technology and African Americans' use of the new technology of the automobile are another important and almost completely overlooked piece of the story. Future studies should consider patterns of segregation and the contributions of African American business owners, drivers, and inventors to American auto culture. *See also* Automobile Workers; Taxicab Operators; Uplift; Primary Document 69.

Further Reading

Gaines, Kevin. *Uplifting the Race: Black Leadership, Politics, and Culture in the Twentieth Century*. Chapel Hill: University of North Carolina Press, 1996.

Rhodes, Lillian. "One of the Groups *Middletown* Left Out." *Opportunity* 11 (March 1933): 75–77, 93.

Schuyler, George S. "Traveling Jim Crow." *American Mercury* 20 (August 1930): 423–32.

Sinclair, Bruce, ed. *Technology and the African American Experience: Needs and Opportunities for Study*. Cambridge, MA: MIT Press, 2004.

Trotter, Joe William, Jr., ed. *The Great Migration in Historical Perspective: New Dimensions of Race, Class, and Gender*. Bloomington: Indiana University Press, 1991.

Kathleen Franz

Aviation Industry, Black Employment in

World War II almost doubled the population of the West Coast. Eight million people moved there between 1940 and 1950. In the South a million black families were surplus or seasonal labor. Between 1940 and 1945 over 4 million southern African Americans headed for the wartime factories.

Black migrants sought economic opportunity in the wartime West. A woman, for example, made $3.50 a week in the South as a domestic servant

but could earn $48.00 a week in Los Angeles as an aircraft worker. When President Franklin D. Roosevelt banned racial discrimination in defense work through executive order and the creation of the **Fair Employment Practices Committee** (FEPC), northern California's new war industries (one Kaiser plant went from 0 in 1940 to 100,000 workers in 1943) were a natural magnet for black migrants. The **San Francisco** Bay Area, for example, saw a 400 percent increase in African Americans, from 14,000 to 60,000, who mostly worked in the region's **shipyards**. Migrants to Southern California sought work in aircraft industries.

After the United States lifted its arms embargo with the Fourth Neutrality Act of 1939, President Roosevelt committed to building 50,000 planes a year, almost ten times the 5,856 planes built in 1940. After the Japanese attack on Pearl Harbor, Roosevelt told Congress in his January 7, 1942, State of the Union Message that he had ordered production to be increased to 60,000, including 45,000 combat aircraft.

Before the war aircraft plants were small job shops, with multiyear apprenticeships and craftsmen. Output was small and specialized, with frequent model changes. In

On the eve of the World War II, North American Aviation refused to hire blacks as a matter of company policy, but after the creation of the Fair Employment Practices Committee in 1941, African Americans, such as the one pictured above in 1943, worked alongside white employees. Courtesy of the Library of Congress.

January 1940 there were fewer than 100,000 men working in the industry. Most were of draft age. Demand for mass-produced planes meant severe shortages of workers. The West Coast plants increased their workforce fifteenfold, from under 37,000 in 1940 to almost 475,000 in 1945.

Aircraft plants employed few blacks. In 1940 the industry employed 107,000 workers, of whom 240 were black. Boeing had 41,000 workers, none black. In spite of the FEPC and protests by black organizations, companies resisted, wanting to preserve their image as technologically sophisticated, highly skilled, and highly paid. North American Aviation hired blacks as janitors only. When the pool of white men disappeared, aircraft plants chose **women** replacements instead of black men. Women were over a third of the industry's workforce in 1943.

By the summer of 1944 blacks had about 100,000 jobs, but they were just 6 percent of the workforce, a lower rate than in other industries. In **Los Angeles** in June 1942 blacks had 7.2 percent of shipbuilding jobs, but only 1.5 percent in the aircraft industry. Shipyard work was much rougher and dirtier. Black women were hired over black men because employers and white male workers assumed that women were there only temporarily. White women's aversion to working with black women meant that black women in the aircraft plants were either segregated or relegated to janitorial work.

Not only could blacks not build the planes, but they could not fly them either. Blacks had flown since Charles "Chief" Anderson and Bessie Coleman in the 1920s. Between 1930 and 1941 the number of black pilots increased tenfold, to about 102.

The federal government, but not the private sector, began to acknowledge that blacks could fly. The Civilian Pilot Training Program came into being over intense opposition in 1939. After the war the Tuskegee Airmen, their mechanics, and most of the black aircraft workers were shunted aside, as were the women. The industry reverted to a predominantly white preserve.

Still, although set aside temporarily, a million black workers did not return to southern agriculture. Rather, they stayed in the urban North and West, where they organized, marched, protested, voted, worked, and reared families. The wartime labor needs of the defense industries outside the South helped move blacks from subservience and poverty and set the stage for the breakthrough in civil rights that came in the 1950s. Economic success was harder to attain. Although the factories integrated, the pilot's chair remained mostly white. In 2001 African Americans were only 2 percent of America's 71,000 commercial pilots. *See also* Black Aviators; Employment, Black Female Patterns of; Employment, Black Male Patterns of; Wartime Mobilization, World War II.

Further Reading

Chamberlain, Charles D. *Victory at Home: Manpower and Race in the American South during World War II*. Athens: University of Georgia Press, 2003.

Eick, Gretchen Cassel. *Dissent in Wichita: The Civil Rights Movement in the Midwest, 1954–72*. Urbana: University of Illinois Press, 2002.

Hardesty, Von, and Dominick Pisano. *Black Wings: The American Black in Aviation.* Washington, DC: Smithsonian Books, 1984.

Sato, Chitose. "Gender and Work in the American Aircraft Industry during World War II." *Japanese Journal of American Studies*, no. 11 (2000). www.soc.nii.ac.jp/jaas/periodicals/JJAS/PDF/2000/No.11-147.pdf.

John H. Barnhill

B

Baker, Ella Josephine (1903–1986)

Civil rights activist Ella Baker was born in 1903 in Norfolk, Virginia. She grew up on a farm on which her grandparents had worked as slaves. Baker's origins shaped her ideas and actions even from a young age. As a student at Shaw University in Raleigh, North Carolina, Baker criticized the college's policies that she felt were unjust. After graduating as the class valedictorian in 1927, she migrated north to **New York City**. Having done so, she could easily relate to the problems that many blacks experienced as a result of the Great Black Migration.

In 1930 she became active in the Young Negroes Cooperative League, founded by journalist George Schuyler, whose members pooled their funds to purchase products and services at a reduced cost on a national scale. She was elected the first national director of the organization a year later. She also devoted time in the 1930s to teaching consumer education in the **Works Progress Administration** (WPA). Baker was greatly affected by the suffering she witnessed in Harlem during the Great Depression.

Baker also became active in various **women**'s organizations and promoted both consumer and literacy education by working for the WPA's Worker Education Project. In 1940 she went to work for the **National Association for the Advancement of Colored People** (NAACP). She was initially hired as a field coordinator and was very successful at recruiting new members, in part because of her own southern, rural background. She went on to serve as director of branches from 1943 to 1946. She was instrumental in expanding the NAACP throughout the South and created a grassroots network that served as the basis for the **civil rights movement** in the 1950s and 1960s. Baker was also instrumental in gradually moving the organization's emphasis away from legal struggles and toward more community-based activism.

Although she resigned from her position at the NAACP in 1946, she continued to volunteer for the organization, serving as the first woman to head its New York branch. In this capacity she led the struggle to desegregate the New York City public schools. After being inspired by the historic bus boycott in Montgomery, Alabama, in 1955, Baker founded In Friendship, an organization devoted to raising money for the civil rights movement in the South.

In 1956 Baker relocated to **Atlanta, Georgia**, to organize the recently formed Southern Christian Leadership Conference (SCLC). She became SCLC's first director, and Dr. **Martin Luther King, Jr.**, served as its first president. Baker largely worked behind the scenes, organizing more than sixty-five local chapters, while King acted as the group's spokesperson. She also oversaw a voter registration organization known as Crusade for Citizenship. Baker remained with SCLC for two years, but she clashed with King over the organization's policy of supporting strong, centralized leadership rather than local, community-based, grassroots politics, which Baker preferred.

After a group of college students in Greensboro, North Carolina, organized a sit-in at various restaurants to protest the exclusion of blacks, she invited young leaders of the civil rights movement to attend a conference at her alma mater in 1960. Several hundred people attended. As a result of the conference, the Student Nonviolent Coordinating Committee (SNCC) was founded. Unlike most other civil rights organizations, SNCC was a decentralized organization, preferred direct-action tactics and politics, and encouraged young people, women, and the poor to assume leadership roles. Baker helped SNCC establish the Mississippi Freedom Democratic Party, which attempted to replace the all-white delegation from Mississippi at the 1964 Democratic National Convention.

Baker returned to New York in 1964 and continued to be a presence in the civil rights movement until her death. She inspired a wide range of political organizations, including the militant **Black Panther Party**, Students for a Democratic Society, and a number of feminist groups. She remained active in the civil rights movement in the 1970s and 1980s, supporting liberation in Africa, fighting against racial intolerance in America, and volunteering for many organizations, especially those in Harlem. Ella Baker died in 1986 at the age of eighty-three. Several organizations have been founded in her honor, including the Ella Baker Child Policy Training Institute and the Ella Baker Center for Human Rights.

Ella Baker had a profound influence on the civil rights movement, in part because of her emphasis on group-centered, grassroots leadership, in which she differed from most other leaders in the 1950s and 1960s. Baker believed in equal participation for all regardless of gender, income, education, or status. *See also* Community Organizing; Desegregation.

Further Reading

Ransby, Barbara. *Ella Baker and the Black Freedom Movement*. Chapel Hill: University of North Carolina Press, 2003.

Gene Gerard

Baker, George *See* Father Divine

Baldwin, James Arthur (1924–1980)

James Arthur Baldwin knew more about hostile, repressive environments and the need to escape them than he did about southern blacks migrating to the North. He did not even visit the South until 1957. But his own search for freedom led him from his home in Harlem to an apartment in Greenwich Village and finally to Paris. The impetus for the moves, both his and those of the migrants, was about the same: a desire to live and work in an atmosphere free from the constraints of a repressive society.

James Baldwin, born in Harlem on August 2, 1924, was an intellectual, social critic, novelist, dramatist, and essayist whose influence was far-reaching. In 1927 his mother married an unbalanced Pentecostal **minister** who hated him for his illegitimacy and who told him that he was too ugly for anyone to ever love.

Suffering from feelings of guilt and inadequacy, as well as from the taunts of peers who nicknamed him "Froggie" for his smallness and protruding eyes, Baldwin did not do well in school, but several instructors, among them poet Countee Cullen, worked closely with him on his writing. By the age of eleven he had published a short story in the church newsletter, and a poem had drawn the congratulations of **New York City** mayor Fiorello La Guardia.

His stepfather's death in 1943 made him the chief caregiver for his eight siblings. He realized that the only way to help his family out of abject poverty was to make a life for himself as a writer, and to do that, he had to get away. He moved to Greenwich Village in 1944 and by 1946 was publishing reviews and essays on literature and race problems in national left-wing periodicals.

Much of his early fiction was autobiographical. *Go Tell It on the Mountain* (1953) ties in most directly with the Great Black Migration. Of the two main characters who had left the South for the North, he said that they had left the darkness and despair but were now in the fire. He also noted that they cannot "escape **Jim Crow**: they merely encounter another, not-less-deadly variety" (Baldwin, *Nobody Knows My Name*, 68).

By 1948 Baldwin's discomfort in an America plagued by racism and homophobia led him to seek refuge in Paris. There he formed close friendships with the resident literati and created a satisfactory life with a Swiss artist, Lucien Happersberger, in an Alpine villa.

The publication of a collection of essays, *Notes of a Native Son* (1955), brought him wide attention. However, the explicit homosexuality in two subsequent novels, *Giovanni's Room* (1956) and *Another Country* (1962), unsettled many, as did another collection of essays, *The Fire Next Time* (1963), with its prophetic warning about violent racial confrontations.

A leading figure in the **civil rights movement**, Baldwin took part in the March on Washington and arranged for a critical meeting with other black intellectuals and Attorney General Robert F. Kennedy to expose him to the raw bitterness and despair among African Americans. By the late 1960s Baldwin had fallen out of favor with black nationalists who scorned his lifestyle and his approach to the problems of racism. Perhaps in response to the criticism, Baldwin began to take a more extreme stance. Talk of a peaceful resolution to conflict gave way to a militant call for change. James Baldwin, an eloquent spokesperson for all races, for all people in search of a good life in a just world, died of stomach cancer in 1980. *See also* Ellison, Ralph Waldo; Himes, Chester; Literature, the Great Migration in; Wright, Richard Nathaniel.

Further Reading

Baldwin, James. *Go Tell It on the Mountain*. New York: Knopf, 1953.
———. *Nobody Knows My Name*. New York: Dial Press, 1961.
Campbell, James. *Talking at the Gates: A Life of James Baldwin*. New York: Penguin Books, 1991.
Leeming, David A. *James Baldwin: A Biography*. New York: Knopf, 1994.

Gay Pitman Zieger

Baltimore, Maryland

In seeking to understand Baltimore's place as a destination for African Americans relocating north during the Great Migration, it is important to bear in mind that the contemporary relocation of Maryland to the mid-Atlantic region does not diminish its history as a slave state, albeit one with a large free black population in the antebellum period. The legacy of slavery and subsequent **Jim Crow** legislation in the postbellum era continued to influence economic and political opportunities for African Americans well into the 1960s. Thus the problems that black migrants were seeking to escape, such as legal segregation and discrimination that circumscribed their lives within the Deep South, also existed in Baltimore and throughout Maryland. Unlike its northern counterparts such as **New York City**, **Philadelphia**, and **Chicago**, Baltimore did not experience a dramatic external increase in its black population until World War II. But the desire to transform racial opportunities that characterized the motivation of the migrants and the larger political and economic role that African Americans began to play in urban life were mirrored in Baltimore.

Because Maryland was a border state that allied with the Union, its slave owners were exempt from the Emancipation Proclamation of January 1, 1863. Slavery did not officially end in Maryland until November 1864. Attempts to reconfigure the racial hierarchy during Reconstruction were undermined by Democratic political leaders who quickly instituted segregation and Jim Crow legislation to maintain racial boundaries in **housing**, education, employment, and entertainment. Although African Americans maintained the right to vote despite a series of state challenges to the Fifteenth Amendment, the electoral power of the community was ultimately stifled, and the process of **desegregation** did not conclude until the end of the 1960s.

Although municipalities such as Philadelphia, **Pittsburgh**, Chicago, **Detroit**, and New York had episodes of racial unrest, African Americans could live without the fears of **lynching** and racial violence. This was not the case in Maryland, where between 1900 and 1911 there were seven lynchings. Mob violence again erupted in the period 1913–1933, when two lynchings and several attempted lynchings on Maryland's Eastern Shore reminded black Baltimoreans that the specter of southern-style racial violence still existed in their state.

The migration patterns of African Americans reveal that Baltimore did not experience a great influx during the first half of the Great Migration. The federal census reports covering the years 1910 through 1930 reported a total net loss of 53,315 blacks throughout Maryland. In 1910, 87 percent of the black population was native to Maryland. Of the 13 percent born outside the state, migrants from Virginia made up 8.7 percent of the total, with all other states contributing less than 1 percent each to Maryland's black population. In 1920, 76 percent of Baltimore's black population of 108,322 were natives of the state, in comparison with Detroit's mere 8.4 percent. Of the 109,000 blacks living in Manhattan, only 20.9 percent were New York natives, whereas 51 percent of the total population registered as being born outside the state, and 21 percent were foreign born. In 1930, out of a total black population of 276,379, there were 201,244 persons who were black Marylanders by birth, constituting 72.8 percent of the total black population. Baltimore also had a high percentage of native-born black residents, 84,410 out of a total population of 142,106, but the 59.4 percent native born marked a decline of 7.4 percent from 1920 and 17.1 percent from 1910.

Baltimore was, however, a part of the Great Migration to the extent that the movement was also marked by the urbanization of the African American population nationwide. In 1930 Virginia continued to serve as the birthplace for the largest number of migrants to the city, 29,332, while an additional 7,757 moved into the state. In addition to migrants coming from Virginia, Baltimore's population increase can be attributed to relocation from rural sections of the state. Higher wages, better education, and psychological freedom were some of the reasons African Americans left Maryland's agricultural areas. Yet many found their employment opportunities in the city limited to unskilled manual labor. While these jobs paid more than agricultural ones, the costs to live in an urban area were higher. The most desirable and highest wages, for skilled work, were elusive for black men. In 1930 there were only 253 black carpenters, 86 machinists, 41 plumbers, and 163 tailors in Baltimore. The largest percentage found jobs in the manufacturing and mechanical industries, but more than half the 22,426 employed were laborers. Of the 8,841 black men who worked in domestic and personal service, the majority listed their occupations as janitors, porters, servants, and waiters.

In addition to a racially segregated labor market, African American **women** also had to contend with gender bias that often limited them to the lowest-paying and least skilled jobs. Of the 35,740 women in Baltimore who listed work in "domestic and personal service," 26,032 were African American, and of that number 18,687 worked at servants and 3,962 as laundresses. There were 1,670 more black laundresses in Baltimore than the total number of black women employed in all the manufacturing and mechanical industries. Unlike their white counterparts, 48 percent of married black women worked, in comparison with 10.3 percent of native white women and 7.2 percent of foreign-born women. Out of 78,886 gainfully employed black Baltimoreans over the age of ten (67.6 percent of the community, as compared with 50.9 percent of the native white community), 95 percent were engaged in some kind of unskilled work in 1930. In addition, although they constituted just over one-quarter of the total workforce, a higher percentage of the black community, 84.8 percent of men and 50.7 percent of women, were gainfully employed.

These patterns of racial segregation in employment continued until the federal government intervened with Executive Order 8802 in 1941, which ordered companies with defense contracts to hire African Americans. Federal intervention in defense industries in Baltimore afforded African Americans new economic opportunities. Working with both the **Fair Employment Practices Committee** and the **Congress of Industrial Organizations**, civil rights leaders were able to break through racial barriers that had historically confined nonwhites to the lowest-paying and least desirable jobs. As a result, there was a noticeable increase in the numbers of African Americans who were employed in skilled and semiskilled positions. In addition to federal intervention, the spread of industrial unions offered black workers new protections, the chance to earn higher wages, and the chance for skilled employment. Even with the shifts in the workplace and increasing opportunities for African Americans, the majority of black men recorded their occupations in three categories—laborers, operatives, and service workers. Black women were still concentrated in domestic service, with service workers listed as the second most available option. Nevertheless, it is important to note that while the majority of black women classified themselves as household workers, many had moved into other service jobs. At the top of the scale, although the professional class was still small, the increase in clerical workers was noticeable. By 1950, although the African American population had increased to 265,425 in the metropolitan area, the occupational structure remained virtually the same.

While the opportunities for high wages were limited in Baltimore, African Americans in the city had the best access to educational resources in the state. In the first half of the twentieth century Baltimore was the site of the state's only institution of higher learning open to African Americans. Originally founded as an Episcopalian seminary in 1867, Morgan College (the name was changed in 1890) was purchased by the state to serve black students in 1939. For those African Americans who found the education at Morgan College lacking, a limited number of scholarships were available for study at universities outside the state.

One of the marked differences between Baltimore and its southern counterparts was its active civil rights struggle that began in the mid-1930s. Influenced by ideas from the **New Negro** and inspired by opportunities in the North, young black Baltimoreans decided to challenge the racial status quo in the city. With an activist newspaper, the ***Baltimore Afro-American***, and a core of politically minded leaders, black activists were able to launch a mass movement that brought together traditional civil rights organizations, like the local branches of the **National Association for the Advancement of Colored People** (NAACP) and the **National Urban League**, with groups including radicals, intellectuals, **fraternal orders**, and labor leaders. In the midst of the Great Depression the Baltimore NAACP launched a series of campaigns in conjunction with the legal defense wing of the NAACP that offered a response to the changing political, economic, and social climate of the times. The middle-class leadership initiated traditional campaigns, such as their suit to equalize the salaries of African American and white teachers in Maryland counties, as well as organizing mass marches against discrimination and racial violence.

The first major campaign initiated by the Baltimore NAACP had widespread implications for higher education across the South. Maryland's state university system barred African Americans from attending its professional schools until 1935, when the landmark case *Murray v. University of Maryland* forced the desegregation of the law school. Representing the plaintiff, Donald Gaines Murray, the legal powerhouses Charles Hamilton Houston and Thurgood Marshall embarked on a campaign to desegregate professional schools throughout southern public university systems.

By the 1940s African American campaigns included the desegregation of the workplace. With the rapid industrial development needed during World War II, the black community in Baltimore, which had been plagued by high rates of **unemployment**, was able to reap the benefits. Thousands of African Americans, both men and women, joined the workforce in industries that had excluded them from semiskilled and skilled jobs. Part of the reason for this success rests with the continued pressure placed on industry by the coalition that included the *Afro-American* and civil rights organizations. With more than 25,000 new members in 1945, the Baltimore NAACP was one of the largest branches in the country. Baltimore's civil rights struggle continued through the 1960s, with desegregation following the guidelines established by the Supreme Court in 1954, as well as patterns laid forth by grassroots movements. By the time the black population was able to use its numerical strength in local politics, the increases in the black population were offset by **white flight**, **deindustrialization**, and economic decay. In many ways the most significant impact of the Great Migration on Baltimore was linked to an emerging urban politic. As black Baltimoreans witnessed what was possible in the North, they were inspired to create a mass movement that eventually laid the groundwork for other southern civil rights campaigns. *See also* Civil Rights Movement; Employment, Black Female Patterns of; Employment, Black Male Patterns of; Political Activism (1915-1945); Washington, D.C.; Primary Documents 4, 40.

Further Reading

Argersinger, Jo Ann E. *Toward a New Deal in Baltimore: People and Government in the Great Depression*. Chapel Hill: University of North Carolina Press, 1988.

Orser, W. Edward. "Neither Separate nor Equal: Foreshadowing *Brown* in Baltimore County, 1935-1937." *Maryland Historical Magazine* 92 (Spring 1997): 4-35.

Reid, Ira De A. *The Negro Community of Baltimore: A Social Survey*. Baltimore: Baltimore Urban League, 1934.

Seawright, Sally. "Desegregation at Maryland: The NAACP and the Murray Case in the 1930s." *Maryland Historian* 1 (Spring 1970): 59-73.

Shoemaker, Sandy M. " 'We Shall Overcome, Someday': The Equal Rights Movement in Baltimore, 1935-1942." *Maryland Historical Magazine* 89 (Fall 1994): 261-73.

Sktones, Andor. " 'Buy Where You Can Work': Boycotting for Jobs in African American Baltimore, 1933–1934." *Journal of Social History* 27 (Summer 1994): 735–61.

Prudence D. Cumberbatch

Baltimore Afro-American

Founded in 1892, the *Baltimore Afro-American* was one of three or four publications that became modern, mass-circulation national newspapers during the 1930s and 1940s as a result of the massive black migrations of the twentieth century. The newspaper barely survived its first few years under the management of its founder, Rev. William Alexander. In 1897 John Murphy, Sr., manager of the printing department and a former slave and Civil War veteran, purchased the newspaper out of bankruptcy. Three years later he merged the paper with George F. Bragg's *Ledger*, and the paper became known for a time as the *Afro-American Ledger*. With Murphy as business manager and Bragg as editor, the paper won a circulation war against five competing black weeklies in **Baltimore** and emerged as the leading black newspaper in the city by 1915. After Bragg's departure that year the *Afro-American* continued to expand its circulation, from 7,500 to 19,200 in 1919, by expanding its distribution outside the city and, after 1917, adopting a more sensational style. Following the pioneering **Chicago Defender**, the *Afro-American* began to make the newspaper more graphically enticing while emphasizing **crime**, sex scandals, and other sensational topics in bold headlines on the front page and continuing to campaign for racial justice in editorials.

When thousands of blacks began the Great Migration out of the Deep South during World War I, the *Afro-American* called on black leaders to demand an end to **lynching**, the building of better schools, and the expansion of civil and political rights. The threat of removing the South's labor force might force whites to agree to such demands. Though the *Afro-American* never advocated migration as enthusiastically as the *Defender*, the paper did support blacks who decided to move. If "the Negro . . . cannot receive fair treatment in the South, his home, then he will have to make a new home for himself elsewhere," the paper editorialized (January 27, 1917, 4). As the black population of Baltimore and nearby cities grew, the *Afro-American* improved its circulation by appealing to different kinds of readers, including the less literate migrants from the Deep South. Murphy's son Carl Murphy took over management of the paper after his father's death in 1922 and became the architect of the new approach. He managed the paper for the next forty-five years.

The *Afro-American* was one of a few newspapers to prosper during the Great Depression because of Murphy's shrewd business decisions. He created editions of the paper in **Philadelphia**, **Washington, D.C.**, and **Richmond** and opened distribution centers along the East Coast and in the Midwest. Circulation exceeded 45,000 by 1930, 100,000 by 1940, and 230,000 by 1945, making it the second-largest black newspaper after the **Pittsburgh Courier**.

Like other black newspapers, the *Afro-American* took on the role of advocate for the black community on both the local and national levels. Nationally, the paper endorsed presidential candidates and sought to hold them to promises on race policy. Unlike most black newspapers, the *Afro-American* was sympathetic to left-wing causes and even provided unofficial endorsements of Communist Party candidates in the 1932 and 1936 presidential elections, while defending **Paul Robeson** and **W.E.B. DuBois** against disloyalty charges during the Red Scare after World War II. Locally, the paper crusaded for jobs, **housing**, fairness in the criminal justice system, and equal educational opportunity. The *Afro-American* organized boycotts of local businesses that discriminated against blacks. It also sought to **uplift** the black community with its moralistic editorials promoting middle-class values.

Like other black newspapers, the *Afro-American* began to decline after the 1940s. Black newspapers found that more black readers were turning to the mainstream press for its more immediate coverage of the **civil rights movement** of the 1950s and 1960s. In addition, mainstream news organizations began to hire the best black journalists away from the **black press**, especially after 1968. By 1977 the *Afro-American*, now publishing three times per week, sold only 34,000 of its two weekday editions and 18,500 of its weekend edition. Still, the paper survived and had a circulation of 120,000 in 2004. *See also* Associated Negro Press (ANP); Primary Documents 4, 25, 40.

Further Reading

"About Us." *Afro-American Newspapers.* July 2004. www.afro.com/aboutus.htm.
Farrar, Hayward. *The "Baltimore Afro-American," 1892–1950.* Westport, CT: Greenwood Press, 1998.

William G. Jordan

Banks and Bankers

The history of black-owned banks in the United States followed the pattern of black-owned businesses in general. Between 1888 and 1971 about 157 black-owned banks were organized. Beginning primarily in the South with the deposits of **fraternal orders** and insurance companies, black-owned banks responded to state regulatory laws by obtaining state charters after 1910. Those that survived the Great Depression did so because of conservative lending practices and limited investment in real estate. Between 1930 and 1960 interest in operating a bank waned among African Americans, but the political and social advances of the **civil rights movement** and large urban populations reawakened interest in banking after 1960. Unlike the early period of black banking, the late twentieth century was not marked by flamboyant or stalwart personalities such as John Mitchell, Maggie Lena Walker, Charles Banks, Jesse Binga, or **Richard R. Wright, Sr.**

In *The Negro as Capitalist: A Study of Banking and Business among American Negroes*, **Abram L. Harris** concluded that although a lack of experience and technical bank training, dishonesty, fraud, and speculation were prevalent among black-owned banks, these were not the primary causes of their failures and weaknesses; black-owned banks were "handicapped by the inherent characteristics of black business enterprise." While black migration to

One of the many loan banks in the African American section of Chicago. Courtesy of the Library of Congress.

urban areas helped black-owned banks by increasing depositors, these depositors were the most economically vulnerable. Therefore, **unemployment** and a poor economy had a more deleterious effect on black-owned banks.

Between 1888 and 1908 fraternal order accounts were large enough to encourage the founding of a number of black-owned banks. In Virginia these banks included the Savings Bank of the Grand Fountain of the United Order of True Reformers, founded by W. W. Browne, the grand worthy master; the Independent Order of St. Luke's Penny Savings Bank, founded by Maggie Lena Walker, the right worthy grand secretary; and the Mechanics Savings Bank, founded by John Mitchell, the grand chancellor of the Virginia Knights of Pythias and grand worthy counsellor of its women's auxiliary, the Order of Calanthe. Mitchell was also the owner and publisher of the *Richmond Planet*, a weekly newspaper. Of the three, only Walker presided over a bank that was not plagued by mismanagement and unprofitable real estate investments. Walker and the St. Luke's Bank and Trust Company took control of the last of the black-owned banks in **Richmond** and became the Consolidated Bank and Trust Company.

Others were making their mark in banking in southern cities as well. In Mississippi, Charles Banks and Isaiah T. Montgomery, founder of Mound Bayou, founded the Mound Bayou State Bank in 1916. Banks had founded the Bank of Mound Bayou in 1904, but it failed in 1914. Banks and Montgomery were shining examples of **Booker T. Washington**'s doctrine of self-help and were instrumental in the founding and operation of the National Negro Business League (NNBL). Banks served as the third vice president of the NNBL from 1901 to 1905 and as first vice president from 1907 until his death in 1923.

Although African Americans in the South can be credited with founding the greatest number of black-owned banks, **Chicago** stands as the undisputed capital of black-owned banking. Chicago had four black-owned banks, but Binga

State Bank and Douglass National Bank, the first black-owned bank with a national charter, were the largest black-owned banks in the country. Their combined resources totaled almost $4,000,000 in 1929, about one-third of the total deposits of all black-owned banks in the country. Compared with the average metropolitan bank, however, these titans of black-owned finance were modest.

Chicago black banking was dominated by one man, Jesse Binga, a real estate broker whose success necessitated his entry into banking. In 1908 he founded the first black-owned private bank outside the South, and thirteen years later he opened the Binga State Bank. Binga's real estate business and his bank profited from the population explosion caused by African Americans migrating to large urban cities outside the South. In 1929 the crowning jewel of his success was the construction of the Binga Arcade, a five-story office complex with a ballroom that he hoped would revitalize a once-thriving black business district, but the Great Depression struck, and Binga's empire crumbled. The Binga State Bank failed in 1930, and Binga was convicted of embezzlement. He served three years of a ten-year term in the Illinois State Penitentiary.

Richard Robert Wright, Sr., became a banker after a long and successful career as an educator in Georgia. After a clerk at the Citizens and Southern Bank in Savannah refused not only to address his daughter as "Miss" but struck her during the argument, Wright lodged a civil and criminal suit against the institution. A less-than-satisfactory settlement encouraged Wright to relocate to **Philadelphia**, where several of his nine children lived. With his son, Bishop **Richard R. Wright, Jr.**, and one of his daughters, Wright opened the Citizens and Southern Bank and Trust Company in September 1920. He was known for his cautious lending practices; one depositor is claimed to have said, "If you need $25, Major Wright want you to leave both eyes, both legs, and all the collateral you can muster."

Eleven black-owned banks survived the Great Depression, and two more were chartered during the 1930s. By 1940, twelve black-owned banks were still in operation. After World War II, three more banks were opened. But it was not until the political and social changes of the civil rights movement that black banking received renewed interest. Between 1963 and 1969, twelve banks were organized, primarily in large industrial cities outside the South. Eight of the twelve operated under national charters. In 1970 and 1971, six more black-owned banks were chartered, bringing the total number of black-owned banks to thirty.

Racial reasons more than economic ones were responsible for the establishment of black-owned banks, but the segregated economy in which they operated determined their success or failure. The creation of black-owned banks and the houses, churches, and buildings they invested in served as proof to the African American community of their success in the American economy. *See also* Black Consumer Market; Insurers and Insurance Companies; Policy Gambling.

Further Reading

Ammons, Lila. "The Evolution of Black-Owned Banks in the United States between the 1880s and the 1990s." *Journal of Black Studies* 26 (March 1996): 467–89.

Harris, Abram L. *The Negro as Capitalist: A Study of Banking and Business among American Negroes*. 1936. Reprint, New York: Negro Universities Press, 1969.

Haynes, Elizabeth Ross. *The Black Boy of Atlanta*. Boston: House of Edinboro, 1952.

Henderson, Alexa Benson. "Richard R. Wright and the National Negro Bankers Association: Early Organizing Efforts among Black Bankers, 1924-1942." *Pennsylvania Magazine of History and Biography* 117 (1993): 51-81.

Kinzer, Robert H., and Edward Sagarin. *The Negro in American Business: The Conflict between Separatism and Integration*. New York: Greenberg Publishers, 1950.

Lemon, Harriet Beecher Stowe, ed. *Radio Speeches of Major R. R. Wright, Sr*. Philadelphia: Farmer Press, 1949.

Lindsey, Arnett G. "The Negro in Banking." *Journal of Negro History* 14, no. 2 (April 1929): 156-201.

Osthaus, Carl R. "The Rise and Fall of Jesse Binga, Black Financier." *Journal of Negro History* 58, no. 1 (January 1973): 39-60.

Pace, Harry H. "The Business of Banking among Negroes." *Crisis* 34 (February 1927): 184-88.

Debra Foster Greene

Baptist Church

The Baptist Church is one of the largest evangelical Protestant denominations in America. The Baptist faith traces its roots back to the Reformation in Europe with the emergence of the Anabaptists, a group that emphasized the Reform tradition of worship, church polity, and the baptism of the voluntary, conscious believer. The first Baptists in America originated from the Separatists and Puritans, two groups that migrated from Europe in the early seventeenth century. Both the Separatists and the Puritans settled in places like Massachusetts to escape the corruption and persecution of the Church of England. Almost 200 years later, African American Baptists, much like their predecessors, left the South in America for places like **Chicago**, **Pittsburgh**, **New York City**, and **Detroit** to escape the economic and political persecution of the southern white ruling classes in America in what is known as the Great Migration.

Origins of African American Baptists

Ironically, those who brought the gospel of the Baptist faith to thousands of African Americans initially came to the shores of America with African slaves. After the American Revolution in 1776, white Baptists became some of the primary missionaries to slave communities in the South. Although many slave owners restricted slaves from converting to Christianity, many within slaveholding societies believed that Christianity would be beneficial to the slave as well as to the institution of slavery. There was a widespread belief that the slave trade was instrumental in converting the "heathen" slave to Christianity. Indeed, the conversion of the slave was seen as a deterrent to slave rebellions and a way to keep slaves docile under the hands of their masters.

Baptist missionaries began sporadically to evangelize slaves throughout the colonies, especially when it was determined that baptism did not free the slaves from their servitude. With the coming of the Second Great Awakening in the 1800s, Baptist missionaries were found to convert slaves to Christianity in the hundreds. Many slaves were drawn to the Baptist form of worship and baptism by water submersion, which mirrored ritual practices within some West African traditions. By the 1840s Baptist missionary efforts had equipped slave and free black communities with their own **ministers** and missionaries.

During Reconstruction the Baptist denomination saw the fruit of its missionary labors among African peoples by the establishment of black Baptist churches throughout the North and South. In 1890, for example, black Baptists numbered more than 1 million in the United States. By 1906 black Baptists had doubled their membership, boasting a nationwide membership of more than 2 million, with many of these members living in southern states.

The organizational structure of the black Baptist church reflected a two-tiered system. The first tier consisted of the local body of black Christians who made up the church's membership, and the second tier was made up of the regional representatives from black Baptist communities across the nation or state. Within the second organizational structure, black Baptists formed a series of national conventions (the Foreign Mission Baptist Convention, U.S.A., and the National Baptist Convention, which formed the National Baptist Convention, U.S.A.) designed to address issues pertinent to black life.

Theologically, the black Baptist church understood God to be a God who was on the side of the oppressed and downtrodden in society. Black Baptists believed that God through Jesus Christ was not just concerned about the eternal salvation of people, but Christ also wanted them to experience physical salvation in this present life. God, according to black Baptists, wanted the freedom and equality of the entire black community. Key biblical images such as the Exodus story and Canaan Land were heralded as divine narratives reflecting black life and God's promise to bring true freedom to African Americans. With these biblical mandates in mind, black Baptists structured the very function of their organization to reflect these divine imperatives.

The Great Migration

The first decades of the twentieth century invoked radical responses from black southerners suffering from the devastation of floods, the tenacious **boll weevil**, corruption within the sharecropping system, and the daily indignities of **Jim Crow**. Black southerners began to resist by leaving the South for the North and its industrial opportunities opened up by World War I. The National Baptist Convention and its local congregations in the North played a key role in creating support systems to aid black migrants.

Black Baptist churches created a sense of solidarity within black migrant communities by providing support networks in which blacks could combat poverty, disfranchisement, and discrimination. Many of these support networks were established in the form of church auxiliaries and ministries that specifically targeted these issues. The formulation of such specialized ministries was based on the belief that those black communities that received support would experience the presence and activity of God. Black Baptists felt that they were instruments of God's providence, enabling God's people to escape the proverbial Egypt and find peace in the "Canaan lands" of the

North. Migrants mirrored this perspective, and thousands flocked to the open doors of black Baptist churches in such places as Chicago, Detroit, **Philadelphia**, Pittsburgh, and New York.

Among migrants, black Baptist churches in the North developed reputations as centers of refuge and aid—the "Moseses" that would help them settle in the "Promised Land." Second Baptist Church of Detroit was one of those centers and held a reputation as the "Home of Strangers" among southern migrants. Union Baptist Church of Philadelphia was the house of worship that the city's black professional and middle classes attended for services. By 1916 both churches had tripled their membership, with Second Baptist jumping from 250 in 1910 to 900 by 1915. Union Baptist's membership increased so much during this period that its membership of 2,100 outgrew the church's facility by 1916, making it necessary to purchase a larger building. In 1903 Olivet Baptist Church in Chicago held a congregation of 600, but by 1921 the church's membership exploded to 10,012 congregants.

The overall attraction of churches like Union and Second Baptist was the congregation's ability to transform the very pews of the church into overnight shelters and housing facilities. Second Baptist of Detroit was known to allow migrants to sleep on the pews in the church overnight. Another church, Union Baptist of **Cincinnati, Ohio**, converted a lecture hall into a shelter for sixty-five migrant men per night. Other churches opened their pews and created programs that specifically targeted the various needs of migrants. Olivet Baptist Church of Chicago, for example, created more than forty programs to assist migrants.

Another attraction of the black Baptist church was in large part the religious affiliation of black migrants. Many migrants were long-standing members of black Baptist churches in the South. Readjusting to northern cities was simply a transplanting of their faith traditions, reestablishing the Baptist denomination in black urban areas. As a result, social agencies such as the **National Urban League** sought out Baptist leadership and services to help alleviate social and cultural problems inherent to black migrants.

In short, the Great Migration created a shift in the theological focus of the black Baptist church, causing it to manifest a more social and political spirituality within urban communities. The good news of the gospel was now about physically manifesting the provisions of God to the migrant, as opposed to preaching that the migrants' Promised Land was only an afterlife experience. For northern Baptists confronting the overflowing river of migrants from the South, the Promised Land was a reality that could be realized with the help of God and the arm of the black Baptist Church. *See also* Bradby, Robert L.; Storefront Churches; Primary Documents 44, 50, 57.

Further Reading

Fisher, Miles Mark. "History of the Olivet Baptist Church of Chicago." Master's Thesis, Divinity School, University of Chicago, 1922.

Higginbotham, Evelyn Brooks. *Righteous Discontent: The Woman's Movement in the Black Baptist Church, 1880–1920*. Cambridge, MA: Harvard University Press, 1993.

Lincoln, C. Eric, and Lawrence H. Mamiya. *The Black Church in the African American Experience*. Durham, NC: Duke University Press, 1990.

Raboteau, Albert J. *Canaan Land: A Religious History of African Americans*. New York: Oxford University Press, 2001.

Robinson-Harmon, Julia. "Reverend Robert L. Bradby: Establishing the Kingdom of God among Migrants, Women and Workers, 1910-1946." Ph.D. diss., Michigan State University, 2002.

Sernett, Milton. *Bound for the Promised Land: African American Religion and the Great Migration*. Durham, NC: Duke University Press, 1997.

———, ed. *African American Religious History: A Documentary Witness*. 2nd ed. Durham, NC: Duke University Press, 1999.

Julia Robinson-Harmon

Baraka, Amiri (1934–)

Amiri Baraka (LeRoi Jones), born Everett Leroy Jones in 1934 in Newark, New Jersey, is a prolific poet, dramatist, novelist, and essayist. He was perhaps the most influential figure in the **Black Arts movement**. His views on the development of black art have changed dramatically, but remain embroiled in the tensions between assimilation, acculturation, and **black nationalism**. Baraka's work repeatedly returns to the migration and its role in the development of American and African American cultures. He argues that the migrants themselves—not large-scale social and economic "push" and "pull" forces—were the most important agents of the twentieth century's cultural changes. In *Blues People: Negro Music in White America* (1963), his principal statement on the migration's cultural implications, Baraka portrays the migration and the black populist aesthetic migrants brought to American cities as the single most important challenge to the dominance of what he describes as an elitist, economically driven Euro-American culture.

Biographer William J. Harris separates Baraka's career into three distinct periods: the Beat Period (1957–1962), the Black Nationalist Period (1965–1974), and the Third World Marxist Period (1974–present). After attending Rutgers University and then **Howard University** for a short time, in 1952 he changed his name to LeRoi Jones and joined the U.S. Air Force. Through these early experiences with formal education and military service, Baraka rejected bourgeois aspirations for respectability and in 1957 left the air force for the bohemian world of Beat writers such as Allen Ginsberg, Frank O'Hara, and Gilbert Sorrentino in **New York City**'s Greenwich Village. During his "bohemian" days Baraka's work explored personal alienation more than the political implications of racial oppression. He did, however, strongly identify with the Cuban Revolution, traveling there in 1960 with a group of black artists and intellectuals. After the assassination of **Malcolm X** in 1965, Baraka turned toward cultural nationalism. In 1967 he changed his name to Imamu Ameer (Amiri) Baraka, moved to Harlem, and started the Black Arts Repertory Theater School. In 1968 he moved again to Newark, where he founded the Black Community Development and Defense Organization and committed himself to Islam. Baraka subsequently rejected nationalism as a racist ideology, embracing instead Marxist critiques of capitalist economic and social relations.

Many of Baraka's poems and his only novel, *The System of Dante's Hell* (1965), explore African Americans' changing relationship to African culture,

the South, and the tensions in modern racial consciousness between assimilation and ethnic nationalism. *Blues People* is the classic statement of the relationship between black music and the changing historical contexts in which
it was made. In this influential work and in his essays in *Black Music* (1968),
Baraka describes the history of black music as it changed through African
Americans' migrations from Africa to America, from the South to the North
and West, from premodern to modern life, and from rural to urban communities. More specifically, the transitions from Africa to American slavery and
later from southern fields and juke joints to **blues** and **jazz** clubs, theaters,
churches, and recording studios in the North changed the music's form and
performance. He argues that the move to modern urban life made it less likely
that black musicians would perform spontaneously, with acoustic instruments, or without a band. Planned performances with written music and
lyrics, he contends, reflected an increasingly bourgeois, homogenized, and
formalized black culture in modern communities. Nonetheless, Baraka describes a dialectical relationship between African-inspired black culture and
modern Euro-American consumer culture. From this perspective, black migrants brought a radical alternative to the dominant Western literary tradition.
See also Black Power; Literature, the Great Migration in; Visual Arts, the Great
Migration in.

Further Reading

Griffin, Farah Jasmine. *"Who Set You Flowin'?" The African-American Migration
    Narrative*. New York: Oxford University Press, 1995.
Hall, James C. *Mercy, Mercy Me: African-American Culture and the American Sixties*.
    New York: Oxford University Press, 2001.
Harris, William J. *The LeRoi Jones/Amiri Baraka Reader*. New York: Thunder's
    Mouth Press, 1991.
Jones, LeRoi (Amiri Baraka). *Black Music*. New York: Da Capo Press, 1998.
———. *Blues People: Negro Music in White America*. New York: William Morrow,
    1963.
———. *Three Books by Imamu Amiri Baraka (LeRoi Jones): The System of Dante's
    Hell; Tales; The Dead Lecturer*. New York: Grove Press, 1967.
Keil, Charles. *Urban Blues*. 2nd ed. Chicago: University of Chicago Press, 1970.
Watts, Jerry Gafio. *Amiri Baraka: The Politics and Art of a Black Intellectual*. New
    York: New York University Press, 2001.
Woodard, Komozi. *A Nation within a Nation: Amiri Baraka (LeRoi Jones) and Black
    Power Politics*. Durham, NC: University of North Carolina Press, 1999.

Jeffrey Helgeson

Barbers

As the popular films *Barbershop* and *Barbershop II* illustrate, the modern
black-owned barbershop not only provides economic opportunity—teaching
young men marketable skills and giving them stable employment and a chance
to own a business—but also provides a space where black men can air their
opinions and debate the issues. The barbers who preside over these shops,

consequently, are important community leaders. They assumed that role by drawing on traditions of enterprise that predated the Great Black Migration, reinventing their businesses to serve an urbanizing African American population. This transformation sheds light on how mutual aid, entrepreneurship, and the politics of identity shaped urban black America.

The commitment of black barbers to mutual aid facilitated African American migration, first by barbers and later by their customers. Because they retained the artisan system that preserved high levels of skill and reduced competition through apprenticeships, black barbers, in contrast to their white counterparts, made the trade into a close-knit network extending across the nation. They represented the vanguard of black migration because talented young barbers moved between cities in the South and the rest of the nation regularly as early as the antebellum period to seek opportunity and a shop of their own. Throughout the nineteenth century, when African Americans were too rural and too poor to support barbershops, black barbers dominated the upscale end of the trade, serving white customers. Their success, in large part, came from exporting deferential traditions of race relations from the South to the rest of the country. In 1879 George Myers relocated from **Baltimore** to **Cleveland**, where he eventually became the owner of the barbershop in the Hollenden Hotel, reputed to be the finest in America. Myers, in turn, relied on southern migrants for barbers, whom he actively recruited after the turn of the century.

African American barber shop, Chicago. Courtesy of the Library of Congress.

By the 1890s, however, African American migration to southern cities established a **black consumer market** that barbers could serve instead of white customers, so the modern black-owned barbershop originated in the South. These barbershops offered their customers access to the barbers' network. According to the childhood memories of James P. Hall of Mobile, early twentieth-century black barbers shared information with their customers about jobs and **housing** in northern cities, helping them decide when and where to migrate north. Historian James Grossman has also uncovered evidence of barbers moving with their customers. In 1916 Robert Horton, a barber in Hattiesburg, Mississippi, recruited nearly forty men and women to join his family in a migration club, which secured a group discount for travel north on the Illinois Central Railroad. Horton established the Hattiesburg Barber Shop in **Chicago** not long after his arrival there, which became a gathering place for migrants from Mississippi.

Barbers joined the movement to create a group economy within segregated neighborhoods that arose in the wake of urban migration. In Chicago, for example, barbershops ranked third among the most numerous black-owned businesses in 1938, underscoring how pervasive these businesses had become on black main streets across the country. Barbers also assumed prominent roles at meetings of the National Negro Business League, an organization dedicated to economic self-help. In several cases, leading barbers ventured into corporate enterprise to better serve their communities. Alonzo Herndon and John Merrick, the wealthiest barbers in **Atlanta** and **Durham**, respectively, founded insurance companies that served African Americans at a time when mainstream firms such as Prudential refused to sell them policies. When African Americans moved to cities for factory work, they traded the security of land for wages. An urban widow could not make up for the death of her husband by taking his place in the fields, so insurance was vital to the well-being of her family.

The identity politics of the 1960s and 1970s signaled the assimilation of black migrants and posed a challenge for barbers. Previously, migrants desired processed hair as a symbol of their transformation and regarded kinky hair as a badge of the countryside. The Afro announced a new aesthetic that tapped into the growth of **black nationalism** in America's cities. Since people just wore their hair natural at first, the Afro also put many barbers out of work. Nathaniel Mathis of **Washington, D.C.**, also known as the Bush Doctor, led a new trend among barbers by specializing in Afros, braids, and other forms of natural hairstyles. Natural hair represented many things—a political statement, a fashion trend, a growing awareness of the damage resulting from chemically processed hair—but it ultimately signaled a fragmentation of the black hair market and a displacement of barbershops as centers of community. *See also* Beauty Culture; Chain Migration; Insurers and Insurance Companies; State Clubs.

Further Reading

Bristol, Douglas Walter. "From Outposts to Enclaves: A Social History of Black Barbers from 1750 to 1915." Ph.D. diss., University of Maryland, 2002.

Grossman, James R. *Land of Hope: Chicago, Black Southerners, and the Great Migration*. Chicago: University of Chicago Press, 1989.

Henderson, Alexa Benson. *Atlanta Life Insurance Company: Guardian of Black Economic Dignity*. Tuscaloosa: University of Alabama Press, 1990.

Walker, Susannah. "Black Is Profitable: The Commodification of the Afro." In *Beauty and Business: Commerce, Gender, and Culture in Modern America*, edited by Philip Scranton. New York: Routledge, 2001.

Weare, Walter B. *Black Business in the New South: A Social History of the North Carolina Mutual Life Insurance Company*. 1973. Reprint, Durham, NC: Duke University Press, 1993.

Douglas Bristol

Barrow, Joe Louis *See* Louis, Joe

Basie, William "Count" (1904–1984)

William "Count" Basie reversed the usual direction of the Great Black Migration, traveling from **New York City** to **Kansas City, Missouri**, to refine his mastery of **jazz** piano and bandleading at one of the music's southern wellsprings. His orchestra subsequently enjoyed a nearly uninterrupted national and international fame.

Basie was born on August 21, 1904, in Red Bank, New Jersey, to working parents. He learned piano and drums, formed a boys' band, and played piano at a movie theater. In the early 1920s he moved to Harlem, where Willie "the Lion" Smith and other pianists tutored him in the new "stride" style. Basie's career stagnated, though, and in 1928 he joined a burlesque show's tour of the Midwest. He took ill and was forced to recuperate in Kansas City, where he later gained work with Walter Page's Blue Devils. The Devils were one of the best local "boogie-woogie" bands, playing a hard-driving dance music against a four-to-a-bar beat. Basie altered his piano style and became a skilled arranger, and in 1929 he joined Bennie Moten's more celebrated band, with which he played until 1934. The next year Basie created a new band with some of his mates, including saxophonists Lester Young and Herschel Evans, trombonist Eddie Durham, vocalist Jimmy Rushing, and drummer Jo Jones.

The young white jazz enthusiast John Hammond heard a radio broadcast of Basie's band; thrilled by its rugged boogie-woogie style, he offered to help Basie achieve national success. Hammond brought the group to **Chicago**, where it made its first recordings, and then to New York, where it polished its sound at the Roseland Ballroom. A recording contract brought the band little income but gained it a successful stint at Harlem's Savoy Ballroom. By 1937, adding the guitarist Freddie Green to the rhythm section, Basie's band achieved fame. Other new musicians also enriched its sound, which (along with **Duke Ellington**'s orchestra) came to embody the African American presence in the "big-band" era.

Unlike Ellington, Basie rarely composed music, instead hiring talented arrangers to provide numbers. His band toured almost unceasingly, even though World War II slowed travel and led to the conscription of musicians. Basie proved almost uniquely skilled at finding and developing new talent. The waning postwar popularity of big bands and the rising costs of touring, though, eventually forced disbandment. In the early 1950s Basie experimented with a sextet and for a time ran a nightclub in Harlem.

In 1952 Basie assembled a new orchestra around his old rhythm unit. New arrangements by Neal Hefti, Quincy Jones, and others blended the band's rhythmic heart with a more lush "pop" sound. Recordings with stars such as Frank Sinatra contributed to Basie's renewed success. Continuous travel across the nation, as well as many European and Asian tours, made Basie's the most widely exposed jazz orchestra in history. The diffident, modest pianist was criticized for remaining silent on racial issues, and his band notably conformed to conservative commercial trends. Basie believed, however, that his very success in the American mainstream made a considerable statement. His career indeed shows that musicians in the black migrant jazz tradition could navigate the music business to find fame and fortune in the years after the migration and the vogue for big bands. Showered with honors in his last years, Basie fought off ill health to continue touring and recording. He died in Hollywood, California, on April 26, 1984. *See also* Calloway, Cab[ell]; Dance Halls and Nightclubs; Recording Industry.

Further Reading

Basie, Count, and Albert Murray. *Good Morning Blues: The Autobiography of Count Basie*. New York: Random House, 1985.

Erenberg, Lewis. *Swingin' the Dream: Big Band Jazz and the Rebirth of American Culture*. Chicago: University of Chicago Press, 1998.

Peretti, Burton W. *The Creation of Jazz: Music, Race, and Culture in Urban America*. Urbana: University of Illinois Press, 1992.

Burton W. Peretti

Basketball

Basketball originated at the Springfield, Massachusetts, **Young Men's Christian Association** (YMCA) in 1891 and soon spread throughout the country. A segregated YMCA in **Washington, D.C.**, fielded a team in 1902, and southern black colleges soon adopted the sport. Interscholastic and adult league play in **New York City** and **Chicago** featured interracial contests, and interregional play between teams in the East, South, and Midwest fostered rivalries and professionalism. African American businesses and churches sponsored both men's and **women**'s teams, and black newspapers extolled the merits of the game as a means of opportunity and racial pride.

Interracial contests allowed African American teams to measure themselves against the social Darwinian perceptions of white superiority. The Monticello Athletic Club team from **Pittsburgh** (also known as the Big Loendi Five), formed in 1910, consistently defeated its white opponents to negate such notions.

The promise of jobs, opportunities, and less overt discrimination led blacks to flee the South in search of better lives elsewhere. Southerners hence formed the nucleus of some of the best northern basketball teams. Robert Douglas, an immigrant from the British West Indies, helped organize the New York Renaissance (Rens) professional team in 1923. Its star player, Clarence "Fat" Jenkins, reputedly earned a salary of $10,000 by 1930 at the height of the Great Depression. In 1939 the Rens won the first world professional basketball tournament.

In Chicago Wendell Phillips High School enrolled the southern migrants who flocked to the city. By 1924 it engaged in interregional play with southern schools, and its star players formed the barnstorming Savoy 5, which later became known as the famous Harlem Globetrotters. Phillips won the Chicago high-school championship with an all-black team in 1930, and within five years its players returned to the South, where they created a basketball dynasty for Xavier University in **New Orleans**. The Globetrotters went on to win the second professional championship in 1940. At a time when professional baseball and **football** excluded African Americans, basketball provided a major opportunity for the display of black athletic talent.

Women's teams also earned fame and respect. The Chicago Romas, Philadelphia Tribune, and Bennett College of North Carolina all produced championship teams by the 1930s. Althea Gibson, born in South Carolina, starred as a basketball player be-

Original members of the Harlem Globetrotters. Courtesy of the Harlem Globetrotters.

fore gaining international renown as a tennis and golf celebrity in New York.

Southern blacks continued to migrate northward and westward throughout the twentieth century, and southern-born basketball players such as Reece "Goose" Tatum, Marques Haynes, Meadowlark Lemon, Bill Russell, Elgin Baylor, Oscar Robertson, Nate "Sweetwater" Clifton, Walt Bellamy, and Walt Frazier led their high-school, college, and professional teams to athletic glory.

The quest for championships even hastened the downfall of segregation practices in the South. When Texas Western College (now the University of Texas, El Paso) won the national basketball championship with a starting lineup composed of African American players in 1966, it signaled a wholesale change in the composition of team rosters and styles of play. By the end of the twentieth century teams had adopted the swift play, deft ballhandling, and crisp passing exhibited by the earliest black teams. Michael Jordan, born in North Carolina, led National Basketball Association's Chicago Bulls to six world titles and worldwide recognition as professional teams featuring other African American stars proliferated throughout the South, a legacy of the Great Black Migration. *See also* Sport; Primary Document 15.

Further Reading

Ashe, Arthur R., Jr. *A Hard Road to Glory: A History of the African-American Athlete, 1919–1945*. New York: Warner Books, 1988.
———. *A Hard Road to Glory: A History of the African-American Athlete, 1946–1986*. New York: Warner Books, 1988.
George, Nelson. *Elevating the Game*. New York: HarperCollins, 1992.

Peterson, Robert W. *From Cages to Jump Shots*. New York: Oxford University Press, 1990.

Gerald R. Gems

Bass, Charlotta *See California Eagle*

Bearden, Romare (1911–1988)

Born in **Charlotte, North Carolina**, in 1911, Romare Bearden is the most critically acclaimed African American artist and one of the most important American modernists of the twentieth century. Because he was born in the South, raised in Harlem, and spent significant time in such places as **Pittsburgh**, Paris, and St. Martin, Bearden's art has a multitude of diverse influences from his life and from art history. His paintings, drawings, and collages cull imagery from black rural life to the ghetto, from Italian Renaissance frescoes to West African masks. Throughout his career his immersion in the world as a migrant colored his work, which often strove to present both a universal and a specifically African American experience.

A true Renaissance man, Bearden succeeded at many professions from professional baseball to songwriting, but art making was his true passion. In 1920 he moved with his parents to Harlem, where his mother Bessye was the **New York City** editor for the ***Chicago Defender***; Bearden occasionally wrote on baseball for the paper. The artist began as a cartoonist. In the 1930s his work appeared in the ***Baltimore Afro-American***, the *Crisis, Opportunity*, and *Collier's*, among other publications. Bearden began taking art classes

Romare Bearden at work in his Long Island City studio in 1980. A photograph of his great-grandparents from Charlotte, North Carolina, hangs above his table. Photo by Frank Stewart.

at the Art Students League in 1933. In the 1940s he developed important relationships with such artists and writers as **Jacob Lawrence**, Norman Lewis, Stuart Davis, Walter Quirt, **Claude McKay**, and Morgan and Marvin Smith. At this time Bearden gained critical acclaim with his early watercolor series, such as *The Passion of Christ* and the *Bullfighting Series*. Travel to Europe in 1950 and 1961 enabled him to see early Italian masters and Gothic cathedrals and to meet such figures as Pablo Picasso.

Living in Harlem most of his life also provided invaluable sources for Bearden's work and life. Despite his mounting success and celebrity status, Bearden continued to be a social worker until 1969. His art thus strove to give voice to the voiceless, be they the working, urban poor of New York City or the tenant farmers of North Carolina. It was this focus on revealing the vibrancy and the spirit of humanity in the face of adversity that made Bearden's paintings, collages, and later some murals achieve such a universal appeal. In 1964, spurred by the turmoil of the **civil rights movement**, he with a small group of African American painters in New York founded the arts collective Spiral, which later helped open one of the first black-owned art galleries, Cinque Gallery.

Though he lived primarily in Harlem for most of his life, he, like many migrants, kept ties to his hometown by returning many summers during his childhood and sometimes as an adult. Bearden's art often reflected his rural roots and return visits to the South. Black rural life was the subject of works such as *Maudell Sleet's Magic Garden* (1978), *Early Carolina Morning* (1978), and *Carolina Shout* (1974). The subject of his breakthrough collage series *The Prevalence of Ritual*, begun in 1965, was based upon the universality of southern black traditions and rituals. It was in this series that he gave African masks to the faces of African American preachers baptizing congregants or to field workers raising their outsized hands. As Bearden remarked regarding the impression of such events on his memory:

> I would say, rather than [religious] training, of seeing the baptisms. . . . I went to a Baptist church and sometimes in the summer they would have the baptisms in the river or little streams. And going South again and seeing this in Virginia or North Carolina, these baptisms as they did in the twenties, of maybe a mass baptism, forty or fifty people at once. And I tried to interpret some of this in my painting. This type of thing, of visual and emotional experiences and its effect on people still interests me. . . . So these types of things that I would say remain with me rather than any Christian doctrine. (Ghent, 7)

Many scholars have also seen Bearden's use of the collage format as a metaphor for the patchwork-quilt quality of African American identity. His whole and fractured images of black bodies, African masks, landscapes, and other objects that he painted and cut from magazines represent the hybridity of this American identity and the broader complexity of the human condition. *See also* Baptist Church; Migrants, Cultural Identity of; Ministers and Preachers; Visiting; Visual Arts, the Great Migration in.

Further Reading

Fine, Ruth, et al. *The Art of Romare Bearden*. Washington, DC: National Gallery of Art, 2003.

Ghent, Henry. Unpublished interview with Romare Bearden, June 29, 1968. Archives of American Art, reel 3196/682.

National Gallery of Art. The Art of Romare Bearden. www.nga.gov/feature/bearden/.

Schwartzman, Myron. *Romare Bearden: His Life and Art*. New York: H. N. Abrams, 1990.

Kymberly N. Pinder

Beaumont, Texas, Race Riot of 1943

On June 15 and 16, 1943, southern whites rioted in Beaumont, Texas. Beaumont, a small city eighty miles east of Houston and near the western Louisiana border, attracted white and black migrants because of jobs created by the need to produce war materiel for the U.S. armed forces during World War II. White workers attacked fellow black migrants. White antiblack violence in Beaumont continued a long-standing southern tradition of white violence against African Americans based on white fear, external distress, and frustration with an increasing black and white population, industrial development, and urban growth.

The little-known Beaumont Riot of 1943 was more than the traditional "southern-style" riot, where angry whites attacked and killed isolated blacks over questions of alleged black male assaults upon white **women** and defense of white supremacy. The Beaumont riot extended the South's ongoing struggle with urban development, industrialization, and the changes these forces of economic development and social distress imposed upon an urban community that suddenly grew from 59,000 to 80,000 between 1940 and 1943. The riot also was a response to white gender relations fueled by the changing status of white women who worked in war industries earning incomes that made them independent of traditional white male protection.

A shipping, petroleum, and manufacturing center, Beaumont witnessed an influx of over 18,000 newcomers in one year, 1942–1943, making it a boomtown under siege. Overcrowded, Beaumont, like most southern cities that experienced transformations, attempted to hold the line on racial separation. Urban growth, the result of migration, eroded the traditional boundaries of segregation. The resulting competition for jobs, public transportation, living space and recreation and just encountering new people in confined spaces increased the friction developing between blacks and whites.

Aggravating the overcrowding were two 1943 summer conventions. The **Ku Klux Klan** invited members to Beaumont to attend the organization's regional convention. Local African Americans invited East Texas blacks to Beaumont for a Juneteenth emancipation celebration. On June 5, 1943, an eighteen-year-old white female telephone operator was allegedly raped and beaten by a black defense employee. One hundred and fifty white men attempted to lynch the black suspect in a local hospital, but he died two days later.

White fears escalated because of rumors that blacks were organizing an invasion of Beaumont aimed at white women. Ten days after the first accusation of rape came a new allegation on June 15 in which a white woman claimed that a black transient had invaded her home near the city limits and raped her. She was the wife of a white war worker and mother of three children who had put the transient to work in her yard. Rumors of this assault mobilized white men, especially 2,000 white men at the Pennsylvania Shipyards who left their jobs to engage in fifteen hours of rioting, looting, robbery, and arson in Beaumont's black neighborhoods. Whites destroyed 200 buildings. Two blacks were killed and one white. Over 2,000 blacks left Beaumont after the riot. *See also* Detroit Race Riot of 1943; Harlem Riot of 1943; Racial Violence and World War II; Shipyards and Shipyard Workers; Zuit-Suit Riots (1943).

Further Reading

Burran, James Albert, III. "Racial Violence in the South during World War II." Ph.D. diss., University of Tennessee, 1977.

Grimshaw, Allen D. "Lawlessness and Violence in America and Their Special Manifestation in Changing Negro-White Relationships." In *Racial Violence in the United States*, edited by Allen D. Grimshaw, 14–28. Chicago: Aldine Publishing Company, 1969.

Johnson, Marilynn S. "Gender, Race, and Rumors: Re-examining the 1943 Race Riots." *Gender and History* 10 (August 1998): 252–77.

Gregory Mixon

Beauty Culture

African American beauty culture as a commercial institution existed before the peak decades of the Great Migration, but the development of the industry owes much to the growth of large black communities in the cities of the Northeast, Midwest, and West and played a vital role in the life of these communities. Beauty business leaders promised African American **women** in particular opportunities for economic independence as hairstylists and sales representatives for one of several black-owned beauty product companies. In fact, women owned three of the largest black-owned firms: Poro, **Madam C. J. Walker** Manufacturing Company, and Apex. Beauty culture also exemplifies the importance of African American participation in the consumer society that was emerging in the first half of the twentieth century in the United States. This development depended to a significant degree on the growth of the urban black population in these decades. At the same time, through its beauty training programs, sales representatives, and advertising, the African American beauty industry was highly successful in the South too, reflecting continuing connections between black migrants and those who remained.

Early in the twentieth century African American beauty entrepreneurs established enterprises that would later profit from the movement of black southerners to urban centers throughout the nation. Louisiana native Sarah Breedlove (Madam C. J. Walker) started her company in **St. Louis** and spent time in **Pittsburgh** and Denver before choosing **Indianapolis** for her headquarters in 1910. Breedlove deliberately selected this central location to facilitate the spread of her sales agent–based business into all the regions of the country into which African Americans were moving. Annie Malone, founder of Poro, also began her

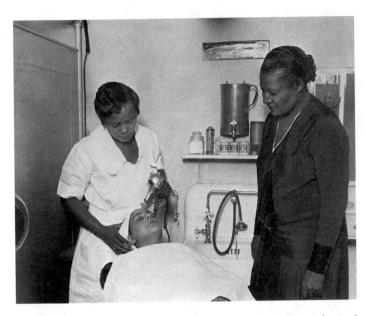

A'Leila Walker, the only daughter of Madam C. J. Walker, inherited her mother's beauty parlor businesses. Here, in the late 1920s, she supervises a facial in one of her many salons in Harlem. © Bettmann/ Corbis.

enterprise in St. Louis. In the late 1920s, at the urging of **Associated Negro Press** founder and marketing expert Claude A. Barnett, she moved her business to **Chicago**'s South Side, the heart of one of the largest black migrant communities in the country. Other companies, such as Overton (Chicago), Johnson Products (Chicago), and Apex (Atlantic City and **New York**), had their beginnings in the urban North. By the 1930s and 1940s most of these companies also ran beauty schools in cities throughout the North, Midwest, and South. By the post–World War II era African American beauty colleges, both independent and beauty company owned, were thriving in southwestern and West Coast cities.

Beauty culture as an occupation for black women developed in tandem with the Great Migration. Most African American women who moved to cities during the first few decades of the twentieth century found it difficult to get employment except as domestics or in other low-paying service jobs. The migration created a concentrated market for beauty salons in many cities, particularly in the years during and after World War II, when the tremendous growth of black populations in northern and West Coast cities and improving incomes for African Americans in these years bolstered demand for luxury services such as professional hair care. Meanwhile, northern-based beauty companies and schools maintained close connections with their agents and beauticians in the South through conventions, newsletters, traveling beauty culture instructors, and, of course, product-distribution networks. Black-owned beauty product manufacturers and beauty colleges promised African American women the opportunity to become economically independent while pursuing more creative and fulfilling careers as beauty culturists. In truth, few owned their own salons or were able to make a comfortable living as product sales agents. Studies by the Women's Bureau and other investigators in the 1930s, for example, found that black beauticians in major U.S. cities made, on average, little more than many domestic servants did. Nevertheless, beauty culture offered African American women more flexible hours than most jobs and independence from the scrutiny of white employers. Those who did own their own salons, as well as the founders and senior executives of beauty product companies, could live comfortably and often became community leaders. Some, such as Madam C. J. Walker, Annie Malone, and head Walker company instructor Marjorie Stewart Joyner, gained national prominence as philanthropists and political activists as well as entrepreneurs and educators.

African Americans were becoming more urban at the same time as mass consumer culture was becoming increasingly important in American life. Black migrants confronted an array of new kinds of products and services, and commercial beauty culture was one of the most visible and lucrative examples of African American female consumerism. It was so lucrative, in fact, that from at least 1910 onward, many white-owned companies successfully marketed beauty products to black women, much to the chagrin of African American business leaders. While rural southern black women had access to professional hairdressers and mass-marketed beauty products in their communities, city-based salons and beauty companies claimed to set the standard for the latest techniques and most fashionable styles. Well aware of the traditional homemade methods of hair care that persisted in rural areas well into the twentieth century, the African American beauty industry promoted commercial products and salon treatments as an integral part of modern city life. *See also* Barbers; Black Consumer Market; Primary Documents 4, 53.

Further Reading

Blackwelder, Julia Kirk. *Styling Jim Crow: African American Beauty Training during Segregation*. College Station: Texas A&M University Press, 2003.

Peiss, Kathy. *Hope in a Jar: The Making of America's Beauty Culture*. New York: Henry Holt and Company, 1998.

Robinson, Gwendolyn. "Class, Race, and Gender: A Transcultural, Theoretical, and Sociohistorical Analysis of Cosmetic Institutions and Practices to 1920." Ph.D. diss., University of Illinois at Chicago, 1984.

Rooks, Noliwe. *Hair Raising: Beauty, Culture, and African American Women*. New Brunswick, NJ: Rutgers University Press, 1996.

Susannah Walker

Bebop

Bebop is a **jazz** idiom whose origins lay in experimentations during the late 1930s that moved the current fad, big-band **swing** music, to new melodic and harmonic ideas, faster tempos, freer polyrhythmic impulses, and a new virtuosity that established improvisation as a norm. Young African American musicians in widely scattered locales rejected the standard 4/4 time of swing and practiced their ideas mostly in isolation or in territorial bands until 1941. Three of the four principal architects of bebop, Kenny Clarke, **Charlie Parker**, **Dizzy Gillespie**, and **Thelonious Monk**, were migrants who arrived in **New York City** between 1936 and 1941. Monk is the lone exception, arriving in the city from his birthplace, Rocky Mount, North Carolina, around age two. Most African American popular music embodies the migration theme. **Blues** and jazz especially have blended elements of African polyrhythms, down-home church beats, bluesmen keening about moving on and meetings at the crossroads, Congo Square dancers and drummers in antebellum America, and redcaps in the modern era, taking each new music from whistle stops to urban areas across the United States.

The Kansas Exodus of 1878 and 1879 and the Great Migration of both the World War I and World War II periods were movements of people and intellectual and creative energy that all made direct contributions to bebop's emergence. A secondary migration spinning out of the Kansas Exodus, the homesteading and settlement of blacks in Indian Territory (Oklahoma, 1907) reinforced the pattern of movement and music. The territorial black jazz bands that operated in Kansas, Oklahoma, Arkansas, and Texas until the 1930s supplied some of the musical ideas, motivations, and personnel to the embryonic music that became bebop.

By the mid-1930s **Kansas City** had become not only the repository of existing black popular music, swing, but also, simultaneously, the incubator of a new musical form: bebop. Bennie Moten's Blue Devils segued into **Count Basie**'s first band, the outfit that brought the Kansas City sound to a nationwide audience. Local bands of startling musicianship crossed musical swords with bands and sidemen of traveling national jazz orchestras like **Duke Ellington**'s. Before Basie's exposure, those traveling ambassadors of black culture, Pullman porters, commented that Kansas City was one long continuous jam session. Their comments reached the hustlers in urban areas: a musically hip black bar audience and white record entrepreneurs who provided a potential audience for Kansas City's musical export. Thus a cross-fertilization of traveling, musical tastes, and a ready reception stimulated Charlie "Yardbird" Parker, one of the significant inventors of bebop, to move from Kansas City to Harlem.

It is ahistoric to credit one individual with the creation of so protean a music as bebop, but Charlie Parker's influence is undeniable. Bird was a product of migratory forces, as were the other founding fathers of the genre, Gillespie, Monk, and Miles Davis, who gravitated to Harlem clubs just before and during World War II. In several crucial ways the migratory impulses generated by the war mirrored the creative forces that provided the grounding for bebop's emergence. War is men, money, and munitions moving across oceans, time zones, and continents, not as permanent residents, but as military forces. Among the civilian musicians, war was also movement, money, and creative outlets in flux. Blacks from every part of the world had flowed into Harlem, New York City's black enclave, particularly since the 1920s. In moving to Harlem, bebop followed a recognizable migratory pattern: the black movement toward urban centers.

From the late 1930s through the early years of World War II, emerging, embattled bebop was a staple at Harlem clubs like Minton's Playhouse, the Chicken Shack, and Monroe's Uptown House. New York–based musicians combined with the newcomers to continue developing their particular sound and concepts. An early version of cultural war ensued as older musicians and critics formed a substantial opposition to the new music. While the harmonic signatures marking bebop's changes were overladen with Euromusical notations and instrumentation, the basic foundation of the music was the blues. This melding of musical ideas was itself a product of migration. Bebop's southern blues staple was influenced by urban sensibilities and reshaped in urban environments.

Harlem was the penultimate stop in bebop's peripatetic birthing. The last stage in its migratory process was geographically shorter than all the other stages, but creatively and socially the most far-reaching. Between 1942 and 1945 white downtown club owners began offering bebop groups in clubs on Fifty-second Street. Broadway and Fifty-second Street became the Jazz Corner of the World. This new locale, the terminus of a journey started almost a decade before from disparate hamlets, towns, and cities like Cheraw, South Carolina, Rocky Mount, North Carolina, and Kansas City, became the venue to present the music to the world. Appearances at Fifty-second Street clubs were followed by exposure on public outlets such as radio stations, journals, popular magazines, and, most important, record contracts. This business and media attention conferred recognition, sometimes acceptance, and usually a more assured livelihood for bebop's practitioners. Not surprisingly, it stimulated at least two secondary migrations. As they became cult figures, master musicians, and public entertainers, the bebop musicians accepted that staple in a musician's life, tours. A new generation of players descended on Fifty-second Street playing bebop spin-offs: hard bop, the birth of the cool, and West Coast jazz. By the mid-1950s bebop's revolutionary motifs had become staid and publicly accepted, and its players who survived became cultural icons as well as musical innovators.

Prevailing racial attitudes in the bebop era have been commented on by the innovators themselves, their contemporaries, and later historians. Bebop's founders faced legal and extralegal segregation. Just as in their pioneering musical contributions, they worked in small ways to overcome racial proscriptions. Not many white musicians were part of the Harlem jam session scene, but pianists like Al Haig, George Wallington, and drummer Stan Levey appeared in several Fifty-second Street groups headed by African American bebop headliners. In the latter years of the swing era black sidemen appeared in white groups led by Benny Goodman, Artie Shaw, and Red Norvo, usually as guest artists, a code for some whites that no racial taboos were being broken, but until the bebop era no white sidemen found employment in groups headed by blacks.

While Harlem became the birthplace of bebop, and Fifty-second Street became its launch pad, the joining of people and musical expression had traveled a nexus that included the South, old **Midwestern states**, and new southwestern territories and states. Bebop's travels, experimentations, and venues demonstrate migration as a central, if not usually remarked, theme in the emergence of African American cultural forms in mid-twentieth-century America. *See also* Recording Industry.

Further Reading

DeVeaux, Scott. *The Birth of Bebop: A Social and Musical History*. Berkeley: University of California Press, 1997.

Patrick, James. "Charlie Parker and Harmonic Sources of Bebop Composition: Thoughts on the Repertory of New Jazz in the 1940s." *Journal of Jazz Studies* 2 (June 1975): 13–23.

Russell, Ross. *Jazz Style in Kansas City and the Southwest*. Berkeley: University of California Press, 1971.

Spellman, A. B. *Black Music: Four Lives in the Bebop Business*. New York: Schocken Books, 1966.

Harry A. Reed

Benson, Al (1910–1980)

Al Benson was the most popular and influential black radio personality in **Chicago** in the 1950s and early 1960s. Using the rural southern dialect on the air, "Ole Mushmouth," as he was called by his listeners, provided a friendly voice to the southern rural migrants in the city. Benson has been called the first black personality disc jockey. He was also active in promoting race pride and civil rights. Benson was involved in **black appeal radio** from 1945 to 1964, when he retired. He died on September 8, 1980.

Benson's real name was Arthur Leaner, and he was born in Mississippi in 1910. Before entering radio, he appeared in traveling music shows, attended Jackson Normal College in Jackson, Mississippi, and worked for the Pennsylvania Railroad. After moving to Chicago during the Great Depression, he worked for the **Works Progress Administration**, as a Cook County probation officer, as a Democratic precinct captain, and as a pastor. His job as a pastor led to a radio career that began in 1945 with a fifteen-minute religious show on Chicago station WGES, which featured a foreign-language format at that time. The Reverend Arthur B. Leaner changed his name to Al Benson and expanded his interests to popular music. By 1947 he had built a radio business that controlled ten hours of airtime a day on three stations. At WGES Benson did not work under the time brokerage system, as **Jack L. Cooper** did, but was a salesperson for the station, receiving a commission for the sponsor airtime sold. Benson later expanded into the music business, promoting concerts and founding a record company.

Benson's audience was the migrant community. He spoke on the air in a thick **Mississippi Delta** accent and used street slang. Benson was the first Chicago disc jockey to feature the popular urban **blues** and **rhythm and blues** music on his shows. He also was involved in race progress and the **civil rights movement**. His trademark saying "And that's for sure" guaranteed that the sponsor would provide quality service to black consumers and that he would redress any grievances. He actively fought segregation by speaking out on the radio and by public actions such as integrating Chicago nightspots. In 1956 Benson protested the treatment of blacks in Mississippi by hiring an airplane to drop leaflets on the state capitol building in Jackson.

Much as Jack L. Cooper provided a programming format model, so Benson transformed the persona of the disc jockey. Younger black disc jockeys nationwide emulated his on-the-air speech, sales pitch, and music playlist. He trained other disc jockeys to work on his shows and sponsored an annual disc jockey contest. In the process, he served the burgeoning migrant population not only in Chicago but in other cities by pioneering a radio personality that had a friendly, familiar voice, catered to their music tastes, and protected their consumer interests. *See also* Black Consumer Market; Chess Records; Recording Industry.

Further Reading

Barlow, William. *Voice Over: The Making of Black Radio*. Philadelphia: Temple University Press, 1999.

Newman, Mark. *Entrepreneurs of Profits and Pride: From Black Appeal to Radio Soul*. New York: Praeger, 1988.

Williams, Gilbert Anthony. *Legendary Pioneers of Black Radio*. Westport, CT: Praeger, 1998.

Mark Newman

Bethune, Mary McLeod (1875–1955)

Mary McLeod Bethune's ample portfolio of public service can be divided into four major areas: education, **women**'s organizations, government and civic affairs, and international concerns. In all these overlapping arenas she established herself as one of the foremost race leaders in American history. With her unusual combination of dedication, skill, charisma, and faith in her destiny, Bethune emerged from the devastation of the post-Reconstruction South to found a school and grow it into a college, lead black women's organizations and found another one, and become an adviser to the president of the United States. In the process, she earned such honorific titles as "mother of the race," "the first lady of black America," and "the female **Booker T. Washington**," among others that have elevated her in public memory. During a career of service that spanned half a century, she valued and maximized her role as racial representative, spokeswoman, and fount of inspiration for her once-enslaved race and exploited sex.

Bethune was born on July 10, 1875, in Mayesville, South Carolina, to Patsy McIntosh McLeod and Samuel McLeod. She was the fifteenth of seventeen children, who were expected and required to work on the small family farm that the McLeods had managed to purchase from their former owners. Bethune, who viewed herself as "different" and "special," was allowed at age ten to attend the nearby Presbyterian mission school for blacks run by Emma Wilson, a Scotia Seminary graduate. Scotia had been established by Presbyterian missionaries for the daughters of freed slaves during Reconstruction. Bethune was given a scholarship to Scotia in Concordia, North Carolina, which she attended from 1888 to 1894. She completed her formal schooling with a one-year stint at Moody Institute for Home and Foreign Missions, aimed at her desire to become a Christian missionary in Africa. After she was turned down because the Presbyterians did not permit black American

Student at Bethune-Cookman College. © Corbis.

missionaries in Africa, she accepted a one-year teaching job with the South's most eminent black teacher, Lucy Craft Laney, founder of Haines Institute in Augusta, Georgia. Bethune polished her teaching skills under Laney, whom she described as a "master" and an "artist" in her work.

In 1904 Bethune moved from Palatka, Florida, to the touristy Daytona Beach to open her school, the Daytona Educational and Industrial School for Negro Girls. In just ten years she turned her beginning balance of $1.50 and land on a garbage dump into a true campus, dedicating the first of its several new buildings, Faith Hall. Her interest in girls' education stemmed from her Scotia experience and its interracial teaching staff, whom she credited with rounding out her rough edges and showing her the value of women working together for positive change. She was also influenced by other female mentors, including her mother, Emma Wilson, and Lucy Laney. Bethune's belief in the potential of black women for leadership and service reflected her own well-honed confidence and was a core tenet of her life's work.

By 1923 her girls' school had become a junior college and was producing teachers for the entire state when it merged with the coeducational Cookman Institute of Jacksonville. Bethune-Cookman College, under the auspices of the Methodist Episcopal Church, developed into an accredited four-year liberal arts college, the first jointly named for a black woman and a white man (Alfred Cookman).

Bethune rose to the presidency of the Florida Federation of Colored Women (1917–1924). She then was elected president of the first national organization started by African Americans, the **National Association of Colored Women** (NACW). During her two terms as president (1924–1928), Bethune led the organization toward institutional stability and visibility, establishing a national headquarters in **Washington, D.C.**, and sponsoring the Frederick Douglass homesite as a national historic site. She used her media savvy to generate publicity, including coverage of a cross-country train trip to Oakland, California, for hundreds of NACW members to attend their national convention in 1926. Bethune's desire for a broader influence in public policy led her to found the National Council of Negro Women in 1935. During World War II she threw the organization behind the war effort and helped establish an officer-training facility for black women in the Women's Army Corps.

After moving back to Daytona in retirement, she continued an active schedule of meetings and international travel, visiting Africa, Haiti, and Switzerland. She promoted black economic development with the Bethune-Volusia Beach project, which was designed to give blacks ownership of beachfront property to which **Jim Crow** laws denied them access. In 1954 she hailed the U.S. Supreme Court decision declaring racial segregation in public schools unconstitutional and looked forward to a more democratic, equal America that she had spent her life fighting to obtain. Before she died of a heart attack at her home in Daytona Beach on May 1, 1955, she made it the official site of the Bethune Foundation in the hope that it would become a gathering place to promote her dream of uniting "all nations, all creeds, all classes...in peace and brotherhood, and to make a better world" (Bethune, "My Foundation," in McCluskey and Smith, 272). *See also* Bond, Horace Mann; Brown, Charlotte Hawkins; Burroughs, Nannie Helen; National Training School for Women and

Girls (NTSWG); National Youth Administration (NYA); Schoolteachers and Teaching; Terrell, Mary Church; Tuskegee Normal and Industrial Institute.

Further Reading

McCluskey, Audrey. "Most Sacrificing Service: Lucy Laney and Mary McLeod Bethune." In *Women of the American South*, edited by Christie Anne Farnham. New York: New York University Press, 1997.
———. "Multiple Consciousness in the Leadership of Mary McLeod Bethune." *NWSA Journal* 6 (Spring 1994): 69–81.
McCluskey, Audrey, and Elaine M. Smith, eds. *Mary McLeod Bethune: Building a Better World*. Bloomington: Indiana University Press, 1999.
Smith, Elaine M. "Mary McLeod Bethune and the National Youth Administration." In *Clio Was a Woman: Studies in the History of American Women*, edited by Mabel E. Deutrich and Virginia C. Purdy. Washington, DC: Howard University Press, 1980.

Audrey Thomas McCluskey

Birmingham, Alabama

By 1916 African Americans constituted 60 percent of the population in Birmingham, Alabama. Attracted by the opportunity to escape the suffocating poverty of the southern sharecropping system, blacks moved to the "Magic City," looking for work in the expanding iron and steel industry. Migrants responded to the promises of **labor agents** sent into the countryside to promote the benefits of industrial labor and to the encouraging appeals of relatives who had preceded them. Life in Birmingham was not exactly as migrants had been led to believe. Black workers in the city encountered a system of job segregation that relegated them to the worst jobs in the iron and steel industry while it preserved preferred jobs for whites. Yet compared with life in the countryside, Birmingham, with a more vibrant black culture and relatively regular paydays, represented an improvement.

Though the black experience in **Jim Crow** Birmingham always fell short of migrants' hopes, black workers did make progress during the first two decades of the twentieth century. Their willingness to move about to find better jobs contributed to the development by major employers of labor policies designed to hold black labor by extending an array of benefits. Some of the largest employers of black labor, including U.S. Steel, always concerned about labor turnover, labor supply, and labor unions, implemented labor policies that provided workers, including blacks, health care, improved **housing**, education, and job training. Employers, who had long chafed under the restrictive rules of **American Federation of Labor** unions, also took advantage of changes in the technology of steelmaking to challenge union regulation of the labor market by adopting the open shop. As the open shop spread, blacks began to move into jobs previously reserved by union rules for whites. Job segregation continued, but black workers did make significant gains before World War I.

As the steel industry began to expand production to fill the demand caused by the outbreak of war in Europe, and labor markets tightened, especially in the steel-producing centers of the North and East, companies sent representatives to Birmingham, where they knew that they could find experienced workers. Black workers, now experienced in working the market and facing a campaign by white workers to roll back any gains blacks had made, began to leave Birmingham for opportunities in **Pittsburgh**, **Cleveland**, **Chicago**, and other northern destinations. After the United States entered the war, and white workers entered the military, the demand for blacks in the northern steel industry expanded accordingly.

In Birmingham the exodus of black workers further exacerbated employers' labor problems. Employers responded to the migration with a combination of incentives and coercion. Black workers who did not migrate received increases in pay and promotion into jobs previously closed to them. Some historians have explained these tactics as part of the ongoing attempt by employers to divide workers along racial lines. But blacks by demonstrating their willingness to seek opportunities elsewhere forced employers to respond to the realities of the market. Thus black workers who stayed behind gained leverage in the local market.

The exodus of black workers from Birmingham exacerbated divisions within the African American community. Since at least the 1890s African Americans in Birmingham had differed over the best strategy to pursue in dealing with the realities of Jim Crow segregation. Some, following the advice of **Booker T. Washington**, attempted to work within the system to advance the interest of "the race." They established businesses that served the black community and invested in chronically underfunded black public schools. These black leaders, sometimes referred to as "race men," maintained relationships with white community leaders, believing that cooperation was the best way to ease the worst effects of segregation. As the number of blacks leaving Birmingham increased, they often cooperated with industry by urging potential migrants to stay in the city, where they might benefit from the tight labor market.

Others in Birmingham's black community, influenced by the more aggressive philosophy of **W.E.B. DuBois**, criticized the strategy and tactics of the "race men," arguing that cooperation within the system reinforced the inequities white paternalism institutionalized. They urged African American workers to abandon a city and a region not likely to change soon for places where they might find economic opportunity and would be able to participate in the political system. Unlike the "race men," they encouraged migration as a protest against the discrimination blacks faced in the city. If city leaders and employers wanted to stem the tide of migration, they argued, they should do something about the conditions that caused blacks to leave.

Those who advocated a more direct-action approach often supported increased unionization among black workers. In the early years of the migration the reduced supply of black labor created conditions more favorable to union organization, and labor leaders tried to take advantage. From 1915 to 1920 the number of strikes in the city increased sharply. A few labor leaders urged blacks who did not migrate to join them as they tried to restore their power. Some blacks responded favorably, especially around the district's coal mines. They either joined white-led unions, becoming second-class members, or formed organizations of their own. Most others, however, were unwilling to commit to organizations that had always stood as obstacles in the way of black progress.

Many African Americans in Birmingham continued to seek ways to compromise with segregation so they could remain in the city. But for a generation the most direct protest against Jim Crow remained migration. In time the black population of the North became a political force to be reckoned with. The influence it was able to bring to bear on national politicians and in the courts proved to be critical to the successful struggle for black equality that killed Jim Crow. *See also* Gulf South; Organized Labor; Steelworkers; Welfare Capitalism.

Further Reading

Kelly, Brian. *Race, Class, and Power in the Alabama Coalfields, 1908-21.* Urbana: University of Illinois Press, 2001.

Letwin, Dan. *The Challenge of Interracial Unionism: Alabama Coal Miners, 1878-1921.* Chapel Hill: University of North Carolina Press, 1998.

McKiven, Henry M., Jr. *Iron and Steel: Race, Class, and Community in Birmingham, Alabama, 1875-1920.* Chapel Hill: University of North Carolina Press, 1998.

Norrell, Robert J. "Caste in Steel: Jim Crow Careers in Birmingham, Alabama." *Journal of American History* 73 (December 1986): 669-94.

Henry M. McKiven

Black Appeal Radio

Black appeal radio is radio programming and advertising aired specifically for African American audiences. The concept of developing radio programming for African Americans originated in **Chicago** on November 3, 1929, when **Jack L. Cooper** premiered his *All-Negro Hour* on station WSBC. It evolved slowly during the 1930s and early 1940s and experienced a boom period from approximately 1945 to 1960. Today, black appeal is a staple of the radio dial. In 2004 more than 800 of the more than 13,800 radio stations in the United States had a black format. In 1998, 168 radio stations were owned by African Americans.

The development of black appeal radio was directly connected to African American migration, especially from the 1920s to the mid-1960s. Radio programming for African Americans emerged in response to changing economic and residential conditions that led to the development of large African American communities and **black consumer market**s in cities, towns, and rural areas. Radio played a multifaceted role in these communities, acting as a medium of culture, consciousness, and leadership that helped bond together the growing and diverse population.

Stations airing black appeal programming developed strong community service functions that included charitable work and initiatives specifically designed for migrants, such as locating long-lost friends and relatives and shows to help former rural dwellers assimilate to urban life. In the 1950s, for example, **Memphis** station WDIA aired programs to help black homemakers and one called *Call for Action* that offered assistance in dealing with government agencies and landlords, among others. News relevant to the African American community was also a featured segment.

Radio and electrical stores such as this one on Chicago's South Side emerged to cater to the city's expanding population of black radio listeners. Courtesy of the Library of Congress.

Entertainment programming followed popular music trends, with radio serving as a medium of creative collaboration for new music forms. Religious and popular music was aired, including spirituals and gospel, as well as big-band **jazz** in the 1930s, **rhythm and blues** and **blues** in the 1940s and 1950s, and **soul music** in the 1960s. The rise of soul music and soul consciousness was directly linked to radio, which promoted race pride, solidarity, and culture. Radio also was involved in the **civil rights movement**, as many stations and on-air personalities assumed activist roles.

A major consideration was advertising. Sponsors of black appeal programs had to treat the listener as a first-class citizen and consumer by touting high-quality goods and services, as well as treating shoppers with respect when they patronized businesses. For example, in 1941 radio station KFFA in Helena, Arkansas, appealed to black audiences with a blues radio show featuring live performances by Sonny Boy Williamson. The sponsor was Interstate Grocer Company, whose white owner had recognized changes in the local black consumer market and developed a high-quality flour and later corn meal for African Americans. The respectful, first-class treatment of the black consumer by radio stations and sponsors also promoted race pride.

Other ways black appeal radio contributed to the development of the community were by providing employment for both men and **women** and acting as a voice for the audience. The appearance of black voices on the air talking to African American audiences in a respectful manner represented a great breakthrough. Through these personalities, radio stations became involved in community activism. The airwaves facilitated transmitting messages to the mass audience. In the 1960s in Chicago, the call letters of the popular white-owned radio station WVON stood for "Voice of the Negro."

The initial phase of black appeal radio's development occurred before World War II and set the pattern for later trends. The first black appeal program was partially a response to mainstream radio programming that adapted blackface minstrelsy shows to radio, such as *Amos 'n' Andy*, which featured white actors lampooning the experiences of two black migrants to the city. Other network programming relegated black actors to roles as servants and domestics. Inspired by the **New Negro** movement of the 1920s that promoted African American self-sufficiency, Jack L. Cooper's *All-Negro Hour* in Chicago produced and presented a program by African Americans for an African American audience.

Throughout the 1930s, programming for African Americans emerged independently in large cities and small towns in the North and South and on the West Coast. In large cities such as Chicago, programming generally was aired on local, independent foreign-language stations that also featured shows for European immigrants. Appealing to African Americans logically extended the ethnic concept to the latest wave of immigrants. Many stations employed a brokerage policy. Those seeking to produce programs bought time from the station and sold advertising airtime to sponsors, with the receipts paying for the programs. The formats at first followed network models but later stressed music, news, and service.

In southern cities and small towns, programming for blacks was aired by small independent stations that were unable to capture a white audience. The shows generally followed music formats, and the sponsors were small retailers.

Changes in agriculture in southern rural areas in the late 1930s stimulated a massive migration that lasted into the 1960s and also contributed to a post–World War II black radio boom. The transition from tenancy to wage labor and increasing mechanization transformed the South. The depopulation of rural areas stimulated a massive black movement into small southern towns and large cities nationwide. It also created large black consumer markets that led to the development of new products and services that catered to African Americans and radio programming designed for them.

The rise of television, which transformed the radio industry, also contributed to the black appeal radio boom. As stations sought new formats, between 1946 and 1956 the number of stations airing black appeal programming rose from 24 to 600. Stations such as WDIA in Memphis and WERD in **Atlanta** devoted their entire schedule to black programming.

The trends established before World War II guided the explosive growth of black appeal radio after 1945. The entertainment-news-service concept pioneered by Cooper became standard, and Chicago was the capital of black radio. The declining foreign-language population led some stations in northern cities to embrace the black appeal format. In addition, the disc jockeys assumed a strong community activism role. Some, like **Al Benson**, the king of black appeal radio in Chicago in the late 1940s and 1950s, spoke to the newly arrived southern immigrants in their dialect, forging strong bonds with their listeners. The brokerage concept remained in place until approximately the late 1950s, meaning that popular radio figures dominated the radio dial. At various times both Cooper and Benson controlled forty hours of airtime a week each on several stations.

By the mid-1950s, reflecting the scope of African American migration, black appeal shows could be heard nationwide. Listeners could tune in programs in Fresno, Oakland, and **Los Angeles**, California; Flagstaff, Arizona; Newman, Georgia; **Gary, Indiana**; Tampa, Florida; **Detroit, Michigan**; and **New York**, among other cities. The largest number of stations was in the South. In 1954, 269 were in the South, 102 in the North, and 27 in the West. Texas had the most outlets with 47. Memphis and Atlanta emerged as major black radio centers. WDIA in Memphis was the first black appeal station to receive a 50,000-watt channel. In 1949 WERD in Atlanta became the second black-owned radio station, having been preceded by a few months by a **Kansas City** outlet.

From the 1960s to the present, black appeal radio's development followed general industry trends, but it never lost its racially defined voice. From the late 1920s to the mid-1960s, its development was intimately connected to African American migration and its impact on the United States. In a sense, black radio resulted from this migration. *See also* Chess Records; Recording Industry; Primary Document 12.

Further Reading

Barlow, William. *Voice Over: The Making of Black Radio.* Philadelphia: Temple University Press, 1999.
Newman, Mark. *Entrepreneurs of Profits and Pride: From Black Appeal to Radio Soul.* New York: Praeger, 1988.
Williams, Gilbert Anthony. *Legendary Pioneers of Black Radio.* Westport, CT: Praeger, 1998.

Mark Newman

Black Arts Movement

The Black Arts movement of the 1960s and 1970s has been described as the aesthetic double of the **Black Power** concept. By transforming their rural southern backgrounds to fit their new urban homes, African Americans created a new black culture. Yet their hopes for equal rights were met by the suspicion of many white northerners and the outbreaks of urban riots. Originating from the social contrasts that the Great Migration had set in motion in northern cities and from the racism that still afflicted those blacks who had not migrated from the South, Black Power expressed African Americans' continuing frustration with the lack of real progress toward general social and economic equality in the country. The nonviolent tactics of the **civil rights movement** were challenged by Black Power leaders who, as Stokely Carmichael wrote in his article "What We Want" (1966), had seen for too many years harmless black Americans march and get shot. At the same time, the protest and petition literature of the civil rights era was rejected by the Black Arts movement. Culture became the weapon to further political and social goals.

From its very beginning, the Black Arts movement, whose leading figures included **Amiri Baraka** (LeRoi Jones), Ed Bullins, Addison Gayle, Nikki Giovanni, and Sonia Sanchez, argued for the fundamental relationship between black art and black consciousness. It demanded that literature and artistic forms in general participate in the revolutionary change of society. The movement, whose symbolic birth is often dated in March 1965 with Baraka's move from Manhattan to Harlem after **Malcolm X**'s assassination, tried to combine a Marxist and a nationalist agenda. The promotion of political freedom and full citizenship for African Americans resulted in the production of politically committed literature with a confrontational rhetoric. Harlem, with its Black Arts Repertory Theatre/School (BARTS), which Baraka helped establish, became the first center of the movement. Other important areas associated with the Black Arts movement were **Chicago**, with its *Negro Digest/ Black World* and Haki Madhubuti's publishing house Third World Press, and the **San Francisco** Bay Area, with the *Journal of Black Poetry* and *Black Scholar*. These journals, together with the development of writers' groups (such as Umbra and the Harlem Writers Guild) and poetry performances, contributed to link Black Arts personalities to the black community. The work of Black Arts artists was also disseminated through several important anthologies, such as *Black Fire* (1968), edited by Baraka and Larry Neal, *The Black Aesthetic* (1971), edited by Addison Gayle, *Understanding the New Black Poetry* (1972), edited by Stephen Henderson, and *The Black Woman* (1970), edited by Toni Cade Bambara, the first black feminist anthology.

Amiri Baraka is generally acknowledged as the founding writer of the movement, and his poem "Black Art" includes a clear definition of literature as militant and revolutionary: "We want 'poems that kill' / Assassin poems, poems that shoot / guns. Poems that wrestle cops into alleys / and take their weapons leaving them dead / with tongues pulled out and sent to Ireland." Black art becomes for Baraka the way to restructure the Western cultural aesthetic. His poems in *Black Magic* (1969) and *It's Nation Time* (1970) are typical of the preferred stylistic features of Black Arts: the use of street slang, the rhythm of **blues**, **jazz**, and gospel music, and the adoption of a polemical and confrontational voice. Within the Black Arts movement writers and intellectuals are seen primarily as educators and agitators. Haki R. Madhubuti and Sonia Sanchez explored too in their poetry the potential of street slang and black music. Sanchez's work, in particular, celebrates African American leaders and music. Her poems denounce white superiority and what she has defined as the "neoslavery" of blacks. People such as Malcolm X, **John Coltrane**, and Billie Holiday were praised by Sanchez because, like the artists of the Black Arts movement, they tried to communicate the black experience through their words. Sanchez's poetry instructs its readers on the struggles of the past and exhorts them to fight for a better future.

Poetry and drama were the two most popular genres with Black Arts writers. Ed Bullins, together with Baraka, was the leading playwright of the group, writing more than fifty plays, such as *Clara's Ole Man* (produced in 1965) and *The Fabulous Miss Marie* (produced in 1971), which denounced the dispossessed conditions of African Americans in urban centers. Like poetry, theater was defined by Baraka in revolutionary, aggressive, and anti-Western terms. In his essay "The Revolutionary Theatre" (1964), Baraka argues for a theater of assault whose heroes will be Crazy Horse, Denmark Vesey, and Patrice Lumumba and that will destroy white America. Several Black Arts writers were also involved in writing essays and pamphlets. Some of them, like Addison Gayle and Sanchez herself, gave new impetus with their monographs for the establishment of black studies programs in universities across the United States.

The split between nationalists and Marxists, as well as repressive government measures, were at the root of the Black Arts breakup. In addition, corporate

America targeted several artists in the movement, making it impossible for the black community to compete with new offers of publication. *See also* Black Nationalism; Literature, the Great Migration in; New York City; Urban Crisis of the 1960s; Visual Arts, the Great Migration in.

Further Reading

Baker, Houston A. *Blues, Ideology, and Afro-American Literature: A Vernacular Theory*. Chicago: University of Chicago Press, 1984.

Jones, LeRoi. "The Revolutionary Theatre." *Liberator* 5, no. 7 (1965): 4–6.

Powell, Richard J. *Black Art and Culture in the 20th Century*. London: Thames and Hudson, 1997.

Salaam, Kalamu ya. "Black Arts Movement." In *The Oxford Companion to African American Literature*, edited by William L. Andrews, Frances Smith Foster, and Trudier Harris. New York: Oxford University Press, 1997.

Smethurst, James Edward. *The Black Arts Movement: Literary Nationalism in the 1960s and 1970s*. Chapel Hill: University of North Carolina Press, 2005.

Luca Prono

Black Aviators

The epic flight of the Wright brothers at Kitty Hawk in December 1903 inaugurated the air age. The new aeronautical technology unfolded in a highly restrictive social context where blacks were routinely barred from active participation. The U.S. Army Air Corps mirrored the tradition of racial exclusion in the American military. The decision of the Air Corps to exclude blacks from pilot training was based on the widely held belief that blacks lacked the aptitude for flying. African Americans were the sole group excluded from the air age on racial grounds.

Despite these barriers, African Americans of the first migrant generation challenged racial exclusion in aviation. **Chicago** became the locale for the organization of the all-black Challenger Air Pilots Association in the late 1920s. Under the leadership of Cornelius Coffey and John C. Robinson, this fledgling group of aviation enthusiasts managed to gain entrance to a local aeronautical school, although on a segregated basis. Another aspiring black aviator in **Philadelphia**, C. Alfred Anderson, overcame the existing racial barriers by purchasing his own airplane and then recruiting a white flight instructor to train him. Despite all these racial restrictions, a small number of blacks qualified as licensed pilots in the 1920s and 1930s.

The exploits of Bessie Coleman inspired this first generation of black pilots. In 1915 she migrated from the rural poverty of Texas to Chicago. After several menial jobs Coleman boldly traveled to France to gain flight training, graduating from l'Ecole d'Aviation des Frères Caudron in 1921. Returning to America, "Queen Bess," as she was affectionately known, pursued a brilliant, if brief, career as a barnstormer. She died in an air crash in 1926. There were few licensed black pilots, except for the flamboyant Hubert Julian, who promoted himself as the "Black Eagle of Harlem." Julian's hucksterism and fanciful schemes for record-breaking flights eventually alienated the small black aviation community.

By contrast, **William J. Powell** emerged as the great visionary for aviation progress in the black community during the Great Depression. Like Coleman, Powell's family had migrated from the rural South to Chicago. A veteran of World War I and successful businessman, Powell had moved from Chicago to **Los Angeles** to promote aviation. As the leader of the Bessie Coleman Flying Club, he sponsored the first all-black air show, promoted record-breaking flights, and wrote *Black Wings* (1934).

In 1932 James Herman Banning and Thomas Allen made the first transcontinental flight by black airmen. The following year C. Alfred Anderson and Albert Forsythe made a round-trip transcontinental flight, which was followed later by their "Pan-American Goodwill Flight" across the West Indies.

In the 1930s black air enthusiasts managed to establish a few flying clubs across the country to offer flight training and mutual support. However, Chicago remained the main hub for black aviation. Cornelius Coffey helped organize the National Airmen Association and set up a training program under the auspices of the federally funded Civilian Pilot Training Program. Willa Brown emerged as a prominent woman pilot. Willie "Suicide" Jones thrilled onlookers at all-black air shows with his parachute jumping. The decade ended with the highly publicized flight of Chauncey Spencer and Dale White to **Washington, D.C.**, to promote black involvement in aviation.

The Army Air Corps responded to the growing pressure to end its racial restrictions by opening the Tuskegee Army Airfield in 1941. The flight training program at Tuskegee, although a real watershed in the military, still operated on a segregated basis. Benjamin O. Davis, Jr., a West Point graduate, took command of the newly formed all-black 99th Fighter Squadron (later part of the 332nd Fighter Group). In World War II the Tuskegee airmen established an impressive record flying escort for bombers of the 15th Air Force in Europe.

During the postwar years blacks expanded their role in both civil and military aviation. Benjamin O. Davis, Jr., became the first African American general in the newly independent air force, to be joined by Daniel "Chappie" James. In both the Korean and Vietnam wars black airmen now flew in integrated air units. Blacks also made significant progress in civilian general aviation, most notably with the flying career of John W. Greene, Jr., who set up his own fixed-base operation in Maryland. Marlon Green played a key role in opening commercial aviation to blacks when he sued Continental Airlines in 1959 for discrimination. The benchmark case eventually went to the Supreme Court, which unanimously ruled that the airline had racially discriminated against Green. Black pilots and mission specialists participated in a sequence of NASA shuttle flights. The twentieth century ended with notable gains in racial equality in the realm of aerospace. *See also* Aviation Industry, Black Employment in; Military Service, Vietnam War; Military Service, World War II; Tuskegee Normal and Industrial Institute.

Further Reading

Davis, Benjamin O., Jr. *Benjamin O. Davis, Jr., American: An Autobiography*. Washington, DC: Smithsonian Institution Press, 2000.

Gropman, Alan L. *The Air Force Integrates, 1945–1964*. Washington, DC: Smithsonian Institution Press, 1998.

Powell, William J. *Black Aviator: The Story of William J. Powell: A New Edition of William J. Powell's; Black Wings.* Edited by Von Hardesty. Washington, DC: Smithsonian Institution Press, 1994.

Rich, Doris. *Queen Bess: Daredevil Aviator.* Washington, DC: Smithsonian Institution Press, 2000.

Sandler, Stanley. *Segregated Skies: All-Black Combat Squadrons of WWII.* Washington, DC: Smithsonian Institution Press, 1992.

Von Hardesty

Black Consumer Market

The evolution of the African American consumer market appeared directly linked to the massive migration and urbanization of blacks during the twentieth century. The millions of African Americans who moved from the rural South to southern, northern, and western cities forced U.S. companies to take African Americans seriously as consumers.

Before the watershed Great Migration of the World War I era, which started significant black migration out of the rural South, most American businesses ignored and disrespected blacks. This is borne out by the proliferation of contemporary products whose trade names included such racially derogatory terms as "mammy," "pickaninny," "coon," and "nigger."

From the standpoint of early twentieth-century U.S. white enterprises, African Americans' overall socioeconomic status legitimized the widespread

Black-owned businesses, such as the Perfect Eat Shop on Chicago's South Side, were among the many new enterprises that capitalized on the Great Migration to cater to an urbanizing, all-black clientele. Courtesy of the Library of Congress.

disrespect shown them. At the time, African Americans were primarily a rural and relatively impoverished segment of the national population. Moreover, any group desire for upward mobility appeared to be thwarted by the existence of American apartheid, popularly known as **Jim Crow**. Nevertheless, as African Americans from 1915 onward began to proliferate in cities and major markets across the country, a once predominantly agrarian people with limited disposable income was increasingly seen as a potentially lucrative market by both black and white businesses.

Although many white companies, because of racism, were slow to recognize the potential profits associated with an increasingly urban black population, black-owned businesses quickly gauged the economic implications of African American migration. In fact, during the 1920s black businessmen, both excited about increasing African American urbanization and cognizant of the white racism that restricted them to serving only black consumers, dreamed of establishing an independent economic structure within U.S. cities.

The National Negro Business League, composed of affiliate chapters across America, assumed an especially high profile during the mid- to late 1920s. One of the league's most important programs during this period was its National Negro Trade Week. Hoping to maximize black consumer support of black-owned businesses, the National Negro Business League, through its local chapters, employed a variety of techniques that urged black shoppers to "Buy Something from a Negro Merchant!"

As the black presence in American cities continued to increase, the evolving "Negro market" increasingly attracted the attention of white writers and researchers. H. A. Haring, a contributing editor of the advertising trade journal *Advertising and Selling*, and Paul K. Edwards, a professor of economics at Fisk University, emerged as notable authorities on black consumers during the 1920s and 1930s.

Haring's pioneering articles, "Selling to Harlem" and "The Negro as Consumer," which appeared in the October 31, 1928, and September 3, 1930, issues of *Advertising and Selling*, respectively, were based primarily upon anecdotal evidence, replete with condescending remarks about African Americans. Paul K. Edwards, on the other hand, was a much more thorough and objective student of African American consumption. In fact, Edwards's 1932 book *The Southern Urban Negro as a Consumer* and his unpublished 1936 Harvard University dissertation, titled "Distinctive Characteristics of Urban Negro Consumption," were the first truly systematic studies of African American consumers.

Although Edwards and Haring differed in their methodological rigor, they both sought to reach the same primary audience, the U.S. white business community. Moreover, the clear thesis of both authors' publications was that the "Negro market" should be taken seriously as a source of potential corporate profits.

Besides a growing body of literature relating to African American consumers, the 1930s featured significant black consumer activism. A generation before the celebrated Montgomery bus boycott of 1955 and 1956, the various **"Don't Buy Where You Can't Work" campaigns** of the 1930s fired the imagination and initiative of the national African American community. Commencing in **Chicago**, this movement quickly spread to other cities.

Besides boycotting and picketing discriminatory white businesses to force them to hire black personnel, some African American consumers during the 1930s ignored white businesses altogether and worked toward enhancing black business development. The Housewives League of **Detroit** epitomized this trend. Convened in June 1930 by Fannie B. Peck, by 1935 the organization had grown from 50 to 10,000 members. To join the league, African American **women** pledged to support black businesses, buy black-produced products, and patronize black professionals. Considering that African American women generally coordinated their families' spending patterns, the league sought to mobilize this power toward community development. Moreover, the "Housewives' League" concept, similar to the "Don't Buy Where You Can't Work" campaign, expanded from Detroit to other U.S. cities.

World War II accelerated the movement of rural southern blacks to southern, northern, and western cities. Stimulated by President Franklin Delano Roosevelt's June 25, 1941, Executive Order 8802, which banned race-based employment discrimination in war-related industries, African American workers proliferated in even greater numbers in cities across the country. Moreover, by 1943 aggregate black spending power stood at over $10 billion.

An important consequence of World War II–era urbanization was the subsequent desegregation of major league baseball. The 1947 baseball season, Jackie Robinson's first full season in the major leagues, represented not only a source of pride for African Americans but a box-office bonanza for Branch Rickey's Brooklyn Dodgers. The **Cleveland** Indians' signing of the legendary pitcher **Satchel Paige** in 1948 produced similar profits by enhancing black attendance at Indians' games. Moreover, the subsequent decline and disappearance of the **Negro Leagues** (as black players and fans began to proliferate in major league ballparks) established an ominous precedent regarding the impact of **desegregation** on historically black community businesses and institutions.

Increased African American urbanization during the 1940s also contributed to the rapid growth of "Negro appeal" radio stations. Between 1949 and 1955 the number of radio stations aimed at black consumers grew from less than 10 to nearly 600. Ironically, while these stations featured music and programming of interest to blacks, the vast majority of them were owned by white entrepreneurs. To help deflect attention away from "Negro appeal" radio stations' ownership, these businesses spotlighted their African American on-the-air personalities (dee-jays). This strategy proved extremely profitable for the white businessmen who owned and advertised on **black appeal radio** because black dee-jays were expected to be both master showmen and salesmen.

During the 1950s and 1960s African Americans' campaign for human dignity, commonly referred to as the **civil rights movement**, commanded America's attention. Significantly, this unprecedented succession of events has become almost synonymous with the public career of Dr. **Martin Luther King, Jr.** Yet while King's place in history has been deservedly illuminated, consumer activism, the most potent nonviolent strategy employed by blacks during this period, has not been similarly spotlighted. Minimizing the central role of African American economic leverage erroneously suggests that civil rights legislation primarily resulted from white "moral transformation," rather than from African Americans' skillful use of their economic clout. In fact, after the famous **Birmingham, Alabama**, campaign of spring 1963, King himself concluded that organized black consumer boycotts represented the best strategy for achieving civil and human rights.

The civil rights movement revealed not only the power of black consumer boycotts, but also the flexibility of American capitalism. Corporate marketers began the 1960s by developing advertising campaigns that catered to African Americans' perceived desire for racial integration. By decade's end, as African Americans moved politically from "We Shall Overcome" to **Black Power**, U.S. corporations promoted the soul market (for example, soul food, **soul music**) both to extol the nuances of African American culture and to retain the allegiance of black consumers.

The early 1970s featured a dramatic overture by the American film industry to the African American community. Hollywood producers, hoping to counteract declining movie revenues, began to aggressively pursue the urban black consumer market. This development, which resulted in the **blaxploitation** film phenomenon, subsequently generated huge profits for whites throughout the film industry.

Although aggregate black income increased from $183 billion to $242 billion between 1978 and 1988, the 1980s were a difficult time for many African Americans. As black social and economic gains associated with the civil rights movement stalled during the conservative Reagan presidency, class distinctions within the African American community became much more pronounced. This market segmentation prompted corporate marketers to develop more class-specific advertising aimed at blacks.

Buppies, the black counterparts of white young urban professionals (yuppies), were actively courted by the producers of upscale consumer items and financial services companies. Conversely, the growing black underclass attracted the intense attention of tobacco and alcoholic beverage companies. Considering the economic deprivation associated with 1980s urban black enclaves, as well as the historic use of alcohol and cigarette consumption as short-term escapes from reality, it appeared to many observers that the accelerated marketing of tobacco and alcohol in 1980s urban black neighborhoods represented a blatant attempt to profit from human misery.

Today's African Americans bear little resemblance to their forebears at the dawn of the twentieth century. Once perceived as primarily a rural group with limited disposable income, blacks are now a free-spending, pronouncedly urban people whose collective spending power is moving steadily toward $1 trillion. Moreover, it is strikingly ironic that white companies, and not black ones, are deriving most of the profits from African Americans' ever-increasing spending power. *See also* American Negro Exposition; Associated Negro Press (ANP); Banks and Bankers; Barbers; Beauty Culture; Black Film; Black Press; Ghettos; Insurers and Insurance Companies; Recording Industry; Sport; Undertakers; Primary Document 9.

Further Reading

Edwards, Paul K. "Distinctive Characteristics of Urban Negro Consumption." Ph.D. diss., Harvard University, 1936.

———. "Selling to Harlem." *Advertising and Selling* 11 (October 31, 1928): 17–18, 50–53.

———. *The Southern Urban Negro as a Consumer.* New York: Prentice-Hall, 1932.

Haring, H. A. "The Negro as Consumer." *Advertising and Selling* 15 (September 3, 1930): 20–21, 67–68.

Hine, Darlene Clark. "Housewives League of Detroit." In *Black Women in America: An Historical Encyclopedia*, edited by Darlene Clark Hine, Elsa Barkley Brown, and Rosalyn Terborg-Penn, vol. 1, 584–86. Brooklyn, NY: Carlson, 1993.

Weems, Robert E., Jr. *Desegregating the Dollar: African American Consumerism in the Twentieth Century.* New York: New York University Press, 1998.

———. "The Revolution Will Be Marketed: American Corporations and African-American Consumers during the 1960s." *Radical History Review*, no. 59 (Spring 1994): 94–107.

Robert E. Weems, Jr.

Black Film

When African Americans began to make films around 1913, they hoped to offer alternatives to the limited and stereotypical representations of black life and character they saw in white-produced films. They also wanted to capitalize on the cinema's exploding popularity, as well as the African American market for mass media and commercial amusements that was expanding dramatically during the years of the Great Migration. Between 1913 and the late 1940s black and white filmmakers produced black-cast films aimed at African American audiences in an effort both to represent and to profit from a racially segregated public sphere. In some ways, these films mirror mainstream film culture by featuring African Americans in familiar genres—newsreels, comedies, westerns, musicals, gangster films, melodramas—moving blacks from marginal, subservient, or nonexistent roles to the center of the action. However, these films vary substantially in style and political orientation in ways that illustrate the difficulty of adapting dominant filmmaking practices to the tastes and social conditions of a distinct but diverse African American viewership.

Black subjects had been featured in films from the inception of the medium in the early 1890s. Early film companies such as Edison and American Mutoscope and Biograph presented "actuality" footage of blacks (e.g., *The Ninth Negro Cavalry Watering Horses*, Edison, 1898). But from the very beginning, black film images were informed by the enduring popularity of the minstrel traditions that shaped black representations in every form of American popular culture, from live musical performance to board games to postcards. Black roles in film were routinely performed by whites wearing blackface makeup, and even actualities of "real" black subjects presented them as performers (*The Pickaninny Dance—From the "Passing Show"/The Pickaninnies*, Edison, 1894), exotics (*Native Women Washing Clothes at St. Vincent, BWI*, Edison, 1903), and/or visual gags (*Whitewashing a Colored Baby*, Lubin, 1903).

In response, a small number of African American men sought to rescue the black cinematic image from the confines of blackface minstrelsy. **William**

Foster, an entertainment writer and theatrical booking agent, produced his first film, *The Railroad Porter*, in 1913, a short comedy depicting **Chicago**'s thriving black middle class. Hunter C. Haynes, founder of the Haynes Photoplay Company in **New York City**, produced *Uncle Remus's First Visit to New York* (1914), which details the comic adventures of a southern black rube and his wife as they navigate the big city. In 1914 Chicago-based portrait photographer Peter P. Jones produced the newsreels *For the Honor of the 8th Illinois Regiment* (1914) and *Colored Soldiers Fighting in Mexico* (1916), which illustrated black achievement through military service. These early black filmmakers capitalized on the vibrant black entertainment cultures that were growing in northern urban centers, as well as increasing black urban populations that enjoyed more disposable income and access to commercial entertainments than African Americans living in rural areas, particularly in the South.

But the economic and social gains made by African Americans, particularly those trickling out of the South during the early 1910s, were attacked on many fronts, notably including D. W. Griffith's epic film *The Birth of a Nation* (1915), a nostalgic commemoration and passionate defense of an aristocratic southern white culture lost during the tumult of the Civil War and Reconstruction. The film's white supremacist celebration of the **Ku Klux Klan** and submissive blacks and its denigration of African Americans seeking to rise above their "place"—by, for example, securing political office or desiring white women—drew major protests from liberals across the color line, largely coordinated by branches of the **National Association for the Advancement of Colored People** (NAACP). Though these efforts could not thwart the film's blockbuster success, the film's unprecedented popular and critical praise demonstrated to many African Americans not only the importance of challenging this increasingly influential medium (now elevated to the status of art), but also the necessity of using the medium itself to voice those challenges.

In the wake of *Birth*, African Americans across the country founded film companies and attempted to present more accurate and positive portrayals of the race. One of the most successful, the Lincoln Motion Picture Company, was established in **Los Angeles** in 1916 by Noble Johnson, a character actor at Lubin and Universal studios, with a group of prominent black businessmen and white cameraman Harry Gant. Lincoln's features, including *The Realization of a Negro's Ambition* (1916) and *The Trooper of Troop K* (1916), were praised by black audiences and race leaders across the country for the quality of their acting, writing, and photography and for their uplifting black representations. Author **Oscar Micheaux** began his long filmmaking career with an adaptation of his third novel, *The Homesteader*, in 1919. In this and subsequent films, including *Within Our Gates* (1920) and *The Symbol of the Unconquered* (1920), Micheaux challenged Griffith by presenting African Americans as industrious, patriotic, and entitled to the rights of full American citizenship.

Lincoln and Micheaux were among the few race film companies owned and operated by African Americans. Many black-cast films were made by white-controlled concerns and demonstrate a range of interracial collaborations. David Starkman's Colored Players Film Corporation and Robert Levy's Reol

Productions starred actors from the legendary Lafayette Players repertory company in dramas exploring the nuances of African American social and private lives. Colored Players was eventually helmed by African American entrepreneur Sherman H. Dudley. On the other end of the spectrum, the Ebony Film Corporation of Chicago specialized in black-cast slapstick comedies marketed to mainstream and African American audiences. Although Ebony publicity played up the executive role of African American general manager Luther J. Pollard, unlike Dudley, he never assumed full control of the company and was accused of being a black front man for an exploitative white firm.

Many race film companies did not survive past their first film or folded before they could get a single production off the ground. Although race film production reached its peak in the early 1920s, competition for the captive but small black audience was quite stiff, and as independents, race film companies faced increasing difficulty competing with better-capitalized studios well on their way to building Hollywood empires. While African American film entrepreneurs made appeals to black audiences with discourses of race pride (going as far as asking viewers to buy stock in their companies), this was often not enough to sustain the increasing costs of producing the longer and more sophisticated films audiences desired, let alone distributing them to a national black audience that was migrating into every section of the country.

African American viewers patronized movie theaters in large numbers throughout Hollywood's "golden age" of the 1920s to the 1940s, despite the fact that most of the films they saw were made by, for, and about whites and had to be consumed in segregated conditions. In large cities such as Chicago, **Atlanta**, and Los Angeles, African Americans attended theaters located in their own communities. In locations with fewer neighborhood theaters, separate screenings were designated for blacks (usually at off-peak hours, such as "midnight rambles"). Some theaters allowed blacks and whites to attend the same screenings, but separated the races by restricting blacks to balconies. In these contexts, black-cast films could function as affirming special events or as problematic novelties, displaying the mixed blessings of migration and modernization. On the one hand, watching black actors in prominent roles on screen as part of an all-black audience could be an affirming cultural experience, enabling black participation in the most popular form of American entertainment. On the other hand, viewing low-budget race films in segregated conditions could serve as a reminder of the persistently separate and second-class status of blacks in American society.

These contradictions intensified with the coming of synchronized sound, which had a number of paradoxical effects on African American film culture. For example, while Hollywood sought out black musical performers to show off the new technology (as seen in Warner Brothers/Vitaphone shorts featuring **Bessie Smith**, **Duke Ellington**, and **Cab Calloway**), many black musicians (like their white counterparts) lost wages they had been earning as accompanists for silent films. Black neighborhood theaters were slow to make the costly transition to sound, and African American filmmakers also struggled with increased production costs. Oscar Micheaux was the only African American filmmaker to survive into the sound era, beginning with his first "all-talking" picture, *The Exile* (1931). Thus while Hollywood presented **jazz** (*The Jazz Singer*, Warner Brothers, 1927, starring Al Jolson) and spirituals (King Vidor's *Hallelujah*, MGM, 1929), most black film theaters and production companies were momentarily unable to take advantage of the most vibrant and popular black cultural forms with which they shared close relations.

By the early 1930s, however, black musical performances became a staple in race films, which routinely featured cabaret scenes and song-and-dance numbers even when they would not seem to fall into the musical genre. Although Hollywood studios siphoned off some of the best-known black entertainers throughout the 1930s and 1940s (including Ethel Waters, Bill Robinson, and the Nicholas Brothers), Micheaux and other race filmmakers offered a wide range of up-and-coming performers and those with local followings exposure to a national black audience, as well as a potential launching pad into the dominant film industry. This was the case for Lena Horne, who made her screen debut in the Ralph Cooper vehicle *The Duke Is Tops* in 1938. When Horne signed a much-publicized contract with MGM in 1942, the film was repackaged as *The Bronze Venus* and circulated again in the national network of black theaters.

As in the silent era, black producers of race films were rare, and a number of white directors, producers, and distributors (such as Jed Buell, Arthur Dreifuss, Richard C. Kahn, Bud Pollard, and Alfred Sack) sought to address and to profit from the segregated African American market. Black-cast films produced by both blacks and whites during the sound era vary more widely than silent race films in their commitment to critiquing black stereotypes and uplifting black audiences. Sound-era race films conform more closely to mainstream generic conventions, particularly Hollywood B movies that were cranked out quickly with smaller budgets. As a result, black-cast westerns (such as *Two-Gun Man from Harlem*, 1938, and *The Bronze Buckaroo*, 1939, featuring vocalist Herb Jeffries as a singing cowboy), gangster films (such as *Dark Manhattan*, 1937, and *Sunday Sinners*, 1940), and horror films (*Son of Ingagi*, 1940) offered welcome variations from the servile roles played by Hattie McDaniel, Louise Beavers, and Stepin Fetchit in Hollywood films of the period, but they did not always self-consciously address issues of racism and inequity presented in earlier race films. Indeed, the idea of **uplift** became something of a cliché for some race filmmakers, as evidenced by Bud Pollard's *The Black King* (1932), a parody of **Marcus Garvey**'s back-to-Africa movement. Oscar Micheaux continued to make social and political commentary in his 1930s dramas, but his didactic messages of thrift and sacrifice, coupled with his reliance upon extended musical numbers and actors with varying degrees of film experience, increasingly alienated black viewers accustomed to Hollywood style.

When the United States entered World War II, civil rights groups pressured the federal government and a host of American industries to live up to the rhetoric of democracy the nation claimed to be defending on an international stage. **Walter F. White**, executive secretary of the NAACP, brokered an agreement with Hollywood studios in which they pledged to include more and more accurate roles for blacks. Lena Horne's groundbreaking MGM contract stipulated that she was not to play maids or jungle natives. While these moves brought about a subtle but significant integration of Hollywood films (such as the incidental appearance of an African American couple in the background of a scene in *The Maltese Falcon*, 1941), blacks were more visible in all-black musicals such as *Cabin in the Sky* (MGM, 1943) and *Stormy Weather* (Fox, 1943), in which black performers are given lavish star treatment, but are restricted to roles as performers and silent on issues of racial discrimination.

During and after World War II theaters began to discontinue their segregationist seating practices, slowly dismantling the conditions for a separate black public sphere (though **Jim Crow** persisted in the South at least through the 1960s). Race films produced during the 1940s, such as the works of actor/director Spencer Williams (including his religious drama *The Blood of Jesus*, 1941, military drama *Marching On*, 1943, and musical comedy *Juke Joint*, 1947), present culturally specific forms and themes such as spirituals and urban migration while acknowledging the influences of Hollywood films and the social and personal issues black Americans share with their white counterparts. Much like the fate of baseball's **Negro Leagues**, race movies and the thriving black film culture of which they were a part declined when the country's moves toward racial integration created new roles for African Americans in the mainstream of American life. *See also* Black Consumer Market; Desegregation; Literature, the Great Migration in; Visual Arts, the Great Migration in.

Further Reading

Bowser, Pearl, Jane Gaines, and Charles Musser, eds. *Oscar Micheaux and His Circle: African American Filmmaking and the Race Cinema of the Silent Era.* Bloomington: Indiana University Press, 2001.

Carbine, Mary. " 'The Finest outside the Loop': Motion Picture Exhibition in Chicago's Black Metropolis, 1905–1928." *Camera Obscura* 23 (1990): 9–41.

Cripps, Thomas. *Slow Fade to Black: The Negro in American Film, 1900–1940.* Oxford: Oxford University Press, 1977.

Everett, Anna. *Returning the Gaze: A Genealogy of Black Film Criticism, 1909–1949.* Durham, NC: Duke University Press, 2001.

Knight, Arthur. *Disintegrating the Musical: Black Performance and American Musical Film.* Durham, NC: Duke University Press, 2002.

Massood, Paula. *Black City Cinema: African American Urban Experiences in Film.* Philadelphia: Temple University Press, 2003.

Sampson, Henry. *Blacks in Black and White: A Source Book on Black Films.* 2nd ed. Metuchen, NJ: Scarecrow Press, 1995.

Stewart, Jacqueline. *Migrating to the Movies: Cinema and Black Urban Modernity.* Berkeley: University of California Press, 2005.

University of Chicago. Black Film Research Online. http://blackfilm.uchicago.edu.

Jacqueline Stewart

Black-Jewish Relations

One of the most intriguing and complex relationships among racial and ethnic groups in America has been that of African Americans and Jews. Steeped in both religious and secular traditions of shared persecution, these two groups have experienced an ambivalent relationship dating back to the colonial period. The basis upon which much of the relationship has been understood and misunderstood draws from a roughly twenty-year period after World War II when both groups were engaged in an alliance for civil rights. Yet the relationship can be analyzed over several distinct periods in American history ranging from the days of slavery to the present time. Just as significant as the relationship itself has been the way journalists, civic leaders, labor leaders, politicians, rabbis, preachers, and scholars have attempted to explain this historical relationship.

Before the beginning of the twentieth century, it would be difficult to point to any particular set of historical circumstances that would have set black-Jewish relations apart within the paradigm of an alliance. Yet there were also incidents that coupled the two groups on the basis of mutual intolerance and violent persecution perpetrated by the larger white, Anglo-Saxon, Protestant majority. Indeed, some Jews engaged in the slave trade and owned black slaves, as did some African Americans in the colonial and antebellum South. Some Jews fought with the abolitionist John Brown and supported the Union during the Civil War. Judah Benjamin was a proslavery senator from Louisiana who became the Confederacy's secretary of state. As for African Americans who were enslaved, but exposed to Christianity, the closest link they expressed concerning any similarity with Jews was seeing themselves held bondage like the Hebrews in Egypt and awaiting some form of emancipation.

After the Civil War and into the early 1900s, a series of events and circumstances symbolized the mutual intolerance each group suffered. For example, during Reconstruction it was not unusual for some Jewish merchants to employ blacks. In one instance in Franklin, Tennessee, in 1868 the **Ku Klux Klan** lynched S. A. Bierfield and Lawrence Bowman, his employee. **Lynching**, organized racism and anti-Semitism, and employer-employee relations each played a major role in shaping the relationship for the next 100 years. The overlap between lynchings and race riots in the American South and pogroms in Russia in the early twentieth century drew the attention of both communities.

By the turn of the twentieth century it was clear that there were significant similarities in the plight of African Americans and Jews, and black leaders like **Booker T. Washington** and **W.E.B. DuBois** were urging blacks to learn from the example of Jews and overcome whatever handicaps they faced. Interaction between the two groups occurred on several levels. One involved the activities of Jewish philanthropists and Progressive Era reformers concerned with the plight of African Americans. Most notable was Julius Rosenwald, who donated millions of dollars to advance black education in the South. Lillian Wald, Jacob Schiff, and E. A. Seligman were several of the leading Jews who represented a growing concern with social and racial prejudice and channeled their efforts into the creation of the **National Association for the Advancement of Colored People** (NAACP) and the **National Urban League**.

Until the 1920s the basis for interaction between blacks and Jews existed within these organizational relationships and involved a very specific group of middle-class and elite Jews. Beginning in 1915 and continuing well into the 1920s, increased contact between the two groups occurred on a mass scale among the working classes as thousands of southern blacks began migrating to the urban North and took up residence in Jewish neighborhoods. Jews were the least likely among European ethnic groups (particularly Irish, Italian, and Polish) to violently protest the arrival of blacks into their neighborhoods.

During the 1920s major demographic changes took place in cities like **New York City**, **Philadelphia**, **Chicago**, **Cleveland**, and **Detroit** as African Americans moved into Jewish neighborhoods. In most cases, Jews moved away to establish new communities, but retained ownership of much of the property, particularly retail establishments. At this same time black entrepreneurs were also attempting to lay an economic foundation within these newly created black urban enclaves. Once the Great Depression hit, the dynamics of the urban economic interaction between Jewish and African American merchants and retailers and a black clientele changed.

The 1930s were a critical decade for black-Jewish relations. Tensions grew as blacks in urban northern cities accused Jewish merchants and landlords of price gouging, inferior **housing** conditions, and selling goods of poor quality. Moreover, many of these merchants refused to hire black employees or relegated them to menial positions. Both grassroots and mainstream black organizations engaged in **"Don't Buy Where You Can't Work" campaigns** that in many cases targeted Jewish merchants, most noticeably in Harlem and the South Side of Chicago. Because of these protests and those of more extremist agitators, Jewish merchants decried what they labeled "black anti-Semitism." These urban economic tensions and conflicts continued well into the 1960s.

Black anti-Semitism was part of a larger pattern of native fascism that took root in the United States at the same time Adolf Hitler came to power in Germany and began his persecution of Jews in that country. By the later 1930s and early 1940s some African American and Jewish journalists and religious leaders began to discuss the similarities in the plight of Jews in Germany and the **Jim Crow** system African Americans suffered in the American South. In light of these developments the first serious dialogue of blacks and Jews forming an alliance for civil rights began. By the end of World War II there was increased cooperation between the NAACP, the American Jewish Committee, Jewish unions like the International Ladies Garment Workers' Union, and other progressive unions like the **United Automobile Workers** to promote civil rights legislation. All of these organizations filed amicus curiae briefs in support of the NAACP's historic case that resulted in the 1954 *Brown v. Board of Education* decision.

Over the next ten years, as the **civil rights movement** moved into full swing, African Americans and Jews forged a civil rights alliance based upon the cooperation of their respective civil rights organizations. Black leaders like Dr. **Martin Luther King, Jr.**, and Jewish rabbis like Abraham Heschel, along with numerous black and Jewish journalists, unionists, intellectuals, and scholars, spoke often about the common bond that African Americans and Jews shared, and that it was fitting that they worked together to create an America free of racial, ethnic, and religious discrimination.

After 1965, however, the civil rights movement took on a decided shift and new approach once major civil and voting rights legislation was achieved. Not only did the movement move to the urban North, but the rhetoric of liberation often became more militant and nationalistic. Groups like the **Congress of Racial Equality** and the Student Nonviolent Coordinating Committee began to call for the removal of whites from their organizations—that the freedom struggle needed to be initiated and carried out by blacks only. Indeed, the next twenty years witnessed a series of events that has led more recent scholars to challenge the notion of an alliance.

Issues such as affirmative action in the 1970s and the comments of the Reverend Jesse Jackson and **Nation of Islam** leader Louis Farrakhan in the 1980s, as well as polling data that implied that there was a significant level of anti-Jewish feeling among middle-class and college-educated African Americans, reflected a growing estrangement since the late 1960s. Recent scholarship suggests that there have always been ongoing and underlying tensions between the two groups despite their cooperation in civil rights initiatives. The relationship has not been totally discarded, though, and since the late 1980s a number of initiatives ranging from interfaith-interracial dialogues to focus groups and the creation of the short-lived but important publication *Common Quest* imply that there are still a number of people from each group who view mutual understanding and cooperation in creating a just society as important. *See also* European Immigrants, Relations with Black Migrants; Primary Document 9.

Further Reading

Franklin, V. P., Nancy L. Grant, Harold M. Kletnick, and Genna Rae McNeil, eds. *African Americans and Jews in the Twentieth Century: Studies in Convergence and Conflict*. Columbia: University of Missouri Press, 1998.

Greenberg, Cheryl Lynn. *Troubling the Waters: Black-Jewish Relations in the American Century*. Princeton, NJ: Princeton University Press, 2006.

Kaufman, Jonathan. *Broken Alliance: The Turbulent Times between Blacks and Jews in America*. New York: Charles Scribner's Sons, 1988.

Salzman, Jack, and Cornel West, eds. *Struggles in the Promised Land: Towards a History of Black-Jewish Relations in the United States*. New York: Oxford University Press, 1997.

Washington, Joseph R., ed. *Jews in Black Perspectives: A Dialogue*. Rutherford, NJ: Associated University Presses, 1984.

Weisbord, Robert G., and Arthur Stein. *Bittersweet Encounter: The Afro-American and the American Jew*. Westport, CT: Negro Universities Press, 1970.

Marshall F. Stevenson

Black Legislators

As they migrated north and west during the First and Second Great Migrations, African Americans found themselves concentrated in majority black districts in America's urban centers. While this situation brought a host of social ills, it also brought significant benefits, including allowing the migrants a role in local politics. Black migrants, particularly in the Northeast and Midwest, rapidly entered into local politics and gradually translated their newfound political power into representation on the national level. Beginning in 1928, when **Chicago**'s Bronzeville sent Alabama-born **Oscar DePriest** to

Washington, black communities across the nation slowly began sending their own to Congress. Because the number of blacks in Congress remained low, black legislators in the migration eras served as representatives of all African Americans. Their legislative agendas reflected the desires of the migrant populations that elected them and the hopes of the southern populations from whence the migrants came for legislative action on civil rights.

The first black legislators after Reconstruction, Oscar DePriest and **Arthur W. Mitchell**, made only tentative steps toward a civil rights agenda. DePriest's victory marked a major consolidation of black political power in Chicago's growing Black Belt. Immediately upon his election blacks across America considered DePriest, a lifelong Republican, "their lone 'watchdog' in Congress" (Drake and Cayton, 369). His representation, though, centered more on his defiance of segregation, such as his frequent speeches in the South that ridiculed **Jim Crow**, than on a legislative attack against segregation. Still, he did sponsor a bill to integrate the House restaurant and fought for a larger appropriation for **Howard University** during his second term. The Black Belt's growing population, however, proved too important for the Democratic Party to ignore, and it established a foothold in the community by supporting Alabama-born Arthur Mitchell in his successful challenge to DePriest in 1934. Unlike DePriest, Mitchell proved unpopular with blacks in Chicago and the rest of America. Even though Mitchell submitted antilynching legislation and a bill to desegregate interstate travel, he also feuded with the **National Association for the Advancement of Colored People** (NAACP), which he called a "vicious" organization. Moreover, political opponents and civil rights leaders criticized Mitchell for having "cozy" relationships with southern segregationist legislators, and one **Associated Negro Press** reporter called Mitchell's position on **organized labor** "ill-advised, reckless, and unenlightened."

As the migration made it clear that blacks would be permanent players in national politics in the 1940s, black congressional representatives began to advocate more forcefully for civil rights. No black legislator during this period, however, was able to submit and pass significant civil rights legislation, for southern Democrats worked with conservative Republicans to block nearly all the civil rights bills submitted by black representatives or their liberal white colleagues. In 1942 Bronzeville sent Georgia native **William L. Dawson** to replace Mitchell, and in 1944 Harlem voters elected **Adam Clayton Powell, Jr.**, to Congress. Though they possessed very different political styles, Powell and Dawson were committed to keeping civil rights on the national agenda. They submitted 119 bills between 1942 and 1968 on a range of civil rights issues, including bills to establish a permanent **Fair Employment Practices Committee**, to desegregate public accommodations, and to abolish the poll tax. Indeed, the entire black delegation—six congressmen by 1968—submitted over 200 civil rights bills during this period, but none made it out of their initial committee assignment.

Although black representatives proved unable to rally the support necessary to pass civil rights bills, they generally succeeded in their "watchdog" role by effectively blocking explicitly racist legislation submitted by other members. For instance, in his first speech in Congress, Dawson spearheaded a drive to prevent Congress from forcing the dismissal of a black employee in the

Treasury Department, William Pickens, for his association with radical organizations. In 1951 Dawson and Powell teamed with liberal whites to defeat a bill to create a segregated veterans' hospital. They were not always successful, though. In 1957 Dawson, Powell, and freshman congressman Charles Diggs of **Detroit** fought against an amendment to the Civil Rights Act of 1957 to allow a jury trial in civil rights cases, arguing that most southern juries would not convict their peers of civil rights violations. Though the NAACP, prominent civil rights leaders, and the three members of the black congressional delegation opposed the amendment, liberal white Democrats focused on the bill overall as a first step toward civil rights legislation, and the strength of their votes passed the amendment.

Despite these instances of cooperation, black legislators during the migration era do not appear to have coordinated their efforts. In 1956, for example, the black delegation split over an amendment to an education bill submitted by Powell that would block funds to any school that practiced segregation. Dawson and many liberal white representatives feared that the controversial Powell amendment would kill any attempt to increase funding for schools, while Powell and Diggs wanted to use the amendment to commit the federal government to equal education. As their numbers increased, the black delegation remained divided over the amendment. When the Powell amendment was added to a vocational education bill in 1963, Louisiana-born Augustus Hawkins, a freshman congressman from **Los Angeles**, joined Dawson in opposition, while Robert Nix of **Philadelphia** sided with Powell in support, and Diggs abstained.

As the number of black legislators grew in the late 1960s, their bills increasingly overlapped and their agendas expanded. In 1969, for instance, Hawkins, Nix, Dawson, and William Clay from **St. Louis** submitted a bill to advance equal employment opportunities. Likewise, most of the black legislators supported Lyndon Johnson's Great Society programs, most of which came into being through Powell's efforts as chair of the House Committee on Education and Welfare. Thus in 1968 John Conyers of Detroit, Shirley Chisholm of New York, and William Clay of St. Louis added their names to a bill to strengthen the Food Stamp Act.

By the end of the 1970s the nine black members of Congress decided to formalize their efforts to represent the nation's blacks. Their new organization, the Congressional Black Caucus, signaled a new era in black national representation. *See also* Black Mayors; Brown, Willie L., Jr.; Electoral Politics; Political Realignment.

Further Reading

Barker, Lucius J., and Mack H. Jones. *African Americans and the American Political System*. 3rd ed. Englewood Cliffs, NJ: Prentice Hall, 1982.

Branham, Charles. "The Transformation of Black Political Leadership in Chicago, 1864–1942." Ph.D. diss., University of Chicago, 1981.

Clay, William L. *Just Permanent Interests: Black Americans in Congress, 1870–1991*. New York: Amistad Press, 1992.

Drake, St. Clair, and Horace R. Cayton. *Black Metropolis: A Study of Negro Life in a Northern City*. Rev. and enl. ed. Chicago: University of Chicago Press, 1993.

Haygood, Wil. *King of the Cats: The Life and Times of Adam Clayton Powell, Jr.* Boston: Houghton Mifflin, 1993.

King, Desmond. *Separate and Unequal: Black Americans and the US Federal Government.* Oxford: Oxford University Press, 1995.

Manning, Christopher. "The Ties That Bind: William L. Dawson and the Limits of Electoral Politics, 1942–1970." Ph.D. diss., Northwestern University, 2003.

Singh, Robert. *The Congressional Black Caucus: Racial Politics in the U.S. Congress.* Thousand Oaks, CA: Sage Publications, 1997.

Swain, Carol M. *Black Faces, Black Interests: The Representation of African-Americans in Congress.* Enl. ed. Cambridge, MA: Harvard University Press, 1995.

Christopher Manning

Black Mayors

Despite the Great Migration significantly increasing black Americans' population in metropolitan areas, black political incorporation at the highest level of local government, the mayor's office, proceeded at an uneven pace. Multiple factors, including the proportion of blacks to the general population and the ability of black politicians to forge alliances with other ethnic groups, influenced this process. Upon obtaining office, black mayors made local governments more sensitive to minority concerns, but they faced large-scale economic and demographic shifts that could not be satisfactorily addressed at the local level.

Population was the first major factor that stimulated the ascendancy of black mayors in large cities. This was the case in **Gary, Indiana**, where black in-migration and **white flight** brought about a black majority by 1966. The following year **Richard Hatcher**, a city council member with a militant reputation, put together a coalition of white radicals, black nationalists, upper-middle-class blacks, and Jewish business elites to defeat the local political machine led by Mayor Martin Katz. Hatcher won what became a divisive election with 91 percent of the city's black vote and approximately 17 percent of the white vote. Also that year **Carl Stokes** became the first African American mayor of a major U.S. city when he was elected mayor of **Cleveland, Ohio**. Blacks had grown to 34 percent of that city's population in 1965 when Stokes made his first unsuccessful attempt for the mayor's office. In 1967, though, Stokes campaigned more heavily for white votes. This strategy proved successful, garnering Stokes 94.5 percent of the black vote and 21 percent of the white vote for a slim 2,500-vote margin.

In the 1970s black politicians led broad coalitions to achieve incorporation in the nation's megacities. Arriving in **Los Angeles** during World War II and the Cold War, blacks had increased their population by 334,000 but still composed only 15 percent of the population in 1973. Black Angelenos first organized among themselves to gain three city council seats in 1962 and 1963. Six years later Tom Bradley, a member of the city council, with the backing of blacks, liberal Jews, Latinos, and Asians, unsuccessfully challenged the city's business-oriented Protestant coalition led by Mayor Sam Yorty. Undaunted, the coalition rallied against the Yorty administration's disregard for progressives and insensitive law enforcement to win the 1973 election. Although it was a very different city, **Detroit** shared some circumstances with Los Angeles in 1973 when **Coleman Young** won city hall. Both cities endured race riots in the 1960s, and in both cities black citizens suffered from **police brutality**. Young, a state senator, successfully addressed public safety and police brutality in his campaign. Moreover, although the migration had already shifted Detroit to a predominantly black population, Young also ran a strong citywide campaign, winning the general election by 17,000 votes.

In both of these cities strong political machines and party systems had allowed only limited black political participation before the 1970s. In other major cities, such as **Chicago** and **Baltimore**, blacks needed both a large population and a strong coalition to defeat local political machines. Upon the death of Mayor Richard J. Daley in 1976, the Chicago machine was left leaderless, and the black community played an important role in Jane Byrne's successful challenge to the machine in 1979. Ironically, the Byrne administration governed in the same manner as her machine predecessors. Thus in 1983 Congressman Harold Washington forged a coalition that included blacks, liberal whites, and Latinos to beat the divided machine and win what turned into a bitter election. In 1971 black Baltimoreans attempted to elect a black mayor, but divided their votes between a black machine and a black civil rights–oriented candidate, allowing white city council leader William Donald Schaeffer to win. Schaeffer worked hard to earn black support, though, and stayed in office until 1986. At this point it was clear that Baltimore would have a black mayor. Focusing on antipoverty and community development, State's Attorney Kurt Schmoke united the black community and liberal whites to defeat the black machine camp during the primary and sweep the general election.

Upon achieving office, black mayors successfully fought entrenched white bureaucrats and politicians to make local governments more sensitive to minority concerns. Coleman Young, for instance, found the mostly white city bureaucracy uncooperative, while in Chicago Mayor Washington spent nearly four years battling remnants of the Daley regime. Both mayors overcame these obstacles and actually heightened their popularity with white and black voters in their subsequent reelections. Young used his mandate to disband the much-hated undercover police program STRESS (Stop Robberies, Enjoy Safe Streets), while Washington created several city commissions that enabled women, Hispanics, gays and lesbians, Asian Americans and others to communicate with local government (Grimshaw, 188). In **Philadelphia** Mayor Wilson Goode, elected in 1983, pushed his city to go beyond parity in its hiring of racial minorities.

While these efforts represented great strides, black mayors came to power when large-scale economic and demographic changes were hurting America's cities. White flight, a removal of business to the suburbs, a decrease in government expenditures for cities during the Reagan era, and the shift from an industrial to a service economy devastated city budgets. Although black mayors were unable to defeat these problems entirely, they reacted imaginatively. For example, **Washington, D.C.**, Mayor Marion Barry created a program that located jobs in the suburbs for city residents. Young used his popularity and an appeal to Detroit's conscience to pass a tax hike during an election year to boost the city's budget. Bradley focused on winning federal grants to redistribute wealth downward in Los Angeles. As budgets tightened, though, most black mayors had to pay increasing attention to downtown business interests, often alienating elements of their own coalitions. This tension between appealing to the business community for its ability to keep wealth in the city and maintaining responsiveness to the city's often lower-class black and minority constituencies will remain a central challenge to black mayors for years to come. *See also* Black Legislators; Deindustrialization; Electoral Politics; Political Realignment; Urban Crisis of the 1960s.

Further Reading

Biles, Roger. "Black Mayors: An Historical Assessment." *Journal of Negro History* 77 (1992): 109–25.

Browning, Rufus P., Dale Rogers Marshall, and David H. Tabb, eds. *Racial Politics in American Cities*. 3rd ed. New York: Longman, 2003.

Colburn, David R., and Jeffrey S. Adler, eds. *African-American Mayors: Race, Politics, and the American City*. Urbana: University of Illinois Press, 2001.

Grimshaw, William J. *Bitter Fruit: Black Politics and the Chicago Machine, 1931–1991*. Chicago: University of Chicago Press, 1992.

Moore, Leonard N. *Carl B. Stokes and the Rise of Black Political Power*. Urbana: University of Illinois Press, 2002.

Rich, Wilbur C. *Coleman Young and Detroit Politics*. Detroit: Wayne State University Press, 1989.

Christopher Manning

Black Metropolis (Drake and Cayton)

Published in 1945 by sociologists St. Clair Drake and Horace Cayton, *Black Metropolis: A Study of Negro Life in a Northern City* detailed the experiences and worldviews of African Americans living in **Chicago** during the 1930s and 1940s. The book depicted the ideal of the African American community in Chicago as a "city within a city." Its character had largely been shaped by the Great Migration of the 1910s and 1920s, as well as by the Great Depression and the mobilization on the home front during World War II. The study showed a bustling and dynamic community amid the struggles experienced on an everyday basis by African Americans in Chicago.

Drake and Cayton cited proponents of the idea of autonomy in the African American neighborhoods as the means of attaining economic and political power. The increases of jobs, businesses, and voters in the black community during the Great Migration gave rise to this hope. This was especially true in the period described by Drake and Cayton as the "fat years," 1924 to 1929. However, economic prosperity was beyond the reach of many African Americans in Chicago, even in the "fat years," and particularly in the "lean years" of the Great Depression. The authors argued that racial discrimination hurt African American advancement. In the workplace there was the "job ceiling," where African Americans were often denied job promotions and pay raises. In the home sphere, white realtors and home owners went to great lengths to prevent blacks from moving into predominantly white neighborhoods.

This forced African Americans to crowd in enclaves located on the South and West sides of Chicago, with tenants paying exorbitant rents and property owners losing money on depressed property values.

Cayton and Drake interviewed a cross section of African American residents from different class backgrounds and worldviews. Consequently, *Black Metropolis* featured many candid observations of African American leaders, institutions, advancement strategies, and values from within black Chicago. In particular, Drake and Cayton's interviews revealed growing frustration and sharper criticism of prominent individuals and institutions in black Chicago. The criticisms underscored divisions along class lines within the African American neighborhoods and were evident in black Chicagoans' contrasting lifestyles, spending practices, political ideology, and social outlook. Purported leaders and voices of authority—particularly the clergy—were challenged and found their motives and actions questioned by many of the other African Americans who were supposed to "follow the leaders." The professionals' and entrepreneurs' promotion of a race-based local economy was ignored by those who found that white proprietors usually offered lower prices and more credit than their African American counterparts. Similarly, many African Americans, in their pursuit of recreation, rejected middle-class mores of "propriety" and "self-restraint" and enjoyed the clubs, cafés, and policy halls.

Drake and Cayton, while documenting the hardships experienced by many black Chicagoans and despite their criticisms of the exclusionary practices of white realtors and neighborhood associations, did not view black Chicago as a **ghetto**. Instead, they saw it as a vibrant hub of social activity. They referred to black Chicago as Bronzeville, an area alive with businesses, shops, clubs, churches, and theaters. Bronzeville was a place where blacks came from other parts of the country—particularly the South—to "better their condition" by being out from under the thumb of white domination. Drake and Cayton stated that while black Chicago included some of the worst neighborhoods of the city, there was still a distinct African American culture and social life in Bronzeville and much for blacks to be proud of in Chicago. The obstacles that African Americans encountered in their attempts to create the Black Metropolis were deeply rooted and underscored the difficulties of achieving an autonomous, self-sufficient local economy. Such issues as **occupational mobility**, job opportunities, and livable **housing** bedeviled the present generation, as well as future generations. Drake and Cayton acknowledged that and also highlighted the progress made by the inhabitants of Bronzeville, the range of diversity in opinion and living experiences of black Chicagoans, and the possibility of future improvements. Published in 1945 with an introduction by **Richard Wright**, *Black Metropolis* was revised and reprinted three times in the years that followed its initial publication. *See also* Chicago Renaissance; Chicago School of Sociology (CSS); Primary Documents 8, 9, 52.

Further Reading

Cayton, Horace R. *Long Old Road*. New York: Trident Press, 1964.

Drake, St. Clair, and Horace R. Cayton. *Black Metropolis: A Study of Negro Life in a Northern City*. New York: Harcourt, Brace and Company, 1945. Rev. and enl. ed. Chicago: University of Chicago Press, 1993.

Hobbs, Richard S. *The Cayton Legacy: An African American Family*. Pullman: Washington State University Press, 2002.

Peretz, Henri. "The Making of *Black Metropolis*." *Annals of the American Academy of Political and Social Science* 595 (September 2004): 168–75.

Gareth Canaan

Black Migration before World War I, Patterns of

The Great Migration of the twentieth century has become the standard by which all African American migration is measured. This approach has validity because the Great Migration fundamentally reshaped not only the experiences of African Americans but the United States as a whole. Yet at the same time, it is important to realize that the northern migration of African Americans in the twentieth century is but one of three distinct migration streams in the years before 1970.

Within a few years of their arrival in British North America, people of African descent began to move westward within the southern colonies. As slavery and staple-crop production began to spread westward within the South, so too did the presence of enslaved African Americans. This pattern of westward migration within the South lasted throughout the centuries of slavery. Western migration within the South continued in the decades after slavery as freedmen looked to find homes where they could farm their own land.

Like the rest of the nation, the South became far more urbanized in the late nineteenth century. African Americans were significant contributors to this urban growth, and their moves to southern towns and cities constituted the second overall stage of African American migration. This phase lasted from approximately 1880 at least through the 1930s. While it can be tempting to see this movement as a precursor to the Great Migration, which in many ways it was, it should not be simply assumed to be a part of African Americans' eventual northward migration. There was really no reason to assume that African Americans would begin to migrate in huge numbers to the North in the 1910s. Indeed, many African American and white commentators even into the 1920s predicted that African Americans would continue to migrate within the South. We can now see that such predictions were wholly wrong, but these views highlight how much the Great Migration fundamentally altered existing patterns of migration in a relatively short period of time.

While African Americans experienced rampant racial discrimination and oppression in the South, both before and after the end of slavery, the overall patterns of their migration were often quite similar to that of southern whites through the early twentieth century. Like the region's African Americans, southern whites primarily moved westward within the South through the late nineteenth century and then began to move to southern towns and cities, moves they continued through the first decades of the twentieth century. This similarity in migration patterns highlights a point that has not been sufficiently appreciated in the study of African American migration: the extent of movement often did not match the desires of African Americans. There was a fundamental contrast between the types of moves that African Americans in the South sought to make and the kinds of moves that they undertook, when they moved at all. The prospective migration destinations that grabbed the attention of African Americans in the centuries before the Great Migration were poor reflections of where they settled. Therefore, any analysis of African American migration before the Great Migration has to address both the movement of people and the multifaceted hopes of African Americans for a better life through migration.

Because African Americans were rarely able to achieve their migratory goals before the Great Migration, it is necessary to establish the dynamic nature of where African Americans sought to move. While they were enslaved, the migratory hopes of African Americans are hard to pinpoint, but available evidence highlights the continued attempts of African Americans to establish a life apart from slavery. As slaves' experiences varied greatly across space and time, the specifics of slaves' migration goals were often locally defined. When slavery was present throughout the colonies, as it was before the American Revolution, slaves sought the closest place where they might be free; for slaves in colonial South Carolina, for example, that would likely have meant escaping to Spanish Florida. After most northern states abolished slavery in the early nineteenth century, many slaves saw the North as the most desired destination. No matter where African Americans sought to go to get away from slavery, only a relative handful ever made successful escapes.

The abolition of slavery in 1865 fundamentally changed the societal position of African Americans in the United States. Whereas they had been chattel, they were now citizens. With this change, however, many African Americans maintained consistent goals—the ability to live independent and decent lives. In the wake of the Civil War, many thought that this was possible in the South, and discussions of wholesale migration from the region were relatively rare. As the political climate of the South deteriorated in the last years of Reconstruction, African Americans across the South began to look for a better home away from their native region. It was in the violence and tumult of the late 1870s that migration to Kansas and Liberia became attractive to many African Americans. In both cases the total number of migrants was relatively small. The few who moved to Kansas or Liberia represented the goals of many thousands of African Americans who were unable to make such a journey because of poverty, white interference, or assorted other obstacles. African Americans continued to look for attractive migration destinations outside the South after these two migrations came to an end. It was not until the Great Migration, however, that there was any sort of match between the interest of African Americans in moving and their ability to conduct such moves. When the interest and ability of movement came together for African Americans with the Great Migration, the African American experience was completely transformed as millions of African Americans moved out of the South seeking a better life in the cities of the North and West. *See also* Emigrationism; Exodusters; Involuntary Servitude; Midwestern States, Black Migration to; Migrants, Expectations of; Northeastern States, Black Migration to; Western States, Black Migration to.

Further Reading

Cohen, William. *At Freedom's Edge: Black Mobility and the Southern White Quest for Racial Control, 1861–1915*. Baton Rouge: Louisiana State University Press, 1991.

Hahn, Steven. *A Nation under Our Feet: Black Political Struggles in the Rural South from Slavery to the Great Migration*. Cambridge, MA: Belknap Press of Harvard University Press, 2003.

Johnson, Daniel M., and Rex R. Campbell. *Black Migration in America: A Social Demographic History*. Durham, NC: Duke University Press, 1981.

Painter, Nell Irvin. *Exodusters: Black Migration to Kansas after Reconstruction*. New York: Knopf, 1977.

Jason Carl Digman

Black Nationalism

The migration of African Americans out of the rural South to urban areas in the North and Midwest and the circulation of African Caribbeans—initially within the **Caribbean** and Central America and eventually to northeastern cities—laid the groundwork for the proliferation of black nationalist movements in the post–World War I United States. Spurred by the promise of better economic opportunities and new environments without legally sanctioned racism, blacks arrived in northern and midwestern cities full of optimism and the belief that they were in control of their own destiny for the first time. Despite the egalitarian promise of migration, however, blacks, especially the working class, still found themselves relatively powerless in the formal arenas of power. One of the results of this persistent powerlessness in the face of optimism was an increasingly race-conscious and radicalized black community. What emerged were organizations and individuals who espoused several different variants of black nationalism, including racial separatism, race-conscious Marxism, and an artistically oriented racial chauvinism.

Along with the African Americans who were fleeing from the legal and extralegal manifestations of white supremacy in the South—disfranchisement, segregation, racial violence—the black population in cities like **New York City**, **Boston**, and **Philadelphia** was augmented by the in-migration of blacks from Jamaica, Barbados, Trinidad, British Guiana, and other European colonies in the Caribbean basin. Their numbers were nowhere near those of African American migrants, but their presence was critical to the development of many of these nationalist movements. While many came from peasant and urban working-class backgrounds, a disproportionate amount of African Caribbean immigrants were professionals and skilled workers. They tended to be, on average, more literate than African American migrants and to have more history of being involved in political organizations and trade unions. These immigrants shared with African American migrants a sense of optimism that was ultimately dashed by the racist backlash directed toward them by white workers, a revitalized **Ku Klux Klan**, and the federal government.

Blacks became increasingly disillusioned with the promise of American democracy in the years after World War I. Demobilization and the return of white veterans to the workforce meant the relative loss of industrial skilled and semiskilled jobs among blacks. Racial violence reached unprecedented levels in the **Red Summer of 1919**. More than seventy blacks were lynched that year, and there were more than twenty race riots—often the result of black-white competition over jobs and **housing**—in cities such as **Chicago**, **Washington, D.C.**, and **Omaha**. With the failure of the federal government to respond to these pogroms—in addition to the horrific **East St. Louis race riot of 1917**—African Americans began to question whether full citizenship was possible. Persistent economic, political, and social marginalization after World War I contributed to the emergence of the **New Negro**, an archetypal personality that rejected the accommodationist and assimilationist politics of the past and embraced a more radical politics of racial consciousness and racial chauvinism.

Perhaps the best-known organization that reflected the New Negro mentality was the **Universal Negro Improvement Association** (UNIA). Founded in Jamaica in 1914 by **Marcus Garvey**, Amy Ashwood, and others, the UNIA mobilized people of African descent around their common racial identity. It stressed race pride and race purity. The organization also adopted the self-help ideology of **Booker T. Washington** (although not his accommodationist politics) and advocated the development of economic self-sufficiency among blacks. Its ultimate goal was the creation of an independent black nation-state in Africa. Although it did not come close to achieving the latter two objectives, the UNIA's mission of cultivating race pride among blacks continued to reverberate throughout the twentieth century.

Emerging concurrently with the UNIA was a group of intellectuals and activists who approached the race question through a class analysis. Grounded in the internationalist politics of Marxism, these individuals argued that addressing class inequality was a necessary precursor to dismantling the racist American and global social order. **Hubert Harrison**, a native of St. Croix who migrated to New York, was a **socialist** activist. He broke with the Socialist Party of America, which he felt was not addressing the needs of black workers, in 1914. In 1917 he established the Afro-American Liberty League, a quasi-nationalist organization that advocated black independent politics, self-help, and armed self-defense. The **African Blood Brotherhood** (ABB), founded by Caribbean native **Cyril V. Briggs** in 1919, was a similar organization. Structured like the UNIA, with a parent body and local chapters, the ABB stressed self-help, the right to armed self-defense, and cooperative economics. The ABB was broader in its scope, linking antiblack racism in the West with colonialism in Africa and Asia and attributing both to global capitalism. The ABB and the Liberty League sought to conjoin radical black nationalism with revolutionary socialism.

Finally, African Americans and African Caribbeans engaged in an intellectual and artistic project of reclaiming the African roots of black culture. This cultural nationalism was expressed, for instance, through historical research societies begun by scholars and bibliophiles like John E. Bruce, J. A. Rogers, and **Arthur Schomburg**. In addition, black writers and artists coalesced in New York, Philadelphia, Washington, D.C., Chicago, and other cities and engaged in cultural production that had at its core a righteous indignation over the racist treatment of blacks, on the one hand, and a celebration of blackness, on the other. Writers such as **Gwendolyn Brooks**, **Langston Hughes**, **Zora Neale Hurston**, and **Claude McKay**, visual artists such as **Aaron Douglas** and **Augusta Savage**, and performers such as **Paul Robeson** and **Bessie Smith** all expressed in their cultural work the importance of love of, and pride in, the black folk. *See also* Chicago Renaissance; Harlem Renaissance; Malcolm X; Nation of Islam; Primary Document 49.

Further Reading

Bush, Rod. *We Are Not What We Seem: Black Nationalism and Class Struggle in the American Century*. New York: New York University Press, 1999.

Cruse, Harold. *The Crisis of the Negro Intellectual*. New York: Morrow, 1967.

James, Winston. *Holding Aloft the Banner of Ethiopia: Caribbean Radicalism in Early Twentieth-Century America*. London: Verso, 1998.

Mitchell, Michele. *Righteous Propagation: African Americans and the Politics of Racial Destiny after Reconstruction*. Chapel Hill: University of North Carolina Press, 2004.

Watkins-Owens, Irma. *Blood Relations: Caribbean Immigrants and the Harlem Community, 1900–1930*. Bloomington: Indiana University Press, 1996.

Martin Summers

Black Panther Party

The Black Panther Party was a revolutionary movement of the urban **ghettos** of more than a dozen cities across the United States in the late 1960s and early 1970s. Despite the presence of a few older members, young adult African Americans, ranging in age from nineteen to twenty-five, constituted the core of the party's membership and leadership. Although the Black Panther Party originated in Oakland, California, the spirit of the organization was born of the children of the Second Great Black Migration. Even if the intellectual ideas that informed the party's ideology came from the creative genius of Huey P. Newton, who drew inspiration from the writings of Mao Zedong and Frantz Fanon, the people who breathed life into the Black Panthers and stamped the party with its personality were the sons and daughters of the black migrants to the North and West of the 1940s and 1950s.

For a variety of reasons, the Black Panther Party resonated with recent migrants from the South. In **Chicago**, for example, the party became much more popular and viable on the West Side—a community of displaced African Americans, 65 percent of whom were from the South—than in the older, more established ghetto of the city's South Side. The Panthers' sincerity, optimism, and numerous acts of bold character promised to rekindle a community spirit that resonated with West Side residents. They saw in leaders such as Fred Hampton, a West Side community activist who had been born near Monroe, Louisiana, a southern-born sense of community and love of people. Much the same could be said for the Panther Party branches that sprang up in **New York City** and Oakland. In Oakland the Hilliard family from Rockton, Alabama, and in New York Afeni Shakur from Lumberton, North Carolina, accentuated their southernism to earn credibility and legitimacy among urban migrants. Party membership then grew as activists drew upon extended networks of kith and kin, still rooted in southern traditions, to enlist new members and broaden the party's reach in the urban community.

The Black Panthers' targets and political tactics also won the party support among the children of recent migrants. The Panthers sought to eliminate the worst manifestations of the growing **urban crisis of the 1960s— prostitutes**, **crime**, illegal drug use, **housing** discrimination, **unemployment**, and **police brutality**—that starkly revealed the limitations of black migration as a path to the promised land. Panther tactics of direct, and often physical, confrontation with **women**

A member of the Black Panther Party in Chicago peers from behind a bullet-riddled door after a police raid in 1969; notice the party's bulletins advertising its free breakfast program for black youths and its commitment to the political education of the black community. © Bettmann/ Corbis.

selling their bodies, pimps, small-time drug dealers, and abusive police made them immediately popular on the West Side of Chicago because their approach was plainly understandable to a community of small-town southern folks. Their approach was neither intellectual nor politically sophisticated, but their confrontational tactics against the people and forces that eroded urban neighborhoods repeatedly demonstrated a deep love for community that urged residents to take pride in themselves. The Panthers thus promised an approach from the heart that would restore community intimacy that migrants had left behind in the South but had been unable to recapture in places such as Chicago's West Side. As West Side community activist Nancy Jefferson explained of the Panthers in an unpublished interview, "They are like the old-time men [in the South], not afraid to get somebody told!"

Chicago Black Panther roots were southern born in other ways. In the early 1960s black Chicagoans formed the Deacons for Defense and Justice, a group of older men who armed themselves to protect their leadership from the depredations of the **Ku Klux Klan** in the South and abusive, racist police in Chicago. Some Chicago police officers on the West Side were openly supportive of the Klan (one Chicago police officer even had "KKK" sprayed on the car he drove to work), underscoring how indistinguishable law enforcement was in the North and the South. The Chicago Deacons were also active in Louisiana. The back-and-forth movement of transplanted southern families to their "down-home" relatives kept the two communities connected and shared their common cause against racial injustice. To Chicago West Siders familiar with the Deacons, the Black Panthers, who also armed themselves and talked about taking up arms against the oppressors, were regarded as a younger version of the Deacons, and some Deacons even joined the Illinois Black Panther Party. The Deacons never established a presence in Chicago's South Side ghetto, nor was that ghetto of urban-born grandsons and granddaughters of an earlier migration as receptive to the Illinois Black Panther Party. There the Panthers encountered resistance from an established black middle class and a black political structure that served the Cook County Democratic Party machine more than it served the black residents of the South Side.

These West Side Panthers came from a Protestant Christian background, and while they spoke of revolution, they did not mean simply revolution in the black community. They meant worldwide evangelical revolution. The Christian tenet of universal brotherhood and sisterhood, regardless of race, which many had learned at small churches in the South, now informed their struggles in the urban North. So between 1968 and 1970 the Illinois Black Panther Party, in the highly segregated city of Chicago, ventured into other ethnic communities to seek out allies. This "Rainbow Coalition" was the brainchild of twenty-one-year-old Deputy Chairman Fred Hampton and Texas-born Illinois Panther Field Lieutenant Bobby Lee. Despite the apparent odds against black youngsters working with Appalachian whites and Puerto Ricans, it was an effective project. Within a year of the Black Panther Party's formation there were organizations, working with the Black Panthers as their guide, in the Puerto Rican community of Humboldt Park, the poor white community of Uptown, the working-class white community of West Lincoln Park, and the white community of Rogers Park as well. The Panthers believed that this could change Chicago and eventually change the world. That optimism perhaps came from the success many of them had seen in ridding the South of **Jim Crow**. They acted with conviction, confronting the most powerful local political institutions, the Cook County Democratic Party and its de facto militia, the Chicago Police Department. Risking their lives, it seemed, could bring about change.

Their potential was apparent, but their party did not exist long enough to do more than begin to achieve it. That they were unable to survive as a group was largely due to the role of the Federal Bureau of Investigation in undermining the party with "ghetto informants" and arranging the assassination of Fred Hampton in December 1969, which destroyed their trust in each other (because it was clear that one of them had set him up) and effectively made the immediate community fear being around them. Over the next decade the changing conditions of the black community—**deindustrialization**, **urban renewal**, **white flight**, and **black suburbanization** among urban blacks of talent and privilege—dissolved the old ties that had held communities together. *See also* Black Power; Civil Rights Movement; Community Organizing; Open Housing.

Further Reading

Guy, Jasmine. *Afeni Shakur: Evolution of a Revolutionary.* New York: Atria Books, 2004.

Hilliard, David. *This Side of Glory: The Autobiography of David Hilliard and the Story of the Black Panther Party.* Boston: Little, Brown, 1993.

Knoohuizen, R. *Police and Their Use of Fatal Force in Chicago.* Chicago: Chicago Law Enforcement Study Group, 1972.

O'Connor, Len. *Clout: Mayor Daley and His City.* New York: Avon Books, 1975.

Rice, Jon F. "Black Radicalism on Chicago's West Side: A History of the Illinois Black Panther Party." Ph.D. diss., Northern Illinois University, 1998.

Jon F. Rice

Black Political Activism *See* Political Activism (1915–1945)

Black Populism

During the final decade of the nineteenth century, southern African Americans formed an independent regionwide political movement, Black Populism. The movement attempted to stem the rising tide of **Jim Crow**, yet had the effect of accelerating the process of legal disfranchisement by the Democratic Party in response to its growing strength. The failure of Black Populism fueled the Great Black Migration at the turn of the twentieth century as tens of thousands of African Americans, landless, financially destitute, and politically marginalized, sought economic opportunities in the North.

Distinct from the white Populist movement, between 1886 and 1898 black farmers, sharecroppers, and agrarian laborers formed their own organizations that drew upon the networks created by the black churches, benevolent associations, and **fraternal orders** during the prior two decades. As part of the movement, African Americans developed their own tactics to gain better economic conditions, secure civil and political rights, and challenge the authority of the Democratic Party, which had taken control of the region with the collapse of Reconstruction.

As Black Populists asserted themselves, they met violence and repression at the hands of the region's white planter and business elite through its affiliated network of courts, sheriffs, and newspapers, collectively known as the Southern Democracy. Despite fierce opposition to their growth, Black Populists carried out a wide range of activities, often in cooperation with white Populists. They established farming exchanges, raised money for schools, published newspapers, lobbied for better legislation, mounted boycotts against agricultural trusts, carried out strikes for better wages, protested **lynching** and convict leasing, demanded black jurors in cases involving black defendants, promoted local political reforms and federal supervision of elections, and ran independent and fusion campaigns for public office.

Black Populism found early organizational expression in the Colored Agricultural Wheels, the Knights of Labor, the Cooperative Workers of America, and the Colored Farmers' Alliance (CFA), which helped consolidate much of the base of the growing movement by 1890. The CFA, founded in Houston County, Texas, in 1886, not only became the largest organization of primarily black farmers and agricultural laborers in the late nineteenth century but Black Populism's principal organization before the establishment of the People's Party.

Within five years of its founding the CFA spread to every state in the South and claimed a membership of 1,200,000, of whom 300,000 were **women**. In the fall of 1891 one faction of the CFA launched a national cotton pickers' strike through the Cotton Pickers League, demanding a minimum of one dollar per 100 pounds of cotton picked. The strike, which had been hastily planned and poorly coordinated, was quickly suppressed by planter militias.

Among the CFA's most notable leaders were Oliver Cromwell, a veteran of Reconstruction-era struggles who led a boycott of goods in Mississippi against exorbitant merchant prices; Richard M. Humphrey, a white **Baptist minister** and cotton farmer, elected general superintendent of the CFA, who served as the organization's principal propagandist; and Jacob John Shuffer, a large landholding farmer in Texas who served as president of the national CFA, which he had helped establish with Humphrey and fifteen other black leaders.

Lobbying efforts, strikes, collectivizing resources, and educating farmers about better agricultural techniques had little impact on reversing the deteriorating state of rural economic affairs among most African Americans in the South. With little success in their attempts to implement needed agrarian reforms—including better wages, more equitable trading terms, government regulation of transportation monopolies, and lowering interest rates for lenders—Black Populists entered the electoral arena and helped launch the People's Party with white Populists. Where possible, Black Populists used the Republican Party in fusion campaigns with the People's Party to advance the interests of African Americans, whose civil and political rights were increasingly being eroded.

The CFA voted unanimously to endorse the Lodge Bill, which would have mandated federal supervision of elections if passed. The Reverend Walter A. Pattillo, a black Baptist minister from North Carolina, CFA state lecturer, and national delegate to the conventions leading to the formation of the People's Party, was among the first to call for the formation of a third party among African Americans. George Washington Murray, a CFA lecturer from South Carolina called "the Republican Black Eagle," ran as a Republican and was elected to Congress (Tindall, 56). Murray led the fight against disfranchisement in the state. John B. Rayner, known as "the silver-tongued orator of the colored race," helped establish a series of Black Populist chapters in Texas and was elected to the state executive committee of the People's Party (Cantrell, 200). Lutie A. Lytle, one of the few black female leaders in the People's Party, originally from Kansas, served as the third party's enrolling clerk (she would also become the first black female to teach law in the South); and the Reverend Henry S. Doyle campaigned on behalf of the People's Party congressional candidate Tom Watson, a controversial white Populist, surviving several assassination attempts in the process.

By the late 1890s, under relentless attack—ranging from propaganda campaigns warning of a "second Reconstruction" and "Negro rule" to physical intimidation and assassination of leaders of the movement—Black Populism collapsed. By that time most states in the South had moved toward the "Mississippi Plan" of rewriting their constitutions to disfranchise African

Americans. Although the collapse of Black Populism marked the end of organized political resistance to the Southern Democracy in the late nineteenth century, the movement stands as the largest independent political uprising in the South until the modern **civil rights movement**.

Black Populism's legacy includes the formation of the **Southern Tenant Farmers' Union**, the Louisiana Farmers Union, and the **Share Croppers Union** in the 1930s. In more recent years the Virginia-based National Black Farmers Association has carried on the economic struggle of rural black farmers. Politically, the efforts of Dr. Lenora Fulani—the first woman and the first African American to appear on the ballot in all fifty states as a candidate for president of the United States, running as an independent—have championed the cause to build an independent political alternative to the Democratic and Republican Parties through the Committee for a Unified Independent Party. *See also* Cotton Belt; Mississippi River Delta; Organized Labor.

Further Reading

Ali, Omar H. "Independent Black Voices from the Late 19th Century: Black Populists and the Struggle against the Southern Democracy." *Souls: A Critical Journal of Black Politics, Culture, and Society* 7, no. 2 (2005): 4-18.

Cantrell, Gregg. *Kenneth and John B. Rayner and the Limits of Southern Dissent.* Urbana: University of Illinois Press, 1993.

Gaither, Gerald H. *Blacks and the Populist Revolt: Ballots and Bigotry in the "New South."* University: University of Alabama Press, 1977.

Goodwyn, Lawrence. *The Populist Moment: A Short History of the Agrarian Revolt in America.* New York: Oxford University Press, 1978.

Tindall, George B. *South Carolina Negroes, 1877-1900.* Columbia: University of South Carolina Press, 1952.

Omar H. Ali

Black Power

Black Power is often depicted as an urban phenomenon that is a continuation of or departure from the **civil rights movement** that lay in the experiences of the Student Nonviolent Coordinating Committee and the **Congress of Racial Equality** (CORE). This view gives total credit to northern white and black participation in the changing of the social and political landscape of the South and North. The Black Power concepts of community control, self-defense, self-determination, and political and social empowerment of African Americans have southern roots as well. Southern activists influenced the roots of Black Power and militancy as much as participants from the North did. This is very evident in the African American politics of World War II and the later years of the Great Migration. Many southern African Americans during the migration after World War II experienced the southern civil rights movement before arriving in the North. They used their experiences and exposure to new black militancy to change the political and social landscape of their new urban homes.

New Black Militancy, 1940–1960

The fight against Nazi Germany during World War II and the hypocrisy of America's fight against fascism abroad and the treatment of African Americans at home ignited a new black militancy across the country, especially among southern black soldiers. For example, in 1941 armed conflicts between black and white troops and civilians broke out in Fayetteville, North Carolina, and Alexandria, Louisiana, because of the failure of black soldiers to adhere to **Jim Crow** laws and practices. Other incidents occurred in Fort Bragg, Gibbon, Camp Davis, and Fort Jackson. On the national level, **A. Philip Randolph** and the **Brotherhood of Sleeping Car Porters** organized the all-black **March on Washington Movement** to protest the unfair treatment of blacks in the armed forces and defense industries. President Franklin D. Roosevelt issued Executive Order 8802 and created the **Fair Employment Practices Committee** to ban discriminatory practices and avoid the march in **Washington, D.C.** Many of the participants in these incidents were black migrants who had moved from rural areas in the South to northern and southern cities. It was clear that many of these migrants would use World War II as a springboard for new black militancy.

The surge of black militancy created by World War II and the frustration of black activists served as the catalyst for the modern civil rights movement. On July 2, 1946, Medgar Wylie Evers led a group of fellow black veterans through the streets of Decatur, Mississippi, to register blacks to vote in the Democratic primary. Evers was known to carry a gun for protection against white supremacists. Robert Williams formed black militias with veterans in Monroe, North Carolina, to confront members of the **Ku Klux Klan** and protect local black neighborhoods. He later became president of the local branch of the **National Association for the Advancement of Colored People** (NAACP) and promoted black history programs for local residents. The well-known civil rights events such as the 1954 U.S. Supreme Court decision in *Brown v. Board of Education*, the Montgomery bus boycott of 1955, and the student sit-in movements of 1960 owed as much of their creation to early southern Black Power activists as they did to the nonviolent strategists who would become popular.

Southern Roots of Black Power in the North, 1960–1970

When millions of southern migrants entered the North after World War II, many of them had already experienced early black militancy and the early years of the civil rights movement. Many of these migrants used their experiences to change the social and political environment of the North. Though CORE started during World War II in **Chicago** and became part of the civil rights struggle in the South, many of its early participants were recent migrants from Mississippi and other southern states. By the mid-1960s many southern migrants formed local chapters of CORE in their communities and used President Lyndon Johnson's **War on Poverty** initiatives to push Black Power agendas for community control and economic development. Southern migrants formed community centers throughout the Midwest and Northeast. For example, members of the Long Island chapter of CORE were instrumental in the development of community centers in the towns of Long Beach, Lakeview, Hempstead, Rockville Centre, Westbury, and other parts of Long Island. Many of these communities catered to white suburbanites and had a hard time accommodating the new population of black migrants. The community centers were used to promote the black arts and development of economic opportunities. The new assertion of power by many African Americans in the North was a product of the Jim Crow era, southern black militancy, and the civil rights movement they experienced in the South.

Other groups during the Black Power movement also had connections to southern migrants. The **Nation of Islam**, known for its **black nationalism** and separatist ideology, was made up of many black migrants from the South. Its founder, **Elijah Muhammad**, was born Elijah Poole on a Georgia farm. His experience with black disfranchisement in the South and the new black militancy made it easy for Muhammad to embrace the concepts of the Nation of Islam. In Chicago, **New York City**, and other cities in the North, the Nation of Islam recruited recent migrants who were dissatisfied with the Jim Crow South and the false promises of prosperity and equality in the North. **Malcolm X** was very good at exposing these inequalities when recruiting recent migrants in Harlem and other parts of New York City. Local branches of the NAACP were also active in promoting black self-determination. Though the national headquarters did not always support Black Power ideologies, many local branches used the organizations to fit their own local agendas. For example, the Long Beach branch in Long Island promoted black history in schools and the development of black and Latino community centers and openly expressed its disagreements with philosophies of the NAACP's national headquarters. The vast majority of its members were recent migrants from the South. In 1967 local members protested against the appearance of national NAACP president Roy Wilkins in Long Beach because of comments he had made against Black Power advocates at the NAACP's 1966 national convention. Black migrants helped promote similar ideologies and tactics in NAACP chapters in **Philadelphia**, Newark, **Baltimore**, and other urban areas. The Great Migration allowed the transference of these ideas across state boundaries, gave the new black militancy greater visibility, and created urgency for black self-determination. *See also* Baraka, Amiri; Black Arts Movement; Black Panther Party; Community Organizing; Double V Campaign; Military Service, World War II; Political Activism (1915–1945).

Further Reading

Carson, Clayborne. *In Struggle: SNCC and the Black Awakening of the 1960s.* Cambridge, MA: Harvard University Press, 1981.

Graham, Patrick C. " 'We've Come This Far by Faith': The Long Beach Martin Luther King Center, Local Black Power, and the Great Migration, 1964–1980." Ph.D. diss., State University of New York, 2002.

Lemann, Nicholas. *The Promised Land: The Great Black Migration and How It Changed America.* New York: Vintage Books, 1992.

Tyson, Timothy B. *Radio Free Dixie: Robert F. Williams and the Roots of Black Power.* Chapel Hill: University of North Carolina Press, 1999.

Van Deburg, William L. *New Day in Babylon: The Black Power Movement and American Culture, 1965–1975*. Chicago: University of Chicago Press, 1992.

Patrick C. Graham

Black Press

The black press, made up of hundreds of small weekly newspapers around the turn of the twentieth century, stimulated and organized the great urbanization and northward migration of the African American population during and after World War I. That migration, in turn, led to the modernization and dramatic expansion of the black press, which became one of the most important institutions in African American life.

John Russworm and Samuel Cornish established the first black newspaper, *Freedom's Journal*, in **New York City** in 1829. During the antebellum period free blacks published more than forty weekly newspapers to provide for the "defense of five hundred thousand free people of color," work toward abolition of slavery, and unify, educate, and **uplift** African Americans (Jordan, 14). With the end of the Civil War, the black press expanded dramatically. According to one estimate, blacks had published 575 different newspapers by 1890. Most of these were short lived; all had small circulations, selling well under 10,000 copies per week. Though emancipation and the rapid expansion of black literacy after the war made black publications more viable, the violence of post-Reconstruction southern states—where most blacks continued to live—made it extremely dangerous to operate a black newspaper there. Mobs and vigilante societies executed or exiled blacks who dared to challenge white supremacy. Journalists often found themselves targets of violence. **Ida B. Wells** fled **Memphis, Tennessee**, in 1892, for example, after a white mob ransacked her newspaper office after she wrote a series of editorials challenging the rationale for **lynching**. In this hostile climate southern black editors increasingly refrained from vigorous agitation against lynching, voter disfranchisement, and segregation. As these papers lost political relevance, their circulations declined. By 1910, although 89 percent of blacks lived in the South, they published only 63 percent of black newspapers.

The smaller number of newspapers published in the North became more influential. An important black newspaper around the turn of the twentieth century, the *New York Age*, published by the "dean of black editors," T. Thomas Fortune, until 1907, printed antilynching articles by Ida B. Wells in the 1890s. Though he was known as an agitator who called on blacks to arm themselves in self-defense, Fortune, like many other northern publishers, increasingly came under the influence of **Booker T. Washington** and his accommodationist doctrine of advocating black economic self-advancement while largely refraining from political protest. Washington made contributions to several financially strapped newspapers so that he could control their editorial content. Angered by this retreat from political activism, William Monroe Trotter established the *Guardian* in **Boston** in 1901 with the purpose of fighting uncompromisingly against all racial injustice and exposing Washington as the "Benedict Arnold of the Negro race" (Jordan, 26). Trotter's paper, along with some others, like Henry Clay Smith's *Cleveland Gazette*,

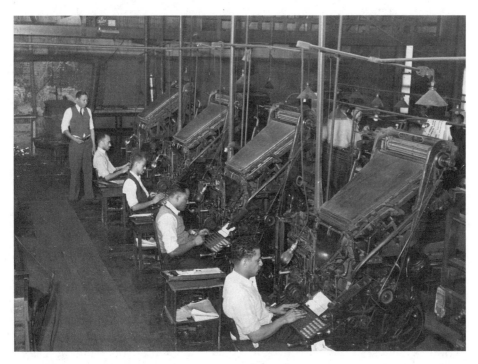

Linotype operators prepare an upcoming edition of the *Chicago Defender*, 1941. Courtesy of the Library of Congress.

carried on the protest tradition of black newspapers during the reign of Booker T. Washington.

Neither Trotter nor Smith, however, combined political protest with financial success. Before 1910 only one black newspaper, the *Indianapolis Freeman*, had a circulation in excess of 10,000. Text-heavy, sedate newspapers of the nineteenth century attracted only educated middle-class readers, who were few in the black population. **Robert S. Abbott**, who established the *Chicago Defender* in 1905, became the first black newspaper publisher to achieve dramatic business success by combining protest with the sensationalism of William Randolph Hearst's newspapers. Not only did the paper publish vivid accounts of injustices against blacks, it also printed sensational stories about sex and violence and disaster in lurid detail. The paper eventually introduced graphic elements as well, expanding the paper's audience to working-class readers, who made up the vast majority of African Americans.

Abbott also found innovative means of distributing the *Defender* beyond the 44,000 black inhabitants of **Chicago**. He recruited agents throughout the South to market the papers and took advantage of Chicago's status as a railroad hub, using black Pullman porters to deliver papers. Abbott also engaged traveling entertainers and preachers as promoters. The *Defender* quickly won an enthusiastic readership throughout the South. In contrast to censored southern newspapers, the *Defender* told the unvarnished truth about racial injustices in the South. The newspaper's circulation rose dramatically. In 1919 about two-thirds of the 130,000 *Defender*s sold weekly circulated outside Chicago in 1,542 southern cities and towns. Contemporaries noted that copies of the *Defender* were liberally passed from reader to reader and were sometimes read out loud to small groups, suggesting a readership much higher than the number of copies sold.

Up to 1916 Abbott criticized the South in unstinting terms while offering a much more favorable view of life for blacks in the North, yet he continued to echo Booker T. Washington's advice—and that of most other black newspapers—that African Americans should remain in the South. By mid-decade business conditions began to change, and as Abbott saw an increase in demand for industrial laborers in Chicago, he changed tactics and began to counsel southern blacks to move north.

While some have credited the *Defender* with setting the migration in motion, many social, economic, and political factors combined to push African Americans out of the South and pull them toward the North. The *Defender* facilitated and accelerated the process. If southern lynchings spurred the black exodus, the *Defender* spread the awareness of each example of a brutal killing beyond the local area where it occurred. If employment opportunities drew migrants, the *Defender* provided a medium through which employers could advertise jobs. The *Defender* portrayed Chicago as more hospitable to blacks than the South. Articles depicted blacks in Chicago participating in the military, owning prosperous businesses, holding public office, attending school with whites, and living with modern accommodations and access to urban entertainment and playgrounds. They reported on the accomplishments of black **sports** heroes like **Jack Johnson**, the first black heavyweight boxing champion, and followed black baseball teams. All this stood in stark contrast to the portrait of life in the South—dominated by racial violence—that appeared in the *Defender*'s pages. The *Defender* reported on the exodus of blacks from the South and generated excitement for the movement, at one point inventing a "Great Northern Drive" to be held on one day in May 1917. The *Defender* continued to promote northward migration throughout the 1920s, but in January 1929, perceiving a downturn in employment prospects, the paper began advising blacks to stay put.

While the black press had a significant influence on the northern migration, the growth of the black population in Chicago and other northern cities had an equally profound impact on the black press. The migration increased the number of blacks—and potential newspaper readers—in northern cities. Circulation of the *Defender* and other black newspapers in northern cities continued to grew accordingly during the war and throughout the 1920s. From 1920 to 1950, four newspapers emerged as the leading mass-circulation black weeklies: the *Defender*, the **Pittsburgh Courier**, the **Baltimore Afro-American**, and, to a lesser degree, the *Amsterdam News* of New York City. The migration accelerated the northward shift of black journalism, but some important southern newspapers emerged too as rural migrants moved into southern cities. The *Journal and Guide* of Norfolk, Virginia, became the most influential southern weekly between the world wars, and in 1932 the *Atlanta Daily World* became one of a very few successful black daily newspapers.

With the exception of the *Journal and Guide*, the leading publications adopted similar formulas, promoting campaigns against racial discrimination and employing a sensational approach to news, focusing on **crime** and sex scandals. These newspapers also kept readership high by providing a varied content, appealing to every segment of the black population. They printed sensational accounts of sex and violence, but also learned discussions of race issues by intellectuals like **W.E.B. DuBois**, **James Weldon Johnson**, **Langston Hughes**, and George S. Schuyler. Newspapers chronicled the accomplishments of leading black figures, followed black sports teams and celebrities, and reported on social life in the city. During the 1930s and 1940s some newspapers sent correspondents overseas to cover Italy's invasion of Ethiopia, the 1936 Berlin Olympics, World War II, and other significant events. They also hired more professionally trained staff members, increasing the quality of the news. Although eighty black newspapers folded during the Great Depression, these few publications made dramatic gains in circulation and revenue.

The *Baltimore Afro-American* became the leading newspaper on the East Coast during the 1930s by establishing local editions in **Richmond**, **Philadelphia**, and **Washington, D.C.**, and distribution centers throughout the Midwest and along the East Coast. The most widely circulated newspaper in the country during most of these years, however, was the *Courier*, supplanting the *Defender* in 1937 with a circulation of 250,000. Resorting less to sensationalism than the *Afro-American* or the *Defender*, *Courier* publisher Robert Vann and his general manager, Ira F. Lewis, improved the paper by introducing a more professional staff and adopting higher journalistic standards. Vann hired Schuyler, who became known as the H. L. Mencken of the black press, to write a weekly column and serve as chief editorial writer. In the 1930s the scholarly Joel A. Rogers wrote a black history column and served as a correspondent to Africa and Europe. In the sports pages the *Courier* followed the rise of **Joe Louis** and played a role in Jackie Robinson's integration of baseball.

Vann used his paper's soaring circulation to leverage political influence. In 1932 he called on blacks to turn Abraham Lincoln's picture to the wall and vote for Democratic presidential candidate Franklin D. Roosevelt. The migration of blacks to a region where they could vote had made them a significant voting bloc, helping FDR create a winning coalition. In exchange for his role in the election, Vann, a lawyer, secured an appointment in the new administration as special assistant to the attorney general. During the war the paper called for a **Double V campaign** for victory against the Axis abroad and racism at home.

After Vann's death in 1940—Abbott died the same year—the paper enjoyed a few more years of growing circulation under Lewis's management, reaching its peak circulation in 1947 at 357,000. Lewis died in 1948, and the paper declined rapidly thereafter. In spite of continued northward migration, the black press entered a period of generally declining circulations, brought about in part by the successes of the **civil rights movement** of the 1950s and 1960s.

Black newspapers found it difficult to compete against the mainstream press in covering the civil rights movement. Most newspapers did not have the resources to send correspondents to all the places where important events of the movement were happening, and weeklies could not match the immediacy of television or daily newspapers. In addition, mainstream news organizations began to hire the best black journalists, especially after 1968. In 1965 John H. H. Sengstacke, Abbott's nephew and successor at the *Defender*, purchased the *Courier* and renamed it the *New Pittsburgh Courier*, making it part of Sengstacke Publications, the largest chain of black newspapers. Circulation of both the *Courier* and the *Defender*, as well as other black newspapers, continued to decline. In 1977 the *Defender* (now a daily), the *Afro-American* (publishing two weekly issues), and the *Courier* sold no more than 34,000 copies per issue. The 300 black newspapers published in 1960 fell to 170 in the 1980s.

As weekly newspapers declined in significance, glossy monthly magazines gained readers and became a highly profitable enterprise. Before 1940 monthlies by and for African Americans were few—limited to journals subsidized by black churches or organizations or appealing to narrow audiences. The **National Association for the Advancement of Colored People** (NAACP) subsidized one of the more influential monthlies, the *Crisis*, beginning in 1910. W.E.B. DuBois edited the journal until 1934, promoting black achievement and publicizing the NAACP's protest activities. The **National Urban League** launched *Opportunity* in 1923, and **A. Philip Randolph** promoted a leftist, pro-labor message with his ***Messenger***, published between 1917 and 1928.

The era of modern glossy magazines by and for African Americans, however, began when John H. Johnson began publishing *Negro Digest* in 1942 and *Ebony* in 1945. Johnson had been a young reader of the *Defender* in Arkansas before his family moved to Chicago in the 1930s. Using shrewd marketing strategies, Johnson beat out a few early competitors and built a publishing empire on the successes of these and other black publications, including *Jet*, *Black World*, and *Tan Confessions*. Johnson's journals took a positive slant on black life, printing news of interest to African Americans, provocative opinion pieces on race issues, feature stories about black celebrities and leaders, and lots of eye-catching photographs. In 2003 *Ebony*, one of the top fifty consumer magazines in the United States, had a paid circulation of 1.8 million. *See also* Associated Negro Press (ANP); Baltimore, Maryland; Black Consumer Market; *California Eagle*; *Houston Informer*; Johnson Publishing Company; Pittsburgh, Pennsylvania.

Further Reading

"Black Press: Soldiers without Swords." PBS Online. August 2004. www.pbs.org/blackpress/.

Bunie, Andrew. *Robert L. Vann of the "Pittsburgh Courier": Politics and Black Journalism*. Pittsburgh: University of Pittsburgh Press, 1974.

Farrar, Hayward. *The "Baltimore Afro-American," 1892-1950*. Westport, CT: Greenwood Press, 1998.

Grossman, James R. *Land of Hope: Chicago, Black Southerners, and the Great Migration*. Chicago: University of Chicago Press, 1989.

Jordan, William. *Black Newspapers and America's War for Democracy, 1914-1920*. Chapel Hill: University of North Carolina Press, 2001.

Ottley, Roi. *The Lonely Warrior: The Life and Times of Robert S. Abbott*. Chicago: Henry Regnery Co., 1955.

Washburn, Patrick S. *A Question of Sedition: The Federal Government's Investigation of the Black Press during World War II*. New York: Oxford University Press, 1986.
Wolseley, Roland E. *The Black Press, U.S.A.* Ames: Iowa State University Press, 1972.

William G. Jordan

Black Suburbanization

Despite popular stereotypes of suburbia as white and middle class, suburbs attracted a steady share of African American migrants during the Great Migration. Reflecting the agency of people who believed that they could make better lives on the outskirts of town than in its center, suburbs were an important setting in which migrants rebuilt communities and adapted to metropolitan life.

Outside the South the first upsurge of black suburbanization coincided with the Great Migration. During the 1910s and 1920s, as many as one in six migrants to the urban North settled in a suburb. Families moved to enclaves of domestic service workers in predominantly white, affluent suburbs such as Montclair, New Jersey, and Pasadena, California; to industrial satellites such as Homestead, Pennsylvania, and River Rouge, Michigan; and to semirural, "all-black" suburbs such as Robbins, Illinois, and Lincoln Heights, Ohio. By 1940, 500,000 African Americans lived in suburban areas outside the South, an increase of 285,000 since 1910.

Like other migrants, most new suburbanites were working-class people who moved directly from the South. They came to suburbs for jobs and to join others who had gone before them. In new surroundings they fashioned communities interwoven with kinship ties rooted in the South. Working-class suburbanites also expressed similar values regarding **home ownership**, economic independence, open space, and family life. Where there was vacant land, they worked to buy it and build homes. Consequently, they were more likely than city dwellers to be home owners—in many suburbs a majority of blacks owned their homes. Even in the most congested suburbs they grew gardens, kept small livestock, and used domestic space for income. **Women**'s labor played key roles in this process. Households relied on extended families for economic as well as emotional support, and many explicitly rejected city living, preferring rustic landscapes reminiscent of the South. Last, they gravitated to black communities not only because of discrimination but because of the comfort and connection they felt among people like themselves. These preferences reflected a coherent vision of better living in the metropolitan United States, a suburban dream that found continued expression despite white efforts to thwart it.

In suburbs and cities alike, migrants' arrival provoked wide-ranging efforts to restrict public and private space. Discrimination in the real estate market and terroristic violence in neighborhoods blocked access to most suburban areas. **Banks** denied credit, real estate agents prevented sales, and municipalities enforced zoning and building codes that limited admission. Thus migrants moved to those few suburbs where job opportunities, the presence of an earlier black community, or the lack of land-use controls opened a door to settlement. These areas were often isolated and subject to municipal neglect or environmental nuisances, such as smoke and floods, but for black migrants, they were a foothold, a stepping-stone to economic security, and a place to call home.

As migration peaked after World War II, black suburbanization grew in step. During the 1940s and 1950s the number of black suburbanites increased by 1 million—15 percent of black metropolitan population growth overall— including several hundred thousand people who became pioneer suburbanites on the West Coast. By 1960 more than 2.5 million African Americans lived in U.S. suburbs, setting the stage for a mass migration that pushed the number of black suburbanites to 6 million by 1980 and 12 million at century's end.

As the number of suburbanites rose, the socioeconomic status of the newcomers also shifted upward; by the mid-1950s the majority of new suburbanites were middle class. If they were southern born, they had lived in the city for some time. More recent migrants, by contrast, faced rising barriers to suburbanization as millions of new white suburbanites blocked access to undeveloped property and curtailed land-use practices that had sustained blue-collar suburbs before the war. Middle-class blacks also faced formidable barriers to suburbanization, but they had greater means at their disposal. Their efforts to buy suburban homes provoked intense, often violent racial conflict over suburban space throughout the postwar period.

In contrast to the thrift-oriented ethos that prevailed in early suburbs, many new suburbanites articulated residential preferences that they shared with the wider suburban middle class. They sought "adequate play space for children, good schools, safety and quiet, good property maintenance, and congenial neighbors of roughly equivalent income and educational background" (Woodson, 119). Although many desired new **housing** in up-to-date subdivisions, in only a few places outside the South, such as Markham, Illinois, Long Island, New York, and Pacoima, California, did developers built substantial numbers of new tract homes for black families. Most suburbanites found homes in older neighborhoods, usually within a short distance of existing black communities. Regardless of the housing to which they moved, postwar suburbanization tended to reinforce a segregated and geographically cumulative pattern of settlement.

Nonetheless, migrants' long-deferred aspiration to have places of their own continued to reverberate in postwar suburbia. Older black suburbs continued to attract migrant families, and patterns of kin-based settlement and productive land use remained common. Perhaps the best-known representation of this ethos was Lorraine Hansberry's 1958 play *A Raisin in the Sun*. The drama's motive force is the unfulfilled desire of "Mama," a southerner living in a **Chicago** tenement, to own "a little place" with space for a garden "like I used to see sometimes . . . down home" (Hansberry, 18). In real life, too, the echoes of southern upbringings resounded in the choices that migrants made and shaped the environment of black suburbia.

Throughout these decades black suburbanites won access to improved housing, schools, and amenities, yet the period saw little change in the cumulative and contested expansion of residential areas that had characterized black suburbanization since early in the century. Even as the pace of suburbanization accelerated after 1960, the process gave rise to dozens of new majority-black suburbs, including East Orange, New Jersey, East Cleveland, Ohio, and Compton, California, and over time black suburbanites fought ongoing battles with redlining, commercial flight, diminishing services, and high taxes. As the Great Migration came to an end, suburbanization became the next frontier, driven by African Americans' abiding—and often thwarted—efforts to overcome racism, to improve their lives, and to build better places to live. *See also* Home Ownership among Migrants; Migrants, Expectations of; Neighborhood Property Owners' Associations; Restrictive Covenants.

Further Reading

Farley, Reynolds. "The Changing Distribution of Negroes within Metropolitan Areas: The Emergence of Black Suburbs." *American Journal of Sociology* 75 (January 1970): 333-51.

Grier, Eunice, and George Grier. *In Search of Housing: A Study of Experiences of Negro Professional and Technical Personnel in New York State*. New York: State Commission against Discrimination, 1958.

Hansberry, Lorraine. *A Raisin in the Sun*. New York: Random House, 1959.

Schneider, Mark, and John Logan. "Suburban Racial Segregation and Black Access to Local Resources." *Social Science Quarterly* 63 (1982): 762-70.

Wiese, Andrew. *Places of Their Own: African American Suburbanization in the Twentieth Century*. Chicago: University of Chicago Press, 2004.

Woodson, Carter G. *The Rural Negro*. Washington, DC: Association for the Study of Negro Life and History, 1930.

Andrew Wiese

Black Swan Records

Black Swan Records is considered by many historians to be the first black-owned record company in the United States. It was founded by Harry Herbert Pace, who, with the assistance of other African American businesspeople, started the company in 1921. Like many other black Americans, Pace was born and educated in the South. He later graduated valedictorian from Atlanta University. Pace developed strong business practices while working in various managerial positions around the **Atlanta** area, but always had a keen appreciation for music. Eventually he moved to **Memphis, Tennessee**, where he worked alongside musician **W. C. Handy** as a music writer. Seeking even more success, Pace soon migrated to the North and settled in Harlem. There he managed an office for his business, Pace and Handy Sheet Music. Despite some success, he had noticed how white-owned record companies were becoming profitable through the use of his music. Phonograph recordings from 1900 until 1920 were controlled solely by companies such as Paramount, Columbia, and Okeh. These labels were also highly reluctant to record black singers and musicians, which limited the exposure and development of talented artists. The only exceptions were **blues** singer Mamie Smith and the multitalented Bert Williams. Pace's frustration eventually drove him to consider starting his own record company.

Less than a year later the Pace Phonograph Company was incorporated with just over $100,000 and set up offices in **New York City**. Racist practices slowed his company's early development when another company would not allow Pace to manufacture records at its pressing plant. The entrepreneur sent

Black Swan recording label. © Hulton Archive/ Getty Images.

his master recordings to another company in the Midwest to be manufactured. Eventually Pace had the discs and the packaging necessary to release his own label. The actual name of Black Swan Records was later chosen by Pace to honor the talented African American singer Elizabeth Taylor Greenfield, also known as "the Black Swan." Pace also prided himself on reminding customers that the label was not a white-owned company featuring black artists but was in fact black owned. He maintained a varied roster of artists as well. Early recordings featured singers who trained in opera and vaudeville, favorites among high-society patrons of New York's arts scene. However, the label had not released the type of music that seemingly appealed to most African American audiences.

During its first year of operation Pace passed on the opportunity to sign the highly popular singer **Bessie Smith**. He originally felt that Smith would not appeal to the fan base of the label. She went on to become the "Queen of the Blues." In the meantime another highly popular singer named Ethel Waters had become a shining star in small clubs all around the New York area. After hearing her sing one evening, Pace offered her the opportunity to make two recordings with Black Swan Records. They were warmly received by many fans, both black and white. When Pace decided to sponsor a tour of Black Swan artists, he planned to send Waters along to headline the show. After he signed Waters to a contract (which included the clause that she would not get married for at least one year and would devote time to singing and recording with Black Swan), the tour began in **Philadelphia** and traveled to twenty-one states. The tour was a hit with fans and with the **black press**. Papers such as the *Pittsburgh Courier* and the *Chicago Defender* praised the performances of Waters and the Black Swan Troubadours. The tour helped establish Black Swan as a major record label and moved the genre of **jazz** and blues into the national spotlight. Soon after, Waters, with the backing of the Black Swan jazzmen, became the first black performer to perform on radio. Pace's company also continued to release a wide variety of music, which included symphony recordings, opera, and orchestra performances.

By 1922 the Pace Phonograph Company and its Black Swan label were posting profitable returns on Pace's investments. The company soon expanded its employee roster and began shipping records overseas. Pace later invested in his own record-pressing plant in Long Island City for the sole purpose of producing Black Swan records. The plant soon increased production to over 6,000 records a day. However, Pace had shown the record business just how lucrative blues and jazz artists could be. The success of his label convinced Paramount, Columbia, and Okeh that black singers and jazz music were hot commodities. Soon it became increasingly difficult to sign any talented black artists because white record labels signed them first. Also during this era radio became even more popular, driving fledgling record companies out of business as more and more consumers purchased radios. Pace and Black Swan Records declared bankruptcy in 1923. One year later Paramount Records controlled the Black Swan music catalog. *See also* Black Appeal Radio; Harlem Renaissance; Recording Industry.

Further Reading

"Ethel Waters." The Red Hot Jazz Archive. A History of Jazz before 1930. http://redhotjazz.com/waters.html.

Schoenberg, Loren. "Race Records." Jazz: A Film by Ken Burns. www.pbs.org/jazz/exchange/exchange_race_records.htm.

Spencer, Jon Michael. *The New Negroes and Their Music: The Success of the Harlem Renaissance*. Knoxville: University of Tennessee Press, 1997.

Suisman, David. "Co-workers in the Kingdom of Culture: Black Swan Records and the Political Economy of African American Music." *Journal of American History* 90, no. 4 (2004): 1295–324.

Waters, Ethel, with Charles Samuels. *His Eye Is on the Sparrow*. Garden City, NY: Doubleday, 1951.

Weusi, Jitu. "The Rise and Fall of Black Swan Records." The Red Hot Jazz Archive: A History of Jazz before 1930. www.redhotjazz.com/blackswan.html.

Darrell Newton

Black Towns

Between 1877 and 1915 southern African American migrants created some sixty all-black towns in the United States, most of which were located in the trans-Mississippi West. When the **Exodusters** migrated to Kansas in the late 1870s and founded the town of Nicodemus, other African American town boosters followed suit and established their own ventures. These black settlers congregated in all-black communities where they could enjoy economic development, self-governance, and racial solidarity.

The entrepreneurs who promoted black town building viewed the towns as capitalist enterprises that would become prosperous and profitable. In the Great Plains of Oklahoma, Kansas, Texas, and elsewhere, they hoped to create separate black economies of farms, businesses, and **banks** enhanced by their own institutions such as churches, schools, **fraternal orders**, and newspapers. Some of these towns, such as Boley, in the Oklahoma Territory, which boasted some 2,500 residents in the early twentieth century, enjoyed modest prosperity. Supporters pointed to the viability of towns such as Boley as an endorsement of **Booker T. Washington**'s creed of economic self-help. Washington, who visited Boley in 1907, raved that the town was "striking evidence" of race progress. Those who settled the Great Plains, he claimed, were "not a helpless horde of black people, but land-seekers and home-builders" who practiced the "art of corporate and united action" (Washington, 430–31).

If boosters created these towns with an eye to profits, racial catalysts attracted settlers seeking freedom and safety from white prejudice, discrimination, and violence not only in the South but in the North and Midwest as well. The height of black town building coincided with the spread of **Jim Crow**, disfranchisement, and **lynching** in the South. Outside the South white residents of towns in the North and Midwest were transforming their communities into **sundown towns** that prohibited African Americans. Thus black settlers seeking a life outside the South but away from urban areas found the prospects of all-black towns attractive. Some of the town builders envisioned these communities as the basis of establishing a black political power base. E. P. McCabe, for example, who founded Langston City, Oklahoma, created a town newspaper, circulated throughout the South by traveling agents who tried to recruit settlers who would help establish a black political bloc in the state.

Whatever the motives of boosters and settlers, problems beset these race enterprises. Towns such as Nicodemus, Kansas, and Langston City failed to attract rail links. Most of the towns had difficulty securing outside investment and experienced troubles luring settlers. Conflicts among leaders undermined their claims that these were places of intraracial harmony. When Oklahoma became a state, whites initiated a series of measures that hurt the viability of the thirty-two black towns in the eastern part of the state. Whites in some counties tried to block black in-migration by pledging not to hire black laborers or rent, lease, or sell land to African Americans. The Great Depression made the situation even worse. Many of these towns, dependent on agriculture and cotton prices, suffered terribly when agriculture on the Great Plains collapsed in the 1930s. With few other options, most residents left, withering the tax base. In 1939 Boley, the town that Washington had praised in 1908, declared bankruptcy.

Despite their troubled history, the black towns that African Americans struggled to create in the early twentieth century were an important part of the larger history of black migration. Southern blacks not only sought new hopes and dreams in the emerging **ghettos**, defined by de facto segregation, in the urban North and West, but pursued economic and political justice in communities of their own. *See also* Home Ownership among Migrants; Midwestern States, Black Migration to; Western States, Black Migration to; Primary Document 24.

Further Reading

Crockett, Norman L. *The Black Towns*. Lawrence: Regents Press of Kansas, 1979.

Hamilton, Kenneth Marvin. *Black Towns and Profits: Promotion and Development in the Trans-Appalachian West, 1877–1915*. Urbana: University of Illinois Press, 1991.

Rose, Harold M. "The All-Negro Town: Its Evolution and Function." *Geography Review* 55 (1965): 362–81.

Taylor, Quintard. "The Emergence of Black Communities in the Pacific Northwest, 1865–1910." *Journal of Negro History* 64 (1979): 342–54.

Washington, Booker T. "Boley, a Negro Town in the West." *Outlook* 88 (January 4, 1908): 28–31.

Steven A. Reich

Blaxploitation

Blaxploitation is a term used to refer to a series of films marketed to African American youth audiences in the early 1970s. *Sweet Sweetback's Baadasssss Song* (1971) was the first film of this genre. *Sweetback*, made for around $150,000, went on to earn more than $11 million at the box office. The success of the film spawned an entire genre of quickly produced films aimed at inner-city African American youth audiences. The films exploited youth audiences that had grown weary of the blatant assimilationist rhetoric of the Sidney Poitier films of the 1960s and that were looking for protagonists willing to challenge that social order.

The success of blaxploitation was primarily due to Hollywood's ability to capitalize on the economic, social, and political tension of the period. Economically, Hollywood was in the midst of a financial crisis. A steady decline in box-office attendance had left many Hollywood studios struggling to stay fiscally sound. The shifting audience demographics left many downtown movie theaters without patrons as moviegoers abandoned the cities for the suburbs. It would take several years before suburban multiplexes could be completed, leaving Hollywood to find a product that would appeal to inner-city filmgoers. Hollywood took notice as *Sweetback* was playing to sold-out audiences with little traditional marketing and despite its X rating. Hollywood rushed to create a similar product.

Shaft (1971), *Super Fly* (1972), and *Slaughter* (1972) were put on the Hollywood fast track and hurried into theaters. These films aroused controversy because they created heroes out of pimps, drug dealers, and street hustlers. This new breed of hero openly challenged the social order and was willing to use violence to solve problems. African American **youth culture** was the target audience for these films as they reflected the tension between parents and youth. Parents saw the **civil rights movement** as a work in progress, while youths were frustrated by the slowness of changes. Organizations like the **Black Panther Party** encouraged youth to take a more active approach in achieving civil rights. For many youth, the **Jim Crow** racism of the past had been replaced by a more insidious form of institutional racism.

The heroes of blaxploitation films created and embraced a code of street justice that resonated with their youth audience. Street knowledge was presented as more valuable than the institutional access that their parents had fought so hard to provide. The films presented graphic depictions of sex and violence as these heroes lashed out against authority. These films created a market that appealed to youth by offering them music, fashion, and vicarious rebellion. The films provided escapism by reducing a biased social system to a series of white villains who were easily eliminated by the end of the film.

Politically, these films reduced complex issues to a simplistic plot of us (African Americans) versus them (white America). The films never offered any significant discussion about the politics of racism or equality. The problems of racism were reduced to the malfeasance of a few individuals whom our heroes could dispose of by film's end. The focus on the individual hero within the narrative also discouraged any sense of the efficacy of collective action as an agent of social and political change. African American militancy was often represented as nothing more than large Afros, **Marcus Garvey** posters, and ineffective leadership.

Blaxploitation came to an end amid changes in the economic, social, and political landscape of the late 1970s. The building of multiplexes throughout suburban America made the inner-city audience less important to Hollywood's bottom line. The economics of producing blaxploitation films also changed as actors began to demand salaries that were commensurate with their status as movie stars. These stars began to demand better production values and a percentage of the films' profits. Rather than acquiesce to these demands, studios begin to look for other products to fill the seats in urban theaters. Blaxploitation was replaced on urban screens with kung fu action films. Imported from Hong Kong, these films were quickly dubbed and released. The films often maintained the revenge narrative that had been a critical component of blaxploitation.

The criticism of blaxploitation had taken a toll on the studios and actors that participated in the films. Both actors and studios were beginning to look for less inflammatory material, which led to films aimed at a more general audience. Films like *Buck and the Preacher* (1974), *Uptown Saturday Night* (1974), and *Let's Do It Again* (1975) offered an alternative to the violence and explicit sex of blaxploitation. These films also appealed to adult audiences by featuring older performers such as Sidney Poitier, Bill Cosby, and Harry Belafonte. In the end blaxploitation provided black youth audiences with a temporary diversion from the social and political angst of the immediate postmigration years. *See also* Black Consumer Market; Black Film; Black Suburbanization; White Flight.

Further Reading

Bogle, Donald. *Toms, Coons, Mulattoes, Mammies, and Bucks: An Interpretive History of Blacks in American Films*. New York: Continuum, 1995.
Guerrero, Ed. *Framing Blackness: The African American Image in Film*. Philadelphia: Temple University Press, 1993.

Eric Pierson

Blockbusting

Blockbusting was the primary means of racial transition for many urban neighborhoods throughout the twentieth century. Blockbusting refers to the methods practiced by realtors and speculators who convinced whites to sell their dwellings at depressed prices and who then resold the properties to blacks at above-market prices. Two conditions made blockbusting possible: inflated demand for housing among African Americans because of racial segregation and the racial fears of whites who so abhorred black neighbors that they willingly sold their property and fled the neighborhood before it transitioned to an all-black community. Blockbusting schemes usually entrapped upwardly mobile African American families who sought to escape the poverty and inadequate living conditions of the inner city by coveting better **housing** in neighborhoods contiguous to black **ghettos**. Despite having similar or superior class status, these black newcomers were not welcomed by their white neighbors, who soon sold out and left the neighborhood.

Realtors fanned the flame of white panic by predicting an invasion of blacks into an area. They subjected white residents to incessant appeals to sell their property before it was too late, sometimes offering cash. Fearing that the value of their property would decline each time a new black family moved into the neighborhood, many white home owners sold quickly. For more reluctant home sellers, some white realtors and their black subagents used more reprehensible methods such as recruiting blacks who most resembled racial stereotypes to pose as potential home buyers or renters. Once they held titles to the properties, these realtors took out ads in black newspapers appealing to African Americans tired of living in overcrowded and deteriorating areas. But the escape was only temporary. The affluent black family that escaped the ghetto to live in an integrated, middle-class neighborhood soon was joined by its lower-income brethren. To accommodate poorer blacks, some unscrupulous white and black realtors divided single-family homes into kitchenettes and charged them exorbitant rent.

Other black middle- and working-class families followed the first "pioneers" seeking larger and nicer houses and yards. Because these home buyers could not secure financing from white-owned **banks** or savings and loans, and the few existing black financial institutions were undercapitalized, they often borrowed directly from the sales agent in the form of land contracts. Under a land contract, a home buyer put a substantial amount down and made monthly payments to cover the inflated housing price and the above-market interest rate. Home buyers did not hold title to the property until they paid off the contract, making it impossible to build any equity. The high monthly payments made them vulnerable to default and subsequent eviction. Given this situation, it was not unusual for blacks to "buy" a home, default, and lose their property, only to be replaced by another housing-starved black consumer attempting to meet the usurious terms.

Blockbusting facilitated the speed of neighborhood change from white to black. While white resistance and realtors' exploitation prevented racial dispersal throughout a city, realtors sanctioned the expansion of the black ghetto block by block. These neighborhoods were only "integrated" between decennial census years, usually within only three to four years. After the 1968 Fair Housing Act some communities banned the use of racial appeals and for-sale signs and sought neighborhood racial balance by recruiting white home buyers. *See also* Home Ownership among Migrants; Neighborhood Property Owners' Associations; Open Housing; Public Housing; Restrictive Covenants; Weaver, Robert C.

Further Reading

Helper, Rose. *Racial Policies and Practices of Real Estate Brokers.* Minneapolis: University of Minnesota Press, 1969.

Hirsch, Arnold R. *Making the Second Ghetto: Race and Housing in Chicago, 1940–1960.* Cambridge: Cambridge University Press, 1983.

Massey, Douglas S., and Nancy A. Denton. *American Apartheid: Segregation and the Making of the Underclass.* Cambridge, MA: Harvard University Press, 1993.

Orser, W. Edward. *Blockbusting in Baltimore: The Edmondson Village Story*. Lexington: University Press of Kentucky, 1994.

Pritchett, Wendell. *Brownsville, Brooklyn: Blacks, Jews, and the Changing Face of the Ghetto*. Chicago: University of Chicago Press, 2002.

Seligman, Amanda Irene. " 'Apologies to Dracula, Werewolf, Frankenstein': White Homeowners and Blockbusters in Postwar Chicago." *Journal of the Illinois State Historical Society* 94, no. 1 (2001): 70–95.

Sugrue, Thomas. *The Origins of the Urban Crisis: Race and Inequality in Postwar Detroit*. Princeton, NJ: Princeton University Press, 1996.

Preston H. Smith II

Blues

Movement, journey, and escape are all essential themes embedded in blues music. From individuals who "had to keep moving while the blues was falling down like hail," as expressed in **Robert Johnson**'s "Hellhounds on My Trail," to the thousands who longed to make the urban North their home, as **Bessie Smith** uttered in "Chicago Bound Blues," the African American migration experience has been a pivotal force in the development, growth, and cultural transmission of the blues.

While the popular image of a blues performer is that of a worldly man belting out his sorrowful tune while accompanying himself on guitar or harmonica, this image is far from representative of the vast legacy of blues music. Blues can be found in the plantation communities of the **Mississippi Delta**, the nightclubs of **Chicago**, or the concert stages of international **jazz** festivals and has been performed by men and women as disparate as Robert Johnson, **Muddy Waters**, Dinah Washington, Bessie Smith, and Taj Mahal. For the past century performers and audiences alike have joined together in their appreciation for the blues—an African American art form that has been a foundation for gospel, jazz, **rhythm and blues**, and rock and roll.

Blues music was born in the late nineteenth century from the combination of the black musical genres of spirituals and work songs. Spirituals are sacred songs sung initially by enslaved Africans and later their freed descendants. They were often sung a cappella, or without instrumental accompaniment. Known for their lyric simplicity, spirituals like "Wade in the Water" or "Ride On, King Jesus" were sung in harmony and often made a personal plea to God, expressed a person's faith, recounted biblical tales, or discussed a longing for an afterlife. Additionally, enslaved Africans often used spirituals as a means of coded communication to hide plans of a clandestine prayer meeting or even an escape attempt from overseers and plantation masters. Work songs differed from spirituals in subject and theme, because they were secular songs used to alleviate the monotony of manual labor and as a way of setting the pace for an individual work task. **Railroad** workers often chanted to move the pace of laying railroad ties along, while street vendors used musical refrains to advertise their products and could create chants about such goods as corn, onions, twine, or tin.

When musicians merged the emotional musical and narrative quality of spirituals with the rhythmic phrasing and practical function of work songs, the genre of blues music began. Yet blues music differed from spirituals and work songs in that blues entertainers moved away from group a cappella singing to accompanied and often individual performance. A harmonized longing to "steal away to Jesus" in a spiritual became one woman's discussion about how "her sweetie" went away in a blues lyric.

The exact location and moment of the development of the blues are difficult to discern, for it is likely that several performers in locations throughout the South in the late nineteenth century experimented with various musical styles that became the precursor to blues music. Written accounts that mention the fledgling sounds of blues music include the autobiography of blues music composer **W. C. Handy**. In his autobiography, *Father of the Blues*, Handy recounted how in 1903 he waited at a train station in Tutwiler, Mississippi, and witnessed a young itinerant male who played a slack-key guitar as he sang about escaping away on a train, and this was the moment that Handy could recall hearing the first strains of blues music.

Country Blues and Classic Blues Styles

Blues became popular throughout the South and started to attract national attention as a result of early black migration movements from rural southern communities to urban southern centers at the dawn of the twentieth century. By the mid-1910s there were two prevailing types of blues—country or down-home blues and classic or vaudeville blues. While the classic vaudeville blues was the first type to be recorded, the country blues predated classic blues in its origins. The country blues was often played on the fiddle, banjo, guitar, jug, washboard, or harmonica and was originally performed by male itinerant musicians who accompanied themselves as they sang. These musicians played and sang songs of their life and travels and focused on themes of love, poverty, loneliness, and escape. Country blues was arguably born in the plantations and farms of the Mississippi Delta region in the 1890s and subsequently sprang up in Texas, Tennessee, and the Piedmont region (lower Virginia, the Carolinas, and Georgia). Soon musicians were playing on street corners, in train stations, and in honkytonks—wherever the traveling musician could take his individual song.

The first country blues appeared on record in 1924 with the blues guitar recording of "Guitar Blues" by Sylvester Weaver. Both **women** and men earned success in the genre, although male country blues performers were more prevalent. Early country blues stars included the incomparable "Mother of the Blues," **Ma Rainey**, singer Lucille Bogan, guitarist and vocalist Memphis Minnie, and guitarists and vocalists Charlie Jackson, Blind Lemon Jefferson, **Huddie "Leadbelly" Ledbetter**, and **William "Big Bill" Broonzy**, among others. The country blues musicians were known for their ability to involve the audience in their performance by using the call-and-response aspect present in many genres of black folk song. A single lyric sung by the performer acted as the call, while the cries, cheers, and other comments made by audience members, in addition to the instrumental refrain that followed the lyric, served as the responses. A skilled musician could make a guitar or harmonica phrase mimic the human voice so that a blues instrumentalist could almost "talk" in the absence of words. In general, the country blues was thought to be more blunt and roughly hewn in both lyric content and phrasing than the vaudeville blues. Nonetheless, it embodied many of the emotions of the Great Depression of the 1930s and hence was extremely popular, especially among working-class African Americans both in their rural homes and in new urban migrant communities.

The classic blues is the earliest recorded form of blues music. Its origins trace back to the first written blues music composer, the noted W. C. Handy, whose piece "St. Louis Blues," published in 1914, was one of the most performed and recorded blues pieces of the time. Handy further made a name for himself as a partner in the Pace and Handy publishing company, one of the first black-owned music publishing companies in the United States, which opened in **Memphis, Tennessee**, in 1913 and as migration progressed was relocated to **New York City** by 1916.

The first classic blues recording was made by black vaudevillian Mamie Smith in 1920. Smith recorded "That Thing Called Love" and "You Can't Keep a Good Man Down" in February 1920 on General Phonographs' Okeh records. Yet when Mamie Smith's "Crazy Blues" recording, made in August 1920, sold several thousand copies to a primarily African American market, the "race record" boom and a classic blues music craze began. By 1923 Mamie Smith was joined by Ida Cox, Alberta Hunter, Victoria Spivey, Ma Rainey (whose style bridged the country and classic styles), and one of the most popular and financially successful blues stars, the "Empress of the Blues," Bessie Smith.

In terms of format, the classic blues often featured a twelve-bar (a bar being a measured unit of music that possessed a certain number of beats or counts of music) AAB format, in which the introductory lyrical line was repeated twice and the end of the third lyric line resolved or rhymed with the last word of the introductory line. It also used call-and-response patterns in which a vocalist would sing a line and the instrumentalist would respond musically. Classic blues often differed from country blues in that it often featured a female vocalist who would be backed by an ensemble of guitar, wind instruments, and drums. Jazz combos of piano, drums, guitar, and a cornet or trumpet sometimes supported early classic blues performers.

The popularity of the classic blues and the success of many blueswomen in the 1920s were bolstered by the establishment of the Theater Owners' Booking Association (TOBA). Formally founded in Chattanooga, Tennessee, in 1920, TOBA consisted of both black- and white-managed theaters that contracted various African American entertainers and organized them into a systematic route of performances. By the mid-1920s TOBA included over eighty theaters and extended into such states as Oklahoma, Missouri, Ohio, Illinois, Arkansas, and Louisiana. Among the predominant theaters were the Howard in **Washington, D.C.**, the Monogram in Chicago, the Eighty-one in **Atlanta**, the Booker Washington in **St. Louis**, and the Koppin in **Detroit**. TOBA theaters were the training grounds for many young African American performers and featured singers and musicians such as Alberta Hunter, Ethel Waters, Clara Smith, Lovie Austin, Ma Rainey, and the Whitman Sisters, comedians such as Butterbeans and Susie, Whitney and Tutt, and Dewey "Pigmeat" Markham, and numerous other variety acts.

TOBA's success was made possible as African Americans flooded into the industrialized regions of the North during the Great Migration period of 1915 to 1930. Blues performers, many of whom were migrants themselves from Tennessee, Louisiana, Mississippi, Texas, or Georgia, belted out songs to other southerners about despair, confusion, and frustration, but also about joy, a need for amusement and escape, and sexual desires—all emotions that might be intensified for southern migrants in their new homes of the urban North. Hence classic blues stars not just entertainers to many in the community, but examples of people who had perhaps survived racial oppression, poverty, or violence and could thus be voices for all the many African Americans who did not have the opportunity to publicly express these same issues.

Postwar Blues

Ultimately, the popularity of the classic blues genre began to wane as a result shifting consumer tastes and a decrease in record sales at the onset of the Great Depression of the early 1930s. The blues music that appeared in the late 1930s and early 1940s was quite similar in style to its classic and country predecessors, yet this postwar blues was often an urban creation that reflected the latest trend in technology, electric amplification, and a change in the instrumentation that backed the vocalist. All these changes could be found in the blues of the northern cities, particularly in Chicago and Detroit. Migrants adapted their blues to their new surroundings, and this post–Great Depression period gave rise to artists such as guitarists and vocalists Robert Johnson, Muddy Waters, David "Honeyboy" Edwards, Willie Dixon, Howlin' Wolf, and the legendary **Riley "B. B." King**. Women such as Koko Taylor also became skilled in the urban blues and performed songs along with an ensemble that now could include an amplified bass guitar, a piano, saxophone, drums, and harmonicas. Themes of the urban blues reflected on the joys and ills of life not on the plantation or farm, but in the **housing** project or the city streets. Unrequited love, unfaithful spouses, domestic abuse, poverty, yearning for travel, and frank discussions of sexual desire and skilled partners also permeated the lyrics of black blues in the post–World War II era, as they had in the 1920s.

The new urban blues gave way to the development of rhythm and blues (R&B), a combination of blues, jazz, boogie-woogie, and gospel influences that rose to prominence in the late 1940s and early 1950s. The early R&B stars like Big Maybelle, Etta James, LaVern Baker, Ruth Brown, Louis Jordan, Bobby "Blue" Bland, and Ray Charles were reminiscent of their blues predecessors in their popularity, technical skill, and powerful vocal styles. These R&B vocalists concentrated on much of the subject matter of the urban blues, yet with a new, amplified rhythmic pulse. Blues-inflected songs like "Candy," "Roll with Me, Henry," "Mama, He Treats Your Daughter Mean," "Further Up down the Road," and "The Night Time Is the Right Time" made the 1950s and 1960s R&B charts.

Blues was a steady foundation for much of the popular American music of the 1950s and 1960s, including both rock and roll and **soul music**. Guitarist-vocalist Chuck Berry, pianist-vocalist Richard "Little Richard" Penniman, and guitarist-vocalist Willie Mae "Big Mama" Thornton were among the pioneers who fused blues, gospel phrasing, and upbeat tempos to create rock and roll.

Thornton's powerful phrasing served as such an influence in the music industry that when Elvis Presley performed a cover version of her 1953 recording of "Hound Dog," he helped sparked a rock-and-roll music craze in mainstream American society. Hence an African American blueswoman helped usher in a genre that redefined American music (although Thornton did not receive much credit or royalties for this contribution at the time). As R&B evolved into the genre of soul music in the late 1960s, blues strains could be heard in the renowned Aretha Franklin's recordings of "Respect," "I've Never Loved a Man," and "Dr. Feelgood" and the incomparable James "the Godfather of Soul" Brown's "I Got That Feeling," "Please, Please, Please," and "I Feel Good."

Contemporary Blues

Between 1970 and the late 1990s the national popularity of blues music seemed to wane in favor of other types of music like soul, funk, rock, pop, and most recently **hip-hop**. While legends like Etta James, Buddy Guy, Koko Taylor, and B. B. King continued to perform to sold-out crowds at blues festivals or in venues like the House of Blues restaurants and clubs, young African Americans were far from the majority of spectators in the audiences. Blues entertainers speculated that some of the disdain for their music might have existed because African American youth overlooked the uplifting aspects of the blues and did not want to be associated with music that reminded them of the oppression, discrimination, and sadness in the African American past, realities that had prompted much migration from the South in the first place.

Fortunately, by the late 1990s new blues performers like Shemeika Copeland and Robert Cray began to show interest and skill in the genre, while neo-soul artists like Jill Scott, Anthony Hamilton, and Angie Stone definitely had blues-inflected tones in their repertoire. Additionally, the importance of blues music in American history reached national prominence when the Senate designated 2003 as the "Year of the Blues" and praised the blues as one of the most influential American art forms, heralded it as a document of twentieth-century African American history, and acknowledged blues musicians as cultural ambassadors of the United States. This platform of national prominence was only possible because of the artistry and skill of thousands of composers, musicians, and vocalists who migrated throughout the United States and the world and took their blues with them. *See also* Black Swan Records; Chess Records; Dance Halls and Nightclubs; Recording Industry; Primary Documents 21, 68.

Further Reading

Barlow, William. *Looking Up at Down: The Emergence of Blues Culture*. Philadelphia: Temple University Press, 1989.

Davis, Angela. *Blues Legacies and Black Feminism: Gertrude "Ma" Rainey, Bessie Smith, and Billie Holiday*. New York: Pantheon, 1998.

Harrison, Daphne Duval. *Black Pearls: Blues Queens of the 1920s*. New Brunswick, NJ: Rutgers University Press, 1988.

Murray, Albert. *Stomping the Blues*. New York: McGraw-Hill, 1976.

Santelli, Robert. *The Big Book of Blues: A Biographical Encyclopedia*. New York: Penguin Books, 2001.

Southern, Eileen. *The Music of Black Americans: A History*. 3rd ed. New York: W. W. Norton and Company, 1997.

Michelle R. Scott

Boll Weevil

Contemporary studies of the Great African American Migration during World War I assigned the boll weevil (*Anthonomus grandis*) a major role in the configuration of causes that pushed African Americans out of the South in response to the pull of better conditions in the North. The boll weevil moved out of Mexico into Texas in 1892 and within three decades had brought devastation to many of the cotton-growing areas of the South. By 1904 the weevil had moved into Louisiana, and within five years the pest had crossed the Mississippi River into Mississippi. The infestation also moved north into Oklahoma and Arkansas and continued eastward into Alabama, Georgia, Florida, and South Carolina.

The boll weevil brought financial ruin to many plantation owners, but the greatest sufferer was the African American farmer. Unable to grow cotton, planters were refused loans and consequently could not provide credit for their tenants. To aggravate the situation, floods in 1915 and 1916 destroyed most of the cotton left by the boll weevil.

The boll weevil infestation was a favorite explanation among those who contended that African American migration was primarily a response to economic forces. This little insect made a good villain, and its depredations could be regarded as an act of God. It was the boll weevil, they contended, that, by destroying the cotton crops, deprived the mass of African American tenants of their income. In addition, proponents of the boll weevil infestation as the primary cause of African American migration argued that this blow to cotton agriculture created an incentive toward more diversified crops. Many African American tenants were left without land to cultivate and without any promise of a place in the new agricultural order.

The boll weevil probably bore too much of the blame for this great northward movement. Actually, migration and the boll weevil spread in opposite directions. While the boll weevil was making its way up through Texas, African Americans in Florida and the Southeast were beginning to move northward. Migration fever moved from east to west, and the movement of the boll weevil was from west to east.

Evidently, boll weevils brought havoc and suffering wherever they appeared, but they did not vent their fury equally and simultaneously upon all parts of the South. The boll weevil's role as a cause of migration, therefore, has often been overdrawn. *See also* Cotton Belt; Great Migration, Causes of.

Further Reading

Myrdal, Gunnar. *An American Dilemma: The Negro Problem and Modern Democracy*. Vol. 1. New York: Pantheon Books, 1972.

Strickland, Arvarh E. "The Strange Affair of the Boll Weevil: The Pest as Liberator." *Agricultural History* 68 (Spring 1994): 157–68.

Woofter, Thomas Jackson, Jr. *Negro Migration: Changes in Rural Organization and Population of the Cotton Belt.* New York: W. D. Gray, 1920.

Arvarh E. Strickland

Bond, Horace Mann (1904–1972)

Horace Mann Bond's career as an educator, researcher, and higher-education administrator spanned the Great Black Migration of the twentieth century. As an African American scholar, Bond personified **W.E.B. DuBois**'s "talented tenth" of college-educated black leaders, authoring four books, eleven book reviews, and more than eighty journal articles during his lifetime. As a participant in and observer of black migrations throughout the twentieth century, Bond was especially interested in the influence of environmental factors, both in the North and in the South, on black Americans' educational attainment.

Bond was born in **Nashville, Tennessee**, to James and Jane Alice Browne Bond, both graduates of Oberlin College. Holding high educational expectations for their son, Bond's parents encouraged his matriculation at Lincoln University (Pennsylvania) at the age of fourteen. After his graduation in 1923, Bond journeyed north to the University of Chicago, where he completed a master's degree in education. After receiving a fellowship from the Julius Rosenwald Fund, Bond began his doctoral work at the University of Chicago, earning a Ph.D. in education with an emphasis in history and sociology in 1936.

During his graduate studies Bond served as principal investigator for a Rosenwald-financed study of the degree of educational achievement among black children in the South, directing the testing of almost 10,000 students from 500 schools. Firmly believing in the potential of science to discredit claims regarding blacks' supposed biological inferiority, Bond wrote a number of stinging criticisms of the racist manipulation of IQ tests and their results. His prolific research in these early years led to the publication of his classic, *The Education of the Negro in the American Social Order.*

Biographer Wayne J. Urban has demonstrated how Bond's career benefited from philanthropic support, especially that provided by the Julius Rosenwald Fund. However, philanthropic pressure also led Bond to reluctantly accept a number of administrative positions in institutions of higher education—assignments that hindered his research and writing efforts. He served as dean of Dillard University in **New Orleans** for a short time before assuming the chair of the Education Department at Fisk University and eventually the presidency of Fort Valley State College in Georgia. He returned to his alma mater, Lincoln University, in 1945, serving as president until 1957. At Lincoln, Bond encouraged ties between the university and prominent African alumni, including Nnamdi Azikiwe, the first president of Nigeria, and Kwame Nkrumah, Ghana's first president. Bond traveled to Africa more than sixteen times between 1949 and 1963, and these trips led him to promote Lincoln's Institute of African Studies, one of the first centers of its kind in the United States.

At Lincoln, Bond also joined a team of scholars conducting research for the landmark Supreme Court case *Brown v. Board of Education*. Before the court's rehearing of the case in December 1953, Lincoln alumnus Thurgood Marshall, head of the Legal Defense and Educational Fund of the **National Association for the Advancement of Colored People**, asked Bond to gather historical evidence proving that the framers of the U.S. Constitution's Fourteenth Amendment had intended to prohibit segregated public schooling. Though the scholars' findings were ultimately inconclusive, the NAACP used Bond's research to bolster its case against racial segregation in public schools.

In 1957 Bond became dean of the School of Education at Atlanta University. He served in this position for five years before assuming the directorship of the school's Bureau of Educational Research. During his fourteen-year tenure as director of the bureau, Bond returned to his central interest in the role of culture, environment, home, and community in black student achievement. His retirement in 1971 came only one year before his death. His marriage to Julia Agnes Washington in 1929 produced three children: Jane Marguerite, Horace Julian, and James. His second child, known as Julian, became active in the **civil rights movement**, served in the Georgia State Assembly for twenty years (first as a representative and then as a state senator), and since 1998 has been chairman of the board of the NAACP. *See also* Bethune, Mary McLeod; Brown, Charlotte Hawkins; Howard University; Schoolteachers and Teaching; Terrell, Mary Church; Tuskegee Normal and Industrial Institute.

Further Reading

Fultz, Michael. "A 'Quintessential American': Horace Mann Bond, 1924–1939." *Harvard Educational Review* 55 (1985): 416–42.
Urban, Wayne J. *Black Scholar: Horace Mann Bond, 1904–1972*. Athens: University of Georgia Press, 1992.
Williams, Roger. *The Bonds: An American Family*. New York: Atheneum, 1971.

Charles Dorn

Bonner, Marita (1899–1971)

During the **Harlem Renaissance** Marita Bonner published stories, plays, and essays in the movement's leading journals, the *Crisis* and *Opportunity*. Her work explores two major topics: the dilemmas faced by the **New Negro** woman and the dislocation southern blacks experienced in northern cities in the early twentieth century. She is among the keenest observers of the latter; her stories depict the disruption of family life, as well as the effect of cultural conflict and exchange between black migrants and European immigrants.

Born on June 16, 1899, in **Boston**, Bonner graduated from Radcliffe College in 1922. She taught high school in West Virginia and in **Washington, D.C.**, where she participated in poet Georgia Douglas Johnson's literary salon. **Alain Locke**, May Miller, Bruce Nugent, and **Jean Toomer** were regulars. In their company, Bonner began to write.

"On Being Young—A Woman—And Colored" explores the psychological cost of racism and sexism and notes the difference that class makes. While acknowledging the advantages she enjoys, Bonner writes against the fear of being trapped in a doubled **ghetto**—the ghetto of race and the ghetto within the ghetto that is the gilded cage of the black middle class. Although it was published in 1925, the same year as Alain Locke's *The New Negro*, Bonner's essay is less optimistic in tone; its images encode stasis and claustrophobia rather than movement and change. Its themes and metaphors resonate with the novels of **Jessie Fauset** and **Nella Larsen**. Unlike those novels, however, Bonner's fiction depicts the experiences of working-class characters.

Bonner's first play, *The Pot Maker: A Play to Be Read* (1927), addresses the theme of marital infidelity, but its subtitle was an omen; none of Bonner's structurally experimental and thematically challenging plays was produced in her lifetime. *The Purple Flower* (1928), like her essay "The Young Blood Hungers" (1928), brims with revolutionary fervor in its attack on racism. *Exit, an Illusion: A One-Act Play* explores the theme of mixed-race identity.

After marrying William Almy Occomy in 1930, Bonner published a series of stories set on and around "Frye Street," an ethnic intersection where Chinese, Russian, and eastern European immigrants lived side by side with African Americans. The trilogy "The Triple Triad on Black Notes" (1933) and the two-part story "Tin Can" (1934) excel at conveying the price the "Promised Land" exacted from all. In 1939 Bonner published "The Makin's," "The Whipping," and "Hongry Fire," which represent the crippling effect of urban poverty on children. Although Bonner was not adept at representing vernacular speech, she invented memorable characters and vivid situations.

Despite publishing more than a score of stories and several plays, Bonner was forgotten by the literary world until 1987, when her writing, including several never-before-published pieces, was collected in a book, *Frye Street and Environs*. Bonner's daughter Joyce Occomy Stricklin, who had kept her mother's notebooks, wrote the introduction. The publication was posthumous. Bonner died in a fire in 1971. *See also* European Immigrants, Relations with Black Migrants; Literature, the Great Migration in; Women.

Further Reading

Bonner, Marita. *Frye Street and Environs: The Collected Works of Marita Bonner.* Edited and introduced by Joyce Flynn and Joyce Occomy Stricklin. Boston: Beacon Press, 1987.

Wall, Cheryl A. *Women of the Harlem Renaissance.* Bloomington: Indiana University Press, 1995.

Cheryl A. Wall

Boston, Massachusetts

Studies of Boston's black community tend to focus on either its pre–Civil War abolitionist tradition or the battles over school **desegregation** in the 1970s. Less has been written about the intervening period, a time when the population grew substantially, the community changed its physical location within the city, and the political and social context shifted dramatically.

In 1900 Boston's black population of 11,500 was 2 percent of the total Boston population, about the same proportion as in other major northern cities. Between 1900 and 1940 the population grew at a relatively slow, steady pace. After 1940 it grew much faster, accompanied by significant community change.

Between 1900 and 1940 the black population doubled to over 23,000 people. Close to half the new residents were from the South, especially the coastal states of Virginia, Maryland, and North Carolina. Another 10 to 15 percent arrived from the West Indies, especially Jamaica and Barbados, and Canada, including descendants of enslaved people who had fled there before the Civil War.

Migrants were attracted to Boston in part by its long history as a free black community and a sense that Boston was racially tolerant. Black representatives were regularly elected to positions in either city or state government in the late nineteenth century, and new arrivals expected that Boston held educational and economic opportunity.

Even with this growth, the black population was still only 3 percent of Boston's total population. The post–World War I expansion that had affected many cities had not played as big a role in Boston. The limits on **occupational mobility** may have played a part in this slower growth. In 1900 a majority of employed black males held jobs as unskilled laborers, servants, janitors, porters, and waiters. In 1940 that proportion was virtually the same. It also had not changed for black men holding white-collar jobs. In reality, black workers faced a stagnant economic picture in Boston.

This steady stream of migrants created a more diverse black community. A small number of longtime Boston black families with a middle- or upper-class consciousness identified with white values and practices and maintained an elite sense by emulating these values. Southern blacks from small towns and poor rural areas came seeking jobs and education. Immigrants from the West Indies and Canada had different experiences and skills and arrived with a stronger economic and educational background.

During World War II, as job possibilities increased, Boston's black population nearly doubled in one decade, rising from 23,000 in 1940 to 40,000 in 1950. Many came to work in industrial plants, army posts, armories, and **shipyards**. The percentage of black men in menial jobs decreased, and more were found in skilled and professional categories.

As the number of black residents increased, the proportion of the black population also increased, reflecting the decline in real numbers of the white population, from 758,700 in 1950 to 524,588 in 1970. Middle- and upper-class whites moved away from the city, in part because of the new highway system and suburban development, in part because of increasing fear and racism. The proportions changed quickly: in 1950 blacks made up 5 percent of the total population; in 1960 they constituted 9 percent, in 1970, 16 percent, and in 1980, 22 percent. These proportions were still lower than those of other urban centers in 1970, such as **Detroit** at 43 percent or **Cleveland** at 38 percent.

During the nineteenth century the black population was located primarily along the north slope of Beacon Hill, in an area between the State House and the docks and industry along the waterfront. The community, clustered around the African Meeting House, lived a self-contained existence there, interacting only as necessary with the white society.

A redistricting plan in 1895 led to the loss of the community's small level of political presence, and residents faced continued crowding by a growing number of Italian and Jewish immigrants settling in nearby tenements. Members of the black community began to move to the South End and Lower Roxbury.

By the 1930s, as the black population passed the 20,000 mark, the black community extended to Dudley Street in Lower Roxbury. Businesses and services lined Tremont Street. This vibrant community sustained two weekly newspapers, the *Chronicle* and the *Guardian*, and four black-owned and operated restaurants. There were drug stores, a florist shop, an appliance store, barbershops, hairdressing parlors, a tailor, and other black businesses.

This neighborhood also created a rich cultural scene. The intersection of Massachusetts and Columbus avenues was the center for performance, especially music. Nightclubs were host to jazz musicians like Lionel Hampton and **Count Basie**, and larger venues, such as the Roseland Ballroom, presented the big bands, including Benny Goodman and Woody Herman. Boston was home to internationally recognized vocal artist Roland Hayes and South End painter Allan Rohan Crite. Elma Lewis established her National Center of Afro-American Artists, with annual performances of *Black Nativity* by **Langston Hughes**.

In the early part of the twentieth century the black population made up too small a proportion of the community to establish a strong political voice. The Irish were the main political power, led by James Michael Curley. A local pharmacist, Dr. Silas F. (Shag) Taylor, established an organization called the Mass Colored League. Shag and his brother Balcom worked with the Curley machine, exchanging votes in black wards for jobs and **housing**. At the same time, black newspaper publisher William Monroe Trotter led protests against the level of discrimination and limitation in the city. He was a founder of the **National Association for the Advancement of Colored People**, and his boycotts and organizing led to the integration of Boston City Hospital.

A number of established and new organizations served community needs, including at least ten churches of various denominations and **settlement houses**, such as Harriet Tubman House. A strong set of **women**'s organizations and service clubs developed. Josephine St. Pierre Ruffin, publisher of the *Woman's Era*, was instrumental in the founding of the **National Association of Colored Women**. Her daughter, Florida Ruffin Ridley, was active in the local League for Community Service. Lucy Miller Mitchell, executive director of Associated Day Care Services of Metropolitan Boston, was active in Robert Shaw Settlement House and in establishing the first Head Start programs. She was the first black board member of the Boston **Young Women's Christian Association**. Melnea Cass, known as "the First Lady of Roxbury," was a tireless activist for civil rights and a pioneer in the day-care movement. Muriel S. Snowden, with her husband Otto, founded Freedom House, a nonprofit community-based organization dedicated to advocacy for African Americans and a vibrant force for interracial cooperation.

Boston began to reinvest in the city after World War II, and the white leadership slated much of the South End for **urban renewal**. As the number of black residents continued to climb, and much of the black neighborhood was taken by eminent domain, the community expanded into other sections of the city, especially Dorchester and Mattapan.

Black leaders were increasingly open in expressing their resentment against social and economic injustices and issued demands for equal rights in housing, education, and economic opportunities. Some white Bostonians who feared these changes chose to move out. Other resisted through school and city politics, so that the change in the black population's ability to act in concert and make a difference happened at the same time as white resistance increased. This dynamic in Boston played out dramatically within the schools and the efforts to achieve educational equity through desegregation in the period after 1960. *See also* Caribbean Migration; Northeastern States, Black Migration to; White Flight; Primary Document 23.

Further Reading

Bailey, Ronald. *Lower Roxbury: A Community of Treasures in the City of Boston.* Boston: Northeastern University Press, 1993.

"Boston by Race." Boston Public Library. www.bpl.org/research/govdocs/bostonrace .pdf.

Cromwell, Adelaide M. *The Other Brahmins: Boston's Black Upper Class, 1750-1950.* Fayetteville: University of Arkansas Press, 1994.

Daniels, John. *In Freedom's Birthplace: A Study of the Boston Negroes.* 1914. Reprint, New York: Negro Universities Press, 1968.

Hayden, Robert. *Faith, Culture, and Leadership: A History of the Black Church in Boston.* Boston: Boston Branch, NAACP, 1983.

Schneider, Mark R. *Boston Confronts Jim Crow, 1890-1920.* Boston: Northeastern University Press, 1997.

Thernstrom, Stephan. *The Other Bostonians: Poverty and Progress in the American Metropolis, 1880-1970.* Cambridge, MA: Harvard University Press, 1973.

Sharlene Voogd Cochrane

Bradby, Robert L. (1877–1946)

As the nineteenth pastor of Second Baptist Church of **Detroit, Michigan**, Robert L. Bradby stood as the forerunner of black self-help in Detroit and an exemplar of the power of the gospel to impact the social and political contexts of its adherents. Reared in the small hamlet of Middlemus, Ontario, Bradby steadily prepared himself for ministry among black **Baptist** communities by attending secondary schools in Chatham, Ontario, and later McMaster Seminary from 1904 to 1906. Traveling to America in 1909, Bradby took a position as the senior pastor of Third Baptist Church in Toledo, Ohio. A year later he took over the pastorate of Second Baptist Church of Detroit. During his thirty-six-year tenure at Second Baptist, Bradby received an honorary doctor of divinity degree from Virginia (Lynchburg) Theological Seminary and a law degree from Wilberforce University.

It was during the Great Migration that Bradby brought all of his education to bear upon his ministerial activities. In meeting the needs of thousands of black newcomers to Detroit, Bradby orchestrated the ministries of Second Baptist to organize men's groups, **women**'s clubs, nurseries, and a kindergarten, as well as sewing, cooking, and music classes to help migrants adjust to urban life. One of Bradby's main ministries that directly targeted migrants was the around-the-clock committees established to meet incoming trains and buses loaded with newcomers to Detroit. Many of them spent their first night in Detroit sleeping on the church pews in Second Baptist's sanctuary. Bradby also organized a home where black migrant women could stay while finding employment and permanent **housing**.

Bradby's uncanny ability to assist black migrants was tied to his powerful connections with such influential figures as Henry Ford, Mayor Frank Murphy, and the Detroit Urban League. Henry Ford of Ford Motor Company solicited Bradby's leadership in supplying the company with black labor during the interwar years. Bradby wrote hundreds of recommendations to Henry Ford on behalf of "trustworthy" migrants seeking employment. His dynamic connection with Henry Ford lasted over twenty-six years and helped change the racial makeup of the automotive industry for years to come.

The Detroit Urban League also called upon Bradby to help address a variety of needs relative to black migrants. Bradby wrote letters to department stores, parole boards, the city treasurer, and the Detroit Board of Education in an effort to support the black migrant community. Politically, men like Mayor Frank Murphy petitioned Bradby for black votes in Detroit elections.

Other notable features of Bradby's life were his activities as one of the earliest presidents of the Detroit branch of the **National Association for the Advancement of Colored People** in 1925, a prominent supporter of Clarence Darrow's defense team in the Ossian Sweet trials of the 1920s, and an active voice during the controversial rise of the **United Automobile Workers** in Detroit. Bradby's life demonstrated the power of the black **minister** to transcend the sacred sphere of the Protestant Church and create avenues of economic and social **uplift** for the black community during times of crisis and change. *See also* Automobile Workers; Political Activism (1915–1945); Primary Document 57.

Further Reading

Robinson-Harmon, Julia. "Reverend Robert L. Bradby: Establishing the Kingdom of God among Migrants, Women and Workers, 1910–1946." Ph.D. diss., Michigan State University, 2002.

Shelly, Cara. "Bradby's Baptists: Second Baptist Church of Detroit, 1910–1946." *Michigan Historical Review* 17, no. 1 (Spring 1991): 1–33.

Wolcott, Victoria W. *Remaking Respectability: African American Women in Interwar Detroit*. Chapel Hill: University of North Carolina Press, 2001.

Julia Robinson-Harmon

Briggs, Cyril V. (1888–1966)

Cyril V. Briggs immigrated to the United States in 1905 from the island of Nevis in the British West Indies and settled in **New York City**. He was among the first wave of Caribbean immigrants who came to the United States contemporaneous with the Great Black Migration. In 1912 he started working as a journalist for the New York *Amsterdam News* and quickly became an editor. However, during World War I Briggs resigned after the U.S. Intelligence Department demanded censorship of his editorials condemning segregation in the armed forces.

In 1915 Briggs began publishing the *Colored American Review*, a cultural and business monthly magazine; and in 1917 Briggs, along with fellow Caribbean immigrant Richard B. Moore, founded the *Crusader* magazine, the official organ of the **African Blood Brotherhood**, a radical political group. In its pages Briggs advocated socialism and revolutionary **black nationalism**, defended Bolshevism, proposed the establishment of an independent black nation-state, and supported cooperative economic ventures and an alliance with revolutionary class-conscious white workers, among other things. By 1922 the magazine was reduced to the *Crusader Bulletin* and went out of existence entirely in 1923.

The African Blood Brotherhood, which Briggs established sometime between 1917 and 1919, was the first Afro-Marxist revolutionary secret organization dedicated to the liberation of Africa and people of African descent. Through this organization and its official organ the *Crusader*, he expanded his ideas concerning racial pride, black nationalism, pan-Africanism, and the economic nature of the African American struggle. Briggs initially aimed at a coalition with **Marcus Garvey**'s **Universal Negro Improvement Association** (UNIA), but Brotherhood members were later expelled from a UNIA convention over the need to establish white alliances and the overall programmatic differences between the two organizations. During the early 1920s and 1930s Briggs published several criticisms of Garvey.

When the Socialist Party split in 1919 over support for the Russian Revolution, Briggs supported the pro-Communist faction. Briggs, along with other members of the Brotherhood, later became the first cadre of African American **Communists** to join the Communist Party U.S.A. He became editor of the Communist *Harlem Liberator* and played a significant role in assisting the Communist Party in organizing the American Negro Labor Congress, formulating the party's proposal for a Black Belt Republic in the southern United States and agitating from within the Party to raise its consciousness on the "Negro Question" and reach out to the African American masses.

During the Great Depression Briggs moved to the West Coast and worked with Charlotta Bass on her *California Eagle* and later with Pat Patterson on her *Los Angeles Herald Dispatch*. He also proffered advice to the **Black Panther Party** in formulating its original program, and the Republic of New Africa adopted some of his ideas for a Black Belt Republic. Briggs was a major contributor to the radical politics of the **Harlem Renaissance** and was part of the core leadership of black Communists in the United States. He committed his entire adult life to building a revolutionary consciousness among African Americans and died in **Los Angeles** in 1966. *See also* Caribbean Migration; Harrison, Hubert Henry; McKay, Claude; *Messenger*; Owen, Chandler; Political Activism (1915–1945); Randolph, Asa Philip; Socialists and Socialism.

Further Reading

Cruse, Harold. *The Crisis of the Negro Intellectual*. New York: Morrow, 1967.

Samuels, Wilfred D. "Five Afro-Caribbean Voices in American Culture, 1917–1929: Hubert H. Harrison, Wilfred A. Domingo, Richard B. Moore, Cyril V. Briggs, and Claude McKay." Ph.D. diss., University of Iowa, 1977.

Vincent, Theodore G. *Black Power and the Garvey Movement*. San Francisco: Ramparts Press, 1971.

Ronald A. Kuykendall

Brooks, Gwendolyn (1917–2000)

Gwendolyn Brooks's second volume of poetry, *Annie Allen*, earned her the distinction of being the first African American recipient of the Pulitzer Prize (1950). Her first collection, however, is the one that dealt most directly with the aftermath of the Great Black Migration. In *A Street in Bronzeville* (1945) she provides an honest depiction of the lives of transplanted southerners in this thriving, predominantly black, South Side **Chicago** community. Bronzeville, as advertised in the **black press**, did prove to be a place of promise, with area churches helping new arrivals find employment in black-owned **banks**, insurance companies, **hospitals**, stores, and recreation facilities. It attracted writers, musicians, artists, and wealthy families not welcome in white districts. There, African Americans could prove to themselves and others that they could be self-sufficient. And there, Gwendolyn Brooks found the setting for much of her work.

Gwendolyn Brooks, granddaughter of a runaway slave, was born in Topeka, Kansas, on June 7, 1917, to David, a blue-collar worker who had planned to be a doctor, and Keziah, a **schoolteacher** who had dreamed of being a concert pianist. The two, caught up in love and practicality, instead settled into marriage, moving to Chicago when Gwendolyn was four.

As a child, Brooks was scorned by her black peers for lacking athletic ability, light skin, and "good" hair, but she had a sense of herself because of deep familial love. She knew that something as superficial as skin pigmentation and kinky hair did not make her less of a person. She did not need the "Black Is Beautiful" concept for validation, knowing already that popular notions of (white)

Gwendolyn Brooks at her typewriter, 1950. © Bettmann/Corbis.

beauty had little to do with her. Early on, she developed racial pride but also gained sensitivity to the agony of those with bad self-perception.

Brooks's parents recognized her talent and encouraged its pursuit. Looking to Wordsworth, Keats, Longfellow, Eliot, Pound, and Cummings for inspiration, she had a portfolio of seventy-five published poems by age sixteen. After graduating from a junior college in 1938 and after a stint at menial work, she became publicity director for the **National Association for the Advancement of Colored People** Youth Council and there found a sense of purpose. She went on to write of the struggles for personal identity of **women** and children who were not suffering from overt racism, but from being ghettoized or marginalized. Through her poetry she gave a concrete vision of what daily life was like for black people and how racism threatened them at their very core. She dedicated herself to helping improve the self-images of young people, working with children's groups and even conducting a series of poetry workshops in 1968 with a Chicago youth gang, the Blackstone Rangers.

Racial pride was key with her, as was racial solidarity. In her only novel, *Maude Martha* (1953), she explores racism and sexism, with the protagonist not so much disturbed by her dark skin as by the perceptions of others of dark skin as ugly. Brooks's highly acclaimed poetry collection *The Bean Eaters* (1960) is peopled with **ghetto** dwellers seeking a purpose in life.

During the 1960s black radicals accused Brooks of writing "white," a charge that may have impelled her to don the mantle of **black nationalism**, her poetry becoming more angry and militant, sometimes even suggesting force. She also dropped her long-term white publisher, determined to support only black presses.

From 1968 until her death in 2000, Gwendolyn Brooks was poet laureate of Illinois, garnishing much recognition for her work. She was awarded a Guggenheim Fellowship, a lifetime achievement award from the National Endowment for the Arts (1989), a lectureship from the National Endowment for the Humanities (1994), and fifty honorary doctorates. *See also* Literature, the Great Migration in.

Further Reading

Melhem, D. H. *Gwendolyn Brooks: Poetry and the Heroic Voice.* Lexington: University Press of Kentucky, 1987.
Mootry, Maria, and Gary Smith, eds. *A Life Distilled: Gwendolyn Brooks, Her Poetry and Fiction.* Urbana: University of Illinois Press, 1987.

Gay Pitman Zieger

Broonzy, William "Big Bill" (c. 1893–1958)

William "Big Bill" Broonzy was a popular **blues** guitarist and vocalist during the Great Migration's middle years (1920s to 1940s) and is best remembered for his role in shaping the emergent barrelhouse blues scene in **Chicago** during the 1930s. A southern migrant himself, Broonzy has been described as "a truly urban bluesman with one foot forever planted in the country"

(Humphrey, 167). Active in the Chicago club scene until World War II, Broonzy recorded over 300 songs of various types: work songs, spirituals, blues, and folk songs. He accompanied some of the leading blues musicians of his time, such as Tampa Red and John Lee "Sonny Boy" Williamson, and fostered emerging stars, including **Muddy Waters** and Memphis Minnie.

While nearly all early blues musicians were rather mobile people, the events of Broonzy's life and the lyrics of his songs reflected the conditions, opportunities, and hardships experienced by millions of black southerners as they migrated to the urban North in the first half of the twentieth century. He sang about southern farm life, migration, war and the draft, the Great Depression and the New Deal, racial discrimination, and personal relationships. Despite the serious themes, Broonzy's music and lyrics were noticeably upbeat, even during the tough times of the depression, and he preferred communal party songs over the brooding, lonely blues of **Mississippi Delta** recording artists like Charley Patton and Son House.

Broonzy was born to a large farming family in the Delta cotton town of Scott, Mississippi. As a sharecropper and **railroad** track layer, Broonzy learned field hollers and work songs and began to perform music in his late teens. By the early 1920s Broonzy had served in the U.S. Army and relocated to Arkansas. He continued to improve his vocal and guitar skills, hoping to use music as a means to escape the limitations of the sharecropper's life.

By 1930 the black population of Chicago had reached nearly 250,000, and the number of black Mississippians living in Illinois had quadrupled in the preceding two decades. Broonzy moved to Chicago in the late 1920s and began recording "race records"—albums designed to appeal to black audiences. He often stayed at blues maestro Tampa Red's place on State Street, where he joined an innovative and interesting group of southern émigrés such as Memphis Slim. These and other southern migrant musicians created the popular Chicago blues scene of the 1930s. Broonzy's music took on elements of boogie-woogie and **swing** as he added piano accompaniments, then drums, and eventually wind and brass instruments. Just before World War II Broonzy adopted the electric guitar. Despite his musical innovations, Broonzy's lyrics often remained rooted in the southern rural experience. His songs "Goin' Back to Arkansas" and "Grandma's Farm" were popular in Chicago among fellow native southerners.

Some blues historians interpret Broonzy's move toward a jazzier, swing blues idiom as a reflection of the chaotic existence of northern urban life, while other observers believe that Broonzy jazzed up his music to win stage appearances in front of white audiences. Whatever the motive, Broonzy's urbanized blues songs of the 1930s bridged the musicological gap between the itinerant blues musicians of the sharecropping South and the mainstream blues celebrities of the 1950s and after.

After World War II Broonzy's musical career declined as the very musicians he helped foster in Chicago—"Big Boy" Crudup and Muddy Waters—thrilled audiences and record executives with their raw, electrified blues. While American audiences found Broonzy's ragtime-like music old fashioned and boring, Europeans heard in his music an authentic, classic blues that enticed them. In 1951 Broonzy's migration away from his native South continued when he relocated to western Europe to tour and record for the remainder of his life. In Europe

Broonzy billed himself as the last true American blues musician and returned to his musical roots by renewing his country and folk blues repertoire, at one time joking: "I guess all songs is folk songs. I never heard no horse sing 'em" (Levine, 202). Broonzy died of cancer in 1958. *See also* Recording Industry.

Further Reading

Broonzy, William "Big Bill." *Good Time Tonight*. Columbia CK 46219. 1990. Audio CD.

Humphrey, Mark A. "Bright Lights, Big City: Urban Blues." In *Nothing but the Blues: The Music and the Musicians*, edited by Lawrence Cohn. New York: Abbeville Press, 1993.

Levine, Lawrence. *Black Culture, Black Consciousness: Afro-American Folk Thought in Slavery and Freedom*. New York: Oxford University Press, 1977.

R. A. Lawson

Brotherhood of Sleeping Car Porters (BSCP)

When the Brotherhood of Sleeping Car Porters (BSCP) became the first national labor union of black workers recognized by the leaders of a major American corporation in 1937, it won more than a shorter work week and higher wages for Pullman porters and maids. Its larger legacy lay with the pro-labor point of view

Black porters relax over games of cards and pool at the Brotherhood of Sleeping Car Porters's headquarters in Harlem, 1944. © Herbert Gehr/Time Life Pictures/Getty Images.

that the union planted within the black community, which helped shape the rise of widespread unionization of black workers. The story of the BSCP also contains the broad outlines of a David and Goliath narrative that began in 1925 when a ragtag group of Pullman porters rose up to challenge the right of an antiunion, corporate giant, the Pullman Company, to unilaterally determine the economic fate and working conditions of its black employees. To understand the BSCP's success, it helps to place the union within the context of the Great Migration and the protest politics that rose to the fore during that era.

From its inception in Harlem in 1925, **Asa Philip Randolph**, the head of the BSCP, envisioned the Brotherhood as a struggle for more than bread-and-butter issues. He hoped to use the BSCP as a vehicle for shaping a protest strategy for claiming civil and economic rights, believing that the union provided a means to carry forward the spirit of the **New Negro**. The Great Migration and the war to make the world safe for democracy had rekindled the ongoing quest for full participation in American society that generated the impulse of the New Negro movement. Randolph helped shape the concept in the pages of the ***Messenger***, a magazine he edited, by applauding New Negroes who made demands and unlike the Old Negro were not able to be lulled into a false sense of security with political spoils and patronage from white America. When five Pullman sleeping car porters approached Randolph about leading the BSCP in 1925, Randolph thought that the organization might be the perfect means for addressing the root cause of racial inequality, which Randolph linked to the social relations of slavery. Until the myth connecting black people with the status of servants was destroyed, black Americans would never enjoy economic rights of citizenship.

Pullman porters exemplified the servile status that was conferred on black men. George Pullman, founder and president of the Pullman Company, created the position of Pullman sleeping car porter in the early 1870s to serve his patrons in a princely manner, evoking the comfort and style slaves provided for the gentry in the antebellum South. Pullman porters were expected to sustain a smile even while they looked submissive to protect sleeping car clients from the discomfort they would feel were a white worker to wait on them in the intimate and limited space of a sleeping car. Thus the organizers of the BSCP, fed up with long hours, low pay, and the servile demeanor demanded for the job, set out to rewrite the master-servant narrative that the Pullman Company's work culture had nurtured for so long.

Although the BSCP's initial organizing campaign in **New York City** was fairly successful, the union's organizing efforts met massive resistance in **Chicago**, headquarters of the powerful Pullman Company and home to more than one-third of the Pullman porters. Through the years Pullman executives had cultivated close relationships with black leaders by pouring money into institutions in black Chicago and promoting the image of Pullman as a friend not just of workers, but of the entire community. As a result, the majority of black leaders, the press, and most **ministers** in Chicago opposed the BSCP.

To counter the resistance, the BSCP launched a major education campaign around the concept of manhood rights to win the hearts and minds of the black community. The BSCP's manhood rights campaign was the link connecting the struggle for a union and resistance to the Pullman Company's company union with the struggle for recognition of black humanity within the larger society. The idiom of manhood rights was used to describe the servile relations that prevailed on the job as well as in black America. Organizers also linked manhood rights to the concept as it had developed in nineteenth-century conflicts over the meaning of suffrage and citizenship in black history. Slowly resistance broke down as the BSCP's network expanded. One of the Brotherhood's first successful alliances in Chicago was with clubwomen who were drawn to the BSCP because they, too, identified with the concept of manhood rights, which they defined in universal, humanistic terms. **Ida B. Wells-Barnett**, internationally renowned antilynching activist, was among them.

The Pullman Company sat down with the BSCP leaders in August 1937 and signed the historic labor contract. From that victory, the BSCP continued for several years to use the union and the networks it had developed throughout black America to mobilize around issues related to the black freedom struggle. Networks connected to the Brotherhood were particularly important in the **March on Washington Movement** of the early 1940s, which successfully challenged discrimination against black workers applying for jobs in defense industries as the nation prepared to fight yet another war for democracy. *See also* Organized Labor; Political Activism (1915-1945); Railroads, Black Employment on; Primary Document 14.

Further Reading

Arnesen, Eric. *Brotherhoods of Color: Black Railroad Workers and the Struggle for Equality*. Cambridge, MA: Harvard University Press, 2001.

Bates, Beth Tompkins. *Pullman Porters and the Rise of Protest Politics in Black America, 1925-1945*. Chapel Hill: University of North Carolina Press, 2001.

Harris, William H. *Keeping the Faith: A. Philip Randolph, Milton P. Webster, and the Brotherhood of Sleeping Car Porters, 1925-37*. Urbana: University of Illinois Press, 1977.

Beth Tompkins Bates

Brown, Charlotte Hawkins (1883–1961)

Charlotte Hawkins Brown was a pioneering school founder, black **women**'s club leader, and activist on behalf of interracial cooperation and racial advancement during the first half of the twentieth century. She founded Palmer Memorial Institute (PMI) in 1902 in Sedalia, North Carolina, and presided over its growth into an accredited and nationally acclaimed college preparatory school for black youth. As an author and lecturer, the aristocratic "first lady of social graces" proudly claimed lineage to the English navigator John D. Hawkins. Brown's dress and decorum were immaculate, and she expected no less from students who came under her tutelage at PMI. Although she urged blacks to cultivate good manners to improve interracial relations, Brown was also an outspoken advocate for civil rights and a tireless worker on behalf of the women of her race.

Lottie Hawkins was born in 1883 in Henderson, North Carolina, and moved with her family to Cambridge, Massachusetts, at the age of seven. She later changed her name to Charlotte Eugenia, which she considered more dignified. After graduating from Cambridge High School, she attended the Massachusetts State Normal School in Salem, helped by a chance meeting with Alice Freeman Palmer, the first woman president of Wellesley College in 1902. She left Salem before graduating to accept a teaching offer from the Bethany Institute, a one-room school in rural North Carolina supported by the American Missionary Association. The Bethany Institute closed the following year when the AMA withdrew its support from the school, but the nineteen-year-old Brown stayed on, encouraged by parents and neighbors who pledged support. She also traveled back to New England to raise funds from supportive whites like Alice Palmer and friends. Unfortunately, Palmer died soon after pledging her support, and Brown named the school in honor of her. Beginning with an industrial education emphasis, PMI evolved into a prestigious precollegiate academic institution that catered to the black "upper crust." A school brochure advertised Palmer as "a little bit of New England in North Carolina."

Brown married Harvard graduate Edward Sumner Brown in 1911. They divorced in 1915. She had no children of her own, but raised several nieces and nephews, all of whom graduated from PMI.

With Palmer as her base, Brown developed into a sought-after author and lecturer on topics related to interracial cooperation, women's issues, and social graces. Her first book, *Mammy: An Appeal to the Heart of the South* (1919), attempted to forge interracial understanding by invoking the trusted figure of the antebellum Mammy. In 1941 her most influential book, *The Correct Thing to Do, to Say, and to Wear*, was published. She explained that her motive for writing the book was to warn black people not to slavishly imitate whites, but to keep their own "heritage of grace." She combined gentility with a tenacious insistence on defending civil rights. She brought lawsuits against **Jim Crow** laws and campaigned against **lynching**.

Brown joined fellow school founders **Mary McLeod Bethune** and **Nannie Helen Burroughs** in the black women's club movement and became a founding member of the National Council of Negro Women, serving as vice president under Bethune. Brown was also active in promoting interracial alliances through the southern women's network and served on the national **Young Women's Christian Association** (YWCA) board. In 1920 she lectured white women and warned them to "control your men," who disrespected and exploited black women.

Brown died in 1961 in Greensboro. North Carolina established the Charlotte Hawkins Brown Historical Foundation in 1983, the first in the state to honor an African American. Today, the Charlotte Hawkins Brown Museum operates on the site of the original Palmer Institute, which closed in 1971 after a devastating fire. *See also* National Association of Colored Women (NACW); Schoolteachers and Teaching; Tuskegee Normal and Industrial Institute; Uplift.

Further Reading

McCluskey, Audrey T. "We Specialize in the Wholly Impossible: Black Women School Founders and Their Mission." *Signs* 22 (Winter 1997): 403–26.

Wadelington, Charles, and Richard Knapp. *Charlotte Hawkins Brown and Palmer Institute: What a Young African American Woman Could Do*. Chapel Hill: University of North Carolina Press, 1999.

Audrey Thomas McCluskey

Brown, Sterling Allen (1901–1989)

Sterling Brown, poet, teacher, anthologist, and self-described "amateur folklorist," was a founding father of African American literary criticism. Born on May 1, 1901, Brown came of age in the segregated worlds of **Washington, D.C.,**'s black middle class and elite white collegiate academies. Brown graduated from college, Phi Beta Kappa, in 1922 and earned his M.A. degree at Harvard University. Brown then embarked upon a teaching career in historically black colleges and universities that spanned over half a century. Between 1923 and 1929 Brown taught at Virginia Seminary and College, Lincoln University (Missouri), and Fisk University. In 1927 Brown married Daisy Turnbull. During the Great Depression he served as an editor for the **Works Progress Administration**'s Federal Writers' Project and began his more than forty-year tenure teaching at **Howard University** in Washington, D.C. According to literary critic Darwin Turner, Brown "wrote the Bible for the study of Afro-American literature" (Henderson, "Sterling Brown," 79).

Among his southern students Brown initiated his "self-education" in black folk culture. His scholarship and poetry bear the marks of the African American oral tradition in form and content, making use of the **blues**, spirituals, ballads, work songs, the folk epic, sermon, and lie. In the tradition of poet Carl Sandburg, Brown, like **Langston Hughes**, developed a democratic black aesthetic, drawing upon the everyday speech and daily life of blacks to create his art. Written in the vernacular language of black folk, Brown's poetry articulates the subjectivity, humanity, and meaning of early twentieth-century African American experience with a depth that sharply defies the dehumanizing stereotypes of blacks prominent in mainstream white American culture and letters, as well as the superficial dialect poetry of **Paul Laurence Dunbar** and **James Weldon Johnson**.

Much of Brown's work engages the Great Migration, frequently employing the road as a complex metaphor of black experience. His books of poetry—*Southern Road* (1932), *The Last Ride of Wild Bill* (1975), and *No Hiding Place* (unpublished until 1980)—illuminate motives for leaving the South: violence, poverty, the **boll weevil**, fugitive status, and impulses toward self-determination. His works envelop deterrents to mobility such as convict labor and sharecropping, the experience of arrival in an urban world, nostalgia for home, and the disillusioning class dynamics of city living. "Odyssey of Big Boy," perhaps his most famous poem, evokes the epic nature of black migration and celebrates the search for autonomy in the United States. Drawing upon black folk idioms, Brown articulates the realities of black movement toward freedom: "This is not Jordan River / There lies not Canaan / . . . Still we are motherless children / . . . dragging travelers / Alone, and a long ways from home" (Brown, 204–5). Brown believed both that "urbanization . . . break[s] up folk culture" and that such a dynamic culture could nurture migrants and their growing communities in racist cityscapes like **Atlanta**, **Chicago**, **Memphis**, Harlem, and Washington, D.C. (Rowell, " 'Let Me Be wid Ole Jazzbo,' " 802). Thus his poetry draws upon the mythic heroes and antiheroes, folktales, music, and spirituality forged to sustain blacks in the aftermath of slavery and grasp of **Jim Crow**: "You had what we need now, John Henry," he writes in "Strange Legacies," "Help us get it" (Brown, 96). *See also* Literature, the Great Migration in.

Further Reading

African American Review 31, no. 3 (1997). Issue contains ten essays on Brown.

Brown, Sterling A. *The Collected Poems of Sterling Brown*. Selected by Michael S. Harper. New York: Harper and Row, 1980.

Callaloo 21, no. 4 (Fall 1998). Special issue on Brown.

Gabbin, Joanne V. *Sterling A. Brown: Building the Black Aesthetic Tradition*. Westport, CT: Greenwood Press, 1985.

Henderson, Stephen E. "The Heavy Blues of Sterling Brown: A Study of Craft and Tradition." *Black American Literature Forum* 14 (1980): 32–44.

———. "Sterling Brown." In *African American Writers*, vol. 1, edited by Valerie Smith. New York: Charles Scribner's Sons, 2001.

Rowell, Charles H. " 'Let Me Be wid Ole Jazzbo': An Interview with Sterling A. Brown." *Callaloo* 14, no. 4 (Fall 1991): 795–815.

———. *A Son's Return: Selected Essays of Sterling A. Brown*. Edited by Mark A. Sanders. Boston: Northeastern University Press, 1996.

———. "Sterling A. Brown and the Afro-American Folk Tradition." *Studies in the Literary Imagination* 7 (Fall 1974): 131–52.

Michelle Yvonne Gordon

Brown, Willie L., Jr. (1934–)

Willie Brown, one of twentieth-century California's most powerful politicians, was part of a sizable migration of African Americans to **San Francisco** during and after World War II. Brown's involvement with migrant organizing for fair access to jobs and **housing** led him into politics, and by the 1960s San Franciscans elected him to the state legislature, where he represented African Americans and other communities of color for nearly thirty years. As Assembly Speaker and mayor of San Francisco, Brown was often an advocate for the economic and social needs of African Americans, and his tenure in both powerful positions signaled the incorporation of African American migrants into California political culture.

Brown was born on March 20, 1934, in Mineola, Texas, a deeply segregated town in East Texas's declining **cotton belt**. His mother's family raised him after his father, Lewis Brown, migrated to **Los Angeles** in 1938 and his mother, Minnie Collins, migrated to **Dallas** to work as a domestic servant. The race riots that convulsed Mineola during World War II shaped both Brown's political consciousness as an opponent of racial discrimination and his desire to escape **Jim Crow** (see **Racial Violence and World War II**). After graduating from Mineola Colored High School in 1951, Brown found few opportunities for higher education in Texas and followed his uncle, Rembert "Itsie" Collins, to San Francisco.

San Francisco was a major center of the wartime migration of African Americans to the Pacific Coast, with nearly 40,000 migrants living there by 1950. In 1951 Brown was admitted to San Francisco State College on a probational basis and worked to overcome the inadequate education he had received in Texas. Brown also joined the Jones Methodist Church in San Francisco, a politically active congregation mostly made up of African American migrants from the South. Along with two other newcomers, Dr. Carlton B. Goodlett and Terry Francois, Brown took a leadership role in the city's branch of the **National Association for the Advancement of Colored People**. After his 1955 graduation from college, Brown attended the Hastings School of Law in San Francisco and was admitted to the bar in 1957. He went into practice with Francois, making a name as an **attorney** willing to defend anyone in the city's African American community.

In 1962 Brown achieved local prominence when he led a protest against a race-exclusive housing development in San Francisco that refused to show him or any other African American a house. Although the protesters failed, Brown became a recognized leader of the militant faction of the NAACP. He advised on protests led by the NAACP and the **Congress of Racial Equality** (CORE) against local hotels and car dealerships that maintained discriminatory practices. Though successful, the protests revealed a growing gap between radical protesters and Brown, who had turned to **electoral politics** to end discrimination (see **Restrictive Covenants**).

Brown had befriended John Burton and his older brother, Phillip Burton, as a student at San Francisco State, and together they formed a durable political alliance that dominated San Francisco politics for the remainder of the century. Brown was elected to the California Assembly in 1964, soon becoming a leader of the growing African American membership of the state legislature and taking an increasingly prominent role in Democratic Party politics. He served as a cochair of Robert F. Kennedy's 1968 presidential campaign in California. In 1980 Brown was elected California's first African American Speaker of the Assembly, a post he held for a record fifteen years. In 1995, forced out of the Assembly by term limits, he was elected to the first of two terms as San Francisco's first African American mayor. *See also* Black Legislators; Black Mayors; Civil Rights Movement.

Further Reading

Broussard, Albert S. *Black San Francisco: The Struggle for Racial Equality in the West, 1900–1954*. Lawrence: University Press of Kansas, 1993.

Richardson, James. *Willie Brown: A Biography*. Berkeley: University of California Press, 1996.

Robert Cruickshank

BSCP *See* Brotherhood of Sleeping Car Porters (BSCP)

Buffalo, New York

Buffalo's African American community dates to the eighteenth century when blacks were attracted to the Niagara frontier because of adventure, its proximity to Canada and freedom, and readily available unskilled and semi-skilled jobs. Blacks settled east of the downtown business district, and their numbers grew gradually. By the eve of the Civil War the fledgling community supported three churches: the Vine Street **African Methodist Episcopal (AME) Church**, the Michigan Avenue **Baptist** Church, and St. Philips Episcopal Church, each of which played leading roles in the development of the free black community.

Slavery was the major catalyst that attracted black Buffalonians to the political arena. George Weir of the Vine Street AME Church joined the Buffalo City Anti-slavery Society in 1838. Ten years later Abner H. Francis, a wealthy black merchant, was elected its treasurer. Buffalo also was the home of William Wells Brown, who transported escaped slaves to Canada.

At the third National Negro Convention that met at the Vine Street Methodist Church in Buffalo in 1843, the Reverend Henry Highland Garnet of Troy delivered an impassioned speech calling upon slaves to overthrow the institution if owners refused to free them. Frederick Douglass urged caution. But it was Buffalo cooper and future pastor of the Michigan Avenue Baptist Church Samuel Davis who introduced the subject and initiated the debate between Douglass and Garnet. Davis told the audience that blacks sought the franchise, education, and their constitutional right to happiness. This convention highlighted the growing disparity between African American reformers and their white supporters and blacks' dissatisfaction with the government responses to their conditions.

Buffalo attracted other intellectuals who also articulated African Americans' concerns during the antebellum days. Poet James Whitfield, a lifelong **barber**, in "America" explained his dissatisfaction with his country and called upon it to adhere to its ideals. He won praise from William Wells Brown and Frederick Douglass and also enjoyed renown in black literary circles nationwide.

Nineteenth-century black Buffalonians waged a major battle against illiteracy. Their Sunday school classes and the lyceums that they founded were creative responses to the inferior education offered to black children. Former slave and barber Henry Moxley initiated a lawsuit against the Buffalo Board of Education in 1867 to force it to eliminate the inferior African School. After a protracted struggle that involved prominent black citizens, including Robert Talbert, Buffalo in 1891 abolished the African School and integrated black children into the public school system. Their success led to the elimination of African schools throughout New York State. Education was too important to be left solely to the public schools, so African Americans continued to use their traditional approaches. Mrs. John Bell operated a cooking school at St. Luke African Methodist Episcopal Zion Church that prepared young women to go into domestic service.

While nineteenth-century Buffalo blacks were restricted mainly to service occupations, some found skilled and professional jobs. Nearly 10 percent found employment in the crafts and professions. Blacks in Buffalo would not enjoy such favorable economic conditions again until long after the post–World War I migration.

Buffalo's black population grew gradually, doubling between 1855 and 1900, and still composed less than 0.5 percent of the city's population. By

1925 it increased to 9,000. Despite its small size, Buffalo blacks had developed a legacy of struggle. By 1900 this population had developed a relationship with white Buffalo based largely upon noblesse oblige. Blacks from the southeastern states began gradually to trickle into the city. With the outbreak of World War I the population expanded as blacks sought to take advantage of opportunities to work in the wartime industries.

Employers in the growth industries initially refused to hire African Americans. Their first major opportunity came in 1916 when some replaced striking white maritime workers. For the first time black workers retained their jobs after the strike was settled. Subsequently, other industries such as the **railroads** and steel mills began to employ them. The job security and higher wages that blacks earned elevated their status in their community.

The pattern whereby employers assigned tasks to workers based upon their ethnicity continued. Blacks worked in the blast furnace areas of the steel mills because employers believed that they had high tolerance rates for heat. Such prejudices assured that blacks would penetrate and retain certain semiskilled and unskilled jobs. Despite this seeming advantage, African Americans still had the highest rates of **unemployment**, with fewer than 50 percent finding jobs.

Women did not benefit from the opening of industrial jobs to blacks and faced severe job restrictions. Most worked, over half in the narrowly defined field of domestic service. Only a few were **skilled workers**.

The black migrants increasingly experienced prejudice. Judges handed down arbitrary decrees or sentenced blacks to prison for minor infractions of laws, such as loitering. Restaurants and other public establishments closed their doors to them.

Although the migration of southern blacks increased demands for **housing**, recreation, and jobs, black migrants brought with them a community infrastructure. Often they migrated in groups from the same town and settled in close proximity to each other upon arrival. Their family and church had formed the core of their southern communities. **Fraternal orders**, civic and social organizations, and business enterprises also were characteristic of the communities from which they came. They knew that blacks were held in high esteem in certain sectors of the South. Their southern culture was reinforced because the migrants constantly returned to their homes in the South for family rituals (see **Visiting**).

The newcomers relied upon this culture to cushion the blows that they received in the external world of work, as well as other assaults meted out to them. Their families, characterized by two parents, were a source of strength. A sizable number of these migrants lived in extended and augmented households where these networks benefited them in finding jobs, housing, and security in the city. Newcomers stated that they had come to Buffalo because they had friends and relatives there already. Not only did these people share their homes with each other, but they frequently worked in the same occupation or at the same company, thereby demonstrating the magnitude of their ties.

In an era of dire economic circumstances and harsh social conditions, race pride and necessity fueled the establishment of several new businesses. The *Buffalo American*, one of these, heralded the establishment of each. Dr. Ivorite

Scruggs, southern born and educated, with his wife Ruth bought an apartment building. Dan Montgomery's Exchange Street supper club was a center for black intellectuals and attracted nationally prominent entertainers. In 1921 Robert Joplin opened the McAvoy Theatre.

In the 1920s and 1930s blacks created cooperatives. This was part of a national trend. The Douglas Grocery was capitalized at $10,000 and included among its early subscribers the Reverend J. Edward Nash, James Gant, a fireman, and a housewife, Irene Allen. George Schuyler, founder of the Young Negro Cooperative League Movement, encouraged local blacks to establish the Citizens' Cooperative League, a grocery store that had weekly receipts of $850 in 1931. Dr. Ezekial Nelson founded the Buffalo Cooperative Economic Society in 1935. It offered seminars on business topics and established a credit union. Blacks responded positively to this organization, which lasted into the 1960s. Such establishments were a source of racial pride, but they also employed blacks in clerical positions that eluded most applicants outside the community.

Blacks began to organize a number of self-help organizations to address the issues that confronted them. The Michigan Avenue **Young Men's Christian Association**, with its large endowment from Julius Rosenwald and George Matthews, was one of them. Founded in 1922, it provided community-based education programs, including courses, public lectures, and recreational programs. It also provided a forum for community meetings.

The **National Urban League** organized a branch to alleviate the job situation. It negotiated with government and businesses to increase employment and educational opportunities for blacks. It initiated the Big Brothers, Negro Health Week, and Visiting Teachers programs. While its successes were mixed, the league addressed broad social issues that Buffalo blacks faced and provided the community with a catalyst committed to change.

The migrants breathed new life into the Buffalo branch of the **National Association for the Advancement of Colored People** (NAACP), which had been founded in 1909, because it addressed issues like peonage, **lynching**, and racial bias in housing, schools, and public accommodations. The NAACP also was an important source for community education and brought prominent African American lecturers to Buffalo.

Blacks began to make inroads into the political process during the 1930s. They received appointments to various boards and commissions. A few blacks became police officers. Sherman Walker and others achieved political prominence. In 1940 the African American population had reached approximately 19,000. Blacks made progress in the political arena in the civil rights era and advocated for voting rights. They were elected as county and city legislators. In 1966 they elected Arthur O. Eve to the State Assembly as the representative of the 141st Assembly District. Eve later became Deputy Speaker of the Assembly, the highest position to which blacks had acceded. His bid to become mayor of Buffalo in 1977 failed.

Several self-help projects, such as the Saul Alinsky–established grassroots organization BUILD, emerged in the 1960s (see **Community Organizing**). The population continued to grow, and blacks made gains in the steel and automobile industries. Yet these rust belt industries began to decline, and many moved out of the region. Buffalo gradually became a city whose economy was based upon the service and high-technology industries. Subsequently, blacks lost economic ground. At the same time some assumed high-ranking positions in government, including council representatives and superintendent of the school board and chief of police. Blacks achieved these advances at a time when financial resources and the population were dwindling. Consequently, their struggle for equality and social justice continues. *See also* Chain Migration; Deindustrialization; Northeastern States, Black Migration to; Talbert, Mary B.

Further Reading

Williams, Lillian S. *Strangers in the Land of Paradise: The Creation of an African American Community, Buffalo, New York, 1900–1940.* Bloomington: Indiana University Press, 1999.

Lillian Serece Williams

Burroughs, Nannie Helen (1879–1961)

Nannie Helen Burroughs, educator, club leader, and social reformer, was part of the post-Reconstruction migration to the city and the generation of institution builders who established organizations to meet the needs of migrants coming to the cities during the late nineteenth and early twentieth centuries. Born in 1879 in rural Virginia, she resettled with her family in **Washington, D.C.**, in 1883. Since education was segregated, her experience at M Street High School exposed her to some of the most educated **women** of her race (**Mary Church Terrell**, Anna Cooper, and Mary Jane Patterson) and developed her interest in the growing field of domestic science.

Her presence in Washington, D.C., and her contact with race leaders led to her attendance at the founding meeting of the **National Association of Colored Women** (NACW) (1896). The NACW represented educated, urban women interested in improving the popular image of black women and uplifting the "lowly and fallen" of their race. Both classes had been thrown together by the spreading legalized **Jim Crow** segregation of cities by the turn of the century. To meet the needs of the race, women had to turn to themselves for answers. Self-help and racial solidarity were means to meet the needs of a segregated race. Nannie Burroughs was part of this generation of female leaders shaping programs and philosophies of racial **uplift**.

Unlike some of her privileged, married mentors, the unmarried Burroughs had to earn a living. Later in 1896 she moved to **Louisville, Kentucky**, to become the bookkeeper and stenographer for the Foreign Mission Board of the National Baptist Convention (NBC), a position she held until 1909. Her organizational skills and education prevailed, and she rose within the organization. At the NBC annual meeting in 1900, Burroughs gained national recognition for her speech, "How the Sisters Are Hindered from Helping." This speech served as a catalyst for the formation of the largest black women's organization of that time, the Woman's Convention of the NBC. By 1907 this organization had over 1.5 million members.

Burroughs saw the needs of her race in the cities. Unlike the white purity crusaders and white clubwomen, who viewed the black urban population as difficult to assimilate, black women were less paternalistic and more realistic in their expectations. In Louisville Burroughs organized the Woman's Industrial Club, which functioned as a **settlement house** for the community. In a rented house the women taught millinery, domestic science, and health care. They served lunches for working people and provided short-term lodging for recent migrants to the city. The women paid dues, held fundraisers, and served as the volunteers at this center.

The experience she had within these organizations provided Burroughs with financial and political resources. She returned to Washington, D.C., in 1909 to establish the **National Training School for Women and Girls**, the first national trade school for black women. She became a national leader within the **National Association for the Advancement of Colored People**, the **National Urban League**, and the International Council of Women of the Darker Races of the World. By the 1920s Burroughs accomplished her goal to organize women for better wages and working conditions through the formation of the National Association of Wage Earners. From 1934 until 1961 she edited the *Worker*, a publication of the Trade School for the Women's Convention describing racial conditions, church leadership, and women's issues. In 1949 Shaw University gave her an honorary doctorate for her lifetime efforts. After her death in 1961, her school dropped industrial education in 1964 to become the Nannie Helen Burroughs School for elementary education. *See also* Baptist Church; Childbirth; Schoolteachers and Teaching; Primary Document 44.

Further Reading

Barnett, Evelyn Brooks. "Nannie Burroughs and the Education of Black Women." In *The Afro-American Woman: Struggles and Images*, edited by Sharon Harley and Rosalyn Terborg-Penn, 97–108. Port Washington, NY: Kennikat Press, 1978.

———. "Religion, Politics, and Gender: The Leadership of Nannie Helen Burroughs." *Journal of Religious Thought* 44 (Winter/Spring 1988): 7–22.

Harley, Sharon. "Nannie Helen Burroughs: 'The Black Goddess of Liberty.'" *Journal of Negro History* 81 (Winter–Autumn 1996): 62–71.

Pickens, William. *Nannie Burroughs and the School of the Three B's*. New York: [s.n.], 1921.

Dorothy C. Salem

C

California Eagle

The *California Eagle*, one of the oldest and most influential African American newspapers in the West, traces its origins to 1879, when John James Neimore, a migrant from Texas, started the paper in **Los Angeles, California**. Offering information on jobs and **housing**, the paper helped ease the transition of black settlers to the region. First known as the *Owl*, later the *Eagle*, and then the *California Eagle*, the paper promoted Los Angeles as a hospitable destination for black migrants because it offered the possibility for **home ownership**, a favorable climate, a relative absence of overt racial violence, and the presence of other minority groups, namely, Mexicans and Asians, who deflected white racism. As these conditions began to change in the 1910s with growth of the black community, the arrival of larger numbers of white southern migrants, and the rise of **Ku Klux Klan** activity in the area, the paper shifted its focus from promotion of the city as a land of opportunity to criticism of rising levels of racial intolerance that belied black migrants' expectations for new opportunities free from the racial hostility they fled in the South.

The *California Eagle* is most often associated with its longtime editor and publisher Charlotta A. Bass (née Spears), who took over from Neimore in 1912 and maintained her position at the helm until 1951. Under her leadership the paper practiced advocacy journalism, informing the African American community about racial injustice and organizing it to combat it. Bass used the *California Eagle* to focus attention on housing and job discrimination, **police brutality**, and racism within the burgeoning motion picture industry centered in Hollywood. As an example, the paper pioneered an effort to stop production of the racist movie *The Birth of a Nation*.

Charlotta Bass, editor of the *California Eagle*, and two members of the production staff stand outside the printing plant in Watts where the newspaper was published between 1929 and 1934. Photo courtesy of the Southern California Library for Social Studies and Research.

With offices located on Central Avenue, the hub of the black community in Los Angeles, the *California Eagle* promoted black businesses and in the early 1930s helped initiate a local **"Don't Buy Where You Can't Work"** campaign modeled after a similar one led by Chicago's black papers. The *California Eagle* lauded local black achievement and informed readers about black community activity elsewhere in the country and throughout the world, regularly carrying syndicated columns from other black papers.

The World War II arrival of scores of new black migrants to Los Angeles prompted Bass to focus the *California Eagle*'s attention on ensuring blacks' access to newly created jobs and adequate housing. Along with local religious leaders and activists, the paper led a successful campaign to integrate black **women** in particular into the local war industries. The *California Eagle* served as a West Coast beacon in the **Double V campaign** pursued by the **black press** throughout the country, seeking victory against fascism abroad and racism at home. At the close of the war Bass took up the fight to ensure that returning black GIs had equal access to veterans' housing in Los Angeles.

The *California Eagle* actively covered **electoral politics**, including Bass's own campaigns for city council and Congress. She eventually ran for vice president of the United States in 1952 on the Independent Progressive Party ticket. Though she lost the election, the campaign's slogan reflects her broader attitude and that of the *California Eagle*—"Win or Lose, We Win by Raising the Issues."

Bass sold the paper in 1951 to Loren Miller, a former city editor of the *California Eagle* and prominent **National Association for the Advancement**

of Colored People attorney, who continued to publish an activist paper. When Miller was appointed to the bench as a municipal court judge in 1964, the paper was acquired by a group of fourteen investors, but quickly deteriorated and ceased publication in 1965. *See also* Associated Negro Press (ANP).

Further Reading

Bass, Charlotta A. *Forty Years: Memoirs from the Pages of a Newspaper*. Los Angeles: self-published, 1960.

"Charlotta Bass and the *California Eagle*." Southern California Library for Social Science Research. www.socallib.org/bass.

Freer, Regina. "L.A. Race Woman: Charlotta Bass and the Complexities of Black Political Development in Los Angeles." *American Quarterly* 56, no. 3 (2004): 607–32.

Regina Freer

Calloway, Cab[ell] (1907–1994)

Jazz singer, songwriter, and bandleader Cab Calloway epitomized the urban hipster between the wars, recording many hits and thriving during the **swing** and jump eras. While bandleaders such as **Duke Ellington** and **Count Basie** exuded aristocratic panache, Calloway cultivated the hip style, in the late 1930s dressing first in white-tie full dress, then adopting a black-belted blue serge suit, and finally, in the 1940s, wearing the baggy, narrow-ankled pants with knee-length jacket that came to be known as the zoot suit. If Calloway did not invent the zoot suit, he made it popular, as he did the wide-brimmed hat, watch chain, and pointy-toed shoes with which he accessorized it. With his zoot suit, Calloway showcased his onstage strutting and dancing prowess. Calloway also collected the jargon of jazz musicians, publishing arcane phrases and vocabulary in *The New Cab Calloway's Hepsters Dictionary: Language of Jive*.

Calloway was an accomplished singer who specialized in scat, nonsense syllables that allow singers to use the voice as an instrument without words. He recorded his theme song, "Minnie the Moocher," early in his career (1931) and thereafter was known as the "Hi-de-ho Man" because of the song's refrain: "Hi-de-hi-de-hi." Although Calloway might have seemed a devil-may-care hipster, in truth he was an exacting leader who demanded punctuality, precision, and propriety from his players, whom he would fine for being late, for playing a wrong note, or for swearing on stage. Soloists who graduated from Calloway's organization included jazz greats Chu Berry,

Jazz musician Cab Calloway. © Bettmann/Corbis.

Ben Webster, and **Dizzy Gillespie**. Calloway took singer Lena Horne out of the chorus at the Cotton Club to introduce her as a soloist, and he said that he taught Nat King Cole how to enunciate when Cole began to supplement his piano playing with singing.

Calloway followed his sister into show business in **Chicago** and moved to **New York City** in 1929 for an engagement at the Savoy Ballroom. Calloway claims that in 1931 he was ordered to succeed Duke Ellington at the Cotton Club, New York's celebrated jazz supper club, when the owners made him an offer he could not refuse. He remained there until 1940. When wartime conditions made touring with big bands impractical and record production was limited, Calloway streamlined his band into a smaller configuration, creating one of the first jump bands of the era and maintaining a working band in an era when larger swing bands were pining for bookings.

Reflecting the accelerating tempo of black life during and after the urban migration, jump bands specialized in tunes whose insistent four beats—often emphasized by a walking bass line (notes that climbed and descended the pitches of the **blues** scale or outlined chords every two measures)—provided an upbeat accompaniment for jitterbugging dancers. By the mid-1940s jump bands were the dance bands of the age and the stylistic refuge for players who did not play **bebop** or sweet popular ballads. Jump bands that added electric guitars and blues singers were prototypical **rhythm and blues** bands, the forerunners of rock and roll. As he had in the 1930s, Cab Calloway kept audiences dancing through the 1940s, building a bridge between swing music and rock. When he disbanded his group in 1948, Calloway continued performing—touring with the Harlem Globetrotters and appearing as Sportin' Life in Gershwin's *Porgy and Bess*, in an all-black version of *Hello, Dolly!*, in the Broadway revival revue *Bubbling Brown Sugar*, and in the film *The Blues Brothers*. *See also* Dance Halls and Nightclubs; Recording Industry.

Further Reading

Calloway, Cab. *Minnie the Moocher and Many, Many More*. 55 min. MPI Home Video, 1987. Videocassette.

Calloway, Cab, and Bryant Rollins. *Of Minnie the Moocher and Me*. New York: Crowell, 1976.

Dance, Stanley. *The World of Swing*. 1974. Reprint, New York: Da Capo Press, 2001.

Gena Caponi-Tabery

Caribbean Migration

Migration in search of work and opportunity, both within the Caribbean Basin and to points beyond its geographic boundaries, has long been a way of life for people of the region. Its causes are deeply rooted in the history of the islands. The legacy of slavery and plantation agriculture, the collapse of the sugar industry in the British-held territories, and crippling natural disasters all made migration necessary in many households. Colonial rule, which imposed a system of color-class stratification in all walks of life, limited opportunities for advancement. Today the limited resources of postcolonial nations,

unemployment, and underemployment leave people with little choice but to look abroad for better living standards and to realize economic and social ambitions. Historically, members of the dissatisfied middle class, as well as working-class people, regarded emigration as an avenue of social and economic mobility. Although the regions' early migration opportunities were generally structured in favor of male labor, **women** have always participated in migrations and especially in the present are often the first in a family network to migrate.

Background in the Caribbean

Between 1880 and 1930 opportunities to earn better wages in foreign countries bordering the Caribbean Sea attracted tens of thousands of Caribbean migrants in interregional movements to U.S.-owned sugar and banana plantations in Cuba, the Dominican Republic, Puerto Rico, and Central America. Centralized production and the expansion of **railroads** and shipping stimulated an unprecedented demand for labor. Panama Canal construction under the French and then the Americans after 1904 attracted several hundred thousand Caribbean workers. Some 240,000 migrated to Panama from Barbados and Jamaica alone between 1881 and 1915. Tens of thousands of others from the British Caribbean and Haiti migrated to Cuba and Central America. Labor conditions were dangerous, and black workers were subjected to the most hazardous jobs. Deaths from accidents and disease were common, and workers endured American imposition of **Jim Crow** wages and **housing**. But because laborers could earn up to three times as much as at home, they continued to emigrate. "Panama money" had great resonance in many households, for workers' wages could provide realistic hope of a better life. Remittances could help purchase or expand family land or finance the migration of family members and perhaps workers' own secondary migration.

Migration to the United States

African Caribbean migration to the United States began in significant numbers around 1900 and is characterized by two significant waves that reflect the deeply rooted migration history of the region. The first wave or "old" immigration occurred between 1900 and 1930 and established many of the institutional characteristics of the second wave or "new" immigration, which began after 1965 and continues in the present. Both movements, in which the majority of the immigrants are distinguished by English language and African descent, are marked by race and until recently have been barely visible in U.S. immigration history or even the history of the Great Black Migration. Caribbean labor migrants have been critical to U.S. capitalist development in the Caribbean, Central America, and Florida, while highly selected U.S. arrivals have played vital roles in the intellectual, social, and cultural development of black communities in America.

In 1930 the U.S. census recorded just under 100,000 foreign-born residents of African descent. A majority of these immigrants, approximately 90 percent, had been born in the Caribbean, while smaller percentages had been born in Africa, mainly the Portuguese-held Cape Verde islands. First-wave immigrants

Three women from Guadeloupe, part of the larger African Caribbean immigration to the United States, arrive at Ellis Island in the 1920s. Courtesy of the New York Public Library.

settled mainly in **New York City**, **Miami**, or **Boston**. More than 80 percent of U.S. arrivals were English-speaking, and this number did not include 8,000 arrivals from the U.S. Virgin Islands. Smaller numbers arrived from the Francophone Caribbean, including Haiti, Martinique, and Guadeloupe, or the Danish colonies of the Caribbean Basin. The immigrants were generally restricted to African American areas of their cities of settlement, where they lived in clusters of compatriots. African Caribbean immigrants also arrived from Hispanic countries such as Cuba, Panama, and Costa Rica and often settled in predominantly English-speaking areas. Notably, some 40,000 Puerto Rican migrants also arrived and, like African Caribbean migrants, were restricted to certain neighborhoods. In New York the presence of all these immigrants of color changed the racial and ethnic landscape of the city.

In the late nineteenth and early twentieth centuries Florida attracted mainly laborers from the nearby islands of the Bahamas and Cuba, whereas almost all of the Caribbean Basin was represented among migrants to New York and Boston. Middle-class, literate, and more prosperous working-class migrants tended to settle in the latter cities after 1900, but Bahamian migration to Florida really began at least two decades before. It was primarily Florida's Bahamian labor—about 10,000 persons in 1930—that transformed a sparsely developed small town into the city of Miami between 1880 and 1920 and made possible the expansion of commercial agriculture in southern Florida. The cost of travel, about five dollars, made the trip affordable, but by 1920 emigration of poor Bahamians to Florida declined when U.S. officials began enforcing the 1917 Literacy Act.

Although potential emigrants could obtain regular transportation via passenger and banana ships to the United States, travel to northeastern cities from more distant islands than the Bahamas required a significant outlay of cash. "Panama money" was one of the most dependable sources of passage money, especially for a first migrant in a family network. Or a bit of family ground might be sold. Once a migration network was established, immigrants sent passage money earned from wages. This money, as well as other remittances, gifts, and even children, who were sent back and fostered by grandparents and other kin, were important symbols of trust built between family at home and those far way. These transnational networks linking places of settlement with home communities were institutionalized among early twentieth-century Caribbean immigrants and remained vital in the first seventy years of Caribbean migration (see **Chain Migration**).

To facilitate their adjustment to the city and to maintain relationships with their homelands, virtually every island group organized benevolent associations after 1900. Women as well as men were important participants and organizers of these community institutions. Their proliferation after 1900 distinguished this migration wave from previous migrations of mostly male students, professionals, and members of the upper class. These smaller migrations could not sustain separate homeland organizations. By 1898 Bermudians in New York were a large-enough group to form the Bermuda Benevolent Association in the San Juan Hill section (Columbus Hill) of New York City. In addition to providing sick and death benefits, benevolent associations provided meeting spaces for their members to socialize and conduct business. A significant aspect of the associations' business was to provide relief in the form of money, goods, scholarships, and books to homeland communities. The benevolent associations also organized relief for victims after natural disasters such as hurricanes or earthquakes.

If creating and maintaining transnational communities were a significant aspect of early twentieth-century Caribbean settlement in New York City, immigrants were also involved in the local and national black public sphere as entertainers, writers, and political leaders. This tradition was not new. Caribbean immigrants, especially well-educated or highly skilled men of the upper and middle classes, found fertile ground for their talents in nineteenth-century African American communities throughout the United States. African Caribbean men played significant roles in the black community as Reconstruction politicians, ministers, and educators. A tiny African American middle class generally welcomed the contributions of this Caribbean-born talented tenth.

However, as the Caribbean community expanded after 1900, cultural and often political distinctions between the new arrivals and African Americans became more apparent. One of the most controversial political leaders was Jamaican **Marcus Garvey**. He arrived in New York in 1916 and established the central branch of the **Universal Negro Improvement Association**, which he had formed in Jamaica in 1914. Unlike the **National Association for the Advancement of Colored People**, which called for full integration of black people into American society, Garvey urged the black masses everywhere to form their own nationalist base in Africa. Other immigrant men and women combined an aggressive approach to civil rights with a firm stand against colonial oppression. Some adopted a **socialist** or **Communist** approach to these political issues. Their periodicals, street-corner meetings, demonstrations, and tenant and labor strikes that occurred during and between the world wars had an important impact on the later **civil rights movement**. Well-established immigrants who early on became naturalized citizens and typically joined the Democratic Party in New York City were also positioned to win electoral offices as the African American electorate switched to the Democratic Party after 1932 (see **Political Realignment**).

The **Harlem Renaissance**, the cultural flowering among writers, musicians, and graphic artists during the 1920s, witnessed the spread of new journals, magazines, and newspapers in which immigrants played critical roles as founders, editors, and feature writers. Although their works are rarely considered in studies of American immigrant literature, the Caribbean writers of this generation also established the first substantial body of black immigrant literature in the United States. These writers include Jamaican columnist and essayist Joel A. Rogers, Jamaican poet and novelist **Claude McKay**, Panamanian and British Guianan novelist Eric Walrond, and Nevis-born playwright Eulalie Spence. **Nella Larsen**, a second-generation writer of Danish Caribbean descent, who published two novels (*Quicksand* in 1928 and *Passing* in 1929) during the Harlem Renaissance, also belongs with this group.

Immigration from the European-held Caribbean was virtually cut off after federal immigration legislation in 1924 applied national origins quotas and racial restrictions to immigrant admissions. For most of the Great Depression more Caribbean immigrants left the United States than arrived, and interregional opportunities for migration also dried up. In the Caribbean, workers, frustrated by low wages, unemployment, and lack of representation under colonialism, violently protested these conditions. Riots erupted in St. Kitts, St. Lucia, Trinidad, Jamaica, Barbados, and elsewhere as politically conscious laborers sought redress for collective economic injustice and demanded widespread political reform. Significantly, these developments led to organized movements for independence from Britain, and Caribbean New Yorkers held solidarity meetings and formed political unions such as the Jamaica Progressive League (1936), an important transnational organization still active today.

Migration after 1930

In the first seventy years of the twentieth century Caribbean migration to the United States never ceased entirely, but between 1930 and 1965 immigrants arrived in comparatively small numbers. Some historians identify this period as a "second wave" of migration, but migration during this period was intermittent rather than steady. During the entire period permanent immigrants' numbers never exceeded 3,000 per year. World War II ushered in the contract labor system in which seasonal workers were recruited to work in sugar cane and other crops. Some of these workers left their contracts and remained in the country. Others immigrated under the British quota system and joined family members who had arrived in the first wave. Another group was mainly students who had entered on student visas. While immigration was never large during this period, the interim years are nonetheless significant. Many youthful first-generation and second-generation immigrants, as well as new arrivals, came of age during this period and by 1970 had entered public life.

Until 1952 Caribbean immigrants could in theory enter the United States under the quota allotments of their "mother" countries, but in that year the McCarran-Walter Act restricted the use of European country quotas by colonial subjects. In the postwar period most African Caribbean migration was directed toward Britain until 1962, when restrictive legislation abruptly halted

Commonwealth migration to the United Kingdom. Notably, an important contingent of mostly upper-class Haitians exiled from the brutal human rights violations of François "Papa Doc" Duvalier arrived in the late 1950s and early 1960s. They were soon joined by a larger Haitian middle class. In 1965 the Hart-Cellar Immigration Reform Act eliminated the national origins quota system established in 1924, opening up large-scale immigration. For the first time in U.S. history new immigrants of color entered the country without restriction based on race.

Comparison of First- and Second-Wave Migrations

There were a number of continuities and changes in the late and early twentieth-century movements. New York remains the beachhead of Caribbean migration to the United States, but Florida has developed as a far more significant center than earlier in the century. In addition, significant Caribbean communities have developed elsewhere in the United States, including **Los Angeles**, **Chicago**, and southern cities such as **Atlanta**. Thus centers of settlement are emerging all over the United States, not just in the traditional migration centers.

The sheer size of the post-1965 wave makes its dynamics quite different from those of the earlier movement. By the early 1980s up to 50,000 English-speaking immigrants arrived each year, with another 6,000 to 8,000 arriving yearly from Haiti. In the first wave, the largest yearly migrations leveled off at between 5,000 and 8,000 per year. The volume of second-wave Caribbean migration has made possible more distinctive residential enclaves than among the old immigrant group. In addition, larger numbers allow Caribbean communities to develop distinct identities and to form political interest groups within the immigrant constituency, especially in New York City. While first-generation immigrants had little incentive to become naturalized citizens in a largely Jim Crow America, today legal immigrants naturalize more quickly. As American citizens, they are eligible to sponsor the immigration of immediate family members. While first-wave migration tended to favor a highly selected middle and working class, virtually every sector of Caribbean society is represented in recent migrations. Poorer and unskilled migrants make up a larger contingent of recent movements than in the first wave. Finally, gender, as in the past, is a major dynamic of the recent migration. While women were a significant minority of the earlier immigration, today women predominate and are typically the first to find jobs in health care and other growing service sectors that attract female wage earners.

Massive African Caribbean migration, within the Caribbean Basin and to the United States, is one of the most remarkable historical developments of the last century. Although historians have rarely linked the southern black migrations to American cities with African Caribbean migrations to the Panama Canal, Cuba, and the United States, these overlapping migrations provide a hemispheric dimension to our understanding of the Great Black Migration. The continuing arrivals of Caribbean immigrants, whose numbers, including first and second generations, now total several million, blur the boundaries of the black diaspora. *See also* African Blood Brotherhood (ABB); Briggs, Cyril V.;

Gulf South; Harrison, Hubert Henry; Schomburg, Arthur Alfonso; Primary Documents 22, 31, 33, 49.

Further Reading

Bryce-Laporte, Roy Simon. "Black Immigrants: The Experience of Invisibility and Inequality." *Journal of Black Studies* 3 (September 1972): 29–56.

Foner, Nancy, ed. *Islands in the City: West Indian Migration to New York.* Berkeley: University of California Press, 2001.

James, Winston. *Holding Aloft the Banner of Ethiopia: Caribbean Radicalism in Early Twentieth-Century America.* London: Verso, 1998.

Johnson, Howard. "Bahamian Labor Migration to Florida in the Late Nineteenth and Early Twentieth Centuries." *International Migration Review* 22 (Spring 1988): 84–103.

Johnson, Violet Showers. "Relentless Ex-colonials and Militant Immigrants: Protest Strategies of Boston's West Indian Immigrants, 1910-1950." In *The Civil Rights Movement Revisited: Critical Perspectives on the Struggle for Racial Equality in the United States*, edited by Patrick B. Miller, Therese Frey Steffen, and Elisabeth Schäfer-Wünsche. Hamburg: Lit Verlag, 2001.

Kasinitz, Philip. *Caribbean New York: Black Immigrants and the Politics of Race.* Ithaca, NY: Cornell University Press, 1992.

Reid, Ira De A. *The Negro Immigrant: His Background, Characteristics and Social Adjustment, 1899-1937.* New York: Columbia University Press, 1939.

Reimers, David. *Still the Golden Door: The Third World Comes to America.* New York: Columbia University Press, 1985.

Watkins-Owens, Irma. *Blood Relations: Caribbean Immigrants and the Harlem Community, 1900-1930.* Bloomington: Indiana University Press, 1996.

Irma Watkins-Owens

Catholics

The first Black Catholic community in the New World was documented in parish registers from 1563 to 1763 in St. Augustine, Florida (in New Spain). The oldest and the first settlement for freed slaves in America was called Gracia Real de Santa Teresa de Mose (Fort Moses), which was sanctioned by the governor of St. Augustine. In sum, colonial blacks worshiped and adhered to Catholic sacraments, as did Daniel Rudd (1854–1933), a former slave in **Cincinnati, Ohio**, who edited *African Catholic Tribune* and in 1889 organized the first National Black Catholic Congress (NBCC) in **Washington, D.C.** The NBCC called for racial inclusion of blacks in Catholic initiatives: **housing**, labor unions, and the establishment of parochial schools, orphanages, **hospitals**, and asylums. Father Augustus Tolton (1854–1897), ordained bishop in Rome in 1886, opened the ceremony with eighty-five delegates from thirteen states. The NBCC held four additional meetings before it ceased holding these national forums after the fifth Black Catholic Congress, which was held in **Baltimore, Maryland**, in 1894.

At the beginning of World War I blacks migrated north and west, where churches became central to shaping their identity and contributed to a resurgent racial and social activism. Black Catholics did much to contribute to that activism. The Black Catholic Lay Congress delegates continued their work in other activist groups after its decline. Frederick McGhee (1861–1912), a criminal **attorney** in St. Paul, Minnesota, and a delegate to three Black Catholic Lay Congresses, collaborated with **W.E.B. DuBois** to organize the legal section of the Niagara Movement. Delegate Lincoln C. Valle and his wife opened the St. Benedict the Moor mission in **Milwaukee** and later helped to persuade the Capuchin order to begin the St. Benedict the Moor Catholic Church of Milwaukee. Spirituality and social activism continued to evolve with Thomas Wyatt Turner's Black Catholic Community Committee against the Extension of Race Prejudice in Washington, D.C., (1913) to protest racial discrimination in the church and society; in 1924 the organization adopted the name Federated Colored Catholics of the United States.

The efforts of Jesuit priests John LaFarge and William Markoe contributed to the inclusion of black institutions in the Catholic Church during the 1950s. LaFarge formed the Cardinal Gibbons Institute, a vocational school in Maryland, and later the New York Interracial Council. Markoe wrote several articles in the Jesuit publication *America* on race relations. They influenced Catholic liberals forming the National Catholic Conference for Interracial Justice in 1958. Racial attitudes within the Catholic Church continued to evolve. In March 1965 Catholics marched in the civil rights protests in Selma, Alabama. With the culmination of Vatican II and the assassination of Dr. **Martin Luther King, Jr.**, in 1968, black priests urged the church to eradicate racial discrimination in the church and to place emphasis on developing the number of black priests. **Black nationalism** progressed within the Catholic Church with the establishment of several national organizations to eradicate racism: the National Black Catholic Clergy Caucus, the National Black Sisters' Conference, and the National Black Catholic Seminarians Association. In 1970 the National Office of Black Catholics became a clearinghouse, creating black Catholic liturgies, led by Reverend Joseph Rivers, and later resulting in the publication of *Lead Me, Guide Me: The African American Catholic Hymnal* (1987).

Rudd's NBCC was resumed in 1987 by Bishop John H. Ricard, where the formal adoption of the National Black Catholic Pastoral Plan formed the platform for evangelizing and ministering in black communities. The 1992 Black National Congress marked the formation of several new organizations calling for recognition and inclusion of blacks in Catholic organizations, for historic recognition of their contributions to the Catholic Church, for the expansion of the roles of black bishops, and for the creation of a viable voice within the church. As a consequence of the Pastoral Plan, the National Office of Black Catholics was organized and presently named the Secretariat for Black Catholics; fourteen bishops were appointed, and the Offices of Black Catholics in numerous dioceses were organized nationally to address black Catholic issues. The Pastoral Plan was affirmed by the Catholic Church and implemented throughout the United States.

Black Catholics historically worked within the theocracy, but in 1990 George A. Stalling, Jr., formed an independent congregation of the Catholic Church. Stalling petitioned the Washington, D.C., diocese to establish a Black Catholic rite and was denied; thereafter the American Independent Orthodox Church ordained Stalling, and he formed the Imani Temple.

Further Reading

The American Catholic History Research Center and University Archives. American Catholic History Classroom. The Federated Colored Catholics. http://libraries.cua.edu/achrcua/FCC/.

Davis, Cyprian. *The History of Black Catholics in the United States.* New York: Crossroad, 1990.

Hayes, Diana L., and Cyprian Davis, eds. *Taking Down Our Harps: Black Catholics in the United States.* Maryknoll, NY: Orbis Books, 1998.

McGreevy, John T. *Parish Boundaries: The Catholic Encounter with Race in the Twentieth-Century Urban North.* Chicago: University of Chicago Press, 1998.

National Black Catholic Congress. NBCC Online. www.nbccongress.org.

T. Alys Jordan

CCC *See* Civilian Conservation Corps (CCC)

Chain Migration

Chain migration, as with other global population movements in world history, framed the basis of the Great Black Migration of the twentieth century. Sociologists John and Leatrice MacDonald define chain migration as a process in which potential newcomers learn of job openings, gain access to transportation, receive food and lodging, and secure references and recommendations to church homes, schools, and business connections. Black migrants relied on elaborate social networks of relatives, friends, acquaintances, church members, newspaper editors, **labor agents**, and **railroad** porters to obtain the vital material support and critical information they needed to travel and relocate.

Chain migrations ran in multiple directions and sustained social ties among African Americans across a variety of places. These migration chains, or migration networks, stretched from farms to small towns, from small towns to medium-sized cities, from medium-sized cities to big cities, and from farms to big cities and from the rural South to the urban South, from the rural South to the rural Southwest, from the rural South to the rural-industrial South, from the South to the North, and from the South to the West. Migrants often moved in stepwise traveling patterns. A farmer from rural San Augustine County in East Texas, for example, might move to nearby Nacogdoches, Texas, a small city, before relocating to **Houston**, perhaps to work in nonfarm employment during lulls in the agricultural season. Upon returning to the farm for the next planting season, this farmer would share information with friends and family members, thus helping facilitate the seasonal, stepwise migrations of others. As historian Peter Gottlieb has argued, this pattern of movement was the "logic from which northward migration developed" (Gottlieb, 25).

Chain migration involved many important intertwining dimensions of assistance. Migrants who made their way to Houston, **New Orleans**, **Memphis**, Norfolk, **Dallas**, **Los Angeles**, **San Francisco**, **Chicago**, **Detroit**, **Cleveland**, **Milwaukee**, **New York City**, and other urban and industrialized centers across the United States used a complex web of communication networks in their search for jobs, homes, schools, churches, social organizations, and business associations. Migrants relied heavily on African American newspapers such as the *Chicago Defender*, the *Pittsburgh Courier*, the *New York Age*, the *Michigan Chronicle*, the *Boston Guardian*, the *Norfolk Examiner*, and the *Houston Informer* for job notices and feature stories and editorials that discussed black demographic patterns and provided readers with sociopolitical commentaries regarding race relations, the economy, and other pertinent issues facing people of color. Railroaders, especially service personnel—Pullman porters, waiters, maids, cooks, and redcaps—provided useful, descriptive, and sometimes deceptive commentary on black life and culture in urban and industrial places of interest. The church setting, too, offered newcomers refreshing perspectives on city life, jobs, schools, and political consciousness. Church services, concerts, churchwide annual events, and statewide, regional, and national conventions all provided occasions for visits from the country to the city, from the South to the North, and from the South to the West. Worship services, pastoral anniversaries, choral concerts, Sunday school district meetings, and National Baptist Conventions allowed for both respites from the reality of poverty and racism and discussions of the Great Migration. Employment agencies and labor agents also provided important services to newcomers. Businesses advertised positions in black weeklies and sent labor agents to recruit workers. Employment agencies like that of the **National Urban League** provided newcomers with a wealth of information on job opportunities, interviewing techniques, training seminars, and literacy.

More than anything else, personal contacts with relatives and friends provided migrants with the core foundations needed in the migration melodrama. Kith and kin put potential newcomers in contact with labor agents, job openings, and educational opportunities; introduced migrants to newspapers, feature stories, and newspaper advertisements; and in letters and visits, and at church picnics, concerts, worship services, and conventions, discussed with family members and friends their expanded options as city residents, voters, high-school graduates, industrial workers, and businesspersons. Without these meaningful family bonds and friendships, return visits to migrants' places of origin would have been impossible. Without question, chain migration networks framed the success of these twentieth-century movements. *See also* Return Migration; State Clubs; Visiting; Primary Documents 10, 42, 61.

Further Reading

Bethel, Elizabeth Rauh. *Promiseland: A Century of Life in a Negro Community.* Philadelphia: Temple University Press, 1981.

Gottlieb, Peter. *Making Their Own Way: Southern Blacks' Migration to Pittsburgh, 1916-30.* Urbana: University of Illinois Press, 1987.

Lewis, Earl. *In Their Own Interests: Race, Class, and Power in Twentieth-Century Norfolk.* Berkeley: University of California Press, 1991.

MacDonald, John S., and Leatrice D. MacDonald. "Chain Migration, Ethnic Neighborhood Formation, and Social Networks." *Millbank Memorial Fund* 42 (1964): 82-97.

Marks, Carole. *Farewell—We're Good and Gone: The Great Black Migration.* Bloomington: Indiana University Press, 1989.

Phillips, Kimberley L. *AlabamaNorth: African-American Migrants, Community, and Working-Class Activism in Cleveland, 1915–45*. Urbana: University of Illinois Press, 1999.

Bernadette Pruitt

Charlotte, North Carolina

During the era of the Great Migration, as thousands of African Americans abandoned the rural areas and small towns of the Carolina Piedmont, the attraction of better opportunities brought large numbers to Charlotte, and although many stayed, others moved on to urban centers in the Northeast and Midwest, largely pulled away by the lure of better job opportunities and the hope of escaping the legal persecution of **Jim Crow** laws. Although many factors influenced individual choices to move during the Great Migration, for black Charlotteans, Jim Crow laws were undoubtedly a highly significant, if not the most important, factor. After the introduction of Jim Crow laws during the 1890s, African Americans were legally deprived of many economic, political, and social rights, and all black Charlotteans were relegated to an official second-class status.

Before the 1890s African American **housing** in Charlotte was mixed among a variety of small or interracial neighborhoods, but with the introduction of Jim Crow laws and segregation, blacks were forced increasingly into a patchwork of well-defined neighborhoods, including Biddleville, Blandville, Brooklyn, Cherry, Greenville, Washington Heights, and the First and Third wards.

Although Jim Crow laws and practices severely restricted the lives of African Americans living in Charlotte, those living in the surrounding rural areas of the Piedmont suffered far more. In the sea of black poverty covering the Carolina Piedmont, Charlotte served as the center of black economic activity, and the city developed a growing African American middle class. One of the ironies of Jim Crow segregation was that blacks increasingly patronized black-owned businesses instead of patronizing those owned by whites, and the number of black-owned businesses in Charlotte increased steadily during the first half of the twentieth century. These businesses were especially centered in Brooklyn, the black business district just off the downtown area. In addition to better economic opportunities than their rural counterparts, members of Charlotte's African American community also enjoyed better social and educational opportunities, with the community's crown jewel being Biddle University (changed to Johnson C. Smith University in 1923).

With its vibrant black community, Charlotte became a magnet for African Americans from the rural areas and small towns of the Carolinas, but it also developed as a staging area for blacks migrating north. Attracted north by perceived economic opportunities and the hope of escaping the legal restrictions of Jim Crow, many migrants maintained contact with friends and relatives left behind. Thus tales of opportunities were repeated, and a steady migration of African Americans continued out of Charlotte.

Although Charlotte's black population grew throughout the twentieth century, as a percentage of the total population in comparison with whites, it actually decreased during the first decades of the Great Migration in the 1910s and 1920s. In 1900, 7,000 African Americans were 40 percent of the city's population. By 1920, the population had doubled, but it was just 30 percent of the population. Although the population continued to swell throughout the period of the Great Migration, reaching 75,000 in 1970, it still hovered at just below 30 percent of the city's population.

The **civil rights movement** of the 1950s and 1960s terminated the legal restrictions of Jim Crow laws, eliminating one of the primary forces that pushed black Charlotteans north. The movement in Charlotte was led primarily by activists from Johnson C. Smith University and the local **National Association for the Advancement of Colored People** branch, with Reginald Hawkins and Kelly Alexander, Sr., being the two most prominent leaders. Unlike some southern cities, most notably Little Rock and Montgomery, Charlotte's reaction to the civil rights movement was relatively nonviolent. Much of the white political and economic leadership was open to civil rights advances and racial harmony, probably more for economic reasons than because of social justice.

During the last half of the twentieth century economic opportunities, as well as social and political conditions, improved progressively for African Americans in Charlotte. Lacking the racist stigma that characterized other southern cities during the civil rights era, Charlotte became an even stronger magnet for blacks moving from the rural areas of the Carolinas, as well as those migrating back to the South, especially from northeastern and midwestern urban areas. *See also* Cotton Belt; Durham, North Carolina; Low Country South Carolina and Georgia; Return Migration.

Further Reading

Greenwood, Janette Thomas. *Bittersweet Legacy: The Black and White "Better Classes" in Charlotte, 1850-1910*. Chapel Hill: University of North Carolina Press, 1994.

Hanchett, Thomas W. *Sorting Out the New South City: Race, Class, and Urban Development in Charlotte, 1875-1975*. Chapel Hill: University of North Carolina Press, 1998.

Stephen H. Dew

Chess Records

For more than two decades **Chicago**-based Chess Records was the premier producer of **blues** music in America. Although the company also enjoyed considerable success with **jazz**, gospel, and even comedy records, blues was the musical mainstay of Chess Records from its formation in 1950 until its demise in the early 1970s. Its roster of recording artists contained a veritable who's who of blues legends, including **Muddy Waters**, Howlin' Wolf, Willie Dixon, Little Walter, Sonny Boy Williamson, Buddy Guy, and John Lee Hooker. Chess also helped usher in the rock-and-roll era with its discovery of rock pioneers Chuck Berry and Bo Diddley. As guitarist Buddy Guy put it, "The blues is at the heart of popular music, and Chess Records was at the very heart of the blues" (Collis, 7).

The company was the product of two Jewish immigrants, Leonard and Phil Chess. Born Lejzor and Fiszel Czyz in Poland, the brothers came to Chicago in 1928, where their father had arrived years earlier. During the 1940s Leonard, the elder brother, went into business in the city's South Side, an area that contained most of Chicago's burgeoning community of African American migrants from the South. After Phil's return from the army, the Chess brothers initially operated a liquor store, then opened a small club on South Cottage Grove Avenue, the Macomba Lounge. Leonard had a knack for identifying musical talent that would draw an audience, as well as the respect of other musicians. Soon the lively jazz music at the Macomba Lounge had become a popular South Side draw. Seeking ways in which to further capitalize on the South Side's vibrant music scene, in 1947 Leonard joined the sales staff of a small Chicago recording company, Aristocrat Records. Within three years he bought out his partners, brought Phil into the business, and renamed the company. Chess Records was born.

Although the Chess brothers recorded a variety of musical artists and styles, blues quickly became the bread and butter of their company. The genre was well established in Chicago by the postwar years, introduced to the city by thousands of African American musicians who joined the migration of southern blacks from the **Mississippi Delta**. But the acoustic blues tradition of the Delta was transformed in the bustle of Chicago, gaining drums, a livelier beat, and electric amplification, a sound personified by such classic Chess recordings as Little Walter's bouncing "Juke" and the driving beat of Muddy Waters's "Hoochie-Coochie Man."

Chess Records found its primary customer base in the black communities of such northern urban centers as Chicago and **Detroit**. But the South also played an important part in the Chess brothers' success. Most of the company's blues artists were native southerners (Waters, Bo Diddley, Howlin' Wolf, and Willie Dixon were born in Mississippi; Little Walter hailed from Louisiana; Chuck Berry was from Missouri); and **Memphis**, **New Orleans**, Shreveport, and **Atlanta** remained key markets for Chess recordings. And while few Chess artists found success among white listeners in America, they were eagerly embraced by a generation of young, white musicians in England in the late 1950s and early 1960s, providing the inspiration (and a sizable part of the repertoire) of bands like the Rolling Stones, the Yardbirds, and other pioneering English rock-and-roll bands.

The 1960s brought changes to Chess Records. While the company continued to issue blues recordings, it branched into other musical avenues as well, enjoying success with jazz artists such as Etta James and Ramsey Lewis, as well as experimental, psychedelic albums by Rotary Connection (a project championed by Leonard's son Marshall). The end of the decade marked the decline of Chess Records. Leonard Chess, the driving force behind the company, died in 1969. Earlier that year the brothers sold the company to California-based General Recorded Tape (GRT), a move that hastened the demise of Chess Records, both economically and artistically. A struggling GRT sold the Chess master recordings in 1975, and after several changes of ownership, they were eventually acquired by MCA, which commenced an ambitious and well-received reissue program in the 1990s. The surviving catalog is an enduring testimony to the partnership between the Jewish immigrants and southern migrants that made Chess Records an icon of American popular music. *See also* Dance Halls and Nightclubs; Recording Industry.

Further Reading

Cohen, Rich. *Machers and Rockers: Chess Records and the Business of Rock & Roll.* New York: W. W. Norton and Company, 2004.

Cohodas, Nadine. *Spinning Blues into Gold: The Chess Brothers and the Legendary Chess Records.* New York: St. Martin's Press, 2000.

Collis, John. *The Story of Chess Records.* London: Bloomsbury, 1998.

Tom Downey

Chicago, Illinois

No city was more central to the twentieth-century flow of African Americans from the South than Chicago, Illinois. In 1910, before the onset of the first wave of the Great Migration, fewer than 50,000 blacks lived in Chicago, roughly 2 percent of the city's population. Sixty years later a million blacks, most of whom were born in the South, resided there, nearly one-third of the total population. By 1970 more blacks called Chicago home than the state of Mississippi, a fact that dramatically illustrates its importance to the southern exodus.

First Wave

The spectacular growth of Chicago in the late nineteenth and early twentieth centuries set the stage for the city's leading role in the Great Migration. The nation's second-largest city, Chicago was a transportation and commercial hub and a manufacturing giant. Its factories and plants had an almost insatiable appetite for labor. Not long after the onset of hostilities in Europe in 1914 halted the influx of immigrant laborers, Chicago's packinghouses, steel mills, and foundries actively sought southern black workers.

The job opportunities in Chicago were decisive in making the city a primary destination for African American migrants, who faced discrimination, violence, and declining prospects in agriculture in the **Jim Crow** South. The migrants largely bypassed cities like Peoria, Illinois, whose major industries did not hire black workers. By taking a job in Chicago's packinghouses, for example, an African American could earn much more than was possible as a southern farm worker (see **Packinghouse Workers and Unions**).

The arrival of between 50,000 and 70,000 black migrants in Chicago between 1916 and 1919 was, however, more than an economic imperative. Southern blacks decided to leave their homes. They longed for better conditions and better prospects. They also decided where to go. They had choices, and many chose Chicago.

Chicago was especially appealing to African Americans in Louisiana, Tennessee, Alabama, and, above all, Mississippi. The Illinois Central Railroad line ran directly from Chicago to **New Orleans**, helping connect the midwestern metropolis to a broad southern hinterland. And the ***Chicago Defender***, a vigorous advocate of the southern exodus and widely circulated in the South, helped link the Windy City with "the land of hope" in the minds of many black southerners.

It is not easy to draw a profile of the typical migrant. A large percentage of migrants were single, young men, but **women** and married couples represented a significant portion too. A substantial number came directly from the rural South, but many left from that region's towns and cities. Some had existing contacts in Chicago; others became the front edge of a network that drew family members, acquaintances, and, ultimately, whole communities. Some southern black **ministers** left for Chicago because that was where their congregations now resided (see **Chain Migration**).

The influx of black migrants transformed black Chicago from a modest-sized enclave into one of the centers of African American life in the country. By 1920 over 100,000 blacks lived in Chicago, most of whom resided in a narrow band on the city's South Side running from Thirty-first to Fifty-fifth streets. On major thoroughfares in this district, blacks far outnumbered whites on the streets, and buildings housed black businesses and organizations. Black Chicago had become a city within a city.

The newcomers found themselves in an unfamiliar urban, industrial world. Though generally restricted to the least desirable work, many migrants—male and female—toiled in processing and manufacturing jobs, the heart of the city's economic life. They were a vital part of a growing black urban working class. Moreover, because of **housing** discrimination, they were packed together and not located near the city's plants and factories. They endured high rents and overcrowding as apartments and tenements were subdivided into smaller units, many of which were known as kitchenettes.

More established black residents could not ignore the changing composition of their community. Some were alarmed by the appearance and manners of the southern migrants, and they did not keep their opinions to themselves. Most black Chicagoans, however, followed the lead of the *Chicago Defender* and lent a supportive hand to the newcomers. The Chicago Urban League was established in 1916 in large part to help migrants adapt to northern big-city life.

Before the Great Migration Chicago's blacks did not face the overt discrimination that southern blacks did. They were not relegated to the back of streetcars, excluded from juries, or prohibited from voting. The newcomers valued the greater freedom in their new city, but they quickly learned that it was also a place of deep prejudice.

The influx of African American migrants triggered even more competition between blacks and whites for housing, jobs, and other treasured resources. Whites in neighborhoods adjacent to the growing Black Belt sought to keep out blacks by the use of **restrictive covenants** and physical intimidation, including bombings of the residences of black pioneers. In the packinghouses and other industries whites viewed blacks suspiciously as rivals for jobs and as enemies of unions.

The rising tensions exploded in late July 1919 in the **Chicago race riot** when a black teenager drowned in Lake Michigan after whites had thrown rocks at him and four friends while their raft drifted near a beach claimed by whites. For the next five days blacks and whites battled one another. When the rioting finally ended, twenty-three blacks and fifteen whites had been killed, and millions of dollars of property had been damaged.

The rioting alarmed black and white leaders, who were determined to prevent another cataclysm. But despite the deep hostility of whites, black Chicagoans, many of whom were newcomers, knew that this upheaval differed from racial outbursts in the South. In Chicago blacks squared off directly against whites. They held their ground in a way almost unimaginable in the Jim Crow South.

The downturn in Chicago's economy after World War I curbed the influx of black southerners for a time, but by 1921 the migration had resumed with great velocity. Nearly 100,000 newcomers arrived in Chicago over the next decade, and by 1930 more than 225,000 African Americans lived in the city.

Nearly all the city's blacks lived in the expanding South Side Black Belt, which was the nation's largest contiguous area of black settlement. The growing, concentrated population, in a time of relative prosperity and optimism, fueled political and cultural ambitions. In 1928 black voters propelled **Oscar DePriest**, a Republican and a native of Alabama, to the U.S. Congress, making him the first African American ever elected to a national office outside the South. Across the South Side black performers gathered in popular venues and developed a Chicago sound to the **blues** and **jazz** music that had followed the migrants. **William Lee "Big Bill" Broonzy** and later **Muddy Waters** of Mississippi gave blues a faster, louder, urban flavor after they moved to Chicago, while **Ferdinand "Jelly Roll" Morton** and **Louis Armstrong** were among those southern black artists who revolutionized jazz while they were in Chicago. At the same time, **Thomas Dorsey** (born in Georgia) and **Mahalia Jackson** (born in New Orleans) pioneered African American gospel music. African American writers like **Richard Nathaniel Wright**, who hailed from Mississippi, and artists like **Archibald Motley, Jr.**, born in New Orleans, helped inspire the **Chicago Renaissance**.

Second Wave

The Great Depression halted the flow of southern black migrants northward as northern factories shed jobs and long lines formed at soup kitchens. The population of black Chicago grew only slightly during the 1930s, but a combination of the growing mechanization of cotton production that displaced hundreds of thousands of black workers and the growing need for industrial labor triggered a second, even larger wave of black migration from the South to Chicago.

Far less is known about this wave—despite its dimensions and importance—than about the first. Historians have only begun to capture its dynamics, though social scientists have investigated a number of its consequences. In *The Promised Land* Nicholas Lemann did more than anyone else to stress the significance of this second wave and to offer a striking, though controversial, framework for understanding it, while at the same time featuring intimate stories of the experiences of migrants heading to Chicago.

From 1940 to 1970, hundreds of thousands of black southerners moved to Chicago, perhaps three times as many as those who were transplanted during

A street in the African American section of Chicago, 1941. Courtesy of the Library of Congress.

the original Great Migration. The networks of the second wave built upon the tracks of the first. Once again, the lower Mississippi River valley sent the most migrants to Chicago. These newcomers had the advantage of already knowing relatives or friends in the midwestern metropolis. Interstate buses and cars were, however, as likely to transport the newcomers as trains. It is difficult to generalize, but it appears that these new migrants, while optimistic about starting new lives, were more aware of the difficulties that African Americans faced in Chicago than the migrants of an earlier generation.

World War II was decisive in igniting the new exodus. Roughly 60,000 black migrants arrived in Chicago from 1940 to 1944. The wartime labor shortage meant that jobs were widely available. Because of the progressive and inclusive orientation of the **Congress of Industrial Organizations**, these newcomers, unlike their counterparts two decades earlier, became more integrated into the world of labor unions. Southern blacks continued to head to Chicago in large numbers for the next twenty-five years. To a greater extent than in the first wave, many of these migrants could be classified as displaced persons because of the dramatic collapse of the agricultural labor market in the South.

The sheer number of black migrants after 1940 helped reconfigure the social geography of the city. While many settled on the established and ever-expanding South Side, others flowed into the growing West Side ghetto. The West Side had been home to roughly 25,000 blacks until 1940, but as Jews and other European ethnic groups left their original settlements for better housing elsewhere, eager black migrants, facing a housing squeeze, packed into the available housing in East Garfield Park, North Lawndale, and Near West Side. By 1960 the West Side was home to more than 200,000 African Americans.

In the 1940s and 1950s, Forty-seventh Street and South Park (now **Martin Luther King, Jr.**, Drive) was the heart of Bronzeville, as the South Side Black Belt came to be known. Here black migrants encountered a whirl of activity as black Chicagoans shopped, dined, and enjoyed a vibrant nightlife. As the number of blacks grew, the Black Belt gradually expanded farther west and south. More affluent African Americans settled in communities like Chatham, which exemplified the rising role of social class in spatial distribution in black Chicago.

The growing concentration of people and wealth ensured that the South Side was home to some of the nation's most important black-owned businesses and institutions. The Olivet Baptist Church was reputed to be the largest black congregation in the country, and its minister, the Reverend **Joseph H. Jackson**, a Mississippi native, was one of the most influential black Americans in the country. The size of black Chicago was one reason **Elijah Muhammad** moved from **Detroit** in the early 1930s. During the postwar era Chicago became a center of **black nationalism**, and Muhammad's **Nation of Islam** attracted a number of black migrants.

White hostility toward black neighbors had turned Chicago into an intensely segregated city in the early twentieth century, but the second wave of black migrants gave rise to much larger **ghettos** maintained by the racism of white residents and the policies of local, state, and federal governments. Black newcomers as well as native black Chicagoans were excluded from the proliferating postwar suburban housing, and many found themselves living in high-rise **public housing** projects stacked within the confines of the ghetto. If blacks sought to live in white neighborhoods in the city or suburbs, they often faced white violence. And the changing neighborhoods on the edges of the expanding black ghettos witnessed ongoing white resistance.

There has been a lively debate about how the new wave of black migrants fared in their new city. In *The Promised Land* Lemann argued provocatively that many migrants brought with them a culture of poverty from the rural South that expressed itself in high levels of out-of-wedlock births, dependency on welfare, and stunted lives. Other scholars, with more empirical evidence, contended that migrants were less likely to be on welfare and in poverty than northern-born blacks. The difficulties that migrants faced, then, were due to their new setting and not their cultural background.

By the early 1960s it was becoming more difficult to extol Chicago as a "City of Progress and Opportunity," as black business executive A. L. Foster had in 1957. The big public housing projects like the Robert Taylor Homes, hailed by its first residents, had become increasingly warehouses of human misery. The low-skill and semiskilled manufacturing jobs that had done much to lure black migrants and raise their standard of living were no longer plentiful. Conditions in the inner city were more grating than ever. That Chicago blacks erupted in two outbursts, one in 1966 and a larger one in 1968 on the West Side, signaled the mounting dissatisfaction. That these uprisings did not bring blacks face-to-face with whites, as in 1919, was a clear sign of how separate the lives of most blacks and whites were in one of the most segregated cities in the country.

In the aftermath of the murder of a young black teenager, Emmett Till, who was visiting relatives in Money, Mississippi, in 1955, black Chicagoans showed their determination to fight violence and discrimination in that state. A decade later Chicago civil rights activists had to turn to a southern organization, Martin Luther King, Jr.,'s Southern Christian Leadership Conference (SCLC), to come north to help combat segregation and discrimination in their city. SCLC concentrated its operations on the city's West Side in part because it felt that this newer region of black settlement, packed with recent migrants from Mississippi, Alabama, and other southern states, would be more receptive to a southern-style movement. The West Side was, according to James Bevel, the head of the SCLC field staff in Chicago and a native of Mississippi, "very much Mississippi in terms of the ethos of the black people" (Ralph, 49). The Chicago Freedom Movement represented a dramatic reversal of the perception of the site of the nation's worst racial problems (see **Open Housing**).

Legacy

After 1970 the confluence of factors that had initiated and sustained the flow of southern migrants to Chicago had dissipated. In fact, more blacks began to leave Chicago than migrated to it. In recent years the South has become a receiving region of blacks from Chicago rather than a sending zone. The dynamics of this **return migration** have yet to be fully studied, but some of the migrants from Chicago followed the networks that had connected black Chicago to communities throughout the South ever since the eruption of the Great Migration. Nearly 60,000 more African Americans left metropolitan Chicago than entered it between 1995 and 2000, but it is still too early to tell if this exodus constitutes a new third wave in the story of black migration and Chicago.

For the past eighty years, because of the Great Migration, Chicago has been home to the country's second-largest black population. Roughly 40 percent of the residents of the city are of African descent. With enterprises like **Johnson Publishing Company**, the publisher of *Ebony* magazine, whose founder moved to Chicago from Arkansas in 1933, Chicago is one of the capitals of black business in the United States. Rainbow/PUSH Coalition is one of the most important activist groups in the country, and its founder and leader Jesse Jackson came to Chicago from the South in 1965. The city is known as a center for African American music, arts, and literature, and this creativity has shaped the broader culture of Chicago, the United States, and even the world. *See also* American Negro Exposition (1940); *Black Metropolis* (Drake and Cayton); Chicago Commission on Race Relations; Midwestern States, Black Migration to; Primary Documents 1, 8, 9, 10, 42, 50, 52.

Further Reading

Black, Timuel D., Jr. *Bridges of Memory: Chicago's First Wave of Black Migration*. Evanston, IL: Northwestern University Press, 2003.

Chicago Jazz Archive. Research Resources on Chicago and the Great Migration. Regenstein Library, University of Chicago. www.lib.uchicago.edu/e/su/cja/greatmigration.html.

Drake, St. Clair, and Horace Cayton. *Black Metropolis: A Study of Negro Life in a Northern City*. New York: Harcourt, Brace and World, 1970.

Grossman, James R. *Land of Hope: Chicago, Black Southerners, and the Great Migration*. Chicago: University of Chicago Press, 1989.

Hirsch, Arnold R. *Making the Second Ghetto: Race and Housing in Chicago, 1940–1960*. New York: Cambridge University Press, 1983.

King, George. *Goin' to Chicago*. San Francisco: California Newsreel, 1994. Videocassette.

Lemann, Nicholas. *The Promised Land: The Great Black Migration and How It Changed America*. New York: Knopf, 1991.

Ralph, James R., Jr. *Northern Protest: Martin Luther King, Jr., Chicago, and the Civil Rights Movement*. Cambridge, MA: Harvard University Press, 1993.

Spear, Allan H. *Black Chicago: The Making of a Negro Ghetto*. Chicago: University of Chicago Press, 1967.

Tuttle, William M., Jr. *Race Riot: Chicago in the Red Summer of 1919*. New York: Atheneum, 1970.

James Ralph

Chicago Commission on Race Relations

The Chicago Commission on Race Relations was appointed by Illinois governor Frank Lowden to investigate the causes of the **Chicago race riot of 1919** and recommend ways to avoid further outbreaks of violence. Consisting of an equal number of African Americans and whites, all of whom were well known as moderates on racial issues, the twelve-person commission published its findings in the 1922 volume *The Negro in Chicago: A Study of Race Relations and a Race Riot*. This study focused on how mass migration of African Americans from the South during World War I and afterward impacted living and working conditions of blacks in **Chicago** and also contributed to racial tensions in the city.

In its report the commission stated that while the act that precipitated the riot was the drowning of an African American youth at a bathing beach, much of the violence occurred elsewhere in the African American neighborhoods. The major participants were white gangs, such as Ragen's Colts, that vandalized homes in African American neighborhoods and attacked blacks traveling in and out of their neighborhoods. According to the commission, African Americans were targeted by Democratic politicians who opposed Mayor William Thompson and believed that blacks made the critical difference in Thompson's election. White residents who opposed African Americans moving into their neighborhoods also joined in the violence.

To understand the racial tensions in Chicago that led to the riot, the commission examined the changes in social and living conditions caused by the expansion of the African American population during World War I. It found that blacks in Chicago faced discrimination in **employment** and **housing**. Surveys of African American neighborhoods on the South and West sides showed that many blacks were paying exorbitant rents for substandard housing with dilapidated roofing and walls, poor ventilation, faulty plumbing, and overcrowding. Hostile actions from residents and real estate boards in adjacent white neighborhoods discouraged many African Americans, and most remained within fixed residential sections while the black population doubled. Researchers from the commission investigated working conditions in the retail and manufacturing sectors and found that most African Americans were employed at lower wages than whites and were often passed over for promotion. They worked the least desirable jobs and had the least job security, with white workers returning from the war usually taking over.

Researchers observed that despite the hardships experienced by African Americans in the North, blacks found their new situation preferable to what they had left behind in the **Jim Crow** South. For this reason, migrants were unlikely to return to the South, and migration surely would continue. The commission recommended that to reduce racial tension and avoid further violence, moderates in the white and black communities actively keep the peace between the races. Through the use of the press, civic organizations, and churches, moderates could promote understanding and cooperation among whites and African Americans.

Perhaps because of its moderate tone, the commission's report was largely praised, particularly in the local press. In the subsequent decades of the 1920s and 1930s there was no repeat of the 1919 riot. During this same time, however, the racial inequities described by the commission persisted, while migration of African Americans to the North continued. *See also* Chicago School of Sociology (CSS); Johnson, Charles Spurgeon; Red Summer of 1919.

Further Reading

Chicago Commission on Race Relations. *The Negro in Chicago: A Study of Race Relations and a Race Riot*. Chicago: University of Chicago Press, 1922.

Tuttle, William M., Jr. *Race Riot: Chicago in the Red Summer of 1919*. New York: Atheneum, 1970.

Waskow, Arthur I. *From Race Riot to Sit-In, 1919 and the 1960s: A Study in the Connections between Conflict and Violence*. Garden City, NY: Doubleday, 1966.

Gareth Canaan

Chicago Defender

The first 300 copies of **Robert S. Abbott**'s *Chicago Defender* unceremoniously hit the streets in May 1905. By 1909 the little paper that started out as an unimpressive, four-page, handbill-sized newssheet evolved into the popular paper of choice among black Chicagoans. By 1916 it had become the largest-selling black newspaper in the United States. Weekly circulation during this period has been estimated to be as high as 250,000 a week, with the large majority of the copies distributed south of the Mason-Dixon Line.

While these circulation figures are impressive in their own right, they do not account for the two informal modes of paper circulation—borrowing and communal reading. The *Chicago Defender* was often shared among family members, friends, church congregations, and even members of other communities who could not afford or procure their own copies. The masses of illiterate black southerners who dreamed of a better life in the North often gathered at local churches, barbershops, and saloons to listen to communal readings of the paper. The communal interaction was so predominant during the years of the Great Migration that John H. H. Sengstacke, Abbott's nephew and chief editor of the *Defender* from 1940 until his death in 1997, estimated that for every one *Defender* purchased, five to seven others were either read or heard aloud.

With its sensationalistic and crusading editorial policy, the paper quickly gained the reputation of being the most radical and race-conscious black newspaper in America. The *Defender* regularly reported and editorialized about southern white-on-black **crimes** and called for open retaliation from its readers. It was the paper's unflinching call for northern migration out of the "Racist and Curupt South," however, that gained the most national attention during this period (December 2, 1916).

The publication and circulation of such inflammatory rhetoric created a panic that reverberated throughout white southern communities. This anxiety was especially felt by white southerners who had grown accustomed to

A newsboy peddles the latest edition of the *Chicago Defender*, 1942. Courtesy of the Library of Congress.

cheap African American labor. In almost every state in the Deep South, the *Defender* generated severe white reaction. Whites attacked and killed two *Defender* distributors in Alabama. An Arkansas judge issued an injunction restraining its circulation in two counties. The governor of Georgia asked the postmaster to exclude the paper from the mail.

These efforts, however, were in vain. The paper, until the summer of 1919, continued to make its impassioned call to the millions of southern blacks suffering from the failures of Radical Reconstruction. This migration campaign may be best understood in three stages.

The first stage of the *Chicago Defender*'s campaign began in 1915 and employed editorials, cover stories, political cartoons, poems, pictures, and investigative reports to highlight the oppressive moral situation in the South. While southern blacks did not need the *Defender* to make them aware of their conspicuous lack of empowerment, the paper's coverage went beyond creating awareness. According to Metz Lochard, a lifelong friend of Abbott, the *Defender* "dared to articulate in print what southern Negroes were afraid to whisper. It gave them courage to acknowledge their dissatisfaction" (Lochard, 125). In issue after issue, patrons read of the systemic racism throughout the South: "Boy Lynched by Mob for Stealing Cow That Returned Later" (January 30, 1915); "Twenty-Thousand Southerners Burn Boy at Stake" (May 19, 1916); and "Sheriff Delivers Live Prisoners to Mob" (January 29, 1916).

In juxtaposition to the oppressive South portrayed in the first stage, the *Defender*'s second stage featured the North as a "land of hope," a place where all the promises of the American Dream waited to be taken. Just as systematically as it detailed the dangers of the South, the paper informed readers that **Chicago** offered them work, freedom, voting rights, new time-saving devices, luxury items, and a nightlife unimagined in Dixie.

Stage three of the *Defender*'s migration campaign began in the summer of 1916, as an increasing number of articles began to overtly encourage a southern exodus away from the oppressive South of stage one and toward the promised land of stage two. By September of that same year this encouragement had evolved into a full-blown crusade. Black southerners read of the thousands who had already said, "Farewell to the South" (January 6, 1917), or of the "2 Million Needed" (October 4, 1916) to work in America's second-largest city. They memorized Ward's poem "Bound for the Promised Land," sang William Crosse's inspirational words to "The Land of Hope," and laughed at Fon Holly's political cartoons "Desertion" and "The Awakening" (September 2, 1916, and August 19, 1916).

In the spring of 1919, however, the *Defender* began devoting less space to the migration campaign. The "Promised Land" of Chicago was undergoing a metamorphosis. This transformation was brought about by a number of related events that seemed to have an intensifying effect on one another. Most notably, the war in Europe had ended. Thousands of white solders returned home to Chicago to find that the jobs, communities, and lifestyles they had left behind had been appropriated by thousands of American American migrants.

This tension ultimately led to the five-day **Chicago race riot of 1919** in July of that year—an event that forever changed the tenor of the *Defender*'s migration discourse. The bold headlines of the paper's August 2, 1919, issue summarized the situation for patrons in the South waiting their turn: "Riot Sweeps Chicago," "Ghastly Deeds on Race Rioters Told," and "Gun Battles and Fighting in Streets Keep the City in an Uproar." When the dust settled, 23 blacks lay dead, with at least 537 others wounded. All calls for southern migration ceased after the racial violence in Chicago and elsewhere during what **James Weldon Johnson** called the **Red Summer of 1919**. Abbott could no longer promise his readers a better life in his once-beloved city of Chicago. While the paper has continued to remain on the front line in the battle for racial justice, the Great Migration campaign of 1915 to 1919 is generally acknowledged as the watershed event that defined the paper's mission and assured its place in American history. *See also* Black Press; *Pittsburgh Courier*; Simmons, Roscoe Conkling; Primary Documents 7, 11, 65.

Further Reading

DeSantis, Alan D. "Selling the American Dream Myth to Black Southerners: The *Chicago Defender* and the Great Migration of 1915–1919." *Western Journal of Communication* 62, no. 4 (1998): 474–511.

Drake, St. Clair, and Horace R. Cayton. *Black Metropolis: A Study of Negro Life in a Northern City.* New York: Harcourt, Brace and Company, 1945.

Grossman, James R. *Land of Hope: Chicago, Black Southerners, and the Great Migration.* Chicago: University of Chicago Press, 1989.

Lochard, Metz T. P. "*Phylon* Profile XII: Robert S. Abbott—'Race Leader.' " *Phylon* 8 (1947): 124–32.

Ottley, Roi. *The Lonely Warrior: The Life and Times of Robert S. Abbott*. Chicago: Henry Regnery Co., 1955.

Ross, Felicia G. Jones, and Joseph P. McKerns. "Depression in 'The Promised Land': The *Chicago Defender* Discourages Migration, 1929–1940." *American Journalism* 21, no. 1 (2004): 55–73.

Alan D. DeSantis

Chicago Race Riot of 1919

On July 27, 1919, a racial altercation at a beach in **Chicago** that resulted in the death of a fourteen-year-old black youth provided the spark that ignited a murderous race war. In five days of pitched battles, 38 were killed, including 23 blacks and 15 whites, and considerably more than 500 of both races were injured. The Chicago race riot was the bloodiest urban riot of the **Red Summer of 1919**.

During World War I, for countless African Americans living in the South, Chicago represented "the top of the world." It was Chicago, renowned among blacks and whites alike for its World Columbian Exposition of 1893 and famous for its mail-order houses, mass-production industries, and vast **railroad** network, that made the city "the most accessible destination for numerous blacks" in the South (Tuttle, 85). In addition, black men in Chicago could vote, and black families could send their children to schools that were vastly superior to their counterparts in the South. To southern blacks, Chicago was not only a city, it was a state of mind. It was "the Promised Land."

During World War I Chicago teemed with jobs. Not only was employment in industry plentiful, but wages were relatively high, especially in slaughtering and meatpacking, iron and steel forging, electrical machinery, and machine-shop products. "The packing houses in Chicago for a while seemed to be everything," an African American man from Mississippi recalled; "...you could not rest in your bed at night for Chicago" (Tuttle, 84). Perhaps the most effective institution in stimulating the migration was the *Chicago Defender*, which was vehement in its denunciations of the southern treatment of southern blacks, as well as its emphasis on pride in race. The newspaper's circulation increased tenfold between 1916 and 1918. "Millions to Leave South" was the *Defender*'s banner headline on January 6, 1917. "Northern Invasion Will Start in the Spring—Bound for the Promised Land" (Tuttle, 91). To the persistent rumor that African Americans would freeze to death in the North, the *Defender* countered that this was "all 'bosh.' IF YOU CAN FREEZE TO DEATH in the north and be free, why FREEZE to death in the south and be a slave" (Tuttle, 92).

Chicago's African American population doubled between 1914 and 1920. Chicago's school census of 1914 counted 54,557 black people; by 1920, according to the federal census, the city's black population had soared to 110,000. Even before the Great Migration Chicago had witnessed growing competition between blacks and whites for jobs and **housing**. Adequate housing, for example, was in short supply, and when black families threatened to move into all-white neighborhoods, white residents responded angrily. "If we can't get them out any other way," one white Chicagoan warned, "we are going to . . . bomb them out." Indeed, bombs did explode: in Chicago in the two-year period from the summer of 1917 to the eruption of the Chicago riot in July 1919, two dozen bombs damaged the homes of blacks and the offices of those realtors who dealt with them.

While jobs in the Chicago stockyards were abundant, black and white workers clashed, sometimes violently, over the wisdom of establishing an industrial union of **packinghouse workers**. When a black worker was verbally assaulted by a union organizer in June 1919, he angrily replied, "No, I would rather quit than join the union." "If you don't join tomorrow, these men won't work with you." "Fuck you." "God damn you." A fight erupted; knives were drawn; and the whites walked out, declaring that they would no longer work with nonunion blacks (Tuttle, 108–9). In Chicago whites and newly arrived blacks confronted each other not only over housing and unions, but also over political power (African Americans tended to vote Republican, while working-class whites tended to vote Democratic), public transportation, schools, parks, and beaches. Moreover, gangs of white youth assaulted blacks in Chicago, and the police, in their dealings with black people, were guilty of harassment, abuse, and outright **police brutality**. As the temperatures in Chicago soared in July 1919, racial tensions threatened to erupt into full-scale rioting. On July 27 the long-dreaded race riot exploded on the streets of Chicago. *See also* Chicago Commission on Race Relations; East St. Louis Race Riot of 1917.

Further Reading

Chicago Commission on Race Relations. *The Negro in Chicago: A Study of Race Relations and a Race Riot in 1919*. 1922. Reprint, New York: Arno Press, 1968.

"The Chicago Race Riot of 1919." Jazz Age Chicago: Urban Leisure, 1893 to 1934. http://chicago.urban-history.org/scrapbks/raceriot/raceriot.htm.

The Killing Floor. Produced and directed by Bill Duke. Orion Home Video, 1985. Videocassette.

Tuttle, William M., Jr. *Race Riot: Chicago in the Red Summer of 1919*. 2nd ed. Urbana: University of Illinois Press, 1996.

White, Walter F. "N.A.A.C.P.—Chicago and Its Eight Reasons." *Crisis* 17 (October 1919): 293–97.

William M. Tuttle, Jr.

Chicago Renaissance

The Chicago Renaissance of African American arts and intellectual production refers to the period between the early 1930s and the late 1940s when black sociologists, philosophers, critics, journalists, novelists, poets, visual artists, civil rights leaders, and politicians flourished in the city's segregated black neighborhoods. The Renaissance—not to be confused with the earlier literary Renaissance dominated by **Chicago**'s white writers and intellectuals—was a vital period in African American cultural and intellectual history, along with the **Harlem Renaissance** of the 1920s, the **Black Arts movement** of the 1960s, and the rise of the **hip-hop** generation in the 1970s.

Scholars who employ the Renaissance as an interpretive device tend to lift Chicago's African American arts and intellectual production of the 1930s and 1940s out of their broader local and national context, while at the same time viewing it separately from Chicago's more established and celebrated **blues** and **jazz** scenes. At its best, however, the notion of a Chicago Renaissance allows us to see the links in the dynamic cultural networks that emerged from the Great Black Migrations. Most Renaissance figures were southern migrants themselves or the children of migrants, and many of the themes they explored were at heart the subjects of migration: migrants' reasons for leaving the South; their travels, arrival, and adjustment in the North; and the effects of migration on African Americans' families, work lives, politics, and culture. The Chicago Renaissance grew out of the depression-era struggle for jobs, **housing**, and racial equality, a struggle most Renaissance figures perceived in terms of the hardships of a transition from rural to urban life.

During the Renaissance black artists and intellectuals drew support from a variety of sources. Organizations such as the University of Chicago, the Julius Rosenwald Fund, the Chicago Urban League, and the Chicago branch of the **National Association for the Advancement of Colored People** and federal government programs, including the Federal Writers' Project, the Federal Theater Project, the **National Youth Administration**, and the **Works Progress Administration** provided crucial income for African Americans who otherwise would have been without resources. Just as important were the enterprises and civic organizations of the Black Metropolis. The *Chicago Defender*, the *Chicago Bee*, and *Negro Story Magazine* all provided outlets for black writers. Black churches and professionals—especially black-owned life insurance and real estate companies—provided entrepreneurial resources. At the same time, the artists' and intellectuals' relationships with grassroots organizers of the **Congress of Industrial Organizations**, the **Brotherhood of Sleeping Car Porters**, the National Negro Congress, the Communist Party, and black politicians added a labor and civil rights flavor to the Renaissance. Finally, **Communist** John Reed Clubs, the South Side Writers' Group, and the South Side Community Arts Center all provided sites for artistic collaboration, as well as audiences for black artists generally excluded from white-owned galleries and media.

In 1986 literary historian Robert Bone invoked the notion of a black Chicago Renaissance in a discussion of the cultural milieu from which novelist **Richard Nathaniel Wright** emerged. Bone highlighted migrants' struggles to find opportunity in their new urban industrial communities. Literary scholar Carla Cappetti expanded on Bone's version of the Renaissance to bring to light the connections between black novelists of the 1930s and 1940s, earlier white Chicago writers, and the **Chicago School of Sociology**. African American studies scholar Craig Hansen Werner has distinguished between the optimism of the 1920s Harlem Renaissance and the Chicago artists' increasing disillusionment with northern urban "promised lands." In the broadest historical view of the Chicago Renaissance, historian Bill V. Mullen argues that the "renaissance" model obscures the diversity of the black South Side's "cultural front." For Mullen, the key point is that the works of the 1930s and 1940s reflected the multiple ideological and political coalitions of the Popular Front era. In this sense, the quintessential Chicago Renaissance event was the **American Negro Exposition** in 1940, the result of cooperation between New Deal politicians, "respectable" black intellectuals, religious leaders, labor unions, civil rights organizations, and intellectuals and artists with Communist or **socialist** backgrounds.

The Renaissance's diverse combination of influences meant that black artists and intellectuals in Chicago during the 1930s and 1940s were especially well prepared to explore the nature of the migration. Chicago School sociologists were intensely interested in the processes of rural-to-urban adjustment, racial contacts, and industrialization. Artists picked up on these sociological themes, dramatizing black southerners' encounter with the North's climate and more subtle but still oppressive race relations. It would be nearly impossible to list all of the individuals who contributed to the Renaissance, but examples of those who directly addressed the migration include **William Attaway**, **Marita Bonner**, Arna Bontemps, **Gwendolyn Brooks**, Margaret Taylor Goss Burroughs, Horace Cayton, Frank Marshall Davis, St. Clair Drake, Katherine Dunham, **E. Franklin Frazier**, **Chester Himes**, **Langston Hughes**, **Jacob Lawrence**, Willard Motley, Margaret Walker, Theodore Ward, Charles White, and Richard Wright.

The Renaissance can safely be said to have ended sometime in the late 1940s when the concentration of black writers and artists decreased, and the anti-Communist politics of the postwar era suppressed prominent work inspired by labor and civil rights struggles. Yet Chicago's postwar arts and intellectual productions were more a continuation of the work of the 1930s than a new development. *See also* Black Consumer Market; *Black Metropolis* (Drake and Cayton); Ellison, Walter; Literature, the Great Migration in; Motley, Archibald J., Jr.; Political Activism (1915–1945); Visual Arts, the Great Migration in.

Further Reading

Bone, Robert. *The Negro Novel in America.* New Haven, CT: Yale University Press, 1958.

———. "Richard Wright and the Chicago Renaissance." *Callaloo* 9, no. 3 (1986): 446–68.

Cappetti, Carla. *Writing Chicago: Modernism, Ethnography, and the Novel.* New York: Columbia University Press, 1993.

Mullen, Bill V. *Popular Fronts: Chicago and African-American Cultural Politics, 1935–46.* Urbana: University of Illinois Press, 1999.

Werner, Craig Hansen. *Playing the Changes: From Afro-Modernism to the Jazz Impulse.* Urbana: University of Illinois Press, 1994.

Jeffrey Helgeson

Chicago School of Sociology (CSS)

In 1892 the University of Chicago created the first sociology department in the United States. The department grew to the height of its influence between the late 1910s and the early 1930s. Since the 1940s sociologists and historians have recognized the Chicago School of Sociology (CSS) as a "school" of sociological thought marked by its empirical and theoretical investigation of rapid urbanization, industrialization, and repeated mass immigrations of racially and ethnically diverse groups into industrial cities. The Chicago School drew on both the empirical work of the Progressive Era social survey movement and German sociological theories of social life in urban settings. The Chicago School's works regarding migrants' adjustment, social organization, urban ecology, and race and ethnic relations shaped how academics, public policy makers, and the broader public understood the perceived problems of black migration. Moreover, CSS models have had unintended consequences as the background for what later came to be seen as neoconservative behavioralist understandings of race, family and community structure, and poverty.

William I. Thomas and Florian Znaniecki's five-volume study of Polish immigrants, *The Polish Peasant in Europe and America* (1918–1920), described the roles of cultural continuity and discontinuity in Polish immigrants' adjustment to cities in the United States, introducing the notion of "social disorganization" as a measure of immigrants' adjustment to their new homes. The causes and criteria of social disorganization have been key points in the debate over the origins of black urban poverty. The political and sociological debate has wavered between a focus on structural conditions—poverty, poor **housing**, and **unemployment**—and a definition that highlights the "pathologies" of single-parent families, juvenile delinquency, and intemperance.

In the 1920s Robert E. Park and Ernest W. Burgess developed and popularized an environmentalist approach to group differences, contradicting what were still dominant biological theories of race and ethnicity. Park also developed a theory of intergroup relations that posited that when different racial or ethnic groups came into contact, they progressed from competition through conflict and accommodation and finally to assimilation. When taken separately from Park's optimistic stages of race relations, the environmentalist perspective has led to controversial arguments that blame black migrants for the disorganization in their "maladjusted" urban communities. Louis Wirth, whose study *The Ghetto* (1928) set the standard for studies of life in segregated, isolated, and underserved urban communities, also helped define the intellectual and popular understandings of the differences between rural and urban life. In his article "Urbanism as a Way of Life" (1938)—a recapitulation of Ferdinand Tonnies's *Community and Society* (*Gemeinschaft und Gesellschaft*, 1887) and Georges Simmel's "Metropolis and Mental Life" (1903) for an American audience—Wirth identified the social psychological challenges of living in cities, defined as large, permanent, dense, diverse, and highly specialized social settlements. The essentialist view of urban life unintentionally reinforced the problematic view of black migrants as backward rural folk.

The Chicago School was also at the center of early efforts to employ empirical research in the construction of public policy. The earliest example was the **Chicago Commission on Race Relations**' massive study of the **Chicago race riot of 1919**, *The Negro in Chicago* (1922), conducted almost single-handedly by black sociologist **Charles S. Johnson** while he was at the University of Chicago. Johnson, who later went on to head Fisk University's sociology department, created the model for evenhanded investigations of racial violence that were especially influential for the "human relations" commissions that flourished in the wake of riots in 1943 and again in the 1960s.

Johnson and other black sociologists, including **E. Franklin Frazier**, St. Clair Drake, and Horace Cayton, all studied and/or worked at the University of Chicago at one time. Frazier's landmark studies *The Negro Family in Chicago* (1932) and *The Negro Family in the United States* (1939), for example, drew on earlier formulations of the immigrant family's experiences and Park's description of the stages of race relations. As historians such as Anthony M. Platt have emphasized, however, these black scholars integrated the Chicago School tradition into their background in an African American intellectual tradition. Black scholars, Platt contends, drew on the previous work of African American intellectual giants **W.E.B. DuBois**, **Carter G. Woodson**, and the many black scholars who worked with Woodson's Association for the Study of Negro Life and History. *See also Black Metropolis* (Drake and Cayton); European Immigration, Comparison with the Great Black Migration; New Negro; Primary Documents 8, 9, 13, 42.

Further Reading

Bulmer, Martin. *The Chicago School of Sociology: Institutionalization, Diversity, and the Rise of Sociological Research.* Chicago: University of Chicago Press, 1984.

Faris, Robert E. L. *Chicago Sociology, 1920–1932.* San Francisco: Chandler Publishing Company, 1967.

Fine, Gary Alan, ed. *A Second Chicago School? The Development of a Postwar American Sociology.* Chicago: University of Chicago Press, 1995.

Frazier, E. Franklin. *The Negro Family in Chicago.* Chicago: University of Chicago Press, 1932.

———. *The Negro Family in the United States.* 2nd ed. New York: Dryden Press, 1948.

Park, Robert E., and Ernest W. Burgess. *The City.* 6th ed. Chicago: University of Chicago Press, 1967.

Platt, Anthony M. *E. Franklin Frazier Reconsidered.* New Brunswick, NJ: Rutgers University Press, 1991.

Wirth, Louis. "Urbanism as a Way of Life." *American Journal of Sociology* 44, no. 1 (July 1938): 1–24.

Jeffrey Helgeson

Childbirth

African American migrant **women** in the urban North chose physician-assisted home or **hospital**-based delivery over the traditional midwife, thereby functioning as agents of change in the movement from social to medical childbirth. In contrast, until 1940 midwives attended more than 75 percent of the births of black women in southern states. By 1935 **physicians** attended 97.9 percent of black births in northern cities, with 61.8 percent of those occurring in a hospital. Women chose physicians in spite of the existence of black midwives and continued beliefs in other **folk medicine** practices. Their experiences differed from those of white women because they were more apt to be used to provide educational experiences for student physicians. Only ward accommodations were available, and mothers rarely shared race with their doctor.

Unlike southern black women, African American migrant women in the urban North received prenatal care, recognized by 1915 as essential in reducing infant mortality rates, and postnatal care from private doctors or privately funded "public health" **nurses** who provided care in neighborhood clinics (often located in **settlement houses**) or in patients' homes. Evidence suggests that prenatal care and medical deliveries reduced the maternal and infant mortality rates among blacks and whites, although black infant mortality rates continued to be 1.5 times higher than white rates for decades.

Local chapters of the **National Urban League**, with the cooperation of black churches, influenced migrants' decisions regarding childbirth. A national organization established during the Progressive Era to aid migrants, the Urban League launched numerous health campaigns. Its national publication, *Opportunity*, included informational articles on preventive health and childbirth.

By the 1950s provision of services in the urban North had changed. Homecare and community-based nursing and medical services, widely used among migrant women, declined because of limited funds, nursing shortages during the war, and changes in hospital hiring practices. Improvements in medical care and the progressive aging of the population forced such agencies to devote more time to care of the chronically ill and elderly. Although publicly funded health agencies, new funding sources, and Medicaid programs tried to make up for the decline in the private agencies, home care never reached the levels seen before World War II. Community-based clinics also declined in number. **Urban renewal**, with its resultant displacement and neighborhood destruction, eliminated doctors' offices, settlement houses, and other clinics, often forcing individuals to move to **public housing** communities and further isolating them from community health services. A 1954 amendment to the Hill-Burton Act of 1946, which granted federal money to states for hospital construction, permitted money to be used for ambulatory care facilities, further reducing the number of community-based clinics. Home physician-attended childbirth delivery services declined in the 1950s because physicians advocated hospital delivery only. By the end of the migration period black northern urban women had their babies in a hospital, assisted by a physician, and received prenatal care in a doctor's office or hospital outpatient facility.

Further Reading

Carson, Carolyn Leonard. "And the Results Showed Promise . . .: Physicians, Childbirth, and Southern Black Migrant Women, 1916-1939; Pittsburgh as a Case Study." *Journal of American Ethnic History* 14 (Fall 1994): 32-64.

Frankel, Barbara. *Childbirth in the Ghetto: Folk Beliefs of Negro Women in a North Philadelphia Hospital Ward*. San Francisco: R and E Research Associates, 1977.

Smith, Susan L. *Sick and Tired of Being Sick and Tired: Black Women's Health Activism in America, 1890-1950*. Philadelphia: University of Pennsylvania Press, 1995.

Carolyn Leonard Carson

Church of God in Christ (COGIC)

The Great Migration was a significant time for the growth of black **Pentecostalism** in northern cities. During these years the Church of God in Christ (COGIC) in particular expanded enormously in the Midwest and the eastern regions of the United States. Bishop C. H. Mason, its founder, sent several **ministers** and **women** into northern cities in order to gain new members and establish churches. Through its spread in northern cities, the Church of God in Christ became a powerful black Pentecostal denomination in America. In **New York City**, **Philadelphia**, **Detroit**, **Los Angeles**, and **Chicago** the larger black Pentecostal groups thrived.

The oldest and largest black Pentecostal body in the United States, the Church of God in Christ (COGIC) existed before the dawning of the Pentecostal movement. The COGIC was part of the **Baptist** Holiness reform movement in the **Mississippi Delta** during the late nineteenth century. This interracial, working-class movement rejected the historic Baptist churches and their middle-class pretensions. The Church of God in Christ is firmly rooted in this nineteenth-century Holiness tradition, and its immersion in this tradition characterizes its spirituality and ethos even though it is now a part of the Pentecostal tradition.

In 1897, after being excommunicated from the Baptist Church, Charles Harrison Mason established a new church in Lexington, Mississippi, that embraced his Holiness beliefs. Mason held his services in an old abandoned gin house. This gin house became the founding meeting place for the future Church of God in Christ, the "mother church" of the denomination.

People filled the little gin house. Mason wanted to provide a name for the church and asked God for a name that distinguished it from other bodies with similar names. As he was walking down a street in Little Rock, Arkansas, Mason said that God spoke to him and gave him the name "Church of God in Christ." Mason found justification for this name in I Thessalonians 2:14, which states, "For ye brethern became followers of the Churches of God which in Judea are in Christ Jesus: for ye have suffered like things of your own countrymen even as they have of the Jews." Mason shared his revelation with the church, and the men of the church unanimously voted to adopt the name. The church thereafter was known as St. Paul Church of God in Christ. Mason also realized that he must have the church recognized as a legitimate body and in 1897 had the new church chartered as a Holiness denomination in **Memphis**. The Church of God in Christ became the first Southern Holiness denomination to legally chartered. In 1907, after a trip to the Azusa Street Revival in Los Angeles, California, Mason rechartered the Church of God in Christ as a Pentecostal denomination. Mason's conversion to Pentecostalism made him pivotal in spreading Pentecostal doctrine and worship in the United States.

The Great Migration became the catalyst for transforming the Church of God in Christ into an urban movement. The Church of God in Christ is part of a larger story of the southernization of the urban North and West and the impact of rural southern culture in the making of a northern, urban African American culture. Mason used his influence and leadership to also expand his southern rural denomination into northern urban cities. Many migrants welcomed the presence of the Church of God in Christ. For them, the Church of God in Christ reminded them of the home they had left. Most of these early missions were led by southern migrants who encouraged family members to join them. They also invited their southern friends to preach to their congregations, as well as agree to look after migrants who were sent to them. Thus there was a continual connection to the South. The music, the worship, the preaching, and the rituals that the Church of God in Christ embodied created a sense of community and security for many dislocated and disillusioned migrants. The church often became the one thing that was familiar to these migrants living in a busy and often isolating city.

Mason envisioned a denomination that would be an extended family. Therefore, he encouraged his followers to regular fellowship locally and nationally. As a result, members of the Church of God in Christ had annual organized events in which they could meet together for worship and recreation. This aspect of the Church of God in Christ appealed to migrants and the working class. It provided a kinship network for its members. This network was not limited to their local membership. Members of the Church of God in Christ were part of a family that was quickly becoming national. Followers often looked forward to and anticipated attending the annual convocation in Memphis, Tennessee, so they could see friends and family members from the South, as well as meet others.

This kinship also created a safe space for migrants and the working class to freely express their pain, joys, and struggles and find not only comfort and encouragement but material support. Having this space was critical for migrants and the working class, who were often criticized for not emulating the politics of respectability or being good reflections of the black race. Within the Church of God in Christ, migrants and the working class did not have to keep face or be concerned about the constant white gaze. If they needed to speak in an unknown tongue, scream, run around the church, or roll on the floor, it was okay. This freedom and emphasis upon Pentecostal power drew significant numbers of followers, so much so that by the 1940s the Church of God in Christ had become a permanent and critical fixture on the urban landscape. As World War II ended and a new wave of migrants began to migrate north and west, migrants no longer found just storefronts bearing the name "Church of God in Christ" but established congregations. The Church of God in Christ was no longer a rural church in an urban world. *See also* Ford, Louis Henry; Migrants, Cultural Identity of; Pentecostal Assemblies of the World (PAW); Storefront Churches.

Further Reading

Clemmons, Ithiel C. *Bishop C. H. Mason and the Roots of the Church of God in Christ.* Bakersfield, CA: Pnuema Life Publishing, 1996.

Lincoln, C. Eric, and Lawrence H. Mamiya. *The Black Church in the African American Experience.* Durham, NC: Duke University Press, 1990.

Mason, Elsie W. *The Man, . . . Charles Harrison Mason, 1866–1961.* Memphis: Church of Christ, 1979.

Pleas, Charles. *Fifty Years of Achievement from 1906–1956.* 1956. Reprint, Memphis: Church of God in Christ, 1991.

Range, C. F., ed. *Official Manual with Doctrines and Discipline of the Church of God in Christ.* Memphis: Board of Publications of the Church of God in Christ, 1973.

Sernett, Milton. *Bound for the Promised Land: African American Religion and the Great Migration.* Durham, NC: Duke University Press, 1997.

———, ed. *African-American Religious History: A Documentary Witness.* 2nd ed. Durham, NC: Duke University Press, 1999.

Taylor, Clarence. *The Black Churches of Brooklyn.* New York: Columbia University Press, 1994.

Shalanda Dexter-Rodgers

Cincinnati, Ohio

Located at the southwestern edge of Ohio on a bend in the Ohio River, Cincinnati has long been an important destination for southern African Americans heading north. Black movement to Cincinnati was sizable even as early as the mid-nineteenth century, though the in-migration hit its most notable peaks during the two world wars. The southern migration to Cincinnati continued in significant numbers through the 1960s. The city's relatively middling size and close proximity to the South meant that the move to Cincinnati was in some ways distinct from a move to a larger or more distant city. In general, however, the story of black migration to Cincinnati is a typical one: migrants came seeking social and economic opportunities and found them, though not without a great deal of individual and community struggle.

In contrast to many northern and midwestern cities, African Americans were a significant part of the city's makeup long before the twentieth-century Great Migration. As the largest city in the mid-nineteenth-century Midwest, Cincinnati was a key stop in the Underground Railroad and a hotbed of anti-slavery activity. African Americans certainly met resistance in pre–World War I Cincinnati, though their responses were quick and varied. Cincinnati's schools were integrated in 1887, the Cincinnati branch of the **National Association for the Advancement of Colored People** (NAACP) was chartered in 1915, and a nationally recognized black newspaper, the *Cincinnati Union*, began publishing in 1907. In 1910 a black population of about 20,000 made up 6 percent of the city. By contrast, only about 2 percent of the population in **New York**, **Detroit**, and **Chicago** was African American at this time. Even before World War I Cincinnati's black community was overwhelmingly southern. More than two-thirds of the city's black population in 1910 had been born outside of Ohio, compared with less than one-third of the local white population.

Although Cincinnati was a significant migrant destination before World War I, the impact of the war was immense. Cincinnati's black population increased by 50 percent between 1910 and 1920. Even though the city bordered on the Upper South, the new black migrants were largely from the farming communities and small towns of the Deep South. In the early 1920s about half of southern black migrants to Cincinnati came from Deep South states, primarily Georgia and Alabama. Even well after World War I kin and friendship connections continued to draw migrants from the most distant southern areas.

The massive influx of World War I–era migrants drove significant changes in African Americans' work and home lives in Cincinnati. Blacks had always been overrepresented in the city's service sector, and it was only during World War I that the majority of black men began to work in the city's key industries—printing, clothing manufacturing, meatpacking, and automobile manufacturing. To be sure, blacks most often filled positions as unskilled laborers in these industries, though that too changed radically between World War I and 1970. More than two-thirds of southern black men in Cincinnati worked in unskilled and service-sector jobs in 1920, but less than one-third did so by 1970. The balance worked in skilled industrial jobs and increasingly over time in clerical and professional jobs.

Southern blacks' integration into the residential world of Cincinnati took place more slowly. Most local African Americans lived in the downtown West End neighborhood before World War I, and the area actually became more segregated during the 1920s and 1930s. The neighborhood's black population increased threefold between the two world wars, whereas its white population declined by 75 percent. The northeastern Walnut Hills neighborhood emerged as a middle-class, African American neighborhood in the early 1920s. Like the West End, however, Walnut Hills underwent a fairly rapid transformation from mainly white residents to mainly black residents during the 1920s and 1930s. The nearby neighborhood of Avondale gradually followed the same pattern during and after World War II. Segregation continued to be a significant fact of Cincinnati black life even as late as the 1970s, when the only significant concentration of blacks outside the main core urban areas was in the northern neighborhood of Lincoln Heights.

Because of both the continuing in-migration of southern blacks and the stagnation of the southern white population, Cincinnati's African Americans were a powerful force in local politics by the 1970s. In 1971 Cincinnati elected its first black mayor, Theodore "Ted" Berry, himself born to southern migrants in the city's West End neighborhood. Southern blacks' integration into the society and politics of the city was hard won. In addition to a vibrant NAACP chapter, active local branches of the **Universal Negro Improvement Association**, the **Congress of Racial Equality**, and the **National Urban League** all worked in their own ways to combat segregation in **housing**, the job market, and public accommodations over the course of the twentieth century. Through these organizations and through their own individual efforts, southern migrants made Cincinnati a city of their own. *See also* Cleveland, Ohio; Indianapolis, Indiana; Midwestern States, Black Migration to; Primary Document 58.

Further Reading

Alexander, J. Trent. "Great Migrations: Race and Community in the Southern Exodus, 1917–1970." Ph.D. diss., Carnegie Mellon University, 2001.

Ohio Historical Society. "The African-American Experience in Ohio, 1850–1920." http://dbs.ohiohistory.org/africanam/index.stm.

Shapiro, Henry D., and Jonathan D. Sarna, eds. *Ethnic Diversity and Civic Identity: Patterns of Conflict and Cohesion in Cincinnati since 1820.* Urbana: University of Illinois Press, 1992.

Taylor, Henry Louis, Jr., ed. *Race and the City: Work, Community, and Protest in Cincinnati, 1820–1970*. Urbana: University of Illinois Press, 1993.

J. Trent Alexander

CIO *See* Congress of Industrial Organizations (CIO)

Civilian Conservation Corps (CCC)

One of the most significant New Deal programs to affect African Americans was the Civilian Conservation Corps (CCC). The CCC was created by an act of Congress on March 30, 1933, that was signed into law by President Franklin D. Roosevelt the following day. The CCC was designed to provide useful employment to young men between the ages of seventeen and twenty-three in work camps, where they were to undertake a variety of jobs in the nation's forests, parks, farmlands, beaches, and wildlife refuges. It was the first of the so-called alphabet agencies established during the New Deal, and it represented the federal government's recognition that American youth had its own unique set of problems to be addressed and overcome. The majority of the 3,000,000 who served in the corps during its nine years of activity were white youths, but 200,000 African Americans also served. A CCC worker received a monthly salary of thirty dollars, twenty-five of which were sent home to his needy family. In addition to regular wages, the enrollee (the

An African American enrollee in the Civilian Conservation Corps operates a roller on a road surfacing project. © Corbis.

official term for CCC participants) received food, clothing, shelter, medical care, and educational opportunities. For black migrants caught in the throes of the Great Depression, the CCC offered an outlet as well as an avenue of escape from **unemployment** in cities or the agricultural crisis unfolding across the rural South.

African American participants were initially assigned to CCC camps without regard to race. However, because of hostility and harassment from local (white) communities and the increased pressure for segregation, racially mixed CCC camps ended. In the summer of 1935 an official policy announcement ordered the "complete segregation of white and colored enrollees. Only in those states where the colored strength is too low to form a company unit will mixing of colored men in white units be permitted." Thus in 1942 when the Civilian Conservation Corps was officially terminated, segregated camps were the norm.

The numerous tasks undertaken and completed by CCC enrollees throughout the nation are well known and documented. They planted millions of trees, constructed hundreds of lookout towers, restored historic sites, cleared camp sites, battled forest fires, and worked on a myriad of other projects. In addition, millions of acres of farmland were saved from the ravages of soil erosion. In the East Bay hills near the city of Richmond, California, enrollees carried out beautification projects in what is today Samuel P. Taylor State Park. The CCC also developed many of the recreational facilities in Washington State parks. In Oregon corpsmen renovated buildings, installed bathrooms, and developed picnic and camping areas in Silver Creek Falls State Park, near Salem, Oregon.

Both white and African American CCC workers were sent to work in the forests, parks, and agricultural regions of America. Less known, however, but nevertheless important, were the duties performed by African American CCC participants. Although most of the African American CCC camps did only routine work, others were associated with specific projects. In the state of California, for example, one African American CCC camp used pigeons to transmit messages during fires. The camp trained the pigeons to fly from fire areas to fire-suppression camps when other ways of communicating were impractical. This was the first CCC camp in the United States to use homing pigeons as messengers.

Community acceptance of camps occupied by African American corpsmen varied throughout the nation. In most cases, however, even outside the South, communities near CCC camps did not welcome African American enrollees. In most states local resentment toward all-black camps was a fundamental problem for CCC officials.

The CCC program provided a type of formal education, which was conducted during off-duty hours on a strictly voluntary basis. The general purpose of the educational program was to enable the enrollee to improve himself so that he might be more employable once his service in the CCC was over. Retrospectively, the CCC educational program was not of much benefit to African American corpsmen. However, the long-term impact of the CCC experience on African American corpsmen was significant because the CCC made it possible for a relatively small group of young African Americans, undereducated, jobless, and without marketable skills or social credentials, to gain access to mainstream American society and thus to attain middle-class status. *See also* Agricultural Adjustment Administration (AAA); National Recovery Administration (NRA); Welfare State; Works Progress Administration (WPA); Primary Document 46.

Further Reading

Cole, Olen, Jr. *The African-American Experience in the Civilian Conservation Corps.* Gainesville: University Press of Florida, 1999.

Kirby, John B., Robert Lester, and Dale Reynolds, eds. *New Deal Agencies and Black America in the 1930s.* Microfilm, 25 reels. Frederick, MD: University Publications of America, 1985.

New Deal Network. "African Americans in the Civilian Conservation Corps." http:// newdeal.feri.org/aaccc/index.htm.

Salmond, John A. *The Civilian Conservation Corps, 1933–1942.* Durham, NC: Duke University Press, 1967.

Olen Cole, Jr.

Civil Rights Movement

In the 1950s and 1960s African Americans throughout the United States formed a mass movement to challenge racial discrimination and push the nation into living up to its promise to ensure freedom, justice, and equality for all its citizens. Activists used boycotts, demonstrations, lawsuits, and nonviolent direct action to draw attention to the unequal treatment of black people in employment, education, voting, and the legal system. Although these efforts met with violent resistance from white supremacists, participants in the civil rights movement eventually succeeded in persuading policy makers to pass legislation outlawing the legalized segregation and disfranchisement of black southerners. The Civil Rights Act of 1964 and the Voting Rights Act of 1965 were the major achievements of this movement.

The civil rights movement was predated by decades of informal resistance and organized political activity by African Americans. Migration often served as a means of protest for black southerners who could not afford to risk more open activism during the **Jim Crow** era. New opportunities for economic advancement and political participation in the North and West helped forge an enlarged black electorate that political leaders could no longer ignore. The second half of the twentieth century also saw significant internal migration within the South as displaced black workers moved from the plantations to cities. Newly liberated black southerners were instrumental in forming local civil rights groups that became the basis of a mass movement for social change.

George B. Morris, vice president of the Philadelphia branch of the NAACP, explains the group's civil rights initiatives to neighborhood supporters in the 1950s. Courtesy of the Library of Congress.

Migration and Civil Rights before World War II

In the early twentieth century black southerners were imprisoned by a system of laws and social customs designed to keep them powerless and poor. The denial of educational and economic opportunities confined most African Americans to plantation labor, domestic service, or other low-wage work. Restrictive voter qualification requirements prevented black people from participating politically. Children attended segregated, poorly equipped schools that often operated for only a few months of the year. Labor laws granted enormous power to employers and enabled them to limit workers' incomes and mobility. Many sharecropping families were perpetually in debt to their landlords, unable to leave their places of employment until the debts had been paid off. Black southerners who dared to protest these conditions faced the threat of eviction, loss of employment, or physical violence.

The Jim Crow system aimed to ensure a stable, dependent workforce for plantation owners. However, white southerners never succeeded in exerting complete control over their black laborers. Throughout the South thousands of sharecroppers left their employers at the end of each year (or sometimes earlier if they feared that their landlords were going to cheat them out of their earnings). Some moved illegally, slipping quietly away during the night. Others were fortunate enough to break even at settlement time or to find another plantation owner willing to pay any debts owed to a previous employer. In plantation records, letters, and diaries, white southerners frequently complained of black workers' lack of reliability. Although employers often attributed this to African Americans' supposedly inherent "shiftlessness," migration was often a carefully considered response to oppression. Just as enslaved black people had demonstrated their desire for liberty by running away, their sharecropper descendants moved to other plantations, counties, or states to seek better living and working conditions.

In the early twentieth century limited resources and the lack of job opportunities outside the South meant that most black migration occurred within and between the southern states. With the start of World War I in Europe in 1914, the geographic scope of migration expanded to include major industrial cities in the North. Immigration from Europe declined to a trickle, prompting northern employers to recruit black southerners as an alternative source of cheap labor. **Labor agents** visited southern communities and urged sharecroppers to take advantage of better-paying jobs that were available in the North. Black newspapers like the ***Chicago Defender*** also encouraged people to migrate by printing job advertisements and letters from migrants describing the higher wages, political rights, and greater personal freedom they enjoyed. Civil rights leaders and migrants themselves viewed the mass movement of African Americans out of the South as a way to express black people's rejection of the Jim Crow system. Explaining their reasons for moving, migrants cited the low wages, inferior education, disfranchisement, and violence that black people suffered in the South. Some African Americans hoped that the exodus would persuade white southerners to improve conditions for black people in the region. Faced with the loss of their labor supply, planters in many communities did begin to offer small concessions such as higher wages and better schools, but the most oppressive features of the system remained intact.

Roughly half a million black people left the South between 1916 and 1919, followed by another million in the 1920s. Although racism limited black opportunities in the North as well as in the South, an important difference was that black northerners could freely express and act upon their political views. Migrants helped boost membership in the **National Association for the Advancement of Colored People** (NAACP), and the circulation of black newspapers and magazines also increased. Larger audiences for black art, **literature**, and music fostered new cultural forms that challenged the key assumptions of white supremacy. Participants in the **Harlem Renaissance** condemned racial discrimination, celebrated black Americans' African heritage, and demonstrated the inaccuracy of racial ideologies that defined black people as inferior. Most important, black northerners registered to vote and participated in elections in high numbers, becoming a political power that demanded attention. In the 1930s most black voters shifted their allegiance from the Republican Party to the Democratic Party in response to President Franklin D. Roosevelt's New Deal reforms. African Americans, working-class white people, and middle-class reformers forged a liberal coalition within the party that pushed for measures to enhance equality and economic opportunity for all Americans.

Migration and Civil Rights after 1940

World War II precipitated another wave of migration out of the South in the 1940s. Black men and women joined the armed forces and their auxiliaries and once again moved from plantations to cities to seek work in defense industries. In addition to the northern destinations that had drawn black people from the South earlier in the century, **western states** like California and Nevada attracted many migrants. New military bases and defense plants located in the southern states also acted as magnets to black people from the surrounding plantation regions. Economic empowerment and liberation from the plantation system led to increasing political activity among black Americans. Former sharecroppers participated in wartime civil rights activism like the **March on Washington Movement** and the **Double V campaign**, pointing out the senselessness of asking black Americans to fight a war for democracy overseas when they lacked basic democratic rights at home. Under pressure from black protesters, federal policy makers enacted antidiscrimination measures to encourage fair treatment of African Americans in the armed services and defense industry employment.

Meanwhile, the southern plantation system was gradually being transformed in ways that undermined the Jim Crow social order in the South and created new problems for African Americans both within and outside the region. Encouraged by federal agricultural policies such as those of the **Agricultural Adjustment Administration** that attempted to raise farm commodity prices by limiting production, many landowners began cutting back crop acreages and laying off workers in the 1930s. Planters also began mechanizing operations, a process that accelerated during the war as employers turned to machines such as the **mechanical cotton harvester** to replace black laborers who left to seek better opportunities elsewhere. These developments lessened plantation owners' dependence on black labor and displaced tens of thousands of agricultural workers throughout the South in the 1950s and 1960s. Although this freed many African Americans from the control of white employers and contributed to the rise of the civil rights movement, it also created massive problems of **unemployment** and poverty in black communities.

In the decades after the war African Americans across the United States organized local protest movements to challenge racial discrimination and push for full equality. Activists worked through their churches, labor unions, **fraternal orders**, and other community institutions to mobilize people for social change. Participants engaged in boycotts of white-owned stores to demand an end to **employment discrimination** and visited their neighbors and friends to encourage them to register to vote. With help from the NAACP, black parents and students filed hundreds of lawsuits to equalize educational opportunities at the college, high-school, and elementary-school levels. These efforts culminated in the Supreme Court's decision outlawing school segregation in *Brown v. Board of Education* (1954). The following year black activists in Montgomery, Alabama, began a yearlong boycott of city buses that gained national publicity and inspired the formation of the Southern Christian Leadership Conference, headed by **Martin Luther King, Jr**. In the late 1950s and early 1960s young black people engaged in sit-ins and other forms of direct action to desegregate restaurants and stores in scores of cities in both the North and the South. The example set by black civil rights activists and growing awareness of the injustices African Americans suffered encouraged white people to become involved in the struggle as well. Hundreds of white and black Americans volunteered to assist with voter registration drives in the South in the 1960s. The combination of all these efforts and the violent responses of white supremacists finally compelled federal legislators to pass the Civil Rights and Voting Rights acts in the mid-1960s.

The new civil rights legislation ended legalized discrimination and disfranchisement, but did little to solve the problems of widespread poverty and joblessness in black communities. Southern political leaders who feared the new voting strength of African Americans responded by cutting social services and blocking antipoverty efforts to discourage displaced plantation workers from staying in the region. Migrants who left depressed rural areas in the South often ended up in deteriorating urban neighborhoods that were rapidly being abandoned by businesses and wealthier white residents who fled to the suburbs. Urban rebellions in cities across the nation in the late 1960s reflected black people's frustration with high unemployment, poor schools, and inadequate public services. These developments altered the meaning of migration in the minds of many African Americans. Black southerners who had once viewed migration as a form of protest now chose to remain in the South and fight to improve their communities instead of moving away. The civil rights movement opened access to the political system and other avenues for expressing their concerns, ending the era when migration was the only way for black people to demonstrate their opposition to the racist social order. *See also* Black Panther Party; Black Power; Community Organizing; Desegregation; Electoral Politics; Political Activism (1915–1945); Political Realignment; Poor People's Campaign; War on Poverty; Primary Documents 23, 43.

Further Reading

Cohen, William. *At Freedom's Edge: Black Mobility and the Southern White Quest for Racial Control, 1861–1915*. Baton Rouge: Louisiana State University Press, 1991.

Grossman, James R. *Land of Hope: Chicago, Black Southerners, and the Great Migration*. Chicago: University of Chicago Press, 1989.

Lemke-Santangelo, Gretchen. *Abiding Courage: African American Migrant Women and the East Bay Community*. Chapel Hill: University of North Carolina Press, 1996.

Morris, Aldon D. *The Origins of the Civil Rights Movement: Black Communities Organizing for Change*. New York: Free Press, 1984.

Public Broadcasting Service. *Goin' to Chicago*. 1995. www.pbs.org/gointochicago/.

Sullivan, Patricia. *Days of Hope: Race and Democracy in the New Deal Era*. Chapel Hill: University of North Carolina Press, 1996.

Greta de Jong

Clay, Cassius Marcellus *See* Ali, Muhammad

Cleveland, Ohio

In 1910, when Cleveland's African American population stood at 8,448, one could scarcely have imagined its subsequent importance for black southern migrants in the succeeding decades. Up to that point, amid massive immigration from Europe, the black share of the city's population had hovered at just over 1 percent. But a massive population influx in the World War I era, fed by labor demand and the cutoff of immigration from overseas, dramatically transformed Cleveland's African American community. The 1920 black population figure of 34,451 represented a growth of 308 percent in ten years, increasing blacks' share of the city's population to 4.3 percent. Migrants kept coming in the 1920s in pursuit of job opportunities or to reunite with family; more **women** than men arrived during this decade, in fact, resulting in a rough gender parity by 1930.

Historians Kenneth L. Kusmer and Kimberley L. Phillips, in their studies of the first Great Migration wave to Cleveland, have both stressed that the decision to migrate should not be regarded as simply an economic one; additional factors such as a desire for better schooling or to escape racial oppression—and perhaps most important, emotional ties to kin and friends— also motivated these journeys. Informational networks stemming from the migrants' social bonds allowed individuals to evaluate their prospects, and these same connections were crucial in helping migrants find **housing** and jobs once they arrived at their destination (see **Chain Migration**). Even so, Phillips has emphasized, migration was a "complicated and protracted" process shaped by gender, among other factors (Phillips, 16).

World War I saw some initial labor recruitment in the South, specifically of black workers for the steel mills and **railroads**. In general, black men had uneven access to industrial work in Cleveland's wartime economy, being prevented from holding higher-paying, skilled positions by managerial notions of racial fitness and white workers' opposition. Strikingly, though, the proportion of African American men working in personal service fell dramatically by 1920, and they maintained a tenuous grasp on wartime gains into the succeeding decade. Black women, in contrast, remained mired in domestic service, with only a small number finding access to the lowliest war-related jobs (see **Railroads, Black Employment on**; **Steelworkers**).

Migration gave impetus to residential segregation, and all-black pockets became evident by 1917 in the vast district running astride Cedar and Central avenues. African Americans living in the area had previously been intermingled with southern and eastern European immigrants. Because black housing options were constrained by low wages and the opposition of white residents in outlying sections, the wartime influx precipitated a severe housing shortage. Although a small number of black southern migrants succeeded in re-creating semirural subsistence living in a handful of outlying enclaves, the overwhelming majority became trapped in the emergent Cedar-Central **ghetto**, which by 1930 had a population density twice the city's average. Landlords divided single- and double-family houses into numerous kitchenette apartments and charged disproportionately high rents, while the less fortunate wartime migrants lived in garages, storefronts, and even boxcars. Phillips has emphasized the importance of extended family arrangements and the prevalence of boarding among migrant families as examples of "adaptive strategies" (Phillips, 136). With racial segregation hardening, Kusmer's revelation that Cedar-Central was stratified by class also needs to be stressed; recent migrants tended to live in the westernmost portion with the oldest and worst-quality housing, geographically separated from the black elites who lived in the district's other end.

Some longtime African American residents viewed the recent arrivals with disdain, fearing that their presence could jeopardize prospects for Cleveland's blacks as a whole; Kusmer distinguished northern-born "old elites" who had forged business and political ties to prominent whites from the often southern-born "new elites" who were less likely to look down on (and often staked their business success upon) the new migrants (see **Intraracial Class Conflict**). Established black churches used outreach in attempting to resocialize southern migrants, in some cases enticing them by offering useful services; secular organizations like the Negro Welfare Association (Cleveland's affiliate of the **National Urban League**) and the Phillis Wheatley Association similarly attempted to inculcate bourgeois values (see **Settlement Houses**).

As Phillips has demonstrated, however, the migrants successfully created a rich associational life of their own. They left existing churches to found congregations incorporating ecstatic southern styles of worship in such proliferation that the number of African American churches in Cleveland jumped from 14 in 1910 to 132 in 1930. Most of these congregations were housed in storefronts or other unconventional quarters. By the latter year the migrants' culture had become the mainstream because they effectively "southernized" the black culture of this northern city with their churches, food, music, and street life. Phillips identifies the Future Outlook League, a civil rights and labor organization founded in 1935, as not only having had an overwhelmingly migrant membership, but also having incorporated a distinctive southern protest style.

In contrast to our extensive knowledge of the First Great Migration, research on the population surge associated with World War II has only just begun, while that on southern blacks' continuing exodus during the succeeding decades is practically nonexistent. Cleveland is no exception in this regard. This disparity looms larger when one considers that the volume of black migration to the North from the 1940s through the 1960s was approximately twice that which occurred from the 1910s through the 1930s, and that African American migration to the West was minimal before the 1940s.

Like other World War II industrial centers, Cleveland again came to rely on southern in-migrant labor as its resident supply was steadily depleted. But discrimination against African American workers seeking jobs in the city's defense industries persisted, and those gains that did occur took place comparatively late in the war. In a "last-hired, first-fired" pattern, black workers (and especially women) did not make inroads into skilled production jobs until the available white workers had been placed. Tellingly, Cleveland was designated as one of the nation's "critical labor shortage areas" in December 1943, and all restrictions on in-migration were removed (see **Skilled Workers**). One sector, foundry work, saw heavy recruitment of African Americans from the outset. "Because the work was unpleasant, heavy, dirty, hot, and with low wages, practically no one would take a foundry job except inmigrant Negroes," the city's public housing agency, the Cleveland Metropolitan Housing Agency (CMHA), stated in 1944 (Michney, 92). Managers recruited black potential employees in the South, brought them to Cleveland, and sought to retain them by writing letters to local housing officials on their behalf. Sometimes these companies even supplied makeshift housing. In one example, a former grocery was divided into five "stalls" made from cardboard and two-by-fours, intended for fourteen black employees of the Aluminum Company of America, which said of the awkward arrangement, "We have never made any promises to men coming here that we could provide them with nice places" (Michney, 109).

Because little housing had been built during the Great Depression, accommodations were already generally scarce, and as defense workers streamed into Cleveland, the city's vacancy rate fell below 1 percent by mid-1942. African Americans, consolidated overwhelmingly in Cedar-Central, saw their dire housing situation grow increasingly worse. The ongoing conversion of properties to multiple-family occupancy—actually encouraged with federal Home Owners' Loan Corporation (HOLC) funding as a way to accommodate more war workers—had devastating effects in this segregated district. Dozens of black renters, seeking to escape overcrowded and deteriorating living conditions and finding agencies like CMHA and the city's War Housing Service ineffectual in meeting their needs, wrote to President and Eleanor Roosevelt to describe their plight. "The place I am now living in there are twelve rooms and twenty use one bath room," one man wrote the president. "I have tried every way to find a house for the place I am in is a kitchenett[e], so see if there is anything you can do to help me," he enjoined. Another woman wrote to say, "The place I have now is not fit for dogs to live in . . . it even rains in the Bath [and] all the Window Frames are Broken & when I speak to the Landlord about it she say I can move if I don't like it" (Michney, 85, 87). Housing officials finally decided to build segregated temporary war housing for black in-migrant workers, but the late start and controversy surrounding one project— Seville Homes, located on the city's southeastern outskirts next to an existing African American enclave—ensured that this approach would not effectively resolve the wartime housing crisis for blacks. Perhaps most significantly, these temporary housing projects long outlasted the war and were communities distinctly stamped by the black migrants' southern origins. Existing newsletters attest to the significance of family visits back home, the transfer of agricultural expertise, and the centrality of churchgoing as a community-based activity. Some tenants moving out of the Seville Homes remained in the vicinity and built their own homes, augmenting the black presence in this outlying area (see **Visiting**).

Statistics from the temporary war housing estates indicate that African American migrants living there were nearly twice as likely as white migrants (85 percent versus 46 percent) to remain in the Cleveland area after the war. Black migration to the city during the next two decades is a history still waiting to be written. In 1940 Cleveland's black population numbered 84,504, 9.6 percent of the total; by 1950 their share grew to 147,847 (16.2 percent), and by 1960, to 250,818 (28.6 percent). One of every five African Americans living in Cleveland in 1960 had not lived in the metropolitan area five years earlier, census data reveal.

One interesting lens through which to view the ongoing postwar migration is the efforts of black middle-class community leaders and social service professionals to evaluate its social effects. Cleveland's branch of the **National Association for the Advancement of Colored People** actually formed an In-Migration Committee in 1956, out of which the Cleveland Citizens' Committee on Newcomers arose the following year with the mission of determining how to "best meet the challenge of new arrivals and the subsequent problems of adjustment associated with them" (Michney, 291). Local black leaders held different opinions on how to handle recent arrivals. While some favored a tolerant approach—like Judge Perry B. Jackson, who proposed using welcome committees and benign measures to eliminate supposedly dysfunctional, rural-origin behavior—others, like the Reverend Wade H. McKinney, advocated strict policing. Councilman Leo Jackson represented a middle view, calling for "more assertive and aggressive" social service programs, "not to force compliance on the in-migrant, but at least to win confidence and participation" (Michney, 291). A 1961 Urban Migration Workshop cosponsored by the Urban League, the Community Relations Board, the Cleveland Welfare Federation, the Cleveland Board of Education, and other organizations evidenced negative stereotypes even as the participants pondered ways to assist migrants. A theme of "urban adjustment" continued well into the 1960s as an undercurrent of the reformist agendas pursued by middle-class blacks at the neighborhood level through the various community councils.

After the publication of Karl E. Taeuber and Alma F. Taeuber's *Negroes in Cities* (1965), which found that migrants arriving in major U.S. cities between 1955 and 1960 were better prepared in terms of employment skills and education than previously assumed, Cleveland researchers Gene B. Petersen, Laure M. Sharp, and Thomas F. Drury uncovered additional evidence that migrants adjusted relatively quickly and relied on kin and friendship networks to secure employment and housing. Like the Taeubers, these sociologists proved that significant numbers of migrants were not leaving rural areas, but rather southern cities. The study surveyed 600 African American migrant households that the researchers had located systematically—many of them in Hough, a neighborhood that had recently exploded in a major urban uprising. Increasing levels of **unemployment**—a symptom of the accelerating pace of **deindustrialization** in the urban North—dampened this ambitious study's generally positive conclusions, however.

As one of the top destinations for black southern migrants between 1910 and 1970, Cleveland's particular experience deserves further study, a task that will be facilitated by the city's particularly rich documentary record. More than anything else, the kind of outstanding scholarly attention that has until now been focused only on the earlier waves of African American migration to Cleveland needs to be paid to the post-1945 period. *See also* Employment, Black Female Patterns of; Employment, Black Male Patterns of; Employment Discrimination; Migrants, Cultural Identity of; Migrants, Expectations of; Migrants, Settlement Patterns of; Public Housing; Storefront Churches; Primary Documents 10, 18, 33, 39, 67.

Further Reading

Kusmer, Kenneth L. *A Ghetto Takes Shape: Black Cleveland, 1870–1930.* Urbana: University of Illinois Press, 1976.

Michney, Todd M. "Changing Neighborhoods: Race and Upward Mobility in Southeast Cleveland, 1930–1980." Ph.D. diss., University of Minnesota, 2004.

Ohio Historical Society. "The African-American Experience in Ohio, 1850–1920." http://dbs.ohiohistory.org/africanam/index.stm.

Petersen, Gene B., Laure M. Sharp, and Thomas F. Drury. *Southern Newcomers to Northern Cities: Work and Social Adjustment in Cleveland.* New York: Praeger, 1977.

Phillips, Kimberley L. *AlabamaNorth: African-American Migrants, Community, and Working-Class Activism in Cleveland, 1915–45.* Urbana: University of Illinois Press, 1999.

Todd M. Michney

Cleveland Gazette

When the *Cleveland Gazette* folded soon after the death of its owner and editor, Henry Clay Smith (1863–1941), it was the nation's longest-running black weekly. Smith viewed the Great Migration as a "sure weapon" against the **Jim Crow** South even as he criticized the behavior and expressive culture of the migrants. Founded in 1883, the *Gazette* came under the youthful Smith's control within three years and thereafter served as a mouthpiece not just for his own views, but for those shared by that segment of **Cleveland**'s black leadership that historian Kenneth Kusmer has designated the "old elite." As a three-term Republican state assemblyman who sponsored civil rights and antilynching legislation in the 1890s, Smith epitomized these ardent integrationists who cultivated business and political connections with prominent whites; at the same time, he exhibited considerable race pride and early on sought to popularize the term *Afro-American*. In 1917 Smith put forth his view that migrants were coming north because they were "tired of being treated like cattle" and because "there is freedom here" (Ross, 534). However, Smith downplayed the prevalence of racial discrimination or went so far as to blame migrants for its existence, on occasion deriding them by using terms like *ignorant*. *See also* Abbott, Robert S.; Associated Negro Press (ANP); Black Press; *Chicago Defender*; *New York Age*; Primary Document 33.

Further Reading

Kusmer, Kenneth L. *A Ghetto Takes Shape: Black Cleveland, 1870–1930.* Urbana: University of Illinois Press, 1976.
Ohio Historical Society. "The African-American Experience in Ohio, 1850–1920. The Gazette." http://dbs.ohiohistory.org/africanam/nwspaper/gazette.cfm.
Ross, Felicia G. Jones. "Preserving the Community: Cleveland Black Papers' Response to the Great Migration." *Journalism Quarterly* 71 (Autumn 1994): 531–39.

Todd M. Michney

COGIC *See* Church of God in Christ (COGIC)

Coltrane, John William (1926–1967)

John Coltrane, one of the greatest saxophonists in history, migrated from a segregated town in North Carolina to **Philadelphia** during World War II, following black laborers, farmers, domestic workers, and other musicians fleeing the depressed southern economy, **Jim Crow** laws, and racist violence. They migrated north in search of employment, better social conditions, and, for some, a music venue to learn, share, and inspire the unrestricted principles of **jazz**.

Coltrane was born in Hamlet, North Carolina, on September 23, 1926. Shortly after, his family moved to High Point, North Carolina. In 1939 a school band teacher persuaded Coltrane's mother to buy her son a saxophone. That same year Coltrane's grandfather, uncle, and father died, leaving his mother to support the thirteen-year-old novice musician. A few years later, unable to support herself and her son in High Point, she left the young Coltrane with family and friends and boarded a train crowded with southern blacks traveling north to find work in the war industries. She was caught in the wave of the Second Great Migration, which swept over a million blacks from the rural South to northern and western industrial cities during World War II. In May 1943 Coltrane graduated from William Penn High School in High Point and in the next month boarded a train with two friends heading north to Philadelphia. His two friends traveled north to find work to pay for college. Coltrane needed to find work to pay for music school.

While working at a sugar refinery, Coltrane attended Philadelphia's Ornstein School of Music, but soon transferred to the prestigious Granoff Studios to study clarinet, saxophone, and composition. During his early years in Philadelphia Coltrane started playing in small cocktail bars and lounges, following in the footsteps of his childhood idols Lester Young and Johnny Hodges and inspired by **Charlie Parker** and **Dizzy Gillespie**. Gillespie had made the same journey from North Carolina to Philadelphia the decade before.

Coltrane, nonetheless, was unable to escape the wartime draft. Luckily, his superiors recognized his talent and assigned him to the navy's black-only Melody Makers, stationed in Hawaii. Coltrane was released from duty and returned to Philadelphia in 1946, where he joined a new battle—an assault on big-band jazz led by Parker, Gillespie, and **Thelonious Monk**. They created **bebop**, a jazz revolt against corporate big bands, European **swing**, and melodic restrictions. Bebop is unrestricted and democratic and highlights an individual's skills. Coltrane and most of the jazz greats grew up in segregated towns and hated the humiliation of "separate but equal." Many blacks tried to escape these restrictions by traveling north, but nonetheless, they had the worst jobs outside the war industries and continued to suffer from police harassment, tenement **housing**, and racist violence. Bebop demonstrated democracy, freedom, and expression. It was a zone where blacks were free to create. Jazz was the music of black urban America.

In 1947 Coltrane met Miles Davis and traveled to **New York City** to play with the great trumpeter. Back in Philadelphia he jammed with Jimmy Heath and other local musicians until the autumn of 1949, when he began touring with Gillespie's band. In the 1950s he journeyed with Earl Bostic, Johnny Hodges, and Monk and later with Davis. By the end of the decade and into the 1960s Coltrane was playing gigs throughout the United States and Europe with various jazz greats, ensembles, and his quartet. Coltrane played benefit concerts for civil rights organizations and dedicated songs to **Martin Luther King, Jr**.

Coltrane's birthday, September 23, 1926, was the day of the autumn equinox— a day of balance. Jazz historians and enthusiasts insist that this contributed to his inspiration and talent. Coltrane was influenced by many legends and contemporaries, but was celebrated for his individualism, ingenuity, and complexity. Nevertheless, he continuously searched for balance and sobriety. Like many jazz musicians, including Parker and Davis, Coltrane was an alcoholic and heroin addict. He died on July 17, 1967, of liver disease, no doubt complicated by his addictions.

Coltrane's most celebrated albums include *Ascension, Meditations*, and *A Love Supreme*—a tribute to his creativity, fierce spirituality, and humility. Coltrane and many blacks migrated north pursuing the opportunities, acknowledgment, and civil liberties they could not find in the segregated and economically depressed midcentury South. The Great Migration did not guarantee everyone who made the journey the same inspiration, recognition, and fame Coltrane enjoyed. Nevertheless, it was a supreme journey for southern blacks who sought respect and resolution. *See also* Dance Halls and Nightclubs.

Further Reading

Duke University. "The Jazz Archive." John Coltrane Student Projects. www.music .duke.edu/jazz_archive/artists/coltrane.john/.

Fraim, John. *Spirit Catcher: The Life and Art of John Coltrane*. West Liberty, OH: Greathouse Co., 1996.

John Coltrane Foundation. John Coltrane Web site. www.johncoltrane.com.

Simpkins, Cuthbert Ormand. *Coltrane: A Biography*. New York: Herndon House Publishers, 1975.

Smith, Martin. *John Coltrane: Jazz, Racism, and Resistance—Extended Version*. London: Redwoods, 2003.

Robert C. Donnelly

Communists and the Communist Party

The relationship between Communism and African Americans, which was most extensive during the 1920s and the 1930s, has usually been described according to critical standards influenced to some degree by the cultural politics of the Cold War. Until the 1990s, when a wider variety of scholarly viewpoints arose, Marxism was conceptualized as an oppressive doctrine that, practiced by the Communist Party USA (CPUSA) under Russian diktats, constrained rather than liberated African Americans. Most critics and cultural historians chose not to focus on how Marxism and the CPUSA may have positively influenced African American lives and instead emphasized how African Americans drifted away from or expressed dissatisfaction with Marxist theory and the racial politics of the Communist Party after a brief infatuation. Political theorists such as Theodore Draper, Harvey Klehr, and Harold Cruse argued that American Marxism had become increasingly manipulated by and dependent on Moscow and Stalinism. As Mark Naison and William Maxwell have emphasized from a critical point of view, manipulation, disillusionment, and betrayal are the three different phases through which the encounter between African Americans and Marxism passed.

Newer scholarship has revised descriptions of the connections between Marxism and African Americans, pointing out the Communist effort for the liberation of African Americans. As wartime migration from the South to the North and returning soldiers from Europe expanded urban **ghettos**, African American leaders started to perceive the liberating potential of Communism for their race. Although the Party had almost no black members when it was founded, it was committed to world revolution, which earned the CPUSA the sympathies of blacks coming from colonized areas such as the West Indies. With its revolutionary potential, Communism responded well to the radical demands of African Americans during the years of the Great Migration. Black Americans challenged their status as second-class citizens under **Jim Crow**. The revolutionary policies of the CPUSA fit in well with the increasing militancy of African Americans who demanded the right to self-determination and rejected the accommodationist programs of some leaders. The masses of urban black proletarians who populated northern cities such as **Chicago** and **New York City** demanded equal rights with white workers and interracial organizing.

Because of the Communist stress on class, rather than race, as the basis of revolutionary change, the CPUSA and the Communist movement in general have been faulted for failing to give due importance to racial issues. Yet at the important Sixth World Congress of the Communist International in 1928, much of the debate was devoted to the role of American blacks in the revolutionary struggle. The position espoused by the Comintern with the support of the African American delegate Harry Haywood conceived American blacks as an oppressed nation. This description was clearly influenced by Lenin's and Stalin's writings on the "national question," comparing African Americans to the minorities in the republics forming the USSR. This thesis, which was also influenced by black American intellectuals such as poet and radical editor **Claude McKay**, conceptualized in nationalistic terms the presence of African Americans in southern states, arguing that African Americans formed a separate nation that was oppressed but that showed vital cultural signs of resistance. While the number of African Americans who were moving north was rising steadily, those who remained in the southern Black Belt needed to be treated as a separate nation that, before allying itself to the white proletariat, needed to reach an emancipated position.

The black contribution to the nation thesis challenges the assumption that the unity of black and white Communists was achieved simply by forcing white policies on African Americans. The Party line on emancipation provoked an important series of antiracist activities such as the campaign in defense of the Scottsboro boys and the organization of sharecroppers' unions. Self-determination was not unanimously accepted as the solution to the "Negro question." It attracted criticism from some black Communists who contended that through migration to the industrial North or to southern urban centers, African Americans were losing their common roots and could no longer be defined as a united nation. Yet the self-determination thesis remained influential. When the transition to the Popular Front strategy in the mid-1930s caused a redefinition of many Party policies, the self-determination of the southern Black Belt continued to remain a central CPUSA strategy.

In northern urban centers such as Chicago and Harlem, a new style of politics emerged during the Popular Front period that stressed interracial solidarity and support, as well as the integration of economic, cultural, and political fields in African Americans' struggle for citizenship. The CPUSA soon targeted in its policies issues that had already been tackled by non-Communist black organizations such as evictions, **employment discrimination**, inadequate public relief, high rents, and **police brutality**. Once again, there was a mutual exchange between whites and blacks within the Party. These exchanges caused the intersection of Communism with black nationalist programs. They also prompted the proliferation of cultural and social centers and institutions, inspired by, yet autonomous from, the Party, that could achieve interracial unity. The Party adopted a more inclusive policy toward non-Communist organizations that reflected the Popular Front effort to unite all progressive forces against the threat of fascism. As a result of this new dialogue, the National Negro Congress was created in the mid-1930s.

The prominence of the "nation thesis" within Communist policies and the characterization of the CPUSA in northern urban centers as the symbol of interracial struggle challenge the assumption that African Americans were simply treated as a different part of the proletariat. Furthermore, black militancy rather than Soviet diktats influenced American Communist policies on African Americans. More important than Comintern directives in forging the Party's racial politics were the rank and file of the grass roots. The Comintern put pressure on American Communists to consider African American rights as a crucial goal. Yet American political events, such as the imprisonment and the death sentences of the Scottsboro boys, were instrumental in involving Communists and their followers in political struggle. During the peak of black migration from the rural South to the industrial North, Communists fought against the oppression of African Americans. They strove to resolve the tension between assimilation and separatism by defining African Americans as an oppressed nation, thus bridging class-based politics and the aspirations of **black nationalism**. *See also* African Blood Brotherhood (ABB); Briggs, Cyril V.; Congress of Industrial Organizations (CIO); Ellison, Ralph; International Longshoremen's and Warehousemen's Union (ILWU); New Negro; Organized Labor; Political Activism (1915–1945); Robeson, Paul; Share Croppers Union (SCU); Socialists and Socialism; Wright, Richard Nathaniel.

Further Reading

Denning, Michael. *The Cultural Front: The Laboring of American Culture in the Twentieth Century*. New York: Verso, 1997.

Foley, Barbara. *Radical Representations: Politics and Form in U.S. Proletarian Fiction, 1929–1941*. Durham, NC: Duke University Press, 1993.

Haywood, Harry. *Black Bolshevik: Autobiography of an Afro-American Communist*. Chicago: Liberator, 1978.

Kelley, Robin D. G. *Hammer and Hoe: Alabama Communists during the Great Depression*. Chapel Hill: University of North Carolina Press, 1990.

Maxwell, William J. *New Negro, Old Left: African-American Writing and Communism between the Wars*. New York: Columbia University Press, 1999.

Solomon, Mark. *The Cry Was Unity: Communists and African Americans, 1917–1936*. Jackson: University Press of Mississippi, 1998.

Luca Prono

Community Organizing

Southern migrants arrived in urban centers with an array of needs. A variety of institutions—including churches, mutual aid societies, social service agencies, racial **uplift** groups, and informal social networks—offered them material aid and advice. Community organizations, which emerged in the late nineteenth century as a tool for neighbors to address local concerns, were one mechanism through which migrants could help themselves. Community organizations' primary activities varied with local concerns but often focused on **housing**, education, or the local environment. Few community organizations concentrated exclusively on migrants. Because of the residential segregation of African Americans, geographically based community organizations and other kinds of activist groups tended to overlap. Three types of community organizing efforts affected migrants: groups of whites, external programs to promote new organizations, and locally sponsored initiatives.

Urban whites often resisted the arrival of African Americans in their neighborhoods with violence or community organizations. In the first half of the twentieth century such groups were typically called "improvement associations." Ostensibly devoted to local physical upkeep, they also discouraged African Americans from seeking homes within their boundaries. In some neighborhoods whites used **restrictive covenants** to ban the sale or rental of housing to nonwhites. In the second half of the twentieth century whites' community organizations experimented with other means of preventing black in-migration. Local groups publicized their members' resolve not to move, displayed hostility to African Americans, lobbied for legal protections against **blockbusting**, and generally promoted their white neighbors' morale. Only a few local organizations, formed in the 1960s, such as the North Avondale Neighborhood Association in **Cincinnati, Ohio**, and the Austin Tenants and Owners Association in **Chicago** made welcoming African American neighbors an object.

Organizations of established northern blacks were eager to help migrants adjust to urban life by fostering their engagement with neighbors. In the 1910s the **Pittsburgh** Urban League pioneered the practice of organizing block clubs. During the 1930s the **St. Louis** and Chicago Urban Leagues also promoted local block clubs and larger federations to foster local beautification and community spirit. Creating and nurturing block clubs required a considerable investment of energy and time as staff workers knocked on doors to identify potential leaders, mailed out meeting reminders, and followed up to ascertain how groups were doing. Some groups with primarily political aims, like the **Universal Negro Improvement Association** and the **Black Panther Party**, engaged in community organizing and service as a strategy for building broad support.

External stimulation of community organizing exploded in the 1960s. The federal government's Office of Economic Opportunity required the "maximum feasible participation" of local residents in its governance and programs. Because migrants usually clustered into neighborhoods of concentrated poverty, they were often included in **War on Poverty** organizing efforts. The East Central Citizens Organization, for example, used federal funding to offer recreation, health, and educational services to residents of a square mile of Columbus, Ohio. In Cincinnati, Ohio, the Mount Auburn Community Council (MACC) was started in part with federal Model Cities funds. Between 1965 and the early twenty-first century MACC addressed both poor housing conditions and gentrification. Broad cultural shifts in the 1960s also inspired private efforts to organize migrant communities. Most notably, a group of leftist white college students billing themselves as the Economic Research and Action Project organized black and white southern migrants in **Cleveland** and twelve other cities. Both federal and private efforts suffered from the pitfalls of top-down organizing, in which the visions of those organizing and those being served did not align neatly. This mismatch made sustaining organizations difficult, exacerbated interclass and interracial tensions, and sometimes hampered improvement efforts.

The organizing methods of Saul Alinsky's Industrial Areas Foundation (IAF) were better suited to creating autonomous organizations. IAF's customary practice was to spend a three-year period gathering existing organizations into a strong federation to challenge local power structures before leaving the new group to be sustained by local people. In Rochester, New York, the Board of Urban Ministry, with African American consent, paid Alinsky's staff to create Freedom, Integration, God, Honor, Today. This group, known by its acronym FIGHT, engaged in a public battle with the Eastman Kodak Company over the creation of jobs for inner-city residents. In **Buffalo, New York**, BUILD (Build, Unity, Independence, Liberty, Dignity) won a variety of job-creation and training opportunities for constituents and founded the BUILD Academy for grade schoolers. Both BUILD and FIGHT elected migrants as president. On Chicago's South Side, The Woodlawn Organization (TWO) also sought dramatic ways to publicize and improve the economic status and educational experiences of area residents. TWO, which evolved into a community development corporation, lasted into the twenty-first century.

On occasion, migrants also organized their own formal groups with neither the interference nor the aid of outsiders. For example, African American residents of urban areas often formed block clubs to signal local expectations for behavior and upkeep. In Cleveland, during the Great Depression, migrants formed the Future Outlook League (FOL). Organized primarily around employment issues and influenced by members' experiences with the radical American Left, FOL agitated for steady work and fair employment practices using a variety of publicity-oriented tactics such as boycotts and picket lines. In **Boston** the Roxbury Action Program, founded in 1968, focused on redeveloping housing for African Americans and celebrating black culture. Locally generated groups were usually smaller and less likely to attract attention than those built by external organizers, perhaps accounting for their general invisibility in historical scholarship. *See also* National Urban League (NUL); Neighborhood Property Owners' Associations.

Further Reading

Fish, John Hall. *Black Power/White Control: The Struggle of the Woodlawn Organization in Chicago*. Princeton, NJ: Princeton University Press, 1973.

Lipsitz, George. *A Life in the Struggle: Ivory Perry and the Culture of Opposition*. Rev. ed. Philadelphia: Temple University Press, 1995.

Melvin, Patricia Mooney. *American Community Organizations: A Historical Dictionary*. New York: Greenwood Press, 1986.

Phillips, Kimberley L. *AlabamaNorth: African-American Migrants, Community, and Working-Class Activism in Cleveland, 1915–45*. Urbana: University of Illinois Press, 1999.

Amanda I. Seligman

Congress of Industrial Organizations (CIO)

African Americans who moved out of the South during the Great Migration had an enormous impact upon the development of the labor movement. In particular, the black struggle for equality in northern cities shaped the battle within the **American Federation of Labor** (AFL) over industrial unionism and in fact spurred the formation of the Congress of Industrial Organizations

(CIO). For a time and in no small part because of the organizing work of many black migrants, the CIO became a champion of the **civil rights movement**. In other words, the Congress's goals and core beliefs meshed tightly with those of black migrants and their children who worked in the mass-production industries and who sought to end American apartheid.

The CIO was conceived in the midst of one of the most transformative periods in U.S. history. During the 1930s, when American capitalism seemed on the brink of collapse and when President Franklin D. Roosevelt's New Deal administration was desperately seeking a formula for recovery, the CIO blazed a path for economic and social justice. In so doing, it became by the late 1940s a progressive and vital force in the economy and in politics. Although the CIO lasted a mere two decades, it nevertheless made stellar—as well as dubious—accomplishments. It organized to a significant extent the mass-production industries, including automotive, steel, and rubber. Among its staunchest supporters were African Americans. Like other industrial workers, blacks recognized the benefits of the CIO's form of organizing and collective bargaining agreements, which provided a higher standard of living for millions. Additionally, the CIO fostered the growth of the modern civil rights movement by advocating civil rights reform. Although it never accomplished all of its social goals, the CIO nonetheless left a progressive legacy that still influences the labor movement today.

The creation of the Congress of Industrial Organizations occurred at the intersection of several dynamic historical forces. The first was a second industrial revolution that began at the dawn of the twentieth century and reshaped modern America by the 1920s. The icon of this economic change was the mass-production factory, such as Henry Ford's **Detroit** automotive plants. On these workshop floors thousands of workers, including hundreds of black migrants, toiled at semiskilled and unskilled jobs. They turned out the consumer items that Americans craved, such as cars, refrigerators, and radios. Although these same workers could sometimes afford these new consumer goods, wages were still low, factories were unsafe, and workers labored under the whims of plant managers. For example, in the late 1920s, Henry Ford laid off his entire workforce of 120,000 without any **unemployment** benefits while he retooled his shops for new models of automobiles. In the 1920s these same managers and owners of the mass-production industries waged an unrelenting, at times violent, and very successful campaign against **organized labor**. Although some employers provided modest wages and benefits—so-called **welfare capitalism**—most offered very little besides the chance to grind away at a factory job. Unions sought to organize the mass-production workers in order to improve wages, benefits, and working conditions, but with the forces of capital and nearly all local, state, and federal governments against them, little progress was made.

The election of Franklin D. Roosevelt changed everything. Part of the New Deal program was to encourage labor unions to organize. The centerpiece of the first New Deal, the National Industrial Recovery Act (NIRA), which established the **National Recovery Administration**, contained two provisions that revolutionized the shop floor. The NIRA's Section 7(a) gave unions the right to organize and bargain collectively. Organizers within the nation's largest labor federation, the AFL, quickly went to work. Thousands rushed to join the federation, but many were soon disappointed. AFL officials were taken off guard at the gigantic demands of workers to join their organizations. Union leaders wanted them to be patient and wait for organizers and business agents to sort them into their proper crafts. Many AFL unions also blatantly barred black workers from membership, thus maintaining a decades-old tradition of organizing only white workers. The AFL's approach not only cooled union sentiment but also made many workers (especially black migrants and other new industrial workers) and some important union officials upset. A few AFL leaders tried to get the federation to change policy and practice and to organize the new unionists into large, industry-based unions. Although such broad-based unions did exist in the AFL, federation president William Green and the AFL Executive Council rebuffed this proposal to expand and create new industrial unions.

Undaunted, a group of AFL members led by John L. Lewis, head of the United Mine Workers of America, decided to take their case to the entire AFL at its 1935 annual convention in Atlantic City, New Jersey. There, Lewis tried again and again to get the federation to adopt the practice of organizing by industry and not by craft alone. Despite several attempts, Lewis's motion for industrial unions was defeated. When he tried to raise the issue in another way, William "Big Bill" Hutcheson of the Carpenters' Union started to heckle him. Having lost his patience with Hutcheson and the entire AFL, Lewis strode over to him, punched him squarely on his chin, and walked out of the convention with his supporters. Thus with a display of union machismo, the CIO was created.

Initially, the CIO—then known as the Committee for Industrial Organizations—was quite small and technically still part of the AFL. The day after the 1935 convention, Lewis met with fifty of his backers, including David Dubinsky of the International Ladies Garment Workers' Union, Sidney Hillman of the Amalgamated Clothing Workers of America, Thomas McMahon of the United Textile Workers, John Sheridan of the Mine and Mill Workers, and Max Zaritsky of the Hatters, Cap, and Millinery Workers. Together they devised a plan to organize workers in mass-production industries. Their efforts were quite successful. In rapid succession the CIO unionized significant parts of the automotive, rubber, and steel industries, where many black migrants worked. Rather than welcome this development, the AFL decided to kick the CIO unions out of the federation. The CIO's leadership took expulsion as a badge of honor and in 1938 established itself as the Congress of Industrial Organizations.

By the time of this great schism in the house of labor, the CIO had already differentiated itself from the AFL. Unlike most AFL unions, many CIO unions, such as the **United Automobile Workers** (UAW), the United Steel Workers, and the United Electrical Workers (UE), adopted open membership policies. In other words, **women** and minority workers were welcome to become full members of the union. This practice was in stark contrast to the AFL, which, if it organized blacks and women at all, put them in separate auxiliary locals. African Americans in the AFL also found themselves in completely separate unions such as the **Brotherhood of Sleeping Car Porters** (BSCP). The CIO was more inclusive because of its belief that workers wielded more power when they combined their interests regardless of race, religion, or sex. Additionally, there were CIO leaders and organizers affiliated with **Communist** politics who stressed class interests over racial and gender divisions. Many new industrial workers found the CIO's message appealing. In particular, African Americans who had moved from the South to midwestern, northern, and western industrial cities in the 1910s and then again in the 1940s discovered that the CIO was a more attractive union federation, and when they were given the choice, they frequently joined the CIO over the AFL.

The CIO's reputation for liberal—if not radical—politics and policies is well deserved. For example, to fight **employment discrimination**, it created the Committee against Racial Discrimination. The CIO and its member unions also promoted African Americans—even some black migrants such as George Crockett—to leadership positions. Moreover, it was intimately involved with the development of liberal politics and policies, particularly in the Roosevelt and Truman administrations. During World War II, for instance, the CIO played crucial leadership roles in the industrial mobilization. Yet the CIO was not always consistent. A case in point was the serious attempt to organize the unorganized in the South. Led by the CIO's Southern Organizing Committee, this unionization drive, dubbed Operation Dixie, purposely avoided civil rights issues in order to avoid upsetting conservative white politicians and workers. Ultimately, the seven-year campaign (1946–1953) ended in failure. Unlike their recently relocated northern counterparts, black southern workers refused to join the CIO in large numbers. Additionally, during the late 1940s and early 1950s, as McCarthyism reached a peak, the CIO leadership engaged in a purge of Communist and left-led unions. Among the unions that were targeted were several, such as the United Electrical Workers and the Food, Tobacco, and Allied Workers Union, that had terrific track records on civil rights issues.

Shortly after the CIO's expulsion of eleven unions, it became static and began to falter in finances and membership, partly because of its organizing failures and internal battles and partly because of a new federal law, the Taft-Hartley Act, which severely curtailed organized labor's ability to operate and push for equity on the shop floor and social and political reform. In 1952 the CIO's president, Philip Murray, who had succeeded John Lewis, died. Under the new leadership of Walter P. Reuther, a dynamo in the UAW, the CIO restarted long-dormant reunification talks with the AFL. In December 1955 the CIO rejoined the AFL. The new organization became the AFL-CIO.

Historians remain absolutely fascinated by the CIO's history, particularly its commitment to interracial organizing and progressive politics. Not all African American union leaders and migrants joined the CIO (for example, **A. Philip Randolph** never left his post within the AFL), but many did. Moreover, for a time, the CIO was a powerful political force. Its Political Action Committee (PAC), which was the first of its kind, helped deliver the vote for several Democratic presidents. And its leaders, such as Sidney Hillman and Walter Reuther, were not only mainstays in the White House but also household names. The CIO thus typified a twenty-year period in American history when organized labor achieved a momentary victory in advancing the cause of the average worker, regardless of race, creed, color, or sex. *See also* Automobile Workers; Industrial Workers of the World (IWW); International

Longshoremen's and Warehousemen's Union (ILWU); Packinghouse Workers and Unions; Steelworkers; Primary Document 5.

Further Reading

Fraser, Steven. *Labor Will Rule: Sidney Hillman and the Rise of American Labor.* New York: Basic Books, 1991.

Levinson, Edward. *Labor on the March.* New York: Harper, 1938.

Lichtenstein, Nelson. *Labor's War at Home: The CIO in World War II.* New York: Cambridge University Press, 1982.

Rosswurm, Steve, ed. *The CIO's Left-Led Unions.* New Brunswick, NJ: Rutgers University Press, 1992.

Zieger, Robert H. *The CIO, 1935–1955.* Chapel Hill: University of North Carolina Press, 1995.

Andrew E. Kersten

Congress of Racial Equality (CORE)

The Congress of Racial Equality (CORE) was an early pioneer of nonviolent direct-action campaigns that took place during the **civil rights movement** during the 1950s and 1960s. The organization grew out of the Christian pacifist student organization the Fellowship of Reconciliation (FOR), which was started during the World War I migration era with the goal of fostering improvement in race relations. CORE's nonviolent direct-action ideology was employed a number of times within urban African American communities during the migration era in their struggle against racial discrimination. These protests developed out of a long-established protest tradition that ranged from the **"Don't Buy Where You Can't Work" campaigns** in **Chicago** and **New York City** during the 1930s, **A. Philip Randolph**'s **March on Washington Movement** of the 1940s, and the more militant mood among African Americans over the obvious contradictions between America's democratic war propaganda and its violation of democratic principles at home. Each of these campaigns came in response to inadequate **housing** opportunities, job segregation, and discrimination in public accommodations and public spaces that resulted from white resistance to the growing number of black migrants moving north in search of better economic and social opportunities in the World War II and postwar periods.

The first CORE chapter, the Chicago Committee of Racial Equality, was formed in 1942 at the University of Chicago. The leaders of this new organization, which included future national directors **James Farmer** and James A. Robinson, were skeptical and critical of conservative actions of older civil rights groups, like the **National Association for the Advancement of Colored People** (NAACP) and the **National Urban League**, which often insisted on lengthy legal battles to fight **Jim Crow**, and instead embarked on campaigns that directly confronted discrimination in housing, employment, and public accommodations.

After changing its name to the Congress of Racial Equality in 1943, CORE expanded its operations and affiliated with other civil rights groups across the country. This proved difficult because CORE affiliates resisted centralized leadership out of the belief that a central structure would deprive local chapters of valuable, and often limited, financial resources. Moreover, problems in northern urbanized areas transcended mere segregation and encompassed a myriad of other issues, in particular, residential and **employment discrimination**, and many chapter leaders believed that creating a bureaucracy unfamiliar with local issues would severely limit the type of activism that could be employed.

Despite this resistance, throughout the late 1940s and early 1950s local CORE groups managed some substantial victories. For example, in 1949 **St. Louis** CORE, operating in a locale whose African American populace had increased during wartime migration, launched a successful campaign to desegregate Woolworth lunch counters through sit-ins and picketing. In another example, CORE operations in **Omaha, Nebraska**, successfully pressured a local Coca-Cola plant to agree to more equitable hiring practices. Unfortunately, the successes of these campaigns were not enough to maintain morale and activism among CORE affiliates across the nation. By 1954, while the NAACP was enjoying success as a result of the *Brown v. Board of Education* case, and 1955, when **Martin Luther King, Jr.**, and the Montgomery bus boycott gained national attention, CORE suffered from organizational disarray and growing anti-Communist investigations. In 1961 CORE reached an important point in its history when James Farmer became its national director. Before Farmer, whose charisma proved invaluable in strengthening CORE's ability to increase its profile within the African American community, CORE had begun to develop a reputation as being a predominantly white organization. With Farmer as its leader, the group moved into a more influential position among African American protest organizations because of its willingness to directly confront racial inequality.

On May 4, 1961, CORE brought its confrontational style to the Deep South when thirteen CORE members departed via bus from **Washington, D.C.**, in two interracial groups as part of the Freedom Rides. On May 13th, outside **Birmingham, Alabama**, an armed mob attacked the buses carrying a group of Freedom Riders and firebombed one of the bus. These incidents prompted CORE activists to abandon the remainder of their trip, and the riders were transported to **New Orleans** under the protection of the Justice Department. These actions, although initially disappointing, stimulated other freedom rides throughout the South and demonstrated how a protest strategy, tested and proven in northern states, could be implemented in the South. In the end, the Freedom Rides, along with its work in voter registration drives in the South, succeeded in moving CORE into a better position to fight racism throughout the North and the South.

The year 1963 ushered in a new philosophy in the civil rights movement— "Freedom Now!" For many activists within CORE, the achievements won between 1960 and 1963 brought only token success. This new philosophy brought organizations like CORE into more substantial debates with the NAACP and Urban League, which were devoting much of their resources to ending segregation in the public space and less attention to economic freedom. Nowhere was this more important than in the 1963 March on Washington. In the initial planning of the 1963 march, CORE was approached by

A. Philip Randolph to cosponsor the event. However, as the event grew and more organizations agreed to participate, the original impetus of the march—jobs—became a secondary focus behind the passage of the 1964 Civil Rights Act. Moreover, the NAACP, the Urban League, and the Southern Christian Leadership Conference (SCLC) openly argued against militant direct action or sit-ins in exchange for CORE's participation. This conflict accentuated an already contentious relationship between CORE and these other groups over such issues as membership, funding, and prestige.

By 1964 civil rights activists found it increasingly difficult to coordinate activities with other groups. For CORE, this cooperation was made more difficult as the organization developed a more militant critique of the Vietnam War and American society and began to publicly distance itself from an integrationist platform and membership such as those in more moderate organizations like the NAACP and SCLC. This conflict gained growing momentum within CORE when Floyd McKissack succeeded James Farmer in 1966. McKissack's ascension marked a shift from an adherence to Gandhian principles of nonviolent direct action to a philosophy of **black nationalism**. *See also* Political Activism (1915–1945).

Further Reading

Meier, August, and Elliott Rudwick. *CORE: A Study in the Civil Rights Movement, 1942–1968*. Urbana: University of Illinois Press, 1975.

Noble, Phil. *Beyond the Burning Bus: The Civil Rights Revolution in a Southern Town*. Montgomery, AL: New South Books, 2003.

Rachal, John R. " 'The Long, Hot Summer': The Mississippi Response to Freedom Summer, 1964." *Journal of Negro History* 84, no. 4 (1999): 315–39.

Lionel Kimble, Jr.

Construction and Building Trades, Black Employment in

The nation's entrance into World War I transformed the slow trickle of blacks from the rural South to the urban North into a steady stream. Black migrants headed north by the hundreds of thousands in search of economic opportunities, swelling the population of various northern cities. Many found jobs in **shipyards**, meatpacking, automobile manufacturing, and various war industries (see **Packinghouse Workers and Unions**; **Automobile Workers**). In the construction and building trades, however, they met with virtual exclusion. The building trades unions affiliated with the **American Federation of Labor** (AFL) effectively maintained their control over access to skilled jobs. This pattern of control and exclusion continued in the coming decades despite militancy and direct action by many individuals and civil rights groups. Without access to new skills and training through traditional apprenticeship programs, blacks could not secure high-paying construction jobs in the urban economy. The inability to secure these jobs resulted in severe consequences for working-class blacks as the decades passed and other employment sources began to abandon the urban core.

During World War I **W.E.B. DuBois** and the **National Urban League** pressured the AFL to expand efforts to unionize black workers, but could not succeed in effectively changing the powerful traditions and local customs of the building trades. Even with an acute wartime labor shortage, the construction industry did not consider black migrant workers as a solution to its labor needs. As well, the federal government did not exert any power over the construction industry to hire black workers.

In the postwar years some urban blacks did experience small, incremental employment gains, only to find those gains eroded by the end of the 1920s. Growing economic instability and the ongoing migration of blacks to northern cities provided tinder for increased racial tension and more determined control over building trades jobs. Although the public works projects launched through various New Deal programs created thousands of construction jobs during the Great Depression, black workers received very few employment opportunities. In cities like **St. Louis**, AFL-affiliated building trades unions stepped up their organizing efforts in the face of competition by the newly formed **Congress of Industrial Organizations**, effectively strengthening their control of building trades jobs. In addition, the passage of the Davis-Bacon Act in 1931 guaranteed prevailing wage rates, thus easing the fear of white construction workers who felt threatened by unemployed black migrant workers willing to accept lower wages. Most blacks who were able to secure jobs in the building industry worked as common laborers despite efforts by the Urban League and the **National Association for the Advancement of Colored People** (NAACP) to open up skilled construction jobs for blacks.

The nation's mobilization for World War II created an unparalleled number of construction jobs to build the infrastructure necessary to wage and win a global military engagement. Expanding numbers of southern blacks migrated to urban centers to secure jobs in construction and the defense industry. Although essential war construction created thousands of new jobs, southern white migrants secured more of these jobs than black migrants. In 1941 **A. Philip Randolph** organized the **March on Washington Movement** to protest job discrimination by defense contractors, resulting in Executive Order 8802. By the time Executive Order 8802 created the **Fair Employment Practices Committee** (FEPC) and then added a 1943 decree requiring nondiscrimination clauses in war contracts, most essential war construction had been completed. The FEPC did little to alter the discriminatory hiring practices of local building trades unions.

Planning by the federal government to move the nation from a war to a peacetime economy and avoid returning to the prewar economic crisis required a national economic stabilization program. Major urban centers became part of this program by embarking on aggressive postwar **urban renewal** and revitalization plans in large part funded by the federal government. The construction jobs created by urban renewal programs, interstate highway construction, and new **housing** starts went primarily to white building trades workers. Local social and political environments determined which jobs would go to blacks, and barring a few skilled jobs, most could only secure jobs as laborers or hod carriers (transporters of bricks and mortar).

The historical practice of job referrals through informal networks, the securing of admission to apprenticeship programs through kinship networks, and solid patterns of segregated housing and education continued to obstruct access to the skilled building trades for urban blacks. Protest and militancy demanding construction jobs in cities across the nation expanded during the civil rights years of the 1950s and 1960s. The NAACP, the Urban League, and the **Congress of Racial Equality** worked both locally and nationally to ensure change. Ongoing denial of basic economic opportunities added strain to existing racial tension in cities like **Chicago**, St. Louis, **Detroit**, **Philadelphia**, and **Los Angeles**. Herbert Hill, national labor director of the NAACP, pointed to the accountability of the federal government through its funding of discriminatory apprenticeship training programs.

President Lyndon Johnson signed into law the Civil Rights Act of 1964 outlawing employment discrimination. Title VII of the act created the Equal Employment Opportunity Commission, which was charged with ending unfair job practices (see **War on Poverty**). Still, in 1967 black workers were noticeably absent from the skilled construction trades. The federal government took measures to require general contractors to show evidence of their minority hiring practices before receiving awards to construct federally funded projects. This action resulted in protests by white building trades workers against federally mandated affirmative action. The debate over affirmative action continued to escalate in the 1970s, but without resolution. *See also* Deindustrialization; Employment, Black Male Patterns of; Employment Discrimination; Organized Labor; Skilled Workers.

Further Reading

Henry, Deborah J. "Structures of Exclusion: Black Labor and the Building Trades in St. Louis, 1917–1966." Ph.D. diss., University of Minnesota, 2002.

Sugrue, Thomas J. "Affirmative Action from Below: Civil Rights, the Building Trades, and the Politics of Racial Equality in the Urban North, 1945–1969." *Journal of American History* 91 (2004): 145–73.

Waldinger, Roger, and Thomas Bailey. "The Continuing Significance of Race: Racial Conflict and Racial Discrimination in Construction." *Politics and Society* 19 (1991): 291–323.

Deborah J. Henry

Convict Leasing *See* Involuntary Servitude

Cooper, Jack L. (1888–1970)

Jack L. Cooper was the father of **black appeal radio**. He aired the first radio program designed for African American audiences and developed a programming format based on entertainment, news, and service that became standard on black appeal outlets. This format helped radio become an integral part of African American communities coping with the strains of migration.

Cooper's radio career spanned the 1920s, 1930s, 1940s, and 1950s. He was the first African American radio newscaster, sportscaster, and station executive. Cooper was perhaps the first disc jockey of any race, and the first to use radio to serve the black community. A representative of the first generation of African Americans who came to northern cities during the Great Migration,

Cooper embraced **Chicago**'s black metropolis and its ethic of racial pride and self-sufficiency.

Cooper was the last of ten children and left school after the fifth grade. Before entering radio, he worked as a newsboy, bellboy, and porter and later was a boxer and a semiprofessional baseball player, entertainer, and journalist.

In 1924 the **Chicago Defender** hired Cooper to open an office in **Washington, D.C.** In Washington he secured a job on a radio show but was frustrated by the color line in broadcasting. After returning to Chicago, he developed a one-hour variety radio show to be aired specifically to blacks on radio station WSBC, which featured foreign-language programming. Cooper's program fit owner Joseph Silverstein's commitment to having radio serve all ethnic groups. On Sunday, November 3, 1929, at five o'clock, the *All-Negro Hour* premiered. The show featured music and comedy and later expanded to short serial skits, such as "Luke and Timber," that chronicled the comic misadventures of two southern rural migrants to Chicago.

During the 1930s Cooper developed the programming format featuring entertainment, news, and service. Under the brokerage system, he bought station time and sold advertising to sponsors to pay for the programming. After World War II Cooper's career reached its zenith. In 1947 he controlled forty hours of airtime a week on four stations. His company employed sixteen people, including several disc jockeys who later achieved their own renown. In 1951 he was voted top radio man in Chicago, but failing eyesight and advancing age led him to cut back his schedule throughout the 1950s.

Cooper's service venues were particularly relevant to African American migration. They included shows to locate missing persons, advice from a social worker, personal counseling from clergy, explaining how Social Security worked, legal aid, and help with getting a job. He also produced a news panel show to discuss issues of concern to the community. Cooper's efforts provided a national model for other stations and helped black appeal programming become an integral part of the radio industry. *See also* Benson, Al; Black Consumer Market.

Further Reading

Barlow, William. *Voice Over: The Making of Black Radio*. Philadelphia: Temple University Press, 1999.

Newman, Mark. *Entrepreneurs of Profits and Pride: From Black Appeal to Radio Soul*. New York: Praeger, 1988.

Williams, Gilbert Anthony. *Legendary Pioneers of Black Radio*. Westport, CT: Praeger, 1998.

Mark Newman

CORE *See* Congress of Racial Equality (CORE)

Cotton Belt

The Great Migration of African Americans from the South had a substantial effect on those who remained behind in the Cotton Belt. Although this impact of the Great Migration is sometimes neglected, it was a key result of the entire

The stress of negotiating a selling price with a white cotton buyer underscored the racial inequalities of the South's Cotton Belt for many African American farmers. Courtesy of the Library of Congress.

movement of African Americans in the twentieth century. The South became less agricultural and more urban. Wages remained lower in the South than elsewhere, but they showed some movement toward those of other regions during and after World War II as the number of workers decreased compared with the demand for them. Economists refer to this movement of wages as wage convergence. In turn, this contributed to wholesale economic and social change in the South.

African American migration from the South was most intense during World War I and the 1920s and again in the 1940s, 1950s, and 1960s. Most of the period from 1910 to 1970 thus implied urbanization of the black population in the South and elsewhere. Just after 1950, for the first time, a majority of southern African Americans lived in urban areas (at a national level, the majority was reached just after 1940). The American white population reached that level of urbanization between 1910 and 1920.

Among the most apparent results of out-migration in the South was that real wage rates—what workers were paid if the value of a dollar could be thought of as unchanged over time—rose in the wake of a decrease in the number of workers relative to the demand for their labor. The early migration of the 1910s was at first fought by southern elites who tried to prevent the exodus by, for example, enforcing vagrancy laws at railway stations. These measures were only partially successful. Still, after the war the rate of migration abated in the 1920s, and farm wages returned to their prewar levels (Wright, 202). The onset of the Great Depression and government agricultural programs to limit crop production—cotton and tobacco in the South—meant that the need for workers stalled, further adding to the flat pattern of wages until World War II. The upsurge in migration during the 1940s caused agricultural wages to rise again. This time, unlike the period following World War I, farm wage rates never returned to their prewar levels. Nonetheless, southern agricultural workers remained poor even after their wages doubled, an index of how poorly they were paid for the first four decades of the century. Still, the effect was that not only wages, but also total income per person began to converge with incomes in other regions in the United States after 1940. In part, this was because the Great Migration left fewer workers compared with the demand for them, but it also reflects the fact that many of the poorest moved out of the South, necessarily resulting in a higher average income among those who remained.

It should be noted as well that there were many other factors that affected wages and incomes, and it is difficult to separate out the precise effect of migration on wages. Progress was not uniform, because other factors—urbanization within the South and the New Deal among them—led to uneven changes in wages and incomes. Timing was crucial. For instance, during World War II the scarcity of workers that resulted from migration not only raised farm wages in the South, but also created pressure for increased school spending in the South. On the other hand, once the war was over and labor markets moved more in favor of those hiring labor again, these pressures tended to subside.

The increase in wages after 1940 indirectly led to rather important shifts in the southern economy and irrevocably altered the entire southern social system. The incentive to harvest cotton mechanically was now greater. Experiments with the seemingly insurmountable problem of replicating human dexterity at a reasonable cost had been going on for years (see **Mechanical Cotton Harvester**). Yet once wages increased, machines invaded the cotton fields, and the social system surrounding cotton cultivation began to crumble. By the late 1960s the rural South was barely recognizable to those who had lived there only two decades earlier. The shacks lining cotton fields throughout the rural South became an anachronism; mules and hand plows were replaced by tractors and tractor-drawn plows, chemical sprayers, and other equipment. Sharecroppers, wage laborers, and tenants were replaced by tractor drivers and mechanics—and there were many fewer of them, since it took only a fraction of the number of machine operators compared with hand workers to cultivate cotton now. In sum, throughout the South the plantation system itself, which had survived for more than a century after the Civil War, gave way to modern mechanized farming methods by the late 1960s. Urban life in turn became more central.

The progress of African American **women** seems to have been fostered by migration. Early in the twentieth century—and in fact for the first fifty years of that century—African American women worked in the fields, but also formed a key source of labor as domestic servants. Many did not report working full-time. But by midcentury that stereotypical form of employment began to break down, although not overnight. Women not only entered the labor force in a greater proportion than before, but also moved into clerical and service occupations and away from farm and domestic labor.

Some commentators have conjectured that the **civil rights movement** was facilitated by out-migration, but the link is tentative, and thus the idea remains controversial. The bargaining position of workers left in the South improved, but there were many battles still to be fought, and migration itself was hardly sufficient to overcome a social system that so long and so fiercely resisted change. A combination of social activism, changes in economic conditions, and federal legislation all worked along with out-migration to transform the region.

In the end, one can ask: to what degree did migration cause the fundamental social changes in the Cotton Belt in the twentieth century? It is impossible to quantify the answer, but clearly the old technologically backward system had long survived on low wages and social subservience for much of the African American population. Low wages were in part a result of a large number of relatively immobile rural workers. These workers were caught in a social system dominated by poverty, segregation, violence, paternalism, and other socially repugnant features of daily life. Migration was a way out, although not one without its own risks and difficulties. In general, those who stayed behind were the beneficiaries of the fact that many of their counterparts departed permanently, leading to wholesale changes in a region that for centuries had taken a different social path than the rest of the country. *See also* Agricultural Adjustment Administration (AAA); Involuntary Servitude; Mississippi River Delta; Occupational Mobility; Primary Documents 36, 63.

Further Reading

Alston, L. J., and J. P. Ferrie. *Southern Paternalism and the American Welfare State: Economics, Politics, and Institutions in the South, 1865-1965.* Cambridge: Cambridge University Press, 1999.

Daniel, Pete. *Breaking the Land: The Transformation of Cotton, Tobacco, and Rice Cultures since 1880.* Urbana: University of Illinois Press, 1985.

Fite, Gilbert. *Cotton Fields No More: Southern Agriculture, 1865-1980.* Lexington: University Press of Kentucky, 1984.

Heinicke, Craig W. "One Step Forward: African American Married Women in the South, 1950-60." *Journal of Interdisciplinary History* 31 (2000): 43-62.

Wright, Gavin. *Old South, New South: Revolutions in the Southern Economy since the Civil War.* New York: Basic Books, 1986.

Craig W. Heinicke

Crime and Criminals

After slavery, crime among African Americans became inextricably bound to the struggle of blacks to achieve full equality in the United States. Black behavior that threatened the economic, social, cultural, or political supremacy of whites, in many instances, became stigmatized as criminal activity and was often met with fierce resistance through new criminal laws, new crime-control policies, and newly popular forms of extralegal racial violence, such as **lynching**, mob attacks, and race riots. From the late nineteenth century through the era of the Great Migration and beyond, African American criminality became one of the most pressing social issues affecting race relations across the United States.

In the immediate aftermath of the Civil War, southern whites created new mechanisms of legal and extralegal control to reverse the newly gained rights of African American freedpeople. The invention of the black codes in 1865, which made racial discrimination essential to new policing practices and crime-control policies in southern states, created new categories of criminal behavior among African Americans that had not existed during slavery. By state and federal law, slaves had not been recognized as citizens and were not therefore punishable by criminal statutes.

The black codes created new vagrancy laws, for example, that criminalized black workers who escaped extreme hardship by ending labor contracts with unscrupulous white employers. These codes not only provided novel legal protections for whites' economic interests within the realm of criminal law versus the old protections of civil law, but upheld white supremacy by newly policing public displays of black pride or black defiance in the face of white contempt. As sheriffs and deputies replaced former masters and overseers as the protectors of white society, African Americans could not simply walk the streets of many southern towns and rural communities while holding their heads high and demanding the same respect as did whites. They lived under the constant threat of arrest and confinement.

Even when African Americans were guilty of minor crimes, such as petty theft, preexisting criminal statutes in the South were revised specifically to increase punishment for blacks. Mississippi's Pig Law of 1876, for example, targeted blacks who stole farm animals (often to feed their families and to counter exploitation by white farmers). Persons who were caught faced excessively high fines, extremely long prison sentences, and/or the possibility of forced labor on chain gangs or as privately leased convicts. Nearly overnight, new racially biased crime-control policies, such as the black codes and the Pig Law, helped completely reverse the demographics of crime and punishment in the South, with blacks replacing whites as the dominant prison population.

No matter why African Americans entered the criminal justice system across the South—whether because of legitimate labor disputes, public order "violations," acts of self-defense, or minor or major crimes—many blacks unjustly faced the possibility of capital punishment. Incarcerated African Americans were frequently worked to death, killed by prison guards and private contractors, or denied access to lifesaving medical treatment after suffering from malnutrition or after prolonged exposure to disease-infested environments. Thousands of southern blacks, moreover, who had been accused of rape or murder had their lives taken by lynch mobs that operated with impunity from law enforcement. Many of those unlawfully executed, investigators later discovered, were innocent of any wrongdoing. The scale of deadly violence perpetrated by, or with the complicity of, agents of the criminal justice system compelled a small but steady stream of black **women** and men to take matters into their own hands by leaving the South in the 1880s and 1890s in hopes of better and safer lives elsewhere.

By the turn of the twentieth century, with increasing black migration, black criminals had become a national obsession. Although migration to the North and West was an act of resistance by African Americans to escape violence and oppression in the South, northern whites viewed this migration with deep suspicion and great anxiety. As part of a growing national debate about "the Negro problem," race experts across the country linked migration to criminality and warned northerners that southern black criminals were headed in their direction. Northern black intellectuals and middle-class reformers added to this debate (to a lesser degree) with expressions of their own class anxieties, couched in the language of the cultural backwardness and bad habits of southerners in their midst (see **Intraracial Class Conflict**). This heightened dialogue brought to the surface latent racial tensions between northern whites and blacks that had occasionally erupted in racial violence and the wholesale stigmatization of free blacks in the North as criminals since the early nineteenth century. The association of criminality with African Americans' efforts to pursue greater social, economic, and political opportunities even in northern cities, in other words, intensified in the years before and during the Great Migration. As was the case in the South, burgeoning black communities in the urban North were isolated, targeted, and shaped to an excessive degree by white notions of black criminality as an inherent threat to white society.

As southern blacks rebuilt their lives in places like **New York City**, **Philadelphia**, and **Chicago**, the three cities with the largest populations of blacks in the urban North throughout the Great Migration period, they encountered increasing hostility from their white neighbors. Part of the hostility, plainly visible in **housing** segregation as well as job and union discrimination, was also evident in crime prevention and crime-fighting within northern black communities. For example, social workers provided limited crime-prevention services to blacks in poor communities, focusing mostly on native whites and European immigrants. Black children were especially hurt by these discriminatory practices. They were excluded, in many cases, from public parks and recreation centers, which were viewed at the time as constructive outlets for preventing juvenile delinquency. When many of these same social workers collaborated with antivice crusaders and police departments to shut down **red-light districts** in major cities across the country, they drove crime out of predominantly white neighborhoods into black ones, adding to the negative influences black families and individuals struggled to overcome.

Under the growing weight of segregation, discrimination, and institutional racism, most blacks persevered, resisting the temptations of vice and crime in the urban North. Those individuals who did not, however, participated in a range of illegal activities, such as gambling, property crimes, prostitution, illegal drug and alcohol distribution, and violent crimes. All of these activities had at one time or another been (and continued to be in many cases) regular features of poor white and immigrant communities.

The fact that crime was disproportionately measured in northern black communities, black social scientists and middle-class reformers explained in the 1920s and 1930s, was a consequence of both the greater inequality blacks experienced and discriminatory police practices, including overpolicing and underprotecting black neighborhoods. In fact, the epidemic of race riots that spread across the North between 1917 and 1919 in response to the Great Migration itself had revealed to many black observers just how significant was the problem of arbitrary policing, **police brutality**, and police complicity in racial violence initiated by whites. From that moment through the 1960s, many blacks believed that southern criminal justice practices had indeed traveled north with the Great Migration. *See also* Involuntary Servitude; Policy Gambling; Prostitutes and Prostitution; Racial Violence and World War II; Red Summer of 1919; Primary Documents 10, 13, 27, 37, 39, 51, 68, 70.

Further Reading

Bailey, Frankie Y., and Alice P. Green. *"Law Never Here": A Social History of African American Responses to Issues of Crime and Justice*. Westport, CT: Praeger, 1999.

Chicago Commission on Race Relations. *The Negro in Chicago: A Study of Race Relations and a Race Riot*. 1922. Reprint, New York: Arno Press, 1968.

Curtin, Mary Ellen. *Black Prisoners and Their World, Alabama, 1865–1900*. Charlottesville: University Press of Virginia, 2000.

Muhammad, Khalil G. " 'Negro Stranger in Our Midst': Origins of African-American Criminality in the Urban North, 1900–1940." Ph.D. diss., Rutgers University, 2004.

Oshinsky, David M. *"Worse than Slavery": Parchman Farm and the Ordeal of Jim Crow Justice*. New York: Free Press, 1996.

Sellin, Thorstein. "The Negro Criminal: A Statistical Note." *Annals of the American Academy of Political and Social Science* 140 (1928): 52–64.

Khalil Gibran Muhammad

CSS *See* Chicago School of Sociology (CSS)

D

Dallas, Texas

Dallas first became a magnet for rural black immigrants when Afro-Texans left farms and plantations in large numbers immediately after emancipation in 1865. Low wages for black farm workers, however, along with violent political repression after the collapse of the Populist movement, instigated increased migration to Dallas and other Texas cities beginning in the late 1890s, making Dallas a century later one of the largest black metropolises in America.

Dallas passed the state's first racial **housing** segregation ordinance in 1916. Although the Texas Supreme Court invalidated the ordinance the following year, other segregation laws quickly followed, and housing remained racially segmented for the rest of the century. In the 1920s Dallas's African American neighborhoods concentrated along floodplains, particularly in the city's north side. Many black professionals settled into North Dallas's State-Thomas neighborhood. Another largely African American district, Deep Ellum, developed into a vibrant center of **jazz** and **blues** music. There, amid a hodgepodge of pawnshops, whorehouses, and bars, African Americans, along with Mexican American, Jewish, Italian, and Greek immigrants, created a national music center, drawing such blues performers as Blind Lemon Jefferson, **Bessie Smith**, **Robert Johnson**, and **Huddie "Leadbelly" Ledbetter**, as well as early white exponents of western **swing**.

This multicultural fusion inspired the rise of a 13,000-member Dallas **Ku Klux Klan** chapter, the largest in the country. The Dallas Klan leader, dentist Hiram Wesley Evans, took over the national Klan in 1922. The 1920s Klan terrorized blacks, Jews, bootleggers, and other targets until sexual and financial scandals destroyed the group in the mid-1920s. In response to this oppression, a Dallas chapter of **Marcus Garvey**'s **Universal Negro Improvement**

Association (UNIA) formed in 1922. The UNIA advocated black migration to Africa, where a nation free of white oppression could be formed. The early 1920s also saw blacks emigrate from Texas to the neighboring states of Oklahoma and Louisiana.

Neither the Klan nor Garvey ultimately changed Dallas's status as a destination for black economic refugees. By 1924 African Americans represented 15 percent of Dallas's population, one-fourth of which lived in rental housing city authorities deemed unfit for habitation. Because of the discovery of nearby oilfields, Dallas emerged as an economic mecca during the depression, and by 1940 the city's 50,407 African Americans (out of a total population of 294,734) crammed into segregated neighborhoods covering a mere 3.5 square miles. Approximately 80 percent now lived in substandard homes. Some black professionals moved into economically declining white neighborhoods, provoking a wave of house bombings in 1940 and 1941 that Dallas officials failed to seriously investigate.

World War II brought industrial jobs even as large numbers of white employees shipped overseas to battle, creating work opportunities and another spike in black migration. Dallas's black population grew by 30,000 from 1940 to 1950. Private builders, however, constructed only 1,000 new dwellings open to African Americans, and Central Expressway construction in the 1940s tore State-Thomas in two. Unsanitary West Dallas slums, meanwhile, suffered outbreaks of typhus, tuberculosis, and polio. Crowding forced relatively prosperous blacks to again venture into the Exline Park neighborhood, scene of earlier bombings. Twelve bombings between 1950 and 1951 targeted homes sold to blacks in formerly all-white South Dallas neighborhoods. A blue-ribbon commission concluded that unnamed **ministers**, labor leaders, and other high-profile Exline Park whites planned the violence, but no one was ever convicted in the attacks.

White flight to Dallas suburbs followed agonizingly slow school **desegregation** in the early 1960s. Blacks climbed from 24.9 percent to almost 30 percent of the city's population from 1970 to 1990. Selective zoning enforcement, resulting disproportionately in the condemnation and demolition of black-owned homes, and city council support for pricey real estate developments facilitated a white movement back to the urban core by the 1990s. Deep Ellum, which had deteriorated into a cluster of empty warehouses, housed chic lofts, music clubs, and avant-garde art galleries. By century's end Dallas drifted into increasingly separate worlds, with more prosperous whites clustered in North Dallas and 83 percent of the city's black population living in poor South Dallas neighborhoods. *See also* Houston, Texas.

Further Reading

Barr, Alwyn. *Black Texans: A History of African Americans in Texas, 1528–1995.* Norman: University of Oklahoma Press, 1996.

Govenar, Alan B., and Jay F. Brakesfield. *Deep Ellum and Central Track: Where the Black and White Worlds of Dallas Converged.* Denton: University of North Texas Press, 1998.

Payne, Darwin. *Big D: Triumphs and Troubles of an American Supercity in the 20th Century.* Dallas: Three Forks Press, 2000.

Michael Phillips

Dance Halls and Nightclubs

As African Americans migrated from the rural South to the urban industrial centers of the Midwest and Northeast, they brought with them the patterns and elements of recreation and leisure necessary to maintain cultural identity in a new environment. One aspect of this identity was music and its expression in dance halls and nightclubs. These music venues provided a touchstone of contact with a lifestyle left behind while at the same time aiding assimilation into new physical and emotional worlds. Particularly for poor and working-class African Americans, from the juke joints of the South to the bars and the enjoyment of music in the North, a cultural validation was established.

The traditional juke joint in the small towns and agricultural areas of states such as Mississippi, Texas, Arkansas, and Alabama historically is identified with African Americans from the 1920s to the 1950s, decades when there was considerable movement back and forth from South to North. Drinking, dancing, gambling, and **blues** music were the features of the juke joint, which quite often operated on the fringes of the law. Bright strings of lights in the trees surrounding what was often a makeshift tavern served to draw in

African American dancers entertain a mostly white audience at a cabaret on Chicago's South Side, 1941. Courtesy of the Library of Congress.

customers, most of whom were local plantation workers, and the juke joint nurtured the modern development of the blues. Particularly after World War II, as more plantations and farms became mechanized and the traditional workers moved to northern cities, the culture of the juke joint was transferred to the urban nightclub.

In **Chicago**, for example, the neighborhoods of Bronzeville and streets like Cottage Grove, State, and Maxwell were the areas where many African American migrants came to live, and the nightclubs they found there provided a release from the daily struggles of eking out a living. Blues music was heard along the streets and in small bars, while nightclubs offered a continually developing **jazz** culture. However, when Phil and Leonard Chess, Jewish immigrant brothers in Chicago who would eventually create a seminal recording studio for the blues, began operating nightclubs in the African American neighborhoods, they used both jazz and blues musicians to offer their clientele music that was a part of their culture, both urban and rural. From their Macomba Lounge and others like it, they introduced to the public what would become urban blues, the electrified music of a rural form personified by performers such as **Muddy Waters**. The music and the dancing were sexually charged, earthy, passionate, and provocative, with partners dancing close together.

At the other end of the spectrum from the working-class urban nightclubs were the dance halls and ballrooms for a higher socioeconomic class of African Americans. By the end of the 1920s these clubs were flourishing. Again in Chicago, the Savoy featured big-band and jazz music, while in the heart of **New York City**'s Harlem there were nightclubs like the Renaissance Casino and Ballroom and another club called the Savoy Ballroom. The pattern was repeated in other major cities such as **Philadelphia**, **Buffalo**, **Pittsburgh**, **Seattle**, and **Los Angeles**. Here the attitude was one of a more genteel, though no less exuberant, nature than that of the roughhewn haunts of the lower classes, and there was a strong distinction in social rank between the African Americans in the middle class and the recently arrived labor class to urban neighborhoods, either from the American South or the West Indies. And dancing in clubs like the Savoy and the Renaissance reflected a different style that was born of the big-band sound and of **swing** music, livelier, more creative, and exhibiting stylized moves either by couples or by individuals in order to establish local reputations as dancers. The most popular dance in these venues was the lindy hop, or commonly "the lindy," which combined the earlier Charleston and two-step. With its offspring, the jitterbug, the lindy incorporated acrobatic, syncopated footwork that reflected the up-tempo music played on the bandstand or stage.

The dance halls served another, nonmusical function for the African American community in that they were the sites of some of the earliest black professional **basketball** teams. African American teams had been around virtually since the invention of the sport in 1891 and were very strong in the larger cities. Robert Douglas, a West Indian immigrant who promoted African American games in New York City in the early 1920s, persuaded the owner of the Renaissance Ballroom in 1923 to erect basketball goals at the ends of his enormous dance floor and allow Douglas's team to play games before late-night dancing. The team became the Renaissance Big Five, and while barnstorming on the road and playing both black and white teams, it galvanized urban African Americans' interest in basketball. This set a pattern of basketball as a crowd warm-up before dancing in many locations, and not many years after the "Rens" debuted, the Savoy Big Five in Chicago was purchased by a promoter named Al Saperstein and renamed the Harlem Globetrotters in imitation of the New York team. Over the next thirty years, into the 1960s, more than a score of other African American teams attached the word "Harlem" to their names because of the fame of the ballroom squad.

Searching for jobs and a new way of life, the transplanted African Americans from the South also had to search for a means of cultural integrity, not only in the face of a new racial environment but in the social stratification of race found within the African American community as well. They found this integrity in the bars and nightclubs that often echoed the juke joints of the rural existence left behind. In the eventual change from an acoustically driven music to an electronic style, more of that past was left behind. Thus in poor, urban, black nightclubs the music and dancing became a way to integrate the past with the present. The more refined dance halls and ballrooms provided dancing and other entertainment that expressed a release from the strictures of trying to make progress in a white world. *See also* Bebop; Chess Records; Migrants, Cultural Identity of; Rhythm and Blues (R&B); Sport; Youth Culture; Primary Documents 1, 13, 37, 51.

Further Reading

Anderson, Jervis. *This Was Harlem: A Cultural Portrait, 1900–1950.* New York: Farrar Straus Giroux, 1982.

Cohodas, Nadine. *Spinning Blues into Gold: The Chess Brothers and the Legendary Chess Records.* New York: St. Martin's Press, 2000.

Davis, Francis. *The History of the Blues: The Roots, the Music, the People from Charley Patton to Robert Cray.* New York: Hyperion, 1995.

Peretti, Burton W. *The Creation of Jazz: Music, Race, and Culture in Urban America.* Urbana: University of Illinois Press, 1992.

South Side Jazz Clubs Project. "Chicago's South Side Jazz Clubs, ca. 1915–40's." Chicago Jazz Archive. www.lib.uchicago.edu/e/su/cja/jazzmaps/ctlframe.htm.

Kevin Grace

Dawson, William Levi (1877–1969)

Born in Albany, Georgia, in 1877, William L. Dawson played a pivotal role in consolidating the political energies of **Chicago**'s black migrant population into the Democratic Party. At the time of his birth, however, southern Democrats were institutionalizing **Jim Crow** through violence and legislation. Despite these circumstances, Dawson's parents sent William to Fisk University in **Nashville**, **Tennessee**, where he excelled as an athlete and intellectual.

The South, though, provided few opportunities to educated black men. Thus after making frequent visits north as a Pullman porter, Dawson joined the growing exodus north to the "Promised Land." Indeed, when Dawson left for Chicago in 1912, he was part of the so-called Migration of the Talented Tenth, which had brought approximately 40,000 blacks to the city by 1910.

In 1915 Dawson matriculated at Kent Law School, but World War I interrupted his training when he enlisted in the U.S. Army in 1917. In the military Dawson's experience with segregation and observations of the apparent valor of black soldiers catalyzed his sense that he could lead blacks in an effort to bring about racial equality through politics.

Consequently, after leaving the army in 1918, Dawson resumed his legal training and became involved in Republican Party politics. Black Chicagoans had played minor roles in the local Republican Party since the 1890s, but their increased numbers resulting from the First Great Migration had led to the development of a powerful black political machine by the 1920s. Asserting the community's growing determination for political representation, Dawson mounted a groundbreaking, albeit unsuccessful, campaign against an incumbent white congressman in 1928. Then, after winning a city council seat in 1933, Dawson spearheaded efforts for **open housing** and community development in the increasingly overcrowded South Side ghetto. Finding himself frequently in agreement with the New Deal, Dawson switched to the Democratic Party in 1938.

After winning a congressional seat in 1942, Dawson sought benefits for his black constituents similar to those that white immigrants had received from the Chicago machine. Consequently, the Dawson machine became a source of social support for South Side blacks. Nationally, he became vice-chairman of the Democratic Party and the first black chairman of a standing congressional committee in 1948. Dawson expended this political capital on pushing the party toward a more progressive stance on civil rights. To this end Dawson worked for the integration of the presidential inaugural ball, strong civil rights planks in the Democratic Party platforms, and a series of voter registration campaigns in the South.

By the mid-1950s, though, Dawson's popularity had begun to decline. As the Second Great Migration enlarged the South Side and led to the development of the West Side black **ghetto**, the black community outgrew the machine's rather meager services. Meanwhile, middle-class blacks pushed Mayor Richard J. Daley for more equitable treatment, particularly in education, and young activists increasingly disparaged Dawson's political orientation. Consequently, Dawson spent much of the 1960s on the defensive and announced his retirement in November 1969. One year later he died of pneumonia. *See also* Black Legislators; DePriest, Oscar; Electoral Politics; Mitchell, Arthur Wergs; Political Realignment.

Further Reading

Branham, Charles. "The Transformation of Black Political Leadership in Chicago, 1864–1942." Ph.D. diss., University of Chicago, 1981.

Dawson, William L. Papers. Archives. Fisk University Library. Fisk University, Nashville, Tennessee.

Drake, St. Clair, and Horace Cayton. *Black Metropolis: A Study of Negro Life in a Northern City*. Rev. and enl. ed. Chicago: University of Chicago Press, 1993.

Grimshaw, William. *Bitter Fruit: Black Politics and the Chicago Machine, 1931–1991*. Chicago: University of Chicago Press, 1992.

Lemann, Nicholas. *The Promised Land: The Great Black Migration and How It Changed America*. New York: Vintage Books, 1992.

Manning, Christopher. "The Ties That Bind: William L. Dawson and the Limits of Electoral Politics, 1942–1970." Ph.D. diss., Northwestern University, 2003.

Rakove, Milton. *Don't Make No Waves, Don't Back No Losers: An Insider's Analysis of the Daley Machine*. Bloomington: Indiana University Press, 1975.

Christopher Manning

Defense Industries, Black Employment in *See* Aviation Industry, Black Employment in; Fair Employment Practices Committee (FEPC); Shipyards and Shipyard Workers; Tolan Committee; War Manpower Commission (WMC)

Deindustrialization

Deindustrialization refers to the decentralization of industry and the overall decline in industrial production throughout the United States during the second half of the twentieth century. From its earliest origins in the late 1940s, deindustrialization proceeded gradually until the sharp decline in U.S. industrial capacity in the mid-1970s. Large-scale industries moved away from their traditional locations in central cities, and the U.S. workforce shifted from industry to the service sector. As a result, during the 1970s economic growth

Deindustrialization contributed to high unemployment rates among inner-city African Americans in the 1960s. Here more than 1,500 blacks from Detroit line up to apply for work at the Ford Motor Company in 1967. © Bettmann/Corbis.

and real wages virtually stalled, while 32 to 38 million jobs were lost to private disinvestment in industry. Coinciding with the post–World War II migration, deindustrialization was perhaps the key underlying process that affected African Americans in cities during the second half of the twentieth century. By the early 1970s African Americans began moving from northern industrial cities in substantial numbers. This **return migration** to the South marked the rise of the centers of the new economy in cities like **Atlanta, Georgia**, and **Houston** and **Dallas, Texas**. Deindustrialization is a key to both the differences between the First and Second Great Migrations and the fate of post–World War II migrants to northern and western cities. From the perspective of migration studies, deindustrialization is a sociological term for the economic causes for the failed promises of postwar cities.

Initially, industrial and labor historians argued that deindustrialization began with the 1973 Organization of Petroleum Exporting Countries oil boycott and the hyperinflation of the 1970s. Barry Bluestone and Bennett Harrison's *The Deindustrialization of America* (1982) was the first of a spate of major studies of industrial decline in the United States. Bluestone and Harrison set the terms of the debate for many years. They highlighted the key corporate actions and legal structures that caused deindustrialization: the struggle between corporations and communities, U.S. corporations' "excess" industrial capacity caused by two decades of extensive foreign investment, the loss of jobs through automation, and the tax structures and corporate regulations that enabled an unprecedented concentration of wealth and mergers of corporate conglomerates. From this perspective, the 1973 oil crisis forced U.S. corporate managers to attempt to maintain the high profit rates they had achieved during the 1950s and 1960s. In order to do so, some corporations gave in to foreign competitors, as in the electronics industry; others, most famously in steel production, stopped investing in production capacity, creating outmoded and uncompetitive facilities; while many corporations pressured local, state, and federal governments to create better "business environments" by lowering taxes, deregulating, and limiting labor unions' power.

Since the early 1990s, historians have emphasized the long-term context for the decline of the 1970s, arguing that corporations began to pull investment and production out of urban centers as early as the 1930s. World War II and the Korean War fueled temporary reprieves, but industrial cities lost jobs, tax bases, union membership, and opportunities for blue-collar workers to achieve middle-class lifestyles over the last half of the twentieth century. Other students of the rise of the "postindustrial economy" point to the federal deregulation of large industries under Presidents Ronald Reagan and George H. W. Bush, the move toward free trade solidified when President William J. Clinton signed the North American Free Trade Agreement, and technological changes to explain the large-scale shifts in U.S. employment markets.

As Bluestone and Harrison point out, disinvestment was not solely a matter of capital flight. In addition to moving production sites to centers of cheaper labor and lower taxes, corporations removed capital from production altogether by focusing instead on speculation. Rather than modernizing existing plants or even moving production to more profitable locations, many managers simply transferred such "productive" capital into the money markets and foreign investment. What this meant was that even those families willing to move to find jobs discovered that there were fewer industrial jobs nationally. Even the South, with the most friendly business climate in the United States, lost nearly 11 million jobs between 1969 and 1976 (Bluestone and Harrison, 31).

The litany of deindustrialization's manifestations includes high **unemployment**, slow economic growth, precipitous drops in union membership, inflation, declines in real wages and the standard of living, and increasing trade deficits. Comparisons between the 1960s and the 1970s are stark. In the earlier decade the national economy grew more than 4 percent annually, and the unemployment rate fell below 4 percent by the end of the decade. From 1970 to 1980, in contrast, the U.S. gross domestic product grew only 2.9 percent, unemployment reached almost 11 percent by 1982, and between 32 and 38 million jobs disappeared in the 1970s alone (Cowie and Heathcott, vii–viii, ix). In addition, European and Asian manufacturers flooded the U.S. market because their newer factories were more efficient and their designs won the loyalty of American consumers.

Deindustrialization's effects have been devastating for African Americans in northern and western cities. The best jobs in the postindustrial economy are generally located in the majority-white suburbs and require high levels of education. In addition, many observers contend that discriminatory hiring and promotion practices maintain the "job ceiling," relegating African American workers to the lowest levels of jobs in high-tech production, white-collar sectors, and service industries. Labor unions, which lost what were their strongest positions in the declining industries and faced increasingly unfriendly legislation, have not been able to protect workers from this discrimination.

Sociologists and historians connect the history of deindustrialization to the rise of an urban African American "underclass," a chronically unemployed, poor, isolated population left in the wake of job loss and disinvestment. African Americans had established a foothold in large industries during the World War I–era migration and reinforced their position in the industrial workforce after the Great Depression. The great union movements of the 1930s and the explosion in black industrial work during the 1940s seemed to bode well for the urban industrial black communities. Just when interracial unions forced industrial employers and unions to stop racial discrimination, however, the very jobs for which they fought began to disappear. In his celebrated study of the disappearance of working-class jobs, *The End of Work* (2004), Jeremy Rifkin describes this large-scale phenomenon as low-skilled African Americans' move from economic oppression to obsolescence.

The 5 million African Americans who left the South after World War II went to cities that were losing high-paid production jobs, and they found little chance to get the education they needed to obtain the best jobs in the postindustrial economy or to join unions that would protect their access to those jobs and their benefits—seniority, pensions, health insurance, and political power. Deindustrialization also famously created a "spatial mismatch" for African American workers; the jobs they might have been able to get had moved beyond the reach of the public transportation lines on which most depended. During the late 1950s and 1960s migrants found that low-skilled jobs that would likely have been available during the 1910s, 1920s, and 1940s were now either held by workers with years of seniority or gone altogether. The effects of this loss of opportunity were tragic. Historian Thomas Sugrue's *Origins of the Urban Crisis*, for example, connects the long history of deindustrialization (dating to the 1940s) to discriminatory **housing** policies, racist defenses of all-white neighborhoods, and the postwar assault on labor unions. Sugrue contends that it was the combination of ongoing discrimination and deindustrialization that caused the mass demoralization of black youth in northern and western cities, ultimately exploding in the riots of the 1960s.

Beginning in the 1970s, the net migration of African Americans reversed direction. Some new migrants left northern cities to reunite families, a prospect that seemed much brighter with the improvements in southern race relations by the end of the 1960s. The promise of jobs drew millions to cities like Houston and Atlanta. In fact, by the beginning of the 1980s Houston had become the fourth-largest city in the United States. Although a full history is yet to be written, this return migration encountered many of the same problems that earlier migrants had faced in booming cities in the North and West. *See also* Demographic Patterns of the Great Black Migration (1940–1970); Employment, Black Female Patterns of; Employment, Black Male Patterns of; Employment Discrimination; Urban Renewal.

Further Reading

Bluestone, Barry, and Bennett Harrison. *The Deindustrialization of America: Plant Closings, Community Abandonment, and the Dismantling of Basic Industry*. New York: Basic Books, 1982.

Cowie, Jefferson, and Joseph Heathcott, eds. *Beyond the Ruins: The Meanings of Deindustrialization*. Ithaca, NY: Cornell University Press, 2003.

Massey, Douglas S., and Nancy A. Denton. *American Apartheid: Segregation and the Making of the Underclass*. Cambridge, MA: Harvard University Press, 1993.

Milkman, Ruth. *Farewell to the Factory: Auto Workers in the Late Twentieth Century*. Berkeley: University of California Press, 1997.

Raines, John C., Lenora E. Berson, and David McI. Gracie, eds. *Community and Capital in Conflict: Plant Closings and Job Loss*. Philadelphia: Temple University Press, 1982.

Rifkin, Jeremy. *The End of Work: Technology, Jobs, and Your Future*. 2nd ed. New York: Jeremy P. Tarcher/Penguin, 2004.

Stein, Judith. *Running Steel, Running America: Race, Economic Policy, and the Decline of Liberalism*. Chapel Hill: University of North Carolina Press, 1998.

Sugrue, Thomas. *The Origins of the Urban Crisis: Race and Inequality in Postwar Detroit*. Princeton, NJ: Princeton University Press, 1996.

Wilson, William Julius. *When Work Disappears: The World of the New Urban Poor*. New York: Knopf, 1996.

Jeffrey Helgeson

Demographic Patterns of the Great Black Migration (1915–1940)

While a trickle of southern blacks had moved north since the mid-1800s, the mass southern exodus known as the Great Black Migration began in earnest during the 1910s. The Great Migration occurred in two fairly distinct waves, the first beginning during the years surrounding World War I, and the second beginning during the years surrounding World War II. Both waves were precipitated by the needs of wartime industries in the North and West, though both continued for decades after the initial rush, emphasizing African Americans' strong desire to leave the South. The wartime eras are viewed as separate waves in a larger movement in part because there was a significant decline in migration between the wars, during the Great Depression. While the years surrounding World War I saw a flurry of migration that continued at nearly the same pace through the 1920s, the 1930s out-migration slowed to about half the pace of the wartime peak. In addition to being a larger group than the pre–World War I stream, the migrants of the 1910s through the 1930s differed from previous migrants in a number of ways. The new migrants were increasingly from the Deep South, and they were a particularly urban and educated subgroup of the southern black population.

The first large-scale Great Migration began mainly as a movement to the North and Midwest in the 1910s. In 1910 about 450,000 southern-born blacks lived outside the South. By the decade's end the migrants' numbers had grown by 75 percent, totaling about 800,000. The migrants' numbers nearly doubled again in the next two decades, totaling 1.5 million by 1940. By the end of the First Great Migration, almost three-quarters of the northern black population had been born in the South. Even these massive increases do not reveal the true magnitude of the out-migration. Large numbers of cyclical and short-term migrants (as well as deceased migrants) certainly remain uncounted in the decennial census data on which most historians rely. Between 1935 and 1940, for instance, one migrant was returning to the South for every six who moved to the North. In total, probably well over 2 million southerners participated in the northward move between 1915 and 1940.

Southern blacks' places of origin changed radically during the World War I era. Whereas earlier migrants had come mostly from the border South states, the new migrants increasingly came from the Deep South. In 1910 the key sending states by far were Virginia (sending migrants mostly up the seaboard) and Kentucky (sending migrants to the Midwest). These two states together sent half the black migrants to the North at that time. By 1940 only about one in ten new migrants were coming from Kentucky or Virginia; most came from Mississippi, Georgia, the Carolinas, and Texas. The migrants' destinations, on the other hand, changed little in the decades leading up to World War II. About half of the migrants moved to **midwestern states**, and most of the rest headed to the **northeastern states**. The major cities of Illinois and Ohio were the key destinations in the Midwest, while urban Pennsylvania and New York were the key destinations in the Northeast. This pattern was evident in 1940, just as it had been in 1900.

Migrants of the World War I era were a relatively urban and educated group. In 1940 about a third of the migrants had a ninth-grade education or more, compared with only about one-sixth of all black adults in the South. Almost half the southern migrants came from the metropolitan South at that time, while just over one-quarter of all southern blacks lived in metropolitan areas. The migrants' urban and educational experiences resulted not simply because urban people were more often drawn to the North, but because even those rural migrants who intended to head north usually followed complex paths out of the South. The route to the North was often a circuitous one, involving work in a variety of rural and urban industries in the South along the way. Still, almost all migrants had close ties to the rural South, and they continued to nurture these connections even after moving north.

As prepared as many of the migrants were for the northward move, northern blacks still possessed some significant advantages over the southern newcomers. The native northerners were slightly more educated than southern blacks, they had slightly better jobs, and they were less likely to live in the least desirable "port of entry" neighborhoods. Yet contrary to the perceptions of many northerners during the World War I era and since, most southern black migrants were an extremely stable and rooted group. Observers ranging from **E. Franklin Frazier** in the 1930s to Daniel Patrick Moynihan in the 1960s have incorrectly suggested that the migrants brought with them the supposed dysfunctional patterns of the southern black family. In fact, about three-quarters of adult migrants were married (or widowed) during the pre–World War II era. The vast majority of migrant children lived in two-parent households—about 90 percent in 1920, for instance. Virtually no migrant children lived with a never-married mother. In all of these ways, southern black migrants exhibited even more traditional family patterns than did northern-born blacks, who exhibited lower marriage rates, lower rates of children living with two parents, and higher rates of out-of-wedlock **childbirth** at all points during the period from 1910 to 1940.

Scholars of worldwide population movement have increasingly come to view the Great Black Migration together with the concurrent out-migration of southern whites. Southern whites moved north at about twice the rate of southern blacks before World War II. By 1940 about 3 million southern-born whites lived in the North and West. Even though whites and blacks appear to have undertaken similar moves in the broadest sense, key patterns differ upon closer examination. For instance, white out-migrants tended to leave the southern fringes, while blacks tended to leave the core Deep South states. In terms of destinations, more than one-third of the white stream headed west before World War II, compared with only about one in twenty black out-migrants. Perhaps most significantly, southern blacks experienced severe discrimination before and after their moves. As recent studies have shown, however, studying these two groups together allows scholars to isolate the impact of race in the migration; the results have been sobering. Despite the fact that southern whites did not have significantly more education or industrial work experience before leaving the South, their northern work and housing opportunities far exceeded those of southern blacks.

The demographic patterns in the Great Migration offer a critical window on one of the most significant events in modern African American history. While the patterns of the World War I era were not set in stone, they clearly influenced the shape of the even larger migration of the post–World War II era. Additionally, understanding demographic patterns in the Great Migration allows for a better understanding of human mobility: the most prepared migrants tend to be the movers in long-distance migrations, though they are often still at a disadvantage at their destination points. Finally, especially in relief of the parallel move of southern whites, understanding patterns in the Great Migration allows us to better understand race in America: despite the fact that southern whites left similar backgrounds and headed for similar destinations, they faced a completely different reality in the North. In all of these ways, the broad patterns of the Great Migration help us understand African American and American history more fully. *See also* Chain Migration; Demographic Patterns of the Great Black Migration (1940-1970); Migrants, Economic Characteristics of; Migrants, Settlement Patterns of; Migrants, Social Characteristics of.

Further Reading

Alexander, J. Trent. "The Great Migration in Comparative Perspective." *Social Science History* 22 (1998): 349-76.

Gregory, James N. "Southern Diaspora and Urban Dispossessed." *Journal of American History* 82 (1995): 111-34.

Johnson, Daniel M., and Rex R. Campbell. *Black Migration in America: A Social Demographic History*. Durham, NC: Duke University Press, 1981.

Tolnay, Stewart E. *The Bottom Rung: African American Family Life on Southern Farms*. Urbana: University of Illinois Press, 1999.

———. "The Great Migration Gets Underway: A Comparison of Migrants and Non-migrants in the North, 1920." *Social Science Quarterly* 82 (2001): 235-52.

J. Trent Alexander

Demographic Patterns of the Great Black Migration (1940–1970)

African Americans left the South during the period 1940 to 1970 for the urban North in numbers and at rates never before experienced. This is referred to by some as the "Second" Great Migration (although that usage is not universal), the first being that during World War I and the 1920s. World War II was the period of greatest migration, although after a pause the population movement resumed in large numbers well into the 1950s and 1960s. Cities, mainly but by no means exclusively outside the South, gained large numbers of African Americans, while southern farms continued to lose population. The West Coast for the first time became a major destination region for African Americans. Smaller cities in the **northeastern** and **midwestern states** grew in importance as destinations during this period. As northern and western cities became more populated with former migrants, concentrated streams of migration developed.

Indirect evidence from the U.S. population censuses provides information on the numbers involved. These must be estimated, since little direct evidence exists to trace actual movements. According to these estimates, approximately 4.5 million African Americans left the South during the period 1940 to 1970 for other parts of the country. This is actually an underestimate of the total number of persons moving, since estimates are of net migration—those moving out minus any migrating in the reverse direction to the main flow. Not only were the numbers large, but the rates (numbers compared to the African American population of origin) were substantial. In the 1940s the migration constituted more than 15 percent of the 1940 African American southern population. That number is highly deceptive, however, because the base population includes states where net migration was actually into those states (Florida, for instance). A more accurate rate would be closer to 25 or 30 percent of the base population.

Often in migration summaries of this period, the Census South is used as the defining region. This is more convenient than representative of the underlying socioeconomic characteristics. For a better picture, we note that migration flows were largest out of the eleven states of the old Confederacy of 1861. Within that region the five states of the Deep South—Alabama, Georgia, Louisiana, Mississippi, and South Carolina—contributed 70 percent or more of the migrants, amounting to more than 1 million people each decade.

That provides a suitable picture of the regional dimension of out-migration. Note that within the South the net migration flow was concentrated from the rural population of the South. Migration rates are thus most informative if the rural South of the old Confederacy is used as the base population. Measured thus, migration was slightly over 25 percent of the rural southern African American population from 1940 to 1950, and 29 percent for the decade 1950 to 1960.

How high is this rate compared with other times and places? To get a sense of this, we refer to the dust bowl years, regarded as among those of greatest hardship in the twentieth century. Even this seemingly catastrophic change produced lower migration rates. For instance, from 1930 to 1940 more than 570,000 people left the states of Oklahoma, Kansas, and Nebraska, but the migration rates of the total (mainly white) populations were barely more than 11 percent of their 1930 populations.

The changing regional distribution of the population that resulted from migration provides another perspective on this issue. The pie charts (see Charts 1, 2, 3, and 4) illustrate the fact that in 1940 more than three-quarters of the U.S. black population lived in the South, but by 1970 that figure was 55 percent. The North (shown including the Midwest) steadily grew, as did the West from a mere 1 percent to 8 percent by 1970.

Urbanization

One should be aware that the migration just described implied a steady urbanization of the African American population. Sometime between 1940 and 1950 America's black population became more urban than rural for the first time in American history. This demographic shift lagged thirty years after similar changes for the U.S. white population.

Chart 1. Percentage Distribution of the U.S. African American Population in 1940

Chart 2. Percentage Distribution of the U.S. African American Population in 1950

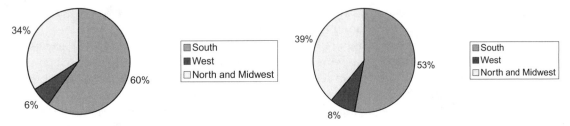

Chart 3. Percentage Distribution of the U.S. African American Population in 1960

Chart 4. Percentage Distribution of the U.S. African American Population in 1970

SOURCE: Calculated from U.S. Bureau of the Census, *Historical Statistics of the United States, Colonial Times to 1970*, Bicentennial Edition (Washington, DC: Government Printing Office, 1975).

Among the northern and western destination cities are familiar names—**Chicago**, **Detroit**, **New York City**, and **Los Angeles**. While the largest number of migrants streamed into these cities, smaller cities also became important destinations. For instance, while Chicago received 166,000 black migrants from 1940 to 1950 (a rate of 56 percent of its 1940 black population), Toledo, Ohio, received 7,600 black migrants, and Rochester, New York, 3,300, both at rates of 51 percent; Peoria, Illinois, experienced 2,000 black immigrants, a rate of 69 percent of its 1940 African American population. While these are not necessarily representative cities, these numbers provide some sense of the magnitudes involved.

Sometimes neglected is the fact that the African American urban population in the South was a net receiving area for migrants, although to a much lesser degree than in the rest of the nation. For example, between 1940 and 1960 more than half a million African Americans moved into southern cities, at rates close to 10 percent per decade of those black urban populations. Many of the larger destination cities tended to be on the coasts and edges of the South; between 1940 and 1950 Norfolk was the destination of 18,000 black migrants, **Houston**, 25,000, and **New Orleans**, 12,000. Thus southern urban immigration of African Americans was significant, although much smaller than the 3 million who moved into the urban North and West.

The social and economic characteristics of the migrants demonstrate that they were hardly representative of the populations from which they came. Among the most notable differences were that migrants tended to be younger and male and to have had more schooling than averages of the populations from which they came. Migration tended to be greatest among the younger age groups. All ages moved, but the twenty to twenty-four age group demonstrated the largest numbers and highest rates of migration, and by far those under the age of thirty tended to be most mobile. Both single individuals and families joined the migration stream. Those with more schooling tended to migrate at greater rates than others.

As with other migrations, both national and international, the paths tended to follow those of early movers. The streams were identifiable. They were heaviest from the Deep South to the cities (although again, some may not have been direct). Those from the Carolinas, for instance, tended to go to New York; those from Mississippi went to Chicago; black migrants from Texas and

Louisiana had a greater tendency to migrate to the West Coast. There were other streams, although less intensely focused.

Migrants seemed to move in steps or stages from farms or very rural areas to cities, gaining urban work experience as they went, although evidence on this is indirect. Thus direct farm-to-factory migration was less common than it first appears. Mixed in, however, were numerous cases of direct moves.

Another interesting feature of the population movement is that whites also moved out of many of these states, but during some of this period whites actually moved into the South. For instance, Arkansas experienced large migrations of blacks and whites. On the other hand, South Carolina and North Carolina evidenced a large out-migration of African Americans in the 1950s at the same time that whites were moving in, in more modest numbers. This no doubt had to do with the fact that the largest industry, textiles, was highly segregated until after enforcement of the 1964 Civil Rights Act.

Causes of Migration

The causes of these great waves of migration were varied. Both long-term factors—those that had been operative throughout the century—and short-term causes were at work. The long-term factors were hostility toward blacks in the South perpetrated by whites, higher wages in the North, and rising education levels in the South. Shorter-term factors were World War II, which drew workers into defense and related industries, and conscription. President Roosevelt's Executive Order 8802 in 1941, establishing the **Fair Employment Practices Committee**, which barred discrimination in defense plants, cleared the way for African Americans to enter the industry in large numbers. Of those entering the military, many fortunate enough to survive the war did not return to the rural South. After 1950 the mechanization of the cotton harvest, the decrease in the importance of cotton overall, and government programs to reduce crop acreage were important factors that encouraged black out-migration.

Among the most underappreciated demographic features of this period was the rising fertility rate of the African American population. The national rate of population growth for the American black population was 17 percent from 1950 to 1960 and 25 percent from 1950 to 1960. Thus the number of individuals moving was greatly affected by this phenomenon. The entire period 1940 to 1970 entailed a dramatic shift in the center of the African American population, and along with it came social, economic, cultural, and political changes of enormous significance. *See also* Great Migration, Causes of; Mechanical Cotton Harvester; Migrants, Economic Characteristics of; Migrants, Social Characteristics of; Wartime Mobilization, World War II; Western States, Black Migration to.

Further Reading

Collins, William. "When the Tide Turned: Immigration and the Delay of the Great Black Migration." *Journal of Economic History* 57 (1997): 607–32.
Davis, G. A., and F. D. Donaldson. *Blacks in the United States: A Geographic Perspective*. Boston: Houghton Mifflin, 1975.

Farley, Reynolds. *Growth of the Black Population*. Chicago: Markham Publishing, 1970.

Gregory, James N. *The Southern Diaspora: How the Great Migrations of Black and White Southerners Transformed America*. Chapel Hill: University of North Carolina Press, 2005.

Heinicke, Craig W. "African-American Migration and Mechanized Cotton Harvesting, 1950–1960." *Explorations in Economic History* 31 (1994): 501–20.

Johnson, D. M., and R. R. Campbell. *Black Migration in America*. Durham, NC: Duke University Press, 1981.

Margo, R. A. *Race and Schooling in the South, 1870–1950: An Economic History*. Chicago: University of Chicago Press, 1990.

Price, D. O. *Changing Characteristics of the Negro Population*. U.S. Census Monograph. Washington, DC: Government Printing Office, 1969.

Craig W. Heinicke

DePriest, Oscar (1871–1951)

Born in Florence, Alabama, in 1871, Oscar DePriest was the first black politician to use the North's growing black vote to achieve both local and national office. A politically active family, the DePriests fled the violent repression of Redemption—a political movement that overthrew the Reconstruction State government in the South—migrating to Salina, Kansas, in 1878 (see **Exodusters**). After completing grammar school and two years of normal school, DePriest left for **Chicago** in 1889.

DePriest quickly achieved success in politics and real estate by using the opportunities created by the migration of southern blacks to Chicago, which had brought 40,000 blacks by 1910 and another 50,000 by 1920. His first major political move came just after the turn of the century when he organized a group of black precinct captains to demand recognition from the white Republican committeeman of Chicago's Second Ward, Martin Madden. This move gained DePriest recognition as a rising leader, and he won his first election, to the Cook County Commission, in 1904. Infighting between machine leaders led to DePriest's removal from the ticket in 1908. Consequently, between 1908 and 1914 DePriest focused on real estate, making a fortune by **blockbusting**—scaring white tenants into leaving an area and charging incoming black migrants even higher rents. Meanwhile, DePriest remained cordial to the Republican machine, supporting three of its candidates for city council even though several qualified black candidates also competed. His support for the machine paid off, though, and as the South Side's black population grew, DePriest, along with Ed Wright and Robert R. Jackson, played a prominent role in organizing blacks into an effective political force.

Their work resulted in DePriest's groundbreaking election to the city council in 1915. As an alderman, DePriest pushed for a civil rights ordinance and worked closely with Republican mayor William "Big Bill" Thompson. Thompson actively recruited black support, which drew him the enmity of his political rivals. Indeed, Thompson's future opponent for mayor, State's Attorney Maclay Hoyne, filed corruption charges against DePriest in 1917. Although DePriest was acquitted, the charges forced him to resign. Yet DePriest retained his political capital by organizing the People's Movement, an independent political party that DePriest could count on for at least 6,000 votes.

Having demonstrated the power of the new black vote at the local level, DePriest by his election to Congress in 1928 signaled the arrival of black migrants to the national political stage. In the 1920s DePriest and his People's Movement reunited with the Republican machine, giving Thompson crucial support in his successful 1928 mayoral campaign. When Republican congressman Martin Madden died unexpectedly that year, DePriest quickly positioned himself to take his place on the ticket and won the election against an independent black candidate by 4,000 votes. Throughout his three terms in office DePriest fought against segregation and urged blacks to push for political organization.

By the 1930s Chicago's Democratic organization had begun to compete for the city's black vote, as indicated by DePriest's failure to win a fourth term. After winning one more term to the city council (1943–1947), DePriest died in Chicago in 1951. *See also* Black Legislators; Dawson, William Levi; Electoral Politics; Mitchell, Arthur Wergs; Political Realignment.

Further Reading

Branham, Charles. "The Transformation of Black Political Leadership in Chicago, 1864–1942." Ph.D. diss., University of Chicago, 1981.

"DePriest, Oscar Stanton (1871–1951)." Biographical Directory of the United States Congress. http://bioguide.congress.gov/scripts/biodisplay.pl?index=D000263.

Drake, St. Clair, and Horace Cayton. *Black Metropolis: A Study of Negro Life in a Northern City*. Rev. and enl. ed. Chicago: University of Chicago Press, 1993.

Spear, Allan H. *Black Chicago: The Making of a Negro Ghetto, 1890–1920*. Chicago: University of Chicago Press, 1967.

Christopher Manning

Desegregation

In an ideal world, the term *desegregation* is defined simply as the elimination of legally mandated racial discrimination, but the reality of racial struggles has complicated that definition in U.S. history. When powerful whites have resisted or delayed the removal of discriminatory barriers, civil rights advocates have responded by pressing for affirmative measures to end racial isolation through integration, particularly in the realm of public schooling. History has blurred the abstract line between desegregation and integration. Furthermore, the political history of these movements has been closely linked to demographic change, particularly the migration of blacks from the South to the North and of whites from cities to suburbs.

In the context of the nineteenth-century abolitionist movement, selected groups of activists challenged racial separation in northern schools. Legal historian Davison Douglas recounts the struggles that resulted in legislative bans against segregated schooling in Massachusetts (1855), Rhode Island (1866), Connecticut (1868), and elsewhere. The last holdout was Indiana, where the state legislature abolished all officially sanctioned school segregation in 1949.

Yet the sudden influx of black migrants during the early twentieth century led many white administrators to defy these laws by establishing racial enrollment practices. School segregation became common in many districts north of the Mason-Dixon Line. For example, **Cleveland** and Columbus, Ohio, which had racially integrated schools in the late nineteenth century, both reversed themselves in the 1910s and 1920s by intentionally assigning most black students to schools by race, gerrymandering attendance boundaries, and refusing to permit black teachers in white schools. When Thurgood Marshall of the **National Association for the Advancement of Colored People** (NAACP) attempted to organize a northern school desegregation campaign in the 1940s, the results were mixed, leading him to refocus attention primarily on the southern campaign instead.

The NAACP's intensive groundwork delivered a tremendous legal victory in the 1954 *Brown v. Board of Education* school desegregation case, which prohibited segregated schooling where it had been codified by law in southern and border states. According to historian James Patterson, initial compliance with *Brown* was most apparent in border-state urban school districts, such as **Kansas City**, **St. Louis**, and Oklahoma City, where 70 percent had biracial classrooms by the 1955–1956 school year. In **Baltimore** the official desegregation of public schools led other authorities to announce similar policies for parochial schools and **public housing**. Yet emerging lower-court decisions enabled southern districts to slow down the pace of racial change. A 1955 federal district-court ruling known as the Briggs Dictum interpreted *Brown* to mean that the Constitution "does not require integration.... It merely forbids the use of governmental power to enforce segregation." A year later a growing white resistance movement rallied under the banner of the Southern Manifesto against federal intervention, then gained national attention by actively defying the desegregation of Central High School in Little Rock, Arkansas, in 1957. Although federal desegregation policy eventually prevailed, many southern districts simply demonstrated "token compliance" by replacing formal segregationist barriers with gradualist student enrollment practices that virtually maintained the status quo. In 1964, a decade after *Brown*, 98 percent of southern black students were still in segregated schools.

Outside the southern spotlight, the 1954 *Brown* ruling emboldened activists in the North. Many insisted that the Supreme Court's ruling that "separate educational facilities are inherently unequal" equally applied to northern cities with their growing, concentrated populations of black migrants. *Brown* reignited smoldering school desegregation protests that had been taken up in earlier years by NAACP branches in **New York City**, **Detroit**, and **Philadelphia**. In 1957 the Chicago NAACP marked a historic shift by challenging the existence of predominantly black schools, regardless of the cause. The battle over de jure segregation (by legal requirement) versus de facto segregation (as a matter of fact, such as by **housing** patterns) had begun in northern courts, though the law would remain unclear on this distinction for years to come. Furthermore, not all northern black communities stood united in these debates. The markers of division sometimes traced back to "old" versus "new" migrants. In **Milwaukee** during the 1950s and early 1960s, established black leaders (who had migrated before World War II) defended predominantly black schools and the teachers' jobs they provided, while black integration activists (who had migrated more recently) criticized these schools as inherently inferior and demanded immediate steps toward mixing students of different races. As Kenneth Goings and Raymond Mohl have suggested, newer histories of African Americans in the urban North have expressed deeper understanding of internal class divisions and contestation, particularly when elite and middle-class blacks have had to deal with waves of southern working-class migrants.

Because of meager changes in racial attendance patterns in the decade after *Brown*, school desegregation advocates lobbied for more affirmative measures to integrate classrooms during the 1960s and early 1970s. President Lyndon B. Johnson's administration began pressuring school districts into compliance by threatening to withhold Title I compensatory funds from the Elementary and Secondary Education Act of 1965. Furthermore, the Supreme Court departed from the "Briggs Dictum" by ruling that previously segregated school districts now had an affirmative duty to eliminate racial discrimination "root and branch" in the *Green v. New Kent County* (Virginia) decision of 1968. Three years later the Court authorized the use of specific policy tools—including mandatory busing, redrawing attendance zones, and limited racial-balance quotas—to counter the effects of segregation in the *Swann v. Charlotte-Mecklenburg Board of Education* (North Carolina) decision. By 1973 the Court's affirmative school desegregation rulings crossed into the northern and western regions with the *Keyes v. Denver School District* (Colorado) case. While historians like Diane Ravitch have criticized the legal trajectory of *Brown* as a shift from a noble goal of color-blindness to a misguided crusade for color-consciousness, other historians like James Patterson have countered that the evolution of desegregation policy has been justified in light of intense white resistance to racial justice.

Yet all agree that the Supreme Court's affirmative desegregation rulings soon came to an abrupt halt at the city-suburban line. In *Milliken v. Bradley* (1974) a sharply divided Court struck down a plan to merge the predominantly black **Detroit** city schools and surrounding white suburban schools into one metropolitan district because of the lack of evidence that the suburban schools had intentionally segregated students. In other northern cities, such as **Boston**, white antibusing protesters violently challenged a federal court plan that mandated the integration of working-class black and white neighborhoods while leaving upper-class whites relatively untouched. Critics of desegregation charged that court mandates threatened to drive whites away from northern cities, but historians countered that suburbanization had long preceded these 1970s events. Nevertheless, conservative shifts in federal administrations and courts since the 1980s have led to a retrenchment of affirmative desegregation policy. Fifty years after *Brown*, reports indicate that school desegregation policies have been most successful in southern and border states, while the Northeast remains the most racially segregated region in the nation.

The politics of school desegregation have become deeply linked to the shifting racial demography of American history. During the Great Migration, when millions of black families left the rural South for the urban North, they did not fully escape segregated schools. Northern whites commonly responded to incoming black migrants by designing policies and practices to maintain white privilege in public education. Sometimes northern whites implemented policies that specifically separated the races, but more often they relied upon the subtler influences of private real estate markets and neighborhood school attendance zones. For nearly two decades after *Brown* the U.S. Supreme Court remained focused on desegregation enforcement in southern and border states. Yet when civil rights advocates successfully pressured the courts to scrutinize the northern cities, the great white migration to the suburbs had already begun. *See also* Open Housing; Schoolteachers and Teaching; Urban Crisis of the 1960s; War on Poverty; White Flight.

Further Reading

Dougherty, Jack. *More than One Struggle: The Evolution of Black School Reform in Milwaukee*. Chapel Hill: University of North Carolina Press, 2004.

Douglas, Davison. *Jim Crow Moves North: The Battle over Northern School Segregation, 1865-1954*. New York: Cambridge University Press, 2005.

Goings, Kenneth W., and Raymond A. Mohl. "Toward a New African American Urban History." *Journal of Urban History* 21 (March 1995): 283-95.

Patterson, James T. *Brown v. Board of Education: A Civil Rights Milestone and Its Troubled Legacy*. New York: Oxford University Press, 2001.

Ravitch, Diane. *The Troubled Crusade: American Education, 1945-1980*. New York: Basic Books, 1983.

Jack Dougherty

Detroit, Michigan

In the first two-thirds of the twentieth century, Detroit was one of the most popular destinations in the nation for African Americans migrating from the South. With the city's booming economy acting as a magnet, the number of blacks living in Detroit shot up from 5,700 in 1910 to 120,000 in 1930, a 2,000 percent increase in just two decades. The Great Depression reduced the flood of newcomers to a trickle, but the Motor City's massive World War II-era mobilization triggered a second migration even larger than the first. By 1970 Detroit was home to 660,000 African Americans, a black population larger than that of any other city but **New York City** and **Chicago**.

Detroit's great migration was inextricably tied to the city's development as the world center of automobile production. The auto industry experienced such phenomenal growth in the first few decades of the twentieth century that manufacturers had trouble finding enough workers to staff their assembly lines. Desperate to meet the labor shortage, automakers paid wages higher than those available in most of industrial America. In their early days, moreover, the largest auto companies did not maintain strictly segregated workplaces, and in the city's working-class neighborhoods blacks and whites often lived side by side. Many African Americans thus saw in Detroit the grand promise of a life free from **Jim Crow**'s grinding poverty and perpetual oppression. One migrant remembered hearing that a Detroit workman could

Residents stroll through the black business district of Detroit in 1942. Courtesy of the Library of Congress.

earn twelve dollars a day. In his native Georgia the man got by on one-sixth that amount. So he packed his bags and headed for Motown.

As the Great Migration intensified, however, Detroit's opportunities constricted. In the immediate aftermath of World War I the auto industry hardened its color line. Although practices varied from factory to factory, employers typically relegated black **automobile workers** to the most demanding, dangerous, and lowest-paying jobs they had to offer. At the Dodge Brothers' sprawling assembly plant they were assigned to the spray room, where they spent their days enveloped in toxic clouds of paint particles. At Cadillac Motors they were slotted into the wet-sanding department. And in plant after plant they were disproportionately represented in the foundries, working in the blistering heat generated by massive furnaces and vats of molten metal.

Segregation also spread through the streets of Detroit in the 1920s. White realtors, developers, bankers, and insurance agents used a variety of mechanisms, from **restrictive covenants** to redlining, to bar African Americans from all but a handful of inner-city neighborhoods. Blacks who managed to break through the businessmen's barriers often met violent resistance from white home owners. In 1925 alone, white mobs attacked five black families who had dared to move across the color line; the clashes resulted in one death and several injuries. Once neighborhoods were segregated, so were public schools and many other public spaces, such as theaters, restaurants, and amusement parks. City officials ignored the needs of the largest African American area, a desperately overcrowded **ghetto** known as Black Bottom, while the almost exclusively white police force ran roughshod over the district's residents.

Still, living in Detroit had its benefits. Despite discrimination at the hiring gate, migrants who found work in the auto industry could indeed bring home paychecks far larger than those earned by most southern laborers. Newcomers also slipped into an extraordinarily rich community life, much of it shaped by southern traditions. Migrants such as Mississippi-born C. L. Franklin infused black Detroit's churches with southern-style religiosity; Mississippians Thad Jones and John Lee Hooker, Texas native Sippie Wallace, and other transplanted artists filled Black Bottom's many nightclubs and juke joints with brilliant **jazz** and the deepest of Delta **blues**; and political activists such as Floridian George Crockett brought to the city's public life a rage for racial justice born amid the brutalities of Jim Crow. Because the growing black population constituted a potentially powerful voting bloc, moreover, African American demands for equal rights could not be ignored or suppressed the way they were in much of the South.

Black Detroit was crosscut with **political activism**. Beginning in the 1920s, African Americans gradually built a base in the Michigan Democratic Party. Other African Americans turned to more radical alternatives: the Communist Party, for instance, enjoyed solid support during the Great Depression and World War II. Once Detroit's auto plants were unionized in the late 1930s, black workers demanded that their unions promote civil rights, both on the shop floor and in the city at large. The local branch of the **National Association for the Advancement of Colored People** (NAACP), the largest in the nation in the 1940s, repeatedly challenged the legal structures that supported Detroit's segregation. And any number of organizations—church groups, block clubs, and even informal gatherings of coworkers and friends—mounted protests against specific acts of discrimination.

Slowly the pressure broke down many of Detroit's racial barriers. During World War II African Americans began to gain access to a much wider range of jobs inside the city's auto plants. In the landmark case *Shelley v. Kraemer* (1948), which originated on Detroit's west side, the NAACP persuaded the U.S. Supreme Court to declare restrictive covenants unconstitutional. Alhough discrimination in the **housing** market continued, over the next quarter century black home owners were able to move into previously all-white neighborhoods across Detroit. African Americans likewise broke the white stranglehold on public office, electing Michigan's first black congressman in 1954, Detroit's first circuit court judge in 1955, and the city's first black city councilman in 1957. Electoral success led to legislative change: after years of agitation, in 1963 African Americans and their white allies finally pushed through a state civil rights law banning discrimination in education, housing, and public accommodations.

Achieving racial justice in Detroit, however, proved to be a mighty struggle. Some problems, such as the segregation of schools and the persistence of **police brutality**, proved impervious to reform. To make matters worse, whites did their best to undermine many of the victories African Americans secured, even to the point of violence. In the 1940s and early 1950s white autoworkers repeatedly walked off their jobs to protest African Americans taking jobs that had been reserved for whites; again and again white home owners attacked blacks who dared to move into their neighborhoods; and on one bitter Sunday in 1943 white gangs clashed with African Americans in the city's largest public park, triggering two days of rioting so vicious that it left thirty-four people dead. Once African Americans battled through such resistance and cracked Detroit's color line, whites fled the city in staggering numbers: between 1950 and 1960, Detroit's white population plummeted by 360,000, from 1,550,000 people to 1,188,000. Most of those who left Detroit moved to its sprawling suburban ring, which barred African Americans with the sharpest of color lines. At the same time, the city's once-enviable economic base began to decay, shedding 100,000 manufacturing jobs in the 1950s alone. **Deindustrialization** hit African Americans particularly hard, since they were more reliant than whites on work in the manufacturing sector. By 1960 black

Detroiters suffered from a 16 percent **unemployment** rate, three times that of whites in the city. Migration continued throughout the period, but Detroit was clearly no longer the promising place it once had been.

The Motor City's racial problems culminated in the latter half of the 1960s. Intensifying poverty, ongoing police harassment, and mounting frustration at the pace of racial change led to a massive outbreak of inner-city rioting in July 1967. The weeklong cataclysm—one of the worst urban disorders of the twentieth century—claimed forty-three lives, destroyed $80 million of property, and left almost 400 families homeless. It also accelerated already rampaging **white flight** from the city: in the twelve months after the riot 80,000 whites left Detroit, almost four times the number who had done so in 1966. The exodus gave African Americans control of city government: in 1973 Detroit's voters—a majority of them now black—elected the city's first African American mayor, Alabama-born **Coleman Young**. But the city's new leadership faced a daunting set of problems. As they fled to the suburbs, whites took a substantial chunk of Detroit's tax base with them. The situation was made even more dire by the continuing erosion of factory work. Detroit lost 19 percent of its jobs between 1969 and 1973 as the deindustrialization of the United States began in earnest. By the mid-1970s a city that had once boasted of the nation's most vibrant economy was locked in a downward spiral, its city services starved for money, many of its neighborhoods scarred by poverty, and its **crime** rate soaring.

Detroit's precipitous decline brought an end to in-migration. In the past two decades, in fact, as the city's struggles have continued, African Americans have started to leave Detroit, which now has a population half that of its 1950 peak. Like their white counterparts, many of the wealthiest black Detroiters have moved to the suburbs. And thousands of the less fortunate have quit the area altogether, some of them, at least, heading back to the South in search of the opportunities that the Motor City no longer provides. *See also* Bradby, Robert L; Detroit Race Riot of 1943; United Automobile Workers (UAW); Primary Documents 2, 5, 57, 66.

Further Reading

Boykin, Ulysses W. *A Handbook on the Detroit Negro*. Detroit: Minority Study Associates, 1943.

Boyle, Kevin. *Arc of Justice: A Saga of Race, Civil Rights, and Murder in the Jazz Age*. New York: Henry Holt, 2004.

Haynes, George Edmund. *Negro Newcomers in Detroit, Michigan*. 1918. Reprint, New York: Arno Press, 1969.

Sugrue, Thomas J. *The Origins of the Urban Crisis: Race and Inequality in Postwar Detroit*. Princeton, NJ: Princeton University Press, 1996.

Thomas, Richard W. *Life for Us Is What We Make It: Building Black Community in Detroit, 1915–1945*. Bloomington: Indiana University Press, 1992.

Thompson, Heather. *Whose Detroit? Politics, Labor, and Race in a Modern American City*. Ithaca, NY: Cornell University Press, 2001.

Wolcott, Victoria W. *Remaking Respectability: African American Women in Interwar Detroit*. Chapel Hill: University of North Carolina Press, 2001.

Kevin Boyle

Detroit Race Riot of 1943

The Detroit race riot of 1943 was undoubtedly the worst truly racial dis-turbance in the United States before the "urban rebellions" of the late 1960s. **Detroit** maintained a small but influential black population throughout the nineteenth century (a little more than 4,000 by 1900, nearly 6,000 by 1910). By the time of World War I, however, with the cutoff of European migration, there was an increased demand for laborers in northern industrial centers. Black southern migrants entered Detroit in record numbers in hopes of se-curing employment in the city's thriving automobile plants. In the period between 1915 and 1920 the black population reached some 40,000, placing considerable strain on the city's **housing** market. While most of Detroit's working-class neighborhoods were never exclusively racially segregated, the 1920s witnessed increased racial tensions as rising middle-class blacks sought to escape the congested east side. Similarly, Detroit was not immune from the racial hostility created by the resurgence of the **Ku Klux Klan** throughout the North during this decade.

Over the next twenty years Detroit developed a distinct history of racial conflict. The two most notable incidents involved black **physician** Ossian Sweet's attempt to move into an all-white neighborhood in 1925. In what became a landmark case in Detroit civil rights history, the Sweets were ac-quitted of murdering a member of a rock-throwing white mob that attempted to force the Sweets to move.

The other event took place in the early 1940s as another wave of black southerners flocked to Detroit in pursuit of employment opportunities in the city's defense industries. In an incident commonly referred to as the Sojourner Truth Housing Controversy, whites and blacks clashed in February 1942 when blacks attempted to move into a federally supported housing project.

Against this backdrop, the Motor City was primed for the violence that erupted the week of June 20, 1943. Amid unusually warm weather hundreds of blacks and whites flocked to Belle Isle amusement park. Throughout the day isolated confrontations between white and black teenagers multiplied. By nightfall, when people began leaving for home, the bridge leading back to the mainland became overly congested, and hundreds of whites, along with sai-lors from the nearby Naval Armory, began an all-out assault against black citizens. Soon the crowd swelled to several thousand whites who continued the attacks.

The violence intensified over the next forty-eight hours, largely be-cause of rumors that accused whites of throwing a black woman and her baby off the Belle Isle bridge, and that a black man had raped and murdered a white woman on the bridge. In response to the first rumor, blacks stormed the streets of the east side **ghetto** known as Paradise Valley and destroyed a number of businesses owned by whites. White mobs roamed the downtown area of the city looking for streetcars and single automobiles with black passengers. Blacks were pulled from buses and beaten, and their automobiles were overturned and set afire. Throughout most of the vio-lence Detroit police stood by as spectators while white mobs ravaged black citizens.

After sustaining a gunshot wound to the stomach, an African American victim of the 1943 Detroit race riot finds his police escort inadequate protection from further harassment from the white mob. © AP/Wide World Photos.

Not until late on the second day of rioting did Mayor Edward Jeffries call for the assistance of federal troops to quell the violence. Some 6,000 soldiers were placed throughout the city to bring the tensions under control. By June 23 the worst of the violence was over, but the injuries, loss of life, and property destruction were tragic. Thirty-four persons were killed—nine whites and twenty-five blacks. Seventeen of the black victims had been shot by white police officers. Estimates of property damage were said to be between $2 and $3 million.

Various perspectives on how and why the riot occurred and who started it were offered by city officials and both the white and **black press**. According to Wayne County prosecutor William E. Dowling, every sector of Detroit's black community was to blame. He specifically pointed to the **National Association for the Advancement of Colored People** and the black press as the "biggest instigators." Mayor Jeffries blamed "Negro hoodlums" and commended the police for their role. Some accused Axis and Japanese agents seeking to disrupt the war effort. Others saw the riot as the result of built-up tensions between black residents of Paradise Valley and Jewish landlords and entrepreneurs. Nearly 75 percent of the business establishments along a two-mile strip of Hastings Street in the heart of the Valley were Jewish owned and had experienced some form of damage.

More than anything else, Detroit's racial climate before and after the riot reflected a complex mixture of social, political, and economic disparities that fueled ongoing tensions. City officials in Detroit formed the Mayor's Interracial Committee to monitor race relations and prevent future violence of the magnitude of the 1943 riot. Nonetheless, institutional racism manifested in the process of **urban renewal** and **police brutality** in the black community in the postwar years led to yet another episode of citywide violence and destruction by the late 1960s. *See also* Beaumont, Texas, Race Riot of 1943; Harlem Riot of 1943; Racial Violence and World War II; Zoot-Suit Riots (1943).

Further Reading

Capeci, Dominic J., Jr., and Martha Wilkerson. *Layered Violence: The Detroit Rioters of 1943*. Jackson: University Press of Mississippi, 1991.

Humphrey, Norman D. *Race Riot*. New York: Dryden Press, 1943.

Shogan, Robert, and Tom Craig. *The Detroit Race Riot*. New York: Chilton Books, 1964.

Sitkoff, Harvard. "The Detroit Race Riot of 1943." *Michigan History* 53 (Fall 1969): 183–206.

Marshall F. Stevenson

Detroit Riot of 1967 *See* Urban Crisis of the 1960s

Division of Negro Economics (DNE)

In the spring of 1918 Secretary of Labor William B. Wilson established the Division of Negro Economics (DNE) within the U.S. Department of Labor and appointed Fisk University professor **George Edmund Haynes** as its director. The DNE was the first federal institutional initiative to address the distinctive problems of African Americans since the liquidation in 1869 of the Freedmen's Bureau, and it represented the national government's most significant response to the effects of the Great Migration. Its charge was to promote the efficient use of black labor in connection with the war effort, to investigate and ameliorate the social and workplace tensions arising out of the migration, and to promote the well-being of black workers, North and South.

The origins of the DNE lay in concerns among southern agriculturalists, trade unionists, and civil rights leaders about the effects of the Great Migration. In 1916, in response to alarms about the economic and social impact of widespread movement northward, Secretary Wilson commissioned a study of the reasons for the black exodus. The resulting report, which stressed the economic roots of the migration and refuted alarmist claims that it jeopardized southern agricultural production, encouraged Wilson to authorize a more ambitious study under the direction of foundation executive Dr. James Dillard, who recruited researchers to examine both the push and the pull factors affecting migration. The Dillard report documented the vast scope of the folk movement, as well as its informal and popular character, and laid the basis for more systematic federal engagement. In February 1918 the Department of Labor held a conference on problems of black labor, involving representatives of the **National Association for the Advancement of Colored People**, the

National Urban League, and other African American leaders. The creation of the DNE shortly after this conference reflected the belief of Secretary Wilson and his chief aide, Assistant Secretary Louis Post, that the migration was permanently transforming the nation's labor-force demographics and as such created a need for ongoing federal interest. In establishing the new agency and in selecting Haynes, a respected scholar sympathetic to the aspirations of northward-bound blacks, Wilson short-circuited the ambitious plans of Giles Jackson, an aspiring African American public entrepreneur. Jackson had found considerable support among southern white politicians and national labor leaders for a scheme that would have discouraged migration in favor of a government-backed program to keep southern blacks on the farms. In deflecting the potent political forces associated with Jackson's initiative, Wilson and Post signaled that they regarded the migration as offering advantages to both the war effort and the African American community, thus aligning themselves with the views of most race leaders.

The thirty-eight-year-old Haynes was a founder and early executive secretary of the National Urban League and the author of an important book on black urban life. He quickly appointed representatives in various states to work with state and local authorities and with biracial committees of notables for the purpose of fulfilling the DNE's mission. Haynes employed only African Americans for DNE work, in part to challenge the widespread belief that blacks could not meet high standards of professional behavior and public service. Field agents conducted detailed studies of industrial and social conditions in states affected by the migration. In addition, Haynes orchestrated a public relations campaign designed to gain the confidence of African Americans, educate the public about the contributions of black workers, and convince southern agriculturalists and northern white workers that the migration did not threaten their own economic interests.

Haynes had to pursue these goals with limited budgetary and personnel resources. As an arm of the Department of Labor reporting directly to the secretary, the DNE was dependent on other department agencies, most notably the U.S. Employment Service, for office and secretarial support. Partly as a result of these limitations, DNE statewide committees functioned in only nine states, five in the South and four in the North. In southern states the DNE countered rumors that blacks were refusing to work or were influenced by radical or pro-German propaganda. At the same time, its representatives sought to persuade employers to improve wages and working conditions. In general, its efforts enjoyed more success in the Upper South than in the Deep South, where white hostility toward black field representatives clothed with federal authority limited the agency's effectiveness. The DNE's most successful southern program was in North Carolina, where an extensive network of local committees and enthusiastic support by white political leaders facilitated the placement of black workers and promoted improved conditions in the state's farms and mills.

In northern states DNE directors conducted surveys of working and living conditions among migrating blacks, stressing the contributions of black workers to the war effort and the need for fairer treatment and improved **housing**. Haynes's own postwar reports of conditions in **Detroit** and strife-torn **Chicago** exemplified sober Progressive Era social observation. Field representatives frequently intervened with landlords and employers on behalf of black workers and their families. In both North and South the DNE cooperated with state authorities, private organizations, and other federal agencies to establish innovative housing projects.

Along with the War Department's appointment of **Emmett Scott** as special adviser and sporadic gestures toward fair treatment in other wartime agencies, the DNE seemed to offer hope of racial progress in a presidential administration otherwise notable for its segregationist policies. Haynes and his associates insisted that problems and opportunities accompanying the Great Migration made permanent federal concern with black workers imperative, a position that Department of Labor officials endorsed. However, southern congressional hostility toward any gesture of recognition for African Americans, along with bipartisan postwar budget cutting, doomed the DNE, which went out of existence in 1921. While no detailed assessment of its tangible accomplishments has ever been made, the DNE did represent an effort to bring characteristically progressive methods of investigation and social amelioration into the otherwise neglected realm of urban race relations. The various reports that Haynes and other DNE staff members produced remain valuable sources for students of the social and economic impact of the Great Migration. *See also* Employment, Black Female Patterns of; Employment, Black Male Patterns of; Employment Discrimination; National War Labor Board (NWLB); Primary Document 38, 76.

Further Reading

Guzda, Henry P. "Social Experiment of the Department of Labor: The Division of Negro Economics." *Public Historian* 4 (Fall 1982): 7–37.

Haynes, George Edmund. *The Negro at Work during the World War and during Reconstruction: Statistics, Problems, and Policies Relating to the Greater Inclusion of Negro Wage Earners in American Industry and Agriculture*. Washington, DC: Government Printing Office, 1921.

———. *Negro New-comers in Detroit, Michigan*. 1918. Reprint, New York: Arno Press, 1969.

U.S. Department of Labor. Division of Negro Economics. *Negro Migration in 1916–17*. Washington, DC: Government Printing Office, 1919; New York: Arno Press, 1969.

Robert H. Zieger

DNE *See* Division of Negro Economics (DNE)

"Don't Buy Where You Can't Work" Campaigns

Ongoing racial discrimination, the ravages of the Great Depression, and the heightened expectations of new migrants intersected to produce employment campaigns in dozens of urban centers in the 1930s. Collectively referred to as "Don't Buy Where You Can't Work" campaigns, these were local efforts, promoted by the **black press** and spearheaded by community groups, to compel white-owned businesses in black neighborhoods to hire black clerical workers. Fair employment efforts predated these campaigns, but after Charles Bibb, editor of the *Chicago Whip*, the Reverend J. C. Austin, and others inaugurated an organized community effort in **Chicago** in 1929, the idea spread, spurred by the depression's hardships.

Generally these protest groups utilized consumer petitions, private meetings with store owners, newspaper coverage, and similarly nonconfrontational strategies to obtain their goals. Organizations like the **National Urban League** often lent their contacts, training facilities, and negotiating experience. Most of these early efforts failed, however, because of both the discriminatory attitudes of many whites and the limited employment possibilities in marginal, underfunded, family-owned stores. But the presidency of Franklin Roosevelt, the political nature of the New Deal, and new pro-labor and antidiscrimination legislation encouraged African Americans, as they did other marginalized groups, to organize and to publicize their grievances.

By the mid-1930s residents of poor black neighborhoods in approximately thirty-five mostly northern and midwestern cities took to the streets, calling on community members to boycott stores that refused to hire black people or to promote them above menial levels. Meanwhile, many black store owners who had long promoted economic nationalism joined the struggle, calling on residents to "buy black." Progressives and **Communists**, uncomfortable with the nationalism of "buy black" campaigns but supportive of black equality, called for fair and equal hiring policies. These antidiscrimination efforts to improve black employment thus enjoyed widespread support, although the goals of participants were not always the same.

Much of the energy of these campaigns came from recent migrants from southern, rural, and Caribbean communities. Moving to cities in order to improve their lives, lured by the absence of legal segregation and the opportunities for economic advancement, these new residents instead confronted entrenched economic discrimination, poorer jobs, and lower pay, inequalities intensified by the economic devastation of the depression. As many noted, blacks, even in the urban North, were "last hired, first fired." Desperate and angry, these migrants made up a substantial proportion of both the urban black population and the protesters themselves.

Migrants were also prominent among the leaders of these protests, from Georgia-born Ira Kemp and Barbadian Arthur Reid of the Harlem Labor Union in **New York City** to Tennessee native William Hastie, who served as counsel for **Washington, D.C.**,'s New Negro Alliance. Others, like Sufi Abdul Hamid, migrated to New York via the **Baltimore** and Chicago Don't Buy campaigns. Sometimes working alongside, other times competing with, locally born activists like **Adam Clayton Powell, Jr.**, of New York's Citizens' League for Fair Play (later the Greater New York Coordinating Committee for Employment) or John Aubrey Davis, New Negro Alliance founder, they pleaded with shoppers to make purchases in nondiscriminatory shops, confronted store owners and managers, held public demonstrations, mounted picket lines, threatened business disruptions, and contacted local newspapers.

Complaints and lawsuits by white merchants in Washington, D.C., **Atlanta**, New York, and elsewhere led state and local courts to declare such boycotts unconstitutional because they were not labor disputes, and much of the early energy of the efforts dissipated or was channeled elsewhere. When these decisions were reversed by the Supreme Court in April 1938 (thanks to the tenacity and legal sophistication of the New Negro Alliance), "Don't Buy" campaigns returned with renewed vigor to northern, western, and even a few southern cities. These later protests also broadened their reach, challenging not only small stores but chain stores, utilities, unions, and large private companies to hire qualified black workers at all levels. Many finally succeeded in getting white store owners, union leaders, and company managers to yield to black pressure. In a few cases infighting between nationalist and integration-minded protesters slowed racial progress, but the tactics and goals of these campaigns, as well as their successes, helped set the trajectory of the larger **civil rights movement** to come. *See also* Black Consumer Market; Caribbean Migration; New Negro; Political Activism (1915–1945).

Further Reading

Greenberg, Cheryl. *"Or Does It Explode?" Black Harlem in the Great Depression.* New York: Oxford University Press, 1991.

McDowell, Winston. "Keeping Them 'in the Same Boat Together'?" In *African Americans and Jews in the Twentieth Century*, edited by V. P. Franklin, Nancy L. Grant, Harold M. Kletnick, and Glenna Rae MacNeil, 208–36. Columbia: University of Missouri Press, 1998.

Meier, August, and Elliott Rudwick. "Origins of Non-violent Direct Action in Afro-American Protest." In *Along the Color Line*, edited by August Meier and Elliott Rudwick. Urbana: University of Illinois Press, 1976.

Cheryl Greenberg

Dorsey, Thomas A. (1889–1993)

Thomas A. Dorsey codified **Chicago** gospel **blues** by crystallizing several divergent elements within African American music into a new sacred music. Dorsey added the pentatonic scales, bent notes, and improvisational embellishments of blues to the older African American traditions of gospel hymns and anthems, sanctified singing, and folk and concert spirituals. Willie Webb, a contemporary gospel musician, explained, "Dorsey wrote down what was 'out there.' He was not the first to use blues elements, but he was the first to write it down" (Kalil, 39).

In 1921 the National Baptist Convention published *Gospel Pearls*, which opened the gates of African American Baptists to a body of music that many old-line churches regarded as "low-down, low-class." *Gospel Pearls* embraced a wide range of songs that included Holiness shouts and traditional anthems such as the lined-out songs of Isaac Watts, Ira Sankey's revival tunes, Charles Tindley's sermon-songs, and "Stand by Me."

In the 1930s, when Dorsey asked several large Chicago **Baptist** congregations to include his blues-inflected gospel songs in their services, he found that *Gospel Pearls* had prepared the way. Throughout the 1920s large, old-line Chicago churches like Pilgrim Baptist featured "musicales" that showed off their trained choirs' European repertoires. Many southern migrants, who had filled these churches' pews, left and started their own, more southern churches. Those who stayed, however, asked for more lively services and music. The ministerial and lay leaders of Olivet, Pilgrim, and Ebenezer Baptist churches sought to balance the desires of both the "shouters" and "nonshouters" in their congregations. Still, in the early 1930s these socially prominent churches relegated the newly created gospel choirs to their basements, while the church chorale and large orchestras practiced in the sanctuary. One old-line choir director remarked critically, "The Negro people liked Gospel, 'cause it goes back to Africa" (Harris, 180).

Georgia-born Thomas A. Dorsey arrived in Chicago as "Barrel House Tom," an accomplished honky-tonk piano player. Like **Mahalia Jackson** from **New Orleans** and Roberta Martin from Helena, Arkansas, Dorsey's migrant experience and his roots in sanctified, southern churches left their imprint on his music. The son of a **minister**, "Barrel House Tom" in the mid-1920s became just "Georgia Tom" when he cut his first record, "Tight like That," with Hudson Whittaker ("Tampa Red"). The success of the recording gave Dorsey financial independence, freeing him from working nights in the steel mills of **Gary** while studying composition and accompanying legendary blues singer **Ma Rainey**. Dorsey brought Rainey into religious music. He admired her "down-home" performance style, which captivated Chicago audiences. "She possessed her listeners," he remarked; "they swayed, they rocked, they moaned and groaned, as they felt the blues with her" (Harris, 89). Rainey led Dorsey to appreciate the Pentecostal adaptation of folk spirituals whose call and response, ecstatic expression, hand clapping, and foot stomping sustained the West African musical tradition in black Christianity. Dorsey recalled, "I always had rhythm in my bones. I like the solid beat. I like the moaning and groaning tone. You know how they rock and shout in church. I like it" (Burnim, "Religious Music," 631).

Dorsey restored the blues to Baptist music. The shouts, embellishments, flattened thirds, pentatonic tones or notes, and improvisation all harked back to West African music that mainline Baptist and Methodist churches, at the urging of white missionaries after the Civil War, had eliminated from black services. Dorsey put the "low-down secular blues" back into African American church music. When the pastors of Chicago's elite Baptist churches, such as Ebenezer and Pilgrim, realized how attached their southern migrant congregations were to the old music, they allowed Dorsey's "moaning," sanctified style back into their sanctuaries.

In 1932 Dorsey suffered a personal tragedy that inspired his first masterpiece. "Take My Hand, Precious Lord" established Dorsey as Chicago's preeminent gospel music composer. Written in the wake of the deaths of his wife and newborn son, "Precious Lord" also led to Dorsey's single-minded dedication to religious music. After 1932 "Georgia Tom" ceased to exist.

Dorsey's voice in "Precious Lord" arose from Chicago's impoverished black community. Its first-person intimacy reached back to the spiritual traditions of the praise houses and the brush arbors of slavery. And with Dorsey's use of a single, haunting blue note with the word *hand*, "Precious Lord" vibrated with Ma Rainey's urban blues. *See also* Pentecostalism; Recording Industry; Tharpe, Sister Rosetta.

Further Reading

Boyer, Horace Clarence. *How Sweet the Sound: The Golden Age of Gospel*. Washington, DC: Elliott and Clark, 1995.

Burnim, Mellonee V. "The Black Gospel Tradition: A Complex of Ideology, Aesthetic, and Behavior." In *More than Dancing: Essays on Afro-American Music and Musicians*, edited by Irene W. Jackson. Westport, CT: Greenwood Press, 1985.

———. "Religious Music." In *Garland Encyclopedia of World Music*. New York: Garland Publishers, 2001.

Dargan, William Thomas. "Congregational Gospel Songs in a Black Holiness Church: A Musical and Textural Analysis." Ph.D. diss., Wesleyan University, 1983.

Harris, Michael W. *The Rise of the Gospel Blues: The Music of Thomas Andrew Dorsey in the Urban Church*. New York: Oxford University Press, 1992.

Heilbut, Anthony. *The Gospel Sound: Good News and Bad Times*. New York: Limelight Editions, 2002.

Kalil, Timothy. "The Role of the Great Migration of African Americans to Chicago in the Development of Traditional Black Gospel Piano by Thomas A. Dorsey, circa 1930." Ph.D. diss., Kent State University, 1993.

Peter M. Rutkoff and William B. Scott

Double V Campaign

The black migrants who relocated to New England, the Midwest, and the Far West dramatically recast not only regional politics but national politics as well. However, they did not share a political philosophy or party allegiance. Black politics ran the gamut from conservative Republican to radical **socialist**. One common theme, however, was the use of pressure politics in the quest for equality. The Double V campaign belonged to that tradition.

The phrase "Double V" had its origins from a January 1942 edition of Robert L. Vann's **Pittsburgh Courier** newspaper. A letter to the editor by a black cafeteria worker, James G. Thompson, criticized the nearly omnipresent racial discrimination in the war effort and called on African Americans to take up the cause of a double victory—the defeat of fascism abroad and racial prejudice at home. Shortly thereafter Vann placed a double V image in the nameplate on the front page of his leading black newspaper and continually through his paper exposed racial bias and encouraged social reform. This four-year campaign to secure civil rights for African Americans spread across the nation and became an emblem of World War II. Sponsored by African American journalists, community leaders, and politicians, especially those from areas of heavy black migration, the Double V campaign sought to end what Swedish sociologist Gunnar Myrdal called the "American dilemma," the widespread existence of invidious racial discrimination in a nation supposedly based upon equality, liberty, and freedom.

Narrowly speaking, the Double V campaign was a journalistic tool to draw public attention to the hardships and indignities suffered by African Americans serving in the military and in the nation's war factories. It was also a prime example of the kind of black pressure politics first pioneered by migrants during the Progressive Era. As in the anti-**restrictive covenant** protests or the **"Don't Buy Where You Can't Work" campaigns**, the supporters of the

Double V mobilized the black community behind their cause. Newspapers like the *Pittsburgh Courier* not only carried the message in print but also distributed bumper stickers, buttons, posters, and pamphlets and held rallies and dances to compel employers, politicians, and bureaucrats on ease racial restrictions on war work and inside the military. But as the war progressed, the Double V took on a life of its own. It was something much larger than a publicity campaign of socially conscious newspaper publishers.

The ideas behind the Double V campaign spurred to action African Americans and others who wished to end American racial prejudice and discrimination. In fact, many African Americans had been working toward the goals of the Double V campaign long before Thompson's letter. In late 1940 **A. Philip Randolph**, president of the **Brotherhood of Sleeping Car Porters** and himself a black migrant to **New York City**, met with President Franklin D. Roosevelt concerning discrimination in the military. With no easing of segregation or discrimination in the armed services forthcoming, a few months later Randolph formed a new civil rights organization, the **March on Washington Movement**, to protest bias in the defense effort. The group's proposed march on **Washington, D.C.**, for jobs and freedom was set for July 1, 1941, and had as its twin goals elimination of **employment discrimination** in defense industries and elimination of segregation in the military. Fearing that a march might disrupt wartime unity and spark a race riot, President Roosevelt met with Randolph again and negotiated a deal to call off the demonstration. In return for Randolph's concession, Roosevelt issued Executive Order 8802, which created the **Fair Employment Practices Committee** (FEPC), a government agency dedicated to stopping job bias in defense factories. The FEPC benefited greatly from the Double V campaign, which energized African Americans in the main cities of the black migration to take up the cause of civil rights. For example, in **Cincinnati, Ohio**, the FEPC worked not only with the local **National Association for the Advancement of Colored People** branch but a new organization, the Double V Council of Cincinnati, as well. Although the FEPC made limited gains against employment discrimination, it was nonetheless a significant advance and a crucial element in the Double V campaign.

The other area that the Double V campaign highlighted was segregation and discrimination in America's armed forces. That democracy's standard bearer in World War II fought with a segregated military was an outrage to civil rights activists in the United States. Randolph's pressure on President Roosevelt had yielded small advances, and very slowly military leaders began to open the doors of opportunity for black servicemen and women. Nearly half a million black soldiers fought overseas, and many units like the 614th Tank Destroyer Battalion, the 99th Pursuit Squadron, and the 332nd Fighter Group distinguished themselves.

Yet equality in the military, just like equality in the "arsenal of democracy," was not realized during the war. Like many other attempts by black migrants to pressure the political, social, and economic systems, the Double V campaign achieved an incomplete victory. Black Americans fought valiantly to defeat fascism in Europe and Asia, but the struggle for victory over race prejudice at home became the paramount goal of the postwar period. *See also*

Military Service, World War II; Organized Labor; Political Activism (1915–1945); Wartime Mobilization, World War II; Primary Document 64.

Further Reading

Bailey, Beth, and David Farber. "The Double V Campaign in World War II Hawaii: African American Racial Ideology and Federal Power." *Journal of Social History* 26 (Summer 1993): 817–44.

Kersten, Andrew E. *Race, Jobs, and the War: The FEPC in the Midwest, 1941–46.* Urbana: University of Illinois Press, 2000.

Skinner, Byron Richard. "The Double 'V': The Impact of World War II on Black America." Ph.D. diss., University of California, Berkeley, 1978.

Washburn, Patrick. *A Question of Sedition: The Federal Government's Investigation of the Black Press during World War II.* New York: Oxford University Press, 1986.

Andrew E. Kersten

Douglas, Aaron (1899–1979)

Aaron Douglas was one of the leading visual artists of the **Harlem Renaissance** and one of the first African American practitioners of modernism. He was born in Topeka, Kansas, in 1899. He worked as a high-school art teacher in **Kansas City, Missouri**, until he decided to quit his job and move to Harlem in 1925. Within two weeks he met Bavarian-born artist Winold Reiss and enjoyed a strong relationship with Reiss, working in his studio. He also met **W.E.B. DuBois**, editor of the **National Association for the Advancement of Colored People**'s monthly magazine *Crisis*, who hired him to work in the mailroom and commissioned him to provide illustrations for the magazine. He found regular work with the **National Urban League**'s magazine *Opportunity* as well, under the editorship of **Charles S. Johnson**, and it was at *Opportunity* that he created one of his earliest images of the Great Migration. Douglas was in fact part of that heritage. After the Civil War many black Mississippians known as **Exodusters** settled in Topeka. This politically active community of African Americans, who numbered 10 percent in a state where blacks numbered only 3 percent of the population, provided inspiration for Douglas's migration images.

Douglas had participated in migration north himself. In 1917, determined to pursue a career as an artist rather than as a lawyer, the young Douglas departed for the urban, industrial North on a **railroad** baggage car arranged by **labor agents**. Unlike the black working-class migrants with whom he traveled, the middle-class Douglas aspired to work in industry for only a few months, hoping to earn enough money to enter college. Though his experience working in a Detroit foundry was brief, his memory of factory work in the North influenced his murals and illustrations in decades to come. He later attended the University of Nebraska and earned his bachelor of fine arts degree in 1922. It was at this time that he became a constant reader of *Crisis* magazine.

In October 1926 Douglas participated in a collaborative issue of *Opportunity* with poet **Langston Hughes**. Douglas contributed five drawings for Hughes's six poems, including his illustration *On de No'thern Road*, which accompanied Hughes's famous poem "Bound No'th Blues." Influenced by cubism and Egyptian art as well as Dan masks of the Ivory Coast, Douglas depicted the silhouette of a long and lanky man looking toward a road that led to the back of the composition toward the promised land, a sun rising on the horizon promising a better future. Douglas's use of African motifs also suggested his effort to connect the migrant with a rich African heritage, a theme common throughout much of Douglas's work.

In 1930 Douglas was commissioned to do a substantial series of murals, actually painted on canvas and fastened to the walls, for Cravath Library at Fisk University. He completed the cycle in the summer of 1930. He included an important element of the Great Migration in the South Room of the library, where he showed the importance of labor as a way out of the confines of agricultural life and slavery, and the railroad, which could transport blacks north, as the vehicle to better opportunities.

His Public Works of Art Project murals for the Countee Cullen branch of the New York Public Library, *Aspects of Negro Life* (1934), also made reference to the Great Migration. The four panels chronicled the life of black Americans from the days of life in Africa through slavery, emancipation, and Reconstruction, and finally to the migration north in *Song of the Towers*. Here Douglas described the escape of black Americans from the clutching hand of serfdom in the South to the urban and industrial life in America after World War I. This movement north contributed to the artistic self-expression of artists, musicians, and writers of the Harlem Renaissance of the 1920s, stifled by the frustration and dejection of the Great Depression. A **jazz** player in silhouette dashes up a giant cog of industry, with precisionist skyscrapers surrounding him, the smokestacks of industry looming near him, always threatened, but through his art and music, hope dominates the composition, symbolized by concentric Orphist circles culminating in the silhouette of the Statue of Liberty just behind the saxophone player. Just like Douglas, the musician has risked all to go to the mecca of the **New Negro**, to Harlem. He has left the confines of the life of the agricultural worker. The city may be troubled, but it is a place of possibilities, too.

Douglas made many images of northern industry. These works include *Power Plant in Harlem*, an undated watercolor, and *The Old Waterworks*, featuring railroad tracks and metal towers that run power lines crossing the composition. In

Song of the Towers from Aaron Douglas's *Aspects of Negro Life* series, 1934. © Schomburg Center, The New York Public Library/Art Resource, NY.

1936 he created *Aspiration*, a painting with arms of enslaved peoples lining the base of the composition. Two men and a woman carry symbols of science and learning, all in silhouette, and look toward the top of the composition. Orphist circles and stars lead the viewer to the outline of a factory and skyscrapers, deco-inspired images of industry and northern migration that suggest hope for a better life.

Douglas became the chairman of the art department at Fisk University in 1939. He received a master of fine arts from Columbia University's Teachers College in 1944, working part-time on the degree for several years. He retired from Fisk in 1966 and died in **Nashville** in 1979. Douglas's images of industry and migration were a part of his own history and appeared in his work throughout his lifetime. *See also* New York City; Visual Arts, the Great Migration in.

Further Reading

Kirschke, Amy. *Aaron Douglas: Art, Race, and the Harlem Renaissance.* Jackson: University Press of Mississippi, 1995.

Amy Kirschke

DuBois, William Edward Burghardt (1868–1963)

At first glance, one could hardly find a less likely spokesperson for the people and emergent consciousness of the Great Migration than W.E.B. DuBois. Yet there is no more salient intellectual figure, no more eloquent and effective writer, no more vigorous and passionate advocate for the rights and welfare of the generations of the Great Migration than DuBois. One must say "generations" because from his young manhood in the late nineteenth century to his death in the 1960s, DuBois's work set the tone and terms of debate not only for much of African America, but for the African diaspora and for all those concerned with questions of race on the international stage. His early great work, *The Souls of Black Folk*, was published in 1903, just as the first waters of the migration stirred. There DuBois anticipated the outlines of an emergent African American identity well before the full impact of the migration could have been imagined. So prescient was DuBois's vision and so powerful his rhetoric that the book continues to be a seminal influence on African American studies in religion, sociology, history, and literature. Yet it is one text in a great library of writing—polemical, literary, and scholarly—that firmly establishes DuBois as the single most important African American intellectual figure of the twentieth century. His readers in the hinterlands and even those who knew him well sometimes referred to him as "the Great Man," his enemies with pointed sarcasm, his friends without irony.

So self-consciously did DuBois set himself to the task of being the spokesperson for the race that it is easy to imagine that DuBois typifies the conscious experience of African Americans in the twentieth century. He titled his second autobiography *Dusk of Dawn: An Essay toward an Autobiography of a Race Concept*, reinforcing the notion that he carried the history of the race in his own person. Yet DuBois was clearly among the most singular of men, black or white. His upbringing, education, cosmopolitan worldview, and even his psychic disposition left him at some distance from those for whom he spoke. This distance colored DuBois's perception of his calling, as well as his perception of the needs, urgencies, and destinies of the migrants.

Born William Edward Burghardt DuBois in Great Barrington, Massachusetts, in 1868, DuBois experienced few of the brutalities of racism common in the post-Reconstruction South from which the headwaters of the migration flowed. His earliest memory of racial identity involved the cruelty of a young white girl who refused his greeting card on Valentine's Day—a sharp thorn for a child, and one he recalled painfully even in his late autobiographies. But not the great prison house of **Jim Crow**. Not until his education at Fisk University did DuBois begin to develop a mature consciousness of the status of the color line as the intractable problem of American civilization. This maturation involved a self-conscious effort to identify with and link his fate to the southern African Americans who would soon make the journey north. To do so, DuBois made his own metaphorical and literary journey south. In *The Souls of Black Folk* "Faith of the Fathers" narrates an odyssey wherein DuBois journeys to a small black church to touch the root of African experience in the Americas. Through this experience DuBois imaginatively immersed himself in the identity of the people for whom he soon became public voice and image.

This immersion is thoroughly literary and poetic in tone. Throughout *The Souls of Black Folk* DuBois links the cultural realities of black people, especially poor black folk with their sorrow songs and wailing religion, their great hopes and disappointments, with the great cultural works of European and American history. This is much more than cultural "me-too-ism," though there is some of that. Rather, it is a form of racial cosmopolitanism through which DuBois not only demonstrates his mastery of Western culture, but also insists that black folk, though doubted at every turn, enter the world stage having their own voice and achievements through which to engage in the universal human conversation. DuBois himself embodied this kind of racial cosmopolitanism. Educated at Fisk and Harvard, then in Berlin as a sociologist, DuBois sought to speak for this people and to equip them to participate in what he saw as the great conversation of culture. Whether as the longtime editor of *Crisis*, as a college professor, or as a novelist and poet, DuBois spoke in this double register, opening the ears of those who might otherwise refuse to hear and working for the racial **uplift** of those otherwise afraid or ill equipped to speak.

This deeply intellectual and erudite cosmopolitanism had two effects on DuBois's perceptions of and relation to the Great Migration. First, DuBois connected the migration of African Americans with global struggles of colonized people in Africa and elsewhere. DuBois was the prime mover behind the first pan-African congresses that brought African peoples together to make common cause. He also envisioned a much broader movement that would bring together persons from the African diaspora with peoples of the Asian continent and elsewhere, a vision delineated in his novel *Dark Princess* (1928). The specifics of DuBois's globalism could sometimes be painfully misguided in practice. For a time he actively promoted Japanese imperialism as a great achievement of people of color, glossing over and implicitly excusing the reports of atrocities in China and elsewhere. Moreover, DuBois's grand vision sometimes seemed to have little to do with the African American in the street, men and **women** more concerned with getting a job or having a decent place to live than with their connection to distant Africans or the military triumphs of the Japanese. Nevertheless, his effort to mythologize the migration and see it in terms of global history contributed enormously to the developing identity of African American peoples. Moreover, his globalism makes his best work, some of which is now more than a century old, seem quite contemporary to our own globalizing society.

DuBois's racial cosmopolitanism also contributed to his unshakable conviction in the primary importance of what came to be known as "the talented tenth." In hindsight we can see that DuBois conceived of the talented tenth as at once a conservative elite and a cultural avant-garde directing the unlettered masses toward full integration into the global culture he envisioned. In this vision the attainment of culture and education above all else would pave the path of African equality in America. In a famous refutation of **Booker T. Washington**'s plan for vocational education and political quietism, DuBois glorified the supposed equality and equanimity of the life of the mind and imagination: "I sit with *Shakespeare*, and he winces not. Across the color line I move arm and arm with *Balzac* and *Dumas*, where smiling men and welcoming women glide in gilded halls. From out of the caves of evening that swing between the strong-limbed Earth and the tracery of stars, I summon *Aristotle* and *Aurelius* and what soul I will, and they come all graciously with no scorn nor condescension. So, wed with Truth, I dwell above the veil" (DuBois, 109). Without endorsing Washington's gradualism, we can recognize this vision as utopian and its vision of racial equality as the province of an elite few, black or white. DuBois's admirable lifelong vocation in advocacy for the downtrodden was always threatened by an inability to fully grapple with the conditions of his own relative privilege.

DuBois died in Ghana in 1963, on the eve of the March on Washington. By the 1940s DuBois had begun to doubt the possibilities of African equality in America and had also begun to doubt some of the basic principles of his talented-tenth point of view. His late-life conversion to Communism and his migration to Ghana spoke to these doubts, even while he lived out his faith in a pan-Africanist vision. Ironically, the March on Washington confirmed the long effort of DuBois's life. An erudite and cosmopolitan **minister**, **Martin Luther King, Jr.**, and his ministry are almost unimaginable without DuBois's precedence, whatever their differences in religious temperament and conviction. The people to whom King spoke were a people whose identity had been forged by social and economic forces far more powerful than any one man's rhetoric or imagination. But they were also forged in part by the imagination and intelligence of DuBois, who saw in them a great and global people before they saw it in themselves. *See also* Fauset, Jessie Redmon; Harlem Renaissance; Intraracial Class Conflict; Johnson, James Weldon; National Association for the Advancement of Colored People (NAACP); White, Walter Francis.

Further Reading

DuBois, W.E.B. *The Souls of Black Folk.* Chicago: McClurg, 1903; London: Constable, 1905.

Lewis, David Levering. *W.E.B. DuBois: Biography of a Race, 1868–1919.* New York: Holt, 1993.

———. *W.E.B. DuBois: The Fight for Equality and the American Century, 1919–1963.* New York: Holt, 2000.

Rampersad, Arnold. *The Art and Imagination of W.E.B. DuBois.* Cambridge, MA: Harvard University Press, 1976.

Peter Kerry Powers

Dunbar, Paul Laurence (1872–1906)

Paul Laurence Dunbar was one of the first African American poets to receive broad critical acclaim, and he gained a large popular readership in turn-of-the-century America for his dialect poems that dealt with plantation life in the Old South. Less well known is his fiction, but it was in novels such as *The Sport of the Gods* that Dunbar registered his mixed feelings about the Great Black Migration.

Dunbar was born in Dayton, Ohio, to Matilda and Joshua Dunbar, both of whom were former slaves. His mother instilled in him a love of reading and storytelling, and he also paid rapt attention to the tales of his father, who had escaped slavery and served in the Union army during the Civil War. Dunbar began writing poetry while still a child, and his years as the sole African American student in his class at Central High School in Dayton were distinguished by membership in the debating society and stints as class poet, editor of the school paper, and president of the literary society. These early literary experiences served him well, since he published his first book of poems, *Oak and Ivy*, at the young age of twenty-one. By the time of his tragic death from tuberculosis and alcoholism at age thirty-four, Dunbar had published numerous essays, volumes of poetry, collections of stories, and novels, including his pioneering novel of the Great Black Migration, *The Sport of the Gods*.

Published in 1902, *The Sport of the Gods* was written in the wake of increasing racial injustices, both in the legally segregated South and in the rhetorically "progressive" northern states. Both regions are subjected to Dunbar's scrutiny, and both are revealed to be problematic for the post-Reconstruction African American community. Dunbar's South—dreamily depicted as a region of beautiful plantation homes amid Virginia creeper and morning glories, on the one hand, and naturalistically exposed as being hopelessly stuck in a racist past, on the other—is a land of contradictions. The human remnants of the plantation aristocracy preach benevolent paternalism, but they quickly withdraw their protection and goodwill when self-interest is no longer served. Similarly, Dunbar's North promises one thing, yet delivers quite another. The freedom of the symbolic North in the African American imagination contrasts sharply with the social and economic realities of the actual North that Dunbar's black characters encounter. Binding the geographic disparities of *The Sport of the Gods* is Dunbar's compelling examination of the ways in which differences of color, caste, and economic class shape and define human motivations, actions, and identity. *The Sport of the Gods* exposes the racist marrow of the South that threatens to rot the promise of a democratic American tradition from the inside out—a core of behaviors, beliefs, and misguided customs about difference so ingrained in the southern white imagination that it renders quite tenuous any positive foundation that may be constructed around it. While northern cities appear to promise blacks a greater degree of freedom than the South, however, Dunbar suggests in the novel that migration to the North can lead African Americans into new and insidious forms of virtual slavery. *See also* Literature, the Great Migration in.

Further Reading

Alexander, Eleanor. *Lyrics of Sunshine and Shadow: The Tragic Courtship and Marriage of Paul Laurence Dunbar and Alice Ruth Moore; A History of Love and Violence among the African American Elite.* New York: New York University Press, 2001.

De Santis, Christopher C. "The Dangerous Marrow of Southern Tradition: Charles W. Chesnutt, Paul Laurence Dunbar, and the Paternalist Ethos at the Turn of the Century." *Southern Quarterly* 38 (2000): 79–97.

Gayle, Addison, Jr. *Oak and Ivy: A Biography of Paul Laurence Dunbar.* Garden City, NY: Doubleday, 1971.

Christopher C. De Santis

Durham, North Carolina

No more than a railroad stop at the end of the Civil War, Durham became North Carolina's richest town by the end of the nineteenth century, one where at least some African Americans also accessed expanding wealth. Located on the Piedmont, the swath of fertile land through the state's midsection, Durham was a center of manufacturing. Tobacco and textiles linked the postbellum South to modern capitalism and the international economy of production and trade. As a southern center of industries that also expanded during economic booms, Durham enticed migrants who wished to pursue aspirations for freedom in the city, and it served as a launch site for migrations to other places, a pattern that had evolved before and intensified during the Great Migration. Just as Durham yielded its experienced laborers to the urban centers of the North and West, it also received migrants moving from field to factory.

At the end of the Civil War, Durham attracted freedpeople seeking family, employment, and distance from whites. African Americans built several separate neighborhoods. The largest, Hayti, pronounced hay'-tie and honoring the independent black nation, flourished with black people's energies, ingenuity, self-help, and cooperative but cunning race relations. Churches, the domain of **women**, anchored a settling population (see **Settlement Houses**). Durham's population grew exponentially as people from other places moved to the city for employment in the professions as well as in skilled and unskilled labor. From Durham, African American migrations moved to the South and West in the 1870s and 1880s and northward by the century's turn. This pattern of in-and-out movement laid the groundwork for and fed into the Great Migration.

In Durham, as in most southern cities, **Jim Crow** defined an intrusive system of laws, rules, and customs that regulated social, political, and economic relations by race. In its most insidious forms Jim Crow engendered distinct white and black communities composed of stable elites, a rising middle class, and a mass of laborers. African Americans managed Jim Crow's oppressions and opportunities in diverse ways. Against the tide of white supremacy, a black leadership group turned some small business ventures into a set of successful enterprises. In 1911 **Booker T. Washington** called Durham the "city of cities to look for the prosperity of Negroes." When his rival **W.E.B. DuBois** hailed the "upbuilding of black Durham" in 1912, African Americans owned and operated an impressive array of organizations, institutions, businesses, manufacturing firms, retail stores, a library, a **hospital,** a college, scores of churches, a number of schools, and a neighborhood of impressive residences.

Symbols of race pride and enterprise, North Carolina Mutual Life Insurance Company, then the largest black business in the world, and its sibling institutions rose against a backdrop of repression and terrorism to make Durham the pecuniary center of black America. "A city of fine homes and middle-class respectability," black sociologist **E. Franklin Frazier** wrote in 1923, dubbing Durham the "Capital of the Black Middle Class." Black professionals, especially women, from both the North and the South found employment in black Durham businesses and institutions (see **Insurers and Insurance Companies**).

Racial segregation created a captive constituency of consumers who supported black businesses, institutions, and services, but its inherent inequalities shaped the city's political economy in ways that affected virtually all African Americans and exploited the most impoverished. Most black neighborhoods suffered the problems of overcrowding and municipal neglect. Notorious for abusing their workforces, American Tobacco and Liggett and Myers employed African Americans by the thousands, mostly women, drawing their workers from the Durham environs and rural and urban districts in North Carolina,

Backs of African American houses, Durham, North Carolina, 1940. Courtesy of the Library of Congress.

South Carolina, and Virginia. The tobacco production schedule ran such that hiring increased sharply at those times during the year when farm families were most able to do without female labor. Women migrated to Durham for other reasons as well, including education for their children, safety for themselves, or because death, disablement, or divorce left them single and struggling on the land. Moving along networks of kith and kin, women's migrations also stimulated community development as settlers' energies created and sustained neighborhoods, institutions, and reform organizations.

Durham operated like a hinge in the black migration process, opening and closing with the push and pull factors of migration, with black aspirations on one side and economic cycles on the other. The image of black affluence combined with the elasticity of the labor market to facilitate black migration from field to factory. Yet the abuses of industrial and service work encouraged Durham's black workers to move on to other prospects, especially when the lure of northern employment called. *See also* Charlotte, North Carolina; Chain Migration; Cotton Belt; Low Country South Carolina and Georgia.

Further Reading

Brown, Leslie. "Common Spaces, Separate Lives: Gender and Racial Conflict in the 'Capital of the Black Middle Class.'" Ph.D. diss., Duke University, 1997.

————. "'The Sisters and Mothers Are Called to the City': African American Women and an Even Greater Migration." In *Stepping Forward: Black Women in Africa and the Americas*, edited by Catherine Higgs, Barbara A. Moss, and Earline Rae Ferguson, 129-40. Athens: Ohio University Press, 2002.

Brown, Leslie, and Anne M. Valk. "'Our Territory': Race, Place, Gender, Space, and African American Women in the Urban South." In *Her Past around Us: Interpreting Sites for Women's History*, edited by Polly Welts Kaufman and Katharine T. Corbett, 207-34. Malabar, FL: Krieger Publishing Company, 2003.

DuBois, W.E.B. "The Upbuilding of Black Durham: The Success of Negroes and Their Value to a Tolerant and Helpful Southern City." *World's Work* 3 (January 1912): 338-39.

Frazier, E. Franklin. "Durham: The Capital of the Black Middle Class." In *The New Negro: An Interpretation*, edited by Alain Locke, 331-41. New York: Albert and Charles Boni, 1925. Reprint, New York: Atheneum/Macmillan, 1992.

Johnson, Charles S. "The Tobacco Worker: A Study of Tobacco Workers and Their Families." Typescript. Industries Section, Division of Review, 1935. Consolidated Reference Materials, National Archives, Records of the National Recovery Administration, Record Group 69.

Murray, Pauli. *The Autobiography of a Black Activist, Feminist, Lawyer, Priest, and Poet.* Knoxville: University of Tennessee Press, 1989. Previously published as *Song in a Weary Throat: An American Pilgrimage.* New York: Harper and Row, 1987.

————. *Proud Shoes: The Story of An American Family.* New York: Harper and Row, 1956.

Washington, Booker T. "Durham, North Carolina, a City of Negro Enterprises." *Independent* 70 (March 23, 1911): 644-48.

Weare, Walter B. *Black Business in the New South: A Social History of the North Carolina Mutual Life Insurance Company.* Urbana: University of Illinois Press, 1973. Reprint, Durham, NC: Duke University Press, 1993.

Leslie Brown

E

East St. Louis Race Riot of 1917

The race riot that erupted in the industrial city of East St. Louis, Illinois, in 1917 was one of the most brutal bouts of urban racial violence of the World War I era. On July 2, mobs numbering hundreds of white men, women, and children swept through the city's streets, beating, shooting, and even hanging African Americans and setting fire to black homes. The rioters were aided by numerous white National Guardsmen—who had been called out to quell the violence but who deserted their posts to join the riot—and by a sympathetic, white-dominated local police department. The violence, which lasted a single day, resulted in the deaths of at least thirty-nine black men, **women**, and children and left countless others injured. The actual death toll is uncertain because authorities failed to account officially for many of the dead. Reflecting the one-sided nature of the aggression, only nine whites died in the riot.

It was a bitter irony that many of the African Americans caught up in the race riot of 1917 were southern migrants who had moved northward in search of improved circumstances. The black community of East St. Louis had been growing rapidly since the first years of the twentieth century, a trend that accelerated in the mid-1910s as local factories, requiring labor to meet war orders from Europe, absorbed black migrant workers. However, as a period of intense industrial conflict between white-dominated unions and employers across the city became increasingly entwined with race between 1916 and 1917, local white workers reacted with increasing hostility toward African Americans. Pressures building over a period of months reached a climax with the defeat of a strike at the city's largest factory, the Aluminum Ore Company, in which management had manipulated racial divisions in order to undermine

National guardsmen escort a black resident of East St. Louis, Illinois, in the wake of the riot in July 1917. © Bettmann/Corbis.

the union's tentative efforts to unite black and white workers. The final defeat of the strike at the end of June coincided with an upsurge in sporadic white racial violence and set the context for the race riot.

If the East St. Louis race riot tragically demonstrated that the North would provide no respite from white racism and racial violence, it also demonstrated that African Americans in the new urban communities of the North would not passively submit to such violence. The African American neighborhood of Denverside, which had grown in East St. Louis because of customary racial segregation, became a social and economic center for black East St. Louis: from this nascent **ghetto**, resistance emerged in the summer of 1917. In actions that would be echoed in other riots of the war years and that continued a tradition of militant self-defense from an earlier period, blacks in East St. Louis defended their community. Responding to sporadic white violence during 1917, black residents of Denverside organized armed patrols of their streets to defend their homes. On July 2, such groups of armed African Americans took up positions in streets on the neighborhood's border. Whites managed to devastate black homes adjacent to downtown, but in Denverside, African Americans created a "no-go" area for whites and held the advancing mobs at bay. Not only did they preserve this black neighborhood, but they also created a sanctuary in which African Americans gathered together for safety. Moreover, this action kept access to a viaduct to **St. Louis, Missouri**, open, providing a route by which numerous African Americans escaped to safety. *See also* Chicago Race Riot of 1919; Elaine, Arkansas, Massacre of 1919; Organized Labor; Red Summer of 1919; Primary Documents 16, 17.

Further Reading

McLaughlin, Malcolm. *Power, Community, and Racial Killing in East St. Louis*. New York: Palgrave Macmillan, 2005.

Rudwick, Elliott M. *Race Riot at East St. Louis, July 2, 1917*. Carbondale: Southern Illinois University Press, 1964.

———, ed. *The East St. Louis Race Riot of 1917*. Frederick, MD: University Publications of America, 1985. Microfilm, 8 reels.

Malcolm McLaughlin

Elaine, Arkansas, Massacre of 1919

In the fall of 1919 sharecroppers in the areas surrounding the Arkansas Delta town of Elaine joined the Progressive Farmers and Household Union of America. Their goal was to secure a fair settlement of their cotton crops. The owners of the large plantations organized vigilantes and secured federal troops to quell what they termed an "insurrection," resulting in the murder of untold numbers of African American men, **women**, and children. The Elaine uprising was part of the **Red Summer of 1919**, when corporations and the federal government sought to rein in workers and African Americans who had been emboldened by Woodrow Wilson's call to fight World War I to "make the world safe for democracy." Fears of returning African American veterans and of an increasingly militant black citizenry led to violent confrontations all over the country in places like **Washington, D.C.**, **Chicago**, Charleston, South Carolina, **Omaha, Nebraska**, and Longview, Texas (see **Chicago Race Riot of 1919**). The events of 1919 signaled African Americans' determination to fight white supremacy, demand social and economic justice, and secure their rights of citizenship.

Sharecroppers in Phillips County, Arkansas, had reaped some of the benefits of wartime high cotton prices. Some had acquired household property, livestock, and automobiles. However, plantation owners persistently cheated them by denying them the right to market their crops outside the plantation where they could secure a just and higher price. Many planters had refused to settle with their croppers, taking their cotton without paying them. The 1919 cotton crop promised to be the most lucrative in southern history, and sharecroppers were determined to secure their fair share. Planters, however, were equally determined to deny the workers a fair return on their crop, and some even sought to steal the personal property that many had acquired. As a result of these injustices, several sharecroppers contacted a lawyer, Ulysses S. Bratton, asking him for help in legally securing a just price for their crops. They also joined the Progressive Farmers and Household Union of America (PFHUA), a benevolent society that may also have passed as a labor union. Led by Robert L. Hill, the PFHUA worked with Bratton to secure legal representation for the members.

In early October several men, women, and children gathered for a union meeting in a church in Hoop Spur. During the meeting shots were fired into the church. Black people returned the fire and killed one of the three white men who had shot at them. The sheriff in nearby Helena immediately sent a 300-man posse to search for the union members. By the next morning, from 600 to 1,000 men from all over the Arkansas and **Mississippi Delta** had arrived to massacre the black sharecroppers. The county judge requested that federal troops be sent from Little Rock to quell what he deemed an insurrection whose goal was to murder the planters, and the following day Governor Charles H. Brough escorted 583 federal troops, including a twelve-machine-gun battalion just returned from France. All telephone lines were cut, and the vigilantes were sent home.

For the next seven days Colonel Isaac C. Jenks led the soldiers in pursuing black people over a 200-mile radius. He ordered his troops to shoot black people on sight. A white citizen from another county described what may have been a typical scene when he saw "twenty-eight people killed, their bodies then thrown into a pit and burned." He also witnessed eighteen black people hanging from a bridge near Helena. Other witnesses described the "cutting off the ears or toes of dead negroes for souvenirs and the dragging of their bodies through the streets of Elaine" (Woodruff, 87). Hundreds of men, women, and children were taken to the Elaine schoolhouse, where they were tortured and interrogated until they were cleared of any wrongdoing and released to their landlords. Later 122 men and women were arrested and indicted by a grand jury, 73 of them for murder. In the end, twelve men were convicted for the murder of three white men: Ed Ware, Will Wordlow, Albert Giles, Joe Fox, Alfred Banks, Jr., John Martin, Frank Moore, Frank and Ed Hicks, Jr., J. E. Knox, Ed Coleman, and Paul Hall. The **National Association for the Advancement of Colored People** (NAACP) fought the convictions and carried the case to the U.S. Supreme Court. In 1923 the Court, in *Moore v. Dempsey*, overturned the convictions of six of the men convicted of murdering Clinton Lee. Justice Oliver Wendell Holmes argued that the defendants' confessions had been secured through torture and that a mob spirit had dominated the trial, thus violating the due process of the Fourteenth Amendment. The Arkansas Supreme Court overturned the remaining defendants' convictions.

In spite of the Supreme Court decision, the planters and politicians held to the narrative of events they had created during the massacre, insisting that black people had sought to murder the planters and managers. However, the Court's decision on some level supported the separate investigations by **Walter F. White** of the NAACP and the antilynching crusader **Ida B. Wells-Barnett** that had revealed that planters had massacred untold numbers of black people to suppress their efforts to secure a just price on their crops. Estimates of the dead ranged from 5 to 25 white men and up to 856 black people. However, an accurate account would require the skills of a forensic archaeologist, and even then, the task would be compromised since many families were burned alive and thus left no trace of their life and death.

The Elaine massacre left a legacy of fear and oppression in the postwar years as Delta planters tightened the reins of terror over their workers. Many African Americans sought refuge in the North, fleeing the region to join other migrants in Chicago, **Cleveland**, **Detroit**, and elsewhere in the industrial Midwest. But for those who remained, the massacre provided other lessons as well, for it demonstrated the ability of black people to fight back, and it linked rural people to national organizations like the NAACP that had successfully defended the sharecroppers and publicized the racism and barbarism of the planter class. In the following decades black people showed remarkable resilience as they continued to form NAACP chapters, organize unions, and use their institutions such as churches and lodges to counter the reign of terror that marked the 1920s and 1930s. Not for nothing had men, women, and children died in Elaine. *See also* Fraternal Orders; Lynching; Organized Labor; Southern Tenant Farmers' Union (STFU); Primary Document 59.

Further Reading

Cortner, Richard C. *A Mob Intent on Death: The NAACP and the Arkansas Riot Cases.* Middletown, CT: Wesleyan University Press, 1988.

Stockley, Grif. *Blood in Their Eyes: The Elaine Race Massacres of 1919*. Fayetteville: University of Arkansas Press, 2001.

Taylor, Kieran. " 'We Have Just Begun': Black Organizing and White Response in the Arkansas Delta, 1919." *Arkansas Historical Quarterly* 58, no. 3 (1999): 264–84.

Whayne, Jeannie M. "Low Villains and Wickedness in High Places: Race and Class in the Elaine Riots." *Arkansas Historical Quarterly* 58, no. 3 (1999): 285–313.

White, Walter F. "Race Conflict in Arkansas." *Survey* 63 (December 13, 1919): 233–34.

Woodruff, Nan Elizabeth. *American Congo: The African American Freedom Struggle in the Delta*. Cambridge, MA: Harvard University Press, 2003.

Nan Elizabeth Woodruff

Electoral Politics

The arrival of southern migrants to cities in the North and West over the course of the twentieth century created new possibilities for black involvement in electoral politics. Between 1890 and 1912 all of the former Confederate states and Oklahoma disfranchised black men. When American **women** acquired the right to vote in 1920 through the Nineteenth Amendment, southern states quickly moved to disfranchise black women as well. By relocating to the North and West, southern migrants regained their stolen voting rights. They also helped create politically active communities that could tip the balance of power in elections and thus force candidates and administrations to take into account the demands of black voters. In this way migration helped set the stage for many civil rights victories during the twentieth century.

The Great Migration expanded the black voting electorate. Here a black woman casts her ballot in the 1964 election in Washington, D.C. Courtesy of the Library of Congress.

The large concentrated black populations that emerged in northern and western cities as a result of migration enabled African Americans to gain a certain amount of influence in local politics that was unobtainable before the twentieth century when their numbers were relatively small and diffuse. In a variety of elections, these large concentrated voting blocs could make or break a candidate. This was especially the case in fiercely partisan contests where victory was achieved by only a small margin and in elections dealing with small political units, such as the district assembly or ward. Black voting strength at the district assembly and ward levels was apparent in **New York City** and **Chicago**, the two cities where the largest number of African Americans re-settled during the Great Migration of World War I. In 1930 African Americans, who were 12 percent of Manhattan's population, made up fully 70 percent of both the Nineteenth and Twenty-First Assembly Districts of Harlem. Similarly, Chicago's growing black population, 7 percent in 1930, constituted the majority of residents in several South Side wards: 86.6 percent of the Second, 79.9 percent of the Third, and 58.8 percent of the Fourth. The swing potential of black votes was also felt acutely during primaries. Until the mid-1930s the majority of African Americans who remained enfranchised cast ballots for the Republican Party, the party of antislavery and radical Reconstruction. In general elections this almost solid black Republican vote was diluted among the entire voting population. By contrast, African Americans constituted a significant portion of those participating in Republican primaries, especially at the local level. When black voters switched their allegiance to the Democrats during the 1930s, they similarly proved pivotal in local Democratic primaries.

As soon as white urban machines in cities like New York, Chicago, and **Cleveland** recognized the new political realities wrought by migration, they began competing for black votes, primarily with the help of black intermediaries. During the 1910s, 1920s, and early 1930s men like Thomas W. Fleming in Cleveland, **Oscar DePriest**, Edward H. Wright, and Louis B. Anderson in Chicago, and Ferdinand Q. Morton and Charles W. Anderson in New York served as intermediaries between white-controlled machines and the sub-machines that they created in neighborhoods with concentrated black populations. Several of these men were themselves originally southerners. These men garnered loyalty by intervening on behalf of residents in law enforcement disputes, offering gifts, and distributing patronage jobs allocated by the white-controlled machine. In New York, for instance, this type of patronage arrangement led by the 1920s to a number of hires in various municipal agencies that had long shut out blacks. At election time submachines used the loyalty they had cultivated to mobilize the black vote on behalf of candidates supported by the larger machine. For example, in Republican primaries between the 1910s and early 1930s, black canvassers regularly helped deliver between 60 and 94 percent of Chicago's Second Ward to candidates supported by the William Hale Thompson machine.

In return for support, white machines not only handed out jobs, they also promoted the political careers of black politicians. Even after the Great Migration of World War I, black urban populations were not large enough to elect black candidates in city and statewide elections without the addition of white votes. With the backing of powerful white-controlled machines, however, black communities were able to secure enough white votes to elect some of their own. In Cleveland the Maschke machine helped Thomas W. Fleming win several runs for city councilman between 1909 and 1929. In 1917 Edward Austin Johnson was the first African American to win a seat in the New York State Assembly. Several others followed in Johnson's footsteps, and in 1919 Charles H. Roberts became the first black alderman of New York City. Nowhere, however, was this combination of an enlarged black electorate and a well-greased patron-client machinery more successful in putting black men into office than in Chicago. Between 1915 and 1928 this combination elected two aldermen, a state senator, several state representatives, a municipal court judge, and a U.S. congressman. This congressman, Oscar DePriest—who in 1915 was also Chicago's first black alderman—became in 1928 the first black American to serve in Congress since 1901. The first black Democrat to be elected to Congress also came from Chicago. This was **Arthur Wergs Mitchell**, who defeated DePriest in 1934.

In the West black communities similarly gained an expanded voice in local electoral politics as their numbers rose dramatically during World War II. For example, **San Francisco**'s black population, which increased by more than 800 percent between 1940 and 1950, was able to extract a number of significant political appointments during the 1950s. African Americans in **Los Angeles** were able to use their new voting strength after World War II to elect city officials—all white or Mexican American—who supported fair **housing** and employment, **desegregation**, and efforts to end **police brutality**. With a few important exceptions and despite multiple tries, however, the relocation of tens of thousands of African Americans to Los Angeles and San Francisco did not immediately lead to the election of black representatives, as witnessed in cities like New York and Chicago after the migrations of World War I. Patron-client-type relationships rarely extended beyond appointments to include support for black office seekers, and the strong interracial, liberal coalitions that in the 1960s would help black candidates win city and statewide elections were still in the making. Local peculiarities also thwarted efforts to capitalize politically on the growth of western urban populations. In Los Angeles, for instance, a combination of redistricting and large city council districts diluted black voting strength and prevented the election of black city council members until 1963.

The 1960s and 1970s witnessed something of a black political renaissance in those cities that had been the destination of migrants for decades. Most notably, **black mayors** emerged in Cleveland, Newark, Oakland, **Detroit**, Los Angeles, and **Gary, Indiana**. Once again, a shift in racial demographics was key. A combination of black urban migration and **white flight** to the suburbs during the 1950s and 1960s created many inner cities where African Americans constituted the majority or near majority. This enabled black independents to seriously challenge party machine candidates. For example, in Cleveland, where African Americans constituted about 40 percent of the population, **Carl Stokes** defeated the machine-supported candidate in the 1967 Democratic primaries with the backing of 96 percent of black voters and 15 percent of white voters. The overwhelming support of black voters enabled Stokes to then carry the general election.

Demographics alone, however, do not explain such victories. These demographic transformations achieved their full potential in the context of the modern **civil rights movement**. Inspired by the ideology and tactics of the southern movement, black candidates and their supporters sought to end discrimination in their own communities by gaining a strong, independent voice in local government. They employed the grassroots organizing and voter registration drives of the southern movement to do so. The pivotal role of grassroots organizing was seen in the election of **Richard G. Hatcher** as the first black mayor of Gary, Indiana, in 1967. Although Gary claimed a black population of about 55 percent, the majority of registered voters were white. Hatcher's election was made possible by an intense campaign to register and mobilize the black vote on his behalf. Grassroots organizing and, especially, interracial coalition building also enabled Tom Bradley to become mayor of Los Angeles, even though the black electorate, about 18 percent, was far from the majority or near majority present in other cities that elected black mayors during these years.

Local politicians were the first to adapt to the new realities caused by migration, but by the 1940s presidential candidates were also forced to address the voting power of large black urban populations in the North and West because these populations were located in states that controlled a large number of Electoral College votes—California, Ohio, Illinois, Michigan, New Jersey, and Pennsylvania. Using votes as leverage, black leaders pushed presidential candidates and administrations to place civil rights on the agenda of the federal government. In the midst of the hotly contested 1948 presidential race, for instance, incumbent Harry Truman signed two executive orders aimed at ending discrimination in the federal government and the armed forces. In return, black voters, especially in California, Illinois, and Ohio, narrowly carried Truman to victory. Seeking votes for the GOP, incumbent President Dwight Eisenhower expressed his support for bills that eventually became the 1957 and 1960 Civil Rights Acts. In 1960 John Kennedy's campaign promises to address racial discrimination and efforts to get **Martin Luther King, Jr.**, released from a Georgia jail gave him the black votes he needed to defeat Richard Nixon by the slimmest of margins. Lyndon Johnson followed through on the assassinated president's promises by working toward the passage of the 1964 Civil Rights Act. A few months later overwhelming black support contributed to Johnson's landslide victory over Republican Barry Goldwater. Although black migration from the South to the urban North and West declined in the 1970s, the relocation of an estimated 6 million southern blacks to these regions in the previous decades had a lasting impact on electoral politics in America. In the last three decades of the twentieth century the growth of black political power in the urban North and West garnered the attention of many local and federal candidates and the ire of a new conservative movement that sought to undo many of the social and political changes of the 1960s. *See also* Black Legislators; National Association for the Advancement of Colored People (NAACP); Political Activism (1915–1945); Political Realignment.

Further Reading

Branham, Charles R. "The Transformation of Black Political Leadership in Chicago, 1864–1942." Ph.D. diss., University of Chicago, 1981.

Colburn, David R., and Jeffrey S. Adler, eds. *African-American Mayors: Race, Politics, and the American City*. Urbana: University of Illinois Press, 2001.

Drake, St. Clair, and Horace R. Cayton. *Black Metropolis: A Study of Negro Life in a Northern City*. Rev. and enl. ed. Chicago: University of Chicago Press, 1993.

Edsall, Thomas Byrne, and Mary D. Edsall. *Chain Reaction: The Impact of Race, Rights, and Taxes on American Politics*. New York: W. W. Norton, 1992.

Gosnell, Harold F. *Negro Politicians: The Rise of Negro Politics in Chicago*. Chicago: University of Chicago Press, 1935.

Katznelson, Ira. *Black Men, White Cities: Race, Politics, and Migration in the United States, 1900-30, and Britain, 1948-68*. New York: Oxford University Press, 1973.

Kilson, Martin. "Political Change in the Negro Ghetto, 1900-1940s." In *Key Issues in the Afro-American Experience*, edited by Nathan I. Huggins, Martin Kilson, and Daniel M. Fox, 167-92. New York: Harcourt Brace Jovanovich, 1971.

Lawson, Steven F. *Running for Freedom: Civil Rights and Black Politics in America since 1941*. Philadelphia: Temple University Press, 1991.

Sonenshein, Raphael J. *Politics in Black and White: Race and Power in Los Angeles*. Princeton, NJ: Princeton University Press, 1993.

Lisa G. Materson

Ellington, Duke [Edward Kennedy] (1899–1974)

One of America's most prolific composers—more than 2,000 compositions—for several decades, Duke Ellington led and played piano for one of the century's most successful **jazz** orchestras. Although he excelled in big-band jazz arrangements, Ellington composed in a variety of forms, including songs, dance tunes, nightclub production numbers, and large-scale, abstract instrumental works. His name became synonymous with the **swing** music that defined the 1930s and provided the soundtrack for America's newly urban African American communities. From 1931, when the **Pittsburgh Courier** declared him the "King of Jazz," to 1971, when he became the first jazz musician invited to join the Swedish Royal Academy of Music in Stockholm, Ellington served as the reference point for twentieth-century American jazz and remains its most significant composer.

From a decidedly southern and fiercely proud black **Washington, D.C.**, community, Edward Kennedy "Duke" Ellington absorbed many of the influences, both social and musical, that would shape the rest of his life and career. At the time of his birth, Washington, D.C., had the largest black population of any city in the United States—about 30 percent of the city's total, segregated from the white community but highly stratified within itself. Ellington's family was not among Washington's wealthy blacks, yet Ellington inherited a sense of privilege, claiming in his autobiography that so beloved was he as a child that his family did not let his feet touch the ground till he was seven. Although aristocratic confidence distinguished his demeanor and deportment on and off stage, Ellington rejected categorization of any kind and called his music simply "the music of the American Negro" (Ellington, 471).

American audiences had another name for the music Ellington's orchestra made famous in the 1930s: swing. It was, after all, Duke Ellington's 1932 "It Don't Mean a Thing (If It Ain't Got That Swing)" that gave the music and the era its name. If audiences had not heard the black swing bands firsthand, they had heard of Ellington, broadcast from the Cotton Club on the CBS and NBC radio networks. In February 1937, when Ellington played for President Roosevelt's birthday ball, that, too, was broadcast on radio. In 1938 Ellington melodies provided themes for thirty-seven different radio programs: "Mood Indigo" played on sixteen, "Sophisticated Lady" on twelve, and "In a Sentimental Mood" on nine. Of the 50 million records of all types sold in 1939, an estimated 17 million—more than one-third—were swing.

As a composer, Ellington emphasized solo parts, and the style of his works often reflected the personality or style of the soloist for whom he was writing. A self-taught pianist and protégé of stride pianist James P. Johnson, he composed at the piano, alone, or with his players in group improvisation, transcribing music after the fact. Perhaps the first true jazz composer, Ellington borrowed heavily and knowledgeably from African American **blues** and Afro-Caribbean traditions. Early blues-based pieces such as "Black and Tan Fantasy" and "East St. Louis Toodle-O" (both 1927) remained part of the band's repertoire throughout the decades, as did his 1937 "Caravan," which paved the way for Cuban jazz of the 1940s. Pieces such as "Concerto for Cootie" (for trumpeter Cootie Williams), "Cotton Tail," and "Black, Brown, and Beige" depended on formal innovations beyond any others at the time yet continue to speak to contemporary listeners.

Although Ellington became famous playing at **New York City**'s mostly white Cotton Club from 1927 to 1930, it was during his years of touring from 1930 to 1942 that he and his orchestra were most creative and most socially significant. Traveling big bands such as Ellington's served as domestic ambassadors for African Americans across the country, bringing news, music, dance, and dress styles from one end of the country to the other, exemplifying dignity and success in a world that tried to deny them both. Towns across the country held dances in auditoriums, stadiums, armories, skating rinks, warehouses, barns, roadhouses, and open fields, and even bands as prominent as the Duke Ellington Orchestra played thousands of one-night stands in black communities throughout the United States. Examples of upward and geographic mobility, the big bands fused African American idiomatic expression with modern sensibilities and improvisation with structure and tradition and merged musical traditions of the rural South with those of the urban North.

In addition to composing the swing music that served the new urbanites, Ellington put the drama of the Great Black Migration on stage in his musical *Jump for Joy*, which ran for three months in **Los Angeles** in the summer and fall of 1941. Collaborating with writer Sid Kuller and lyricist Paul Francis Webster, Ellington conceived of a musical that would officially put **Jim Crow** and Uncle Tom to rest. The **black press** raved about the show, and *Jump for Joy* introduced the term *zoot suit* to America in a sketch performed by dancers Pot, Pan, and Skillet. The show included a deathbed scene in which Uncle Tom's children danced around him as he lay dying. The first song, eventually eliminated from the show because of death threats, was "I've Got a Passport from Georgia (and I'm Sailin' for the U.S.A.)." The title song, "Jump for Joy," also bids good-bye to the South, as the opening lines declare, "Farewell, land of cotton." The song ends with a full orchestral four-beat chugging rhythm while Ellington's trademark "train whistle" blares on top. The music moves the listener northward, away from the Mississippi River bottom, with train whistles in full cry to signal the unembarrassed escape.

The musical *Jump for Joy* remains an important marker of a cultural watershed, a moment when the concentration of African Americans in new urban centers such as Los Angeles could nurture and boost community consciousness and expression. Although the show never opened on Broadway, as Ellington had hoped, the musical launched careers for many of its performers and gained greater respect for black artists across the country as they turned their backs on old theatrical stereotypes. In the 1960s, when San Francisco demonstrators challenged Ellington to make a statement on civil rights, he answered, "I made my statement in 1941 in *Jump for Joy* and I stand by it" (Willard, 31). To the end of his life, Ellington claimed *Jump for Joy* as his proudest extramusical accomplishment. *See also* Basie, William "Count"; Calloway, Cab[ell]; Dance Halls and Nightclubs; Recording Industry.

Further Reading

Dance, Stanley. *The World of Duke Ellington*. New York: Da Capo Press, 2000.
Ellington, Duke. *Music Is My Mistress*. Garden City, NY: Doubleday, 1973.
Hasse, John Edward. *Beyond Category: The Life and Genius of Duke Ellington*. New York: Da Capo Press, 1995.
Tucker, Mark. *Ellington: The Early Years*. Urbana: University of Illinois Press, 1991.
———, ed. *The Duke Ellington Reader*. New York: Oxford University Press, 1993.
Willard, Patricia. *Jump for Joy*. Washington, DC: Smithsonian Institution, 1988.

Gena Caponi-Tabery

Ellison, Ralph Waldo (1914–1994)

Ralph Ellison was an African American fiction writer and essayist whose novel *Invisible Man* (1952) is one of the definitive literary responses to the early years of the Second Great Migration. His second novel, *Juneteenth* (1999, published posthumously), explores migration to the **western states**, particularly Texas and Oklahoma, in the early part of the twentieth century. His first novel, set in Harlem, documents the struggles of the young male protagonist just up from the South, the otherwise unnamed Invisible Man, to establish his identity in **New York City**, specifically Harlem. Ellison uses the metaphor of invisibility to invoke the realities of a historical African American experience that takes on new urgency in this period. The nation as a whole, because of the schism between democratic theory and practice, can only deal with this contradiction by rendering its victims invisible in an act of repression or, ironically, by making them visible in ritual acts of violent exorcism such as **lynching**. As Ellison writes in the novel, much of African American experience resides in a spoken history—in a body of folklore—that parallels and speaks to American history, though it is often unacknowledged. For the Invisible Man and others, as **W.E.B. DuBois** powerfully stated, to be both black and American is to suffer double consciousness and to struggle to acquire a true and integrated self-consciousness.

Ellison was born in Oklahoma City, Oklahoma, to southern parents who had moved to this frontier region in search of greater freedom. Ellison, like the Invisible Man, spent several years at the **Tuskegee Normal and Industrial Institute** before moving to Harlem in 1936. From 1938 to 1942 he worked with the Federal Writers' Project, recording the history of African Americans in New York and collecting folktales and children's rhyming games. In recording these tales and games, Ellison was engaged in collecting what workers on the project understood to be history from the bottom up. The oral expressions that Ellison transcribed in the tellers' idioms, many of whom were from the South, are part of the documentary record of the migration experience. What fascinated Ellison, and what entered into his fiction, were the ways in which these speakers transformed the motifs and insights of folktales developed in response to their labor on southern soil and the omnipotence of the southern white man into responses to the conditions of the urban industrial environment of the North. These tales and the cultural impulse to create out of what was at hand—which Ellison understood to define African American vernacular culture (and American culture as a whole)—were evidence of the survival and adaptation of the migrant folk in the city.

This perspective clashed with that of **Richard Nathaniel Wright**, whose work of the same period forecast the necessary disappearance of folk strategies for assertion and survival as African Americans became industrial workers in the North. In *Invisible Man* the zoot suit becomes a sign of a creative and political energy at work among the African American urban masses. It makes visible and tangible the impulse behind folklore: to, as Ellison writes, improvise upon the given and create something new that expresses an African American attitude toward, and assertiveness in, the world at large. It is the zoot suit that Ellison makes central to his protagonist's contest with the Brotherhood—also known as the Communist Party—which in the novel will not acknowledge the unpredictability and complexity of black cultural expression and the willful presence of African Americans in the North. Like the work of other black writers of this period, Ellison's work demonstrates the tension between forms of cultural nationalism arising from the experience of the migrants themselves—forms that make them visible—and the class-based political strategies of the Left.

The protagonist of *Juneteenth*, like the Invisible Man, must undergo a series of physical and spiritual journeys in an effort to come to terms with his racial, cultural, and ultimately American identity. Ellison also articulates the will and history of the migrant generation to the West, particularly as these are expressed in oral tales and music, both religious and secular. Music is central to much of Ellison's writing, and in it he traces the history of the African diaspora in the Americas. "Richard Wright's Blues" (1945) contains his famous definition of the **blues** as a record of personal and implicitly communal catastrophe and pain that is both tragic and comic in its unflinching worldview. In the period in which he wrote *Invisible Man*, Ellison wrote that the African American music of the South—where, he argued, the **jazz** band was the only available expression of democracy for blacks—was transformed by the migration north: the syncopated rhythms of **bebop**, for example, reflected the rhythms of industry and urban life. Ralph Ellison's work remains a rich record and exploration of the experience of the Second Great Migration. *See also* Communists and the Communist Party; Literature, the Great Migration in; Zoot-Suit Riots (1943).

Further Reading

Scruggs, Charles. *Sweet Home: Invisible Cities in the Afro-American Novel*. Baltimore: Johns Hopkins University Press, 1993.
Sundquist, Eric J., ed. *Cultural Contexts for Ralph Ellison's "Invisible Man."* Boston: Bedford–St. Martin's, 1995.

Robin Lucy

Ellison, Walter (1899–1977)

Walter Ellison's experience, like those of many of the African Americans who migrated north and who studied art, expands and nuances the meaning of opportunity. The journey north was certainly about jobs and better and relatively safer living conditions, but it was also about another and equally necessary condition for a fulfilled life—creative expression.

When Ellison arrived in **Chicago** from Eaton, Georgia, in the 1920s, he found in the post–World War I environment of the midwestern city a place in conflict because of the need for African American labor and the concomitant determination to restrict their existence to one densely populated area known as the Black Belt or, sometimes, Bronzeville. It has been described as a city within a city, comprising a narrow tongue of land, seven miles in length and one and one-half miles in width. During the height of the Great Migration more than 300,000 blacks lived there. They created businesses, ran churches, and maintained cultural institutions. They also, to a very limited degree, were allowed to participate in mainstream institutions. Ellison's life reflected this pattern.

In the 1930s Ellison attended the School of the Art Institute of Chicago (SAIC). The SAIC was one of the few art academies in the United States that admitted African Americans. Artists such as Richmond Barthé, Elizabeth Catlett, Charles White, and **Archibald J. Motley, Jr.**, studied at the SAIC. Nevertheless, these artists, including Ellison, realized the need for their own academy and founded the South Side Community Art Center in 1941, which provided training and exhibition opportunities for black artists. It is one of the few **Works Progress Administration** projects still operating today, although it did close briefly during the McCarthy era. During the early 1940s Ellison's work was featured in two prominent exhibitions: The Art of the American Negro (1851 to 1940), held in Chicago, and the first Negro Annual Exhibition at Atlanta University (now Clark Atlanta University) in 1942.

Ellison's most memorable contribution to the theme of migration is his painting of 1935 titled *Train Station* in the collection of the museum of the Art Institute of Chicago. A small painting (eight by fourteen inches), it nevertheless manages to capture a significant moment in African American history and to make it monumental. Traditionally, painting had depended on one point perspective to unify a composition, with all the action working to

Train Station by Walter Ellison, 1936. © The Art Institute of Chicago.

support a single focus. Instead, Ellison has used divergent sight lines to layer the painting with meaning. Divergent sight lines make the painting seem larger; they also chronicle the segregation of the **Jim Crow** South, as whites go in one direction and blacks in an opposite direction. Ellison subverts the tradition of one point perspective to emphasize the everyday, mundane, dehumanizing horrors of racism.

The black porters are distinguishable by their orange uniforms. On the left is a sign marking the southbound trains. Black porters carry the luggage of well-dressed whites who are on their way to vacation destinations in the South, such as **Miami**. The white passengers emerge from waiting rooms, unmarked, but designated by their very lack of signage. Like the lack of signage, "white" has been taken for granted, normalized, and unquestioned until recently as a racial category. Ellison, however, was already sensitive to this fact. In the center of the composition, a confused black passenger who is well dressed and has his body oriented toward the South is instructed by a porter that he should be headed north. On the right are the northbound trains. Passengers emerge from the clearly marked "colored" waiting rooms. They are boarding trains destined for Chicago, **New York City**, and **Detroit**. No porters help them with their luggage, and yet it was the porters who were in large part responsible for bringing the news south about opportunities in the North— about jobs in factories, steel mills, and stockyards.

The source for Ellison's *Train Station* was probably his own journey as a teenager from his hometown in Georgia to Chicago. In fact, his initials are marked on the luggage of one of the northbound passengers. The train has been an important metaphor for blacks, signifying freedom, rebirth, exodus, and deliverance. Thus the Underground Railroad used the metaphor of trains, stations, and station masters. Finally, the humor of the artist shines through, for the divergent sight lines form the letter "W"—the first letter in his first name. *See also* Chicago Renaissance; Railroads; Visual Arts, the Great Migration in.

Further Reading

Chicago Public Library. Digital Collections. Chicago Renaissance, 1932–1950: A Flowering of Afro-American Culture: Images and Documents from the Vivian G. Harsh Research Collection. www.chipublib.org/digital/chiren/index.html.
Drake, St. Clair, and Horace R. Cayton. *Black Metropolis: A Study of Negro Life in a Northern City.* Rev. and enl. ed. Chicago: University of Chicago Press, 1993.
Johnson, Jamie W. "Journeys through Art: Tracing the Great Migration in Three American Paintings." *Art Education* 55, no. 1 (January 2002): 26–31.

Kirsten Pai Buick

Emigrationism

The Great Migration can appear as a reaffirmation of the American Dream as African Americans left the oppression and poverty of the South for new lives in the North, a place where they could participate in the political arena and have a chance to earn a decent livelihood. Scholars have long questioned this view of the Great Migration for a simple reason—the experiences of African Americans in the North were far from perfect. As much as the North might have appeared to offer, reality was often far different because African Americans found that they had to begin their new lives amid segregation at least as pronounced as it was in the South and in a job market that was only slightly more open than that of the South. There is another reason to challenge this idealized version of the Great Migration as well. This view of the Great Migration supposes that African Americans would only want to move within the United States. This was not the case. Throughout the centuries leading up to the start of the Great Migration and continuing afterward, African Americans hoped to and did successfully move beyond the borders of the United States for better lives in places such as Canada, Liberia, and Mexico.

It would certainly be a mistake to claim that African American interest in emigration was always widespread. It was not. Yet at the same time, emigration remained a consistent part of African Americans' dialogue about their future since at least the start of the nineteenth century. For while there were always African Americans who saw what they thought was the light at the end of the tunnel, there were also those who were sure that such a light, if it existed at all, was an oncoming train. The number of people in each camp often varied within the larger political climate, but both views were present throughout African Americans' time in the United States.

While it is certainly true that African American discussions of emigration were common, especially at a few key points in time, the tumultuous 1850s and the end of Reconstruction being prime examples, one should not suppose that large numbers of people actually left this country. In reality, the total number of African Americans who left the United States was small. How small we really cannot say with utmost certainty, for the United States never kept good records about the departure of people, only those arriving at its ports. Although it is impractical to prove how many emigrants left, available evidence is clear that the total was small—likely fewer than the size of major southern cities' expanding black populations in the late nineteenth century or the growth of prime northern cities' black populations in the first decade or so of the Great Migration. In short, emigration's importance should not be judged on the basis of the number of people who moved, for this was always relatively trivial; its import lay in the continuing presence of the dialogue about emigration among black residents of the United States.

As the Great Migration grew near, those African Americans who were seriously considering movement beyond the United States were a rarity. The first decade of the twentieth century was a low point for emigrationism, largely because in the preceding decades so many had invested so much of themselves in trying to emigrate to little effect. After decades of saving money, forming clubs, and trying to organize for Liberia, few African Americans had left the United States, and the racial oppression that many sought to leave had only grown more pronounced. Emigrationism had been a most disappointing goal for many in the last decades of the nineteenth century, and it remained a weak movement through the start of the Great Migration.

While it may seem counterintuitive, it was the increasing amount of movement among African Americans within the United States in the first decades of the twentieth century that again placed the idea of emigrating in the minds of many African Americans. This was, in fact, a common pattern. Throughout the nineteenth century emigration often became a common goal in communities where there were a large number of recent migrants. In the 1880s, for example, Arkansas became a hotbed of emigrationism. This state had been a primary migration destination for African Americans in the 1870s. As African Americans realized that the hopes they brought to Arkansas for a better life were not likely to materialize, many gave up on the United States entirely. Kansas too experienced a similar growth of emigrationism in the wake of the **Exoduster** movement of the late 1870s. When African Americans saw freedom and hope in Oklahoma in the late nineteenth and early twentieth centuries, a similar process took place there. Starting in the 1890s, there was a growing correspondence from what became Oklahoma with the American Colonization Society, the primary means of financial support for African American emigration in the nineteenth century. The interest of Oklahoma blacks in emigration continued into the twentieth century. In the early 1910s African Americans signed up with Chief Alfred Sam's Akim Trading Company. With the purchase of stock in the company, African Americans were entitled to join in emigration to the then Gold Coast Colony in West Africa. Sam sailed from Galveston with sixty emigrants, and many more were waiting for later voyages. They would continue to wait, because this initial sailing of Sam's ship proved to be its sole voyage.

The goal of leaving the United States was not confined to dreams of African repatriation. In the late 1910s and early 1920s there was a movement among African Americans in California focused on emigrating to Baja, Mexico. Many African Americans believed that Mexico was a country where their race would not be held against them and a place where they could control their own destiny. This was not the first attempt of African Americans to leave for Mexico, as a number of Alabama blacks had relocated there in 1894. The Baja emigrants were more successful than their predecessors who struggled to establish homes and support themselves. The Alabamians fled Mexico with assistance from the U.S. government after dozens died in outbreaks of various diseases in the months following the emigrants' arrival in Mexico. It was not that the Baja emigrants completed their plans, for the area would not support the type of agricultural settlement first envisioned. At the same time, the Baja emigrants did not die in mass numbers, and many remained in the area well into the second half of the twentieth century, a modest success, to be sure, but this was far more than many emigration ventures accomplished.

The start of the Great Migration fundamentally altered where in the United States African Americans lived. It did not, however, change the long-standing pattern whereby African Americans who migrated long distances within the United States with high hopes for a better life soon began to discuss emigration. In the case of the Great Migration the emigration movement was broader, because **Marcus Garvey**'s **Universal Negro Improvement Association** (UNIA) had more far-reaching goals than just emigration. Indeed, one could say that the UNIA was an atypical emigrationist group because it was about connecting African and African-descended people across the Western Hemisphere. Garvey and the UNIA formed a springboard for emigrationist discussion in the late 1910s and early 1920s. This dialogue did not end with the prosecution and deportation of Garvey. In the wake of the UNIA's collapse, some of its leaders remained active. New organizations sprang up as well, such as the Peace Movement of Ethiopia, led by Mittie Maul Lena Gordon. Gordon formed the Peace Movement of Ethiopia as a grassroots organization to support the public financing of African Americans' relocation to Africa in the 1930s. The group launched a petition drive aimed at highlighting African Americans' interest in emigration, and it claimed to have over 400,000 signatures to that effect only a few months after beginning the campaign. Like most emigrationist ventures, the Peace Movement of Ethiopia did not help with the relocation of many African Americans.

The Great Migration can be seen as a revolutionary change in the lives of hundreds of thousands of African Americans and as a force that fundamentally altered the United States as a nation. For all it changed, however, the Great Migration remained another example of a long-standing pattern among African Americans. For many, the prospect of moving great distances provided the opportunity for a new life within the United States. After that journey had been completed, the goals behind the move often remained unrealized. From this realization, a number of African Americans began to conclude that their lives could only be improved by leaving the United States for good. The number of African Americans who were able to begin a new life outside the United States was always small. This fact should not diminish the realization that emigration was a continuing presence among African American communities even if its presence was only felt through dialogue. Emigration may have been little more than the stuff of dreams for all but a few African Americans, yet it was a dream that shaped the lives of African Americans throughout their presence in the United States. The Great Migration changed much about the experiences of African Americans in this country; it did not, however, diminish thoughts and hopes among many for better lives apart from the oppression that seemed to define African American life in the United States. *See also* Black Migration before World War I, Patterns of; Turner, Henry McNeal.

Further Reading

Barnes, Kenneth C. *Journey of Hope: The Back-to-Africa Movement in Arkansas in the Late 1800s*. Chapel Hill: University of North Carolina Press, 2004.

Fitzgerald, Michael W. " 'We Have Found a Moses': Theodore Bilbo, Black Nationalism, and the Greater Liberia Bill of 1939." *Journal of Southern History* 63 (May 1997): 293–320.

Hahn, Steven. *A Nation under Our Feet: Black Political Struggles in the Rural South from Slavery to the Great Migration*. Cambridge, MA: Belknap Press of Harvard University Press, 2003.

Mitchell, Michele. *Righteous Propagation: African Americans and the Politics of Racial Destiny after Reconstruction*. Chapel Hill: University of North Carolina Press, 2004.

Redkey, Edwin S. *Black Exodus: Black Nationalist and Back-to-Africa Movements, 1890–1910*. New Haven, CT: Yale University Press, 1969.

Vincent, Ted. "Black Hopes in Baja, California: Black American and Mexican Cooperation, 1917–1926." *Western Journal of Black Studies* 21 (Fall 1997): 205–13.

Jason Carl Digman

Employment, Black Female Patterns of

Employment opportunities shaped the migration patterns of African American **women** throughout the twentieth century. Migration routes led from rural areas in the South to cities of the South, the North, and to a lesser extent the West. Migration paths often involved intermediate stops in the towns and cities of the South as women moved from farm or domestic labor in rural areas to town-based service economies. Throughout their lifetimes African American women had longer work lives than other American women, and the typical life cycle of the early twentieth century included unpaid work on farms followed by paid labor in agriculture or domestic service. The majority of women stopped work sometime after they married, but then returned to work after a period of time as unpaid homemakers. Because African American families overall were the nation's poorest, widows or divorcées were forced back into the labor force when they became household heads. Throughout the century African American women received lower wages than either white women or African American men. Although the wage gap narrowed somewhat after 1940, the differences remained substantial to the end of the century.

As women moved from farms to towns, they left agricultural work largely for household service. Southern urban growth also created a variety of employment opportunities for African American women, although domestic work remained the dominant urban employment sector until World War II. In the first half of the century African American women in the South succeeded in finding a few industrial jobs, notably in tobacco processing, but their workplaces remained racially segregated, and they were employed for the lowest-paying jobs in the industry.

For African American women, in particular, entry into domestic service often meant living in the homes of their employers, a working situation that deprived workers of privacy, isolated women from their families, and meant long hours because employers demanded near twenty-four-hour availability. Women migrated alone out of the rural South to take service jobs, and many left husbands and children behind. At first, African American servants struggled

Employment opportunities for most African American women in the South before World War II were restricted to domestic service. Courtesy of the Library of Congress.

not to leave household service for better jobs, but to leave live-in circumstances for day work that guaranteed time off and allowed workers to reunite with their families. Young single women, some still children, left the South when older relatives in the North offered to take them in and help them find jobs.

From the late nineteenth century onward women participated in gendered occupations such as cosmetology, boardinghouse keeping, and hand sewing, marketing their services or wares to meet the tastes of African American communities in towns and cities of all sizes. By World War I both Annie Turnbo Malone and Sarah Breedlove Walker (**Madam C. J. Walker**) had amassed sizable fortunes in the beauty industry. Newly acquired African American wealth supported black artists and entertainers, some of whom, like **Bessie Smith**, gained large white audiences as well.

Migration to cities outside the South accelerated with World War I as African American women finally began to obtain manufacturing jobs, although they failed to secure office and retail employment outside of black-owned businesses. While the war's end meant dismissals of white and black women from better-paying occupations traditionally pursued by men, African American women held on to most of the industrial jobs they had gained. Between 1910 and 1920 the number of African American women employed in agriculture declined by 40 percent, while the number of women in manufacturing rose by more than 50 percent. Both **Jim Crow** laws and de facto segregation closed black women out of most office, retail, and professional jobs, but racial prejudice also guaranteed the emergence of parallel educational, medical, and retail businesses within black communities. Women gained jobs as **schoolteachers**, **nurses**, and restaurateurs throughout the country, but these opportunities were highly restricted, and the rewards were inferior to those

During World War II, this former domestic servant obtained work in a supercharger plant in Milwaukee, Wisconsin, after acquiring skills through a National Youth Administration training course. Courtesy of the Library of Congress.

secured by white women. Despite the modest earnings of most black Americans, African American commerce continued to thrive through the 1920s before retrenching amid the Great Depression.

Already at the bottom of the American wage scale, ordinary African American women were hit especially hard by the depression, when they lost jobs in all sectors of the economy. As federally funded jobs programs opened in the Roosevelt administration, black women were included, but programs in the South were totally segregated by race, and programs for African Americans were less numerous and less well funded than those that employed whites. Both New Deal job-training programs and public relief organizations set lower wages or benefits for African Americans than for whites in the South. The national picture was not much brighter for African Americans than life on the southern front. While the employment of white women increased between 1930 and 1940, 80,000 African American women left the workforce during the decade as their employment opportunities shrank.

World War II primed the economy in ways that New Deal programs or policies had failed to do, and the labor shortages of the early 1940s greatly enhanced the work opportunities and the wages of African American women. More than 4,000 African American women found jobs in the military during the war, but unlike civilian black women employed in defense industries outside the South, military women failed to cross race or gender boundaries. For most of the war, African American women were accepted only into the Women's Army Corps, with none serving in the Marines and fewer than 100 in other branches of the services by war's end. Charity Adams Earley proved exceptional, beginning her military career as a second lieutenant in the Women's Army Corps and rising to the rank of colonel, but she too commanded African American women exclusively until the **desegregation** of the military.

Like those of World War I, World War II labor demands drew southern African Americans to towns and cities throughout the nation. Gladys Feeney of **Houston, Texas**, was perhaps typical. When the economy began to heat up in 1940, she left her home to seek employment in Connecticut, writing back not long after her arrival: "Tell folks this is the place to make plenty of money and I'm going to do my best to get my portion. Every thing is nice here no prejudice every man created equal except with cash (smiles)" (Blackwelder, *Styling Jim Crow*, 115–16). San Antonio, Texas, resident Anna Graves, who had trained to be a clerical worker, remained in Texas during the war. Graves broke the race barrier after World War II when she became the first civilian black woman to work in an office at a federal military base in the Alamo City. Circumstances for black women seeking office work were different outside the South, where women gained hundreds of thousands of white-collar civilian jobs in federal, state, or municipal agencies.

The demand for farm labor surged during the war, but women continued to leave the countryside for urban jobs. Some women migrated to follow husbands who were serving on American military bases, but most moved on their own in search of good jobs. Race and gender hurdles had been cleared, and African American as well as white women became trained welders and crane operators, although the poorest jobs as laborers and janitors were filled disproportionately by black women. The West Coast at last proved an attractive migration destination as **shipyards** and defense plants expanded there. More than World War I, World War II broke racial barriers in the North. For the first time, in large numbers, African American women employed in offices and in factories found themselves working alongside white women, and often they were employed at rates comparable to those earned by their white coworkers. African American women in industrial jobs outside the South were presented with their first opportunities to join labor organizations. While union gains were limited during the war, the experience of membership provided a basis for interracial labor actions after the war.

As the end of World War II approached, industries began to lay off workers, and the majority of job cuts occurred among female workers. The vast majority of women who lost jobs were employed in war-related production jobs, and white-collar workers suffered fewer terminations. African American women employed in offices, schools, and **hospitals** were relatively insulated against the downturn, and these wartime jobs permanently altered the occupational options of women and solidified their movement away from agricultural and domestic labor. While residents of the South shared in this occupational shift, white-collar opportunities for black Americans, along with an underlying demand for industrial labor, remained a predominantly northern phenomenon until the late 1960s. Thus the promise of bright futures continued to draw African American women to the cities of the Northeast and the Midwest, with lesser migrations to the Pacific Coast.

In comparison with past decades, the 1950s proved a time of prosperity for African Americans as full employment undergirded family stability and many families enjoyed the luxury of mothers remaining home to raise children, a choice denied to virtually all families during the 1930s and 1940s. African American women and black families narrowed the income gap between themselves and white Americans during the 1950s, as they had in the 1940s. African American women more than doubled their representation in nursing and in clerical positions over the decade.

World War II, partly by introducing increasing numbers of African Americans to employment experiences comparable to those of white Americans, fueled a grassroots **civil rights movement** that delivered real changes in the civil status of blacks. From an employment standpoint, the most significant rewards of decades of rights activism for women of all races were Title VII of the Civil Rights Act of 1964 and Title IX of the Education Act of 1972. Title VII increased African Americans' representation in white-collar jobs within and outside the South in the public and private sectors. Title IX broadened athletic opportunities in secondary schools and colleges for all women, but the more important impact of the legislation was that it eradicated racial and gender quotas or bans in professional programs and, for the first time in American history, permitted large numbers of African American women to become **attorneys**, **physicians**, and professors.

The civil rights movement truly transformed the American landscape by creating open access to public accommodations and education and expanding the employment options of African Americans. African Americans of humble background, like Texas attorney and legislator Barbara Jordan, rose to leadership positions and gained high elective office even within the former Jim Crow South. The death of Jim Crow and rapid economic growth drew many African Americans back to the South they had left as children or young adults. By the 1970s more African American women were coming into the South than were leaving it as brighter prospects beckoned both men and women from the decaying inner cities of the North (see **Return Migration**).

While the civil rights movement delivered economic improvements to educated African Americans, the uneducated had been largely left behind. In the 1970s, as many of the promises of Lyndon Johnson's Great Society programs turned to disappointment for the poor, the poverty rights movement emerged, with major leadership in black communities, but successes were limited and short lived. Among African Americans as well as others, the share of households headed by women continued to grow after a brief decline in the 1950s. Unable to earn sufficient wages to offset the costs of child care, increasing numbers of women turned to welfare programs to support their families. The "welfare reforms" of the Ronald Reagan administration initiated a long-term decline in welfare benefits. By the end of the century the vast majority of single mothers were back in the labor force, but the living conditions of their families had not necessarily improved. Women with little education and few job skills found themselves confined to low-wage jobs in the ever-expanding service sector, and the vast majority of these jobs delivered neither job security nor the health and retirement benefits most needed by the working classes. In contrast to unskilled women, well-educated African American women had moved ahead in business and the professions, thus broadening the base of the African American middle class in all regions of the country. *See also* Beauty Culture; Employment, Black Male Patterns of; Employment Discrimination; Occupational Mobility; Primary Documents 4, 6, 20, 32, 35, 53.

Further Reading

Blackwelder, Julia Kirk. *Now Hiring: The Feminization of Work in the United States, 1900–1995.* College Station: Texas A&M University Press, 1997.

———. *Styling Jim Crow: African American Beauty Training during Segregation.* College Station: Texas A&M University Press, 2003.

————. *Women of the Depression: Caste and Culture in San Antonio, 1929–1939.* College Station: Texas A&M University Press, 1984.

Clark-Lewis, Elizabeth. *Living In, Living Out: African American Domestics in Washington, D.C., 1910–1940.* Washington, DC: Smithsonian Institution Press, 1994.

Feeney, Gladys. Letter to Abbie Franklin Jemison, April 7, 1940. Box 34, folder O. Franklin School of Beauty Papers, Houston Public Library.

Honey, Maureen. *Bitter Fruit: African American Women in World War II.* Columbia: University of Missouri Press, 1999.

Jones, Jacqueline. *Labor of Love, Labor of Sorrow: Black Women, Work, and the Family from Slavery to the Present.* New York: Basic Books, 1985.

Robnett, Belinda. *How Long? How Long? African-American Women in the Struggle for Civil Rights.* New York: Oxford University Press, 1997.

White, Katherine J. Curtis. "Women in the Great Migration: Economic Activity of Black and White Southern-Born Female Migrants in 1920, 1940, and 1970." *Social Science History* 29, no. 3 (2005): 413–55.

Julia Kirk Blackwelder

Employment, Black Male Patterns of

Changing employment patterns among black workers have played an important role in their economic advance. Many of these changes have coincided with sharp economic growth and periods of government involvement in combating **employment discrimination**. Since emancipation black workers have been able to secure substantial income gains relative to the fast-growing incomes of white workers. Between 1870 and 1940 the ratio of black to white earnings grew from 0.25 to about 0.50 and has grown to about 0.70 today. Sharp changes in occupational and industrial employment patterns were a contributor to the relative income gains.

Changing Patterns of Segregation in the Northern States from Census to Census, 1910–1950

The Integrated Public Use Microdata Series (IPUMS) can be used to examine the employment patterns of northern black males across nonagricultural industries and compare them with those of native-born white males for the years 1910, 1920, 1940, and 1950. The sample used contains all employed male wage and salary earners (excluding the self-employed and unemployed) from the ages of nineteen to sixty-four. Table 1 shows the distributions of black and native-born white employed male wage and salary earners in the sample across twenty-six nonagricultural industry classifications. Table 2 contains a dissimilarity index (the Duncan Dissimilarity Index, DDI) that gives the percentage of black or native-born white workers in the sample that would have had to change industries to bring the distribution of black workers across the twenty-six nonagricultural industries into equality with that of whites.

In 1910, 26.7 percent of the black workers would have had to change industries to bring the black distribution across nonagricultural industries into equality with that of whites. Black workers were underrepresented in almost

TABLE 1: Distribution of Black and Native-Born White Workers across Nonagricultural Industries in the North

Industry	1910 White	1910 Black	1920 White	1920 Black	1940 White	1940 Black	1950 White	1950 Black
Mining	4.0	2.7	4.6	2.6	3.0	1.5	2.2	0.6
Logging and wood products	3.8	2.1	2.8	1.2	2.0	0.9	1.9	0.8
Glass and glass products	0.8	0.4	0.5	0.6	0.5	0.3	0.5	0.2
Clay and stone products	1.8	3.3	0.9	1.8	1.1	0.7	1.1	1.0
Primary metal	7.2	6.6	8.3	17.4	8.1	8.4	8.4	13.6
Machinery and equipment	7.6	1.1	13.4	7.5	11.9	5.9	15.6	12.1
Food	2.8	2.1	2.6	3.4	3.4	2.2	3.3	3.8
Tobacco	0.8	0.1	0.4	0.2	0.1	0.1	0.1	0
Textile and clothing	3.4	0.9	3.3	1.1	3.6	1.2	3.1	2.5
Paper	0.9	0.5	1.2	0.6	1.5	0.5	1.6	1.0
Printing	5.2	2.2	2.2	0.5	2.4	0.7	2.2	0.8
Chemicals	0.7	0.6	1.0	1.6	1.6	0.8	1.9	1.9
Petroleum and coal products	0.2	0.2	0.6	0.5	0.8	0.5	0.8	0.7
Rubber and leather	2.6	0.2	3.1	1.7	2.1	1.1	1.9	1.6
Construction	9.8	11.9	7.5	8.4	10.0	22.0	6.9	8.0
Transportation	16.2	16.3	15.6	17.7	7.9	8.1	8.5	9.5
Telecommunications	1.1	0	0.9	0.1	0.9	0.1	1.0	0.2
Utilities and sanitation services	2.0	2.0	1.3	1.3	2.3	1.6	2.3	1.8
Wholesale trade	3.3	1.1	3.6	1.1	3.2	1.7	4.4	3.0
Retail trade	10.5	12.1	9.1	7.4	12.7	11.9	11.7	11.5
Finance, insurance, and real estate	3.0	4.5	2.9	1.8	4.0	3.9	3.4	2.6
Business and repair services	1.4	1.8	3.7	2.8	2.3	3.0	2.9	3.1
Personal services	2.6	21.0	1.9	10.9	2.5	12.5	1.7	6.6
Entertainment and recreation services	0.9	2.0	0.7	1.3	1.3	1.8	0.9	1.2
Professional and related services	3.6	2.5	3.1	2.6	4.7	3.9	4.8	4.2
Public administrative	4.0	1.8	4.7	3.9	6.1	4.7	6.9	7.7

For the years 1910, 1920, 1940, and 1950, this table shows the percentage of all white or black workers in the sample employed in each of the twenty-six industries. The data are from the 1910, 1920, 1940, and 1950 IPUMS. The sample was restricted to employed male wage and salary earners between the ages of nineteen and sixty-four for the years 1910, 1940, and 1950. The 1920 IPUMS does not contain information on whether a worker was employed or not. Since 1920 was a low unemployment year, restricting the sample to wage and salary earners in the labor force is likely sufficient. The sample consists of data for nonagricultural industries in the following northern states: Connecticut, Maine, Massachusetts, New Hampshire, Rhode Island, Vermont, New Jersey, New York, Pennsylvania, Illinois, Indiana, Michigan, Ohio, and Wisconsin.

TABLE 2: Duncan Dissimilarity Index

Year	All Nonagricultural	Manufacturing and Mining
1910	26.7	27.6
1920	23.9	30.9
1940	24.2	16.1
1950	13.9	18.8

The data are from the 1910, 1920, 1940, and 1950 IPUMS. The sample was restricted to employed male wage and salary earners between the ages of nineteen and sixty-four for the years 1910, 1940, and 1950. The 1920 IPUMS do not contain information on whether a worker was employed or not. Since 1920 was a low unemployment year, restricting the sample to wage and salary earners in the labor force is likely sufficient. The sample consists of data for nonagricultural industries in the fourteen most northeastern states.

all the manufacturing and mining industries and were significantly overrepresented in the personal services industry. Among nonagricultural workers, 37.8 percent of white workers and only 20.3 percent of black workers were working in the manufacturing sector. In 1910 the degree of overrepresentation in the personal services sector was particularly striking. Only 2.6 percent of the white workers were employed in the personal services industry, compared with 21.0 percent of black workers.

The DDI for all twenty-six nonagricultural industries was remarkably stable for the years 1910, 1920, and 1940, decreasing only from 26.7 to 24.2 between 1910 and 1940. During the 1940s, however, the differences in the black and native-born white distributions across nonagricultural industries fell substantially. The DDI was nearly cut in half, to 13.9. By 1950 the proportion of black workers employed in manufacturing had risen to 40.0 percent, nearly reaching the white proportion of 42.4 percent. Black workers were still significantly overrepresented in the personal services industry, but this difference too had decreased substantially, from a gap of 18.4 percentage points in 1910 to 4.9 percentage points in 1950.

This significant decrease in the industry employment differential within the twenty-six nonagricultural industries during the 1940s is consistent with other work showing that the 1940s were a period of significant relative gains for black workers. Black workers benefited substantially in terms of higher relative wages and occupational advance. About 37 percent of the increase in the black-white weekly wage ratio from 1940 to 1980 occurred during the 1940s. Much of the increased opportunities for black workers likely resulted from the pressure that tight wartime labor markets placed on employers to employ them. Evidence suggests that the executive order signed by President Franklin D. Roosevelt establishing the **Fair Employment Practices Committee** during World War II, making it against the law for defense contractors and government agencies to discriminate on the basis of race, religion, or national origin, may have helped black workers obtain greater representation in the war industries. Institutional change and competition among unions during the late 1930s and 1940s may also have helped open some industries to black workers.

Annual Changes in Black Industry Employment: Pennsylvania, 1916–1950

Contemporary observers believed that it was important for black workers to obtain greater representation in the manufacturing sector. Race-specific employment data on wage earners (excluding salaried employees) published by the state of Pennsylvania allow a detailed investigation of annual changes in black employment across industries. The decennial snapshots afforded by census data do not provide enough information to determine the timing and causes of the employment changes. Evidence suggests that the Pennsylvania industry employment patterns were indicative of those of the North.

During booms the black share of Pennsylvania manufacturing and mining wage earners tended to approach their share in Pennsylvania's urban population, while during downturns the gap between the shares widened. In 1910, 3.4 percent of Pennsylvania's urban population was black, but black workers were less than 2 percent of the employed manufacturing and mining wage earners. By 1920 the gap between the two shares had fallen; the black share of manufacturing workers had risen to 3.7 percent, nearly reaching the 4.3 percent black share of Pennsylvania's urban population. During the recession of 1921 the black manufacturing and mining share quickly dropped to 2.6 before reaching 4 percent in the mid-1920s. During the Great Depression the share declined below 3 percent again, even though the black percentage of Pennsylvania's urban population rose to 5.8 in 1930 and 6.4 in 1940. During the wartime boom of the 1940s, black workers' proportion of the manufacturing and mining sector rose to about 6.5 percent. After the war the percentage fell some but remained above 5 percent for the rest of the decade, compared with a black urban share of 8.4 percent in 1950.

The degree to which the distribution of black workers across industry differed from that of whites was partly a function of the business-cycle activity of the interwar period. During periods of expansion the fast-growing manufacturing industries disproportionately hired black workers. Regardless of race, workers in the industries that disproportionately expanded during times of boom found their jobs relatively insecure during periods of bust. During the Great Depression black workers suffered a disproportionate share of the declines in employment. One of the causes of this unemployment differential was that blacks were employed by these disproportionately cyclical industries.

Unionization is another factor that may have affected which industries employed black workers. In Pennsylvania black employment was negatively associated with industries organized by the craft unions affiliated with the **American Federation of Labor** (AFL) and positively associated with industries organized by unions affiliated with the **Congress of Industrial Organizations** (CIO). AFL policies openly discriminated against black workers, while CIO policies openly condemned discrimination. *See also* Employment, Black Female Patterns of; National War Labor Board (NWLB); Occupational Mobility; Organized Labor; Strikebreaking; War Manpower Commission (WMC); Primary Documents 4, 5, 6, 10, 14, 19, 22, 30, 36, 38, 61, 66, 74, 76.

Further Reading

Collins, William J. "African-American Economic Mobility in the 1940s: A Portrait from the Palmer Survey." *Journal of Economic History* 60, no. 3 (2000): 756-81.

———. "Race, Roosevelt, and Wartime Production: Fair Employment in World War II Labor Markets." *American Economic Review* 91, no. 1 (2001): 272-86.

Donohue, John J., and James Heckman. "Continuous versus Episodic Change: The Impact of Civil Rights Policy on the Economic Status of Blacks." *Journal of Economic Literature* 29 (1991): 1603-43.

Fishback, Price V. "Operations of 'Unfettered' Labor Markets: Exit and Voice in American Labor Markets at the Turn of the Century." *Journal of Economic Literature* 36 (1998): 722-65.

Higgs, Robert. "Black Progress and the Persistence of Racial Economic Inequalities, 1865-1940." In *The Question of Discrimination: Racial Inequality in the U.S. Labor Market,* edited by Steven Shulman and William Darity, Jr. Middletown, CT: Wesleyan University Press, 1989.

Johnson, Ryan. "The Economic Progress of American Black Workers in a Period of Crisis and Change, 1916-1950." Ph.D. diss., University of Arizona, 2002.

Maloney, Thomas N. "Wage Compression and Wage Inequality between Black and White Males in the United States, 1940-1960." *Journal of Economic History* 54, no. 2 (1994): 358-81.

Maloney, Thomas N., and Warren C. Whatley. "Making the Effort: The Contours of Racial Discrimination in Detroit's Labor Markets, 1920-1940." *Journal of Economic History* 55, no. 3 (1995): 465-93.

Margo, Robert. "Explaining Black-White Wage Convergence, 1940-1950." *Industrial and Labor Relations Review* 48, no. 3 (1995): 470-81.

Smith, James P., and Finis R. Welch. "Black Economic Progress after Myrdal." *Journal of Economic Literature* 27 (1989): 519-64.

Ryan Johnson

Employment Discrimination

The racist actions of northern white employers, workers, and consumers were an impediment to the success of black workers seeking economic success in the North. Among other things, the disparate treatment of black workers potentially lowered their wages, restricted their job and educational opportunities, put them at greater risk of industrial accidents, and raised their rate of **unemployment**. Economists researching employment discrimination usually do so in the context of the market forces and institutions that come to bear as economic agents make decisions. Some acts of racism conflict with economic incentives and thus may be uncommon, while other racist actions may actually be encouraged by market institutions and forces. The interplay between markets and racism continues to be an important area of inquiry and debate for economic research.

One of the central theoretical insights of economist Gary M. Becker's pioneering work on employment discrimination is that employers that discriminate do so at a loss of profit. To see this, consider the incentives a firm in a competitive industry faces when it is choosing whether to hire black or white workers. If there is widespread discrimination in the market, the demand for black workers will be less than the demand for white workers, leading to black workers earning a lower wage than whites. However, if black and white workers are identical in every respect except for the color of their skin, a firm can increase its profits by employing the underdemanded black workers since they are paid a lower wage. To successfully compete with this firm, other firms will also have to employ the low-wage black workers. As firms respond to these competitive market pressures by hiring black workers, the wages of black workers will be bid up. This suggests that wage differentials among black and white workers in a competitive market should be uncommon. Consistent with this, economic historian Robert Higgs found that in Virginia in 1900 and 1909, a place and time with substantial amounts of racism, black and white low-skilled workers performing the same job in the same firm almost always were paid the same wage. Higgs's observation has been substantiated by the large volume of research that followed this provocative finding. It suggests that as unskilled black and white workers competed for jobs, market forces mitigated racial wage differentials between comparable workers.

However, there were substantial income differences between black and white workers. In 1940, for instance, the typical black worker earned less than 50 percent of what the typical white worker earned. Two possible sources of these income differences were differences in human capital (such as education and developed skills) and segregation. The racist actions of employers or white workers often resulted in segregated markets, preventing black workers from competing with whites for certain jobs. The actions of white workers were especially suspect because in some situations, rather than incurring a cost for discriminating, white workers benefited economically if they prevented blacks from competing.

Strong social norms may also have motivated white workers. Economist Donald Dewey argued that the first law governing the employment of black workers was that "Negro workers seldom hold jobs which require them to give orders to white workers" (Dewey, 283). As one of many examples of Dewey's first law, economic historian Price Fishback found that black workers in early twentieth-century West Virginia coal mines were in management positions only when they managed all-black workforces. Similarly, economic historian William Sundstrom argued that social norms in the form of a "racial etiquette" governed interracial interactions in the workplace, creating segregation. The norms prohibited black workers from obtaining jobs superior to those of white workers or jobs that required intimate social interactions with whites, thus dividing labor markets by occupation.

In many instances unionization aided white workers in excluding black workers from certain trades or industries. In Pennsylvania between 1916 and 1950, black workers were significantly underrepresented in manufacturing and mining industries with a relatively large proportion of their national workforces affiliated with labor unions. Like employers, unions too responded to economic incentives. The unions that organized workforces in which the vast majority of workers were white subsequently excluded black workers. However, in order to be successful, unions that organized industries with a relatively large number of black workers promoted the interests of the black workers. An example of this is the industrial unions affiliated with the **Congress of Industrial Organizations** (CIO), which adopted a policy against discrimination in the late 1930s and early 1940s as they sought to organize a number of industries, such as steel and automotive, that employed a large number of black workers. In contrast to the CIO's policy of eschewing discrimination, the **American Federation of Labor** and its affiliates continued to explicitly restrict black membership in unions.

Another form of disparate treatment that may have had a negative impact on black employment opportunities is statistical discrimination. This happens when a person's membership in a particular group carries with it information that is applied to the individual. The information about the group may or may not be correct. Historically, it was common for the trade journals to associate certain skills and natural abilities with a certain race or ethnic group. For instance, employers in the steel industry often touted black workers as being well adapted for hot and heavy labor but thought that they were less well suited for other types of work. As this information was applied, black workers were given a chance to excel in steelwork but were not given opportunities to excel or even gain the experience to compete in other sectors. Thus the statistical discrimination could become a self-fulfilling prophecy. *See also* Aviation Industry, Black Employment in; Construction and Building Trades, Black Employment in; Employment, Black Female Patterns of; Employment, Black Male Patterns of; Fair Employment Practices Committee (FEPC); International Longshoremen's and Warehousemen's Union (ILWU); Occupational Mobility; Organized Labor; Packinghouse Workers and Unions; Skilled Workers; Primary Documents 4, 5, 6, 10, 14, 19, 22, 35, 38, 62, 64, 66, 70, 74, 76.

Further Reading

Becker, Gary S. *The Economics of Discrimination*. 2nd ed. Chicago: University of Chicago Press, 1971.

Dewey, Donald. "Negro Employment in Southern Industry." *Journal of Political Economy* 60, no. 4 (1952): 279-93.

Fishback, Price V. "Segregation in Job Hierarchies: West Virginia Coal Mining, 1906-1932." *Journal of Economic History* 44, no. 3 (1984): 755-74.

Higgs, Robert. "Black Progress and the Persistence of Racial Economic Inequalities, 1865-1940." In *The Question of Discrimination: Racial Inequality in the U.S. Labor Market*, edited by Steven Shulman and William Darity, Jr. Middletown, CT: Wesleyan University Press, 1989.

———. "Firm-Specific Evidence on Racial Wage Differentials and Workforce Segregation." *American Economic Review* 67, no. 2 (1977): 236-45.

Maloney, Thomas N. "Degrees of Inequality: The Advance of Black Male Workers in the Northern Meat Packing and Steel Industries before World War II." *Social Science History* 19, no. 1 (1995): 31-62.

Maloney, Thomas N., and Warren C. Whatley. "Making the Effort: The Contours of Racial Discrimination in Detroit's Labor Markets, 1920-1940." *Journal of Economic History* 55, no. 3 (1995): 465-93.

Sundstrom, William A. "The Color Line: Racial Norms and Discrimination in Urban Labor Markets, 1910-1950." *Journal of Economic History* 54, no. 2 (1994): 382-96.

Whatley, Warren C. "Getting a Foot in the Door: Learning, State Dependence, and the Racial Integration of Firms." *Journal of Economic History* 50, no. 1 (1990): 43-46.

Ryan Johnson

Europe, James Reese (1880–1919)

James Reese Europe was one of the most famous and influential black musicians in the United States during the 1910s. An articulate advocate of African American music, he was the founder of the Clef Club, the first effective union for black musicians in **New York City**. In 1912 he conducted the 100-member Clef Club Orchestra in a program of music written by black composers at Carnegie Hall. It was one of many firsts. Europe was the first black bandleader to record in the United States, and his records provide essential evidence of the transition from **ragtime** to **jazz**. During World War I he distinguished himself not only as the leader of the most widely acclaimed band in the American Expeditionary Force but also as the first African American officer to lead troops into combat in the Great War. His life ended tragically, however, when at age thirty-nine he was murdered by a deranged member of his own band during a concert in **Boston**.

Although he was born in the South, Europe came of age in **Washington, D.C.**, the son of southern black, middle-class migrants. He was born in Mobile, Alabama, in 1880 to parents of musical talent who provided their five children with musical instruction. His father, a former slave, active Republican, and devout **Baptist**, held a position with the Internal Revenue Service branch at the Port of Mobile during Reconstruction. In 1889 he moved his family to the nation's capital to take a clerkship with the National Postal Service.

Having completed school and having decided upon a musical career, Europe left Washington in 1902 for brighter prospects in the North. New York City was seen as the mecca for black professional musicians and entertainers at the time, and many of Washington's aspiring talents had already joined the pilgrimage, among them violinist-composer Will Marion Cook and Europe's piano-playing older brother John. American popular taste in music, dance, and song had begun to shift away from traditional European models toward more native influences, and this meant new opportunities for black musicians, particularly in New York City. New York was then the center of musical theater and popular music publishing and would soon become the center of recording, film, and radio. Symbolically, "King of Ragtime" **Scott Joplin** became a New Yorker in 1907, and "Father of the **Blues**" **W. C. Handy** followed in the next decade.

It did not take long for Europe to become established, and over the next eight years he became well known as a composer of popular songs and instrumentals and as a successful musical director for a number of major shows that featured such stars as Ernest Hogan, Bob Cole, George Walker, and Bert Williams. In April 1910, to take advantage of the vogue of black musicians (who were thought superior to white musicians in furnishing dance music), Europe became the principal organizer and first president of the Clef Club of New York, the first truly effective black musicians' union and booking agency in the city. He was also appointed conductor of the club's large symphony orchestra, which he envisioned as a vehicle for presenting the full range of African American musical expression. It was this aggregation that Europe brought to Carnegie Hall in 1912 for a Symphony of Negro Music, a concert that was so successful that they returned in 1913 and 1914. By the earlier date

Europe had already joined a historic tide of black New Yorkers who had begun leaving the middle West Side of Manhattan for a new "promised land" just to the north called Harlem.

It was also about this time that Europe became the musical director for Vernon and Irene Castle, the charming couple who, with the help of Europe's music, revolutionized American attitudes toward social dancing and much else in the years just before World War I. In 1917 Europe was prevailed upon to organize and direct the New York 15th Infantry Regimental (Colored) Band. Mobilized as the U.S. 369th Infantry, sent to France, and integrated into the French army, Europe's band excited multitudes of French, English, and American soldiers and civilians with their lively music, introducing to Europe some of the characteristically American sounds that would later be called jazz. When the reports of his musical successes reached the papers back home, Europe was proclaimed America's first "King of Jazz," and when the heroic exploits of the 369th Regiment (now dubbed "the Hellfighters") in battle were similarly broadcast, a renewed sense of pride and determination was felt by black Americans across the country. "How Ya Gonna Keep 'Em down on the Farm (After They've Seen Paris)," one of the Europe band's favorites, had a special meaning for thousands of black American soldiers who had experienced the absence of racial bigotry for the first time while serving in France. During the course of a national tour just three months after leading the 369th Regiment up Fifth Avenue in its historic victory parade, Europe was stabbed to death during an argument with one of his drummers. *See also* Military Service, World War I; Organized Labor; Recording Industry.

Further Reading

Badger, Reid. *A Life in Ragtime: A Biography of James Reese Europe*. New York: Oxford University Press, 1995.

Brooks, Tim. *Lost Sounds: Blacks and the Birth of the Recording Industry, 1890–1919*. Urbana: University of Illinois Press, 2004.

Gracyk, Tim. "James Reese Europe: Songs Brought Back from the Battlefield." The Red Hot Jazz Archive. A History of Jazz before 1930. Online multimedia presentation. www.redhotjazz.com/europe.html.

Reid Badger

European Immigrants, Relations with Black Migrants

The relationship between black migrants and immigrants from Europe in the cities, towns, and workplaces of the North has only lately become a subject of active scholarship. These studies, though hardly unified in their analysis, have nonetheless demonstrated that the relationship was complex and subject to change.

Of particular interest has been the relationship of "new immigrants" from eastern and southern Europe to black migrants. This is so for a number of reasons. The older immigrant groups—the Irish, Germans, British, and Scandinavians—had been arriving in relatively small numbers by the beginning of World War I. However, the large wave of black migration from the

South came right on the heels of the most intense period of new immigration, which lasted from about the turn of the century until 1914. Because the new immigration resumed for a few years after World War I, it overlapped with the Great Migration.

Because both new immigrants and black migrants took up work at the bottom rungs of U.S. industry, there was occupational contact between them. The first relationship between black migrants and new immigrants, therefore, was a connection based on their shared status, in the late 1910s and 1920s, as predominantly unskilled, low-paid labor. This brought with it a certain degree of direct contact, for example, in **Chicago**'s meatpacking industry or Pennsylvania's steel mills. In this setting both new immigrants and black migrants often faced the hostility of skilled "American" labor.

The shared position in U.S. industry refracted itself in **housing** and neighborhood into a more limited degree of contact. Undoubtedly a certain level of residential mixing among new immigrants and black migrants occurred. While both groups tended to live in poor and crowded housing, however, the situation for black migrants was often more segregated and more strictly and overtly enforced, as, for example, with Chicago's Black Belt. Much more common than shared neighborhoods, however, was a high degree of residential proximity—areas where different neighborhoods came into contact with each other. This proximity then translated itself into shared public spaces, public transportation, and public schools. While rivalry, competition, and even violence between new immigrants and black migrants occurred, oral histories conducted in both groups suggest that friendships and cooperation were also frequent. In sum, the divisions between new immigrants and black migrants appear to have been more porous than the divisions that separated blacks from native whites, although not as permeable as the barriers between new immigrants and native whites.

Both new immigrants and black migrants experienced great antagonism from native whites. Meanwhile, "old immigrants" from northwestern Europe, even if not fully assimilated, were often referred to as "American" or "native white." Their position in the American racial hierarchy had been lifted by the presence of the new immigrants, who faced deep nativism and racist monikers such as "hunky," "polack," "dago," and "wop." Because black migrants faced similar, albeit more intense, racism, the relationship between the two exploited groups of migrants holds added interest.

In a well-known essay historians James R. Barrett and David Roediger have argued that new immigrants' racial status in the United States was "in-between." The new immigrants were neither fully "white" nor unambiguously nonwhite. Moreover, on arrival they had yet to "learn" prevailing U.S. racial outlooks, a process that would require considerable experience. For example, evidence suggests that relatively few new immigrants participated in the **Chicago race riot of 1919**, despite constituting a large percentage of the city's population. Instead, much of the violence appears to have been between Irish "athletic clubs" and black workers, with the Chicago Police Department often siding with the former. One failed attempt by an Irish street gang to inflame the new immigrants against black migrants involved young men donning blackface, entering the Polish and Lithuanian neighborhood

Back-of-the-Yards at night, and burning a number of homes. The Polish and Lithuanian meatpackers, whose traditional antagonists in Chicago had been the Irish, did not take the bait.

However, despite comparable group positions as oppressed, racialized, low-paid, and unskilled labor, examples of cooperation between new immigrants and black migrants were relatively few. In 1918 meatpacking workers in Chicago resisted the large packinghouses' attempt to inflame racial divisions, and black workers joined Poles and Lithuanians in a successful union organization. However, the packers used the excess of available labor after World War I to exploit racial divisions and roll back the union's gains.

During the massive 1919 steel strike, which stretched from Chicago to New Jersey and involved some 250,000 workers, new immigrant involvement was exceptionally high, so much so that the struggle was contemptuously referred to by contemporaries as a "hunky strike." Evidence suggests that black **steelworkers** did not join the strike in large numbers, and that a considerable number of black strikebreakers used it as an opportunity to gain a foothold in Northern industry. However, the majority of native whites also resisted the call to strike, and many joined in **strikebreaking** themselves.

The general absence of cooperation between new immigrants and African Americans in labor and political struggles in the 1910s and 1920s was the product of a complex history. While the **American Federation of Labor** (AFL) had traditionally been indifferent or hostile to both groups, by the 1910s the necessity for organization had become clear. Evidence suggests that for new immigrants, however, the labor struggles of the era were about more than traditional trade union issues, and indeed, their strikes and community struggles often escaped the boundaries of AFL tactics and were denounced by the upper echelons of the union bureaucracy. Meanwhile, the black community had already by World War I experienced the treachery, racism, and opposition of the trade unions. These lessons were not easily forgotten. Moreover, even the most progressive unions refused to embrace the most deeply felt political goals of black workers, which centered on equality and an active struggle against institutional racism. For all of these reasons, the trade union movement did not become a center of black migrant and new immigrant cooperation until the **Congress of Industrial Organizations'** systematic efforts of the 1930s finally paid dividends.

No political organization was able to fill the void left by the unions. The municipal politics of the northern cities were based on a system of patronage, by which, depending on whether Democrats or Republicans dominated city hall, certain national and racial communities would be rewarded for their political loyalty. In this schema black migrants often supported the Republican Party, while the loyalties of the new immigrants varied from group to group and from city to city. This was not an avenue through which extensive black migrant and new immigrant cooperation might emerge until the materialization of Franklin Roosevelt's New Deal coalition in the 1930s.

U.S. radicalism proved a dead end as well. The **Industrial Workers of the World** (IWW) enjoyed significant support in a number of new immigrant communities. However, though the IWW proudly championed racial equality and even experienced a degree of success in jointly organizing black and white workers, World War I oppression crippled it just at the moment when large numbers of black workers arrived in northern cities. **Socialists**, meanwhile, steadfastly insisted that the question of racism and inequality remained purely economic, and no special appeals were made to black workers. And though new immigrants composed a large percentage of all Socialist Party membership, they had organized themselves into separate foreign-language federations inside the party, where their frequent denunciations of U.S. racism could not lead to joint action with black workers. **Communists** in the United States began to address black oppression head-on only by the mid- to late 1920s.

In the absence of joint labor or political struggles, the door was left open for a turn inward in the 1920s. The various new immigrant groups and black migrants embraced nationalism and communally centered politics in large numbers during those years. This atmosphere was well suited for the horse-trading of municipal politics, but was not conducive to the building of amicable intercommunity relationships. An excellent example occurred when Italy occupied Ethiopia, the last independent African nation, in 1936. Many Italians in the United States—the largest single new immigrant group—cheered this predatory act, which inevitably led them into conflict with the black community, which supported Ethiopia.

Equally as important, the ending of new immigration in 1924 with the passage of the chauvinist Johnson-Reed Act allowed for the beginnings of the slow and contradictory assimilation of new immigrants, as well as their elevation as whites over blacks in the urban industrial hierarchy. Now black migrants often found themselves "the last hired, the first fired," once the typical lot of new immigrants. *See also* Attaway, William; Black-Jewish Relations; Employment, Black Female Patterns of; Employment, Black Male Patterns of; European Immigration, Comparison with the Great Black Migration; Organized Labor; Packinghouse Workers and Unions; Political Activism (1915–1945).

Further Reading

Barrett, James R., and David Roediger. "Inbetween Peoples: Race, Nationality, and the 'New Immigrant' Working Class." *Journal of Ethnic History* 16, no. 3 (1997): 3–44.

Bodnar, John, Roger Simon, and Michael P. Weber. *Lives of Their Own: Blacks, Italians, and Poles in Pittsburgh, 1900–1960*. Urbana: University of Illinois Press, 1982.

Guglielmo, Thomas A. *White on Arrival: Italians, Race, Color, and Power in Chicago, 1890–1945*. New York: Oxford University Press, 2003.

Thomas Mackaman

European Immigration, Comparison with the Great Black Migration

Scholars have shown that migration is triggered by both "push" and "pull" factors—forces that at once attract migrants to a new location and repel them from what had been home. Analyzed at this level, the Great Migration and

European immigration bear a striking resemblance, albeit with important differences. Most notably, the de facto ending of European immigration caused by World War I served as the most forceful impetus for the Great Migration. When northern industry's traditional European sources of labor were blocked at the very moment of the wartime crescendo in production, hundreds of thousands of black southerners moved north to take work. This migration continued in the wake of the Johnson-Reed Act (1924), which virtually prohibited further eastern and southern European immigration.

Among similarities, economic factors stand out. Both the American South and the southern and eastern parts of Europe existed as agricultural peripheries to a transatlantic industrial core that embraced the northern United States and northwestern Europe. Increasingly, the economy of the rural periphery in both Europe and the United States related itself to the industrialized areas through the production of agricultural commodities and natural resources for export. However, as production increased, commodity prices dropped, which in turn triggered constant efforts to increase agricultural production. This resulted in a number of changes that, in both Europe and the United States, caused a sharp increase in the number of landless agricultural workers.

Landowners consolidated small holdings into ever-larger parcels and introduced machinery and other agricultural technologies to the production process. The share of labor and land dedicated to subsistence farming dropped, forcing more and more small farmers and laborers to the market in order to procure basic commodities. Simultaneously, the growing availability of cheap consumer goods from the industrial core, coupled with the emergence of a cash economy, undermined the small-scale cottage production that had, in various places and to varying degrees, been used to supplement agricultural labor. Finally, monoculture—the large-scale production of single cash crops for export—made large populations vulnerable to sudden environmental changes. This can be seen as early as the Irish potato blight of the 1840s, which sent hundreds of thousands of destitute emigrants to the United States, or in the damage wrought by the **boll weevil** in the U.S. South from 1914 to 1917—one of the triggers of the Great Migration.

Of course, the same processes of market penetration also allowed for a hitherto unknown knowledge of the outside world in what had frequently been isolated agricultural communities. In both Europe and the U.S. South, more intense levels of commodity exchange required new lines of communication and transportation, which brought with them more and better information on migrant destinations—information printed in newspapers, letters, and advertisements and carried by train and steamship and over telegraph and telephone wires.

In the United States faster railway links running south-north, such as that between **New Orleans** and **Chicago**, greatly facilitated travel, as did the combination of railways and steamships from Europe. In both instances this provided the single most important source of information—the firsthand knowledge of those who had left for the industrial centers of the U.S. North. The information returned to the South and to Europe often related to jobs and to housing, but might involve any number of subjects, including knowledge of new customs, discussion of freedom and hostility encountered in the new environs, and valuable information on culture and politics. This direct information triggered, in both the U.S. South and in Europe's rural periphery, the process known as **chain migration**, whereby a single departure might later result in the emigration of a significant proportion of the same community. This in part explains the apparently strange fact that while some areas of Europe and the U.S. South saw entire communities emigrate, others were left virtually untouched by migration.

The difference in timing between the new immigration and the Great Migration is partly attributable to changes under way in the southern U.S. economy. The New South, as its boosters called it, also experienced a rapid industrial expansion in the first years of the twentieth century, even if it was tiny compared with that of the North. For a time, therefore, it absorbed much of its own surplus agricultural population in expanding industrial centers such as **Atlanta**, **Birmingham**, and New Orleans. Although similar processes of industrial expansion were under way in eastern and southern Europe, the growth of Naples, Budapest, Warsaw, and St. Petersburg did not keep pace with the even more rapid growth of landless peasants.

Of course, in both the case of European immigration and the Great Migration, a central attraction, or pull, was also economic—the rapid growth in demand for unskilled industrial labor in the factories, mills, and mines of the North, which then deepened demand for labor in all sectors of the economy. If we compare the Great Migration to the new immigration from eastern and southern Europe (c. 1890 to 1914), this similarity is cast into stark relief. In both instances migrants occupied unskilled and relatively low-paid labor. Both groups tended to live in substandard and crowded **housing**, and both faced the antagonism, albeit to varying degrees, of the host society.

Indeed, there is clearly a direct relationship between the new immigration and the Great Migration. As noted, it was the ending of the former by World War I and the Johnson-Reed Act (1924) that was a prime catalyst to the latter. A similar process can also be seen in reverse: in the older, more established cities with close proximity to the South, such as **Baltimore**, **Cincinnati**, and **St. Louis**, the population of new immigrants was relatively low, and the population of black migrants was relatively high. Black migrants moved more easily from the South to these cities and tended to fill the requirements of industry first.

Much more difficult to compare is the important push-pull factor of freedom. While numerous nationalities in eastern Europe found themselves under the yoke of imperial domination, only the Jews in Russia's Pale of Settlement experienced a legal and political disfranchisement that, in its severity, approached the systematic oppression faced by blacks in the U.S. South. This included severe restrictions on movement, occupation, and political rights. Also like blacks, Jews frequently faced state-sanctioned violence that was sometimes massive in scope. Among the old European immigrants, only the Irish confronted comparable oppression, facing numerous laws that codified an inferior communal standing, including laws against miscegenation. This is why, among all the European immigrant groups, only the Irish and the Jews had very low rates of **return migration**.

Scholarship has cast light on the deep nativist and even racist hostility that numerous groups of European migrants faced in their new U.S. industrial settings. This included discrimination in the job market and in housing and the hostility of much of the American trade union movement. Among the old immigrants, this was especially true of the Irish, while among the new immigrants it was a universal phenomenon. Yet the racism faced by black migrants was deeper, more intense, and better established. Segregation was both more official and complete, **occupational mobility** was more limited (particularly as the twentieth century wore on), and violence was more frequent and brutal. Before the mass migration of Italians or Poles, for example, dominant attitudes toward them had not been well established. For black migrants, on the other hand, a great deal of shared U.S. history had helped cultivate prevalent attitudes of racism and prejudice well before their mass migration.

Once they were established in significant numbers, both new immigrants and black migrants tended to be overwhelmingly working class, with large majorities of each population engaged in unskilled industrial or menial labor. Within each community a small middle class exerted a disproportionate influence because of its resources, stability, literacy, and connections to powerful native white institutions. These middle-class residents tended to be clergymen, small businessmen, and professionals.

In both cases migrants brought with them much of the culture of their birthplaces, which suggests that the process of migration was far more a process of transplanting than uprooting. European immigrants brought with them important musical, literary, theatrical, and culinary contributions to U.S. culture. The significance of these contributions is outstripped, however, by the impact that black migrant culture has had on U.S. history, a process most obviously seen in the revolutionizing of American music in the twentieth century. The greater cultural influence that black migrant music exercised on U.S. culture is due, in part, to the absence of a language barrier, which made music much more accessible. New immigrant theater, for example, remained a favorite recreation of numerous immigrant communities, but was prevented by language from reaching a broader audience.

Somewhat contradictorily, despite greater linguistic, religious, and cultural barriers, the assimilation of new immigrants into white America has been much more complete. Scholars have hotly debated both the extent and timing of this change, but the greater degree of new immigrant assimilation is beyond dispute. A prime factor in this change has undoubtedly been the closing of new immigration in 1924, which ended the physical rejuvenation of the various immigrant communities while at the same time allowing for the further penetration of the English language and a certain level of occupational mobility. Upward mobility was also made possible by the growing presence of black and Latino migrants, who increasingly took over the unskilled work at the bottom rungs of U.S. industry. *See also* Asian Immigration, Comparison with the Great Black Migration; European Immigrants, Relations with Black Migrants; Hispanic Migration, Comparison with the Great Black Migration.

Further Reading

Bodnar, John, Roger Simon, and Michael P. Weber. *Lives of Their Own: Blacks, Italians, and Poles in Pittsburgh, 1900–1960.* Urbana: University of Illinois Press, 1982.

Dinnerstein, Leonard, and David M. Reimers. *Ethnic Americans: A History of Immigration.* 4th ed. New York: Columbia University Press, 1999.

Golab, Caroline. *Immigrant Destinations*. Philadelphia: Temple University Press, 1977.

Thomas Mackaman

Exodusters

The first mass movement of African Americans out of the South after the Civil War came in 1879 when over a period of six months some 6,000 migrants, called the Exodusters, left Louisiana, Mississippi, and Texas for Kansas, and an estimated 40,000 moved into the Middle West. The movement to Kansas had been going on for a number of years. In the late 1860s, as the post–Civil War **railroad** expansion reached Arkansas, Missouri, and Kansas, a small number of African Americans from Kentucky and Tennessee went to Kansas seeking employment in railroad construction. At about the same time, Benjamin "Pap" Singleton, who referred to himself as the Moses of the Colored Exodus, began urging African Americans in Tennessee to seek a new life in Kansas. Tennessee did not undergo the stringent Reconstruction process required of other former Confederate states and was readmitted to the Union relatively early. Consequently, the great majority of white Tennessee landowners were less accommodating to the former slaves and were adamant in their refusal to sell land to the freedpeople. Those who would sell were asking prohibitive prices. Singleton believed that landowning was the key to a better life for the former slaves. Singleton began promoting migration to Kansas, where he believed that African Americans could acquire land at affordable prices and find better living conditions. Singleton established three settlements in Kansas—Singleton, Dunlap Colony, and Nicodemus. He claimed credit for the migration of 7,432 settlers to Kansas before the mass movement began.

Henry Adams of Shreveport, Louisiana, was another leader in the migration to Kansas. Adams, who served in the Union army until 1869, was motivated by the suffering he witnessed among African Americans at the end of Reconstruction. When the movement by white southerners to regain control of state governments reached Mississippi, Louisiana, and Texas, they used violence, economic pressure, and intimidation to drive African Americans out of political participation. Adams and his supporters formed a committee to canvass conditions and to work among the freedpeople to help relieve their suffering.

Adams and his fellow veterans organized a committee whose membership reached about 500 to look into conditions. Members of the committee traveled throughout the South exploring conditions and working among the rural people. They found conditions to be deplorable. Southern whites tried to keep African Americans dependent upon them for employment by refusing to sell or lease land to them. Adams, like Singleton, became a promoter of migration to Kansas.

From February to May 1879 the so-called Kansas fever motivated hundreds of African American migrants to leave Mississippi, Louisiana, and Texas to seek a better life in Kansas. At the high tide of the movement, groups of men,

women, and children gathered along the banks of the Mississippi River in Mississippi and Louisiana to board boats headed for **St. Louis**. From there they hoped to board other boats on the Missouri River to take them on to Kansas.

During the early stage of the migration it appeared that white landowners would be willing to change some of the conditions that African Americans complained about. Fearing a labor shortage, the governor of Mississippi and leading planters called the Mississippi Valley Labor Convention in May 1879 to stop the exodus. Those in attendance acknowledged that oppressive conditions associated with the tenancy system and the withdrawal of their political and civil rights were the primary reasons for the African American migration. Nevertheless, only empty promises of better treatment came from the convention.

Moreover, the exodus to Kansas was a short-lived mass movement. The migrants expected assistance from the federal government. They hoped that they would finally get their "forty acres and a mule." The anticipated governmental help did not materialize, and many of the migrants underwent great suffering. Aid societies were organized in St. Louis and in several northern states to help relieve their suffering. Conditions were so bad that some migrants returned to the South, but others stayed to become residents of Missouri and Kansas. *See also* Black Migration before World War I, Patterns of; Black Towns; Emigrationism; Midwestern States, Black Migration to; Western States, Black Migration to; Primary Document 24.

Further Reading

Athearn, Robert G. *In Search of Canaan: Black Migration to Kansas, 1879–80.* Lawrence: Regents Press of Kansas, 1978.

Library of Congress. African-American Mosaic. Online Exhibition. Nicodemus, Kansas. www.loc.gov/exhibits/african/afam010.html.

———. Western Migration and Homesteading. www.loc.gov/exhibits/african/afam 009.html.

Painter, Nell Irvin. *Exodusters: Black Migration to Kansas after Reconstruction.* New York: Knopf, 1977.

Strickland, Arvarh E. "Toward the Promised Land: The Exodus to Kansas and Afterward." *Missouri Historical Review* 49 (1975): 376–412.

Arvarh E. Strickland

F

Fair Employment Practices Committee (FEPC)

The Fair Employment Practices Committee (FEPC) was created in the summer of 1941 by President Franklin Roosevelt (through Executive Order 8802) to limit discrimination in U.S. defense industries. Throughout its existence until 1946, however, the FEPC lacked any real legal grounds for prohibiting racial discrimination in U.S. defense industries. Although the FEPC led to the increased employment of black workers in industries with federal defense contracts, it suffered from a general lack of cooperation among southern industries, which resisted the challenge to **Jim Crow** in the labor market and on the shop floor. As a result, the FEPC's failure to gain voluntary compliance in the South incited many black workers to migrate west and north, where the enforcement of FEPC policy created greater economic opportunities for African Americans.

The FEPC existed in three distinct phases. The first phase lasted from the summer of 1941 to August 1942, during which the committee held hearings on discrimination in defense industries in **Los Angeles**, **Chicago**, **New York City**, and **Birmingham, Alabama**. During this period the FEPC's investigative field staff solidified liberal labor and civil rights networks across the United States. In the second phase, from August 1942 to August 1943, the FEPC languished as President Roosevelt reduced its powers and staff for political reasons. Yet in August 1943 Roosevelt issued Executive Order 9346, which reconstituted the FEPC for its third and most effective period. From 1943 to 1946 the FEPC existed as an independent agency with twelve regions across the United States. Each region maintained an investigative office and field staff, which actively sought out complaints and testimonies from defense workers who experienced discrimination. During this third period FEPC staff put together thousands of cases against defense contractors and employers.

A Fair Employment Practices Committee sign hangs above the sewing table at which African American, Mexican, and white female employees of the Pacific Parachute Company in San Diego work together in 1942. Courtesy of the Library of Congress.

Many of these cases were resolved and classified as closed cases, but many other cases remained unresolved until the end of the FEPC's existence.

Historians have debated the achievements of the FEPC, and no consensus exists. On the one hand, the FEPC faced many barriers because it required only voluntary compliance by industries, and it lacked legal grounds to enforce its mission of promoting fair employment in the defense program. Despite these limitations, the high number of closed cases from 1943 to 1946 reveals that many defense industries complied with the FEPC when the complaints came forth.

Generally, industries in the West and Northeast were the most open to ending discrimination, and likewise, FEPC administrators in the West and the North were the most politically aggressive in their pursuit of the FEPC's goals. **Robert Weaver**, as former director of the Negro Manpower Division of the **War Manpower Commission**, noted that the greatest cooperation between the FEPC and industries occurred in the industrial Midwest and New York. Industries on the West Coast, because of their general labor shortage, could hardly afford to ignore the FEPC mission and thus cooperated with the FEPC more than those in the South. This greater enforcement of FEPC policy outside the South certainly lured southern workers to these regions and contributed to the large-scale migration of African Americans throughout the nation during the war.

As southern industries refused to comply with the FEPC, the more ambitious black workers left the region for greener pastures. The story of defense worker Arthur Chapman bears out this phenomenon. During the fall of 1941 Chapman, a young and experienced African American carpenter from **New Orleans**, sought defense employment in his trade locally. To Chapman's dismay, federal officials at the U.S. Employment Service office in New Orleans tore up his application for skilled work on the spot despite the recent executive order. Not to be deterred, Chapman then sought a position as lead carpenter in the U.S. Navy Yards at Pearl Harbor, Hawaii, where FEPC rules were enforced. Because, according to Chapman, "[the Navy Yard] hired a man if he was qualified for the job," he left New Orleans for Pearl Harbor. Because the FEPC policy was applied in many western and northern industries, its lack of enforcement in the South underscored the push and pull effect of mobilization on African American workers during World War II. *See also* Employment Discrimination; March on Washington Movement (MOWM); Shipyards and Shipyard Workers; Skilled Workers; Western States, Black Migration to; Primary Document 5, 35, 74.

Further Reading

Chamberlain, Charles D. *Victory at Home: Manpower and Race in the American South during World War II.* Athens: University of Georgia Press, 2003.

Collins, William. "Race, Roosevelt, and Wartime Production: Fair Employment in World War II Labor Markets." *American Economic Review* 91, no. 1 (March 2001): 272–86.

Friend, Bruce I., and Charles Zaid, eds. *Selected Documents from Records of the Committee on Fair Employment Practice.* Microfilm, 213 reels. Glen Rock, NJ: Microfilming Corp. of America, 1970.

Kersten, Andrew E. *Race, Jobs, and the War: The FEPC in the Midwest, 1941–46.* Urbana: University of Illinois Press, 2000.

Reed, Merl. *Seedtime for the Modern Civil Rights Movement: The President's Committee on Fair Employment Practices, 1941–1946.* Baton Rouge: Louisiana State University Press, 1991.

Charles D. Chamberlain

Farmer, James L., Jr. (1920–1999)

James L. Farmer, Jr., was one of the founders of the **Congress of Racial Equality** (CORE) in 1942 at the University of Chicago, which incorporated nonviolent direct-action campaigns to confront issues of segregation and discrimination that often grew out of the pressures black migrants placed on resources, already limited because of patterns of legal and de facto racism; led voting and **desegregation** drives throughout the Deep South; and was one of the primary organizers of the 1961 Freedom Rides. During his early career as an activist, Farmer worked for two **Chicago** organizations, a pacifist group, the Fellowship of Reconciliation (FOR), in 1941 and later CORE from 1942 to 1945. With FOR, Farmer helped draft responses to such social ills as war, violence, bigotry, and poverty. With CORE, where he served as the group's first chairman, Farmer proposed a new strategy based less on religious pacifism and more on the principle of nonviolent direct action that was used in northern urban areas during the Great Migration and World War II eras as African Americans increasingly questioned the contradictions between American racism and the nation's war for democracy. In 1943 Farmer and CORE employed this new strategy in a series of sit-ins that successfully ended discriminatory service practices in two Chicago restaurants and participated in other campaigns against housing and **employment discrimination**—all of which had negatively shaped the experiences of African American during the migration period.

Born in Marshall, Texas, on January 12, 1920, Farmer entered Wiley College in Marshall, Texas, at the age of fourteen. After graduating, Farmer attended **Howard University**'s Divinity School until 1941 but refused ordination as a Methodist **minister**, citing that he could not preach in a church that practiced discrimination. He briefly returned to Texas but grew unwilling to endure the **Jim Crow** system. He subsequently left Texas and worked for pacifist and **socialist** groups that, like him, opposed the war and the segregated armed forces. When the United States entered World War II, he applied for conscientious objector status and was deferred from the draft because of his divinity degree.

Farmer briefly left CORE to work for the **National Association for the Advancement of Colored People** (NAACP) but returned to become CORE's national director in 1961. In May, Farmer finally launched the Freedom Rides, a demonstration that he had long pushed the NAACP to undertake, which aimed to challenge southern segregation in interstate travel. Throughout his tenure Farmer was considered one of the "Big Four" in the **civil rights movement**, along with Roy Wilkins, Whitney Young, and **Martin Luther King, Jr.**, and was considered by most to be the spiritual leader of the movement.

He left CORE again in 1966 and unsuccessfully ran for Congress. From 1969 to 1971 Farmer worked for the Nixon administration but resigned after complaining that the administration moved too slowly in changing race relations. He broke with CORE over its pro-leftist position during the civil war in Angola and began lecturing and teaching. On January 15, 1998, Farmer was awarded the Medal of Freedom. He died seventeen months later, on July 9, 1999, in Fredericksburg, Virginia, after a battle with diabetes. *See also* Double V Campaign; Political Activism (1915–1945).

Further Reading

The Congress of Racial Equality Web site. 2004. www.core-online.org.

Farmer, James L. *Freedom, When?* New York City: Random House, 1966.

———. *Lay Bare the Heart: An Autobiography of the Civil Rights Movement*. Fort Worth: Texas Christian University Press, 1985.

Meier, August, and Elliott Rudwick. *CORE: A Study in the Civil Rights Movement, 1942–1968*. Urbana: University of Illinois Press, 1975.

Lionel Kimble, Jr.

Farm Security Administration (FSA)

The Farm Security Administration (FSA) existed as a federal farm agency from 1937 to 1943. When the New Deal agricultural plow-up programs in the

South led to the eviction of share-croppers, most of whom were African American, liberals in the Roosevelt administration urged the creation of the Resettlement Administration in 1935 to address the problems of small farmers, sharecroppers, and agricultural workers. The FSA succeeded that agency in 1937 and held multiple functions related to agriculture. Many FSA programs affected African Americans directly, including the agency's homesteading, resettlement, and model community programs. Yet the FSA's programs directed at migrant farm workers (and eventually defense industry workers) had a direct impact on African American migration during the 1930s and 1940s.

The Nauck FSA trailer camp project for African Americans in Arlington, Virginia. Courtesy of the Library of Congress.

In the 1930s nearly a million migrant farm families (most of whom were African American) traveled in and out of the American South picking cotton, vegetables, and fruit at harvest times. By 1937 the FSA hoped to reform the exploitative system of labor contracting and to improve migrant worker **housing**, health, and working conditions that existed throughout the South and the Southwest. In its effort to streamline the recruiting of farmworkers for peak harvest times for agricultural growers in Florida, Louisiana, Texas, Arizona, and California, the FSA worked hand in hand with the U.S. Employment Service (another New Deal agency) to recruit farmworkers for peak harvest times. Through this program of federal labor recruiting and the creation of a national farm labor recruitment network, FSA assisted African American farmworkers in leaving the South during the late 1930s.

As the Great Depression transformed into the economic boom of World War II during 1940 and 1941, New Deal programs covering worker housing, welfare, employment services, migrant labor, and health care were directed toward the care of displaced or migrant war workers. Within the FSA the prewar farm labor recruitment programs evolved into the **War Manpower Commission**'s sophisticated interregional recruitment networks that placed southern African American workers in western and northern defense industries. Naturally, the FSA also took on responsibilities related to the proper care and housing of migrant defense workers in communities with few existing resources. For example, when the federal government evicted farmers in the South from rural lands to be used for military purposes, the FSA took responsibility for assisting displaced families (many of which were African American) by building temporary housing colonies and providing cash grants to those who wished to leave the area.

In some urban areas the FSA also provided housing for migrant war workers, usually in the form of federal trailer courts or villages. In Arlington, Virginia, for example, an FSA trailer village housed African American workers and their families who worked at nearby defense industries in Alexandria and **Washington, D.C.** This particular trailer court became the basis for the Nauck village and community, which still exists in South Arlington. The Nauck FSA trailer village is documented in the FSA/OWI (Office of War Information) photograph collection of wartime defense communities and FSA housing programs housed at the Library of Congress.

While the FSA/OWI photograph collection is best known for Dorothea Lange's images of white dust bowl migrants in California, the FSA photographers also captured numerous images of black migrants throughout the United States during the depression. Likewise, after 1941 photographers in the OWI succeeded the FSA in documenting migrant communities across the nation. In the field OWI photographers generally visited white migrant camps and defense worker trailer parks, but they rarely photographed black migrants and their camps. Within the FSA/OWI collection, Marjorie Collins's photographs of the Nauck FSA trailer village in Arlington during April 1942 offer a rare, candid, and unglamorous, yet intriguing, snapshot of black defense workers and their families in an FSA migrant housing camp during the war. *See also* Agricultural Adjustment Administration (AAA); Public Housing.

Further Reading

"America from the Great Depression to World War II: Photographs from the FSA-OWI, 1935–1945." American Memory. Library of Congress. http://memory.loc.gov/ammem/fsowhome.html

Baldwin, Sidney. *Poverty and Politics: The Rise and Fall of the Farm Security Administration*. Chapel Hill: University of North Carolina Press, 1968.

Hahamovitch, Cindy. *The Fruits of Their Labor: Atlantic Coast Farm Workers and the Making of Migrant Poverty, 1870–1945*. Chapel Hill: University of North Carolina Press, 1997.

Kirby, John B., Robert Lester, and Dale Reynolds, eds. *New Deal Agencies and Black America in the 1930s*. Microfilm, 25 reels. Frederick, MD: University Publications of America, 1985.

Lange, Dorothea, and Paul Taylor. *An American Exodus: A Record of Human Erosion*. New York: Reynal and Hitchcock, 1939.

Lesy, Michael. *Long Time Coming: A Photographic Portrait of America, 1935–1943*. New York: W. W. Norton, 2002.

Mertz, Paul. *New Deal Policy and Southern Rural Poverty*. Baton Rouge: Louisiana State University Press, 1978.

Charles D. Chamberlain

Father Divine (c. 1880–1965)

Father Divine—born George Baker—was one of the most flamboyant, larger-than-life personalities of depression-era Harlem. Father Divine drew upon diverse religious traditions to develop his own ministry, which later became known as the Peace Mission movement. From its base in Harlem, the

Peace Mission attracted thousands of adherents nationwide during the 1930s with its teachings of racial equality and economic self-sufficiency. Although he is sometimes dismissed as a cult leader and a fraud, Father Divine and his movement were one of many inventive expressions of African American religion made possible by the Great Migration.

Several early experiences shaped Father Divine's adult theology. As the son of ex-slaves, born on Hutchinson Island, near Savannah, Georgia, in 1880, he was exposed as a youth to the eclectic style that was the slave-quarters Christianity of his mother. His later religious convictions would emerge from a similar sifting "through different faiths and creeds" (Watts, 12). Growing up in rural Georgia and living in **Baltimore**, where he migrated as a young adult, also exposed him to the injustices of racial discrimination. But he also admired the close social bonds of black communities, which convinced him to espouse an ethic of economic independence as a path to racial **uplift**, an idea that would become central to his ministry.

George Baker's career as a religious missionary began in 1899 when he partnered with Sam Morris, a preacher of an independent religious group who suggested that God lived in everyone. Baker subscribed to this spiritual philosophy, and both men became "reborn" and took new names. Samuel Morris became Father Jehovah, and George Baker became the Messenger. With the addition of a third man, John Hickerson, who became St. John the Vine, the three men preached in the Baltimore area for five years before going their separate ways in 1913. The Messenger, who declared himself a God, left Maryland for Georgia and caused much anxiety in some of the Georgia natives because of his declaration. The Messenger was taken to court, pronounced insane, and forced to leave the State. But the publicity caused him to gain a few followers who believed that he was indeed a God. The experience emboldened him to continue with his religious practices and to further develop his ministry. The episode also reveals what became a recurring pattern in his life of popular support for his unorthodox religion that eventually led to legal entanglements amid accusations of insanity, misappropriation of money, and sexual promiscuity.

He and his band of disciples journeyed to Brooklyn, New York, in 1917, where he founded his Peace Mission movement. The movement's salient features included the worship of Divine as God incarnate. It espoused communal living—through cooperative labor without pay and the surrender of their possessions, members enabled Divine to provide them with food and shelter at little cost, thus strengthening their faith in his miraculous powers. With vows of the strictest morality, celibacy, and charity, members were enjoined to make restitution for past sins, perform remarkable acts of penance, and observe racial equality. In 1919 Divine purchased a home in a white community in Sayville, New York, on Long Island under the name of Major J. Devine. He made his home a communal dwelling and called it his first "heaven."

The Peace Mission movement became so successful that it spread beyond **New York City** to other cities in the United States and abroad. Eventually there were 178 "heavens." He preached messages that were drawn from

Father Divine's Grocery Store in Harlem. © Bettmann/Corbis.

various Christian traditions. He had worship services on evenings and Sundays, and his disciples became model citizens as he increased his enthusiastic supporters throughout the 1920s, especially among the poor. His neighbors complained of the growing crowds and were particularly concerned over the impact on property values brought on by the large number of blacks attracted to Divine's theology. By 1930 his movement was increasingly interracial and had attracted more middle-class followers. He renamed himself Father Divine and referred to himself as God, and as such, he said that he could provide physical cures and inflict retributive illness and death.

In 1931 he was indicted on charges of maintaining a public nuisance. Subsequently, police raided his home and arrested Divine and his followers for disorderly conduct. A jury found him guilty, but the verdict was reversed by an appeals court that found that the trial judge was prejudiced against Divine. The trial gave Father Divine a national reputation, and two years later he moved his base to Harlem, where he was received by thousands. Cooperative businesses staffed with his followers and underwritten with their money allowed him to house his apostles and feed them during the depression. Followers surrendered their money to him and renounced their families, and he gave them new names. In 1942 he relocated to **Philadelphia**, where his movement had major real estate holdings, as well as ones in New York City and Newark, New Jersey, that were worth millions. Because of ill health, Divine faded from the limelight by the mid-1940s.

Although he is often dismissed simply as a cult leader, Father Divine's role as an early civil rights activist should not be taken lightly. Recent scholarship has not only taken his theology seriously but also appreciated his activism in leading antilynching campaigns, instituting economic cooperatives, and organizing against racial discrimination. In addition, his movement symbolized the progressive spirit in the black church and helped define the church's active role in the **civil rights movement**. *See also* Ministers and Preachers; Powell, Adam Clayton, Sr.

Further Reading

Burnham, Kenneth E. *God Comes to America: Father Divine and the Peace Mission Movement*. Boston: Lambeth Press, 1979.

Watts, Jill. *God, Harlem, USA: The Father Divine Story*. Berkeley: University of California Press, 1992.

Weisbrot, Robert. *Father Divine and the Struggle for Racial Equality*. Urbana: University of Illinois Press, 1983.

Fred Lindsey

Fauset, Jessie Redmon (1882–1961)

Jessie Fauset was born in New Jersey in 1882 and was raised in **Philadelphia**, where the family Bible traced her forebears' residence to the eighteenth century. Educated at Cornell University, the University of Pennsylvania, and the Sorbonne, she did not share much in common with the black southerners who migrated northward after World War I. But she tried intermittently to make common cause as she dedicated herself to the struggle for racial equality, **women**'s activism, and artistic excellence.

While studying at Cornell, Fauset wrote **W.E.B. DuBois** to thank him for writing *The Souls of Black Folk*; she later arranged to spend a summer at Fisk University in **Nashville, Tennessee**, because she wanted to learn more about her "people." DuBois became her mentor, and while teaching high school in **Washington, D.C.**, she began to publish poems and short stories in the *Crisis*, the official journal of the **National Association for the Advancement of Colored People**, which he had founded. In 1919 Fauset moved to Harlem and became literary editor of the *Crisis*; she published work by Countee Cullen, Georgia Douglas Johnson, **Langston Hughes**, **Nella Larsen**, Anne Spencer, and **Jean Toomer**. In 1921 she joined DuBois in editing *The Brownies' Book*, a pioneering children's magazine.

In 1924 her first novel, *There Is Confusion*, was published; it was followed by *Plum Bun* (1929), *The Chinaberry Tree* (1931), and *Comedy American Style* (1933). During the heyday of the **Harlem Renaissance**, Fauset was the most prominent woman writer.

All four novels are set in the North; their plots are conventional and end in the marriage of a beautiful heroine and noble hero. But before they marry, the female protagonists—despite the lack of public recognition and financial and moral support—aspire to be artists. Moreover, the novel's subplots explore tough social and cultural issues. For example, one female character in *There Is Confusion* travels south to investigate **lynching**s. Set mainly in Harlem and Greenwich Village, *Plum Bun* depicts an interracial group of art students; it protests the lack of opportunities available to blacks even as it applauds their idealism. It also features a romanticized portrait of a black servant and demeaning representations of West Indian migrants. In *The Chinaberry Tree* Aunt Sal, an ex-slave, has followed her former owner and lover, Colonel Holloway, north. The novel represents the love between them as mutual, but it does not explore the characters' psychology; Aunt Sal rarely speaks. Fauset's final novel introduces a new type of character in African American literary tradition, the self-hating black woman, whose prejudices against lower-class, darker-skinned people destroy her.

Fauset herself struggled against such prejudices. She traveled to the southern United States, Europe, and Africa. She attended pan-African conferences and met women from the continent and the Caribbean. She translated Haitian poetry into English. Ultimately, however, her understanding of the diverse people of the African diaspora was more abstract than personal. She died in 1961. *See also* Caribbean Migration; Intraracial Class Conflict; Literature, the Great Migration in; New York City.

Further Reading

Fauset, Jessie. *The Chinaberry Tree and Selected Writings*. 1931. Reprint, Boston: Northeastern University Press, 1995.
———. *Plum Bun*. 1929. Reprint, Boston: Beacon Press, 1990.
McLendon, Jacquelyn Y. *The Politics of Color in the Fiction of Jessie Fauset and Nella Larsen*. Charlottesville: University Press of Virginia, 1995.
Wall, Cheryl A. *Women of the Harlem Renaissance*. Bloomington: Indiana University Press, 1995.

Cheryl A. Wall

Federal Surveillance of Black Migrants

When African Americans inaugurated the Great Migration, their movement increasingly caught the attention of the Justice Department's Bureau of Investigation (BI). Between 1916 and 1919 federal agents mobilized to investigate a series of allegations that purported to explain the sudden exodus of blacks from the South. One such conspiracy theory held that the Republican Party orchestrated migration in a plot to colonize black voters in **midwestern states** to swing the electoral vote in their favor in the 1916 presidential election. When the United States entered World War I in 1917, rumors ran wild throughout the South that German agents engineered migration to disrupt the country's labor supply, to recruit blacks into the kaiser's army, and to undermine black support for the war effort. Southern whites, increasingly fearful of the migration's deleterious effects on the region's supply of cheap labor, demanded that the federal government deploy its powers of surveillance to check black migration out of the South. Although the Justice Department found little evidence to substantiate any of these conspiracy theories or uncover that black migrants violated federal law, the investigations themselves reveal the widespread fears that black migration generated, as well as the dangerous political climate in which black migrants moved.

In the months before the 1916 presidential election, pro–Democratic Party newspapers charged that the Republican Party had lured black migrants to the Midwest so that they would vote Republican. Although President Woodrow Wilson had received some significant black support in the 1912 election, his standing among African Americans had deteriorated. He consented to racial segregation of federal office buildings in **Washington, D.C.**, and raved about the racist film *The Birth of Nation* after a private screening in the White House. In a well-publicized investigation, clearly designed to benefit the Democrats, the government charged that 60,000 southern blacks had resettled in Ohio, Indiana, and Illinois in the four months before the election and had registered to vote in violation of state election laws. The president himself indirectly substantiated these claims when he declared on the eve of the election that "conscienceless agents of sinister forces" were at work "in opposition to progressive principles and popular government" (Ellis, 32). The probe generated more publicity than evidence, and when Illinois and Indiana voted Republican, but Wilson won reelection, the Justice Department suspended the investigation.

Black migrants fell under renewed suspicion a few months later when the United States declared war against Germany in April 1917. The southern press gave widespread coverage to allegations that black migration was the work of German spies who infiltrated the rural South. Some stories alleged that foreign agents were recruiting blacks to join a German army gathering in Mexico. Federal agents working for the BI placed black migrants and whites who appeared to be recruiting migrants under surveillance. In **Cincinnati**, for example, a BI investigation speculated that the recent arrival of 700 black migrants with free train tickets might have been the work of German spies. Other federal agents investigated two whites, allegedly representing the Wisconsin Orphan Home, who addressed "crowds of negroes at night" in York, Alabama, "urging them to leave and go to Mexico" (Reich, "Great War"). Although the agents found nothing incriminating, they kept them under surveillance. Federal agents in **Memphis** detained 150 black migrants on their way to Chicago when rumors surfaced that they were really on their way to join the German army in Mexico. Out of these elaborate investigations, the Justice Department found no evidence of a German plot, prosecuted no alleged agitator, and found no black defectors. Stories of German intrigue subsided by summer, but the episode indicated the readiness of the federal government to see black migration as a threat to the war effort.

Southern whites continued to appeal to the Justice Department for help in stopping black migration. Newer allegations tended to charge migrants, and particularly those who encouraged migration, with sedition. The two biggest targets were **labor agents** and the black newspaper the *Chicago Defender*, which had widespread circulation in the South and which ran bold editorials urging southern blacks to come north. The Justice Department consistently reported that labor recruiters never violated federal law, and despite dozens of reports that they filed on labor agents, they never took any action to suppress their activities. Federal agents were less sympathetic to the *Defender* and other periodicals of the **black press**. Many of the investigators endorsed the views of one Arkansas planter who demanded that the federal government take the *Defender* out of circulation for inciting black migration, which he called "a serious national problem" and an "insidious and ingenious plan . . . for crippling the South and its resources" (Ellis, 25). The Justice Department, working with the Military Intelligence Division and the Post Office Department, compiled extensive files on the content of scores of black newspapers and magazines, as well as on the political views of their editors. Despite the alarmist character of investigators' files, the Justice Department refrained from seeking widespread indictments of the editors of the black press.

The federal surveillance apparatus directed at black migrants and the black press during the war years left a legacy of suspicion within the halls of the Justice Department about the loyalty of African Americans. Federal investigators demonstrated a consistent record of dismissing the legitimacy of black dissent. They investigated African American migration because they saw it not as the movement of thousands of people in search of economic and social justice, but as the work of party political operatives, German spies, labor agents, or Bolsheviks. The extensive files of the federal surveillance of African Americans offer substantial evidence of how southern whites and government officials saw black migration as dangerous and disruptive of the social, economic, and political order. Despite their bias, the files remain a rich resource for the study of black migration during the World War I years. *See also* Military Service, World War I.

Further Reading

Ellis, Mark. *Race, War, and Surveillance: African Americans and the United States Government during World War I.* Bloomington: Indiana University Press, 2001.

Kornweibel, Theodore. *"Investigate Everything": Federal Efforts to Compel Black Loyalty during World War I.* Bloomington: Indiana University Press, 2002.

———. *Seeing Red: Federal Campaigns against Black Militancy, 1919-1925.* Bloomington: Indiana University Press, 1998.

———, ed. *Federal Surveillance of Afro-Americans (1917-1925): The First World War, the Red Scare, and the Garvey Movement.* Frederick, MD: University Publications of America, 1985. Microfilm, 25 reels.

Reich, Steven A. "The Great War, Black Workers, and the Rise and Fall of the NAACP in the South." In *The Black Worker: Race, Labor, and Civil Rights since Reconstruction*, edited by Eric Arnesen. Urbana: University of Illinois Press, 2006.

———. "Soldiers of Democracy: Black Texans and the Fight for Citizenship, 1917-1921." *Journal of American History* 82 (March 1996): 1478-504.

Steven A. Reich

FEPC *See* Fair Employment Practices Committee (FEPC)

Folk Medicine and Folk Magic

The African American system of folk medicine and magic known variously as hoodoo, rootwork, and conjure (not to be confused with Voodoo, a religion) has been in existence since colonial days, though until the early twentieth century it was largely confined to the South. Once large numbers of African Americans began migrating to major urban centers, such as **Chicago** and **New York City**, they carried their folk practices with them, using herbal medicines to remedy shortages in health care and relying on magic as a means of bettering the harsh conditions they faced in their new environment. The rise of northern urban conjure resulted in the growth of manufactured hoodoo products. In addition, the transformation of rootwork into a national phenomenon convinced many intellectuals of its value as an expression of black culture.

Traditional rural southern hoodooists fashioned love charms, told fortunes, and conferred good luck. In addition, rootworkers used their craft to combat racism. Antebellum African Americans, for instance, treated ailments with herbal remedies on occasions when whites denied them access to trained **physicians**. Similarly, practitioners could supposedly prevent whippings, help runaways, and deal with cruel masters and enemies. After emancipation hoodoo retained its medical aspect. In place of spells to help slaves cope with their condition, however, conjurers introduced others to help clients acquire jobs and protect themselves from criminal prosecution.

After large numbers of African Americans began moving into northern cities during the second decade of the twentieth century, rootwork became a feature of everyday black life in major urban centers. In part, poverty kept medical care out of the reach of African Americans. De facto segregation and discrimination kept blacks from joining the larger white culture, which denigrated folk practices, especially magic.

Rootwork retained its traditional functions. By the 1960s physicians in cities from **Philadelphia** to New Haven were reporting cases of hoodoo-induced illnesses and their related cures. One 1977 study identified 285 folk beliefs centering on **childbirth** alone, all collected over a one-year period in a single **hospital**. The use of hoodoo in job acquisition, love charms, and the like also persisted.

Hoodoo experienced rapid internal urbanization in the North. As demand for rootworkers' goods and services skyrocketed, a form of manufactured hoodoo arose to meet demand. Companies producing what came to be known as spiritual supplies appeared in several northern cities. Their products differed from traditional hoodoo goods in that they contained few herbs, such as John the Conqueror root, replacing them with commercial oils, incenses, and eventually aerosol sprays. Manufactured supplies soon spread to the South, supplanting traditional items, even where they remained available in nature.

Although hoodoo lost some traditional aspects because of the Great Migration, it earned an increased level of respect once it was adopted by members of the urban African American intelligentsia as a symbol of blackness. During the **Harlem Renaissance**, **Zora Neale Hurston** was attracted to the topic, becoming the first major author to describe hoodoo in a positive manner. Her impact on perceptions of hoodoo can be seen today in the works of Ishmael Reed and Toni Morrison, who frequently depict rootworkers as positive figures. *See also* Migrants, Cultural Identity of.

Further Reading

Anderson, Jeffrey Elton. *Conjure in African American Society*. Baton Rouge: Louisiana State University Press, 2005.

Frankel, Barbara. *Childbirth in the Ghetto: Folk Beliefs of Negro Women in a North Philadelphia Hospital Ward*. San Francisco: R and E Research Associates, 1977.

Hurston, Zora Neale. *Mules and Men*. With a preface by Franz Boas, foreword by Arnold Rampersad, and afterword by Henry Louis Gates, Jr. New York: Harper Perennial, 1990.

Long, Carolyn Morrow. *Spiritual Merchants: Religion, Magic, and Commerce*. Knoxville: University of Tennessee Press, 2001.

Jeffrey Elton Anderson

Football

The failure of Reconstruction, the enactment of **Jim Crow** legislation, and the perception of better opportunities elsewhere caused many African Americans to flee the South in the latter part of the nineteenth century. That ongoing exodus coincided with the explosive growth of football throughout the nation. In northern locations football showcased the opportunities available to elite African Americans and demonstrated the physical prowess, **masculinity**, and racial comparisons denied them in the South. Among the first and most prominent of the early black players, William Henry Lewis refuted the social Darwinian perceptions of African American inferiority. Born in Virginia to former slaves who moved northward, Lewis played center for Harvard University in 1892–1893, earning all-American honors before embarking on a sterling legal career that culminated in the role of assistant U.S. attorney general.

In 1892 Biddle (Johnson C. Smith) University and Livingstone of North Carolina engaged in the first contest between black colleges, but segregation in the South denied any possibility of interracial play. Other African American players left the South and found roles on college teams in New England. By the turn of the century transplanted southerners demonstrated their physicality throughout the North, Midwest, and West. Some African Americans even integrated the ranks of the professional teams that grew out of the town rivalries in Ohio and Pennsylvania.

The Pollard family left its roots in Virginia and eventually settled in **Chicago**, where the sons enjoyed stellar athletic success. Fritz Pollard became the first African American to play in the Rose Bowl (for Brown University in 1916), the first black quarterback, and the first black head coach in the National Football League. He recruited numerous other African American athletes to play in the fledgling pro league. Among them, **Paul Robeson**, the son of an escaped North Carolina slave, earned all-American recognition at Rutgers University and international fame as a singer, actor, and social activist.

Crop failures in the South, continued repression, and **lynching**s swelled the black emigration. Spurred by African American newspapers in the North and the restricted immigration of Europeans during World War I, relocation to urban centers promised work and a better life. Here migrants produced a rich urban, popular culture that exhibited the vibrancy of African American life. This liberation fostered the **New Negro** movement that spawned a strong racial consciousness, but also engendered a white backlash.

After the 1933 season the National Football League owners refused to hire African American players, and southern colleges invoked "gentlemen's agreements" when facing integrated northern teams, which temporarily suspended black players for games in the South. In 1937 Wilmeth Sidat-Singh, born in **Washington, D.C.**, but playing for Syracuse University, was benched for a game at Maryland. The following year at Syracuse he got revenge in a 51–0 victory over the southerners. Top stars from black colleges in the South traveled to **New York City** or Chicago to play for a variety of Brown Bombers contingents that engaged in interracial games. Others moved to California, where integrated teams competed in the Pacific Coast League. Among them,

Jackie Robinson, born in Georgia, gained greater fame as an integrating force in major league baseball.

In 1946 black teams in Virginia started their own league, and professional teams in California hired a number of prominent African American players from southern schools as the post–World War II years eased racial tensions outside Dixie. Four blacks appeared on the roster of the Cleveland Browns of the new All-American Football Conference, including Marion Motley, born in Georgia. Joe Perry, a native of Arkansas, also found opportunity in the West with the San Francisco 49ers. After Charles Pierce, playing for Harvard, appeared on the University of Virginia gridiron for a 1947 game, segregation slowly began to erode in the South. To maintain their cherished honor, southern teams eventually had to accept the challenges of northern foes in the all-important bowl games. In the 1950s natives of the South such as Ollie Matson (University of San Francisco) and Jim Brown (Syracuse) led non-southern teams to prominence. By the 1960s southern colleges began recruiting African American players to remain competitive, and stars like Walter Payton, Lawrence Taylor, and Herschel Walker stayed home to lead their state schools to victory. By that time the **civil rights movement** had brought a measure of change to the South and a diminution of the conditions that precipitated the Great Migration. *See also* Basketball; Sport.

Further Reading

Carroll, John M. *Fritz Pollard: Pioneer in Racial Advancement*. Urbana: University of Illinois Press, 1992.

Gems, Gerald R. *For Pride, Profit, and Patriarchy: Football and the Incorporation of American Cultural Values*. Lanham, MD: Scarecrow Press, 2000.

Gerald R. Gems

Ford, Louis Henry (1914–1995)

Born on May 23, 1914, in Clarksdale, Mississippi, Bishop Louis Henry Ford creatively connected faith and politics in **Chicago**. Ford represented the progressive strain in black **Pentecostalism** that has become more dominant over time. His career exemplified the concrete meanings of black Pentecostalism's becoming urbanized and mainstreamed. Despite inevitable tensions, the outcome was a matured movement that in the 1960s and 1970s became a vital force in black Christianity and the neighborhoods surrounding progressive Pentecostal churches.

Orphaned as a child, Ford grew up in the **Church of God in Christ**. At age twelve Ford felt that God had called him to the ministry. In 1927, a year after his call to ministry, he attended Saints Junior College in Lexington, Mississippi, the secondary school supported by the Church of God in Christ. Ford moved to Chicago in 1933 to join his sister and began serving as assistant pastor of a Church of God in Christ in Evanston, Illinois. In 1934 Bishop William Roberts ordained him. After his ordination Ford desired to lead his own church. He therefore started preaching on street corners. Ford believed strongly in Pentecostal power. He believed that the Holy Spirit was given to empower the recipient to overcome every obstacle in one's life. Ford also taught that this power was for the common man and woman. This power would provide the ability for one to achieve greatness. Ford never forsook his southern roots and crafted his ministry to reflect the ethos and spirituality of the denomination's founder, Charles Harrison Mason. He so admired Mason that he named his son after him.

His charismatic preaching drew many followers. Initially, Ford drew those who were members of the working class and those who were black Pentecostal migrants. His early congregation met in members' homes and in a tent in a vacant lot until he rented a storefront on Wabash Avenue in 1936. He named the mission St. Paul Church of God in Christ in honor of Bishop Mason's original church in Lexington. In 1937 he began broadcasting his services on the radio. Four years later, in 1941, Ford purchased Chicago's oldest house and grounds, a city landmark, as a parish house for himself and his family to live. As Ford's reputation and congregation grew, he began to draw those who had rejected the Church of God in Christ because of its conservatism and southern character. Ford offered a different black Pentecostalism that appealed to urban blacks.

In the competitive religious landscape of Chicago, Ford understood that he had to tailor his message to his audience. He used his weekly radio broadcast *Jesus Never Fails* to encourage his listeners never to lose hope. He wanted to reach those who found the city to be a place that provided anonymity and thus no accountability. In contrast to **Elijah Muhammad**, who emphasized **black nationalism**, Ford continued to stress the importance of Christ and the power of the Pentecostal baptism. Ford believed that Pentecostalism was not a separatist movement focused on the otherworldly. Ford also did not prohibit his female members from wearing makeup or pants. He described the key to Pentecostal power as residing in one's lifestyle and relationship with Christ and not through external markers or adhering to a list of doctrinal commands. He sought to combine the Pentecostal emphasis on power with a commitment to social justice.

Therefore, Ford became very active in Chicago and national politics during the 1960s and 1970s. In 1966 he became an executive committee member of the **National Association for the Advancement of Colored People** and a consultant on urban opportunities for the city of Chicago. In 1970 Mayor Richard J. Daley, the powerful machine politician in Chicago, asked Ford to be his adviser on race relations in the city. In addition, Ford was seen playing golf with political friends and encouraged his members to participate in sports.

In many ways Ford became a politician himself. He was a bold man who was not easily intimidated. Though Ford was connected to politicians and entertainers, he never wavered in his commitment to the Church of God in Christ. He built a progressive church that addressed the spiritual, emotional, and physical needs of his members. In 1978 he began plans for a senior citizen home complex. The following year he opened the Chaney Ford Day Care Center. His church also became a satellite location for the C. H. Mason Bible Institute, where people could study the Bible and theology. Every summer Ford held a weeklong tent service right outside his church, located near a black **housing** project. He wanted the people of the community to feel welcome to come to the church and know that he was there to help them.

In 1963 Ford was elected to the executive board of twelve bishops in the Church of God in Christ. This board was made up of men who assisted the presiding bishop and initiated legislative policies in the church. After the death of Bishop J. O. Patterson in 1990, he was elected presiding bishop of the Church of God in Christ. As international presiding bishop, Bishop Ford began a series of innovations, which included efforts to address problems of senior citizens, the young and disabled, **crime**, **homelessness**, education, and drug abuse. Ford also began two major development projects. One was the re-modeling and refurbishing of Mason Temple, the former church of Bishop Mason and a national landmark. The other was Saints Academy and College in Lexington, Mississippi. The school had been closed because of a lack of funds and enrollment. He reopened the school in September 1993. Ford's leadership propelled the denomination into greater visibility internationally. *Ebony* magazine annually selected Ford as one of the One Hundred Most Influential Blacks in America. His sudden death in 1995 aborted many of his plans, but his emphasis on social justice and holistic ministry continues to inspire leaders in the Church of God in Christ. *See also* Ministers and Preachers; Mississippi River Delta; Pentecostal Assemblies of the World (PAW); Smith, Lucy M.; Storefront Churches.

Further Reading

Clemmons, Ithiel C. *Bishop C. H. Mason and the Roots of the Church of God in Christ*. Bakersfield, CA: Pnuema Life Publishing, 1996.

DuPree, Sherry Sherrod. *Biographical Dictionary of African-American, Holiness-Pentecostals, 1880-1990*. Washington, DC: Middle Atlantic Regional Press, 1989.

Pleas, Charles. *Fifty Years of Achievement from 1906-1956*. Memphis: Church of God in Christ Publishing House, 1991.

Shalanda Dexter-Rodgers

Foster, Andrew "Rube" (1879–1930)

Andrew "Rube" Foster was one of the earliest promoters and organizers of black professional baseball. Because professional organized baseball, which included both the major and minor leagues, excluded the participation of African Americans, talented players and entrepreneurs such as Foster struggled to create a separate, viable, all-black professional baseball league. A native of Texas, where he started his baseball-playing career, Foster followed where his baseball talents led him, and he moved to **Chicago** around the turn of the century, where a growing population and fewer restrictions appeared to open more doors for black athletes of promise. Foster's talents extended beyond just pitching, and in Chicago he turned his management skills to developing not only his own club but also the Negro National League, the first black professional baseball league, which he founded in 1920.

Foster was born on September 17, 1879, in the small town of Calvert, Texas. His parents brought him up in a devout Christian household. Foster's father served the **African Methodist Episcopal Church** as an elder and passed on his religious ideals to his children. About his mother little is known except that she was a gospel singer and that she cared for Foster, who had asthma as a child. To help clear up his breathing, health care workers urged his parents to let him play outside, where the young Foster first discovered baseball. After dropping out of school in the eighth grade, about the time his mother died, Foster began playing baseball more seriously. He began his baseball career with the Austin Reds of Tillotson College in 1897.

Foster then pursued a career as a professional player. Although numerous black professional ball clubs existed at this time, black baseball lacked formal organization and teams lacked league affiliation. Foster first joined the Yellow Jackets ball club, a barnstorming black team in Texas, in 1898. His success led him north to play for the Chicago Union Giants and then the Philadelphia Giants by 1902. In **Philadelphia** Foster led his club to what was then referred to as the Black World Series, defeating the Cuban X-Giants in a three-game series.

Rube Foster's real talents, however, lay in organizing and administrating the game of baseball. He got involved in the managing end in Chicago with fellow migrant Frank Leland and his Leland Giants. Leland had come north from Georgia. Soon Foster saw that Leland did not have the best interests of his players at heart, and he knew that he could negotiate higher guarantees for the ballplayers. He also thought that Leland did not always share the profits evenly with his team. By 1907 Foster moved into the role of player/manager with the Chicago Leland Giants, which had a successful first season under his guidance. Foster believed that the 1910 Leland Giants were the best team ever put together. The club is credited with a record of 122 wins against only 10 losses. Foster contributed at least 13 wins to his team's overall total. John Henry "Pop" Lloyd, Frank Wickware, Pete Hill, Bruce Petway, and Grant "Homerun" Johnson all helped Foster's club win regularly. Foster taught his men the importance of a strong defense, solid pitching, and a running game. Foster wanted his teams to be able to scrape out a run as easily as Johnson could tie a game with a home run.

By 1910 Foster and black owner Frank Leland had a falling out, and Foster wrested control of the team from Leland. He kept the name, while Leland formed the Chicago Giants. In 1911 Foster moved on to form a partnership with white tavern owner John C. Schorling. Many black baseball teams at this time, lacking financial resources and access to credit, and black baseball promoters such as Foster struck deals with whites who provided playing facilities and could schedule games against white semipro teams. Schorling was also the son-in-law of Charles Comiskey, owner of the Chicago White Sox. Together they created the Chicago American Giants, a powerhouse in the Chicago area and later in the **Negro Leagues**.

In 1920 Foster organized a meeting of lawyers, reporters, and baseball men to develop the first permanent Negro League, the Negro National League (NNL). By 1920 things had started to change in areas like Chicago as a result of the black migrations that had begun during World War I. Chicago and other northern industrial cities became part of the Promised Land for African Americans looking for a new start. As many families moved north, a black middle class began to form. This group wanted and needed services that the white community would not provide for them, and so they built their own separate institutions in the black economy of the South Side **ghetto**. The Negro Leagues developed to fill the entertainment needs of the emerging migrant community.

Chicago became the opportune place to start a new league because of the great sporting tradition that already existed there with amateur, semipro, and professional teams playing throughout the city and surrounding areas. Baseball was not the only **sport** that captured the interests of Chicagoans. **Basketball** and **football** also developed strong followings. By the end of the 1919 season, however, semipro ball in Chicago declined. This hurt African American clubs that depended on these teams as opponents. Foster saw the opportunity for a new league to provide regular opponents and paychecks for players.

Foster displayed his business acumen in forming the Negro National League and remained its president through 1926. He became ill in 1926 after a stay in a hotel with a gas leak. As a result of this exposure, Foster began to suffer from a variety of problems that led to his being institutionalized for the last years of his life in Kankakee, Illinois. Foster died on December 9, 1930. Without Foster's guiding hand and connections throughout baseball, the NNL floundered and eventually collapsed with the onset of the Great Depression. Black baseball did not die, however, because new entrepreneurs continued to come north and revived the leagues in the 1930s. *See also* Gibson, Joshua; Paige, Leroy Robert "Satchel."

Further Reading

Cottrell, Robert Charles. *The Best Pitcher in Baseball: The Life of Rube Foster, Negro League Giant*. New York: New York University Press, 2004.

Heaphy, Leslie A. *The Negro Leagues, 1869-1960*. Jefferson, NC: McFarland and Company, 2002.

Lanctot, Neil. *Negro League Baseball: The Rise and Ruin of a Black Institution*. Philadelphia: University of Pennsylvania Press, 2004.

Whitehead, Charles E. *A Man and His Diamonds: A Story of the Great Andrew (Rube) Foster, the Outstanding Team He Owned and Managed, and the Superb League He Founded and Commissioned*. New York: Vantage Press, 1980.

Leslie A. Heaphy

Foster, William (1884–1940)

Dubbed "the Dean of the Negro Photoplay" by George P. Johnson of the Lincoln Motion Picture Company, William Foster released the first black-produced film, *The Railroad Porter*, in 1913. Before founding his film company, Foster had a long career in show business as a vaudeville publicity and booking agent and as business representative for Robert Motts's legendary Pekin Theater in **Chicago**. The nationally known Pekin was celebrated as the first black-owned and operated venue of "legitimate" theatrical entertainment, featuring a stock company of black dramatic actors and appearances by the country's leading vaudeville and musical performers. Foster not only cultivated black talent on the Pekin stage, but also wrote extensively about the black theatrical scene (under the pen name Juli Jones) for black newspapers such as the **Chicago Defender** and the *Indianapolis Freeman.*

The Foster Photoplay Company specialized in nondegrading black-cast comedies, seeking to use moving pictures as an instrument of **uplift**. As Foster wrote in the December 20, 1913, issue of the *Freeman*, "Nothing has done so much to awaken race consciousness of the colored man in the United States as the motion picture. It has made him hungry to see himself as he has come to be." In comedies like his debut, *The Railroad Porter*, and newsreels such as *The Colored Championship Base Ball Game* (1914), Foster represented elements of black life that African Americans had cultivated in northern cities, but that were largely ignored in white-produced films—particularly the lifestyles of the black middle class. *The Railroad Porter* (starring former Pekin Stock Company members Lottie Gradie and Howard Kelly) portrays the wife of a Pullman porter who has an affair with a waiter/dandy at the fashionable Elite Café, one of the leading gathering places along Chicago's State Street "Stroll."

Reviews in the *Defender* suggest that Foster's films enjoyed great popularity among black urban audiences. As a result of *Porter*'s success, Chicago's States Theater offered Foster an exclusive contract for the premieres of his subsequent films, including *The Butler* and *The Fall Guy* (both 1913). Foster's success reached another peak in November 1913 when *The Railroad Porter* was screened to white audiences at the Majestic Theater, Chicago's famous vaudeville house. Beyond making films, Foster tried to persuade African Americans to buy stock in black-owned film companies, and to organize a distribution and exhibition network of black-owned theaters. Despite these efforts, after producing at least eleven short films his company folded in 1916.

Foster continued to play an important role in Chicago's **black film** culture when he was hired in 1917 to manage another black-owned State Street theater, the Star, a movie house operated by businessman and gambling lord Henry "Teenan" Jones, reprising the role he had played at the Pekin. Foster worked as circulation manager for the *Defender* during the late 1910s, notably during the summer riots of 1919. During the late 1920s Foster moved to **Los Angeles**, where he attempted unsuccessfully to found another film production company. Still, his early "race film" efforts paved the way for the handful of black filmmakers of the silent era such as George and Noble Johnson, Peter P. Jones, and **Oscar Micheaux**. *See also* Black Consumer Market.

Further Reading

Butters, Gerald. *Black Manhood on the Silent Screen*. Lawrence: University Press of Kansas, 2002.

Reid, Mark. *Redefining Black Film*. Berkeley: University of California Press, 1993.

Sampson, Henry. *Blacks in Black and White: A Source Book on Black Films*. 2nd ed. Metuchen, NJ: Scarecrow Press, 1995.

Stewart, Jacqueline. "William Foster, 'Dean of the Negro Photoplay.'" *Oscar Micheaux Society Newsletter* 9 (Spring 2001): 1–2.

Jacqueline Stewart

Fraternal Orders

A significant presence in African American communities before the Great Migration, fraternal orders such as the Elks, the Knights of Pythias, the Odd Fellows, and the Prince Hall Freemasons performed a variety of roles for both migrants and established urban black communities. In some cases they facilitated the migration of southerners and provided an opportunity for cooperative interaction among southern migrants, African **Caribbean** immigrants, and the existing black residents in urban areas. In other cases fraternal lodges allowed the established black population, or "old settlers," to cultivate a respectable, bourgeois, middle-class identity and to subsequently distance themselves from the mass of "unrespectable," working-class black migrants.

Prince Hall Freemasonry is the oldest of the major fraternal orders among African Americans, dating back to the late eighteenth century. Elks, Odd Fellows, and Knights of Pythias did not become fixtures in black communities until after the Civil War, in most cases, the 1880s and 1890s. These voluntary associations provided mutual aid for their members in the form of insurance policies, relief funds, payment for burial expenses, and financial assistance to widows and orphans. They also served as entrepreneurial and professional networks and provided charitable service within their communities.

The interregional networks that were formed by fraternal orders facilitated migration and community development in a number of ways. Members of southern lodges often visited northern cities in order to attend national conventions. Their exposure to black communities with well-developed institutional infrastructures and established entrepreneurial networks often enticed these southern brothers to move north. Once in their new environments, migrants who belonged to fraternal orders could count on their brethren to serve as social, business, and professional connections. Lodges also served as important vehicles for professional and entrepreneurial African Caribbean immigrants to embed themselves socially, politically, and economically within African American communities.

Fraternal orders also provided assistance to migrants who were not members. Odd Fellows and Elks tended to offer aid to working-class and what they might consider, unrespectable migrants on a more consistent basis than Masons. This was largely because Odd Fellows and Elks were more "rehabilitative" lodges than Masons, with part of their mission being to **uplift** those African Americans who did not exhibit "proper" middle-class sensibilities. Masons, on the other hand, were typically more exclusive, restricting their membership to individuals who demonstrated a commitment to the self-ascribed values of the bourgeoisie: thrift, regularity, work ethic, and sobriety. They did not see the objective of their venerable order as one of reform; rather, Masons propped themselves up as models of progress to be emulated by the unrespectable working class. Masonic assistance to migrants became less restricted as the twentieth century advanced, but for much of the early part of the century, aid was limited to members, their families, and civic organizations.

Membership in fraternal orders offered more than just professional and business opportunities and financial assistance in times of need. Membership, especially in Masonic lodges, also brought with it a putative bourgeois status. Men within the established black elite and the emergent middle class clung to their identity as Masons as a way of distinguishing themselves from southern migrants, many of whom were deemed by both whites and blacks to be unrespectable and unassimilable because of their rural, working-class backgrounds. Fearful that whites might lump all newcomers and old settlers together in an undifferentiated mass and therefore fail to recognize their own assimilability, Masons pointed to their economic status, respectability, and civic participation. Moreover, they regularly sought to expose "bogus" Masons—individuals who erroneously claimed to belong to the order—and often conflated the illegitimate status of "bogus" Masons with their working-class background. In this sense, Masonic lodges reflected and contributed to social stratification within urban black communities. This was not the case in all cities, however. In some urban areas with smaller black populations, like **Milwaukee**, fraternal orders, including Prince Hall Freemasonry, tended to be more inclusive of the working class.

By the 1930s fraternal orders became less important to the institutional life of black communities. The social functions that they had once performed were being fulfilled by new forms of mass culture such as the radio and motion pictures. The mutual aid benefits that had been a hallmark of fraternalism were increasingly being replaced by commercial insurance companies. And the associational identity and networks that had attracted many black men to lodges in the nineteenth century could, by the 1930s, be found in professional societies, Greek-letter organizations, and civil rights groups. *See also* Intraracial Class Conflict.

Further Reading

Grossman, James R. *Land of Hope: Chicago, Black Southerners, and the Great Migration*. Chicago: University of Chicago Press, 1989.

Muraskin, William A. *Middle-Class Blacks in a White Society: Prince Hall Freemasonry in America*. Berkeley: University of California Press, 1975.

Trotter, Joe William, Jr. *Black Milwaukee: The Making of an Industrial Proletariat, 1915-45*. Urbana: University of Illinois Press, 1985.

Watkins-Owen, Irma. *Blood Relations: Caribbean Immigrants and the Harlem Community, 1900-1930*. Bloomington: Indiana University Press, 1996.

Martin Summers

Frazier, E. Franklin (1894–1962)

The history and consequences of the Great Black Migration were a central theme in the research and publications of sociologist E. Franklin Frazier. He was an important member of a cohort of African American activist intellectuals who, after World War I, formed the cutting edge of a social, political, and cultural movement that irrevocably changed conceptions of race and the politics of race relations in the United States.

The son of working-class parents, Frazier grew up in segregated **Baltimore**, graduated from **Howard University** in 1916, and received his doctoral degree in sociology from the University of Chicago in 1931, all the while supplementing his income with various teaching positions. Between 1922 and 1927 he taught sociology at Morehouse College and directed the Atlanta School of Social Work, which he transformed into a professional program that attracted black students from all over the country. Frazier returned to the South in 1929 to take a job teaching sociology at Fisk University in **Nashville**, in part because academic doors in the North were closed to him. In 1934 he assumed leadership of Howard University's Sociology Department, where he remained for the rest of his career. For all his accomplishments—the first African American president of the American Sociological Association (1948), author of the first in-depth study of the black family (1939) and the first comprehensive textbook on African Americans (1949), and consultant on global race relations to UNESCO (1951–1953)—Frazier was never offered a tenure-track job in a predominantly white university. Near the end of his life he was targeted and harassed by the FBI and other intelligence agencies for his public support of progressive political causes.

In his wide-ranging sociological studies Frazier was particularly interested in the impact of forced migration on the cultural, social, and economic life of southern blacks. He made several contributions to our understanding of this process.

First, Frazier's research on black families included the meticulous collection of oral histories that chronicled the day-to-day experiences of ordinary people as they struggled to leave the caste system of the rural South and accommodate to urban, industrial life in other parts of the country. He vividly documented how "the sudden descent of this vast human tide upon a few northern cities constituted a flight, replete with dramatic episodes, from medieval to modern America" (Frazier, *Negro Family*, 291).

Second, Frazier honestly addressed a wide range of social problems—such as high delinquency and **unemployment** rates and the breakdown of family stability—that characterized the first and second generations of black migrants. With his continued reference to the chaos and disorganization in urban black family patterns, Frazier had a tendency to underestimate the resources and ingenuity of "demoralized" families, as well as to assume that gender roles are naturally constituted. But he was motivated to demonstrate how the combined impact of forced relocation, economic exploitation, and institutionalized racism caused havoc and "disorganization" in northern **ghettos**. Frazier was innovative in demonstrating that the problems of black urban families were socially constructed rather than culturally inherited, and that personal pathologies were created within and by Western civilization, not by the failure of Africans to live up to American standards.

Moreover, he did not regard the black family as permanently and uniformly deformed by its uprooting from the South. Frazier's family is in fact a broad spectrum of families, constantly in a process of change and reorganization, depending on a complex interrelationship of economic, cultural, and social forces. Frazier was interested in the family as an institution that, at different times and under different conditions, was sometimes disorganized and demoralized, sometimes tenacious and resourceful. His perspective was genuinely interdisciplinary, and his solutions to family problems were similarly complex and multifaceted. Though he was more of an economic determinist than a social psychologist, he was opposed to one-dimensional approaches to social policy.

Third, Frazier was among the first sociologists to locate the movement of black people to and within the United States in an international political-economic perspective. "The integration of the Negro into American society," he wrote in 1949, "will be determined largely by the reorganization of American life in relation to a new world organization. The so-called 'Negro Problem' is no longer a southern problem or even an exclusively domestic problem" (Frazier, *Negro in the United States*, 703). In his important work *Race and Culture Contacts in the Modern World* (1957) Frazier analyzed how the "color line" was a global phenomenon, shaped by economic and social forces. He was hopeful that "as imperialism and colonialism based upon color disappear, racial and cultural differentiation without implication of superiority and inferiority will become the basic pattern of a world order" (Frazier, *Race and Culture*, 338).

Since Frazier's death in 1962, diaspora studies, ethnography, and feminist history have enriched the study of the Great Migration. But his pioneering research is worth revisiting because it broke the domination of racialized paradigms within sociology and opened up African American communities to the possibility of serious historical and sociological investigation. Moreover, the problems that he reported in the middle of the last century—the impact of racism on family life, the interconnection between economic inequality and personal problems, and the difficulty of preserving human relationships in a society based on exploitation and inequality—remain ever present. *See also* Chicago School of Sociology (CSS); Haynes, George Edmund; Johnson, Charles Spurgeon; Migrants, Economic Characteristics of; Migrants, Social Characteristics of; Wright, Richard Nathaniel.

Further Reading

Frazier, E. Franklin. *The Negro Family in the United States*. Notre Dame: University of Notre Dame Press, 2001. Originally published in 1939.

———. *The Negro in the United States*. New York: Macmillan, 1949.

———. *Race and Culture Contacts in the Modern World*. New York: Alfred A. Knopf, 1957.

Platt, Anthony M. *E. Franklin Frazier Reconsidered*. New Brunswick, NJ: Rutgers University Press, 1991.

Tony Platt

FSA *See* Farm Security Administration (FSA)

Funeral Directors *See* Undertakers

G

Garvey, Marcus Mosiah, Jr. (1887–1940)

Marcus Mosiah Garvey, a native of St. Ann's Bay on the island of Jamaica, came to the United States in 1916 originally to confer with **Booker T. Washington** and his associates. But having arrived after Washington's death, Garvey proceeded to build a **Universal Negro Improvement Association** (UNIA) chapter in Harlem, an organization he had first launched in Jamaica in 1914 as the Universal Negro Improvement and Conservation Association and African Communities League. It was in Harlem that Garvey refined the general purpose, program, and tactics of the organization, and between 1916 and 1919 he considerably enhanced his appeal through the publication of the *Negro World*, the official organ of the UNIA, and through nationwide tours where he espoused such phrases as the "**New Negro**," "the Renaissance of the Negro Race," and "Africa for the Africans."

As the organization gained momentum, Garvey proposed a variety of programs and plans, including the Black Star Line, a project for a fleet of steamships for commercial and travel purposes; a paramilitary marching society; fleets of moving vans; Black Cross Nurses; and the Negro Factories Corporation, an economic cooperative that would include grocery stores, restaurants, laundries, garment factories, and a publishing house, among other things. But in order to accomplish this, Garvey needed to establish and organize mass-based power that would cement international race unity and African American solidarity. To secure this end, Garvey convened a world convention to meet in **New York City** in August 1920, the largest assembly of persons of African descent ever to meet. Delegates from throughout the United States and around the world were in attendance representing a variety of religious and political persuasions. The convention drafted grievances and a Declaration of Rights for the Negro People of the World, and special committees reported on various

Marcus Garvey. Courtesy of the Library of Congress.

subjects of specific concern to people of African descent. The convention also provided a social milieu for people of African descent from around the world to learn and discuss common problems.

Garvey, through the UNIA, espoused a brand of **black nationalism** and pan-Africanism that combined elements of social and political separatism with demands for civil rights and equal opportunity. However, Garvey's appeal was a result not just of what he was saying but when he was saying it. What later became known as Garveyism was nourished, strengthened, and sustained by the atmosphere of promise and confidence among African Americans that flourished during and after World War I. The migration of African Americans to urban centers throughout the United States and particularly the Midwest and Northeast raised the political consciousness of African Americans. The new awareness inflamed a new militancy that broadened the migrants' perspective and helped develop race consciousness. Into this milieu stepped Garvey, who, along with other social and political groups, addressed the new problems of urban life. The African American masses were now ripe for a movement of the kind Garvey was advocating. The tremendous interest of the African American masses in Garvey's program was magnetic and stimulated the first mass movement among African Americans. So compelling and inspiring was Garvey that many of his followers saw Garvey and the UNIA as a religion and Garvey as the "Black Moses." Unsurpassed by any organization of its time, the UNIA was an expression of black militancy that transformed by uplifting the image of the African and instilling pride in blackness. Its appeal was a testimony of the social ills and frustration that characterized many African Americans.

However, by 1922 financial and legal problems, dissension and factions within the UNIA, and emboldened organized opposition on the outside finally brought about the decline of the movement. The UNIA began its decline in 1922 after Garvey met with a representative of the **Ku Klux Klan** in **Atlanta**. As a consequence, several prominent members broke with the organization, and some joined the anti-Garvey movement. **A. Philip Randolph** and his associates with the *Messenger*, **W.E.B. DuBois** and the **National Association for the Advancement of Colored People**, and **Cyril Briggs** and the **African Blood Brotherhood** were some of the strongest critics of Garvey. Within the UNIA discontent was also brewing over money, fiscal corruption, declining membership, and the direction of leadership. Matters came to a head when Garvey, along with three officers of the Black Star Line, was charged with mail fraud. Garvey was convicted of mail fraud in 1923 in relationship to his steamship line and imprisoned in 1925 to serve a five-year term. He was pardoned by President Calvin Coolidge in 1927 and then deported to Jamaica as an undesirable alien. Although Garvey continued his advocacy on behalf of people of African descent, he never again accomplished the organizational stature of the UNIA. In 1935 Garvey moved to London, where he lived and worked until his death in 1940. Originally interred in London, Garvey's remains were brought to Jamaica in 1964 and ceremoniously reinterred at National Heroes Park.

Garvey's influence on African American social and political history is indisputable. As noted by historian John Hope Franklin, "Although few of the black writers [during the **Harlem Renaissance**] would concede it, there could be no denying that Marcus Garvey was one of the great energizers of the New Negro Movement. By raising the consciousness of millions of black Americans . . . and by creating so much excitement in Harlem . . . Garvey stimulated a variety of forms of expression" (Franklin and Moss, 363). Theodore G. Vincent also revealed that "Garveyites subsequently conceived and popularized a host of new approaches to the struggle for black freedom. . . . As ideologues, they formulated almost every version of **black power** to gain currency in the United States in the twentieth century" (Vincent, 13). Garvey and the UNIA provided an alternative type of struggle among African Americans during the post–World War I era. Garvey was able to capture the imagination and secure the following of the African American masses at a time when they were most suspicious of organizations composed of middle-class African Americans and liberal whites who failed to adequately address the stress and strain of living in hostile urban communities. *See also* Caribbean Migration; Harrison, Hubert Henry; Political Activism (1915–1945); Primary Document 49.

Further Reading

Franklin, John Hope, and Alfred A. Moss. *From Slavery to Freedom: A History of African Americans*. 7th ed. New York: McGraw-Hill, 1994.

Hill, Robert A., ed. *Life and Lessons: A Centennial Companion to the Marcus Garvey and Universal Negro Improvement Association Papers*. Berkeley: University of California Press, 1987.

The Marcus Garvey and Universal Negro Improvement Association Papers Project. A Research Project of the James S. Coleman African Studies Center, UCLA. www.international.ucla.edu/africa/mgpp/.

Martin, Tony. *Race First: The Ideological and Organizational Struggles of Marcus Garvey and the Universal Negro Improvement Association*. Westport, CT: Greenwood Press, 1976.

PBS Online. "Marcus Garvey: Look for Me in the Whirlwind." The American Experience. www.pbs.org/wgbh/amex/garvey/index.html.

Stein, Judith. *The World of Marcus Garvey: Race and Class in Modern Society*. Baton Rouge: Louisiana State University Press, 1986.

Vincent, Theodore G. *Black Power and the Garvey Movement*. San Francisco: Ramparts Press, 1971.

Ronald A. Kuykendall

Gary, Indiana

The southern black migrants who set foot in small communities like Gary, Indiana, during the twentieth century shaped and transformed urban America as much as those who worked, built institutions, and fought for their rights in **New York City**, **Chicago**, or **Philadelphia**. The city of Gary was founded in 1906 by the U.S. Steel Corporation as part of the plan to erect a modern steelmaking complex. In 1930 more than 100,000 individuals—a large portion of whom were immigrants from southern and eastern Europe—had chosen Gary as their home. Representing nearly one in five Garyites at this time, African Americans completed a family migration that most often began in **Memphis**, **Birmingham**, or **Nashville**. When **Richard Gordon Hatcher** was elected mayor in 1967, decades of black in-migration and **white flight** had produced a demographic transition in this midwestern locale of 175,000 residents that put African Americans in the majority.

The black population of Gary increased sharply when World War I and the federal immigration restrictions passed in the 1920s disrupted the flow of cheap labor from Europe, or when the world economy gave American industries the opportunity to run at full capacity. The material advantages that the steel mills of Gary offered to African Americans born in the **Jim Crow** South, however, were inadequate to offset the ambivalent stand of black leaders during the 1919 strike, the paternalist position of U.S. Steel, the reduction of shifts during the Great Depression, the privileges of whiteness cherished inside local unions, the struggle of American steel to compete in the Cold War global economy, and the environmental and health problems produced by years of proximity to a polluting and hazardous industry.

With the foundation of the United Steelworkers of America (1937), African Americans who had showcased their experience and skills directly to employers were now dealing with them through powerful, yet divided, unions. This chapter in the history of Gary symbolized the main challenge that confronted African Americans in the migration process: local black leaders needed to overcome ideological differences among themselves, as well as succeed in closing ranks with whites, if they hoped to win the fight against racism. The black **women** of Gary were at the center of this network of activists that connected working-class families and young professionals. The battles they waged, for instance, revealed how segregation kept African Americans in the neglected and poorest sections of the Central District, and their children in overcrowded and inferior schools. The Combined Citizens Committee on Open Occupancy and the Human Relations Commission were two of the postwar collective efforts to eradicate injustice and discrimination in Gary.

To protest the tokenism to which they were subjected inside political parties, African Americans criticized Republicans ready to make deals with the **Ku Klux Klan** during the 1920s, became enthusiastic Democrats in the following decades, founded organizations such as Muigwithania ("We are together" in Swahili), and elected as mayor one of the local leaders of the **civil rights movement**. Environmental politics complicated matters even more for migrants and dashed the hopes of African Americans who believed in the promises of **black power**. As pressure groups insisted that U.S. Steel and other industries use clean technologies, African Americans still looking for signs of the Promised Land were told that environmental regulations meant loss of jobs for the community, a situation that compelled leaders to tone down their criticism of U.S. Steel even if it meant bargaining with the lives of thousands. *See also* Deindustrialization; Midwestern States, Black Migration to; Political Realignment; Steelworkers.

Further Reading

Hurley, Andrew. *Class, Race, and Industrial Pollution in Gary, Indiana, 1945–1980.* Chapel Hill: University of North Carolina Press, 1995.

Mohl, Raymond A., and Neil Betten. *Steel City: Gary, Indiana, 1906–1950.* New York: Holmes and Meier, 1986.

Needleman, Ruth. *Black Freedom Fighters in Steel: The Struggle for Democratic Unionism.* Ithaca, NY: ILR Press, 2003.

Nelson Oullet

Ghettos

A ghetto is a residential area in which a racial or ethnic group is forced to live; the vast majority of that group resides in the ghetto and dominates its population. The term's origins are European, but in the United States scholars use it to refer to geographic areas where most African Americans and other racial minorities were forced, by legal and illegal means, to live. The first ghettos appeared in large northern cities before 1930; a second ghetto type emerged after World War II in cities across the United States. Ghetto emergence and the Great Migration are linked, but ghettos appeared because of racist actions by whites individually and collectively. Although different black social classes separated spatially within the ghetto, few African Americans could escape residence there, often in the oldest, inner-city areas. Scholars agree on the forces that created ghettos; they disagree over the ghetto's impact.

Historical Origins and Context

The term *ghetto* originated from the name of a Jewish neighborhood in Venice, Italy. Initially Jews voluntarily selected it as a residence area; by the fifteenth century European nations and the Roman Catholic Church enacted laws compelling Jews to live within walled compounds (ghettos) within cities and restricted their behavior. In the United States scholars initially applied the term to the early 1900s voluntary, wall-less enclaves of southern and eastern European immigrants. Despite discriminatory restrictions, many immigrants were soon able to leave these areas.

Late nineteenth-century black residents of northern cities experienced limited residential restrictions and lived in dispersed clusters. Although they were small in numbers, they supported residential and public accommodation integration; civil rights laws, although often not enforced, provided legal protections. Some urban African Americans obtained professions or significant economic positions serving white clients. Black northerners established an array of religious, social, cultural, and civic organizations. These patterns began to change around 1900 when black migration increased, as did white hostility. Southern migrants, imbued with **Booker T. Washington**'s ideology of self-help, had less concern for integration.

Causes of the First Ghettos

Private-sector local forces largely produced the first ghettos. As black migration to **New York City** and **Chicago** increased from the 1890s on, so did white violence and discrimination. Some scholars have used the term "tipping point" to explain how the growing racism in northern cities at the turn of the century produced the first ghettos. Whites accepted small black populations, but as the numbers of African Americans increased, whites grew more hostile, which led to increased discrimination and violence, including white race riots in New York in 1900 and in many cities in the **Red Summer of 1919**.

White northerners grew tired of the Civil War and civil rights struggles. They increasingly adopted racist views of the world's darker-skinned peoples to justify or oppose U.S. imperialism in the 1898 Spanish-American War; they also sought accommodation with white southerners on racial issues generally. Previously integrated churches encouraged black members to form their own, while the **Young Men's Christian Association** discouraged black members from using white facilities and built black-only branches. Between 1910 and 1917 many southern and border cities enacted segregation ordinances to prohibit African Americans from living in white neighborhoods; a few northern cities, such as **Indianapolis**, followed suit. Despite efforts by black and white progressives in the **National Association for the Advancement of Colored People**, who successfully challenged this legal segregation in *Buchanan v. Warley* (1917), most white urbanites appeared ambivalent at best on racial issues. Private and public efforts combined, as in black **physician** Ossian Sweet's 1925 murder trial for defending his home against a violent white **Detroit** mob.

Private, local nongovernmental groups produced the segregation from which the first northern ghettos emerged. Real estate and financial institutions, along with property owners, managers, and **neighborhood property owners' associations**, actively pursued policies, legal and illegal, that restricted African Americans to ghetto **housing**. White realtors refused to show or rent properties to blacks outside the ghetto; white financial organizations refused loans for black home building or purchase. White neighborhood improvement or protective associations, real estate interests, and home owners placed racially **restrictive covenants** on neighborhood properties, prohibiting blacks and others from buying or renting in those areas. By 1940 covenants covered over five square miles of **St. Louis**; suburbs also used these devices. Protective associations sought to buy out black residents who moved into white areas and used intimidation and violence to keep blacks out. State and local governments often failed to enforce antidiscrimination laws, although police ignored physical attacks against blacks and encouraged or led these attacks in some cases.

First Ghettos: Formation and Problems

U.S. ghettos lacked walls, but whites' legal and illegal actions made the boundaries nearly as strong despite black efforts to break out. Ghettos appeared first in New York, Chicago, and **Philadelphia** by 1915; **Cleveland**'s emerged between 1915 and 1930. As migration increased, especially after 1916, migrants and native black residents found that housing was available only in ghetto areas. By 1920 Chicago's South Side ghetto stretched along State Street from Thirty-first to Fifty-fifth streets; African Americans made up more than 75 percent of these ten census tracts. By 1930 over 90 percent of black Clevelanders lived between Euclid and Woodland avenues and between downtown and East 105th Street. Save for some all-black suburban enclaves, few blacks lived in suburbia.

Population growth and constricted living areas produced skyrocketing housing costs; in 1917 black workers in Cleveland paid almost twice the rent that whites did, despite housing that was among the city's oldest and least desirable. During World War I black men gained access to industrial occupations but experienced massive layoffs afterward; most black **women** remained in poorly paid domestic work. Nonetheless, institutional development within the ghetto exploded; newspapers, businesses, and professionals increased to serve the expanded population, as did the numbers of organizations from churches to protest groups. Alabama-born **Oscar DePriest**'s 1928 election to Congress reflected the growing black political organization and power. In Harlem and elsewhere, a cultural renaissance by artists, writers, and musicians demonstrated a vitality that contrasted with the worsening housing and living conditions caused by high rents, low wages, and unstable employment, **crime**, and overcrowding. Ghetto residents revealed other positive adaptations to difficult conditions by taking in borders and holding parties to raise the rent money; they also joined **fraternal orders** that promised sickness and death benefits, as did **Marcus Garvey**'s **Universal Negro Improvement Association**.

Second Ghettos

Migration, reignited by World War II, dramatically expanded existing ghettos in population and spatial size. New ghettos emerged in other northern cities, the West, and the South. Second ghettos resulted from a combination of the local forces that produced the first ones and new federal government programs intended to aid urban residents. While the black populations exploded, the housing supply and ghetto boundaries increased slowly, again driving up rents and overcrowding, while white violence and restrictive covenants limited spatial growth.

Federal **urban renewal** and redevelopment programs that were intended to improve inner-city areas instead became instruments of "black removal" by tearing down both good and bad housing; public agencies then turned the land over to private institutions such as universities and **hospitals**. **Public housing** offered homes for the displaced but seldom matched the numbers of units lost; high-rise public housing proved inappropriate for families with children. Local public housing authorities segregated facilities and restricted black buildings to the ghetto. Federal Housing Authority and Veterans Administration home loan programs aided white suburbanites but benefited few African Americans. Federally funded highways cut off the ghetto from other parts of the city and increased its segregation and isolation. Federal programs raised expectations but not the realities of a better life; the decline in good-paying industrial jobs added to the ghetto dwellers' frustration, which led to major riots in **Los Angeles** (1965), Cleveland (1966), Detroit (1967), and elsewhere (see **Urban Crisis of the 1960s**).

Ghetto Impact

Scholars have long debated the ghetto's impact and meaning for its residents and the nation. Initially they emphasized the environmental factors that affected ghetto dwellers, describing ghettos as disorganized slums that produced a wide range of social pathologies, including crime, substance abuse, family breakdown, illegitimacy, and dependency. More recently scholars have noted the extent of social organization, support networks, and successful survival strategies. Christian and Muslim religious groups and other organizations, including civil rights groups, spoke to needs of ghetto residents, as did the **black press**. In both first and second ghettos the increased population and concentration aided the formation of black businesses, professionals, organizations, and black political power, such as Clevelander **Carl Stokes**'s 1967 election as the first **black mayor** of a major U.S. city. By 1970 yet another ghetto form took shape as middle- and upper-class African Americans left and ghetto disinvestment increased. *See also* Black Consumer Market; *Black Metropolis* (Drake and Cayton); Blockbusting; Hypersegregation; Migrants, Settlement Patterns of; Primary Documents 2, 8, 9, 10, 26, 27, 28, 31, 42, 67, 71.

Further Reading

Borchert, James. *Alley Life in Washington: Family, Community, Religion, and Folklife in the City, 1850–1970*. Urbana: University of Illinois Press, 1980.

Hirsch, Arnold. *Making the Second Ghetto: Race and Housing in Chicago, 1940–1960*. New York: Cambridge University Press, 1983.

Katzman, David. *Before the Ghetto: Black Detroit in the Nineteenth Century*. Urbana: University of Illinois Press, 1973.

Kusmer, Kenneth L. *A Ghetto Takes Shape: Black Cleveland, 1870–1930*. Urbana: University of Illinois Press, 1976.

Osofsky, Gilbert. *Harlem: The Making of a Ghetto; Negro New York, 1890–1930*. New York: Harper and Row, 1966.

Philpott, Thomas Lee. *The Slum and the Ghetto: Neighborhood Deterioration and Middle-Class Reform, 1890–1930*. New York: Oxford University Press, 1978.

Racial Residential Segregation Measurement Project, University of Michigan. [August 2004]. http://enceladus.isr.umich.edu/race/racestart.asp.

Spear, Allan H. *Black Chicago: The Making of a Negro Ghetto, 1890–1920*. Chicago: University of Chicago Press, 1967.

Vergara, Camilo José. *The New American Ghetto*. New Brunswick, NJ: Rutgers University Press, 1995.

James Borchert

GI Bill *See* Serviceman's Readjustment Act (GI Bill)

Gibson, Joshua (1911–1947)

A gifted catcher and overpowering slugger, Josh Gibson entertained legions of black baseball fans with his larger-than-life heroics on the ballfield in the 1930s and 1940s. His towering home runs and defensive skills helped his teams win several Negro League championships. Despite Gibson's unquestionable abilities, he could only compete in the segregated, financially strapped, and often mismanaged **Negro Leagues**. Gibson's career thus embodied both the promises and limitations of life in the North for black migrants.

Gibson was born in Buena Vista, Georgia, in 1911. After World War I his father left the South to work in the mills of Carnegie-Illinois Steel in **Pittsburgh**. Following a pattern similar to that of other black migrants, Gibson's father lived and worked in the North for three years before sending for his wife and three children. Josh attended school briefly in Pittsburgh before working in the steel mills himself. As a teenager, Gibson began playing baseball on the sandlots of Pittsburgh's Northside. At six feet tall and 190 pounds, Gibson was an imposing presence on the field. He quickly caught the attention of **Cum Posey**, the owner of the Homestead Grays, who recruited Gibson to catch for his team, which consistently dominated the Negro

Josh Gibson slides across home plate in the 1944 Negro League East-West All-Star baseball game at Chicago's Comiskey Park. © Bettmann/Corbis.

National League. In his rookie year Gibson established himself as the premier slugger of the Negro Leagues, batting .461 and hitting seventy-five home runs against pro and semipro opponents. In 1932 Gibson signed with the Grays' crosstown rivals, the Pittsburgh Crawfords, who were owned and operated by **Gus Greenlee**, the city's notorious "numbers king."

Gibson became something of a legend in black Pittsburgh. Because records and statistics of Negro League baseball are incomplete, his exploits are shrouded in myth. Fantastic stories abound of Gibson's slugging feats, such as hitting a ball out of Yankee Stadium, knocking a one-handed home run in **Indianapolis**, and smashing a 700-foot blast out of Wrigley Field in **Chicago**. Although Gibson lacked the showmanship of **Satchel Paige**, his frequent tape-measure home runs drew large crowds that helped sustain the Negro Leagues through the uncertainties of the Great Depression. In 1936 Gibson rejoined Posey's Grays, and over the next nine years he helped lead the club to nine successive Negro League titles.

Although the Negro National League afforded a black migrant such as Gibson the opportunity for athletic glory that he would not have had in the South, the league was plagued with problems that denied him the career he could have had. Salaries, playing facilities, umpiring, and scheduling were substandard and inconsistent. Like other Negro League players, Gibson often played winter league ball for better pay in Latin America, where he was often more appreciated and drew a bigger following than in the United States. The hardships of playing segregated ball took their toll on his career, which went into decline by his early thirties. High blood pressure, the loss of his wife to early death, and subsequent heavy drinking and rumors of drug use all combined to diminish his skills. When major league baseball began to integrate in the mid-1940s and started recruiting stars of the Negro Leagues, teams passed him over. Bitterness at this rejection may have brought on the stroke that took his life in January 1947 at the age of thirty-five. In 1972, however, he was inducted into the Baseball Hall of Fame. *See also* Paige, Leroy Robert "Satchel"; Sport.

Further Reading

Brashler, William. *Josh Gibson: A Life in the Negro Leagues*. New York: Harper and Row, 1978.

Ribowsky, Mark. *The Power and the Darkness: The Life of Josh Gibson in the Shadows of the Game*. New York: Simon and Schuster, 1996.

Ruck, Rob. *Sandlot Seasons: Sport in Black Pittsburgh*. Urbana: University of Illinois Press, 1987.

Snyder, Brad. *Beyond the Shadow of the Senators: The Untold Story of the Homestead Grays and the Integration of Baseball*. New York: McGraw-Hill, 2003.

Steven A. Reich

Gillespie, John Birks "Dizzy" (1917–1993)

Born in Cheraw, South Carolina, John Birks "Dizzy" Gillespie was, like three of the four most prominent beboppers, a migrant to the Harlem music scene. During the very late 1930s and more specifically in the years 1941 through 1945, Gillespie, along with **Charlie Parker**, Kenny Clarke, **Thelonious**

Monk, and others, experimented with time, harmonics, and improvisation to forge the musical idiom of **bebop**.

Gillespie's musical career was immediately shaped by migration. His early musical training was acquired in neighboring North Carolina at the Laurinburg Institute. By 1935, with his training in theory and harmony completed, he moved to **Philadelphia**. Later, while freelancing around **New York City**, he took the place of his idol, Roy Eldridge, in the Teddy Hill band. The twenty-year-old Gillespie, who was beginning to construct his zany personality, toured England and France with the band. His playing became noticed by older established musicians, who did not always respond positively to his experimentations. This first exposure to the big-band musician's life stamped a pattern that Gillespie followed until the end of his career. He became one of the most traveled musicians of his generation and certainly the most traveled of his fellow beboppers.

After the European tour he returned to freelancing in New York. In the fall of 1939 he began touring as one of the featured players in **Cab Calloway**'s popular orchestra. Leaving Calloway after a two-year stint, Gillespie played and arranged in big bands of Les Hite, Lucky Millinder, Benny Carter, and Earl Hines. He played in small combos on Fifty-second Street and jammed in Harlem clubs. In June 1944 he took a chair in the Billy Eckstine band, one of the youngest and most progressive bands at the time. His recordings with Charlie Parker in 1945 established Gillespie and Parker as the definitive bebop instrumentalists. After Eckstine, he formed his first big band. This venture was short lived, and he organized and led small combos, including a group with Charlie Parker that introduced bebop to West Coast audiences. The trip was a disaster; Parker was admitted to Camarillo State Hospital, and Gillespie returned to New York and reorganized his big band.

This band toured Scandinavia, and he later returned to Europe fronting small combos in 1952 and 1953. Gillespie founded his own record company, Dee Gee, in 1951. With his name and reputation established, even his detractors admitted his talent as a composer, arranger, and superb musician. Among his compositions, "Salt Peanuts," "A Night in Tunisia," and "Manteca" are staples in the **jazz** repertory. He was not only the ambassador of bebop but also a world-renowned musician, taking his big band on State Department tours to Pakistan, Lebanon, Syria, Turkey, and Greece. Later he did similar tours of Latin America under State Department auspices. Migration, movement, and touring permeated Dizzy Gillespie's career, and he is principally responsible for making bebop a world musical form. *See also* Dance Halls and Nightclubs; Recording Industry; Swing.

Further Reading

DeVeaux, Scott. *The Birth of Bebop: A Social and Musical History.* Berkeley: University of California Press, 1997.

Gillespie, Dizzy. *To Be, or Not . . . to Bop: Memoirs.* Garden City, NY: Doubleday, 1979.

Shipton, Alyn. *Groovin' High: The Life of Dizzy Gillespie.* New York: Oxford University Press, 1999.

Harry A. Reed

Great Migration, Black Opposition to

The harsh predicament in which black southerners found themselves after the overthrow of Reconstruction meant that emigrationist sentiment was never far from the surface. With plans initiated as early as the mid-1860s, some 20,000 black southerners made their way to Kansas as early as 1879. A separate scheme brought a relatively small number of Afro–South Carolinians to Liberia in 1877 under the leadership of well-known black politicians, but the results reflected inadequate organization rather than an absence of enthusiasm. "Had there been a well-organized, amply financed emigration project," one close observer suggested, "the South would undoubtedly have lost much of its black population to Africa during this period" (Taylor, 53). These early migrations, like a number of similar movements in the late nineteenth century, elicited a varied response among black community leaders: while some opposed emigration, other prominent figures were to be found at the head of such schemes. Invariably they found their strongest support among the black working classes. During a turbulent period in which the jubilation and optimism of the immediate postemancipation period were being rapidly replaced by pessimism about the prospects for assimilation, African Americans were willing to embrace a number of strategies aimed at securing safety, autonomy, and the prospect of landownership.

By the turn of the century, however, one particular approach had emerged to dominate black politics: **Booker T. Washington**'s accommodationist strategy. In a context of widespread black disfranchisement and increasing racial brutality, Washington urged African Americans to make their peace with the South's racial status quo, to forsake politics, and to concentrate on moral and economic **uplift**. Announced before a mostly white audience in 1895 at the Cotton States and International Exposition in **Atlanta**, Washington's strategy was based, in part, on black southerners proving themselves indispensable as the unskilled labor force of the region. "To those of my race who depend on bettering their condition in a foreign land," he said, "Cast down your bucket where you are" (Washington, 219).

The first two decades of the twentieth century proved that the black masses were unconvinced of the propriety of staying put, however, or of submitting to the wages and conditions on offer in the South. Washington's formula for racial uplift reflected the laissez-faire outlook then dominant throughout American society, and it reflected in particular the conservative outlook of the South's emerging black middle class. Eschewing politics, committed to an entrepreneurial strategy for racial advancement, and deeply imbued with middle-class standards of morality, the black elite enjoyed an ambiguous relationship with **Jim Crow**: subject, like all African Americans, to discrimination and the constant threat of racial violence, they nevertheless benefited from the sheltered markets created by the color line and were frequently dependent on the goodwill and financial support of wealthy whites for their business success. Though Washington's leadership and the strategy of racial accommodation that he represented were energetically promoted by elements in the South's white ruling class and by northern capitalists and philanthropists, the degree to which he represented black opinion was never clear.

The resurgence of emigration brought on by crop failures and the onset of World War I demonstrated just how tenuous Washington's hold over the black masses was and incited fierce intraracial conflict. For the most part, southern black business and religious leaders used their influence to restrain or bring a complete halt to emigration out of the South. "It is hoped," a typical editorial in the *Reporter*, a black **Birmingham** newspaper, warned in December 1916, "that as the time goes on our people will settle down and become satisfied with conditions" (*Reporter*, December 2, 1916). Its editor, Oscar Adams, blamed emigration on the fact that "not only the American Negroes, but the American people, have formed a habit of living beyond their means" (*Reporter*, January 22, 1916). Adams and other black editors throughout the South attempted to counter the new restiveness among the black working classes with admonishments about self-responsibility and eulogies of the friendly race relations and favorable conditions that, they insisted, were on offer in the South.

The close relations between black elites and leading employers of black labor were crucial in building a coordinated effort to restrain exodus out of the South. When, concerned about the desertion of its labor force, the **Jacksonville, Florida**, Chamber of Commerce invited black "professionals and businessmen" to an interracial "joint conference" in July 1916, "[n]ot a word was spoken at the conference about improving the living conditions" of the city's African American workforce (Ortiz, 136). In Louisiana employers reported conditions "somewhat disturbed on account of a movement...to entice colored laborers to emigrate north," and in response they employed a small coterie of black lay and religious leaders to tour the Gulf States "convinc[ing] Negroes that they are better off under existing conditions in the South than they would be if they should move." Texas lumber operators sponsored at least three black-edited newspapers valued for their efforts to "combat the evil influence of the radical Negro papers and magazines published in the north" and "counteract the northern migration movement" (Kirby Lumber Company Records). The *Negro Advocate*, published by a black **minister** in Fordyce, Arkansas, to "keep the colored laborers of the South... satisfied with their conditions" and "advise against the exodus of neighbors," was distributed throughout industrial operations in the region and heavily supported by employer contributions (Fickle, 67).

One of the most distinctive features of the wartime exodus was its class character, often expressed in the press in terms of its "leaderlessness." "The colored race, known as the race which is led," a Georgia preacher noted, "has broken away from its leaders" ("Negro Migration," 428). The migrants "rarely consult the white people, and never those who may exercise some control over their actions," another sympathetic observer reported. "They will not allow their own leaders to advise them against going north. A Rev. Mr. Carter, of Tampa, Florida, who was brave enough to attempt such advice from the pulpit, was stabbed next day for so doing. They are likely to suspect that such men are in the employ of white people" (Williams, 306). Similar suspicions permeated intraracial tensions in Birmingham, where race leaders' authority deteriorated sharply. Emigrants were departing "against the advice of many of the best men of our race who are able to give them wise and wholesome instruction," the *Reporter* fretted. They had "broken off from consulting the men of the colored race, and . . . learned to scorn the advice of men of the white race" (*Reporter*, September 30, 1916).

As surveillance and repression against the black community gathered force in the wartime South, the close ties between black elites and the white establishment became an object of ridicule for the black masses, deepening the gulf in black politics. Vagrancy ordinances enforced throughout much of the urban South inevitably produced clashes between the black poor, newly confident of the possibility of confronting white authority, and traditional race leadership, which advised caution and compliance with the law. In Jacksonville an already compromised local race leadership was completely overwhelmed by rioting that accompanied the release of a white suspect in the rape of a young black girl, making itself the object of popular scorn in the black community. In Birmingham it was the more general failure of accommodation to deliver results that elicited derision: "The Negro papers which you subsidize and the Negro leaders whom you pay, cannot hold [us]," one emigrant warned the city's white rulers before heading north. "Two [or] three years ago you promised us schools; you have not given them to us. The only thing you have offered us is an old Jail for our children" (National Urban League Records).

The wartime migration substantially eroded the authority of the accommodationist race leadership that had established itself in the difficult years at the end of the nineteenth century, and it opened up space for black working-class self-assertion. That trend was further enhanced by the dispersal of African Americans throughout the United States, where the possibilities of a new, more confident outlook were greater. The Great Depression would induce another substantial movement out of the South, as would World War II, but after 1920 the ability or willingness of black elites to stand in the way of movement out of the South was negligible. *See also* Emigrationism; Exodusters; Great Migration, White Opposition to; Intraracial Class Conflict; Moton, Robert Russa; Nadir of Race Relations; Primary Documents 36, 65.

Further Reading

Fickle, James E. "Management Looks at the Labor Problem: The Southern Pine Industry during World War I and the Postwar Era." *Journal of Southern History* 40, no. 1 (1974): 61–76.

Gaines, Kevin K. *Uplifting the Race: Black Leadership, Politics, and Culture in the Twentieth Century*. Chapel Hill: University of North Carolina Press, 1996.

Harlan, Louis R. *Booker T. Washington: The Wizard of Tuskegee, 1901–1915*. New York: Oxford University Press, 1983.

Jordan, William G. *Black Newspapers and America's War for Democracy, 1914–1920*. Chapel Hill: University of North Carolina Press, 2001.

Kelly, Brian. "Sentinels for New South Industry: Booker T. Washington, Industrial Accommodation, and Black Workers in the Jim Crow South." *Labor History* 44, no. 3 (August 2003): 337–58.

Kirby Lumber Company Records. Forest History Collection, Stephen F. Austin State University, Nacogdoches, Texas.

Litwack, Leon. *Trouble in Mind: Black Southerners in the Age of Jim Crow*. New York: Alfred A. Knopf, 1998.

National Urban League Records. Manuscript Division, Library of Congress, Washington, DC.

"Negro Migration as the South Sees It." *The Survey* 38 (August 11, 1917): 428.

Ortiz, Paul. *Emancipation Betrayed: The Hidden History of Black Organizing and White Violence in Florida from Reconstruction to the Bloody Election of 1920.* Berkeley: University of California Press, 2005.

Scheiber, Jane L., and Harry N. Scheiber. "The Wilson Administration and the Wartime Mobilization of Black Americans." *Labor History* 10, no. 3 (1969): 433–58.

Taylor, Arnold H. *Travail and Triumph: Black Life and Culture in the South since the Civil War.* Westport, CT: Greenwood Press, 1976.

Washington, Booker T. *Up from Slavery.* With an Introduction by Louis R. Harlan. New York: Penguin Books, 1986.

Williams, W.T.B. "The Negro Exodus from the South." In *Black Workers: A Documentary History from Colonial Times to the Present*, edited by Philip Sheldon Foner and Ronald L. Lewis. Philadelphia: Temple University Press, 1989.

Brian Kelly

Great Migration, Causes of

Mobility has long been one form of expressing African Americans' deep-rooted desire for freedom and equality. At once it was a means for an individual to secure greater personal autonomy, as well as for African American communities to seek out less oppression and greater economic, social, political, or personal opportunity. Through migration African Americans hoped to create a world less circumscribed by the reality of racism in America. Through migration African Americans not only expressed a profound dissatisfaction with the conditions in their lives, but also a powerful belief in their own agency and a sense of hope for the future. In moving from one location to another, African Americans sought to find a Promised Land, or at least a better land.

The Nineteenth Century

During the era of slavery, for many African Americans, running away was one of the most powerful expressions of the desire for freedom. Historians have estimated that over 100,000 blacks were able to successfully abscond to a freer North. For others, their dreams of freedom through mobility were tempered by the vigilance of their slave masters as much as by their ties to family. While it is difficult to know how many African Americans actually ran away or even attempted to do so, the constant flurry of runaway notices in southern newspapers and the Fugitive Slave Act of 1850 suggest the frequency with which African Americans attempted to escape slavery, no matter their success. Whether African Americans fled with the hope of leaving the South for good or of only securing a few days of respite, mobility and migration remained powerful symbols of their desires for freedom. Indeed, the large number of African Americans who abandoned their former lives on plantations and households throughout the South during the Civil War to join Union lines, if not the army itself, demonstrates the willingness of southern blacks to act upon any opportunity to move. Yet in 1861, 91 percent of all African Americans lived in the South, representing nearly 36 percent of the southern population.

Even before the ratification of the Thirteenth Amendment abolishing slavery in 1865, mobility remained central to African Americans' larger strategies of empowerment and autonomy in the postwar era. The impetus that led African Americans to build churches, to obtain an education, or to determine how much and when to work were all part of the same desire for freedom that led African Americans to view mobility as key to defining the meaning of freedom in the Reconstruction era. Throughout the late 1860s African Americans moved to southern cities or neighboring plantations as a way to test their newfound freedom. If one of the hallmarks of slavery was an inability to come and go as one chose or control one's own body, then one of the greatest symbols of freedom for African Americans was to go anywhere one pleased. Moreover, for many African Americans in the age of emancipation, mobility provided a means to seek out and reconnect families torn apart during slavery.

Many African Americans' experiences during slavery, working, living, and bleeding into the land, forged a strong sense of connection to the South. As many African Americans set about the work of forging new communities by establishing independent schools and churches, taking control over their labor, and engaging in formal politics, others chose to leave the South. Although the Civil War proved that the nation was antislavery, over time the nation's stance against slavery did not translate into a willingness to secure genuine freedom for African Americans. With each passing year the passion to reform the social institutions of the South waned. An era that was once viewed as an opportunity to literally reconstruct the South gave way to an era historian Rayford Logan termed the "**nadir of race relations**" in the United States, an era defined by the rise of **Jim Crow** segregation, disfranchisement, the emergence of sharecropping, and **lynching**.

In the face of the rising tide of racism in the South and the nation, some, such as the African American **minister Henry McNeal Turner**, advocated emigration to Africa (see **Emigrationism**). Although Turner believed that Africa would offer the possibility of better conditions and the opportunity to forge a "respectable civil and Christian negro nation," during the nineteenth century as a whole, only 12,000 to 20,000 African Americans ever migrated to Liberia. While Africa may have been a more remote option for many African Americans, others found the chance to move to Kansas more of a potentiality. Before the 1870s nearly 10,000 African Americans in Kentucky, Missouri, and Tennessee moved to Kansas in search of freedom and opportunity. As the South capitulated to racism, another 5,000 blacks from the Deep South joined these **Exodusters** despite the resistance of many southern whites and the apathy of many northern whites. Yet the opportunity for escape was limited at best, and the majority of the black population in the United States remained in the South.

1910–1940

Still, for many African Americans, the North remained a beacon of hope throughout the Jim Crow era. The Land of Hope, the Promised Land, and Jim Canaan were but a few of the names that African Americans termed the North during the early part of the twentieth century. At a time when sharecropping began to bind blacks as tightly to the land as slavery, disfranchisement was made possible by a series of Supreme Court decisions, and racialized violence proliferated in the form of the **Ku Klux Klan** and increasingly brutal lynchings, migration to the North symbolized many African Americans' desire for freedom and equality. Yet nearly 90 percent of African Americans remained in the South until World War I stemmed the tide of European immigration to the North and eliminated the primary source of industrial labor. The pull of labor shortages in northern industry and the lack of white male labor combined with the push of the devastation of the cotton crops so many blacks labored on by flood and **boll weevils** to create conditions for migration. Facilitated by **labor agents** who combed the South looking for black workers and provided one-way **railroad** tickets to the North, the *Chicago Defender*, an African American newspaper that broadcast the relative freedom of the North throughout the South, and African Americans' own networks of kin and desire for freedom, more than 1.5 million blacks abandoned the South between 1915 and 1921. Ironically, given the racism, violence, and widespread belief in black inferiority, southern whites, fearful of a labor shortage of their own, attempted to halt the movement.

African Americans moved in hopes of securing a brighter future to northern cities such as **New York City**, **Chicago**, **Philadelphia**, **Cleveland**, and **Pittsburgh**, doubling the black population outside the South by 1940. The black population of Chicago grew 148 percent, from 44,103 to 109,458, while in New York the black population grew 66 percent, from 91,709 to 152,467. There southern blacks joined an influx of immigrants of African descent from Cuba and the West Indies at the dawn of a cultural revolution that would transform Harlem into the black capital of the world. Through kinship networks migrants often arrived with detailed information about **housing** and employment. Many African Americans arrived in the North with the knowledge that the average black worker in the South earned between fifty cents and two dollars per day in wages, compared with the two to five dollars many expected to earn in the North. As much as African Americans moved with the hope of securing better employment, they also moved North with the hope of escape from the shadow of slavery and racism. Some African American **women** used migration as an opportunity to escape sexual violence in the South. Blacks often found improved race relations in the North, better opportunities in education and employment, and the right to vote. However, they were also greeted with contempt by old settlers in previously established black communities, cramped housing, job prospects limited to menial labor, and a series of race riots that led them to question whether the North was in fact a Promised Land. Despite the segregation blacks faced, in the end many embraced the greater opportunity available in the North.

Though the North no longer seemed to be the Promised Land of the past, for many African Americans mobility remained central to the idea of attaining freedom. On the whole, nearly 90 percent of African Americans remained in the South, tied to agricultural labor, mired in poverty, and circumscribed, but not defined by, the reality of Jim Crow. The economic crisis of the Great Depression began earlier and lasted longer for blacks. As an attempt to deal with the economic plight of the agricultural South during the Great Depression, the New Deal's **Agricultural Adjustment Administration**'s effort to reduce crop production induced planters to reduce the number of tenants and sharecroppers they employed. During the 1930s African Americans were forced off farms and plantations throughout the South, losing their livelihood in the process. Unlike the previous Great Migration during the earlier part of the twentieth century, during which planters throughout the South lamented African American migration as a loss of labor, landowners fueled black migration themselves through widespread evictions.

1940–2000

In large measure the displacement of black workers and families had no outlet until World War II. Even as war production increased, creating widespread labor shortages in industry, African Americans remained largely excluded from the revitalization of the U.S. economy until labor leader **A. Philip Randolph** initiated the **March on Washington Movement** in 1941 to secure African American employment in defense industries. Though Franklin Delano Roosevelt issued Executive Order 8802, which established the **Fair Employment Practices Committee**, outlawing discrimination in defense industries, it was largely ignored until 1943. More than 5.5 million African Americans took advantage of the new opportunities for employment in defense industries and left the South for the North and West.

As a result, the African American population in the North substantially increased in cities such as **Detroit**, Chicago, New York, and Philadelphia, while in the West the black population grew exponentially. Within a decade the black population in Chicago grew 77 percent, from 277,731 to 492,635, and in Detroit the population doubled from 149,119 to 298,875. But the African American population increased 168 percent, from 63,774 to 170, 880 in **Los Angeles**; 341 percent in **Seattle**, 3,780 to 16,734; 462 percent in Oakland, 8,462 to 47,610; and 796 percent in **San Francisco**, 4,846 to 43,460, forging new black communities throughout the West. Even though African Americans were the last hired and first fired in defense industries, in the western cities such as Seattle African Americans earned wages 53 percent higher than African Americans throughout the nation. Nonetheless, the arrival of large numbers of African Americans also resulted in greater racial animosity on the part of whites. While larger numbers of African Americans migrated to the West and North, there were also approximately 4,300,000 intrastate migrants and 2,100,000 interstate migrants in the South. While some among those migrants eventually made their way to the North or West, others chose to relocate in southern defense centers such as Charleston, Norfolk, Mobile, or **Louisville**. That nearly half the black population remained in the South suggests that when blacks left the South, they were not fleeing the South per se, but were fleeing the racism, violence, and lack of opportunity white supremacy had created there. But by staying in the South African American migrants effectively claimed the South as their own. Yet North, West, or South, migration facilitated a shift from rural to urban. Nearly 73 percent of all African Americans lived in cities by 1960.

African American migration held profound consequences for the struggles for freedom. First, African American migration to the North radically altered the political landscape in America. In the past their political concerns had been largely ignored in the national political arena since they could not vote. Where African Americans could vote, both in the North and in the South, they were often tied to the Republican Party, not so much because it was the "Party of Lincoln," but because there was little alternative. In the South the Democratic Party was closely allied with white supremacy and was often the only party in town. Nationally, few Democrats were willing to risk political power by alienating white southern voters by advocating black equality. However, through migration black voters in the North and West became a constituency that could no longer be ignored. Second, in part because of their political pressure and the prominence of a northern **black press**, civil rights increasingly became a national issue. Moreover, many migrants in the North remained tied to the plight of their family and friends in the South. For instance, the murder of Emmett Till in Money, Mississippi, in 1955 became a national concern because of the black press, *Jet*, the *Amsterdam News*, the ***Pittsburgh Courier***, and the *Chicago Defender*, as well as the vocal response of African Americans in the North.

At a time when roughly half the black population left the South seeking greater opportunity and freedom in the North and West, that same desire was often a catalyst for others to remain in the South. Whether in the Carolinas, Georgia, Alabama, Mississippi, or Kentucky, a number of African Americans throughout the South proved more than willing to stay and battle for freedom. The era of the Second Great Migration was not only an era of mass exodus, but was also a era of increased civil rights activism within the South. As Hollis Watkins, a civil rights activist with the Student Nonviolent Coordinating Committee (SNCC), noted during a 1964 voter registration campaign in Greenwood, Mississippi, "As long as we continue to go up North and run away from the situation, we will never make it any better" ("Mass Meeting").

African American migration out of the South dwindled to a trickle by the late 1960s as a result of civil rights victories in the South and the racial climate of the North. As African Americans regained the right to vote and access to better schools and public accommodations, if not equal employment, **open housing**, or an end to **police brutality**, the prime motivation for migration, the desire for freedom and equality, was lessened. At the same time, **deindustrialization** short-circuited the limited economic opportunities African Americans found in northern industries. Moreover, African Americans were increasingly confined to overcrowded housing located in deteriorating inner cities across America as they encountered residential segregation even more pronounced in the North than in the South. As work disappeared and racism in the North and West seemingly increased with the influx of migrants, many African Americans questioned whether migration from the South was in fact a road toward greater freedom or a better life.

By 2000 more than 86 percent of all African Americans lived in cities, with nearly 37 percent and 9 percent located in the North and West respectively. However, despite the large numbers of migrants throughout the era of the Great Migration, the majority of African Americans remain in the South. Ironically, increasing numbers of African Americans are returning to southern cities such as **Atlanta**, **New Orleans**, **Charlotte**, and **Houston** still seeking better lives, freedom, and equality. *See also* Black Migration before World War

I, Patterns of; Demographic Patterns of the Great Black Migration (1915–1940); Demographic Patterns of the Great Black Migration (1940–1970); Migrants, Economic Characteristics of; Migrants, Expectations of; Migrants, Social Characteristics of; Return Migration; Primary Documents 7, 10, 20, 22, 25, 30, 32, 33, 41, 42, 44, 47, 56, 61, 65, 66, 68.

Further Reading

Griffin, Farah Jasmine. *"Who Set You Flowin'?" The African-American Migration Narrative.* New York: Oxford University Press, 1995.

Grossman, James R. *Land of Hope: Chicago, Black Southerners, and the Great Migration.* Chicago: University of Chicago Press, 1989.

Hine, Darlene Clark. "Rape and the Inner Lives of Black Women in the Middle West: Preliminary Thoughts on the Culture of Dissemblance." In *Unequal Sisters*, edited by Ellen Carol Du Bois and Vicki L. Ruiz. New York: Routledge, 1990.

Lemke-Santangelo, Gretchen. *Abiding Courage: African-American Migrant Women and the East Bay Community.* Chapel Hill: University of North Carolina Press, 1996.

"Mass Meeting and Prayer." In *Sing for Freedom: The Story of the Civil Rights Movement through Its Songs.* Washington, DC: Smithsonian/Folkways Records, 1990.

Painter, Nell Irvin. *Exodusters: Black Migration to Kansas after Reconstruction.* New York: Knopf, 1977.

Taylor, Quintard. *The Forging of a Black Community: Seattle's Central District, from 1870 through the Civil Rights Era.* Seattle: University of Washington Press, 1994.

Trotter, Joe William, Jr. *Black Milwaukee: The Making of an Industrial Proletariat, 1915–45.* Urbana: University of Illinois Press, 1985.

———, ed. *The Great Migration in Historical Perspective: New Dimensions of Race, Class, and Gender.* Bloomington: Indiana University Press, 1991.

Luther J. Adams

Great Migration, White Opposition to

The mass exodus out of the South in the years straddling World War I exposed the fundamental paradox in southern white attitudes to the large African American population with which they shared the region: pervasive racial hostility, codified in **Jim Crow** legislation and frequently manifested in callous violence, existed side by side with the white South's deep dependence on an abundant supply of cheap black labor. "Politically speaking there are far too many negroes," a white South Carolina politician had remarked at the turn of the century, during an earlier exodus, "but from an industrial standpoint there is room for many more" (Tindall, 177). New South boosters had long acknowledged the essential role of black agricultural and industrial labor in their plans to lift the region out of backwardness, describing black workers as the "most important working factor in the development" of the South, a factor that would eventually make it possible for the region to "take the lead in the cheapest production on this continent" ("Southern Bessemer Ores," *Manufacturers' Review*, October 25, 1890). But even self-styled southern progressives had seemed distinctly unconcerned about the absence of democratic rights for African Americans, sharing the hostility and prejudice that permeated

Southern white opposition to the Great Migration ran deep, such as in this cartoon from the *Memphis Commercial Appeal* in 1923, which insisted that African Americans had no legitimate reasons for leaving the South. Tuskegee Institute News Clipping File, reel 20, frame 893.

every level of white society during this period. The region's white civic and industrial leaders had done little to curb the racial violence that settled upon the region from the mid-1880s onward, and its press had been intermittently obsessed with the so-called Negro problem since the end of slavery.

The German immigrant Carl Schurz, sent south by President Andrew Johnson to survey the region immediately after the conclusion of the Civil War, remarked upon "the prevalent desire among the whites [that] if they could not retain their negroes as slaves, to get rid of them entirely" (Schurz, 21). Between 1865 and the beginning of the Great Migration white southern employers experimented with a number of solutions aimed at accomplishing just that, but every such attempt ended in miserable failure. Early on, they hoped that the importation of large numbers of "docile" Chinese laborers (labeled "coolies" in the press) would displace their troublesome black field hands. Later, southern state governments and employers tried unsuccessfully to lure European immigrants southward, but few were inclined to accept the wages and conditions on offer. By the beginning of the twentieth century the region's employers were compelled to reconcile themselves to black labor as the fundamental element in their supply.

Prominent whites at first seemed unconcerned by the early stirrings of black migration in 1915 and 1916. Industrial employers reeling in the midst of a national slump were relieved, initially, at the siphoning off of surplus labor. Across the Deep South cotton planters hit hard by a series of natural and market calamities were unable to feed or clothe those field hands they had formerly employed. Federal relief workers reported from Alabama's **Cotton Belt** in early 1917 the sight of hundreds of "hungry, half-naked, bare-footed poor Negroes huddled on the frozen ground, waiting their turn to get a little ration of meat and a peck of meal" (Tower, 12). Few planters objected when those they had turned out of employment began making the trek from the plantations to the urban South, and in some cases they actively drove them off.

As their crisis worsened, however, white southern elites began to express apprehension over the dire implications of a prolonged exodus. Voicing their frustration that "everybody seems to be asleep about what is going on right under their noses," editors at the *Macon Telegraph* (Georgia) attempted to alert the region to the peril that threatened it. "We must have the Negro in the South," they warned. "He has been with us so long that our whole industrial, commercial and agricultural structure has been built on a black foundation. It is the only labor we have . . . if we lost it we [would] go bankrupt" (*Reporter*, September 30, 1916). It was a "mistake," agreed the *Montgomery Advertiser* (Alabama), "not to induce our Negroes to stay. . . . If they go, where shall we get labor to take their places?" (*Montgomery Advertiser*, August 24, 1916). Others expressed themselves even more bluntly: "We must have their labor," a Charleston planter proclaimed, "and wherever the niggers go, I'd go too. If I had to work my land with whites, I'd quit" (Litwack, 118).

Destitute African Americans expressed little sympathy for the predicament that their newfound mobility had presented to southern whites, of course, and continued largely undeterred in their attempts to escape their conditions. Nor were they oblivious to the hypocrisy revealed in the new campaign. "Why should the South raise [objections] when it has held [blacks] up to the ridicule of the world as trifling, shiftless and such a burden? Now that the opportunity has come to relieve the South of some of its burden . . . a great hue and cry is started that it must not be allowed" (*Montgomery Advertiser*, September 26, 1919). The patterns of black migration showed two distinct trends: large numbers of those already resident in the urban South, along with rural blacks situated close to the main north-south rail lines, made their way northward to cities such as **Chicago**, **Detroit**, **Cleveland**, and **Pittsburgh**, while another, internal migration brought large numbers from the outlying plantation districts into southern cities seeking industrial employment.

This dual migration resulted partly from the deliberate efforts of white employers to stem the exodus of industrial labor out of the region through energetic recruitment of a new supply in the plantation districts. Employers in **Birmingham, Alabama**'s coal and ore mines, steel plants, and iron foundries dispatched **labor agents** throughout the Black Belt seeking to replenish the ranks of those who had made the trek northward, but in bringing in a new supply of cheap labor and thus holding the line on wages, they gave added incentive to those experienced black and white workers who were considering migration. Similarly, lumber operators in Texas and Louisiana who had long depended on black labor in their logging camps and sawmills dispatched recruitment agents throughout the Southwest and across the rural South as far as Florida and the Carolinas in an effort to tap new sources of black labor. This could lead, at times, to confrontations between industrial and agricultural employers competing over the same dwindling supply of black labor.

The lumber interests supplemented their trawl of the plantation South with an energetic campaign to bring Mexican immigrants into their operations and exerted their influence with federal officials to remove barriers against drawing upon labor from across the Rio Grande. It was in the context of this severe shortage that the head of the region's largest timber company reported in 1918 that "Negro **women** are being employed to do light tasks about the mills," and within weeks the *Gulf Coast Lumberman* reported "the employment of the first woman sawmill engineer in the history of the Texas lumber industry" (Fickle, 64, 65). Just as the demands of war production had induced northern employers to consider large-scale employment of African Americans, out-migration compelled the South's largest white employers to tap into labor reserves that they had previously barred from employment.

In other ways, too, the labor shortage produced by the exodus forced concessions from white southern elites. Broadly speaking, they adopted two main strategies in their attempts to counter the hemorrhaging of their labor supply: inducement and coercion. Though they deeply resented doing so, southern employers understood that the simplest approach to retaining their labor supply was to match the wages on offer in northern industry, and in both industry and agriculture the war brought significant wage gains. "It has been necessary," an Alabama coal operator reported, "to offer inducements to our miners to prevent more of them from migrating northward, where manufacturers . . . are making very attractive offers to southern labor" (Kelly, 138). Under pressure, some employers understood that only the tangible amelioration of the oppression experienced by blacks at the hands of the police and others would persuade laborers to stay put, a recognition that led individual employers to oppose the worst excesses of Jim Crow law and order.

Where such incentives failed to stem the tide, however, southern whites seldom hesitated from resorting to more coercive measures. "Shut the barn door before the horses get out," a bulletin issued by the Southern Metal Trades Association urged its members, and some appear to have followed the directive enthusiastically (*Birmingham Labor Advocate*, June 21, 1917). The largest steel manufacturer in the South refused to cash checks sent south to "finance the 'darky's joyride,' " using its influence to limit **railroad** access for African Americans and leaning on its "friends" in the black community to dissuade their laborers from moving northward (Norrell, 244). The two main employers' organizations in the lumber industry developed an elaborate network to monitor northern migration, stationing agents in northern cities to report on wage levels, unionization, and the growing influence of **black nationalism**. They beseeched the press to devote more coverage to race riots and other negative aspects of African American life in the North and at one point established an employment office in Chicago aimed at inducing a **return migration**.

Southern whites were aided in the coercive thrust of their efforts by federal intervention. U.S. officials attached to the **National War Labor Board** had provoked the ire of many prominent southern whites, who resented their impact in raising wages and fastening the eight-hour day upon the region, but on the whole federal officials shared their desire to maintain the status quo during a tumultuous period of social and economic upheaval. In particular, federal authorities and southern white elites shared deep concerns about the emergence of new, militant forms of black nationalism, embodied most visibly in the rise of **Marcus Garvey**'s **Universal Negro Improvement Association**. Together, white employers and federal marshals engaged in widespread surveillance of black southerners, but these often farcical efforts were generally unproductive. More detrimental to their newfound freedoms were the various federal and local directives aimed at restricting black mobility: local vagrancy ordinances, federal "work or fight" orders, and energetically enforced conscription orders. In short, white southerners attempted by every means at their disposal to reassert control over their formerly compliant black labor force, but the profound social and economic changes that underpinned the Great Migration meant that white southerners emerged from the post–World War I period with their social order severely shaken. Among other things, it would require the revival of the **Ku Klux Klan** to restore the stability they cherished so dearly.

The onset of World War II brought another dramatic rupture in the southern social order, but this time under changed conditions. The mechanization of agriculture from the late 1930s onward had encouraged a further dispersal of rural blacks across the South and along the now-familiar paths northward. Now saddled with a surplus of black labor made redundant by machinery, however, planters put up little resistance to the intensified migration brought on by the war. From the mid-1940s onward they and their urban counterparts were concerned with the problem of how to maintain their grip on a social order whose social and economic foundations had shifted under their feet. *See also* Federal Surveillance of Black Migrants; Great Migration, Black Opposition to; Primary Documents 11, 34, 38, 47, 65.

Further Reading

Cohen, Lucy M. *Chinese in the Post-Civil War South: A People without a History.* Baton Rouge: Louisiana State University Press, 1984.

Ellis, Mark. "Federal Surveillance of Black Americans during the First World War." *Immigrants and Minorities* 12, no. 1 (March 1993): 1–20.

Fickle, James E. "Management Looks at the 'Labor Problem': The Southern Pine Industry during World War I and the Postwar Era." *Journal of Southern History* 40, no. 4 (February 1974): 61–76.

Hahn, Steven. *A Nation under Our Feet: Black Political Struggles in the Rural South from Slavery to the Great Migration.* Cambridge, MA: Belknap Press of Harvard University Press, 2003.

Keith, Jeannette. *Rich Man's War, Poor Man's Fight: Race, Class, and Power in the Rural South during the First World War.* Chapel Hill: University of North Carolina Press, 2004.

Kelly, Brian. *Race, Class, and Power in the Alabama Coalfields, 1908-21.* Urbana: University of Illinois Press, 2001.

Litwack, Leon. *Trouble in Mind: Black Southerners in the Age of Jim Crow.* New York: Alfred A. Knopf, 1998.

Meier, August, and Elliott Rudwick. *From Plantation to Ghetto.* 3rd ed. New York: Hill and Wang, 1976.

Norrell, Robert J. *James Bowron: The Autobiography of a New South Industrialist.* Chapel Hill: University of North Carolina Press, 1991.

Schurz, Carl. *The Condition of the South: Extracts from the Report of Major-General Carl Schurz.* Philadelphia, n.p., 1865.

Tindall, George S. *South Carolina Negroes, 1877–1900*. Columbia: University of South Carolina Press, 1952.
Tower, J. Allen. "Cotton Change in Alabama, 1879–1946." *Economic Geography* 26, no. 1 (January 1950): 6–28.

Brian Kelly

Great Retreat

In the antiracist euphoria of Reconstruction, African Americans moved almost everywhere across America. By 1890 blacks were living and working in river valleys of northeast Pennsylvania, in every Indiana county save one, deep in the northwoods of Wisconsin, and in every county of Montana and California. In that year the proportion of black Illinoisans living in **Chicago** (25 percent) was less than that of whites (29 percent).

Then, from 1890 to the 1930s, a period that historian Rayford Logan termed the "**nadir of race relations**" set in, triggered by three developments: the massacre of Wounded Knee, ending American Indian independence; the new Mississippi Constitution, which removed African Americans from citizenship and drew no protest from the federal government; and the failure by one vote of the U.S. Senate to pass the Federal Elections Bill. At that point the Republican Party largely abandoned its commitment to the civil and political rights of African Americans. Since the Democrats already labeled themselves "the white man's party," African Americans now found themselves friendless.

In the traditional South whites copied Mississippi by passing laws that took away the voting and citizenship rights of African Americans. Elsewhere, whites took a different tack. From town after town, county after county—even from whole regions—African Americans were driven out by white opposition, eventually settling in expansive **ghettos** in northern cities. This Great Retreat left in its wake a new geography of race in the United States. From Myakka City, Florida, to Kennewick, Washington, the nation is dotted with thousands of all-white **sundown towns** that are (or were until recently) all white by design. By 1930, six counties in Indiana, for example, had no blacks and another fourteen had fewer than ten, even though many more African Americans now lived in the state. Eleven counties in Montana had no blacks, and the proportion of African Americans of that state's population fell from 1.13 percent in 1890 to 0.23 percent in 1930. While Oregon's white population tripled in the decades between 1890 and 1930, its black population remained constant, and 70 percent of them settled in **Portland**, having been banned from Ashland, Grants Pass, Medford, Eugene, Tillamook, and other Oregon towns and cities.

This Great Retreat was preceded by a dress rehearsal in the West from the mid-1870s to about 1910, as whites forced Chinese Americans from many towns and entire counties. This "Chinese Retreat" resulted in the concentration of that minority in Chinatowns in **Seattle**, **San Francisco**, **Los Angeles**, and a few other cities. Chinese fled from almost every town in Wyoming and from at least forty in California. Their retreat from Idaho was especially striking: in 1870 Chinese made up one-third of that state's population, but by 1910 almost none remained.

Similarly, the Great Retreat of African Americans resulted in such huge ghettos as Harlem in **New York City**, **Cleveland**'s Hough, the South Side of **Chicago**, and Watts in Los Angeles. Somehow, Americans came to accept that a mostly rural population of black southerners would wind up concentrated in the inner cities in America's largest metropolitan areas. Thus the Great Retreat antedated and channeled the flows of the Great Migration.

The Great Retreat left large areas of the United States virtually free of African Americans. Among these are the Ozarks, the Cumberlands, a thick band of sun-down counties and towns on both sides of the Iowa-Missouri border, virtually every town and city along the Illinois River except Peoria, most of western Oregon, and a 4,000-square-mile area southwest of Fort Worth, Texas. Since the 1980s African Americans have been venturing into these areas, sometimes encountering civility and even goodwill, sometimes continued hostility. *See also* Jim Crow; Midwestern States, Black Migration to; Migrants, Settlement Patterns of; Northeastern States, Black Migration to; Western States, Black Migration to; Primary Documents 54, 55.

Further Reading

Loewen, James. *Sundown Towns: A Hidden Dimension of Segregation in America.* New York: New Press, 2005.

James W. Loewen

Greenlee, William Augustus "Gus" (1897–1952)

Showman and **sport**s promoter William Augustus "Gus" Greenlee achieved widespread notoriety by catering to the entertainment needs of urban blacks during the Great Migration. He operated several popular **Pittsburgh** night-clubs, ran the city's largest daily numbers lottery, and managed a group of talented prizefighters. During the 1930s he owned the Pittsburgh Crawfords, one of black baseball's most successful clubs, and served as chairman of the National Negro League, which attained unprecedented levels of fan support and financial stability under his stewardship. Greenlee's ventures capitalized on the growing demand for affordable amusements among black migrants as they moved north, experienced industrial life, and built up their growing urban communities.

Born in 1897, Gus Greenlee grew up in Marion, North Carolina. His father, a successful masonry contractor, strongly encouraged his son to play baseball and go to college. While the younger Greenlee developed a lifelong passion for the summer pastime, he had far less interest in higher education. In 1916, after completing one year of college, he joined the migration northward, hopping a freight train to Pittsburgh, where an uncle lived.

After arriving in Pittsburgh, Greenlee worked a variety of jobs. He shined shoes, labored as a fireman at the Jones and Laughlin steel mill, and drove a taxicab. During World War I he served overseas with the 367th Army

Regiment. Returning to Pittsburgh after the war, Greenlee began establishing himself as one of the city's most powerful racketeers, transporting cases of illegal liquor around town in his taxicab. Soon he expanded his operations by opening several speakeasies. His best-known establishment, the Crawford Grill, was Pittsburgh's jazziest nightspot. Its all-night jam sessions were legendary, attracting not only top black musicians but also large crowds of both black and white patrons. The nightclub also served as a hub for Greenlee's unlawful but enormously popular and highly lucrative daily numbers lottery.

Greenlee invested much of his racketeering revenues in baseball. In 1931 he acquired a black sandlot team known as the Pittsburgh Crawfords and transformed it into one of the era's premier baseball clubs. Spending freely on salaries, he signed future Hall of Famers Oscar Charleston, Judy Johnson, Cool Papa Bell, **Satchel Paige**, and **Josh Gibson**. To showcase the talents of his players and save them the indignity of playing in white-owned stadiums, Greenlee also funded the construction of a stadium for the Crawfords. Opened in 1932, Greenlee Field was the nation's foremost black-owned baseball stadium. Between 1933 and 1936 the Crawfords won three league championships.

As owner of the Crawfords, Greenlee worked to revive professional black baseball at the national level. In 1933 he helped resurrect the Negro National League and served as its chairman for the next five seasons. Despite the difficult economic times of the depression, the new league surpassed all previous efforts at organized black baseball and survived until the late 1940s. During this period Greenlee also promoted the careers of nearly a dozen black boxers. Black sports fans everywhere celebrated when Greenlee's star fighter, John Henry Lewis, defeated white boxer Bob Olin for the light-heavyweight championship in 1935. Lewis's victory made Greenlee the first black man in boxing history to manage a black champion.

In 1939 Greenlee sold the Crawfords after Bell, Paige, Gibson, and several of their teammates left to play in the Dominican Republic. He briefly reentered black baseball in 1945 by partnering with Brooklyn Dodgers general manager Branch Rickey to form the United States League, but it folded after two seasons. In subsequent years Greenlee lost much of his numbers operation to white racketeers while federal investigators pursued him over unpaid income taxes. A fire destroyed the Crawford Grill in 1951. Greenlee died in Pittsburgh on July 10, 1952. *See also* Dance Halls and Nightclubs; Negro Leagues; Policy Gambling; Taxicab Operators; Primary Document 51.

Further Reading

Bankes, James. *The Pittsburgh Crawfords: The Lives and Times of Black Baseball's Most Exciting Team.* Dubuque, IA: Wm. C. Brown Publishers, 1991.

Ruck, Rob. *Sandlot Seasons: Sport in Black Pittsburgh.* Urbana: University of Illinois Press, 1987.

Scott A. Newman

Gulf South

The yearning for greater freedom that lured African Americans to northern cities also made the Gulf South a desirable destination. Moreover, the Gulf region was an easier destination to reach for many rural migrants hampered by the money, distance, and dangers associated with migration out of the South. Despite the rhetoric of advocates of a New South dedicated to the modernization of the region's economy, the South remained an exporting region. As the South entered the twentieth century, the Atlantic and Gulf ports were the key growth points for an expanding commercial and manufacturing sector. The Gulf South uniquely benefited from the emergence of timber and textile mills, turpentine plants, petroleum, and shipping that created new jobs and stimulated expansion in ports such as Tampa and **Houston**, while older ports such as Mobile and **New Orleans** saw their established trade economies change to accommodate new commercial enterprises and manufactured products. As the southern economy grew, Gulf cities challenged Atlantic Coast cities as economic leaders by the 1920s.

Economic depressions, massive **unemployment**, and deflation combined with the increased mechanization of southern agriculture to force African American laborers to seek jobs in the coastal port region. The development of Tampa in the Gulf east and Houston in the Gulf west highlighted the multiracial development of the Gulf South. Tampa was defined by the presence of a

Many African American men worked as long-shoremen on the docks of the Gulf Coast, including the port of Houston, pictured above. Courtesy of the Library of Congress.

cigar industry that attracted émigrés from Latin America. The city had 159 cigar factories with over 12,000 employees in 1927. In Houston a multiethnic city grew that included both Mexican American and African American migrants. As the Gulf South developed, race, politics, and economic concerns were complicated by conflict and compromise between different cultural groups.

African American émigrés found that their arrival in Gulf port cities generated conflict just as it had in the North. Indeed, the growth of economic opportunities in transportation, long-shoring, manufacturing, **construction**, and public works in fast-growing cities such as Houston was juxtaposed with social tensions created by struggles to maintain segregation as black migrants disturbed social boundaries and challenged racial customs. African American workers barred from white labor organizations created black counterparts and pushed for changes in labor practice in Houston, New Orleans, and Tampa. Indeed, in the 1920s Tampa had the highest rate of union growth for a city its size in the United States. Despite the benefits offered by a strong job market and unionism, however,

Jim Crow segregation, poor education, voting restrictions, and limited employment opportunities marred life in the Gulf South. Several Gulf states banned African American participation in voting primaries, prompting the **National Association for the Advancement of Colored People** to join with black workers in Houston to challenge political exclusion throughout the 1930s. Ironically, the Gulf South's unique racial landscape complicated the struggle for equality as whites' belief in African American inferiority was weighed against an equal scorn for Mexican Americans in Houston or Italians in Tampa Bay. Multicultural communities created bruising competition among oppressed groups. Interracial conflicts limited opportunities for blacks as traditional deference and close primaries worked in concert to limit political, economic, and social participation for all minorities. African Americans realized shared goals in Tampa and Houston and worked to build coalitions based on common labor concerns that challenged white discrimination.

In the midst of the Great Depression, this struggle made the Gulf South a hotbed as New Deal programs emerged that bolstered African American labor activism. Indeed, the struggle to get the benefits associated with new federal jobs programs helped ignite political activism in Tampa as African American residents increased their voting turnout to challenge white leadership. The ability of African Americans to organize politically and fight against unfair employment practices with other minorities in longshoremen's unions represented not only a challenge to white control of the labor market, but a strong political force that voiced support for broader social issues. Black longshoremen in the Gulf South supported antilynching legislation in the 1930s while pressing political leaders to support fair labor practices. Yet the New Deal programs disrupted southern practice more than they transformed it. By 1939, the southern region's economy remained dominated by agricultural production, despite state-sponsored industrial development programs and New Deal reform initiatives.

When the United States prepared for war in 1940, the South's economic stagnation played a big part in the federal government's decision to place training and defense facilities in the South. With strategic reasoning supporting the dispersion of military bases and industrial plants, the Gulf South again expanded economically as **shipyards** and aircraft plants were built throughout the region. The effects were undeniable. The area from Houston to Tampa Bay received an infusion of money and men that significantly changed southern development patterns. The absence of white labor opened the door to African American workers like never before as the entire region became less rural and more urban. Tampa's shipyard employed 16,000 men, while Houston benefited from wartime demand for petroleum products. Nonetheless, the region's lack of infrastructure left many cities facing pressing **housing** and sanitation problems that helped heighten racial tensions. While anger toward African Americans was a staple of southern reaction to change, municipal officials in Houston also complained about the dangers posed by delinquent girls and rural whites drawn to the city. Such concerns marred the economic benefit of wartime investment for Mobile and other Gulf South cities. These growing pains were immaterial to African Americans who attempted to capitalize on labor needs.

African American efforts to gain industrial employment and expand civil rights led to mixed results in the 1940s. Black **schoolteachers** in Tampa challenged the school system as part of a federal lawsuit and won equal pay regardless of race. Yet federal agencies fought an uphill battle to expand hiring practices and increase wages for African American workers in many wartime industries. All-white unions continued to show their resentment of black workers by negotiating closed-shop agreements with southern shipbuilders that barred new African American and Mexican American workers and excluded established black workers from many skilled positions in Houston and elsewhere. African Americans countered these restrictions by joining the **Congress of Industrial Organizations** in an attempt to end segregated unionism. White response to African American labor demands was typified by the 1943 riot at the Alabama Dry Dock Company in Mobile, where white workers exploded in violence after seven African American workers were hired. Indeed, the mixture of black and white workers in wartime industries proved dangerous in southern communities such as Beaumont, Texas, which joined Los Angeles and Harlem in experiencing antiblack riots in 1943 (see **Beaumont, Texas, Race Riot of 1943**; **Harlem Riot of 1943**; **Zoot-Suit Riots [1943]**).

In the aftermath of the war the Gulf South continued to reap the benefits of government spending. In postwar America federal expenditures, a low tax base, open-shop labor policies, a warm climate, and an aggressive business class continued to transform the Gulf South. In Houston the growing importance of gasoline to America's suburban lifestyle made that city the center of thriving petroleum-related industries. The presence of a military base in Pensacola made the Gulf region a destination for both business and government resources. Tampa Bay expanded as massive federal expenditures on defense placed more resources at MacDill Air Force Base. Equally important were federal money provided for **urban renewal**, the real estate and construction boom, and the promotion of tourism and leisure industries. African American workers pushed to expand on minimal wartime gains by pressing the **Fair Employment Practices Committee** to guarantee black workers equal access to defense industry jobs. The Gulf South continued to attract African American migrants even as racism and turmoil associated with the **civil rights movement** and out-migration to other areas increased.

The Gulf South's importance as a destination for African Americans throughout the twentieth century separates it from the South as a whole. Indeed, the multiracial nature of Gulf cities, the economic development, and the rapid pace of change put this subregion at the forefront of southern development. The benefits provided to the black communities allowed them to achieve better lives than the limited prospects they found in the southern hinterlands, and over time the roots established in this region attracted African Americans back to the South. African American **return migration** in the late 1970s helped define the Sunbelt cities phenomenon and was a direct outgrowth of economic, political, and social benefits that made the Gulf South region unique. *See also* Aviation Industry, Black Employment in; Caribbean Migration; Hispanic Immigrants and Hispanic Americans, Relations with Black Migrants; Miami, Florida.

Further Reading

Doyle, Don H. *New Men, New Cities, New South: Atlanta, Nashville, Charleston, Mobile, 1860-1910*. Chapel Hill: University of North Carolina Press, 1990.

Goldfield, David. *Region, Race, and Cities: Interpreting the Urban South*. Baton Rouge: Louisiana State University Press, 1997.

Kaplan, Barry J. "Houston: The Golden Buckle of the Sunbelt." In *Sunbelt Cities: Politics and Growth since World War II*, edited by Richard M. Bernard and Bradley Rice, 191-211. Austin: University of Texas Press, 1983.

Montes, Rebecca. "Working for American Rights: Black, White, and Mexican American Dockworkers in Texas during the Great Depression." In *Sunbelt Revolution: The Historical Progression of the Civil Rights Struggle in the Gulf South, 1866-2000*, edited by Samuel C. Hyde, Jr., 102-32. Gainesville: University Press of Florida, 2003.

Mormino, Gary R. "Tampa: From Hell Hole to Good Life." In *Sunbelt Cities: Politics and Growth since World War II*, edited by Richard M. Bernard and Bradley Rice, 138-61. Austin: University of Texas Press, 1983.

Nelson, Bruce. "Organized Labor and the Struggle for Black Equality in Mobile during World War II." *Journal of American History* 80, no. 3 (1993): 952-88.

Obadele-Starks, Ernest. *Black Unionism in the Industrial South*. College Station: Texas A&M University Press, 2000.

Wiese, Andrew. *Places of Their Own: African American Suburbanization in the Twentieth Century*. Chicago: University of Chicago Press, 2004.

Julian C. Chambliss

H

Handy, W. C. (William Christopher) (1873–1958)

W. C. Handy, the so-called Father of the **Blues**, was an African American composer, bandleader, and music publisher who achieved international fame as the author of "St. Louis Blues," a widely recorded composition. Southern born but northward-yearning, Handy wrote in his 1941 autobiography, *Father of the Blues*, of his "restless spirit"—a migrant's spirit that ultimately propelled him out of the South into an illustrious career centered in Harlem and **New York City**'s Tin Pan Alley, a loosely knit fraternity of professional songwriters.

Born in Florence, Alabama, on November 16, 1873, Handy was the son of former slaves. Both his father and grandfather were Methodist **ministers**, respected members of the black middle class, and Handy was expected to follow their lead. Instead, he defied expectations and followed his wayward muse into the world of popular entertainment. He saved his pennies to buy a guitar ("One of the devil's playthings," cried his outraged father [Handy, *Father of the Blues*, 10]), hoboed to the 1893 Chicago World's Fair with the fellow members of his Lauzetta Quartet, and slept on a cobblestoned levee next to the Mississippi River in **St. Louis** with hundreds of down-and-out migrants, an episode that later found its way into his best-known blues song.

The chief formative experience of Handy's life was the seven years (1896–1903) he spent crisscrossing America as a cornet player and bandleader with Mahara's Minstrels, an Irish-owned theatrical troupe. Although such minstrels, who wore blackface makeup and performed song-and-dance routines, were looked down upon by upwardly striving African Americans, Handy and his colleagues saw themselves as proud, resourceful, and skilled professionals. Touring the South that both celebrated and disdained them, repeatedly resisting white violence as they barnstormed through the land of **Jim Crow** segregation, black minstrels lived the bluesiest of lives.

In 1903, as black Americans were beginning to trickle northward in search of opportunity, Handy swerved south into Mississippi and encountered blues music for the first time. One night in Tutwiler, a **Mississippi Delta** town, he heard an older black guitarist at a train station singing a monotonous ditty about catching a train and taking it to a nearby crossing. This song of restlessness and longing galvanized Handy. Over the next few years he began to write blues-inflected music for the dance bands he led in Mississippi and **Memphis**. A campaign song Handy composed in 1909 for Memphis politician E. H. Crump became a hit as "Memphis Blues" in 1912. In 1914 Handy sat down in a Memphis rooming house, thought back over the road-weary life he had survived, and composed "St. Louis Blues," a song that voiced both his own restless spirit and the spirit of the Great Migration:

> Feelin' tomorrow lak ah feel today
> Feel tomorrow lak ah feel today
> I'll pack my trunk, make ma gitaway.

In 1918, embittered by the **lynching** of a black man on Beale Street, Handy became a northward migrant himself, heading to Harlem to relocate his Pace and Handy music publishing company. Although Handy visited Memphis in later years and Beale Street bears a park with his name, he never again lived in the South. Handy composed several other well-known songs in the course of his career, including "Hesitating Blues" and "Beale Street Blues," but it was "St. Louis Blues," recorded by **Louis Armstrong**, **Bessie Smith**, and many other performers, that helped transform him from locally known bandleader into an American icon. Handy died in New York on March 28, 1958. *See also* Black Swan Records; Europe, James Reese; Joplin, Scott; Ragtime; Recording Industry; Swing.

Further Reading

Gussow, Adam. *Seems like Murder Here: Southern Violence and the Blues Tradition.* Chicago: University of Chicago Press, 2002.

Handy, W. C. *Father of the Blues.* 1941. New York: Da Capo Press, 1991.

———, ed. *Blues: An Anthology.* 1926. New York: Da Capo Press, 1990.

Hurwitt, Elliott S. "W. C. Handy as Music Publisher: Career and Reputation." Ph.D. diss., City University of New York, 2000.

University of North Alabama Libraries. "W. C. Handy, 'Father of the Blues.'" www2.una.edu/library/handy/.

Adam Gussow

Hansberry, Lorraine *See A Raisin in the Sun* (Lorraine Hansberry)

Harlem Renaissance

The term "Harlem Renaissance" usually refers to the flowering of African American arts and letters between 1919 and 1929, even though the genesis and influence of the Renaissance covers a much broader period and even though a good deal of the cultural work occurred outside Harlem. A "renaissance" can suggest either a radical new beginning or a rebirth of an older cultural tradition. Both definitions apply to the Harlem Renaissance. Between the publication of **W.E.B. DuBois**'s *Souls of Black Folk* in 1903 and that of **Claude McKay**'s *Harlem Shadows* in 1922, new works of literature by African Americans had been rare. The twenty-year drought was punctuated by a scattering of unmemorable periodical literature, by two obscure novels from Sutton Griggs, and by DuBois's well-received but still obviously minor achievement, *The Quest of the Silver Fleece*. Further, almost no one perceived the lasting significance of forms of popular art that were developing among rural and working-class African Americans who had begun migrating to the northern cities. **Jazz**, **blues**, and even highly popular and inventive forms of dance flowing out of southern juke joints and northern clubs were largely viewed as subartistic, if not morally and intellectually degrading. Thus when Harlem in the jazz age saw the production by African Americans of several dozen works of literature, innumerable periodical publications, and a multitude of works in dance, music, drama, and the plastic arts, African American contributions to the traditional forms of high culture seemed reborn indeed.

At the same time, the Harlem Renaissance was a radical attempt at a new beginning. The signature literary collection of the period, edited by **Alain Locke**, was titled *The New Negro*. In the first two decades of the twentieth century this phrase had come to define and promote an emergent African American identity shaped by the demographic and cultural changes of the Great Migration. The Old Negro designated the humble, self-effacing, and always accommodating Uncle Tom of plantation myth and fiction. The **New Negro**, by contrast, was self-assertive, independent, and resistant to domination. In his anthology and essays on the idea of the New Negro, Locke turned these images toward distinctly aesthetic ends. Negro art would now no longer toil submissively in the white fields of the literary and artistic traditions. Arts and letters would instead serve the specific task of raising racial consciousness on a global scale. They not only would draw on European models but would look to the African diaspora and especially to the African experience in America for models, forms, and themes. Particular versions of the aesthetics of the New Negro varied widely. Locke himself was something of an aesthete and continued to place the highest value on European forms, though he wanted these forms Africanized in theme and purpose. Countee Cullen, sometimes called the black Keats, was his exemplar. DuBois also championed Cullen, but growled decidedly that art, and especially Negro art, must be propaganda. Younger artists like **Langston Hughes**, **Wallace Thurman**, Richard Nugent, **Zora Neale Hurston**, and **Dorothy West** were by turns Wildean bohemians and cultural nationalists, sometimes both at once. However different these writers and thinkers may have been, they agreed on the basic premise that a new day had dawned and that old models of African American cultural work would no longer suffice.

This assertion of cultural newness inevitably drew from the facts of the ongoing migration of rural southern African Americans to the northern cities. The newness of the New Negro was not only one of aesthetic consciousness;

it appeared in almost every aspect of daily life. In the space of decades an entire population transformed itself from rural to urban, from agricultural to industrial, moving from a quasi-feudal society under white domination in the South to what appeared to be the possibility of individual achievement and racial self-realization in the North. The demographic shifts alone produced massive changes in cultural patterns associated with religion, **housing**, family life, and economics. Writers and artists recognized, reflected, and recorded these changes. From Zora Neale Hurston's *Their Eyes Were Watching God* to the poetry of Langston Hughes, movement, migration, and change were the inescapable themes of Renaissance art and literature.

At the same time, the cultural activity of the Renaissance, rooted as it was in the cultural aspirations of what DuBois described as the talented tenth, bore a complicated and even attenuated relationship to the actual lives and aspirations of the migrants themselves. The initial energy for the Renaissance in the 1920s sprang from the organizational energy and foresight of men like Locke and **Charles S. Johnson**, editor of *Opportunity* magazine. In 1924 Johnson organized a dinner to honor recipients of a literary prize. This led to a special issue of *Survey Graphic* titled "Harlem: Mecca of the New Negro," which was ultimately republished as Locke's collection *The New Negro*. Other prizes, dinners, and collections followed. So self-conscious was the effort to create an African American artistic movement out of whole cloth that historian David Levering Lewis describes the Renaissance as "a somewhat forced phenomenon, a cultural nationalism of the parlor" (Lewis, *Portable Harlem Renaissance Reader*, xiii). Lewis's judgment has been disputed. Nevertheless, Lewis rightly points out that the engines of aesthetic renewal turned at some significant remove from the daily grind the immigrants found as factory workers and chambermaids.

The relationship of the Renaissance to the Great Migration is all the more complicated because of the degree to which white sponsorship played a determinative role. Prize monies almost always came from white benefactors. White philanthropists like Charlotte Osgood Mason supported many of the main artists and thinkers of the Renaissance. Mason also operated out of an unshakably romantic and primitivist view of race, and she insisted on considerable control over the kind of work her minions could publish. Finally, publishing houses, galleries, and museums were largely controlled by white Americans and marketed to white audiences. The degree to which this affected the artistic work itself is almost impossible to determine. However, personalities as different as W.E.B. DuBois and Zora Neale Hurston wrote disgusted essays rebuking white publishers for their limited vision of Negro life, and both believed that the dictatorial power of white publishers undermined and hampered the African American artist. All of this again suggests an aesthetic program that is at some distance from the day-to-day concerns of the mass of African Americans. It is little wonder that Langston Hughes believed that the average African American had not even realized that a Renaissance had occurred.

A final factor in this complicated scenario is that few of the writers and artists were actually participants in the migration. Only **James Weldon Johnson** of the older generation of writers and Zora Neale Hurston of the younger generation actually grew up in the South and made the great trek north. Even for these two, the prime motivation in the journey was educational or professional advancement, a luxury unimaginable to the average street sweeper. Every other major writer of the period grew up in the North or West, and many were part of what **E. Franklin Frazier** famously described as the "black bourgeoisie." W.E.B. DuBois was from Great Barrington, Massachusetts, Countee Cullen was from New York, and Langston Hughes and Wallace Thurman were from Kansas and Utah, respectively. **Jean Toomer**'s family hailed from **New Orleans**, but he grew up in the midst of a high-toned **Washington, D.C.**, middle class that barely recognized itself as Negro. The racialization of American culture obscures the fact that religion, class, educational attainment, and even geographic homelands often created a wide cultural divide among African Americans.

This distance could be expressed in various ways. Cullen and others found the attention that Hughes gave to the lowest-down Negro to be distasteful, a failure of both art and racial **uplift**. On the other hand, many artists felt the need to make a self-conscious identification with the southern masses. The story of **return migration**, wherein the northern Negro makes the trek south, became a virtual staple of Renaissance experience and imagination. DuBois framed this story in *The Souls of Black Folk*, in which two different chapters chart the alienation that an intellectual formed in the North feels upon journeying or returning to the South. Hughes and Toomer both made pilgrimages to the Deep South, journeys that became central to both Toomer's *Cane* and Hughes's *Mulatto*. Often these tales were cautionary. In **Nella Larsen**'s *Quicksand* a talented young African American woman receives her education and leaves the South, only to be dragged back inexorably into the muck and mire of the Negro peasantry with their poverty, patriarchy, and superstitions. Ironically, Zora Neale Hurston, who participated in the migration, failed to write a novel in which the journey north played a central role. Her great novel, *Their Eyes Were Watching God*, remains located in the South and is more a tale of the native intelligence and cultural vitality of the South on its own than of the alienated northern intellectual. Hurston openly disdained depictions of the South attempted by the northern writers, perceiving in even apparently positive images a kind of romantic and condescending exoticism. Only Hughes, in her estimation, came close to realizing the vitality of the migrants' culture.

It may be that this cultural distance accounts for the failure of the Renaissance to develop and connect to an African American audience that could sustain its efforts. During the Great Depression patronage and the interest of publishing houses slowed to a dribble. Artistic energy and focus flagged. What could reasonably be called a Harlem Renaissance drifted to a conclusion sometime in the 1930s. Critics of the Renaissance have tended to focus on its failures, on the way it was compromised by white patronage or missed opportunities to address the crucial political and social problems faced by African Americans. These judgments seem unfair because, for a failure, the Renaissance continues to draw the obsessive interest of scholars and critics. Moreover, this judgment is peculiar given the continued vitality of the best work from the period: much of Hughes's poetry, the novels of Hurston and

Toomer, and the best work of Cullen and McKay all continue to be read with pleasure and profit in classrooms and beyond around the country. But whatever the relative success of the Renaissance itself, it might be said that the Renaissance was one great success of the Great Migration. However distant the writers and artists of the talented tenth remained from the migrants themselves, the excitement of the migration proposed the need for a great literature to match a great people and a great historical movement. The vocation of a writer or artist or intellectual on any significant scale depended on the massive institutional and cultural transformations that were still ongoing as the Renaissance drew to a close. Finally, the facts of the migration itself provided a great artistic theme through which artists began to articulate the consciousness of a new African American century. This theme proceeded from the writers of the Renaissance to inheritors like **Richard Nathaniel Wright**, **James Baldwin**, and **Ralph Ellison** and on to the novels of Toni Morrison in the present. With the singular exception of the story of slavery, the Great Migration has been the mythic narrative of African American arts and letters, a myth first recognized and shaped by the artists and writers of the Harlem Renaissance. *See also* Bonner, Marita; Douglas, Aaron; Fauset, Jessie Redmon; Johnson, William Henry; Literature, the Great Migration in; New York City; Visual Arts, the Great Migration in; Primary Documents 26, 27, 31, 49.

Further Reading

Favor, J. Martin. *Authentic Blackness: The Folk in the New Negro Renaissance.* Durham, NC: Duke University Press, 1999.

Huggins, Nathan J. *Harlem Renaissance.* New York: Oxford University Press, 1971.

Hutchinson, George. *The Harlem Renaissance in Black and White.* Cambridge, MA: Belknap Press of Harvard University Press, 1995.

Lewis, David Levering. *When Harlem Was in Vogue.* New York: Knopf, 1981.

———, ed. *The Portable Harlem Renaissance Reader.* New York: Viking, 1994.

Nicholls, David G. *Conjuring the Folk: Forms of Modernity in African America.* Ann Arbor: University of Michigan Press, 2000.

Peter Kerry Powers

Harlem Riot of 1935

In the midst of the worst economic depression the nation had endured, **New York City**'s Harlem erupted into riot in 1935. If white New Yorkers faced **unemployment** rates approaching 25 percent, up to one in two black New Yorkers could not find work. Many more were underemployed, unable to find full-time jobs or those appropriate for their level of training. The rate was especially high for new migrants, for whom racial discrimination and poorer education, coupled with lower seniority, ensured that they were "last hired, first fired." While government relief in the city was closer to equal between the races than in most southern areas, strict residency requirements left more migrants than longtime residents desperate for aid. Meanwhile, discrimination, lack of political experience, higher rents, and poorer services meant that black neighborhoods fared more poorly than white ones. There were not enough **hospital** beds, classrooms, or homeless shelters; police protection was more arbitrary and occasionally more violent.

At the same time, however, the concentration of African Americans of all classes, histories, and politics in small areas like Harlem provided a base for both a sense of communal grievance and political organizing. Migrants to Harlem, attracted by its relative freedoms and economic opportunities, banded together in mutual aid societies and political clubs based on their community of origin. The **National Association for the Advancement of Colored People** had its headquarters there, several black newspapers competed for readers, and soapbox orators importuned passing crowds. Harlem's history of protest dated back to its emergence as a center of black American life: a "Parade of Muffled Drums" lamented the 1917 **East St. Louis race riot**; mass meetings protested southern **lynching** and northern racism; depression-era church congregations marched to city hall insisting on more, and more equitable, aid; impromptu protests challenged evictions. Harlemites not only suffered the indignities of poverty and racial discrimination, but were well aware of those facts and of political efforts to challenge them.

Black activism and the contributions of Mayor Fiorello La Guardia and President Franklin Roosevelt's New Deal helped ease the worst of the depression for Harlem residents, but by early 1935 things had worsened once more, and ongoing protest movements had slowed from both internal dissent and external repression. Tensions ran high. When a Harlem department store manager caught a sixteen-year-old black boy shoplifting on March 19, 1935, he called the police. Although they released him, a rumor quickly spread that he had been beaten or killed. Past incidents between police and residents both in New York and across the country made the story plausible, and a crowd quickly gathered in front of the store. That night local residents, mostly young, mostly male, broke store windows and looted along 125th Street, Harlem's main thoroughfare. The violence, which produced $2 million of property damage and loss, two deaths, sixty-four injuries (fifty-seven civilian, seven police), and seventy-five arrests, did not ease for two nights.

Although early newspaper reports blamed communists and "hoodlums" for the riot, investigations mounted by the mayor's office and by black and white political organizations concluded that the riot was in fact caused by the hard economic times, the persistence of racial injustice, and the relentless struggle for survival and dignity by a black community so often denied both jobs and aid. Black people had been poor and discriminated against for time out of mind; what had changed were expectations. The relative egalitarianism of New Deal programs, the increasing clout of black political organizations, and the aspirations of West Indian and southern migrants searching for greater opportunity provided hope for a different future. When that future seemed to retreat as hardship worsened and traditional political efforts seemed to stop bearing fruit, frustration burst into violence against the apparent oppressors: the police and white store owners.

Although no specific statistics about the rioters document the proportion of migrants to the native-born, the limited information available suggests that migrants certainly participated. Rioters who were arrested, about whom information is available, represented an economic and demographic cross section of Harlem's black population (although with more males and fewer elderly). More than half of all Harlemites were recent migrants from the South or the West Indies, and certainly they made up the majority of those poor and underemployed or unemployed. They had had experience with **police brutality**. The grievances that sparked the riot were most deeply perceived by them. And it was that population whose decision to migrate reflected raised expectations, and whose expectations had been most cruelly dashed by the depression's hardships and continued racial inequities.

Partly in response to the tensions the riot plainly revealed, New Deal programs and local services improved. Still, their inadequacy, the persistence of black poverty and inequality, and continued tensions between black residents and white police led to another Harlem riot only eight years later. *See also* Caribbean Migration; Harlem Renaissance; Harlem Riot of 1943; New Negro; Political Activism (1915–1945); Primary Document 28.

Further Reading

Greenberg, Cheryl. "Politics of Disorder." *Journal of Urban History* 18 (1992): 395–441.

Mayor La Guardia's Commission on the Harlem Riot. *The Complete Report of Mayor La Guardia's Commission on the Harlem Riot of March 19, 1935*. 1936. Reprint, New York: Arno Press, 1969.

Cheryl Greenberg

Harlem Riot of 1943

On August 1, 1943, a dispute between a white police officer and a black soldier sparked an uprising by the black population of Harlem. The riot that ensued caused $3 to $5 million in damage and resulted in 6 dead, 189 injured, and 606 arrested before it was finally suppressed the following morning. Harlem's shops and businesses were the target of the crowd's rage, with the majority of those vandalized being white owned. This crisis stemmed from the social and economic hardships encountered by black Harlemites, which were exacerbated by the racial divisions within the city and the actions of the city government.

The Great Depression disproportionately affected **New York City**'s black population as job opportunities dwindled and racial tensions intensified. The city's black population had increased by 145,000 during the 1930s, and many of these migrants from the South and the Caribbean found their way to Harlem (see **Caribbean Migration**). By the early 1940s Harlem was not a site of massive migration for blacks because of its poor job market and lack of war contracts; industrial centers such as **Detroit** offered more job opportunities. Nevertheless, migrants continued to flow into and out of Harlem, where they encountered difficulties finding employment and decent **housing** in this area's impoverished economy and overcrowded housing market.

Decisions made by the city government compounded this situation. In the months leading up to the riot, the city closed the Savoy Ballroom, the famous Harlem **dance hall** popular among black Harlemites. The city government

Bystanders gather to examine the destruction of a pawn shop in the aftermath of the Harlem riot of 1943. © AP/Wide World Photos.

also approved the use of city facilities for a segregated program run by the navy, as well as the construction of a white-only housing project, Stuyvesant Town. These decisions fueled black anger in Harlem, and, coupled with the poor socioeconomic conditions facing Harlem residents, considerably increased racial tensions.

The incident that instigated this riot was a dispute between a white police officer and a black woman at the Hotel Braddock in Harlem. The officer, James Collins, attempted to calm a disturbance caused by Marjorie Polite, a black woman who was arguing with the clerk over a refund. A confrontation ensued, and Polite resisted arrest. A black soldier, Robert Bandy, intervened in her defense, as did his mother. Accounts differ as to what happened in the ensuing scuffle; however, Bandy was shot by Collins in the arm, which resulted in a slight wound. Although the injury was not life-threatening, word quickly spread on the streets that a white policeman had shot and killed a black soldier in uniform—a symbolic affront to the African American community. Soon crowds began to gather at the hospital where Bandy was being treated, as well as at the Twenty-eighth Police Precinct and the Hotel Braddock. The situation quickly escalated into a massive riot by the black population of Harlem.

The crowd grew in size and began to shatter storefront windows and start fires, damaging over 1,450 stores. This formed the initial upsurge, which was followed by another period of looting in which many stores were emptied and destroyed. This attack against property constituted the main focus of the riot, which separated it from its contemporaries, such as the **Detroit race riot of 1943**. In Detroit, as in Beaumont, Texas, and Mobile, Alabama, racial tensions resulted in physical confrontations between blacks and whites. In Harlem the relatively small white population did not facilitate this more traditional form of race riot, and interracial violence was limited to that between blacks and white police officers.

This prompted New York City mayor Fiorello La Guardia to declare that "this was not a race riot." Instead, La Guardia emphasized the role of "hoodlums" and young malcontents in the riot, shifting the focus away from the underlying social and economic strains on the black population that fueled the uprising. Many black community leaders agreed with La Guardia, shifting the blame onto undisciplined youth and southern migrants. The class background of participants varied widely, however, because both middle- and lower-class blacks were involved. This brief abandonment of class differences during the uprising reflected the racial undertones of the riot. The accumulated social and economic grievances affected a large segment of Harlem's black population that crossed class boundaries. This riot, which occurred only eight years after the **Harlem riot of 1935**, was indicative of the increasing willingness of the black population to challenge the restrictive environment it encountered in the North as well as the South, and this confidence would fuel the emerging **civil rights movement**. *See also* Beaumont, Texas, Race Riot of 1943; Crime and Criminals; Police Brutality; Racial Violence and World War II; Zoot-Suit Riots (1943).

Further Reading

Capeci, Dominic J., Jr. *The Harlem Riot of 1943*. Philadelphia: Temple University Press, 1977.

Greenberg, Cheryl Lynn. *"Or Does It Explode?" Black Harlem in the Great Depression*. New York: Oxford University Press, 1991.

Johnson, Marilynn S. "Gender, Race, and Rumors: Re-examining the 1943 Race Riots." *Gender and History* 10 (August 1998): 252–77.

Michael J. Murphy

Harris, Abram Lincoln (1899–1963)

Abram Lincoln Harris was the first African American economist to gain prominence in academia. His ideas on how African Americans could gain economic advancement were extensively argued in the period after the Great Black Migration.

Harris was born in 1899 to a family that, though not rich, enjoyed a level of economic security. This greatly aided his education and allowed him to become fluent in German, thanks in large part to the German family for which his father worked as a butcher. In 1924 Harris completed his M.A. from the University of Pittsburgh. His master's thesis, "The Negro Laborer in Pittsburgh," examined the condition of African Americans in the coal and steel industries, a work that was later followed by two articles in *Opportunity*, the monthly journal of the **National Urban League**. Harris believed that the best thing for the economic advancement of African American workers was the establishment of a multiracial labor unit that could confront the class-based grievances of all Americans.

After a year of teaching at West Virginia University, Harris moved to Minnesota to take a position as director of the Minneapolis Urban League. His main achievement in Minnesota was to prepare a detailed report, *The Negro Population in Minneapolis* (1926), on the condition of what was largely a new African American population due to in-migration. He found dramatic levels of inequality on the basis of evidence from surveys and census reports. In the report Harris also used a variety of resources to show an extensive pattern of wage and **employment discrimination** faced by African Americans. Harris remained hopeful that this racially divided workforce, an aftermath of the migration, could be solved.

Harris completed his Ph.D. at Columbia University in 1930. He merged his thesis with work of political scientist Sterling Spero to produce *The Black Worker*, first published in 1931. In it Harris laid out what he saw as the only viable option for the advancement of African Americans: the establishment of an interracial working-class political party. Of course, this would mean first examining and solving the problems that prevented the races from uniting even at work, let alone in politics.

In *The Black Worker* Harris argued that there were three significant, though solvable, problems that caused racial antagonism among workers. First, white distrust of African Americans could be traced back to the time of slavery. Second, most African American industrial workers were recent urban immigrants and thus ignorant of the value of trade unionism. Third, many middle-class leaders of African American groups such as the National Urban League fostered racial hostility among the working classes. Harris argued that time would solve the first two problems with the help of labor education from progressive labor groups. The third problem would be solved by new education patterns for young African Americans who would replace the old leaders.

Harris joined the faculty at **Howard University** in 1927, even before he finished his Ph.D. He continued to promote his radical class analysis of the social status of blacks in the United States, writing a famous report that bore his name at the Armenia Conference in 1933 held by the **National Association for the Advancement of Colored People** (NAACP). In his report he argued that the NAACP should switch its basis from race to class.

In 1945 Harris accepted a teaching position at the University of Chicago, which he held until 1950. For the remainder of his career Harris softened his economic radicalism and wrote very little about the economic problems facing African Americans. He died in 1963. *See also* American Federation of Labor (AFL); Frazier, E. Franklin; Organized Labor; Reid, Ira De Augustine; Wesley, Charles Harris.

Further Reading

Harris, Abram. *Economic and Social Reform*. New York: Harper and Brothers, 1958.
——. *The Negro as Capitalist*. Philadelphia: American Academy of Political and Social Science, 1936.
Holloway, Jonathan Scott. *Confronting the Veil: Abram Harris, Jr., E. Franklin Frazier, and Ralph Bunche, 1919–1941*. Chapel Hill: University of North Carolina Press, 2002.
Spero, Sterling D., and Abram Harris. *The Black Worker: The Negro and the Labor Movement*. New York: Columbia University Press, 1931.
Wilson, Francille Rusan. "The Segregated Scholars: Black Labor Historians, 1895–1950." Ph.D. diss., University of Pennsylvania, 1988.

Brian Stokes

Harrison, Hubert Henry (1883–1927)

Born in St. Croix, Danish West Indies, Hubert Henry Harrison was a brilliant and influential writer, orator, editor, educator, and radical political activist. After immigrating to **New York City** in 1900, he became a major intellectual force in Harlem in the 1910s and 1920s when, spurred by migrants from the South and the Caribbean, it developed into an international center of radical black thought and literary influence. Harrison played unique signal roles in what became the largest class-radical movement (socialism) and the largest race-radical movement (the **New Negro** and Garvey movement) in U.S. history. His followers included activists such as **A. Philip Randolph**, **Chandler Owen**, **Cyril Briggs**, and **Marcus Garvey**. Randolph referred to him as the father of Harlem radicalism. Historian J. A. Rogers, in *World's Great Men of Color*, described Harrison as the foremost African American intellect of the era.

From 1911 to 1914 Harrison was America's leading black **socialist** writer, theoretician, campaigner, and speaker, and he initiated the Socialist Party's first major effort at organizing African Americans, the Colored Socialist Club. He criticized capitalism, pointed to the revolutionary implications of democracy and equality for African Americans, and stressed the need for socialists to reach African Americans and oppose racism. He also supported the egalitarian and direct-action practices of the **Industrial Workers of the World** and urged southern blacks to take direct action—including armed self-defense and migration—in order to end **lynching**.

In the summer of 1917, as the Great War raged abroad, as race riots, lynchings, segregation, discrimination, and white supremacist ideology increased at home, and as Harlem's black population approached 70,000 with thousands of migrants and immigrants from the South and the Caribbean, Harrison founded the Liberty League and the *Voice*, the first organization and first newspaper of the militant New Negro movement. His street-corner talks and weekly newspaper emphasized political and literary education of the masses, and he called for a race-conscious internationalist approach, enforcement of civil and voting rights, federal antilynching legislation, armed self-defense, political independence, and utilization of an organized black vote. The *Voice* was soon followed by other New Negro publications, including Randolph and Owen's *Messenger*, Garvey's *Negro World*, and Briggs's *Crusader*. Harrison's New Negro movement marked a major shift from the white-patron-based leadership approach of **Booker T. Washington** and the talented-tenth orientation of **W.E.B. DuBois**, it prepared the ground for the growth of Garvey's **Universal Negro Improvement Association**, and it was qualitatively different from the more middle-class, more arts-based literary movement associated with the 1925 publication of **Alain Locke**'s *New Negro*.

In 1918 Harrison cochaired (along with William Monroe Trotter) the Liberty Congress, the major wartime protest effort of African Americans. In 1919 he edited the monthly *New Negro*, and in 1920 he became the principal editor of Garvey's *Negro World*, reshaping it into a powerful international political and literary force. With its Harrison-initiated "Poetry for the People" and book-review sections, *Negro World* fostered a mass interest in literature and the arts to an extent unrivalled by any other black newspaper of the era. In the 1920s Harrison also lectured for the New York City Board of Education, wrote widely for the **black press** and many of the nation's leading periodicals, worked at building the International Colored Unity League and the *Voice of the Negro*, and helped found and build the 135th Street Public Library's black studies collection, which developed into the internationally famous Schomburg Center for Research in Black Culture. Harrison was a popular figure in Harlem, and his funeral was attended by thousands. *See also* African Blood Brotherhood (ABB); Caribbean Migration; Harlem Renaissance; McKay, Claude; Political Activism (1915–1945); Schomburg, Arthur Alfonso; Primary Document 49.

Further Reading

Harrison, Hubert Henry. *When Africa Awakes: The "Inside Story" of the Stirrings and Strivings of the New Negro in the Western World*. With an introduction by John Henrik Clarke. Baltimore: Black Classics Press, 1997.

James, Winston. *Holding Aloft the Banner of Ethiopia: Caribbean Radicalism in Early Twentieth-Century America*. New York: Verso, 1998.

Perry, Jeffrey B., ed. *A Hubert Harrison Reader*. Middletown, CT: Wesleyan University Press, 2001.

Jeffrey B. Perry

Hatcher, Richard Gordon (1933–)

Lawyer, civil rights leader, and politician, Richard Gordon Hatcher attracted national attention in 1967 when he became, along with **Carl Stokes** of **Cleveland**, the first African American mayor of a major U.S. city. His twenty years as mayor of the city of **Gary, Indiana**, earned him the respect of his peers, admiration from the urban poor, and honors and awards from civil rights organizations, universities, and the national press. As a leading figure of black political power, he inspired a generation of African Americans to see the wonders of blackness and left a rich legacy for those looking to strike a balance between idealism and pragmatism.

The son of a Georgia factory worker who migrated to the North, Richard Gordon Hatcher was born in Michigan City, Indiana, the youngest of thirteen children. After graduating from Indiana University in 1956, he received a doctor of jurisprudence degree and honors in criminal law from Valparaiso University. Admitted to the bar in 1959, he was appointed deputy prosecuting attorney in the Lake County Criminal Court, a position that expanded his civil rights activities and led him to Muigwithania ("We are together" in Swahili), a local organization he helped found that became a progressive force for change in the black community. In 1963 he was elected as member-at-large, and soon president, of the city council. Working to reform the city and end segregation, he sponsored and authored legislative and policy changes that provided fundamental tools to attack discrimination in education, employment, public accommodations, and **housing**.

After Lake County residents gave George Wallace, the segregationist governor from Alabama, a resounding victory in the 1964 Democratic presidential primary, Gary's blacks turned to Hatcher for new political leadership and urged him to enter the 1967 mayoral race. The political and legal roadblocks he crossed on his way to city hall proved as challenging as those civil rights activists met in the **Jim Crow** South before the 1965 Voting Rights Act. A spoils system with deep local roots also meant that he inherited a treasury in shambles whose state of bankruptcy was compounded by nervous private investors whose decision to hedge against black political power eroded the local tax base and stimulated the growth of suburbs in which whites had already chosen to build new communities. **Deindustrialization** and the dwindling funds of Great Society programs left his office with few resources and allies to change the system and transform Gary into the Promised Land migrants coming from the South since World War I had hoped to find in northwest Indiana. Yet the grassroots support he garnered in Gary allowed him to keep expectations high among his constituents and use his position as a platform to fight for civil rights. In 1972 he welcomed to Gary thousands of delegates who participated in the First National Black Political Convention, which he cochaired. In the 1980s he was campaign director during Jesse Jackson's quest to gain the presidency. His leading role inside national urban interest organizations also revealed that black politics did not operate in a local vacuum. *See also* Black Mayors; Electoral Politics; Political Realignment; Young, Coleman Alexander.

Further Reading

Catlin, Robert A. *Racial Politics and Urban Planning: Gary, Indiana, 1980–1989.* Lexington: University Press of Kentucky, 1993.

Lane, James B. "Black Political Power and Its Limits: Gary Mayor Richard G. Hatcher's Administration, 1968–87." In *African-American Mayors: Race, Politics, and the American City*, edited by David R. Colburn and Jeffrey S. Adler, 57–79. Urbana: University of Illinois Press, 2001.

Poinsett, Alex. *Black Power, Gary Style: The Making of Mayor Richard Gordon Hatcher*. Chicago: Johnson Publishing Co., 1970.

Nelson Oullet

Hawkins, Coleman (1904–1969)

During the Great Black Migration Coleman Hawkins was the king of **jazz** saxophone. A cultured and versatile performer, Hawkins brought the tenor sax, his preferred instrument, from smoky **ghetto** dens to the world's concert halls.

Hawkins was born on November 21, 1904, in St. Joseph, Missouri, to middle-class parents. Although St. Joseph geographically could be called a northern town, it segregated the races by law, and young residents such as Hawkins left to pursue more liberal environments in the urban Northeast. Ostensibly studying the cello at Washburn University in Topeka, Kansas, Hawkins snuck away to play the C-melody saxophone in theaters in **Kansas City, Missouri**, a crossroads for early black jazz musicians. In 1921 he joined Mamie Smith's touring **blues** show, and two years later he settled in **New York City**, playing at Connie's Inn in Harlem. Hawkins was then hired by bandleader Fletcher Henderson. Switching to

Coleman Hawkins, c. 1946. © Metronome/Getty Images.

the lower-registered tenor sax, he quickly became the most popular soloist in Henderson's orchestra, which gained fame for its exquisitely arranged recordings and residency at the Roseland Ballroom.

Hawkins stayed with Henderson into the 1930s. He developed a signature sound, blending a booming timbre with improvisation that exploited the notes within the chords of a tune (rather than varying the rhythm of the tune itself, as was then common). Hawkins's big sound demonstrated the influence of his former bandmate, **Louis Armstrong**, while his harmonic sophistication reflected Hawkins's interest in classical music and his involvement in the general intellectual life of the **Harlem Renaissance**. Young saxophonists widely imitated Hawkins, turning away from the lighter, more melodic alto saxophone style pioneered by Frankie Trumbauer—although, in turn, the sparer tenor style of a new rival, Lester Young, became an alternative to "Hawk" (as he was called). In 1934 Hawkins left Henderson and toured Europe with Jack Hylton's British band. He stayed abroad for five years, frequenting Paris and The Hague and serving as a model for the many black jazz expatriates of the following generation. On the eve of World War II Hawkins returned to New York, where he formed a big band and made new recordings. One session concluded with Hawkins's spontaneous improvisation on "Body and Soul," which became his most famous performance. Departing from the original melody after only a few notes and embarking on a flawless display of Hawkins's improvisational thought, "Body and Soul" immediately became one of the most celebrated statements in jazz history, influencing **Charlie Parker** and other important saxophonists of the 1940s.

In that decade Hawkins experimented with the new **bebop** style and made lengthy musical visits to California and Europe. His 1948 album *Picasso* was an unaccompanied tour de force, the first ever recorded by a "blowing" jazz soloist. For the remaining two decades of his life, despite increasing difficulties with illness and alcoholism, Hawkins remained a revered and active elder statesman of jazz. He had, however, made his greatest musical statement in the 1930s. Incorporating his rich musical education and cultural interests into his saxophone playing, Hawkins became one of the central jazz voices expressing the social and spiritual optimism of the Great Black Migration. *See also* Dance Halls and Nightclubs; Gillespie, John Birks "Dizzy"; Monk, Thelonious Sphere; Recording Industry; Swing.

Further Reading

Chilton, John. *The Song of the Hawk: The Life and Recordings of Coleman Hawkins.* Ann Arbor: University of Michigan Press, 1990.

DeVeaux, Scott. *The Birth of Bebop: A Social and Musical History.* Berkeley: University of California Press, 1997.

Burton W. Peretti

Haynes, George Edmund (1880–1960)

George E. Haynes was a leading contemporary student of the Great Migration, believing in the opportunities it offered for racial advance. Indeed, even before it began in earnest, he published *The Negro at Work in New York City* (1912), which highlighted the opportunities and problems associated with the expansion of the northern urban black population. Haynes combined a belief that industrial work offered a unique opportunity for African American advance with a commitment to ameliorative approaches to attendant social problems. In 1918 his appointment as director of the U.S. Department of Labor's new **Division of Negro Economics** (DNE) provided him briefly with a national forum in which to focus public attention on the migration's character and possibilities.

Born in 1880 to working-class parents in Pine Bluff, Arkansas, Haynes earned a bachelor's degree at Fisk University in 1903 and an M.A. in sociology at Yale in 1904. In 1912 Haynes became the first African American to earn the Ph.D. at Columbia University, in the New York School of Social Work. Active in reform organizations, he was a cofounder of the **National Urban League** (1911) and served as its executive secretary until 1917. In 1910 he joined the Fisk faculty and began building programs in applied sociology and social work, particularly focusing on the emerging industrial role of African Americans.

In May 1918 Haynes accepted the position of director of the DNE. Both white southern agriculturalists, seeking retention of cheap labor, and northern white workers, fearing job competition, urged the government to discourage migration. Haynes, however, stressed the new agency's role in helping blacks make the transition to industrial and urban life. Under Haynes's direction, DNE agents conducted field studies in northern states. They documented the wartime contributions of black workers, examined social problems and workplace frictions, and urged ongoing federal efforts to ease racial tensions. In his own reports Haynes expressed both optimism about the migration's potential for race improvement and the need to combat prejudice and inequality. Despite Haynes's pleas that the government continue to assist both blacks and whites to adjust to the vast changes that the migration had wrought, the DNE quickly fell victim to postwar budget cuts.

After his government service Haynes became executive secretary of the Department of Race Relations of the Federal Council of Churches. For the next four decades he played an active role in encouraging black cultural activities, promoting American understanding of Africa, furthering interracial understanding, and contributing to the development of New York State's system of higher education. In 1910 he married Elizabeth Ross, a fellow Fisk graduate. They had one adopted son, George Edmund Haynes, Jr. Two years after her death in 1953, he married Olyve Love Jeter, his long-term literary assistant. He died on January 8, 1960. Haynes's studies of urban life remain valuable sources of information on the Great Migration, as do those he commissioned during his directorship of the DNE. A Christian progressive, Haynes believed in progress and in the key role that trained social observers could play in promoting it. *See also* Chicago School of Sociology (CSS); Frazier, E. Franklin; Harris, Abram Lincoln; Johnson, Charles Spurgeon; New York City; Reid, Ira De Augustine; Scott, Emmett Jay; Wesley, Charles Harris; Woodson, Carter Godwin; Primary Document 38.

Further Reading

Haynes, George Edmund. *The Negro at Work during the World War and during Reconstruction: Statistics, Problems, and Policies Relating to the Greater Inclusion of Negro Wage Earners in American Industry and Agriculture.* Washington, DC: Government Printing Office, 1921.

———. *The Negro at Work in New York City: A Study in Economic Progress.* New York: Columbia University and Longmans, Green and Co., 1912.

———. *Negro Newcomers in Detroit, Michigan.* 1918. Reprint, New York: Arno Press, 1969.

———. Papers. Amistad Research Center. Tulane University.

Weiss, Nancy J. *The National Urban League, 1910-1940.* New York: Oxford University Press, 1974.

Robert H. Zieger

Henderson, George Wylie (1904–1965)

George Wylie Henderson published seventeen stories and two novels during the 1930s and 1940s. His fiction explores the conditions in Alabama's Black Belt, the opportunities and disappointments migrants faced in **New York City**, and the ambivalent feelings many migrants held toward the rural life they had left behind. He wrote for popular publishers in a straightforward, lyrical style. A migrant from Alabama to Harlem himself, Henderson clearly drew on his personal journey for his imaginative work.

Henderson was born in 1904 in Warrior Stand, Alabama, a small farming community where his grandparents sharecropped for many years before buying their own farm. His father was then a recent graduate of nearby **Tuskegee Normal and Industrial Institute**. A preacher, Henderson's father brought the growing family (there were eventually eleven children) to Wetumpka, Alabama, for a decade before returning to Tuskegee in 1915, when he was appointed pastor of the Butler Chapel AME Zion. In 1918 the young Henderson followed his father's lead by matriculating at Tuskegee Institute. There he followed the practical curriculum that founder **Booker T. Washington** thought would prepare African Americans for prosperity in the industrial era. When he graduated in 1922, though, Henderson was a champion orator and aspired to be a lawyer; he certainly had ambitions beyond factory work.

Henderson married a classmate, and they had a son in 1926. Around the same time, the family migrated to New York City. Henderson found work as a linotype operator for the *New York Daily News*, thereby joining the industrial workforce. Yet he also began writing during this era, and his job at the *Daily News* likely helped him see this work into print. In January 1932 he published the first of nine short stories in the paper's series "Daily Story from Real Life." Like others in the series, Henderson's stories were written plainly yet sensationally; his distinctive contribution was to feature African American characters, mostly in southern settings. Having gained recognition for his writing, Henderson began to publish regularly in *Redbook* magazine in 1933. Engaging the affluent, urbane audience of *Redbook*, Henderson set most of his new stories in New York City. Many of them explore the ambivalent feelings that beset migrants; a common theme is the challenge to female virtue posed by urban mores. He published his last story in the magazine in 1947.

One story from the Daily News, "'Thy Name Is Woman,'" served as the prototype for Henderson's celebrated first novel, *Ollie Miss*. Published in 1935, the novel won critical acclaim for its sensitive use of dialect, its evocative description of rural Alabama, and its compelling portrait of the lead character. Henderson's heroine is a young field hand who finds fulfillment by acquiring a farm where her labor will allow her to raise her son. Henderson's 1946 sequel, *Jule*, marks a changed assessment of prospects for fulfillment in Alabama: the hero is Ollie Miss's son, who flees the **Jim Crow** South to find success in New York City. *Jule* is an important fictional treatment of the Great Migration and is often studied in relation to the protest novel.

Henderson played a key role in rendering the Great Migration into aesthetic form. His publications in the *New York Daily News* and *Redbook* and his two important novels engaged broad, popular audiences. That these literary successes were fostered by one who was himself a migrant, who was born on a tiny farm and emerged as a New York author, makes Henderson a compelling figure in the study of the Great Migration. *See also* Harlem Renaissance; Literature, the Great Migration in; Migrants, Cultural Identity of; Primary Documents 4, 36, 63.

Further Reading

Henderson, George Wylie. *Harlem Calling: The Collected Stories of George Wylie Henderson*. Edited and with an introduction by David G. Nicholls. Ann Arbor: University of Michigan Press, 2006.

———. *Jule*. 1946. Reprint, Tuscaloosa: University of Alabama Press, 1989.

———. *Ollie Miss*. 1935. Reprint, Tuscaloosa: University of Alabama Press, 1988.

Nicholls, David G. *Conjuring the Folk: Forms of Modernity in African America*. Ann Arbor: University of Michigan Press, 2000.

———. "George Wylie Henderson: A Primary and Secondary Bibliography." *Bulletin of Bibliography* 54, no. 4 (December 1997): 335–38.

David G. Nicholls

Himes, Chester (1909–1984)

Chester Himes was the only African American writer of his generation to extensively document in fiction the experience of African American migrants to **Los Angeles** during World War II. The move to the Far West and the Pacific Coast during the Second Great Migration was part of the general movement of the American population to these areas, particularly California. The state had over half the nation's shipbuilding and aircraft industries, and the former was a major employer of black workers, many of whom came from Texas, Louisiana, and Oklahoma. The black population of Los Angeles almost doubled, and many migrants found themselves inhabiting areas along Central Avenue and, after mid-1942, the area known as Little Tokyo, which had been forcibly emptied because of the Japanese internment. That people can be summarily imprisoned because of race haunts Himes's fictional characters. *If He Hollers Let Him Go* (1945) delineates the changing demography of the city; in both this novel and *Lonely Crusade* (1947) a black male war worker must contend with escalating racial tensions in the city and on the job, including conflicts within labor unions.

The **zoot-suit riot of 1943**, when white servicemen and civilians attacked Mexicans and African Americans, was the subject of an essay in which Himes argued that race relations on what many had hoped was a new frontier had already been shaped by those southern patterns of segregation and violence that had also affected northern urban centers. In this essay and in much of his fiction of the period, Los Angeles, because of its broad racial and ethnic composition, becomes a synecdoche for colonized nations as well as the American nation itself.

In *If He Hollers* the protagonist, Bob Jones, is made foreman of a segregated **shipyard** work crew that had previously been supervised by a white employee; he has been given this job to keep down racial tensions. His men, as was typical for many black workers, perform hot, dirty, and dangerous work, in this case, below decks. A false accusation of rape leads to his being forced to join the segregated army. In *Lonely Crusade* Lee Gordon is a union organizer at an aircraft plant that employs African Americans and white southerners; neither group trusts the union to deal with it fairly, and **Communist** infiltrators manipulate this volatile situation. Though considerable scholarship has begun to reevaluate the relationship between the Communist Party and African Americans, these novels are often grouped with those of Himes's contemporaries, **Richard Nathaniel Wright** and **Ralph Ellison**, because they exhibit a negative or ambivalent position on the Party's attitude toward newly proletarian black workers.

Contemporary readers can draw connections between the hero of **Walter Mosley**'s Easy Rawlins mystery series and Himes's protagonists. Rawlins, a veteran, moves to Los Angeles from **Houston, Texas**, after World War II, and because he cannot accept the racial status quo in the aircraft plant where he works, he quits and eventually becomes a private detective. The series goes on to trace African American life in Los Angeles over several decades. *See also* Literature, the Great Migration in; Organized Labor; Western States, Black Migration to.

Further Reading

Muller, Gilbert H. *Chester Himes*. Boston: Twayne–G. K. Hall, 1989.
Skinner, Robert E. "The Black Man in the Literature of Labor: The Early Novels of Chester Himes." *Labor's Heritage* 1, no. 3 (1989): 51–65.

Robin Lucy

Hip-Hop

Hip-hop is a set of culture forms that emerged in the late 1970s out of the experiences of working-class, mostly African American, West Indian, and Puerto Rican youth in the South Bronx, New York. The emergence of hip-hop corresponded with larger social changes, such as suburbanization and **white flight**, that further marginalized these communities. The four elements that make up hip-hop culture are recognized as MC-ing/rapping, DJ-ing, break-dancing, and graffiti writing. Other cultural practices such as beatboxing, street fashion, street language, street knowledge, and street entrepreneurialism are also attributed to hip-hop.

Hip-hop culture reflects the twentieth-century urbanization of black youth that resulted from the Great Black Migration of African Americans out of the Deep South to northern and western cities. Its lyrical and stylistic content confronts the urbanized circumstances experienced by black youth after the **civil rights movement**; often condemning **police brutality**, unequal access to city services, the prevalence of **crime** and drugs, and job discrimination. At the same time, as hip-hop culture has become commercialized, its consumer base has been transformed from urban youth of color to white suburban youth and continues the trend of the popular culture industry's appropriation of black music and culture.

Rapping is the oral-poetic expression of hip-hop culture and is often a rapid, aggressive, and creatively innovative style of wordplay performed to the rhythm of the music. Originally, in the context of competing with other rappers, rapping was characterized as boastful and powerful, with a degree of showmanship. Rappers told stories that were often politically motivated, violent, and hypermasculine in the tradition of toasting, its Afro-diasporic predecessor. The strong expression of rapping made it hip-hop's central mode of expression.

DJs supplied the music over which MCs rapped. Using two turntables and large stereo speakers, DJs combined several sounds, samples, and beats from previous recorded records to make new soundtracks. DJs often looped or manipulated the record to repeat a specific part of other songs in order to create a new song. In addition, DJs "scratched," a practice in which they literally scratched the record in conjunction with the established beat. DJ-ing especially displayed the manipulation of technology by working-class youth to culturally express the experiences of the hip-hop generation.

Breakdancing facilitated the competitive nature of the crews that sustained hip-hop culture. When DJs during the disco music era completed the task of transferring from one song to another, called break points, they added sound techniques to highlight the change. During the break points, breakdancers or b-boys/girls would imitate the break and rupture exhibited when switching from one song to another. Out of this practice a variety of dance moves such as freezes, where a break with the beat was creatively exhibited by the dancer by posing, were developed. Competitively based, breakdance crews would compete against one another, attempting to enact the most daring flips, freezes, and acrobatic moves to gain the crowds' approval. Other moves included backspins, head spins, and the helicopter. These dances are often performed in circles called ciphers. Dance crews still abound in urban areas in the United States and all over the world, but have also been used for commercial advertising to youth.

Graffiti writing surrounded many of the neighborhood parties where DJ-ing, MC-ing, and breakdancing originated and evolved. Although graffiti writing has a longer history preceding the 1970s, it took on more artistic styles that complemented the other cultural elements of hip-hop. Often spraying art pieces depicting b-boys/girls, hip-hop slang, rap lyrics, and hip-hop street fashions, graffiti writing was early hip-hop's mobile expression. By "bombing" trains and buildings in different neighborhoods, graffiti writers spread the bragging messages and elaborate hip-hop style across the city and beyond.

By late 1979 independent record labels were able to release groups such as the Sugar Hill Gang and MC Kurtis Blow on the commercial airwaves, introducing rap music and hip-hop culture to the world. Urban youth of color from inner-city neighborhoods across the country embraced the sounds and culture, creating localized versions of hip-hop culture in cities like **Los Angeles**, **Houston**, **Detroit**, and **Atlanta**. By the mid-1980s crossover acts such as rap group Run D.M.C.'s performances with rock group Aerosmith facilitated the move of rap into the mainstream. Hip-hop's rise to pop status has brought it to the far reaches of the world and continues to set trends in popular music and resonate with aggrieved groups. Still, the association of rap music and hip-hop culture with urban youth of color has been cause for congressional hearings and media accusations that the music is a negative influence on society, is essentially misogynistic and violent, and glorifies crime. *See also* Recording Industry; Youth Culture.

Further Reading

Fricke, Jim, and Charlie Ahearn. *Yes, Yes, Y'all: The Experience Music Project Oral History of Hip-Hop's First Decade*. Cambridge, MA: Da Capo Press, 2002.

George, Nelson. *Hip-Hop America*. New York: Viking, 1998.

Rose, Tricia. *Black Noise: Rap Music and Black Culture in Contemporary America*. Middletown, CT: Wesleyan University Press; Hanover, NH: University Press of New England, 1994.

W.E.B. DuBois Institute for Afro-American Research. The Hiphop Portal Archive. www .hiphoparchive.org/archive/index2.htm.

Jimmy Patiño, Jr.

Hispanic Immigrants and Hispanic Americans, Relations with Black Migrants

Relations between Hispanic and black migrants during the twentieth century varied according to whether interaction was at the national or individual level. At the national level, for example, civil rights organizations, such as the League of United Latin American Citizens (LULAC), a Mexican American civil rights organization, or the Rainbow Coalition, in pursuit of a common agenda, issued numerous statements of collaboration. However, when the interests of each ethnoracial group were threatened, bases for cooperation failed. At the individual level, competition over resources and social status and cultural differences created tensions between both groups. Because Hispanics and blacks have been exploited and have suffered from poverty and discrimination, and because both were racialized minorities, the easy assumption is that there existed alliances between both groups. This assumption, however, does not reflect reality. Historically, there has been competition between Hispanics and blacks that has resulted in conflict.

The rapid growth rate of the Hispanic population in the twentieth century heightened tensions at play primarily because immigrants were perceived as an economic threat. Blacks believed that Hispanics took jobs away from them. They were convinced that some employers favored Hispanic workers over blacks mainly because they could be hired more cheaply than blacks. Working for lower wages, Hispanics transitioned into the service industry with relative ease. As a result, they took jobs that had traditionally been filled by blacks. Hispanics also held fast to the idea that only blacks landed the best jobs and that they suffered more workplace discrimination from both whites and blacks alike. In **Los Angeles**, for example, blacks dominated the public employment sector and kept Hispanics at bay. This competition for jobs occurred only in the lower-paying occupations, and so the idea that Hispanics affected the occupational status of blacks excluded the middle and upper classes. Nevertheless, the most obvious explanation for poor relations between the two groups revolved around competition for economic resources. Whether in Los Angeles, **Houston**, **Chicago**, or new locales such as South Carolina or Georgia, the problem for blacks was the same: resentment toward Hispanic immigrants. Blacks did not merely oppose Hispanic advancement; they simply opposed any advancement that occurred at the expense of the black working class.

Race also played into the dynamics of Hispanic-black relations. Hispanics, for example, believed that race relations in the United States were primarily a black-and-white issue. Compared with blacks, Hispanics felt ignored with respect to civil rights issues and were convinced that only blacks were deemed worthy of fair treatment. During Houston's school **desegregation** campaign, for example, Hispanic activists argued that blacks never included Latinos in their integration plans. Blacks responded by stating that they knew little of the Hispanic civil rights efforts and further charged that Hispanics simply tagged along as "Johnny-come-latelies." Many Hispanics also felt that they experienced more discrimination and had fewer opportunities for advancement than blacks. Furthermore, they felt that blacks were just as prejudiced against them as were whites, although, in cities such as Houston, it was not just whites who imposed **Jim Crow** policies; Hispanics also barred blacks from their public facilities. Felix Tijerina, a former national president of LULAC and founder of the Little Schools of the 400, for example, owned a local restaurant that refused service to blacks, although he, as well as most Hispanic business owners, changed his policies after the passage of the Civil Rights Act of 1964. In California the Los Angeles County Chicano Employees Association was involved in more than 20,000 cases of discrimination against Hispanics by blacks. Its actions prompted the Equal Employment Opportunity Commission to launch an investigation of the allegations, but the end results proved inconclusive.

Even the government, Hispanics believed, initiated programs designed to benefit only blacks. This perhaps was due to the fact that Hispanics, many of whom were not citizens, were ineligible to receive government services. Blacks insisted that government programs did not favor them but argued that Hispanics had not fought for civil rights in the ways they had. In fact, many believed that Hispanics benefited from the struggles led by blacks. Perhaps blacks believed that Hispanics were not deserving of civil rights protection because they suffered more discrimination than Hispanics and contributed more than Hispanics to the civil rights efforts. The end result was that Hispanics believed that blacks were considered the country's first racial minority group and that Hispanics occupied second place. But with the increasing growth of the Hispanic population, any future talks on race relations will no longer be restricted to a black-white binary but will also include talks on the effects of Hispanics as well.

Cultural differences, specifically language, also played a part in the friction and misunderstanding between blacks and Hispanics. As Spanish was transmitted with increasing frequency over the airwaves, in the workplace, and on the streets, it generated a backlash among some groups, including blacks. The most prominent example of negative reaction against the speaking of Spanish was the English Only movement, which sought legislation aimed at amending the U.S. Constitution to make English the official language of the nation. Some Hispanics took language problems to mean indifference or dislike of them, while blacks, on the other hand, experienced frustration because they viewed Spanish as an additional barrier to economic mobility, especially because bilingualism was fast becoming a factor in the employment process.

Political power, like cultural differences, also played into the conflict between the two groups. Hispanics and blacks, for example, were not only competing against whites for political positions, but sometimes against each other as well. In Los Angeles Hispanics and blacks competed over representation on the city council. Hispanic influence on **electoral politics** in the city was weak because many were either undocumented immigrants who were unable to vote or were legal residents who paid little attention to politics. In **Miami**, however, it was blacks who felt frustration at being passed over and nearly shut out by the Hispanic, mainly Cuban, population. By the 1960s Hispanics controlled most of the city's major political, economic, and educational institutions. Furthermore, they seemed indifferent about sharing any of that control with blacks. Yet although they were not major players in the political arena, blacks still influenced the city's politics. In 1981 they helped determine the outcome of Miami's mayoral race. Determined to keep a Cuban American out of office, blacks gave 95 percent of their vote to Maurice Ferre, the Puerto Rican–born incumbent.

But Hispanics and blacks also shared a history of cooperation and coalition building. In many cases they supported each other's candidates. They often formed alliances in support of common issues at nearly all levels of government, including city councils, school boards, and state legislatures. They both historically voted Democrat. Still, despite the political commonalities, there have been many instances of conflict between the two groups, specifically when a Hispanic and a black candidate sought the same position. In December 2001 Houston's potential first black mayor, Lee P. Brown, faced a heated runoff election against Orlando Sanchez, a Cuban American city council member. A Hispanic victory would represent a huge symbolic triumph over both conservative whites and moderate, anti-Latino blacks. Hispanic Democrats cared little that Sanchez was a conservative Republican; they were concerned more with defeating an African American candidate than with keeping a Republican from office. Brown eventually pulled off a victory, but for all the brown-black political conflict that had been brewing since the start of the campaign, any potential conflict between both groups after the election virtually disappeared.

There have also been a few instances in which white candidates divided Hispanic and black voters, thereby causing strains between the two groups. In Houston again, the selection of a superintendent of the city's largest school district stirred a controversy like no other. When a white superintendent resigned from the Houston Independent School District to relocate to another state, many Hispanics expected that one of their own would be considered for the position. But when the district named Dr. Rod Paige, a current board member and a non-Hispanic, but perhaps more important, a black candidate, to take over as district superintendent, Hispanics, stunned by this decision, strongly disapproved the board's move. They argued that Hispanic candidates were deliberately shut out of the selection process. Enraged, community members created the Hispanic Education Committee (HEC), a grassroots organization designed to challenge the selection process. The HEC demanded a state investigation and, along with the Teachers' Association of Chicanos in Higher Education, filed a suit to have Paige dismissed. Immediately the city's local branch of the **National Association for the Advancement of Colored People** intervened and filed a petition on behalf of the school board and Paige. In the end, the Texas Education Agency conducted an investigation and found no misconduct in the selection process. Paige was allowed to remain as district superintendent. What should have been celebrated as an important moment in Houston's civil and political rights history instead created tensions between blacks and Hispanics. In regard to voting power and the number of political positions held, Hispanics lagged behind blacks; still, they were fast becoming a major political force in the United States and a challenge to blacks.

Fortunately, there were also various similarities between Hispanics and blacks that served as a basis for consensus, cooperation, and coalition building. Both groups, for example, became residents of the United States through force, both were physically and culturally different from whites, both experienced discrimination, both suffered from poverty, and both were victims of unfair judicial practices. Both also shared a subordinate status at the lower end of the country's racial hierarchy and felt that the government should do more to help the poor and disadvantaged, especially as it pertained to combating discrimination. Regarding education, both groups worked together toward reducing the dropout rate, increasing the number of college graduates, and improving the quality of educational services, as happened in 1970 when Hispanics and blacks posed an open challenge to a proposed pairing plan for Houston schools. However, Houston schools also had their share of conflict between the two groups. In the early 1960s, for example, Hispanic activists worked against attempts to have their children lumped with black students, arguing that they were white and therefore did not fall under definitions of the state's segregation laws. In Compton, California, also, during the spring of 1989, Pedro Pallan, a longtime Hispanic activist, was removed from his position as personnel commissioner of the Compton school district on the ground that he was not a resident of that district. Pallan, however, believed that the true reason for his dismissal was his critique of a primarily black district's failure to hire bilingual teachers and for its discrimination against Hispanics in general.

For the most part, however, blacks and Hispanics shared a history of combating discriminatory barriers in education, employment, **housing**, politics, and health care. The Mexican American Youth Organization, an avant-garde Hispanic civil rights organization in Texas, for example, supported and participated in conferences held by the Southern Christian Leadership Conference and walked in the **Poor People's Campaign** to **Washington, D.C.**, to network with black activists. Hispanics and blacks interacted more with each other, were more sympathetic to each other's issues, were more familiar with each other's history, and faced similar obstacles. What this meant was that they were more likely to build on those similarities in hopes of forming long-lasting alliances.

The future of relations between Hispanics and blacks is unclear. What is clear, however, is that the numbers now belong to Hispanics. This means that Hispanics will hold more power and influence at multiple levels, especially politically. What is also clear is that growth of the Hispanic population will continue during the next decades, and in regions where their presence is new, they will certainly change the dynamics of race relations and possibly create friction. And as the Hispanic population continues to grow, it will remember its former place behind blacks and remember also its feeling of exclusion. This fact alone has already begun to cause stress for the black community. This is perhaps the hardest fact to swallow because accepting this means accepting the fact that it is now time to share, for the moment at least, center stage with another group. The reality is that a Hispanic tsunami is sweeping across the United States, and sooner rather than later, it will affect the rest of the country. Among those already affected are black Americans. *See also* Asian Immigrants and Asian Americans, Relations with Black Migrants; Black-Jewish Relations; Civil Rights Movement; European Immigrants, Relations with Black Migrants; Hispanic Migration, Comparison with the Great Black Migration.

Further Reading

Mindiola, Tatcho, Yolanda Flores Niemann, and Nestor Rodriguez. *Black-Brown: Relations and Stereotypes.* Austin: University of Texas Press, 2002.

Piatt, Bill. *Black and Brown in America: The Case for Cooperation.* New York: New York University Press, 1997.

Vaca, Nicolás C. *Presumed Alliance: The Unspoken Conflict between Latinos and Blacks and What It Means for America.* New York: HarperCollins, 2004.

Willie, Charles V., ed. *Black/Brown/White Relations: Race Relations in the 1970s.* New Brunswick, NJ: Transaction Books, 1977.

Jesse J. Esparza

Hispanic Migration, Comparison with the Great Black Migration

Hispanic migration to and within the United States has an old and regular pattern that makes it one of the greatest movements in the world. A decline in tenant farms throughout the Southwest, the expansion of a market economy of seasonal crops, and the movement of large-scale agribusiness all generated large-scale migration patterns. Among the groups to follow this pattern were Hispanics. Hispanic migration can be divided into three waves. The first wave consisted of Mexican Americans and Puerto Ricans. The second wave was made up exclusively of Mexican-origin migrants who settled in the midwestern and northwestern parts of the country. The final wave had a majority of Mexican-origin migrants with some Filipinos, blacks, and poor whites, all of whom worked the agricultural centers of Arizona. Although the destinations varied, most settled in the Southwest, namely, in Texas, California, New Mexico, and Arizona. Other regions, however, were also hotbeds for Hispanic migration, such as the Midwest, New England, the Deep South, and the Pacific Northwest. And although Hispanic migrants were a diverse group, the majority were of Mexican origin. How many migrated northward before 1900 is unknown, but perhaps the larger issue is that this regular flow established the pattern of migration for the twentieth century.

A combination of economic boom in the United States and violent unrest in Mexico created a push-pull factor that prompted a massive exodus northward of Hispanic immigrants. The Mexican Revolution of 1910, for example, created waves of incoming migrants to the United States. During World War I the need for laborers increased, and soon thereafter small groups of migrants began to settle in cities such as **Chicago**, **Gary**, **Detroit**, Toledo, and **Minneapolis–St. Paul**. Most landed agriculture-related jobs, but by the 1920s northern industries—meatpacking plants, steel mills, and automobile assembly factories—began actively recruiting Hispanic migrants for their expanding industrial economy. Still, hundreds of thousands of unskilled and semiskilled migrants joined the seasonal migratory labor force that harvested the booming U.S. agricultural industry. When the Great Depression hit, however, most Hispanic migrants, having been last hired, were among the first fired.

The depression also brought a sudden, but temporary, halt to the influx of migrants. The U.S. government, bent on relieving domestic **unemployment**, supervised a massive deportation program of Hispanic migrants. A decade later migrants were able to make further inroads on industrial jobs because of the increase in labor demands created by World War II. To replace the ranks of farmworkers who had gone into military service, U.S. industry once again called on migrant laborers. In 1942, for example, Mexico and the United States initiated the Bracero Program whereby thousands of Mexican workers were brought across the border on temporary labor contracts to work in agriculture. By the 1950s, as the number of migrants increased, the United States initiated another massive deportation program known as Operation Wetback during which more than a million Hispanic migrants were rounded up and deported.

Despite the repressive deportation efforts, economic recessions, and militarization of the U.S.-Mexican border, migration to and within the United States continued in great numbers. Welcomed during times of economic progress but repelled during hard ones, Hispanic migration ebbed and flowed in cycles. It depended, for the most part, upon the strength of the U.S. economy and on the anti-immigrant sentiment present at that time. Most immigrants also lived in rural areas and worked seasonal agricultural jobs, making them easy to identify, round up, and deport. They also considered their stay in the United States temporary. Currently, however, the Hispanic migrant community is settled on a permanent basis, and although many continue to toil in the fields, the majority now live and work in urban centers.

Involved in what is known as the Great Migration, a movement of people from the rural South to the urban North, black migrants were another group involved in migration patterns. This movement began as a trickle after the Civil War but became a flood by the second decade of the twentieth century. After emancipation poor economic conditions trapped the majority of blacks in the South. Some moved from farm to farm in search of better land, but only a few were fortunate enough to find prosperity. By 1900 thousands of blacks fled poverty, powerlessness, and brutality. World War I created an economic boom that contributed to increased migration northward. Slowed momentarily by the depression, migration received fresh impetus from World War II. In fact, the largest wave of black migration occurred during World War II, when an increase in industrial production reduced mass unemployment and created new opportunities for black workers.

Since the 1870s, however, thousands of blacks, a small number in comparison with the migration from Europe, had migrated north, mostly to large urban centers, in search of greater economic opportunities. These sojourners moved for many reasons. Ultimately, they were both pushed from their rural circumstances because of floodwaters and ravaged crops and pulled toward urban areas and an abundance of jobs. Economic necessity was not the only reason for moving north. For blacks frustrated with the accumulation of injustices—**lynching**, segregation, disfranchisement, poor schools, and **housing** restrictions—the Great Migration represented not only embracing the North but a rejection of the South as well. Nevertheless, for the majority of black southerners, migration was not a realistic option. Possessing mainly agricultural skills, they were ill equipped to find work in large cities of the North.

As in the South, workers in the North were restricted to domestic service if they were **women** and common labor if they were men, or were relegated to certain low-wage, unskilled jobs. Nevertheless, black migrants were quick to take advantage of available economic opportunities that had not existed before. Economic profit and necessity, it seemed, trumped racial prejudice and gender discrimination.

For the most part, whites accepted black migrants, but only on **Jim Crow** terms. In fact, black migration in some cases provoked a violent white backlash. The problem for whites was that newcomers produced unwelcome competition for jobs. White workers especially feared and resented black migrants, viewing them as threats to their own social status, political influence, and living standards. Essentially, the Great Migration created a renewed effort on the part of whites to keep blacks in their place.

A few blacks also migrated west, establishing and settling into several all-black towns in Kansas and Oklahoma. Other black migrants settled in Nebraska, the Dakotas, Colorado, and elsewhere on the Great Plains and along the Rocky Mountains. Substantial black migration into California did not occur until the 1930s and 1940s.

This migration pattern is considered one of the largest movements of the modern age. To many white northerners, the flow of black southerners seemed like a raging, uncontrollable flood. And for many black migrants also, the promise of moving north was quickly vanishing as race rioting, ghettoization, **employment discrimination**, and the exclusion of blacks from certain industries convinced them that white northerners were no more willing to accept blacks as equals than whites in the South.

In short, Hispanics and blacks migrated in search of economic opportunities. Sometimes they were recruited by U.S. industries, particularly during times of economic crisis. Hispanics constituted the majority of agricultural workers as opposed to blacks, who worked in factories. Women from both groups were confined to domestic work. After 1915 the northward trickle by both migrant groups swelled. It is uncertain exactly how many traveled north, but what is sure is that migration patterns were the direct result of larger transnational and global events such as the world wars, the depression, and economic booms.

Unlike black migrants, Hispanic immigrants have the Southwest borderlands area and even Mexico as sanctuaries or places to recuperate and escape from the harsh realities throughout the rest of the country. Furthermore, the labor power of Hispanic migrants remains the preferred choice, perhaps because they earn less than non-Hispanic laborers. Also, Hispanic migrants are subject to deportation policies. The anti-immigrant hysteria generated during the depression era led directly to massive deportation of Hispanic migrants, specifically of Mexican migrants. The economic recession after the Korean conflict also caused a backlash and led to the most reactionary anti-immigrant policy instituted by the United States, Operation Wetback. Although Operation Wetback officially targeted illegal migrants, many legal residents were caught up in the dragnet and ended up victims of deportation.

In the end, migration transformed rural blacks into a northern-based, industrial working-class group; Hispanics, on the other hand, remain primarily a southwestern-based, agricultural working class. The single greatest difference between the two migrant groups, however, is the fact that Hispanic migration continues to pour into and surge within the United States in great numbers and influence government policy and promises also to change the dynamics of working-class people throughout the country. *See also* Asian Immigration, Comparison with the Great Black Migration; European Immigration, Comparison with the Great Black Migration; Hispanic Immigrants and Hispanic Americans, Relations with Black Migrants.

Further Reading

Fernández, Gastón, Beverly Nagel, and León Narváez. *Hispanic Migration and the United States: A Study in Politics*. Bristol, IN: Wyndham Hall Press, 1987.

Goodwin, E. Marvin. *Black Migration in America from 1915 to 1960: An Uneasy Exodus*. Lewiston, NY: Edwin Mellen Press, 1990.

Lemann, Nicholas. *The Promised Land: The Great Black Migration and How It Changed America*. New York: Alfred A. Knopf, 1991.

Millard, Ann V., and Jorge Chapa. *Apple Pie and Enchiladas: Latino Newcomers in the Rural Midwest*. Austin: University of Texas Press, 2004.

Jesse J. Esparza

Homelessness

Homelessness affected many black migrants at different stages of their journey. Many working-class African Americans took to the rails, participated in migrant labor, and lived in hobo camps in the early twentieth century. Other migrants encountered a very tenuous **housing** situation when they arrived in northern industrial cities. The Great Depression left large numbers of black migrants without jobs and prompted many to actively resist evictions, establish shantytowns, and live in federal and municipal shelters. Slum clearance, **urban renewal**, and federal highway projects promoted from the 1930s through the 1960s frequently targeted black migrant neighborhoods and left many of those displaced by the projects without homes. The urban triage policies of the 1970s, coupled with ongoing **deindustrialization** and the rapid expansion of the criminal justice system, resulted in working-class African Americans becoming the fastest-growing group among the expanding numbers of homeless people across the United States in the 1980s and 1990s.

Many black migrants took to the road via freight train in the early twentieth century. While several used this method of free transportation as a means to get to a more permanent destination, others joined the pool of seasonal

A homeless African American man sleeps on the steps of a movie theater in New York City, 1938. Courtesy of the Library of Congress.

migrant laborers who traveled from lumber camps in the South and upper Midwest and Northwest to wheat harvests in the Great Plains and the orchards and produce fields in California. The black "hobo" became a key figure in many **blues** lyrics from the period. Other contemporary accounts suggest that hobo camps outside the South were for the most part racially integrated. Black hoboes, however, faced significant obstacles from **railroad** and local police. Most famously, nine black teenagers, later known as the Scottsboro boys, were pulled off the Southern Railroad freight run from Chattanooga to **Memphis** and charged with the alleged gang rape of two white girls on March 25, 1931. The case became one of the most memorable incidents of racial injustice in the 1930s.

Many black migrants who moved to industrial cities in the North faced a precarious housing situation as overcrowding typified increasingly segregated black residential areas. Most private charities, such as the Salvation Army, refused to open their shelters to black people without housing. The for-profit lodging houses in skid row areas across the North also frequently denied access to blacks. While some municipal shelters were open to black males, nearly all cities strictly segregated their services for homeless **women** during the 1920s and 1930s. As a result of this segregation, several lodging houses and hotels opened up in African American neighborhoods, creating a parallel skid row to the white skid row districts in many northern cities. Several black social workers sought to establish agencies that could serve unhoused black men and women, while numerous landlords took advantage of the situation by leasing sheds, boxcars, and even chicken coops to black migrants.

The Great Depression left many black migrants without jobs or housing. Unemployed African Americans were frequently the most active participants in the unemployment councils organized by the Communist Party in the early 1930s. Across the country these groups organized to curb evictions. Many of the most spectacular, violent, and deadly clashes between the police and protesters during the 1930s occurred at the site of evictions in working-class black neighborhoods. Those left without housing often formed camps and shantytowns near landfills and dumps, along railroad tracks and rivers, and on abandoned lots. The majority of these camps were racially segregated. The largest black shantytowns often had mayors, elaborately constructed dwellings, and even an occasional church. Throughout the depression African Americans were overrepresented in the resident populations of municipal and federal transient shelters. The Federal Transient Program, run from 1933 to 1935, operated both racially integrated and segregated shelters across the country.

Federally sponsored slum clearance, urban renewal, and federal highway programs aggravated an already precarious housing situation for working-class blacks. Urban neighborhoods occupied by newly arrived migrants were often the first areas targeted for removal. Furthermore, as large numbers of African Americans continued to come to northern cities after World War II, blacks began to make headway into white skid row areas. As these areas developed larger black populations, urban renewal projects demolished the cheap hotels and rooming houses to expand central business districts in the 1950s, 1960s, and 1970s. These inexpensive housing alternatives had provided a key component in the infrastructure that made working-class migration possible. Throughout this period black home owners engaged in numerous legal battles to save their property. Black tenants and home owners frequently continued to occupy their homes after they had been legally taken over by urban renewal and highway development agencies. Homelessness, however, did not become widespread because former white residential areas in northern cities opened up to black occupancy in the postwar period.

The urban renewal projects of the 1950s and 1960s gave way to the federally sponsored triage policies of the 1970s. As migration from the South slowed down with the onset of deindustrialization in many northern cities, housing markets in working-class black neighborhoods began to collapse by the early 1960s. As a result, landlords began to disinvest from their properties and increasingly abandon them. By the early 1970s abandonment and arson in black urban areas had become an epidemic across the country. The Housing and Community Development Act of 1974 officially abolished the urban renewal program and in its stead established the Community Development Block Grant (CDBG) system. Instead of pursuing the ambitious, yet highly problematic efforts to rebuild urban slums, the federal government encouraged the withdrawal of most public and private funds from the hardest-hit urban areas. Cities across the country moved away from plans to build low-income housing and instead used their CDBG allocations to demolish millions of housing units in the hope of clearing the way for private future development. Furthermore, the expansion of the criminal justice system in the 1970s, 1980s, and 1990s left a disproportionate number of African Americans with criminal records. These ex-offenders found it increasingly difficult to access stable housing or jobs. The combination of deindustrialization, landlord disinvestment, federal triage policies, and the expansion of the criminal justice system made African Americans the fastest-growing segment of the homeless population in the 1980s and 1990s. *See also* Crime and Criminals; Employment Discrimination; Hypersegregation; Open Housing; Public Housing; Unemployment; Urban Crisis of the 1960s; White Flight; Primary Documents 2, 29, 67.

Further Reading

Hopper, Kim. *Reckoning with Homelessness.* Ithaca, NY: Cornell University Press, 2003.

Kerr, Daniel. "Open Penitentiaries: Institutionalizing Homelessness in Cleveland, Ohio." Ph.D. diss., Case Western Reserve University, 2005.

Kusmer, Kenneth L. *Down and Out, on the Road: The Homeless in American History.* Oxford: Oxford University Press, 2002.

Daniel Kerr

Home Ownership among Migrants

Among the values that African American southerners carried cityward was the desire to own homes of their own. Like other Americans, black migrants saw home ownership as a means to domestic comfort, economic security, and social status, yet their unique history shaped distinctive meanings and aspirations.

As black southerners, migrants' value of property had a long history. After the Civil War property ownership was closely linked with freedom in the aspiration of former slaves. Throughout the late nineteenth and early twentieth centuries property ownership persisted among the chief values of blacks in the rural South. Proprietorship symbolized hard work and ambition. It provided a basis for upward mobility, shelter for immediate and extended families, and a foundation in a society that systematically marginalized African Americans. Last, it meant a greater degree of independence, that is, freedom, than any form of tenancy.

In addition to fulfilling historic desires for property ownership, a home of one's own represented an economic and social strategy for families making the transition to urban industrial life. Home ownership allowed migrants to evade high rents, to economize, and to supplement their incomes. Migrant home owners planted gardens and raised small livestock, family members took in work or ran home-based businesses, and where they could purchase land, thousands built houses of their own, contributing the labor of friends and family to build "sweat equity." Many families, too, shared their homes with more recent arrivals. Some owners, especially **women**, opened their homes to renters as an occupation. Others let space as needed or gave shelter to recently arrived kin and friends from the South. Thus owned homes not only yielded economic benefits, but played a significant role in maintaining family ties in the midst of regional migration. Last, for migrants who faced insecurity in the labor market and racist threats in public space, home ownership was a kind of "social security," a haven in old age, a safe harbor for family life, and a cushion against the rough edges of industrial capitalism.

Despite these aspirations, migrants faced extraordinary resistance in their quest to purchase homes. Segregation and exclusion were standard practice in the U.S. real estate industry through the late 1960s. Few banks loaned money to African Americans for housing, and prohibitions against lending to blacks in white neighborhoods were almost universal. White real estate agents blocked access to available homes, and most builders refused to sell new houses to blacks. White residents and neighborhood organizations reinforced these practices with force. Arson, house bombings, and other violent disturbances greeted families who moved into white neighborhoods. Federal housing programs, too, tended to reinforce segregation and the redlining of older neighborhoods and minimally assisted African Americans in buying homes. Between the 1930s and the early 1960s Federal Housing Administration and Veterans Administration mortgage programs assisted more than 200,000 black home buyers, but this was only about 2 percent of total agency support for home ownership during the period.

Given these obstacles and migrants' aspirations to overcome them, home ownership became a focal point for legal and political struggle during the migration years. Civil rights groups such as the **National Association for the Advancement of Colored People** battled **housing** discrimination in public and private life, winning court victories against racial zoning (1917), race-restrictive deeds and **restrictive covenants** (1948), and, ultimately, all forms of public and private discrimination (1968). At the grassroots level, housing discrimination engaged thousands of black citizens in acts of racial protest, forcing families who wanted to buy a home to violate white social customs, and sometimes the law, to do so. Throughout this period the decision to buy a home and the selection of its location were political as well as personal matters.

Separate statistics for migrants are not available, but rates of overall black home ownership rose during the Great Migration as African Americans improved their social and economic conditions. Nonetheless, these rates lagged persistently behind those of whites, remaining a key piece of unfinished business in the struggle for equality. Home ownership increased slightly during the 1920s—from 24 to 25 percent—before slipping as a result of the Great Depression to 23 percent in 1940. In keeping with nationwide trends, black home ownership climbed during the 1940s and 1950s, to 38 percent by 1960; however, this compared poorly with concurrent growth among whites from 40 percent to 62 percent. For hundreds of thousands of African American migrants, home ownership was a long-deferred dream, and for many it remained only a dream. *See also* Black Suburbanization; Migrants, Expectations of; Neighborhood Property Owners' Associations.

Further Reading

U.S. Commission on Civil Rights. *Housing, 1961: Report of the U.S. Commission on Civil Rights*. Washington, DC: Government Printing Office, 1961.

Wiese, Andrew. *Places of Their Own: African American Suburbanization in the Twentieth Century*. Chicago: University of Chicago Press, 2004.

Andrew Wiese

Hopkins, "Lightnin'" Sam (1912–1982)

Known for his adept guitar playing, quick ability to learn **blues** chords, and great improvisational style, "Lightnin'" Sam Hopkins was a notable figure in the American music industry and African American culture. He was a guitarist, songwriter, and blues singer and one of the few blues musicians with a six-decade career. Hopkins had a diverse following of African Americans, southern whites, and international fans through concerts and recordings. His songs primarily depict the turmoil of migrant life—relocation, poverty, **unemployment**, and the end of love relationships.

Born on March 15, 1912, in Centerville, Texas, Hopkins built his first guitar from a cigar box and chicken wire at the age of eight. Using the few blues chords that he learned from his brother Joel, Hopkins initially performed at the Baptist Church Association in Buffalo, Texas, with the Texas blues player Blind Lemon Jefferson. Encouraged by Jefferson and his desire to become a musician, Sam Hopkins took his performances to the streets of Leona and Buffalo, Texas.

During the beginning of his professional career in the late 1920s, Hopkins played with his cousin, Alger "Texas" Alexander, in the black entertainment sections of **Houston** and eastern Texas. They performed blues music and frequently used Hopkins's autobiographical lyrics, which reflected the harsh economic times and the search for prosperity. Hopkins and Alexander drew a large audience of migrant, working-class African Americans who sympathized with their message. With this success, Hopkins wanted to branch out into the national music venues and moved to Hollywood with a piano player named Wilson "Thunder" Smith in 1946.

Adopting the nickname of "Lightnin'," Hopkins recorded his first single, "Katie Mae Blues," with Aladdin Studios. Fans praised Hopkins's unique style, usually marked by his rugged voice, bass of variable rhythms, and high-scale runs. As his career advanced, Hopkins included improvisational chords on his acoustic and electric guitars and spontaneous lyrics that enticed the audience to share in his painful narratives. Music critics and followers also took notice of Hopkins's "boogie rifts" and laments in "T Model Blues" and "Travellers Blues." These songs reflected the woes and mixed material gains of the large numbers of African Americans who had migrated from the South to the cities of the North from the 1900s to the 1930s in the Great Migration.

At the height of his career, Hopkins performed regularly throughout the South. He especially enjoyed singing in Houston and preferred to work in the area's less prestigious musical establishments. His attachment to this region demonstrated his affinity to his humble Texan origins and his commitment to his stronghold of southern fans. Many southerners not only watched but eagerly contributed to a "Lightnin'" Hopkins performance. As part of his legendary improvisational style, Hopkins often inserted or changed lyrics depending on the "feel" of the audience.

By 1954 and the arrival of rock and roll, the public lost interest in classic blues music. Hopkins stopped recording professionally, but continued to play on the blues club circuit throughout the South. In 1959 Hopkins's popularity reemerged when he made an appearance in Houston at the Alley Theater. New and old fans were pleased to hear Hopkins's legendary sound and were drawn by his soulful themes of "moving on" and needing love. From the 1960s to the 1980s Hopkins performed and recorded continuously. Hopkins died of cancer of the esophagus in Houston on January 30, 1982, leaving many to treasure his great legacy of blues music and value his voice of migratory themes. *See also* Broonzy, William "Big Bill"; Dance Halls and Nightclubs; Johnson, Robert; King, Riley "B. B."; Ledbetter, Huddie "Leadbelly"; "Muddy Waters"; Recording Industry.

Further Reading

Charters, Samuel Barclay. *The Country Blues*. New York: Rinehart, 1959.

Oakley, Giles. *The Devil's Music: A History of the Blues*. New York: Da Capo Press, 1983.

Palmer, Robert. *Deep Blues*. New York: Viking, 1981.

Dorsía Smith

Hospitals

The years 1920 to 1945 of the Great Migration paralleled the period of the black hospital movement, a nationwide reform movement to improve the educational and medical programs at black hospitals. The reform movement had been launched by **physicians** associated with two black professional organizations, the National Medical Association (NMA) and the National Hospital Association (NHA). The physicians feared that new developments in medical practice and education such as mandatory internships, medical specialization, hospital accreditation, and advances in medical technology would lead to the elimination of black hospitals. Because of the racial discrimination that then existed in medicine, the demise of these institutions would have had detrimental consequences for black medical professionals and black patients.

By 1919 approximately 120 black hospitals existed, 75 percent of them in the South. Most were small facilities of questionable quality that lacked training programs. At the time, black hospitals consisted of two broad categories—segregated and black controlled. Segregated hospitals had been established by whites to serve African Americans and were located predominantly, but not invariably, in the South. Black physicians, **fraternal orders**, and churches founded the black-controlled institutions. The efforts of the black hospital reformers focused primarily on the black-controlled hospitals.

Chicago's Provident Hospital, the nation's first black-controlled hospital, opened its doors in 1891. Dr. Daniel Hale Williams, a black surgeon, established the institution because of the racially exclusionary practices of the city's **nurse** training schools. In addition to Provident Hospital, several other black-controlled hospitals opened during the last decade of the nineteenth century, including Tuskegee Institute and Nurse Training School at the **Tuskegee Normal and Industrial Institute** in Alabama in 1892, Provident Hospital in **Baltimore** in 1894, and Frederick Douglass Memorial Hospital and Training School in **Philadelphia** in 1895.

Williams created Provident Hospital not as an exclusively black enterprise, but as an interracial one that would not practice racial discrimination. Indeed, white financial assistance played a key role in the hospital's founding. White businessmen supported the hospital in order to help keep their black workforce healthy. Despite its founder's original intentions, by 1915 the hospital had indeed evolved into a black institution. This evolution reflected the rise in racism that greeted the growing numbers of black migrants from the South. Residential segregation confined Chicago's burgeoning black population primarily to the city's South Side, where Provident Hospital operated. By 1920 Provident Hospital had become one of the most highly regarded black hospitals and a model for black hospital reformers. It was one of the few black hospitals to be accredited by national medical organizations and had become a mecca for black health care professionals. In 1929 it became the site of a pioneering affiliation with the University of Chicago, the first between a black hospital and a white university.

The efforts of the black hospital reformers to establish and improve black hospitals did not escape censure. Critics argued that such activities perpetuated segregation and that the emphasis should be on the integration of hospitals. In **Cleveland**, for example, before 1915 hospitals admitted patients on a nondiscriminatory basis. After the increased influx of African American migrants to the city, hospitals adopted more discriminatory policies, including separating black and white patients and limiting the number of beds available to black patients. Because of these practices, in 1921 black physicians began a campaign to open a black hospital in the city. However, the campaign failed because of harsh criticism that such an endeavor would escalate segregation in the city.

The leaders of the NMA and NHA remained undaunted in their efforts. They argued that their programs represented a practical response to the racial realities of contemporary American life and that the advancement and the health of the race depended on the existence of quality black hospitals. The black hospital reformers engaged in various activities to improve hospitals. They provided technical assistance to hospitals, sponsored professional conferences, and produced literature about the proper operation and administration of hospitals. The reformers also lobbied the major health care organizations, such as the American Medical Association (AMA) and the American Hospital Association (AHA), to play active roles in the black hospital movement. Their appeals, for the most part, received lukewarm receptions. The black hospital reformers also worked to raise funds for black hospitals, but funds were not readily forthcoming. Indeed, throughout the 1920s and 1930s all hospitals grappled with the problem of financing. For black hospitals, financial problems were particularly severe because their patients were predominantly poor. Philanthropies such as the Julius Rosenwald Fund and the Duke Endowment did play key roles in assisting the hospitals.

The black hospital movement led to some improvements in black hospitals by World War II. One prominent black physician optimistically hailed these changes as the "Negro Hospital Renaissance." But the renaissance was limited to only a few hospitals. In 1923 approximately 200 historically black hospitals operated. Only 6 provided internships, and none had a residency program. By 1944 the number of hospitals had decreased to 124—9 with approved internships and 7 with approved residencies. Moreover, the quality of some approved hospitals was suspect. Representatives of the AMA freely admitted that a number of these hospitals would not have been approved except for the need to supply at least some training opportunities for black physicians. This attitude reflected the then accepted practice of educating and treating black people in inferior facilities.

Several factors restricted the scope of the black hospital movement, including limited financial resources and lack of support from the major white medical organizations. The rise of integrationism also contributed. By World War II the black medical organizations that had launched the black hospital movement shifted their energies from developing separate black institutions to desegregating the health care system. Despite its limitations, the black hospital movement played a critical role in forestalling the extinction of the black hospital and thus enabled black health care professionals to practice and black patients to receive care at a time when discrimination severely restricted their options. *See also* Childbirth; Primary Document 66.

Further Reading

Buckler, Helen. *Daniel Hale Williams, Negro Surgeon*. 2nd ed. New York: Pitman, 1968.

Gamble, Vanessa Northington. *Making a Place for Ourselves: The Black Hospital Movement, 1920–1945*. New York: Oxford University Press, 1995.

Kusmer, Kenneth L. *A Ghetto Takes Shape: Black Cleveland, 1870–1930*. Urbana: University of Illinois Press, 1976.

Vanessa Northington Gamble

Housing and Living Conditions

Throughout the twentieth century black migrants to northern and western cities in the United States had a difficult time securing safe and affordable housing. Upon their arrival in these cities they settled in the neighborhoods that had the oldest and cheapest housing, usually located nearby either downtown or industrial areas. In these neighborhoods black migrants were more likely to find kin and fellow migrants who shared their culture and helped them find employment and housing. Black migrants encountered a crisis of available housing when they arrived, and it lasted throughout their time in the city. Little housing was available to black migrants for several reasons. Low and irregular incomes limited their buying power. They competed with immigrant workers for housing, which was limited by deterioration, demolition, and scant construction. Finally, black migrants' search for adequate and affordable housing was circumscribed by de facto residential segregation. Not surprisingly, the housing shortage caused overcrowding in inner-city neighborhoods.

The overcrowding resulted from both too little land for housing and too many people jammed into too little space. When black migrants earned good wages, especially during wartime production, and could afford better accommodations to rent or buy in so-called white neighborhoods, they were still forced to live in or near areas that received black newcomers every day. Racial discrimination thus proscribed black migrants' ability to live where they desired, creating an inflated demand for housing open to blacks. Landlords took advantage of the situation by charging black tenants more rent for the same accommodations that whites rented. In **Detroit** in the 1940s, blacks paid 20 to 40 percent more in rent than whites paid for equivalent dwellings. In **Milwaukee** in the 1920s, blacks paid between 30 to 200 percent more after

Children play outside a typical apartment in the African American section of Chicago in 1941. Courtesy of the Library of Congress.

they moved into a formerly white neighborhood. This exploitation was particularly glaring given the fact that black workers earned less than white workers.

African American newcomers were restricted to living in wood-frame tenements or shacks near railroads. These jerry-built structures had already served previous generations of European immigrants and earlier black migrants. The buildings' deterioration from age and neglect was very apparent when the next wave of black migrants came to inhabit them. Landlords were content to take rent from the newcomers while neglecting to make repairs or maintain the property. Overworked or corrupt municipal building inspectors could not or would not hold the landowners accountable. Overcrowding put more stress on the dilapidated buildings and antiquated infrastructure. After World War II, in the heart of **Chicago**'s South Side **ghetto** an estimated 375,000 blacks lived in an area capable under normal conditions of housing no more than 110,000 people. Unplanned and speculative growth in the late nineteenth and early twentieth centuries meant that wooden tenements were built on top of each other and in any other available space, especially alleyways. These dilapidated tenements provided inadequate light, air, sunshine, space, water, and heat to their residents. Many of these buildings did not contain private baths or toilets, which contributed to unsanitary conditions and the highest rates of disease in the city. In **Pittsburgh** black migrants who settled near steel plants during World War I and after were particularly dismayed by the amount of dirt that covered their homes and neighborhood. During the mid-1920s in the Steel City, only 20 percent of black houses had bathtubs and

50 percent had inside toilets. A study of 275 homes conducted by the Milwaukee Urban League in 1926 found that most residences occupied by African Americans lacked basic amenities such as gas, baths, and adequate lighting. Damp basements, leaky roofs, and falling plaster were common features of the homes surveyed in the study. In 1940 half of all blacks in northern cities lived in homes that needed major repairs or had serious plumbing deficiencies, compared with one-quarter of all white dwellings. The dangerous combination of more residents and inadequate garbage collection created dirty, foul-

The kitchen of a typical apartment in Chicago's South Side Black Belt. Courtesy of the Library of Congress.

smelling, and unsafe yards, alleys, and streets. Inadequate garbage disposal led to rodent infestation, and many children suffered from rat bites. Many of these ramshackle wooden tenements were firetraps. Between 1947 and 1953 in Chicago, 180 residents died from fires, at least 63 of whom were under the age of ten. Streets were dirty and crowded with people escaping depressingly tight quarters.

Given the severe housing shortage and restrictions on their mobility due to income and racial discrimination, black migrants had to find shelter where they could. The normal housing shortage worsened during the world wars and the Great Depression. Black migrants found housing in hallways, attics, basements, railroad boxcars, tents, sheds, garages, converted stables, and even an old city bus. Perhaps the type of housing that most symbolized black migrant workers' residence was "kitchenettes." African American sociologists St. Clair Drake and Horace Cayton found that since the Great Depression in Chicago, most black migrant workers lived in kitchenettes. Novelist and social critic **Richard Nathaniel Wright** treated kitchenettes as a metaphor for the cramped, frustrated, and oppressed existence awaiting black newcomers to northern cities. For him, the root of all black social problems, such as **crime**, juvenile delinquency, desertion, and out-of-wedlock births, could be traced to "kitchenette living."

White and African American property owners and absentee landlords responded to an incessant black housing demand by taking larger houses or apartments and dividing them into smaller units, called kitchenettes. They would take a six-room house with one bath and create six apartments. Where the house had once rented for $50 a month, each new "apartment" rented for

$8 a week, netting the owner $192 monthly. These units were usually one room with a converted closet to accommodate a gas stove used for cooking and heating. Sometimes an icebox and bed were supplied. The whole family ate, slept, and lived in the same room. The bathroom was shared by the other families on the floor. Many of these kitchenettes lacked indoor plumbing and running water. The beaverboard partitions that separated the living units were flammable, and the warrenlike structure made it difficult for residents to escape from a fire. Although illegal conversions had been around since before World War I, they increased during wartime and the depression when building materials were scarce. During World War I in **Cleveland**, white property owners contiguous to the ghetto who were pressed by housing-starved blacks chose to divide their houses into kitchenettes to make substantial profits rather than resist black occupancy. Observers in Chicago noted increased conversions during the depression because of falling incomes and demolition of neighborhoods in the path of encroaching industry. There were 80,000 conversions in Chicago in the 1940s, increasing the number of dwellings with no private bath facilities by more than 36,000.

While the majority of black migrants lived in hovels, shacks, or kitchenettes, those with steadier incomes were able to secure large apartments for their families. These migrant families usually housed newly arrived relatives from the South or border cities and helped them get a foothold in a new city. Unable to make the rent by themselves, these families took in boarders and lodgers to pay the exorbitant rents they were being charged. While they constituted a captive housing market with few options, these older and stable migrant families, dissatisfied and exploited, were determined to search for adequate and affordable housing within racial boundaries. Many of the boarders were single migrants who did not have or were estranged from family in the city. Sometimes this housing was closer to where migrants worked. In Pittsburgh during and after World War I, some black migrants owned boarding and lodging houses near steel and iron mills. Black male migrant workers preferred living with a black family to the company-owned bunkhouses or migrant camps. Single black **women** migrants had a difficult time finding suitable housing, unlike immigrant women, prompting the creation of institutions like the Phillis Wheatley Home in Cleveland.

Not all black migrants lived in overcrowded inner-city neighborhoods. Some sought successfully to settle in "black enclaves" on the periphery or outside the city limits. This was the case for black migrants in Detroit who settled in the vacant land around the Eight Mile area. While this area had high **home ownership**—more than two-thirds of the heads of households owned these hovels—it also had very poor conditions in the late 1930s. More than two-thirds of the homes were considered substandard, and only 45.5 percent had a toilet and bath. Some black migrants new to Cleveland in the 1920s settled in an area called Miles Heights just outside the city. Many of the migrants liked this location for its privacy, availability of land for planting large gardens, and population of neighbors reminding them of Alabama. Still, this community lacked paved roads, streetlights, and sewers until the 1950s.

Because black migrants resided in the worst sections of the city, many of these areas were designated as blighted. This designation meant that the majority of the dwellings were in need of major repair or lacked plumbing. In the Brownsville neighborhood in Brooklyn over half the buildings were more than thirty-five years old in 1934, and 87 percent were in fair to poor condition. Before World War II Chicago had an estimated twenty-three square miles of blighted conditions containing 242,000 housing units. An additional 100,000 units were considered blighted outside the designated area. More than half of Chicago's Black Metropolis was considered a slum and slated for clearance. In 1944 the entire black district in Milwaukee was considered blighted. After an area had been designated for slum clearance, no financial institution or property owner would invest in it, contributing to its inevitable decline. Slum clearance in many cities in the 1930s caused black migrants to move into better sections of black communities. In response, property owners began to divide up large apartments to accommodate the newcomers who were surrounding resentful older working- and middle-class residents. More affluent black professionals, businessmen, and **skilled workers**, thwarted by **restrictive covenants** and redlining, sought to escape these southern migrants by moving to the periphery of the Black Belt or into the better neighborhoods within it, setting up patterns of class residential stratification.

Black migrants, while pleased with their larger incomes in the North, were dissatisfied with their shabby housing and depressed living conditions. Many likened their new quarters to those they had left down South. Hemmed into black ghettos, they responded by moving from one dilapidated dwelling to another. Since there was little private construction for black workers, the only relief to the chronic housing shortage was **public housing**. But public housing was inadequate since it barely replaced those private units that had been demolished through slum clearance. Black workers saw an upgrade in their housing only when whites abandoned their neighborhoods for the outlying sections of the city or the suburbs. The explosion of housing construction after World War II in white-only suburbs freed up better housing in neighborhoods contiguous with the ghetto. Black "pioneers" in Chicago got an estimated 4,000 housing units a year between 1945 and 1949 through racial turnover. The number increased to 7,100 units per year between 1950 and 1954 and 7,800 units per year between 1955 and 1959. The acquisition of better housing through racial conversions upgraded the quality of housing for upwardly mobile African Americans. In Detroit substandard buildings were reduced from almost 30 percent in 1950 to 10.3 percent ten years later. Finally, the housing shortage subsided in the 1960s at a time when the flow of migrants coming north slowed. In the aftermath, an unmistakable geography of class had emerged in which working-class and middle-class blacks moved outward, leaving the poorest strata concentrated in deteriorating private housing and neglected public housing projects. This scenario replicated the wretched housing and living conditions of earlier generations of black migrants to the city. *See also* Black Suburbanization; Blockbusting; Farm Security Administration (FSA); Neighborhood Property Owners' Associations; Open Housing; *A Raisin in the Sun* (Lorraine Hansberry); Serviceman's Readjustment Act

(GI Bill); Settlement Houses; Urban Renewal; Weaver, Robert C.; White Flight; Primary Documents 2, 18, 29, 45, 67, 71.

Further Reading

Drake, St. Clair, and Horace R. Cayton. *Black Metropolis: A Study of Negro Life in a Northern City*. New York: Harcourt, Brace and Company, 1945.

Gottlieb, Peter. *Making Their Own Way: Southern Blacks' Migration to Pittsburgh, 1916–30*. Urbana: University of Illinois Press, 1987.

Grossman, James R. *Land of Hope: Chicago, Black Southerners, and the Great Migration*. Chicago: University of Chicago Press, 1989.

Hirsch, Arnold R. *Making the Second Ghetto: Race and Housing in Chicago, 1940–1960*. Cambridge: Cambridge University Press, 1983.

Kusmer, Kenneth L. *A Ghetto Takes Shape: Black Cleveland, 1870–1930*. Urbana: University of Illinois Press, 1976.

Phillips, Kimberley L. *AlabamaNorth: African-American Migrants, Community, and Working-Class Activism in Cleveland, 1915–45*. Urbana: University of Illinois Press, 1999.

Philpott, Thomas Lee. *The Slum and the Ghetto: Neighborhood Deterioration and Middle-Class Reform, Chicago, 1880–1930*. New York: Oxford University Press, 1978.

Pritchett, Wendell. *Brownsville, Brooklyn: Blacks, Jews, and the Changing Face of the Ghetto*. Chicago: University of Chicago Press, 2002.

Sugrue, Thomas. *The Origins of the Urban Crisis: Race and Inequality in Postwar Detroit*. Princeton, NJ: Princeton University Press, 1996.

Trotter, Joe William, Jr. *Black Milwaukee: The Making of an Industrial Proletariat, 1915–45*. Urbana: University of Illinois Press, 1985.

Weaver, Robert C. *The Negro Ghetto*. New York: Harcourt, Brace and Company, 1948.

Wright, Richard. *12 Million Black Voices*. 1941. Reprint, New York: Thunder's Mouth Press, 2002b.

Preston H. Smith II

Houston, Texas

Between 1900 and 1950 an estimated 50,000 blacks moved to Houston, Texas, principally from eastern Texas and Louisiana, for socioeconomic autonomy and sociopolitical liberation. In time these newcomers helped transform both their communities and their chosen city. Black migrants particularly contributed to the socioeconomic, sociopolitical, and cultural vitality of Houston, a city that by World War II had become the center of civil rights activism in the nation and in the twenty-first century is the world's energy capital, America's fourth-largest city, the South's largest metropolis, the most populated metropolitan area along the Upper Texas Gulf Coast (UTGC) industrial region, the city with the South's largest black community, one of the world's leaders in medicine, space exploration, science, and engineering, and the "Golden Buckle" of the Sunbelt.

Blacks who migrated to Houston for jobs, a quality education, and social justice followed the same routes as their nineteenth-century predecessors. African Amerians as slaves had traveled southwestward from the South Atlantic seaboard and the Deep South, and after the Civil War as freedpeople, from place to place within the eastern two-fifths of the state—the Texas Cotton Belt. The industrial revolution of the Gulf of Mexico coastal area— notably the UTGC—fueled increased migrations to the area. While **railroads** in 1900 employed 6,000 Houstonians, including hundreds of African Americans, the discovery of crude oil at the Spindletop oil field near Beaumont, Texas, in 1901 stimulated unprecedented rural-to-urban migration streams to the industrializing Texas Gulf. At the same time, the global demand for cotton and oil products during World War I encouraged burgeoning manufacturing growth in the Bayou City. The completion of the Houston Ship Channel in 1914 and its expansion as a deepwater port by the 1920s, the growth of cotton compress warehouses, the opening of steel foundries, like the Hughes Tool Company in 1918, the development of oil-equipment firms, and the building of refineries along the channel by the mid-1920s motivated further migrations among blacks, whites, and browns from surrounding areas, including northern Mexico, who sought the thousands of new jobs in the growing industrial, technical, civilian, professional, and personal service sectors. Even in the aftermath of the bloody Houston riot of 1917, manufacturers, companies, businessmen, and white households sought menial black workers.

Industrial growth sustained Houston's economic vitality well into the depression, World War II, and postwar decades. By 1930 the UTGC industrial region, including its principal city, Houston, led the world in oil production, shipping out 300,000 barrels a day. The total number of manufacturing firms along the Port of Houston increased from 80 in 1900 to 450 three decades later; equally astonishing, total tonnage along the Houston Ship Channel grew from 1.3 million to 27 million by 1941. In the wake of World War II and the growing global demand for rubber products, manufacturing development continued. By 1942 the city had become the leading global producer of petrochemicals. And people, of course, continued to pour into the city.

Houston's burgeoning economy set in motion the city's population growth. Migrants came from eastern and central Texas, southern and central Louisiana, the borderland communities of South and West Texas, and northern Mexico (Mexican nationals and Mexican Americans made up only 5 percent of the city's overall population until 1950 and less than 10 percent until 1970). The city's population catapulted from 44,633 in 1900 to 596,163 in 1950, an increase of 1,236 percent. Like the city, the African American community grew exponentially from a mere 14,608 at the start of the century to 124,760 fifty years later. Houston, a city that matched Yonkers, New York, at the century's beginning, by midcentury surpassed **New Orleans** as the most populated city of the region and became number fourteen overall in the nation. Houston's incredible population surge of the twentieth century was second only to that of **Los Angeles** in the entire United States.

While most newcomers moved to Houston from eastern Texas, one-quarter fled Louisiana, particularly central and southern Louisiana, especially in the 1920s. In 1922, 500 southern Louisiana migrants founded a small, ten-block neighborhood known as Frenchtown inside Fifth Ward, Houston, a working-class community northeast of the city's downtown business and commercial district. Frenchtown migrants, the products of former slaves, biracial free blacks, and white slaveholders and landowners, named the quarter for their proud French or Creole pedigree; some of the newcomers traced their ancestry to the free "Creoles of color" of Colonial Louisiana (Brasseaux, Fontenot, and Oubre, ix). Frenchtown quickly grew as southern Louisiana refugees from the Mississippi River flood of 1927, which drowned hundreds of farmers, killed livestock, and destroyed thousands of acres of farmland, came to Houston. The Frenchtown settlers, as well as other Louisiana black migrants, would in time leave a lasting imprint on the Bayou City and its African American residents by way of cuisine, dance, music, technical skills, work ethic, and religion.

Overwhelmingly, black migrants moved into menial positions, working as porters, stevedores, draymen, redcaps, sextons, common laborers, and personal servants; like men, African American **women**, too, moved into unskilled positions, mostly working as domestic servants. Ironically, one group within the unskilled workforce dominated its craft and secured a permanent place for black men of color. African American males made up over 60 percent of the city's longshoremen. In the late 1930s a reputation for excellence, coupled with the outstanding lobbying efforts of the local International Longshoremen's Association, successfully persuaded the city to enact the Fifty-Fifty Plan, a citywide statute that gave black and white longshoremen equal work along the Port of Houston (Obadele-Starks, 50). By World War II the black rank and file, with the aid of its middle-class allies, a few Mexican American civil rights groups, a small number of white radicals, lukewarm federal agencies, and the courts, challenged class and racial discrimination in the workplace.

Although unskilled workers made up 80 to 85 percent of the black workforce, others labored in the technical, skilled crafts, civil service, business-sector, and professional areas of the workforce as craftsmen, clerks, mailmen in the postal service, tailors, **barbers**, **physicians**, dentists, **attorneys**, journalists, **undertakers**, realtors, musicians, beauticians, seamstresses, educators, grocers, business owners, and philanthropists. The city's maturing black middle class, which in growing numbers lived in the Third Ward near Houston College for Negroes and the University of Houston, increasingly used its financial clout and influence within the larger African American community to execute racial advancement. In 1943 the city's African American public **schoolteachers** won a major victory when the group persuaded the district to award them equal pay with their white peers. Products of the Great Migration and retired educators Thelma Scott Bryant, Lullelia Harrison, and Hazel Young maintain that the victory ushered in a new period of activism for black Houstonians. A year later the U.S. Supreme Court in *Smith v. Allwright* struck down the racist white Democratic primary law, which banned nonwhites from participating in the state's primary elections. In many ways this important political and legal victory signaled the start of the modern-day **civil rights movement**. Without question, the steady migration streams that poured into the city between 1900 and 1950 set the stage for later activist efforts among many factions of Houston's African American community, including recent newcomers to the city.

After World War II, continued migration streams poured into the city from the surrounding area and influenced newer movements. By the late 1970s and 1980s the economic downturns of midwestern and western manufacturing centers led to interregional migrations that, in reverse order, mirrored the Great Migrations from the South. By the post–Great Migration period the children and grandchildren of earlier settlers from the South moved to Houston and other Sunbelt cities for rewarding career possibilities, educational opportunities, and retirement purposes. The city's growing service-sector industries, notably the emerging Texas Medical Center, National Aeronautics and Space Administration (NASA), engineering firms, computer technology businesses, and Houston-area institutions of higher learning, also attracted transatlantic immigrants from the West Indies and West Africa, particularly Nigerians, who in time both formed their own ethnically unique enclaves and made themselves a part of the city's larger African American community. Indeed, the internal migration streams of the first half of the twentieth century in many ways shaped and supported later interstate, interregional, and international movements of the last half of the twentieth century and on into the twenty-first. In some ways the immigration streams of West Africans into Houston have allowed native-born African Americans, the products of both the Great Migration and the African diaspora, to come full circle with their lost mother continent, Africa. *See also* Gulf South; Hispanic Immigrants and Hispanic Americans, Relations with Black Migrants; Hispanic Migration, Comparison with the Great Black Migration; Hopkins, "Lightnin' " Sam; *Houston Informer.*

Further Reading

Beeth, Howard, and Cary D. Wintz, eds. *Black Dixie: Afro-Texan History and Culture in Houston.* College Station: Texas A&M University Press, 1992.

Brasseaux, Carl A., Keith P. Fontenot, and Claude F. Oubre. *Creoles of Color in the Bayou Country.* Jackson: University Press of Mississippi, 1994.

Bullard, Robert D. *Invisible Houston: The Black Experience in Boom and Bust.* College Station: Texas A&M University Press, 1987.

De León, Arnoldo. *Ethnicity in the Sunbelt: Mexican Americans in Houston.* 2nd ed. College Station: Texas A&M University Press, 2003.

Hine, Darlene Clark. *Black Victory: The Rise and Fall of the White Primary in Texas.* With a new introduction by Darlene Clark Hine and essays by Steven F. Lawson and Merline Pitre. Columbia: University of Missouri Press, 2003.

Obadele-Starks, Ernest. *Black Unionism in the Industrial South.* College Station: Texas A&M University Press, 2000.

Pitre, Merline. *In Struggle against Jim Crow: Lulu B. White and the NAACP, 1900–1957.* College Station: Texas A&M University Press, 1999.

Pratt, Joseph A. *The Growth of a Refining Region.* Greenwich, CT: JAI Press, 1980.

Bernadette Pruitt

Houston Informer

The *Houston Informer*, later the *Houston Informer and Texas Freeman*, was a black weekly newspaper that at its zenith in the late 1940s sold a total of 43,000 papers weekly in a number of rural areas, small towns, and cities across the United States, including **Houston**, Texarkana, Mobile, **New Orleans**, **Memphis**, and San Diego. During the pivotal years of the Great Migration to

Houston from 1920 to 1950, the weekly served as one of the city's chief migration networks for African Americans.

Clifton F. Richardson, a recent Bishop College graduate from Marshall, Texas, along with his wife, Ruby, moved to Houston in 1914. Richardson, the son of a working-class couple from small-town Marshall in the Piney Woods of East Texas, in 1919 resigned from the black weekly the *Houston Observer* as its managing editor and soon afterward founded the *Informer*. The new weekly soon bolstered socioeconomic and sociopolitical consciousness among its readership in Houston, eastern Texas, and southern Louisiana. Like the ***Chicago Defender***, the ***New York Age***, and the ***Pittsburgh Courier***, the *Houston Informer*, "the South's Greatest Race Newspaper," advocated the **New Negro** ideology of race pride, self-help, economic empowerment, integration, and political autonomy. Richardson especially challenged his readers to take a stand against **police brutality**, degradation, and violence. The paper also, through its employment advertisements and civic endorsements, promoted the Bayou City as a haven for displaced farmers, farm laborers, unskilled workers, domestic servants, artisans, high-school and college students, the expanding black middle class, and innovative businesspersons. Richardson, the *Informer*'s publisher and editor, in his editorials, attacked all forms of racial discrimination, especially disfranchisement and violence; he also challenged his out-of-town readers to sell their belongings and migrate to nearby Houston. He also used his newspaper as a forum to publicize his political campaigns of the 1920s and lawsuits against the Texas Democratic Party. Undoubtedly, these viewpoints triggered interest in Houston among potential in-migrants. Routinely threatened by the **Ku Klux Klan** and criticized by white civic leaders, Richardson, in the *Informer* and later a second newspaper, the *Houston Defender*, remained vigilant, politically astute, and a supporter of both racial justice and the Great Migration to Houston until his untimely death in 1939.

In 1931 Houston native Carter Wesley took over the newspaper. The Northwestern University–trained **attorney** and World War I officer expanded both the newspaper and its circulation. First, he merged the weekly with another Houston-based community paper, the *Texas Freeman*, founded in 1893 by Charles N. Love and **Emmett Jay Scott**. Wesley, a shrewd businessman, then bought struggling black newspapers across the state and region, hired full-time and part-time reporters from different cities, and by 1946 circulated nearly 50,000 papers weekly across the United States. Like Richardson, Wesley used the paper as a political vehicle against racial injustice. He faithfully promoted the rights of black rank-and-file workers, salary equalization for African American **schoolteachers**, the eradication of the white Democratic primary, black business expansion, and, of course, migration as a weapon against racial discrimination. According to scholar Amilcar Shabazz, Wesley's *Informer* also highlighted the contributions of blacks outside the city. Beginning in the early 1930s, the paper's "News from Texas Towns" generated a genuine bond among rural/small-town and big-city families, church members, **fraternal orders**, and organizations. Stories of racial pride, accolades, socioeconomic attainment, and gossip highlighted church events, high-school graduations, weddings, banquets, college socials, community events, regional conferences, weather forecasts, deaths, and even divorces in both Houston and its surrounding areas.

Circulation, however, fell in the 1950s as other forms of media outlets, especially television, emerged on the scene. George McElroy, emeritus associate professor of journalism at Texas Southern University, took over the newspaper in the 1970s after the deaths of Wesley and his widow, Doris. Circulation in recent years has stood at 3,000. *See also* Associated Negro Press (ANP); Black Press.

Further Reading

Beeth, Howard. "A Black Elite Agenda in the Urban South: The Call for Political Change and Racial Economic Solidarity in Houston during the 1920s." *Essays in Economic and Business History* 10 (1992): 41–55.

Shabazz, Amilcar. "Sounding the Ram's Horn for Human Rights." In *The Human Tradition in Texas*, edited by Ty Cashion and Jesús F. de la Teja. The Human Tradition in America, no. 9. Wilmington, DE: SR Books, 2001.

SoRelle, James M. "The Emergence of Black Business in Houston, Texas: A Study of Race and Ideology." In *Black Dixie: Afro-Texan History and Culture in Houston*, edited by Howard Beeth and Cary D. Wintz. College Station: Texas A&M University Press, 1992.

———. "Race Relations in 'Heavenly Houston,' 1919–1945." In *Black Dixie: Afro-Texan History and Culture in Houston*, edited by Howard Beeth and Cary D. Wintz. College Station: Texas A&M University Press, 1992.

Bernadette Pruitt

Howard University

The abolition of slavery by the Emancipation Proclamation and the Thirteenth Amendment resulted in a large influx of freedmen into **Washington, D.C.**, until they formed one-third of its population, thus constituting the largest urban group of African Americans in the United States in the late nineteenth century. The educational problem presented by this group, as realized by various freedmen's organizations and philanthropic individuals, grew beyond the primary and secondary education that existing grammar schools could offer. These civic leaders called for the establishment of an institution of higher learning to fulfill the need for training of black **schoolteachers** and **ministers**. It was with a view to supplying this need that Howard University was founded in 1866, immediately after the Civil War, under the direction of General Oliver Otis Howard. On March 2, 1867, by an act of Congress, Howard was chartered to perform a dual mission: "the education of 'youth' and of the 'disadvantaged' Negro" (Hunter, 54).

In the beginning Howard was only an elementary school and social center for the teaching of reading, writing, and religion. The recitations were held in a rented frame building on the east side of what is now Georgia Avenue, previously used as a German dance hall and saloon. The first student body, in May 1867, consisted of five young white women, the daughters of the school's trustees. But by later that year practically all students were African American,

Chemistry lab at Howard University, c. 1900. Courtesy of the Library of Congress.

and the nearly all-black racial composition of the student body has continued to the present day, fulfilling the university's dual mission.

The school depended on nominal annual appropriations of Congress. However, Howard began to grow rapidly as a center for black learning. Although it acquired land for its permanent location on which it erected several buildings for academic programs and for the housing of students, the university's growth placed it in financial difficulty. Ephemeral leadership and financial uncertainty in the mid-1870s coincided with the end of Reconstruction and the nation's waning commitment to expanding and protecting the rights and opportunities of African Americans. These developments put Howard in precarious circumstances.

The election of William Patton as president of the university in 1876 inaugurated a period of recovery and consolidation and an era of good feeling. Much of Howard's development and organization as a university took place under his twelve-year presidency. Previously, however, the various departments made an interesting history. In its first five years Howard University built a curriculum that included the Normal and Preparatory, Musical, Theological, Military, Industrial, Law, and Commercial departments and the College of Medicine. By 1868 the Colleges of Liberal Arts, Medicine, and Pharmacy and the School of Religion had been organized. The School of Law began a year later. The College of Dentistry, originally a department within the School of Medicine, was created in 1881 during President Patton's time. The School of Engineering and Architecture took form in 1910, when Wilbur P. Thirkield was president. The College of Fine Arts emerged in 1914 under the leadership of President Stephen M. Newman.

In 1867 all teachers were white except George B. Vashon, a tutor. Twenty-two years later, seven of thirty-eight teachers with six to twenty years of service were colored. A substantial increase in the number of colored teachers began in 1903. Many of these teachers received their baccalaureate and master's degrees at Howard, but those with doctoral degrees, except in medicine and dentistry, earned them at the leading "white" universities. Howard attracted such notable faculty as Ralph Bunche, **Sterling Brown**, Montague Cobb, Charles Drew, **E. Franklin Frazier**, Charles Hamilton Houston, Ernest Just, **Alain Locke**, Rayford Logan, Kelly Miller, Dorothy Porter, and **Emmett J. Scott**.

During the early years of the university there were only two black deans. John Reeve served as dean of the Theological Department from 1871 to 1876, and John Langston was dean of the Law Department from 1868 to 1875. But by 1967 all the academic and personnel deans were black. Similarly, all seventeen original trustees were white. By the end of President Howard's term in 1874, there were twenty-one trustees, four of whom were black. By June 1967, eleven of nineteen were colored.

Until Dr. Mordecai W. Johnson, the first black president of the university, was elected in 1926, all of Howard's chief executives, with the exception of John M. Langston (who served as vice president and acting president from 1873 to 1875), were white. Under the influence of the **New Negro** movement in the 1920s, students and alumni of schools like Howard, Fisk University, Hampton University, and the **Tuskegee Normal and Industrial Institute** insisted upon greater black representation among the faculties and administrations of these schools. During Johnson's long presidency, which coincided with the peak years of the Great Migration, Howard became a mecca for distinguished black academics. Under his direction Howard inaugurated the Graduate School (1934), the School of Social Work (1945), and programs leading to the doctor of philosophy degree (1955), brought in qualified black educators to replace the white faculty, expanded its facilities, received accreditation for all its schools and colleges, and graduated most of the leading scholars of the race in the fields of medicine, law, engineering, social work, education, and many others. *See also* Attorneys; Bethune, Mary McLeod; Bond, Horace Mann; Terrell, Mary Church.

Further Reading

Holmes, Dwight O. W. "Fifty Years of Howard University: Part I." *Journal of Negro History* 3, no. 2 (1918): 128–38.

———. "Fifty Years of Howard University: Part II." *Journal of Negro History* 3, no. 4 (1918): 368–80.

Hunter, Gregory. "Howard University: 'Capstone of Negro Education' during World War II." *Journal of Negro History* 79, no. 1 (1994): 54–70.

Logan, Rayford W. *Howard University: The First Hundred Years, 1867–1967*. New York: New York University Press, 1968.

Komanduri S. Murty

Langston Hughes in 1943, in an image by the famous African American photographer Gordon Parks. Courtesy of the Library of Congress.

Hughes, James Mercer Langston (1902–1967)

James Mercer Langston Hughes, one of the most influential, prolific, and beloved writers to emerge from the **Harlem Renaissance**, was born in Joplin, Missouri, though, like those of many black migrants, his childhood and adolescence were marked by movement. By the time he reached adulthood, Hughes had lived in Kansas, Mexico, and Ohio, but it was **New York City** that he eventually considered both his spiritual and actual home.

Hughes's artistic presence in Harlem, a section of New York, actually preceded his physical migration to the burgeoning center of black artistic and intellectual activities. When he was only eighteen years old, he gained the attention of **Jessie Redmon Fauset**, the literary editor of the youth-oriented *Brownies' Book* and the **National Association for the Advancement of Colored People** (NAACP)'s prestigious *Crisis* magazine, with several poems written for children that he submitted for publication in the fall of 1920. While these pieces hinted at a youthful literary talent, it was the publication of "The Negro Speaks of Rivers" that helped establish Hughes as a significant voice in African American **literature**. First published in *Crisis* in 1921, the poem's unique blend of self-revelation and historical consciousness reflected a young poet with firm control of the English language and a deep appreciation of the culture on which he would subsequently focus his creative talents. The poem also served to introduce Hughes to important contacts in New York City. Having arrived in New York in September 1921 to enroll for classes at Columbia University, Hughes was quickly invited by Fauset to visit the offices of the NAACP and to meet **W.E.B. DuBois**. Fauset and DuBois proved to be very important to Hughes at the start of his career, publishing his writings in the *Crisis* and introducing him to many NAACP dignitaries, especially those who were part of the literary and artistic community at the center of the Harlem Renaissance.

If "The Negro Speaks of Rivers" was the watershed poem that signified Hughes's maturing literary vision, it was *The Weary Blues* that cemented his reputation as one of the preeminent poets of the Harlem Renaissance. Published by Alfred A. Knopf in 1926 to nearly unanimous critical acclaim, *The Weary Blues* convincingly represented the rhythm, tone, and emotive qualities of **jazz** and the **blues** on the page. The poems in *The Weary Blues*, to many readers, also captured the sheer excitement and energy that characterized Harlem, a community rich in the culture of black migrants from many parts of the world, including the American South. Hughes's first book introduced the world to a poet who clearly loved black culture and was unafraid to represent aspects of that culture in his writings. In 1927 Knopf published Hughes's second book, *Fine Clothes to the Jew*, and while some critics responded harshly both to the book's title and to the themes of the poems, his reputation as the "Poet Laureate of Harlem" was firmly established.

Although the Harlem Renaissance as an artistic movement began to wane during the early years of the Great Depression, Hughes remained committed to his early goal of making a living as a writer. Far removed from the sense of optimism that characterized many of his poems and essays of the 1920s, however, Hughes's writings of this period reflect a deep concern for increasing racial tensions both in the United States and abroad. In response to the plight of the Scottsboro boys—nine African American youths who, in 1931, were wrongly accused of raping two white women in Alabama—Hughes wrote a powerful series of essays and poems that revealed the hypocrisies of the justice system in the South. After the Scottsboro trials Hughes traveled to the Soviet Union and Spain, fueling his literary imagination with ideas and images that would later emerge throughout his writings. In the Soviet Union Hughes was impressed by the peaceable manner in which people of all races lived, and though he never became a member of the Communist Party, he was convinced that revolutionary **socialist** ideas could help the racial situation in the United States. Similarly, Hughes's six-month tenure in Spain as a correspondent for African American newspapers during the Spanish Civil War enabled him to draw connections between the situation of blacks in the United States and the ways of life of oppressed people throughout the world, subsequently generating writings that were at once impassioned and optimistic in their critiques of fascism abroad and **Jim Crow** conditions at home.

While Hughes retained his commitment to representing in writing the dreams and frustrations of oppressed peoples during the 1940s and 1950s, pressures from reactionary groups opposed to his ideas resulted in a tapering off of the overtly radical edge that characterized his earlier writings. Required to testify before Joseph McCarthy's Senate Permanent Subcommittee on Investigations in 1953 to explain and account for his "anti-American," radical past, Hughes offered a prepared statement that effectively repudiated his radical writings and saved him from serious charges by the subcommittee.

Despite the formidable obstacles that McCarthyism posed, Hughes continued to be active as a writer. Though he was getting on in age, the turbulent 1960s saw no decrease in the prolific creative output that had always distinguished his professional writing career. With several collections of short fiction and two powerful books of poems published during the last decade of his life, Hughes contributed a significant and influential voice to American literature up to the time of his death in 1967. *See also* Literature, the Great Migration in; Locke, Alain Leroy; New Negro; *The New Negro: An Interpretation* (Locke).

Further Reading

Bloom, Harold. *Langston Hughes: Comprehensive Research and Study Guide*. Broomall, PA: Chelsea House, 1998.

Gates, Henry Louis, Jr., and K. A. Appiah. *Langston Hughes: Critical Perspectives Past and Present*. New York: Amistad, 1993.

Hughes, Langston. *The Collected Works of Langston Hughes*. 16 vols. Edited by Arnold Rampersad. Columbia: University of Missouri Press, 2001–2004.

Rampersad, Arnold. *The Life of Langston Hughes*. Vol. 1, *1902–1940: I, Too, Sing America*. New York: Oxford University Press, 1986.

———. *The Life of Langston Hughes*. Vol. 2, *1941–1967: I Dream A World*. New York: Oxford University Press, 1988.

Christopher C. De Santis

Hurston, Zora Neale (1891–1960)

Like many African Americans during the Great Migration, folklorist and novelist Zora Neale Hurston made the journey north in stages. Born in Notasulga, Alabama, in 1891, she soon moved with her family to the all-black town of Eatonville, Florida, which her writing would make famous. After her mother's death in 1904, Hurston was sent to **Jacksonville, Florida**, to attend school. Then she began "the series of wanderings" that would define her life. She lived with a brother in **Memphis**, worked as a maid in a traveling theater troupe, then settled in **Baltimore**, where she studied at what is now Morgan State University. For several years she lived in **Washington, D.C.**, where she attended **Howard University**. There she began to write the fiction that caught the eye of **Alain Locke**, a philosophy professor who edited *The New Negro*, the signal anthology of the **Harlem Renaissance**. "Feeling the urge to write," as she wrote in her memoir, *Dust Tracks on a Road*, Hurston arrived in New York City in January 1925 with "$1.50, no jobs, no friends, and a lot of hope" (Hurston, *Folklore*, 682).

Hurston was one of the few Harlem Renaissance writers who knew the migration experience firsthand. Unlike champions of the **New Negro**, she did not believe that the northward migration represented unadulterated progress for the race. She empathized with the cultural and psychological dislocation many migrants suffered. Moreover, she respected the cultural legacy rooted in the rural southern communities the migrants had left behind. In four novels, two volumes of folklore, and the memoir, as well as numerous stories, plays, and essays, Hurston preserved that legacy. Crisscrossing the South, she collected folktales, sermons, children's games, hoodoo rituals, work songs, and **blues**. She later expanded her travel to the Bahamas, Jamaica, Haiti, and Honduras. From this research she developed theories of language and cultural performance that continue to influence scholars today. Ultimately, Hurston distilled the black vernacular English she transcribed from her fieldwork into the lyrical language that constitutes the core of her literary legacy.

Hurston's earliest stories, including "Drenched in Laughter," "The Eatonville Anthology," and "Spunk," are set in her hometown, where men sat on the store porch telling folktales, rich in humor and wisdom, that encoded the people's worldview. Her later fiction partook increasingly of critique as well as celebration, prompted in part by **women**'s exclusion from the porch's "lying sessions." "Sweat," for example, takes up the theme of marital conflict that would become a prime concern. "Muttsy" explores the alienation a southern-born woman experiences in Harlem. The essay "How It Feels to Be Colored Me" contrasts the response the child Zora received to reciting folktales in Eatonville and the response to **jazz** musicians in a Harlem cabaret.

At the height of the Renaissance, Hurston traded Harlem high life for southern hamlets; she lived mainly in the South until her death in 1960. She was persuaded that the "unlettered Negro" had made the race's most important contributions to American culture. Anthropology, which she studied at Barnard College from 1925 to 1927, provided the theoretical framework for her research. *Mules and Men*, a treasure trove of folklore, documents the unwritten, collective history of African Americans; to a substantial degree it captures their uncensored perspectives. As a scholar, Hurston concluded that drama was the primary characteristic of Negro expression; the "folk" improvised impromptu ceremonies for everyday events, including casual conversations, courtship rituals, and worship practices. Its complement was the "will to adorn," which was expressed both through the form of the ceremonies and their linguistic content.

Hurston's novels enacted the aesthetic principles she derived from her fieldwork. The preacher protagonist of *Jonah's Gourd Vine* achieves poetic mastery in the pulpit—his art is the heightened form of communal expressive culture—but fails to sustain his relationship with his wife. In the classic *Their Eyes Were Watching God*, Janie Crawford masters poetic metaphor and after three marriages claims ownership of her self and her voice. Drawing on the long-standing identification of black American slaves and the biblical Israelites, *Moses, Man of the Mountain* retells the biblical story of Exodus in Negro idiom. *Seraph on the Suwanee* uses the same idiom to tell a story of white Floridians, thus dramatizing Hurston's belief that black speech had influenced the way white southerners spoke.

One of her few stories set in the North, "A Story in Harlem Slang," mocks urban blacks who try in vain to deny their southern roots. A virtuoso performance piece, the story consists mainly of "woofing," as Hurston defined the "aimless talking" with which people entertained themselves. But as she represents "woofing" in this story and throughout her writing, it also offered the means through which African Americans spoke themselves into selfhood. *See also* Literature, the Great Migration in; Migrants, Cultural Identity of.

Further Reading

Boyd, Valerie. *Wrapped in Rainbows: The Life of Zora Neale Hurston*. New York: Scribner, 2002.

Hurston, Zora Neale. *Folklore, Memoirs, and Other Writings*. Edited by Cheryl A. Wall. New York: Library of America, 1995.

———. *Novels and Short Stories*. Edited by Cheryl A. Wall. New York: Library of America, 1995.

Cheryl A. Wall

Hypersegregation

In 1993 sociologists Douglas Massey and Nancy Denton published their study of residential segregation, *American Apartheid: Segregation and the Making of the American Underclass*, adding to and qualifying the work of William Julius Wilson's landmark 1987 book *The Truly Disadvantaged*. Wilson argued that poverty in black central cities was the result of jobs moving to the suburbs, accompanied by a shift from a manufacturing-based to a service-based job market requiring high information and symbolic skills and thus greater education than black youth were likely to receive in underfunded inner-city schools. In their demographic analysis of the U.S. census, Massey and Denton emphasized that racial segregation was the single most important factor contributing to black poverty and relative immobility (financial, occupational, and residential) for educated, middle-class blacks. In sum, racial segregation compounded the impact of **deindustrialization** on central-city black neighborhoods.

Massey and Denton's demographic research showed that on the basis of four out of five standard measures of residential segregation, African Americans, unlike Asian Americans or Latinos, were the only group that was extremely isolated, or "hypersegregated," from whites. African American hypersegregation existed in sixteen cities in 1980, of which thirteen were in the North, Midwest, or West and three were in the South. In a separate study published in 1994, using 1990 census data, Denton showed that African American hypersegregation existed in twenty-nine cities, of which nineteen were in the North, Midwest, or West and ten were in the South. Reproducing Massey and Denton's research, Rima Wilkes and John Iceland found that in 2000, on the basis of that year's census, African Americans were hypersegregated in twenty-three cities (even extremely hypersegregated on all five measures in **Chicago**, **Cleveland**, **Detroit**, **Milwaukee**, Newark, and **Philadelphia**), of which fourteen were in the North, Midwest, or West and nine were in the South. Hispanics were hypersegregated from whites in **New York City** and **Los Angeles**. Additionally, census analysis by other social scientists of black **return migration** to the South suggests a relationship to increasing hypersegregation in southern cities. Beginning in the 1970s, as northeastern and midwestern cities lost industry and experienced net losses of black residents to out-migration, the South experienced net gains in black in-migration. Finally, research by other social scientists shows that as of 1990, thirty-seven U.S. cities had become what demographers refer to as "multiethnic," with percentages of the local population higher than that of the national population for at least two of three minority groups (Latinos, Asians, and blacks). While these multiethnic urban conditions further complicate a more comprehensive understanding of racial inequality, research shows that African Americans remain the most segregated of all Americans.

During the 1990s social scientists conducted one of the most comprehensive studies of urban inequality ever undertaken (consisting of 8,916 interviews in five languages with black, white, Asian, and Latino workers and employers, analysis of census data, and ethnographic participant observation, to name a few of the methods used). For each of the four cities studied

(**Atlanta**, **Boston**, Detroit, and Los Angeles), the Multi-city Study of Urban Inequality focused on "changing labor market dynamics," "racial attitudes and relations," and "residential segregation." One of the major conclusions of the study, as Lawrence Bobo and his colleagues put it in the published results of the Los Angeles study, *Prismatic Metropolis*, was that "urban inequality is still heavily racialized . . . that social inequality and the dynamics that produce . . . it are clearly related to racial and ethnic group distinctions" (Bobo, 5).

Persistent hypersegregation of African Americans in **housing** results from continued discriminatory practices by owners, real estate agents, property managers, **banks** and financial institutions, and insurance companies. In 1968 Congress passed the Fair Housing Act to promote the goals of **open housing**. The act also prohibited racial discrimination in the sale, rental, or advertising of housing, realtor statements about the availability of property for sale or rental, and realtor statements about the race of neighbors or those moving in. Such discrimination has been identified through housing audit surveys wherein white and black auditors are sent to the same realtors posing as home buyers or renters to determine whether they are given the same information about housing availability. Many studies conducted in the 1970s and 1980s revealed that housing was consistently made more available to whites, and that realtors spend considerably less time and effort advertising and promoting houses for sale in mixed-race neighborhoods. It is precisely these kinds of discrimination that have continued to channel black home buyers and renters into already black neighborhoods, thereby increasing African American segregation. These discriminatory practices continued even after passage of the 1968 Fair Housing Act because the legislation lacked adequate provision for enforcement. Studies conducted as recently as 2005 show that such discrimination still exists. In addition, as the tenor of congressional politics shifted away from a social democratic orientation to a probusiness, neoconservative orientation, politicians and federal officials further weakened enforcement of housing policies. During the Reagan administration the number of Fair Housing Act cases prosecuted dropped, while the number of discrimination cases filed with the Department of Housing and Urban Development (HUD) increased.

Such discrimination occurs on the basis of prejudice based on stereotypes. Significant here in terms of the history of the urban crisis, and highlighting the shortcomings of the report compiled by the **National Advisory Commission on Civil Disorders** that attributed inequality to a simple definition of prejudice as individual dislike, evidence from the Multi-city Study of Urban Inequality shows that prejudice has more to do with maintaining socially learned commitments to group status and group position. Prejudice stems from a sense of hierarchical group positioning in relation to other groups (status), but also from the degree to which individuals develop an affective/emotional sense of group position on the basis of participation in racially homogeneous communities, friendship networks, and family structures. Rather than individual dislike, this evidence shows that prejudice is based on perceived and experienced structural advantage. Prejudice and stereotyping have an equal impact in the job market. Employers make hiring decisions in the same way. Thus racial inequalities in hiring and promotion for all people of color (as well as between nonwhites) are especially harmful to hypersegregated African Americans affected by the decreasing availability of jobs in central cities.

During the 1990s policy makers and city officials, recognizing the significance of location (industrial, residence, and neighborhood) as a factor contributing to social isolation, concentration effects, and racial segregation, began to rethink **public housing** policy. Seeking an alternative to the dense population concentrations that resulted from the massive high-rise and megablock public housing built during the mid-twentieth century, during the Clinton administration in 1993 Congress passed the Urban Revitalization Demonstration Program, now known as HOPE VI (Housing Opportunities for People Everywhere). Taking advantage of HOPE VI grant policies of "housing mobility" and "mixed income," cities began to demolish older public housing buildings, replacing them with flats, town homes, and scattered-site developments. Encouraging a mixed-class population of residents in these new developments, housing agencies sought to decrease isolation and concentration of poverty.

The success of new housing policies has been mixed. Some have charged that because HOPE VI housing reduces the overall amount of public housing and because a portion of the new housing is for middle-income residents, the program amounts to a new version of **urban renewal**. Few residents displaced by the destruction of older public housing developments were relocated to new public housing. Instead, they were given rent subsidies in the form of Section 8 housing vouchers to enable them to rent housing in urban and suburban locations beyond the inner city. This put displaced families at the mercy of market competition for housing and discriminatory real estate practices. Families who used Section 8 vouchers or who chose to move to scattered-site and/or HOPE VI mixed-class developments did find greater opportunities for their children in their new location. However, they experienced a loss of the valuable social networks they had formerly drawn upon for social support, especially child care and socialization. Those families that chose to move from one public housing site to another public housing site also experienced a loss of their social networks but found themselves in the same situation of concentrated poverty with no new opportunities for their children. In short, changes in housing, while they may offer better options for a few (especially those with high-school degrees), do not adequately address the need for more low-income housing. *See also* Black Suburbanization; Home Ownership among Migrants; Migrants, Settlement Patterns of; Urban Crisis of the 1960s; War on Poverty; White Flight.

Further Reading

Bobo, Lawrence D., ed. *Prismatic Metropolis: Inequality in Los Angeles*. New York: Russell Sage Foundation, 2000.

Clampet-Lindquist, Susan. "HOPE VI Relocation: Moving to New Neighborhoods and Building New Ties." *Housing Policy Debate* 15, no. 2 (2004): 415–47.

Denton, Nancy A. "Are African Americans Still Hypersegregated?" In *Residential Apartheid: The American Legacy*, edited by R. Bullard, C. Lee, and J. E. Grigsby, 49–81. Los Angeles: UCLA Center for Afro-American Studies, 1994.

Massey, Douglas, and Nancy Denton. *American Apartheid: Segregation and the Making of the Underclass.* Cambridge, MA: Harvard University Press, 1993.

O'Connor, Alice, Chris Tilly, and Lawrence D. Bobo, eds. *Urban Inequality: Evidence from Four Cities.* New York: Russell Sage Foundation, 2001.

Oliver, Melvin, and Thomas Shapiro. *Black Wealth/White Wealth: A New Perspective on Racial Inequality.* New York: Routledge, 1995.

Wilkes, Rima, and John Iceland. "Hypersegregation in the Twenty-first Century." *Demography* 41, no. 1 (February 2004): 23–36.

Michael N. Willard

I

ILWU *See* International Longshoremen's and Warehousemen's Union (ILWU)

Indianapolis, Indiana

Located about 100 miles from the Kentucky border, Indianapolis has long been an important destination for southern African Americans heading north. Black movement to Indianapolis was substantial beginning in the late nineteenth century, though the in-migration hit its peaks during the two world wars. The southern migration to Indianapolis continued in significant numbers through the 1960s. The city's relatively middling size and easy accessibility to the South meant that the move to Indianapolis was in some ways distinct from a move to a larger or more distant northern city. In general, however, the story of black migration to Indianapolis is a typical one: migrants came seeking social and economic opportunities and found them, though not without a great deal of individual and community struggle.

In contrast to many northern and midwestern cities, African Americans were a significant part of the city's makeup long before the twentieth-century Great Migration. Indianapolis grew rapidly over the course of the late nineteenth century, from a population of under 20,000 in 1860 to 230,000 by 1920. It was known as the "100 Percent American City," and most of its growth came from the nearby countryside and from the South. Between 1890 and 1910 African Americans made up a steady 10 percent of the population of the burgeoning city; blacks made up only about 2 percent of the population of **New York**, **Detroit**, and **Chicago** at this time. In 1910, two-thirds of Indianapolis's black population were migrants to the state, compared with less than one-third of the rest of the city's population.

African Americans certainly met resistance in pre–World War I Indianapolis, though their responses were many and varied. The Indianapolis branch of the

National Association for the Advancement of Colored People (NAACP) was among the first in the country, chartered in 1909. Even before the existence of the NAACP, new African American **women** migrants got short-term housing, job training, and help looking for work from the Flanner House, a private social service organization initiated to help black women beginning in 1903. Indianapolis had numerous black newspapers before World War I, including the *Indianapolis Leader*, the *Freeman*, and the nationally recognized *Indianapolis Recorder*, first published in 1897.

While Indianapolis was an important migrant destination before World War I, the impact of the war was immense. Indianapolis's black population increased by 60 percent between 1910 and 1920. Since the World War I–era move to Indianapolis drew on kin and friendship connections of the city's earlier migrants, more than three-quarters of the city's new African Americans came from nearby western Kentucky and Tennessee. Over time, the city gradually drew migrants from further and further south. By 1970 Mississippi was the most common birthplace for new migrants to Indianapolis, though Kentucky and Tennessee still sent a combined total of almost half of Indianapolis's migrants.

The massive influx of World War I–era migrants drove significant changes in African Americans' occupational opportunities in Indianapolis. The high demand of World War I provided local blacks with many opportunities in the city's key industries in automobile parts, machine production, and meat-packing. To be sure, African Americans most often filled positions as unskilled laborers in these industries, though that too changed radically over time. While nearly two-thirds of southern black men in Indianapolis worked in unskilled labor and service jobs in 1920, only about one-third did so by 1970. The balance worked in skilled industrial work and, increasingly over time, clerical and professional jobs.

As was the case in most northern cities, southern blacks' integration into the schools and neighborhoods of Indianapolis was a long-term process. In education, Indianapolis was among the few northern cities to actively segregate schools during the Great Migration, opening the all-black Crispus Attucks High School in 1927. The high-quality faculty and academic programs at Attucks were a source of pride for local African Americans. The school remained segregated well into the 1960s, however, serving as a physical reminder of the degree to which blacks remained in a separate world in Indianapolis. With regard to residential segregation, most local African Americans lived either just northeast or northwest of downtown in the World War I era. The areas surrounding northwest Indiana Avenue, known as the Avenue, were the social and economic hub of black Indianapolis. In the early Great Migration the Avenue was home to African American newspapers, the **Madam C. J. Walker** theater and professional building (constructed in the 1920s), and a lively social district. Most of the city's African Americans continued to live in the neighborhoods just north of downtown through the 1960s.

Southern blacks' full integration into the political life of Indianapolis remained in some ways incomplete by the end of the Great Migration. Indianapolis's black population grew steadily over the course of the Great Migration, from about

35,000 in 1920 to more than 100,000 in 1970. Yet the 1969 political initiative known as Unigov (shorthand for Unified Government) severely diminished African Americans' influence in local politics. Unigov consolidated the policy-making bodies of the city (which was about 30 percent black) and the surrounding county (which was almost entirely white), effectively diluting the African American vote in the process. Because of the city's annexation of areas that included more than 300,000 mostly white suburbanites, Indianapolis's black community has never been able to attain the sort of voting bloc that was typical of other major northern and midwestern cities of the Great Migration. *See also* Cincinnati, Ohio; Gary, Indiana; Louisville, Kentucky; Midwestern States, Black Migration to.

Further Reading

Alexander, J. Trent. "Great Migrations: Race and Community in the Southern Exodus, 1917–1970." Ph.D. diss., Carnegie Mellon University, 2001.

Gibbs, Wilma, ed. *Indiana's African-American Heritage: Essays from Black History News and Notes*. Indianapolis: Indiana Historical Society, 1993.

Pierce, Richard B. *Polite Protest: The Political Economy of Race in Indianapolis, 1920–1970*. Bloomington: Indiana University Press, 2005.

J. Trent Alexander

Industrial Workers of the World (IWW)

The Industrial Workers of the World (IWW) is a militant, left-wing union committed to overthrowing the capitalist wage system by organizing workers on the job rather than as citizens at the voting booth. Though still around today, the IWW is far smaller in numbers and influence than it was during its heyday, 1905 to 1925. From its inception the IWW has been committed to racial equality, though African Americans have played a relatively small role in the organization. Local 8, a branch of Philadelphia longshoremen, possessed the union's largest contingent of African Americans and was impacted dramatically by the first wave of the Great Migration.

The IWW advocated equal treatment for African Americans. Article I, Section I, of the IWW Constitution declared that all workers, regardless of color or creed, were welcome in the IWW. The Wobblies—the nickname of the IWW's members—were committed to this egalitarian—and unusual—stand because of their ideology. Simply put, the IWW believed that all wage workers, regardless of their ethnic, national, or racial heritage (or, for that matter, craft, gender, or religion), should identify as workers in opposition to their employers, with whom they shared "nothing in common," according to its famous preamble. The IWW castigated the more mainstream **American Federation of Labor** (AFL) for denying admission to blacks and treating them as second-class.

Despite this highly principled stance against racism, the IWW rarely organized African Americans. There always were blacks in the organization, but their numbers were tiny. The first large-scale effort to organize blacks occurred in the woods of Louisiana and Texas, where the IWW incorporated a mixed-race union called the Brotherhood of Timber Workers (BTW). How-ever, massive violence, blacklistings, and government repression resulted in the BTW's collapse. Some blacks joined other branches of the IWW. Sterling Spero and **Abram Harris** claimed that 100,000 African Americans belonged to the IWW at one time or another, but most scholars consider that number quite exaggerated. The IWW organized in many industries and parts of the country where there were few blacks, such as northeastern textile factories, Mountain West mines, Great Plains farms, and northwestern woods.

Without a doubt, the best way to examine the IWW's relationship to African Americans generally and the Great Migration specifically is through its largest interracial branch, Local 8. In 1913 several thousand deep-sea longshoremen struck. Their demands included a pay raise and recognition of their new union. Although the AFL's International Longshoremen's Association also vied for their allegiance, they joined the IWW because the IWW was a fully in-clusive organization that had proven that its militant direct-action tactics could succeed. Moreover, though he took a conspicuously low profile, a black man by the name of Ben Fletcher also proved pivotal.

Benjamin Harrison Fletcher was the most prominent black Wobbly in the entire IWW. Born in **Philadelphia** in 1890 to African American parents who, typically, had migrated from the Upper South states of Maryland and Virginia, Fletcher joined the IWW around 1910. He already toiled as a longshoreman and quickly became a leader in the city's IWW. Fletcher was not the only African American among Local 8's leadership. Many of its leaders were African Americans: natives of Philadelphia, migrants from other parts of the nation, and even some black migrants from the **Caribbean**. Blacks were present in every leadership position in Local 8, including business agents, meeting chairs, and secretaries.

World War I was a transformative experience for African Americans, and the Philadelphia waterfront was no different. With newfound job opportunities, tens of thousands of African Americans streamed into Philadelphia during the last half of the 1910s. Blacks could get jobs at many of the city's industrial employers who categorically had denied blacks jobs previously. The Delaware River docks were different, for there blacks already worked in large numbers, but even on the waterfront their numbers increased. In 1910 the U.S. census reported 1,369 black longshoremen out of 3,063. In 1920 the census counted 2,388 black longshoremen out of 4,036. Nearly the entire increase was among African Americans, no doubt facilitated because of Local 8, for without mem-bership, a man quite simply could not get work on the river.

These new arrivals dramatically affected Local 8. While the migrants happily joined Local 8 because it was the ticket to employment, few had prior ex-perience with unions and none had participated in the union's formation. Hence southern black members, who formed a significant minority, had al-most no commitment to the principles of the IWW or unionism. Thus, after the war, when Local 8 battled countless times against their employers, these migrants were the weak link in the union's chain.

Most important, in 1922 employers took advantage of the changing dy-namics of labor and race relations in postwar America and locked out all Wobbly longshoremen. The conflict was bitter, and employers consciously targeted Local 8's interracial alliance by bringing in black strikebreakers (some from the South) and appealing to the black unionists to return to work. As it turned out, some of the (older) blacks stuck with the union, as did most of the European Americans and European immigrants. When the union's hold on the city's longshoremen was broken, it was done by driving a wedge between white and black longshoremen, among whom the southern black migrants were particularly soft in their union allegiance.

In general, African Americans played relatively little role in the IWW, and thus the Great Migration was not that significant. The most important exception was the Philadelphia waterfront. There many hundreds of African Americans appeared during and after World War I and found employment, not only because of the war but also because of Local 8's membership, power, and ideology. However, after the war these same migrants sided with employers when labor conflicts erupted. African Americans continued to join the IWW after this period, and countless people have found the story of the IWW to be quite compelling, particularly the discovery that there was such a prominent black Wobbly as Ben Fletcher. *See also* Congress of Industrial Organizations (CIO); Organized Labor; Strikebreaking.

Further Reading

Cole, Peter. *Black Wobbly: The Life and Writings of Benjamin Harrison Fletcher.* Chicago: Charles H. Kerr Press, 2006.

———. *Wobblies on the Waterfront: Interracial Unionism in Progressive Era Philadelphia.* Urbana: University of Illinois Press, 2006.

Foner, Philip. "The IWW and the Black Worker." *Journal of Negro History* 55 (January 1970): 45–64.

Industrial Workers of the World. "Colored Workers of America: Why You Should Join the I.W.W." c. 1912. Industrial Workers of the World Collection. Walter P. Reuther Archives. Wayne State University.

———. "Justice for the Negro—How He Can Get It." c. 1919. Industrial Workers of the World Collection. Walter P. Reuther Archives. Wayne State University.

———. "To Colored Workingmen and Women." c. 1919. Industrial Workers of the World Collection. Walter P. Reuther Archives. Wayne State University.

Kimeldorf, Howard. *Battling for American Labor: Wobblies, Craft Workers, and the Making of the Union Movement.* Berkeley: University of California Press, 1999.

Kimeldorf, Howard, and Robert Penney. "'Excluded' by Choice: Dynamics of Interracial Unionism on the Philadelphia Waterfront, 1910–1930." *International Labor and Working-Class History* 51 (Spring 1997): 50–71.

Spero, Sterling D., and Abram L. Harris. *The Black Worker: The Negro and the Labor Movement.* 1931. Reprint, with a new preface by Herbert G. Gutman, New York: Atheneum, 1968.

Peter Cole

Insurers and Insurance Companies

The history of African American insurance companies is intrinsically connected to the history of mainstream insurers. Before the late nineteenth century the American insurance industry represented a relatively insignificant portion of the national economy. Yet because of insurance's compatibility with societal changes resulting from urbanization and industrialization, individual companies' assets grew by 12,000 percent between 1850 and 1900. Specifically, insurance provided all economic classes a semblance of the family-based security that had been an integral part of preindustrial society.

In their quest to attract the working-class market, American insurance companies initially offered protection to newly emancipated blacks and whites for the same cost. Yet in 1881 the Prudential Life Insurance Company of Newark, on the basis of an excessive black mortality rate, established a rate structure whereby blacks paid higher premiums than whites for the same coverage. Other major insurance companies soon followed Prudential's lead and established their own separate actuarial tables for blacks.

Prudential carried its differential treatment of African Americans one dramatic step further in 1896. The company's statistician, Frederick L. Hoffman, published a widely disseminated study titled *Race Traits and Tendencies of the American Negro*, which, among other things, predicted the eventual destruction of blacks by whites. Prudential, apparently on the basis of Hoffman's work, subsequently severed all ties with black consumers. Once again, other major insurance companies followed Prudential's lead.

The abandonment of black policyholders by some white companies contributed to the development of black insurance companies. Some of the first African American–owned insurance companies were North Carolina Mutual, established in **Durham, North Carolina**, in 1898; the Afro-American Life Insurance Company, established in **Jacksonville, Florida**, in 1901; and the Atlanta Life Insurance Company, founded in Georgia in 1905.

The birth of the black insurance industry has decidedly southern roots because, at the turn of the twentieth century, the vast majority of African Americans resided in the South. Yet commencing with the World War I–era Great Migration, America witnessed a dramatic geographic relocation of its black citizens. Moreover, as rural southern blacks migrated to such places as **New York City**, **Chicago**, **Philadelphia**, **Cleveland**, and **Detroit**, black entrepreneurs in these northern locales established enterprises to cater to migrants' needs.

One of the most pressing needs of these black migrants was that for insurance. Census data for the year 1930 convey astronomical death rates of blacks in northern cities. For instance, in Chicago, the overall death rate from tuberculosis was 57.3 out of every 100,000 inhabitants. However, the tuberculosis death rate for whites was 42.6 out of 100,000, but for blacks the figure rose to 233 out of every 100,000 African Americans in the city. Similar racial disparities were present in other northern enclaves.

As northern blacks moved from the Great Migration to the Great Depression, most black insurance companies, unlike their counterparts in the banking industry, were able to survive this national economic calamity. In fact, the U.S. insurance industry as a whole fared much better than other commercial enterprises. For example, in 1932 alone there were 32,000 business failures, yet only thirty-nine insurance companies ceased operations during the entire decade. Conservative investment policies, coupled with conservative, stable leadership, seemed to explain the insurance industry's relative immunity to this financial disaster.

Office employees of a black-owned insurance company in Chicago, Illinois, 1941. Courtesy of the Library of Congress.

It is worth noting that while economic racial discrimination contributed to the establishment of black-owned insurance companies, these firms, ironically, still competed with discriminatory white insurers for black policyholders. Although the Prudential Insurance Company severed all ties with black consumers, the Metropolitan Life Insurance Company still insured blacks (at higher premium rates than whites). Moreover, Metropolitan Life refused to hire black agents to sell to black customers. Nevertheless, because of Metropolitan Life's prestige in the insurance industry, it attracted a considerable number of black policyholders (to the obvious chagrin of black insurers).

Considering that African American insurance companies, even during enforced racial segregation, never controlled the **black consumer market**, mid-twentieth-century developments related to blacks had a dramatic impact upon the future of black insurers. The mass movement of southern blacks to northern cities, which commenced during the World War I Great Migration, accelerated considerably during World War II. Between 1940 and 1950 the number of African American city dwellers increased from 6,253,588 to 9,120,000, a 46 percent increase. Thus by the 1950s African Americans represented an increasingly visible and attractive consumer market in America's major cities.

The post–World War II period also witnessed a dramatic decrease in African American mortality rates. Decades earlier, insurance industry giants (such as the Prudential Life Insurance Company and the Metropolitan Life Insurance

Company) used higher black mortality rates (which were linked to the ongoing oppression of postemancipation blacks) as a rationale either to exclude blacks from coverage or to charge blacks more for insurance coverage. Yet by the 1950s an increasingly urban and healthier black population caused mainstream insurers to rethink their policies regarding black consumers.

The mainstream insurance industry's subsequent interest in securing black policyholders posed two distinct challenges to African American insurers. First, many black consumers, because they had been denied equitable coverage with industry giants, viewed prospective policies with mainstream companies as attractive status symbols. Second, large insurance companies decided to recruit black agents from black companies to service the African American market. Consequently, mainstream giants, with promises of financial reward, were able to secure many trained black insurance agents.

From the standpoint of black insurance companies, the defection of many of their customers and employees has had a devastating effect on their operations. Recent data illustrate the nearly total marginality of African American insurers in today's society. Between 1996 and 2001 African Americans spent $38 billion on insurance. Yet during the same period the premium income of the top ten black insurance companies was a relatively paltry $899.1 million.

In conclusion, long-standing trends suggest that black-owned insurance companies are heading for extinction. Yet regardless of what the future holds for African American insurers, their past accomplishments (which included providing needed insurance coverage to early twentieth-century black southern migrants in northern cities) deserve respect and recognition. *See also* Banks and Bankers; Metropolitan Mutual Assurance Company (MMAC); Supreme Liberty Life Insurance Company.

Further Reading

Fletcher, Linda. *The Negro in the Insurance Industry*. Philadelphia: University of Pennsylvania Press, 1970.

Gloster, Jesse. *North Carolina Mutual Life Insurance Company: Its Historical Development and Current Operations*. New York: Arno Press, 1976.

Henderson, Alexa B. *Atlanta Life Insurance Company: Guardian of Black Economic Dignity*. Tuscaloosa: University of Alabama Press, 1990.

Puth, Robert C. *Supreme Life: The History of a Negro Life Insurance Company*. New York: Arno Press, 1976.

Weare, Walter B. *Black Business in the New South: A Social History of the North Carolina Mutual Life Insurance Company*. Urbana: University of Illinois Press, 1973.

Weems, Robert E., Jr. *Black Business in the Black Metropolis: The Chicago Metropolitan Assurance Company, 1925–1985*. Bloomington: Indiana University Press, 1996.

———. "A Crumbling Legacy: The Decline of African American Insurance Companies in Contemporary America." *Review of Black Political Economy* 23 (1994): 25–37.

Robert E. Weems, Jr.

International Longshoremen's and Warehousemen's Union (ILWU)

The radical International Longshoremen's and Warehousemen's Union (ILWU), which emerged out of the Pacific Coast District of the International Longshoremen's Association (ILA) after the historic 1934 maritime strike in **San Francisco**, was the first sizable labor union in the area to admit black workers to membership. While blacks labored on the docks throughout the twentieth century's first few decades, because of the Great Black Migration in the early part of the century, blacks migrated in substantially smaller numbers to the California Bay Area cities of San Francisco and Oakland than they did to northern cities such as **Cleveland**, **New York City**, **Philadelphia**, and **Chicago**. This lower level of migration resulted from the great distance blacks had to travel from the South to these West Coast cities, as well as the dearth of family and job contacts in the region.

From the beginning of the twentieth century, blacks in the Bay Area were employed predominantly on the **railroads** and at Oakland's port. However, during the Great Depression of the 1930s black **unemployment** soared, with an estimated 13.7 and 15.3 percent unemployed among San Francisco's and Oakland's black laborers by 1937. Because of the depression, blacks became radicalized, participating actively in both union and left-wing pursuits. In San Francisco at this time, the Communist Party USA (CPUSA) emerged as the earliest active interracial group, playing a major leadership role during the 1934 maritime strike and eventually becoming the guiding force for many decades in the ILWU.

Located in San Francisco, ILWU Local 10's history of racial equality dated to the 1934 strike, in which two black longshoremen who were CPUSA members served on the San Francisco strike committee. During the next strike in 1936–1937, fifteen blacks served on the strike committee. In addition, three black workers were elected to the local's executive board in 1936, and in that year the local organized an antidiscrimination committee to ensure that employment discrimination based on race or color was eliminated. In 1938 a black longshoreman was elected to the powerful position of job dispatcher. Throughout World War II Local 10 continued its antidiscrimination policies, vigorously fighting against any vestige of racism and providing antiracist leadership for the International as a whole, except for the segregationist Portland local. By the end of the war black members accounted for approximately one-third of the local's composition.

In the postwar wave of anti-Communism that engulfed the nation, in May 1950 significant numbers of black longshoremen, along with their white leftist counterparts, were identified by the Coast Guard as "security risks" and were removed from working the military docks. Nevertheless, Local 10 remained a bastion of racial equality well after World War II. Later waves of black migration to the Bay Area enabled a new generation of black workers to obtain work on the docks. In the early 1960s the local conducted a massive and successful recruitment drive for black workers in the black communities of the Bay Area. Thus by the end of the 1960s, and toward the end of the Great Black Migration, black members became the numerical majority in Local 10, constituting 55 percent of the local's membership and playing an important role in the life of this militant and democratic union. *See also* Communists and the Communist Party; Organized Labor; Western States, Black Migration to.

Further Reading

Kimeldorf, Howard. *Reds or Rackets? The Making of Radical and Conservative Unions on the Waterfront.* Berkeley: University of California Press, 1988.

Nelson, Bruce. *Workers on the Waterfront: Seamen, Longshoremen, and Unionism in the 1930s.* Urbana: University of Illinois Press, 1988.

Wellman, David. *The Union Makes Us Strong: Radical Unionism on the San Francisco Waterfront.* Cambridge: Cambridge University Press, 1995.

Victor G. Devinatz

Intraracial Class Conflict

The pattern of intertwining race and class terms that defined the legal and economic status of African Americans emerged during slavery. Under the system of slavery in the United States, the categories of "free" and "slave" defined an economic, social, and political dichotomy that hid a complex of classlike differentiations. Among the free black population in the North, the emergence of political and cultural institutions marked the birth of a radical politics that was inseparable from expressions of class consciousness. In the South economic negotiations and financial independence played a larger role in defining status in African American communities. Within the slave community a distinction emerged between unskilled and skilled slaves, who possessed knowledge of a trade and who were able to hire themselves out and keep a portion of their wages. Some used this economic freedom to buy themselves or members of their family, an option that was unavailable to unskilled slaves. The discourse of African Americans was decidedly antislavery, which fused the issue of race and class under the headings of free and unfree. The hidden dynamics of intraracial class conflict emerged with the death of slavery and the reconstruction, through migration, of black communities throughout the United States.

Black migration in the early twentieth century was part of a longer continuum of African American mobility. Beginning after the Civil War and continuing through the twentieth century, African Americans in the South were motivated to relocate by their desires for better lives, **housing**, and educational opportunities. Decreasing hopes for economic independence propelled African Americans into urban areas, searching for pre- and postharvest seasonal employment. This cycle of intrastate rural-to-urban migration loosened ties to the land, preparing many for the longer journey to the North. While the percentage of blacks who left the South increased dramatically after 1900, the idea of relocating was not new, and many rural blacks either had some personal experience with travel or knew someone who did. Proportionally fewer African Americans left the rural South for northern cities. Instead, surveys conducted at the time of the Great Migration found that nearly three-quarters had spent some time living in the urban South. Economic forces, such as increased job competition in southern cities, pushed African Americans out of the South, while northern labor needs pulled them to areas above the

Mason-Dixon Line. Other factors that influenced the decision to relocate to urban areas were the escalation of racial violence, disfranchisement, and the formalization of their second-class status through **Jim Crow** laws.

For those migrants who remained in the South, the postwar industrialization of southern municipalities opened new economic opportunities, while at the same time, urbanization marked the emergence of a black working class. While most black **women** were confined to domestic employment, and many black men worked as servants and manual laborers, increases in manufacturing and industrial work provided them a variety of job opportunities. Although they might have been confined to the hottest and dirtiest occupations, black workers employed in urban industries reported higher wages than those who remained in agricultural pursuits. Additionally, employment in factories, even as unskilled labor, provided African Americans with knowledge that would ease their transition to life in the North.

African Americans who moved into cities at the turn of the century entered a society that was undergoing dramatic economic and social changes. Along with thousands of recent immigrants from Europe, the new arrivals joined in the competition for jobs, schools, and housing that emerged as cities struggled to meet the increasing needs of their rapidly expanding populations. Old antagonisms based on racial and ethnic differences often intensified as European immigrants and black migrants settled into their new lives in the North. In addition to white racism, African American migrants also had to contend with the concept of class differences, which had been sublimated in the antebellum era.

By the late 1800s the discourse within the black community had shifted from freedom to racial **uplift** through economic and educational gains. As more African Americans moved into northern cities, the numbers of migrants often doubled the existing black populations, and in certain areas migrants outnumbered those who were natives. Thus, as the size of the black working class outpaced any increases in the middle class, many of the latter tried to maintain their distance, socially and economically. One of the first major sociological studies of African Americans by an African American, **W.E.B. DuBois**'s *The Philadelphia Negro: A Social Study*, was published in 1899. DuBois compiled data on **Philadelphia**'s Seventh Ward, which housed the city's black population, covering all aspects of black life from housing, education, and employment to health care, voting, family life, and criminality. Breaking free of the assumptions by the mainstream that African Americans "compos[ed] one practically homogenous mass," DuBois's research carefully outlined class differentiations that had been hidden by the larger category of race and subsequent racial discrimination (DuBois, 309). Within this study he identified four classes of African Americans: the elite or well-to-do, the "respectable working-class," the working poor on the edge of the economic system, and the "submerged tenth," composed of those who made their living from illegal trade and those who simply did not participate in the economy in any significant way, the "loafers" (DuBois, 310–11).

While African American leaders such as **Booker T. Washington** and W.E.B. DuBois debated what path to take toward black achievement, working-class migrants tried to carve out their own spaces in their new urban homes.

Initially, discussions on how to "uplift the race" were based on how best to represent the African American community. Ideas stemming from Progressive Era philanthropy were disseminated among black intellectuals, as well as the civic-minded, producing a variety of institutions to assist in areas such as housing, education, and employment. In the cities migrants entered established black communities, which included institutions such as churches, schools, and **fraternal orders**. Class differences were represented by membership in clubs, religious organizations, and sites and types of entertainment, in addition to neighborhoods and occupations. Distinctions were obvious in comparing the members of older, established churches with those who attended religious services in **storefront churches**. Fraternal organizations functioned as meeting places, mutual aid societies, social gatherings, and in some cases sites of political discourse, but they also bore the hallmarks of class, with many of the black natives belonging to the more established and oldest orders, while the migrants joined those with less history.

Generally, there were two types of responses to the migrants: resentment and entrepreneurship. Some African Americans native to the North believed that the migrants were too deferential to whites. They were unaccustomed to life in the city, unclean, naïve, and ignorant of proper behavior. Black fears that the influx would drag down the quality of life in their neighborhoods were realized when living quarters became more and more cramped. Native black workers complained, along with white workers, that the new migrants undermined their relationships with employers. Some resorted to a rewriting of race relations in which they claimed that the relationships between blacks and whites had been better before the migrants relocated to their cities. Underlying these complaints was a resentment of the fact that African Americans were classified as a "homogenous mass," where the "Negro problem" was one that affected the entire race, with no distinctions made for class or regional differences. While initially the migrants did not seem to be concerned with class differences, they were concerned about the quality of their neighborhoods, educational opportunities, and exercising their new political freedom. Some migrants charged that the native African American communities suffered from political apathy, were submissive to whites, and were complacent, while they were infusing new life and economic opportunities into their adopted cities.

If an older class of black elites resented southern migrants, an emergent class of black entrepreneurs welcomed the newcomers. Migration produced a need for a range of services in black neighborhoods offered by people such as **barbers**, beauticians, grocers, **attorneys**, **undertakers**, and **insurers**. In contrast to the occupational structure of native black elites, many of whom served a white clientele, this new class, a distinct black bourgeoisie, carved out a place to specifically service the African American community. In large metropolitan areas such as **New York City**, **Chicago**, and Philadelphia, the dramatic increases in the black population created new opportunities for black-owned commercial enterprises to meet the needs of the relocating migrants. As the numbers of skilled black elites serving whites declined through competition with white immigrants, the status and numbers of black entrepreneurs increased throughout northern communities. Individuals with capital, education, and training were able to generate a small, but autonomous caste, independent from white customers. As their numbers expanded, this new black bourgeoisie began to challenge the older black elite for community leadership. By the end of World War I the black business class was able to capitalize on its relationship with the migrants in the political arena because of its history in the development and growth of black communities in the North. The divide between the black middle and working classes was not as great as the gulf between these groups and the elite, first because of the shared economic relationship, and second because they lived in the same communities, and it was not uncommon for them to attend the same churches and clubs. Family legacies were not as important as personal initiative and monetary standing in this segment of the black population. By the 1950s the black bourgeoisie had eclipsed the black elite with regard to political power and community recognition.

Mobility was an expression of the economic and social ambitions of African Americans that, in the beginning, unintentionally challenged the established structures of the black elites. With their roots in the antebellum era, class differences within the black community found expression during the Great Migration in social and political debates about the future of the race. The population increases in urban black communities that provided new opportunities also heightened differences among their residents. The subject of intraracial class conflict continues to cause a great amount of discomfort among African Americans. Even in the twenty-first century race remains a more acceptable subject for public debate and continues to obscure deep economic, social, and political divisions within the black community. *See also* Black Consumer Market; Employment, Black Female Patterns of; Employment, Black Male Patterns of; European Immigrants, Relations with Black Migrants; Occupational Mobility; Primary Documents 39, 40.

Further Reading

DuBois, W.E.B. *The Philadelphia Negro: A Social Study*. 1899. Reprint, with a new introduction by Elijah Anderson, Philadelphia: University of Pennsylvania Press, 1996.

Kusmer, Kenneth L. *A Ghetto Takes Shape: Black Cleveland, 1870–1930*. Urbana: University of Illinois Press, 1976.

Marks, Carole. *Farewell—We're Good and Gone: The Great Black Migration*. Bloomington: Indiana University Press, 1989.

Spear, Allan H. *Black Chicago: The Making of a Negro Ghetto, 1890–1920*. Chicago: University of Chicago Press, 1967.

Prudence D. Cumberbatch

Involuntary Servitude

When emancipation ended slavery, it uprooted a system founded on the conviction that whites had the right to control black movement. It is hardly surprising, then, that the post–Civil War era was marked by continuing struggle over the right of blacks to move about freely. With little resistance, whites acquiesced to the reality that they could no longer buy and sell slaves, but accepting the corollary view that African Americans were entitled to move about freely was another matter entirely. In June 1865 an Alabama planter, J. B. Moore, spoke for many when he said, "I look upon slavery as gone, gone, gone beyond the possibility of help." Immediately, however, he went on to add, "We have the power to pass stringent police laws to govern the negroes—This is a blessing—For they must be controlled in some way or white people cannot live amongst them" (Cohen, *At Freedom's Edge*, 28).

Thus from 1865 to 1867 southern whites set about constructing black codes to fill the legal void created by the destruction of slavery. While the specifics varied from one state to another, all aimed at restoring white control, albeit in a context where the freedpeople would no longer be owned as personal property. The codes recognized the legitimacy of black families and gave blacks legal standing in the courts, but their central thrust was about limiting black movement. Vagrancy statutes virtually required that the freedpeople show evidence of having gainful employment (a labor contract), while enticement statutes penalized employers who might hire those already under contract to another employer. Georgia's 1866 enticement law made it an offense to entice a laborer under contract "by offering higher wages or in any other way whatever" (Cohen, "Negro Involuntary Servitude," 35). Other statutes made the mere act of abandoning a labor contract a criminal offense. Anticipating later legislation aimed against **labor agents**, Mississippi levied special penalties against those who might entice laborers to leave the state.

Reconstruction nullified most such enactments, but even before the era ended, former Confederate states began reinventing the black codes. Moving slowly at first and using language that was now race neutral, they erected a fabric of law designed to give planters a broad measure of control over their black laborers. As before, vagrancy, enticement, and contract laws were mainstays of the system, but soon they were supplemented by measures such as emigrant agent laws (licensing statutes aimed at crippling the activities of labor agents) and "false pretenses" laws that treated contract breaking as an intentional criminal activity. Some of these measures led directly to the creation of conditions of peonage.

Reinforcing statutes aimed at limiting black mobility were laws and practices pertaining to criminal punishment. Prime among these were the state criminal surety systems that allowed planters to pay court costs and fines when their employees became embroiled with the law. At one level, the practice might be a way of humanizing the impact of the law. However, since the money paid to the court by the employer was then treated as a binding contractual obligation, this assistance often served as yet another coercive tool for the control of resistant laborers.

Beyond the surety system, the postbellum era witnessed the development of a variety of draconian state convict labor systems aimed at delivering maximum punishment and deterrence at minimal taxpayer expense. Postwar convict leasing began in 1866 when Florida authorized its counties to lease convicts out to individuals. Not long thereafter North Carolina made it legal for counties to hire their prisoners out to **railroads** and other corporations. At about the same time Arkansas, Tennessee, and Virginia legalized the hiring out of state convicts. Alabama, Georgia, Mississippi, and Texas started by sanctioning leasing at both the state and county levels. While many of these laws originated during Reconstruction in cash-strapped Republican regimes, such practices continued apace once the Redeemers took power. The leasing of convicts for work on railroads and levees was particularly common, and increasingly the labor of black prisoners was seen both as a means of disciplining recalcitrant black workers and as a foundation for southern internal development. For a variety of reasons, both economic and noneconomic, the early twentieth century witnessed the decline of convict leasing, and in 1928 Alabama became the last state to abolish the system.

But leasing had never been the whole story of southern convict labor. County chain gangs were everywhere, and county governments often made direct use of prisoners as an unpaid source of labor for road construction and repair, swamp drainage, and a variety of other public purposes. In Chatham County, Georgia, in 1892, Judge William D. Harden won high praise for his long-standing practice "of imposing long periods of penal servitude on persons guilty of crimes involving moral turpitude." By doing this rather than imposing fines, Harden was said to have facilitated "the great work of draining the country . . . a work which has increased the value of the taxable property of our county by hundreds of thousands of dollars" (Cohen, *At Freedom's Edge*, 225).

By the turn of the century vagrancy roundups had emerged as a means of impressing black labor into service for use either on public projects or to supplement the farm labor force at picking time. In September 1901 it was reported that some Mississippi towns were driving "idlers and vagrants" into the cotton fields. In September 1904, when Texas farmers were desperate for labor, it was reported that in Waco, Texas, police had "commenced a determined war on idlers and vags generally" (Cohen, "Negro Involuntary Servitude," 50). There is no way of knowing the precise frequency of these vagrancy drives, but it appears that from the time of the Great Depression onward they became increasingly rare.

Given all this, it is tempting to conclude that for African Americans in the early twentieth century, the South was simply one vast prison camp, but there were significant crosscurrents, and the truth is more complicated. Certainly whites had created a dense fabric of law aimed at limiting black movement, and certainly the convict labor systems of the southern states stood as a sharp warning to anyone who might challenge the system. Moreover, the enactment of the laws of involuntary servitude in the late nineteenth and early twentieth centuries was fully congruent with the parallel passage of a host of other southern laws aimed at strengthening segregation and destroying the last vestiges of black political participation.

But whites were far less successful in regulating African American movement than they were in imposing social segregation and political disfranchisement. While it is true that migration to the North remained at minimal levels during the first fifty years after the Civil War, the fact remains that there was significant internal black migration from one southern state to another. By itself, this belies the notion that the laws of involuntary servitude were effectively preventing African American movement. This idea is further undermined by the fact that from 1916 to 1918, once real job opportunities became available in the North, perhaps half a million southern blacks surged northward in the First Great Migration. To be sure, southern whites tried to stop the migration, but their attempts appear to have been largely unsuccessful.

What explains the apparent discrepancy between the existence of so many laws aimed at limiting movement and the population statistics that show blacks moving about relatively freely within the South? The answer appears to rest largely on the fact that while whites were in substantial agreement on issues like social segregation and political exclusion, no such consensus existed on black mobility. While those who were heavily dependent on black labor did all they could to immobilize black workers, labor-hungry planters in places like Arkansas and Mississippi did not scruple to hire the very emigrant agents who were such anathema to other employers. Beyond this, up-country whites often opposed any measures that would stand in the way of an African American exodus out of their counties. In 1889 a North Carolina Populist journal spoke for many when it declared that so long as the black remained in the country, he would be a "festering sore on our body politic." Further, it said, "we would hail with delight and rejoicing his peaceful departure" (Cohen, *At Freedom's Edge*, 237).

The laws of involuntary servitude represented very real efforts to limit black mobility, and they were indeed used, but not most of the time and not in most places. What needs to be remembered is that these statutes existed against a free labor backdrop that made it difficult to maintain labor immobility over prolonged periods of time. The tension between conflicting white interests created a zone where blacks could assert their freedom by seeking better conditions, and this is precisely what they tried to do. At the same time, when local labor shortages were acute enough, the laws of involuntary servitude gave planters the legal and social framework for holding or impressing the labor they needed. The laws of involuntary servitude persisted on the books well into the second half of the twentieth century, but it would appear that like **lynching** and peonage, the actual practice of holding people to labor against their will went into a significant and continuing decline in the years after World War I. *See also* Black Migration before World War I, Patterns of; Great Migration, White Opposition to.

Further Reading

Alilunas, Leo. "Statutory Means of Impeding Emigration of the Negro." *Journal of Negro History* 22 (1937): 148–62.

Ayers, Edward L. *Vengeance and Justice: Crime and Punishment in the 19th Century American South.* New York: Oxford University Press, 1984.

Cohen, William. *At Freedom's Edge: Black Mobility and the Southern White Quest for Racial Control, 1861–1915.* Baton Rouge: Louisiana State University Press, 1991.

———. "Negro Involuntary Servitude in the South, 1865–1940: A Preliminary Analysis." *Journal of Southern History* 42 (1976): 31–60.

Daniel, Pete. *The Shadow of Slavery: Peonage in the South, 1901–1969.* Urbana: University of Illinois Press, 1972.

Lichtenstein, Alex C. *Twice the Work of Free Labor: The Political Economy of Convict Labor in the New South.* New York: Routledge, 1996.

Mancini, Matthew I. *One Dies, Get Another: Convict Leasing in the American South, 1866-1928*. Columbia: University of South Carolina Press, 1996.

Ransom, Roger L., and Richard Sutch. *One Kind of Freedom: The Economic Consequences of Emancipation*. New York: Cambridge University Press, 1977.

William Cohen

IWW *See* Industrial Workers of the World (IWW)

J

Jackson, Joseph Harrison (1900–1991)

Joseph Harrison Jackson was an African American **minister** who at the height of the second phase of the Great Migration was both pastor of Olivet Baptist Church in **Chicago** and president of the National Baptist Convention, U.S.A., the largest black religious organization in the United States. He was born to Henry and Emily Jackson in Rudyard, Mississippi, on September 11, 1900. A lifelong member of the black **Baptist Church**, Jackson professed Christianity at an early age and was licensed to preach while still a teenager. After serving as a "circuit rider," preaching in rural Mississippi and finishing his A.B. degree at Jackson College in the late 1920s, Jackson moved to **Omaha, Nebraska**, to accept his first pastorate. He remained there until 1934, when he moved to **Philadelphia** to assume leadership of Monumental Baptist Church. It was during his time in Philadelphia that Jackson gained in prominence in black Baptist circles, becoming known for his brilliant preaching style and administrative acumen. It was largely in recognition of these abilities that he was chosen in 1941 to take the pastorate at Olivet Baptist, which was at the time considered to be the largest Protestant church in the world.

Jackson brought greater renown to Olivet Baptist, increasing the church's stature in Chicago and around the nation. He liquidated church debt, increased the ministerial and administrative staff, and launched numerous programs to serve Chicago's African American community. Black southern migrants were particularly attracted to the church for its large resources, community outreach, and lively worship services. Because he had received a master's degree in educational administration while in Nebraska and had started doctoral studies at the University of Chicago, Jackson's preaching style was refined and scholarly, on the one hand. On the other hand, it was revivalist and fiery, reflecting the "mixed-type" sermonic style of many migration-era African

American ministers. For his administrative and preaching abilities, Jackson was granted lifetime tenure at Olivet. He consolidated his power by becoming involved with national organizations such as the Baptist World Alliance and the Federal Council of Churches. He also abolished tenure limits for the presidency of the National Baptist Conference not long after he was elected president in 1953, a move that allowed him to serve in that capacity for nearly thirty years.

Jackson is perhaps best known for his conflict with **Martin Luther King, Jr.** The two Baptist clerics had been friends and coworkers in the National Baptist Convention until they disagreed about the **civil rights movement** and about the role of the Convention in the movement. Although Jackson launched a few progressive initiatives during the movement, such as lobbying for an "Anti-discrimination Day" and campaigning for the presidency of John F. Kennedy, his approach to civil rights was conservative and gradualist. He considered King's nonviolent tactics to be subversive, disloyal, and unpatriotic. King, for his part, wanted to wrest control of the National Baptist Convention from Jackson to use it in the struggle to obtain African American civil rights. King failed in his attempts and eventually left the organization to form the Progressive Baptist Convention in 1961. The rift never healed, and when King was assassinated in 1968, Jackson refused to attend his funeral, claiming that he was busy.

A complex and paradoxical minister, J. H. Jackson made an indelible mark on black Chicago during the second phase of the Great Migration. He is in part responsible for making Olivet Baptist Church the seat of black Baptist power for most of the post–World War II era. Jackson was the only African American cleric granted an audience with Pope Paul XXIII and to attend the Second Vatican Council. In addition to writing three books, he traveled to many places in the world, where he extended the reach of Olivet Baptist Church as well as the National Baptist Convention, U.S.A. *See also* Bradby, Robert L.

Further Reading

Best, Wallace. *Passionately Human, No Less Divine: Religion and Culture in Black Chicago, 1915-1952*. Princeton, NJ: Princeton University Press, 2005.

Branch, Taylor. *Parting the Waters: America in the King Years, 1954-63*. New York: Simon and Schuster, 1988.

Lewis, David Levering. *King: A Biography*. Chicago: University of Chicago Press, 1970.

Tribble, Sherman Roosevelt. "Images of a Preacher: A Study of the Reverend Joseph H. Jackson, Former President of the National Baptist Convention, U.S.A., Inc." Ph.D. diss., Northwestern University, 1990.

Wallace D. Best

Jackson, Mahalia (1911–1972)

Mahalia Jackson was the undisputed "Queen of Gospel Song." The third child born to John A. Jackson and Charity Clark, she grew up in the Black Pearl section of **New Orleans, Louisiana**. Although she began singing as a child in her father's Plymouth Baptist Church, Jackson was heavily influenced by the music of the Sanctified Church, developing an energetic singing style that became her trademark. When her mother died in 1916, she was sent to live with her aunt and namesake, Mahalia "Duke" Paul. While living in her aunt's home, Jackson was able clandestinely to hear the music of such **blues** greats as **Ma Rainey** and **Bessie Smith**, two **women** who also greatly influenced her singing style.

At age sixteen Jackson joined the waves of migrating African Americans who were leaving the South for northern destinations such as **Chicago** in the hope of a better life. Upon her arrival in Chicago in 1927 she affiliated with Salem Baptist Church, singing in the church's choir. Jackson's booming contralto soon garnered her a reputation and following, and she began singing solo with the Johnson Singers, one of the first professional gospel quartets in the country. By the mid-1930s her reputation for singing gospel stretched from coast to coast.

A contract from Decca Records in 1937 confirmed Jackson's popularity and launched her professional solo recording career. The song she recorded for Decca, "God's Gonna Separate the Wheat from the Tares," was only modestly successful, so Jackson took a hiatus from recording. She did not stop singing, however, becoming even more popular as a gospel concert artist, performing before large and small audiences throughout the country. By this time Jackson had also met **Thomas A. Dorsey**, the "Father of Gospel Music," and she became the most recognized "demonstrator" of his songs. Dorsey wrote "Peace in the Valley" just for Jackson.

In 1946 Jackson returned to professional recording with a contract from Apollo Records, this time with record sales that made history. Her recording of W. Herbert Brewster's "Move On Up a Little Higher" sold more than 2 million copies, the first gospel song ever to do so. By this time Jackson also received greater recognition from the African American middle-class establishment, which had previously been lukewarm to her vivacious singing and "down-home" manner. The powerful National Baptist Convention elected Jackson as its official soloist in 1947.

Throughout the 1950s Jackson's star rose even higher. She was a popular guest on Chicago journalist Studs Terkel's television show, and her appearances led to her own radio and television programs. She signed a lucrative contract with Columbia Records in 1954 and began to tour internationally. Performing more frequently in large concert halls than in churches during this time, Jackson suffered some criticism from the African American community. Although her song repertoire often relaxed into trite standards, however, Jackson stayed true to her word that she would never sing secular music. She was influential enough to get the organizers of the 1957 Newport Jazz Festival to feature only gospel music at the prestigious annual event. Jackson's rain-soaked duet with **Louis Armstrong** singing "When the Saints Go Marching In" is one of the more enduring images of her entire career.

Jackson was a lifelong supporter of African American civil rights and used her fame to further the cause of black advancement. **Martin Luther King, Jr.**, was a close friend of Jackson's and sought her advice and support on occasion. She is forever linked with King historically, having sung another Brewster song, "How I Got Over," just before King delivered his immortal "I have a dream" speech at the March on Washington in 1963. At King's request, she sang at his funeral in 1968. He had requested Dorsey's classic, "Take My Hand, Precious Lord."

As the "Queen of Gospel Song," Mahalia Jackson reigned supreme. Her many accomplishments included being awarded the first Grammy for gospel and becoming the first millionaire gospel artist. Jackson's personal life, however, was marked by loss and disappointment. Although she loved children, she was unable to have her own. Her two marriages ended in divorce, and Jackson was plagued by health problems throughout her life. Having left an indelible mark in the world of gospel music, Mahalia Jackson finally succumbed to heart failure at her home outside Chicago in 1972. *See also* Baptist Church; Recording Industry; Tharpe, Sister Rosetta.

Further Reading

Goreau, Laurraine. *Just Mahalia, Baby: The Mahalia Jackson Story*. New York: Pelican Publishing Company, 1984.

Harris, Michael W. *The Rise of the Gospel Blues: The Music of Thomas Andrew Dorsey in the Urban Church*. New York: Oxford University Press, 1992.

Schwerin, Jules. *Got to Tell It: Mahalia Jackson, Queen of Gospel*. New York: Oxford University Press, 1992.

Wallace D. Best

Jacksonville, Florida

Jacksonville is an important city in the story of the Great Black Migration. Although the Great Migration is often regarded as the movement of people from the rural South to the urban North, a close look at Jacksonville complicates that picture of this important population shift. Jacksonville entered the age of the Great Black Migration in 1888. During that year a yellow-fever epidemic devastated the city and caused the migration of a large number of whites. In the wake of this white exodus, thousands of black migrants from rural Florida and southeastern Georgia moved to the city to fill the economic vacuum left by the fleeing whites. Continuous in-migration of blacks between 1888 and 1920 made Jacksonville a black-majority city. For many of these black migrants, Jacksonville was simply one stop on a longer journey to the North; for many others, it remained their final destination. No matter their reasons for coming or the duration of their stay, black migrants transformed the political, social, and economic life of the city.

Black migration to Jacksonville had a great impact on city politics. Blacks in Jacksonville had voted since Reconstruction; however, by the 1890s new laws restricted the ability of most poor blacks and whites to vote. After 1888, when the city's black population began to surge, the majority-white city council persuaded state legislators to pass a law that gave power to the governor to appoint the mayor and city council until new state laws to disfranchise black voters were passed. Even after the disfranchisement laws, numerous black politicians continued to hold local offices in Jacksonville. With a small electoral base, blacks managed to maintain a voting majority along with white

Republicans in Jacksonville's Sixth Ward. Since migration made such an impact on the city, Sixth Ward voters elected at least one black politician, sometimes two, to the city council until 1907, when the city council gerrymandered the Sixth Ward with two predominantly white wards so that it would no longer have a black majority.

Black migration to Jacksonville also had an impact on segregation and civil rights activism. After the great fire of 1901 a rush of white and black migrants moved to the city to help rebuild and to participate in the new economic opportunities available. Black and white professional and political leaders all agreed that black migrants who came to the city after the fire had a habit of testing racial etiquette and manners on the streetcars by sitting next to whites. In response, whites on the city council passed the first in a series of measures to segregate the races on the city's streetcars in 1901. Black leaders protested these measures, and since the black population was so large, they organized a series of effective boycotts that persuaded city authorities to abandon their enforcement of the ordinance. When the city passed another ordinance in 1905, African Americans in Jacksonville staged another boycott and filed a lawsuit charging that the statute violated the Fourteenth Amendment. Although the court ruled in favor of the black petitioners, this victory for the city's African Americans did not last long. The courts upheld the constitutionality of subsequent state and local streetcar segregation laws. Discouraged by these court rulings, African Americans abandoned their boycotts.

There is probably no other area where migration left a more indelible mark on the city than in race relations. **James Weldon Johnson**, in his autobiography *Along This Way*, recorded his experience as a resident of Jacksonville under the backdrop of increased racial tensions and violence within the context of a growing black population. Johnson reflected on the respectful relationship whites and blacks had in the city after Reconstruction, but as blacks and **Jim Crow** came to the city, race relations deteriorated, transforming Jacksonville into what he described as a "one hundred percent cracker town." The city's first recorded **lynching**—of two black men in 1919—brought to a climax the racial animosities that had intensified during the previous three decades.

Many contemporary observers and historians regarded Jacksonville as a southern point for migration out of the South. **Emmett J. Scott**'s compendium of letters of black migrants published in 1919 in the *Journal of Negro History* included numerous letters from current and former Jacksonville residents decrying discrimination and racial tensions in the city. Historian Jerrell Shofner, in his study of the Great Migration in Florida, concluded that Jacksonville was hampered by a high rate of black out-migration. Although Scott and Shofner may have been correct in their description of some black migrants, a majority of migrants looked to Jacksonville as a final destination. So many did so that by World War I black strikebreakers were used against black strikers, and white labor leaders throughout the 1910s demanded that local industries use white labor before resorting to black labor because there were so many black laborers available in the city. Thus Jacksonville was a nexus for black migrants going north, as well as a destination for those wanting to remain in the South. *See also* Gulf South; Miami, Florida; New Orleans, Louisiana; Strikebreaking.

Further Reading

Akin, Edward N. "When a Minority Becomes the Majority: Blacks in Jacksonville Politics, 1887–1907." *Florida Historical Quarterly* 53 (October 1974): 123–45.

Crooks, James B. *Jacksonville after the Fire, 1901–1919: A New South City*. Jacksonville: University of North Florida Press, 1991.

Johnson, James Weldon. *Along This Way*. 1933. Reprint, New York: Viking Press, 1968.

Meier, August, and Elliott Rudwick. "Negro Boycotts of Segregated Streetcars in Florida, 1901–1905." *South Atlantic Quarterly* 69 (Spring 1970): 525–33.

Shofner, Jerrell H. "Florida and the Black Migration." *Florida Historical Quarterly* 57 (January 1979): 267–88.

Robert Cassanello

Jazz

The emergence and development of jazz were fundamentally intertwined with the Great Black Migration. Many musicians participated in the rural-to-urban and southern-to-northern migrations early in the twentieth century. Jazz benefited from the development of educational and entertainment networks that served burgeoning black communities, and when these communities went into decline in subsequent decades, the jazz community experienced hardships as well. Yet jazz remained a vehicle for community building and cultural identification among black urban people throughout the period of migration and urbanization. This music remains a unique index of the social transformations and conflicts that defined the Great Black Migration.

The often-told story of major artists like **Louis Armstrong** and King Oliver beginning their careers in **New Orleans** and then bringing the music upriver to **Chicago** and eventually other cities is symbolic of, but ultimately obscures, a more complicated history of musical networks and interactions. Although the multicultural port city of New Orleans was singularly important to the development of jazz, it was only one of many southern, northern, and western cities where, early in the twentieth century, musicians of different social backgrounds, including many migrants, encountered each other in schools, sidewalks, people's homes, and formal performance spaces. Itinerant **blues** musicians, members of dance orchestras, barroom piano players, and classically trained composers learned from one another and developed a variety of instrumental and vocal musical styles. By the late 1910s these styles had been fused together into syncopated dance music that musicians and others regularly referred to as jazz.

The development of jazz was not solely the product of musicians' encounters and creative energies. Jazz also prospered because black people were part of a new moment in U.S. history marked by urbanization, advances in technology, and access to new kinds of leisure activities and consumer goods made available to a mass audience. Despite the problems black urban dwellers encountered in segregated and hostile cities, many workers had money in their pockets and leisure time during which to spend it. Record companies marketed their wares to black consumers, and black entertainment districts where people could dance to and listen to jazz in nightclubs, **dance halls**, and theaters emerged in many urban centers.

Jazz served a vital social function during these early years of the Great Black Migration. The development of the music went hand in hand with African Americans defining themselves as urban people. Although jazz was created primarily for enjoyment, even as a vehicle of pleasure the music served an important function in the struggle against racial, class, and gender domination. Classic blues artists such as **Ma Rainey** and **Bessie Smith**, often backed by prominent jazz instrumentalists, recorded songs that addressed issues facing black migrants, especially black **women**. They spoke of natural disasters and racism in the South, the hardships of traveling from the South to the North, the oppressive nature of domestic work, and a host of issues pertaining to modern gender roles and sexualities. These blues singers played a liberating social function for people who listened to them. Women could identify with the stories they told and find confirmation of their decisions to leave the South, a means of understanding their position in the labor force, and affirmation of their sexual desires. The classic blues were also a vehicle for black gays and lesbians to explore their sexual identities. A number of blues songs explored the possibilities of homosexual relationships, and several blues singers participated in the development of a gay, African American subculture in Harlem during the 1920s and 1930s.

Whether one listened to blues singers or instrumentalists, recordings or live bands, jazz played an important role in building a sense of community in urban areas. Listening to or dancing to jazz at a club may not have significantly changed an industrial or domestic worker's status in the labor force, but it did allow people to escape temporarily the routine and degradation of work and reclaim their bodies for themselves. Migrants and other urban dwellers developed a sense of collective identity through shared, participatory rituals on the dance floors, and when musicians like Smith or Armstrong became popular icons, they were embraced as symbols of black cultural achievement. Jazz provided African Americans a means for understanding themselves as modern, urbane people who had left behind the legacy of slavery. This function was not lost on black nationalist organizations like the radical **African Blood Brotherhood** and **Marcus Garvey**'s **Universal Negro Improvement Association**, which organized jazz performances as a means of generating support for their programs.

Community building was a precarious enterprise, and the jazz world reflected many of the tensions that were brewing in urban communities during the Great Black Migration. Conflicts between entrenched residents and new arrivals dovetailed with divisions between working-class and middle-class people. Many members of the established black middle class viewed working-class blacks, especially new arrivals from the South, as crude and a threat to their own precarious position in society. So while some middle-class African Americans joined working-class folks in dance halls and nightclubs, others considered jazz something of an embarrassment, symbolic of the unsophisticated culture of working-class or southern people. Jazz also received a fair amount of disdain from churchgoing people of all classes who considered it "devil's music." Thus it is important to keep in mind that although music had the power to bring black people together, it was also a vehicle by which they distinguished themselves from one another.

Although jazz served a particular function in black communities, it was a widespread phenomenon, wildly popular with whites and others and performed by musicians of all hues. During the 1920s this music had a tremendous cultural impact, figuring prominently in the work of writers and visual artists and standing at the center of debates about transformations in U.S. society. The often hysterical reactions to jazz had much to do with anxieties about urbanization, technological developments, immigration, the emergence of the "new woman," the breakdown of cultural hierarchies, Bolshevism, and a host of other issues. But the reaction to jazz, whether positive or negative, also reflected anxieties about the growing presence of black people in urban centers, their political demands, their effect on American culture, and their potential influence on modern sexualities.

During the **swing** era of the 1930s and 1940s an increasingly professionalized African American musicians' community honed its skills in urban entertainment and educational institutions. Migrant musicians and the musical exchanges that followed their arrivals in cities influenced the development of swing. **Count Basie**, for example, energized the **New York City** jazz community upon his arrival from **Kansas City** in 1936. Jazz continued to play an important social function in black communities, though the divisiveness around it decreased somewhat as the music became more entrenched at the center of popular culture during the late 1930s and the controversies around jazz subsided.

The 1940s witnessed something of a decentering of jazz from the center of black migrants' musical experience. The virtuoso **bebop** movement of that decade, which reflected the worldly orientations of musicians and the militancy and expectancy of the larger community, included many migrants among its practitioners and listeners. However, bebop's modern sounds helped redefine jazz from what was primarily dance music to music for listening. From the 1940s on, musical genres such as urban blues, **rhythm and blues**, rock and roll, and **soul** competed with jazz for a working-class black audience, and it was increasingly around these genres that migrant musicians and audiences defined their social worlds.

The arrival of musicians in new cities still had a generative effect on jazz, and while their audiences were often getting smaller, jazz musicians provided a sense of collective identity to recent arrivals and other urban dwellers. In **Los Angeles**, for example, migrants such as Ornette Coleman and Melba Liston played a crucial role in the development of avant-garde jazz in that community before a dedicated audience on Central Avenue in the 1940s and 1950s.

The decline of jazz during the 1960s was related to and symbolic of the decline of the urban centers that had witnessed the Great Black Migration. The reasons for the jazz business's failings include competition from other genres and media, but also the disintegration of music education networks and the scarcity of performance opportunities in African American communities that were directly related to the degeneration of urban infrastructures and the immiserization of urban communities at the tail end of the migration period. As a response to the predicaments facing artists and their communities alike, musicians in various cities formed collective organizations during the 1960s and 1970s. The memberships of organizations such as the Union of God's Musicians and Artists Ascension in Los Angeles and the Association for the Advancement of Creative Musicians in Chicago included people who had recently moved to these cities, as well as those whose families had participated in earlier phases of migration. These groups were noteworthy in their attempts to provide professional services for working musicians and improve the cultural lives of community members. To the latter end, they offered music lessons, music history courses, and free concerts and generally tried to reestablish the communal function jazz had performed in earlier decades. *See also* Calloway, Cab[ell]; Coltrane, John William; Ellington, Duke [Edward Kennedy]; Gillespie, John Birks "Dizzy"; Harlem Renaissance; Monk, Thelonious Sphere; Parker, Charlie "Yardbird"; Primary Document 1.

Further Reading

Bryant, Clora, ed. *Central Avenue Sounds: Jazz in Los Angeles*. Berkeley: University of California Press, 1998.

Chicago Jazz Archive. Regenstein Library, University of Chicago. www.lib.uchicago.edu/e/su/cja/.

Davis, Angela. *Blues Legacies and Black Feminism: Gertrude "Ma" Rainey, Bessie Smith, and Billie Holiday*. New York: Pantheon, 1998.

Griffin, Farah Jasmine. *"Who Set You Flowin'?" The African-American Migration Narrative*. New York: Oxford University Press, 1995.

Jones, LeRoi (Amiri Baraka). *Blues People: Negro Music in White America*. New York: William Morrow, 1963.

Kenney, William Howland. *Chicago Jazz: A Cultural History, 1904–1930*. New York: Oxford University Press, 1993.

Lott, Eric. "Double V, Double-Time." *Callalloo* 11, no. 3 (1988): 597–605.

Ogren, Kathy. *The Jazz Revolution: Twenties America and the Meaning of Jazz*. New York: Oxford University Press, 1989.

Peretti, Burton W. *The Creation of Jazz: Music, Race, and Culture in Urban America*. Urbana: University of Illinois Press, 1992.

Porter, Eric. *What Is This Thing Called Jazz? African American Musicians as Artists, Critics, and Activists*. Berkeley: University of California Press, 2002.

Public Broadcasting Service. "Jazz: A History of America's Music." www.pbs.org/jazz.

Eric Porter

Jim Crow

The term *Jim Crow* has come to designate the system of institutionalized discrimination against African Americans that southern states began to operate from the late 1890s and practiced until the late 1950s. The laws that constituted the backbone of the Jim Crow system were designed to keep whites and blacks as separate as possible in public spaces such as schools, transports, and accommodation and to prevent African Americans from exercising their right to vote. This system of segregation was fully validated in southern states by the 1910s. For white southerners, Jim Crow was a way to reinstate their supremacy, which had been challenged by their defeat in the Civil War. The harsh acts of violence that characterized this brutal system of segregation and the exploitative sharecropping system prompted many African Americans to leave the South and migrate to northern cities. Starting in the 1880s, this process peaked during the 1910s and the 1920s, when many southern black sharecroppers migrated from the rural South to urban centers. Yet as these migrants soon discovered, segregation, albeit in less violent form, also existed in the North. For the people who left behind the cruel Jim Crow system, the North had a mythic dimension of "freedom land." However, they soon found that discrimination was still part of their lives and that segregation and run-down but high-priced **ghettos** were entrenched in the North too.

The name Jim Crow has its origins in the shows of a white minstrel actor, Thomas "Daddy" Rice. During the 1830s, his face blackened by charcoal, he performed the song "Jump Jim Crow" while dancing a silly jig. Some say that Rice invented this character after seeing a southern crippled, elderly black man (or some say a young black boy) dancing and singing. Probably a Mr. Crow owned the slave who suggested the character to Rice, thus the name in the song. By the 1850s Jim Crow had become a standard character in minstrel shows. The stereotype became one of the many embodiments of the idea of African American inferiority in American nineteenth-century popular culture, along with Sambos and Coons. The words "Jim Crow" soon developed into a white insult referring to blacks and, by the 1890s, were used to describe acts of racial discrimination against blacks.

Although Jim Crow laws were passed in the 1890s, attempts to restrict the economic and social freedom of former slaves in southern states started immediately after the Civil War. The first attempts in this direction were called black codes. In them, the word "slaves" was replaced by "freedmen," but the codes still forced former slaves to carry passes, comply with curfews, and live as property of their landowners. These acts were soon declared illegal by the federal government and unconstitutional thanks to the approval of the Fourteenth and Fifteenth Amendments. These two amendments, together with the Civil Rights Acts of 1866 and 1875, helped African Americans achieve important early political successes. Yet these were universally rejected in southern states and prompted a backlash from white supremacists who acted through secret groups such as the **Ku Klux Klan**. Starting in Tennessee as a veterans' club, the Klan soon spread throughout the South, becoming a terrorist organization. Violence erupted throughout the South, and the responses of the federal government to stop this bloodshed were far too weak. Klansmen, whose attacks became more organized from the late 1860s, targeted the more inclusive politics of Reconstruction. They persecuted both those blacks who were willing to fight for their rights and those Republican politicians, black and white, who had ousted Democratic politicians from power. The election of Rutherford B. Hayes to the presidency in 1877 marked the retreat of federal efforts to protect the rights of blacks. It inaugurated decades of racial terror in the South, where **lynching**, chain gangs, rape, and the brutal exploitation of black sharecroppers became part of everyday life.

From the late 1870s, a series of rulings from the Supreme Court paved the way for southern states to pass laws that institutionalized the division between blacks and whites. In 1883 the Court repealed the 1875 Civil Rights Acts, which had banned segregation in public facilities. Public transports started to be equipped with separate Jim Crow sections where African Americans were forced to sit. In protest of the law, blacks in Louisiana challenged the norm's constitutionality when a light-skinned African American, Homer Plessy, was quickly arrested for sitting in a car reserved for whites on a train. A local judge ruled against Plessy, and in 1896 the Supreme Court endorsed the ruling in *Plessy v. Ferguson*. According to the Court, Plessy's rights had not been infringed since the separate accommodations given to blacks were equal to those for whites. It also ruled that "separate but equal" accommodations did not stamp the "colored race with a badge of inferiority." This sentence became the precedent for many other Supreme Court rulings that, under the principle of "separate but equal," masked blatant discriminatory measures against African Americans. The "separate but equal" doctrine was applied to schools in 1899 in the ruling *Cummins v. County Board of Education*. Laws on miscegenation that banned interracial marriages were also passed in many southern states. Historian William Cohen has described these bans as the "ultimate segregation laws" because they clearly implied that whites were superior to blacks and that any mixing of the two races endangered white status and the purity of whites.

To keep the races separate, it was instrumental to disfranchise black voters so that their voices and opinions were not represented on the political scene. This began systematically from the 1890s when voter registration restrictions, such as literacy tests and poll taxes, were imposed. Through these new electoral rules, white registrars could legally deny voting rights to blacks. The effects were distressing. More than half the blacks who voted in Georgia and South Carolina in 1880 had vanished from the polls by 1888. In places such as Alabama, where blacks represented almost half the population, no African Americans were elected representatives to the legislature after 1876.

By 1910 every state of the former Confederacy had approved laws that segregated all aspects of public life so that blacks and whites were prevented from mingling. Streetcars had a special area for blacks at their rear. Water fountains, restrooms, waiting rooms, the entrances and exits at courthouses, libraries, theaters, and public buildings started to exhibit "Whites Only" and "Colored." Even **hospitals** and cemeteries rigidly imposed the division of the color line. Segregation was also applied in some states to the workplace, forbidding whites and blacks to work in the same room. Several states also established curfews for blacks, thus restricting their movements. The army created segregated units, too. Black men were drafted, but they were then assigned to menial labor, and racism became common in military camps. Jim Crow laws marked the failure of Reconstruction and its hope to create a more inclusive society. Those African Americans who remained in the South reacted to racial discrimination by creating their own cultural, religious, and social institutions. Yet their legal rights were disregarded until the late 1950s, and their conditions did not significantly improve until the 1960s.

While laws discriminating against blacks abounded, there was no tutelage to assist former slaves and allow them to earn a decent living. As a result, the vast majority of southern blacks soon became indebted agricultural workers who were controlled by white landlords. This system of land tenancy became

The segregated waiting room at the railroad depot in Jacksonville, Florida, 1921. Courtesy of the Florida State Archives.

known as sharecropping because landless workers were paid a share (usually one-third) of the crop that they had cultivated. In most cases the farmer's share could not cover the debts owed to the local store for supplies or to the landlord for rent. African American farmers found it increasingly impossible to avoid dependency and impoverishment. Southern sharecroppers had a legal status that differed little from that of their slave ancestors. In *12 Million Black Voices*, his folk history of the Great Migration, **Richard Nathaniel Wright** significantly defined sharecropping as "a new kind of bondage" (36) and even the "harshest form of servitude" (38): "We present ourselves to the Lord of the Land and ask to make a crop. We sign a contract—usually our contracts are oral—which allows us to keep one-half of the harvest after all debts are paid.... The Lords of the Land assign us ten or fifteen acres of soil already bled of its fertility through generations of abuse.... If we have been lucky the year before, maybe we have saved a few dollars to tide us through the fall months, but spring finds us begging an 'advance'—credit—from the Lords of the Land" (38). Scarred from the social, economic, and psychological effects of Jim Crow laws, African Americans moved north: "Perhaps never in history has a more utterly unprepared folk wanted to go to the city; we were barely born as a folk when we headed for the tall and sprawling centers of steel and stone. We, who were landless upon the land, ... were such a folk as this when we moved into a world that was destined to test all we were, that threw us into the scales of competition to weigh our mettle" (93).

The Jim Crow system remained firmly in place for the entire first half of the twentieth century. Only in 1956 did the Supreme Court declare Alabama's Jim

Crow laws unconstitutional, bolstering the **civil rights movement** led by **Martin Luther King**. The following year the Civil Rights Act created a federal commission to investigate systematic forms of discrimination, but it was only in the 1960s that civil rights took the center stage of American politics and segregation and disfranchisement of African Americans were legally abolished. Yet the legacy of Jim Crow still lives in sectors of American society, as shown in the sudden eruptions of race riots. Unequal access to well-paid jobs, quality education, and **housing** constantly reminds America of its Jim Crow past. *See also* Involuntary Servitude; Nadir of Race Relations; Wilmington, North Carolina, Race Riot of 1898; Primary Documents 68, 69.

Further Reading

Ayers, Edward L. *The Promise of the New South: Life after Reconstruction*. New York: Oxford University Press, 1992.

Brundage, W. Fitzhugh, ed. *Under Sentence of Death: Lynching in the South*. Chapel Hill: University of North Carolina Press, 1997.

Cohen, William. *At Freedom's Edge: Black Mobility and the Southern White Quest for Racial Control, 1861-1915*. Baton Rouge: Louisiana State University Press, 1991.

Hale, Grace Elizabeth. *Making Whiteness: The Culture of Segregation in the South, 1890-1940*. New York: Pantheon Books, 1998.

Litwack, Leon. *Trouble in Mind: Black Southerners in the Age of Jim Crow*. New York: Knopf, 1998.

Perman, Michael. *Struggle for Mastery: Disfranchisement in the South, 1888-1908*. Chapel Hill: University of North Carolina Press, 2001.

Woodward, C. Vann. *Origins of the New South, 1877-1913*. 3rd rev. ed. Baton Rouge: Louisiana State University Press, 1997.

———. *The Strange Career of Jim Crow*. 3rd rev. ed. New York: Oxford University Press, 1974.

Wright, Richard. *12 Million Black Voices*. 1941. Reprint, New York: Thunder's Mouth Press, 2002.

Luca Prono

Johnson, Charles Spurgeon (1893–1956)

As a sociologist, educational leader, and reformer, Charles Spurgeon Johnson worked quietly but relentlessly to improve race relations throughout America, but especially in the southern states. His career led him to experience the Great Migration as both a participant and an observer.

Born in Bristol, Virginia, on July 24, 1893, Johnson grew up in the South as **Jim Crow** laws took root. Literate parents encouraged Johnson to pursue his education. He attended boarding school at Wayland Academy in **Richmond** and earned his B.A. at Virginia Union University. After serving in the army during World War I, Johnson himself joined the Great Migration northward as he pursued his studies at the University of Chicago under the well-known sociologist Robert E. Park, who had been a publicist and ghostwriter for **Booker T. Washington**. With Park's encouragement and under his guidance, Johnson researched and wrote his classic work *The Negro in Chicago* (1922), a study triggered by the race riots that exploded in that city with the return of soldiers from Europe. From **Chicago**, Johnson moved to **New York City**, where he served as the founding editor of *Opportunity*, the journal of the **National Urban League**, from 1923 to 1927. In the pages of *Opportunity* Johnson published the work of many of the African American writers, poets, and artists who gained recognition during the **Harlem Renaissance**. The renowned poet **Langston Hughes** believed that Johnson did more than anyone else to promote the cause of black writers in the 1920s.

In 1927 Johnson returned to the South, where he gained prominence during his long tenure at Fisk University in **Nashville**, first as professor of sociology (1927–1946) and then as the school's first African American president (1946–1957). A prolific researcher and author, Johnson produced sociological studies on his own and in collaboration with others that assessed the effects of the changes wrought by the Great Migration in the North and South alike. Johnson documented the lives of southern black farmers in *Shadow of the Plantation* (1934); he included white tenant farmers as well in *The Collapse of Cotton Tenancy* (1935, with Will Alexander and Alan Embree). He explored the opportunities and the limitations of the most educated African Americans in *The Negro College Graduate* (1938). In *The Negro in American Civilization* (1930) and *Patterns of Negro Segregation* (1943) Johnson looked at the nature of black life throughout the country. He offered an assessment of the specific effects of segregation on children in *Growing up in the Black Belt: Negro Youth in the Rural South* (1941). Johnson's interest in improving race relations in the South and in the nation as a whole was made evident in such works as *A Preface to Racial Understanding* (1936), *To Stem This Tide: A Survey of Racial Tension Areas in the United States* (1943), and *Into the Main Stream: A Survey of Best Practices in Race Relations in the South* (1947). Now, as then, these works provide useful insights into the lives of African Americans as they faced the realities of segregation during the years of the Great Migration.

Johnson's influence expanded well beyond the readers of his sociological treatises. As an active member of the Commission on Interracial Cooperation (established in Atlanta in 1919 to promote racial peace in the South) and as a founding member of the commission's successor organization, the Southern Regional Council, and as a sponsor of the Race Relations Institutes hosted annually at Fisk University beginning in 1944, Johnson worked with liberal southerners, black and white, in an effort to improve race relations in the region. Never considered radical but never satisfied with the status quo, Johnson emphasized the ongoing need to pursue logical "next steps." Johnson's sociological background informed his efforts. He sought objective information to present to the public; he encouraged interracial cooperation to solve the problems identified; and he hoped that in this way liberals and their allies could chip away at the foundation of segregation in the South. Although the Commission on Interracial Cooperation and the Southern Regional Council did, over time, take a somewhat more aggressive stand on racial issues, northern blacks in particular criticized black council members for their seeming gradualism. Johnson disagreed with the notion that any significant gap divided northern and southern blacks. He observed that the great majority of blacks in the North were originally from the South. If northern blacks could protest more vehemently against segregation, it was not because of a difference in background or ideals. Johnson complained that fights among blacks about approaches served as distractions when, in fact, efforts to undermine segregation anywhere and in any way contributed to the effort everywhere. *See also* Chicago Commission on Race Relations; Chicago Race Riot of 1919; Chicago School of Sociology (CSS); Frazier, E. Franklin; Primary Documents 29, 30, 42, 60, 63.

Further Reading

Dunne, Matthew William. "Next Steps: Charles S. Johnson and Southern Liberalism." *Journal of Negro History* 83 (Winter 1998): 1–34.

Gilpin, Patrick J., Marybeth Gasman, and David Levering Lewis. *Charles S. Johnson: Leadership beyond the Veil in the Age of Jim Crow*. Albany: State University of New York Press, 2003.

Robbins, Richard. *Sidelines Activist: Charles S. Johnson and the Struggle for Civil Rights*. Jackson: University Press of Mississippi, 1996.

Matthew W. Dunne

Johnson, Jack (1878–1946)

Born in Galveston, Texas, in 1878, Arthur John "Jack" Johnson became the first black heavyweight boxing champion of the world in 1908. Johnson won the title in Australia, thereby providing America with what it most feared, a Negro fighter as the epitome of physical preeminence. Notions of white supremacy and black inferiority were hard to defend in the face of his deeply symbolic victory. Yet concern about Johnson did not reach hysterical proportions until he defended his title on American soil against the former white champion, Jim Jeffries. The two met on July 4, 1910, in Reno, Nevada, in one of the most important fights of the twentieth century. Johnson humiliated Jeffries, thereby inciting an extraordinary spate of racial disturbances across the country as whites sought revenge on innocent blacks. In the wake of the violence, fight films were censored and calls for boxing to be banned became shrill, while the search for a "white hope" to defeat Johnson began.

It was Johnson's behavior outside the ring that made his physical prowess all the more intolerable to white Americans. Johnson was a lover of fast cars and the owner of a **Chicago** nightclub, but his major sin was a series of relationships with white women, the ultimate taboo in American society. In 1913 Johnson was convicted under the White Slave Traffic Act, which banned the transportation of women across state lines for immoral purposes. Johnson escaped to Europe after the highly publicized trial, though the authorities were not disappointed at his flight. When Johnson lost his title—perhaps deliberately—to the white American Jess Willard in 1915, the *Chicago Tribune* admitted that the result enabled "millions of [Willard's] fellow citizens to sit down to their dinners ... with renewed confidence in their eight inch biceps, flexed, and twenty-eight inch chests, expanded" (Jaher, 156).

The archetypal "Bad Nigger," Johnson became the focus of white fears at a time when black migration to the North was beginning to gather pace. On the one hand, he challenged stereotypes of black men as unsophisticated and unsuccessful. On the other hand, and more important, he embodied the urban dangers facing white working women should black men abandon the rural South in large numbers. Privately, whites knew that Johnson's relationships with women across the color line had been consensual. Given this recognition, Johnson's punishment and exile stood as a warning to black males leaving sharecropping and segregation for opportunities in the North. Any black thoughts regarding the possibilities of interracial sex had to be quashed.

Johnson's notoriety, therefore, clouded the ambitions not just of black fighters but of the race in general. After Johnson, the color line was drawn more tightly in boxing until men like Tiger Flowers and **Joe Louis** earned shots at world titles by behaving antithetically to their predecessor. Unable to compete against white opponents in the **Jim Crow** South, black boxers still needed to act demurely in the Northeast or Midwest to avoid white fury. At the same time, black migrants were careful to avoid the former champion's inflammatory behavior outside the ring.

However, while Johnson was a bogeyman for some, many working-class blacks revered him as a folk hero, telling stories about his superhuman achievements and displaying his photograph in their homes. Johnson proved that migrants could be successful and enjoy greater freedoms above the Mason-Dixon Line. Equally, intellectuals like **W.E.B. DuBois**, who were often suspicious of the attention garnered by sportsmen, were nonetheless quick to highlight the white hypocrisy that attended the vilification of Papa Jack. *See also* Great Migration, White Opposition to; Sport.

Further Reading

Hietala, Thomas R. *Fight of the Century: Jack Johnson, Joe Louis, and the Fight for Racial Equality.* Armonk, NY: M. E. Sharpe, 2002.

Jaher, Frederic Cople. "White America Views Jack Johnson, Joe Louis, and Muhammad Ali." In *Sport in America: New Historical Perspectives*, edited by Donald Spivey. Westport, CT: Greenwood Press, 1985.

Johnson, Jack. *Jack Johnson—in the Ring—and Out.* 1927. Reprint, New York: Citadel Press, 1992.

PBS Online. "Unforgivable Blackness: The Rise and Fall of Jack Johnson." www .pbs.org/unforgivableblackness/.

Roberts, Randy. *Papa Jack: Jack Johnson and the Era of White Hopes.* New York: Free Press, 1983.

Andrew M. Kaye

Johnson, James Weldon (1871–1938)

Poet, novelist, lyricist, historian, educator, activist, and diplomat, James Weldon Johnson was a household name in black and white households of the 1920s. He was best known as a lyricist and poet—having written the lyrics to "Lift Ev'ry Voice and Sing" and the collection of poetic sermons *God's Trombones*—and as an activist in national politics as field secretary and later executive secretary of the **National Association for the Advancement of Colored People** (NAACP).

A native of **Jacksonville, Florida**, Johnson later described his permanent move in 1901 to the North, to **New York City**, as part of the Great Black

Migration. As he described the experience years later in his autobiography, *Along This Way*, he was nearly lynched by a mob of militiamen when, in 1901, Jacksonville was placed under martial law after a great fire had swept through the city. On the basis of this experience, Johnson was sure that he could not advance in the South.

Johnson abandoned his position as principal of Stanton School in Jacksonville for the uncertain career of lyric writing in New York City, collaborating with his brother, J. Rosamond Johnson, and Bob Cole. As part of Cole and Johnson Brothers, he witnessed firsthand the prejudices and racism directed at the touring group and noted the "freedom in motion" he felt in Europe in contrast to the American South and Southwest. He resolved to abandon lyric writing because of these American constraints (Johnson, *Along This Way*, 238).

From these experiences and those he observed of other black men, Johnson embarked on a new career: that of prose writer. His first book-length work, *The Autobiography of an Ex-Coloured Man* (1912), gathered together these experiences into one of the first fictional migration narratives. In this work Johnson used a narrator who could "pass" to explore the cultural meaning of blackness in the American North and South, as well as in Europe. Johnson described this work in his manuscript notes as a "biography of the race."

As in his own life, Johnson's protagonist in this work made clear divisions between life in the North and in the South: freedom of motion, urban modernist culture, and ambiguous racial identity belonging to the North and vast cultural and artistic stores belonging to the South. Most important, he created a harsh portrait of the reality of violence for black people in the South: after the narrator witnesses the **lynching** of a black man, he flees to the North, simultaneously abandoning his pursuit of black folk culture and his quest for identity as a black composer in exchange for becoming "an ordinarily successful white man" who makes money, not music. This narrator sees his failure and feels his weakness acutely, closing his narrative with the observation that while many black leaders are "making a name for themselves and for their race," he has sold his birthright "for a mess of pottage" (Johnson, *Autobiography of an Ex-Coloured Man*, 154).

Johnson bore no resemblance to his protagonist's final disposition; he held much in common with the "race leaders" against whom the narrator measures himself. In his investigative writing for the NAACP, Johnson was always quick to point out the southern mentality and populace that shaped segregationist practices. He regularly made speeches addressing the impoverishment of black schools in the South and the disproportionate funding of their peer white schools, thus contesting the policy of "separate but equal." He also found, when he visited Haiti during its occupation by the United States, that the majority of marines were southern, poorly trained, and poorly educated in all attitudes except their extraordinary hatred of black people—a hatred that motivated the very instances of extreme brutality that Johnson was investigating.

In 1918 Johnson helped make the NAACP a national power, single-handedly increasing the organization's membership by unprecedented numbers. In 1919, on behalf of the NAACP, Johnson waged his second great attack on the South that had forced him from Jacksonville: he made a sustained effort to enact a federal antilynching law. He underscored the importance of a national conscience when he referred to the "shame of America": the brutal practice of lynching was described as a uniquely American practice. (The antilynching bill failed, passing in the House but dying in the Senate.) As the bill's lobbyist, Johnson shaped the issue as one of southern, mob-rule mentality, not merely murderous, but "anarchic"—defiant of federal law: "a mob sets itself up in place of the state and acts in place of due processes of law to mete out death as a punishment to a person accused of crime" (Johnson, "Lynching," 77).

Johnson made white brutality and mob mentality the implicit theme of his social history of blacks in New York. In *Black Manhattan* (1930) Johnson studied the impact of migrating populations of blacks on the nation's artistic and political capital. In this, his fullest acknowledgment of the broad population of blacks in New York, Johnson described how black migrants from the South, the **Caribbean**, and Africa assumed the collective, urban black identity of Harlemite. Harlem was figured as the capital of America, the cultural and social foundation upon which the nation's reputation as a great civilization rested. In making this argument that the distinctive features of American culture were in fact black ones, Johnson used his social outlook that he termed "cosmopolitanism." Harlem was a cosmopolitan center because of its diverse population of blacks, unified in their American identity. Importantly, this American cosmopolitanism was not simply placed on blacks newly migrated to the city; they defined the very nature of this new identity and therefore actively defined the nation and its ideals.

Johnson's worldview and ideal of cosmopolitanism prevented him from observing and writing about more of the specific features of black migration from the American South. In his political activities and in his writing he was more interested in the broader concerns of the black diaspora—African decolonization, Haitian self-determination, and so on—from a defiantly nationalistic, American perspective. His personal experience of nearly being lynched sparked in him a desire to fight for, and write about, the rage and dejection that black Americans felt toward their condition, particularly toward the mob mentality that governed life for blacks in the South. He sought to remind his readers of their thoughtlessness when they took it "as a matter of course that American Negroes should love their country," showing instead their great strength and faith against the American record of lynching and brutality, a main cause for the black South's migration northward (Johnson, *Along This Way*, 362). *See also* DuBois, William Edward Burghardt; Harlem Renaissance; Literature, the Great Migration in; Passing; White, Walter Francis; Primary Documents 25, 41.

Further Reading

Johnson, James Weldon. *Along This Way: The Autobiography of James Weldon Johnson*. New York: Viking, 1933.

———. *The Autobiography of an Ex-Coloured Man*. 1912. Reprint, New York: Knopf, 1927.

———. *Black Manhattan*. 1930. Reprint, New York: Da Capo Press, 1991.

———. "Lynching—America's National Disgrace." In *The Selected Writings of James Weldon Johnson*, vol. 2, edited by Sondra Kathryn Wilson. New York: Oxford University Press, 1995. First published in *Current History* 19 (1924): 596–601.

Levy, Eugene. *James Weldon Johnson: Black Leader, Black Voice*. Chicago: University of Chicago Press, 1973.

Noelle Morrissette

Johnson, Robert (1911–1938)

Robert Johnson was a member of a small group of guitarist-vocalists including Charley Patton and Son House whose music helped define the prewar **blues** of the **Mississippi Delta** and whose recordings influenced later generations of blues musicians from **Muddy Waters** to Eric Clapton. Toward the end of his life in the late 1930s, Johnson scored one major hit, "Terraplane Blues," but other recordings such as "Cross Road Blues" and "Sweet Home Chicago" became blues standards for the generation of British musicians in the 1960s who learned their trade, in part, from Johnson's recordings.

For several decades after the blues revival of the 1960s, many Johnson fans and scholars regarded him as a mythical figure who had gained his musical ability in a midnight crossroads deal with Legba, the West African trickster-devil spirit. This Faustian tale drew credibility from the odd circumstances of Johnson's death in Three Forks, a farm community outside Greenwood, Mississippi. In the early summer of 1938 Johnson drank poisoned whiskey slipped to him by a lover's jealous husband during a performance in a Three Forks juke joint. Several days later, weakened and bedridden, Johnson died of pneumonia. For the Johnson mythmakers, his murder seemed a divine payback for his diabolical talents. Less sensational, but more significant, Johnson's career illustrated several important aspects of the Great Migration, and his experience resembled that of thousands of other southern African Americans who were on the move during the 1920s and 1930s.

As implied in the lyrics of his 1936 track "Ramblin' on My Mind," Johnson spent the majority of his years making a series of micromigrations from one southern plantation town to the next. He was born in Hazlehurst, Mississippi, about fifty miles south of the state capital, Jackson. While he was a child, his family lived for two years in **Memphis, Tennessee**, but his teen years were spent sharecropping with his mother and stepfather on the Abbay and Leatherman plantation near the Delta cotton town of Robinsville, Mississippi. In general, the sharecropping system was meant to immobilize African American laborers and keep them relatively unskilled. In music, Johnson found a skilled trade that allowed him personal freedom and some independence from white landowners and authorities. Making his base in Helena, Arkansas, during the 1930s, Johnson toured the plantation towns of the Delta regions in Tennessee, Mississippi, and Louisiana, following in the footsteps of the original Delta bluesman, Charley Patton. Johnson's "Traveling Riverside Blues" (1937), like Patton's "High Water Everywhere" (1929), recounted cross-Delta travels through Vicksburg, Rosedale, and other cotton towns. These blues musicians depicted lifestyles based on constant movement despite **Jim Crow** laws and customs that equated black mobility with criminal vagrancy.

Many observers attribute the migration of black southerners to the lure of better-paying jobs in urban America, but itinerant musicians such as Johnson demonstrated that the performing professions, too, afforded African Americans rewarding career opportunities.

Johnson's musical aspirations carried him to destinations beyond the Deep South, though he never settled outside his home region. In 1936 and 1937 Johnson made important trips to San Antonio and **Dallas, Texas**, to record with producer Don Law of the American Record Corporation. In five sessions with Law in makeshift studios, Johnson cut twenty-nine songs (and twelve additional alternate tracks) that became the sole recorded evidence of this young master's career. Inspired by his experience with the record company, Johnson took his show on the road. In 1937 and 1938 Johnson teamed up with fellow blues musician Johnny Shines, and the two made a long-distance journey up the Mississippi Valley to **St. Louis** and **Chicago**, east to **Detroit** and Windsor, Ontario, and down the eastern seaboard through **New York City** and New Jersey. In all of these places Johnson encountered fellow southerners who had found new homes and jobs, but Johnson's sojourns were transitory, illustrating the Great Migration's impermanent quality.

Johnson's lyrics evoked restlessness. From "Traveling Riverside Blues" to "Hellhound on My Trail," Johnson's audiences could sense the impulsive mobility that underlay his music. Like that of many popular African American performers such as **Bessie Smith**, **Gertrude "Ma" Rainey**, and **Huddie "Leadbelly" Ledbetter**, Johnson's music was closely tied to his ability to move. Blues music generally, and Robert Johnson specifically, promoted freedom of the body. In so doing, his music was testament to the mood among black southerners during the first half of the twentieth century when the African American population brought about one of the great demographic upheavals in the history of American minority groups. *See also* Broonzy, William "Big Bill"; Hopkins, "Lightnin' " Sam; King, Riley "B. B."; Recording Industry.

Further Reading

Johnson, Robert. *Robert Johnson: The Complete Recordings*. Columbia C2K 46222/ 46223. 1990. Audio CD.

Pearson, Barry Lee, and Bill McCulloch. *Robert Johnson: Lost and Found*. Urbana: University of Illinois Press, 2003.

R. A. Lawson

Johnson, William Henry (1901–1970)

Artist William Henry Johnson was born in Florence, South Carolina, in 1901. In 1918 he moved to **New York City**, where, like many young black men and **women** migrating north, he took menial jobs such as hotel porter, cook, and stevedore. In 1921 he began taking art classes at the National Academy of Design and quickly became engaged in the cosmopolitan life of Harlem and its burgeoning African American community. By 1926 he had received numerous awards and scholarships as a painter. With the help of his white mentor, Charles Webster Hawthorne, he traveled to France to absorb the rich art history of Europe. While abroad he met, among others, **Henry Ossawa Tanner**,

Edvard Munch, **Paul Robeson**, and Carl Kjersmeier, an African art collector. In 1930 Johnson settled in Kerteminde, Denmark, the home village of his new bride, Holcha Krake.

After a decade of living abroad and a brief transformative trip to Tunisia in 1932, Johnson returned to the United States in 1938 for a "homecoming" to explore his own cultural roots in African traditions and the black communities of Harlem and South Carolina. Painting the black rural South as a subject after 1935 corresponded to a stylistic "homecoming" also. Many family portraits and depictions of southern life appear in this period in such works as *Going to Church* (1940-1941), *Mom and Dad* (1944), and *Chain Gang* (c. 1939). In these paintings rural icons like the shotgun home, the church steeple, and the planted fields, reminiscent of pieced **quilts**, recur. The vibrant juxtaposition of primary colors against the many tones of brown skin in these works and those inspired by the Bible and Negro spirituals, such as *Swing Low, Sweet Chariot* (c. 1944) and *Jesus and the Three Marys* (1939-1940), capture the vitality that Johnson felt was an appealing and enduring aspect of southern rural life. Influenced by cubism, German expressionism, and African sculpture, Johnson used the elongation and the exaggeration of forms to emphasize the large, hardworking hands of laborers and worshipers. He had begun to experiment with this style, not coincidentally, while living in a Danish rural fishing town with his wife's family. He often referred to an affinity he saw between these rural Europeans and rural inhabitants in other parts of the world. He once remarked, "Primitives can be found all over the world, even in Kerteminde, where the fishermen, as human beings, have preserved the [essential] characteristics of their nature, people in whom there is an element of tradition" (Powell, 78).

Johnson's rural origins were a source of pride and racial identification for him because he saw southern, black culture as what connected him to a specific yet also universal authentic life experience. He attempted to return to Kerteminde and live after his wife's death in 1944, but his in-laws sent him back to the United States after he contracted syphilis-induced dementia. In 1947 he entered a mental hospital in Long Island, New York, where he stayed until his death in 1970. *See also* Harlem Renaissance; Low Country South Carolina and Georgia; Migrants, Cultural Identity of; Visual Arts, the Great Migration in.

Further Reading

Powell, Richard J. *Homecoming: The Art and Life of William H. Johnson*. Washington, DC: Smithsonian Institution; New York: Rizzoli, 1991.

Smithsonian American Art Museum. African American Masters: Highlights from the Smithsonian American Art Museum. http://americanart.si.edu/highlights/main .cfm?id=AA.

Kymberly N. Pinder

Johnson Publishing Company

The birth and development of the **Chicago**-based Johnson Publishing Company was intrinsically linked to the reverberations of the Great Migration and the birth and development of an identifiable **black consumer market**.

Moreover, its founder, John H. Johnson, has been described as personifying the American Dream.

Born in Arkansas City, Arkansas, in 1918, Johnson moved with his mother to Chicago in 1933. As a student at Du Sable High School, he first demonstrated his journalistic skills as editor of the student newspaper and yearbook. Johnson further developed as a journalist during his tenure at the black-owned **Supreme Liberty Life Insurance Company**. Moreover, Johnson, while working at Supreme Life, developed the idea for his first commercial publication, *Negro Digest*.

As managing editor of Supreme Life's in-house publication the *Supreme Liberty Guardian*, the young Johnson's duties included culling through magazines and other publications to compile a list of articles related to African Americans (which Johnson subsequently published in the *Supreme Liberty Guardian*). While performing this task, Johnson quickly realized that there existed a great deal of information about African Americans that remained underreported. Moreover, he concluded that there existed a potentially lucrative market for such information. Consequently, in 1942, with a $500 loan from his mother (she used her furniture as collateral to get this sum), Johnson established *Negro Digest*.

Within three years rising sales from *Negro Digest* emboldened Johnson to publish *Ebony*, a monthly magazine reminiscent of the popular mainstream magazines *Look* and *Life*. In 1951 the Johnson Publishing Company introduced African American readers to *Jet*, a pocket-size weekly magazine.

At the same time that the embryonic Johnson Publishing Company began establishing its presence in the landscape of American business, there was a simultaneous explosion of interest in black consumers. Fueled by African Americans' dramatic urbanization during the first decades of the twentieth century, U.S. businesses by midcentury increasingly fixated upon getting their share of the then "Negro Market." In this setting, John H. Johnson and his publications appeared perfectly situated to provide businesses access to this increasingly important consumer group. Moreover, Johnson, an extremely astute businessman, never missed an opportunity to remind fellow businessmen of what he had to offer.

By the 1960s *Ebony* had established itself as a major American magazine, and John H. Johnson stood as one of the country's top executives. Johnson's success as a publisher appeared linked to his ability to gauge the mood and interests of his readers. Therefore, to white corporate leaders seeking insights about black consumers, Johnson appeared to be an ideal ally. In fact, in his autobiography, *Succeeding against the Odds*, Johnson described himself as holding "the unofficial position of special ambassador to American whites" during "the decade of the long hot summers" (Johnson and Bennett, 277).

It is worth noting that Johnson's role as "special ambassador to American whites" also had financial benefits for his Johnson Publishing Company. Although Johnson's autobiography asserts that he did not directly approach white corporate leaders about advertising in *Ebony* during the 1960s, the magazine's advertising revenue nearly tripled between 1962 and 1969.

Another manifestation of Johnson's service to American corporations during the 1960s was the Johnson Publishing Company's 1966 publication *The Negro*

Handbook. This book, on the surface, appeared to be a reference book aimed at a general audience. Considering Johnson's interest in assisting corporate America, as well as U.S. companies' desire for any and all information about blacks, *The Negro Handbook* may, in actuality, have represented a guide to black America for white corporations.

Among other things, *The Negro Handbook* denigrated the role of black-owned businesses in the African American community. Historically, these companies, many of which could trace their origins back to the Great Migration, provided a variety of services to black consumers. Yet *The Negro Handbook* implied that in an increasingly desegregated world black-owned businesses (catering exclusively to blacks) had become passé, especially when white-owned companies could provide similar (and better) services to black customers for less cost.

Ironically, by the 1970s some white companies began to question the efficacy of using black publications to reach the black consumer market. This reassessment appeared to be based upon the premise that because large numbers of blacks read such mainstream periodicals as *TV Guide* and *Reader's Digest*, white corporations did not need to spend extra money advertising in black magazines. Predictably, John H. Johnson spent the rest of the decade trying to reconvince corporate marketers of the black media's unique and indispensable role in reaching black consumers. The Johnson Publishing Company's continued viability suggests the success of Johnson's efforts in this regard. *See also* Black Press.

Further Reading

Berry, William E. "Johnson, John Harold (1918–)." In *Encyclopedia of African American Business History*, edited by Juliet E. K. Walker, 331–35. Westport, CT: Greenwood Press, 1999.

"Black Media Less Efficient, Y & R Says." *Advertising Age*, April 3, 1972, 1, 68.

Johnson, John H., and Lerone Bennett, Jr. *Succeeding against the Odds*. New York: Warner Books, 1989.

Office of Minority Business Enterprise. "Publishing Empire Demonstrates How Minorities Can Succeed." *Commerce Today* 2 (September 18, 1972): 13–16.

Weems, Robert E., Jr. *Desegregating the Dollar: African American Consumerism in the Twentieth Century*. New York: New York University Press, 1998.

Robert E. Weems, Jr.

Jones, LeRoi *See* Baraka, Amiri

Joplin, Scott (c. 1867/1868–1917)

Scott Joplin, known as the "King of Ragtime Composers," created the most sophisticated piano **ragtime** of the original ragtime years (mid-1890s to 1917). The second of six children, he was born in northeast Texas between June 1, 1867 and mid-January 1868 and grew up mostly in Texarkana, on both the Texas and Arkansas sides. His father, a former slave, was a laborer; his mother, freeborn, worked as a domestic servant. Anecdotes relate that he learned piano in the home of a white family where his mother worked. Many years later, in his opera *Treemonisha* (1911), he celebrated his mother's efforts to gain him an education by depicting a parallel situation for the opera's heroine: Treemonisha's parents work for a white woman in exchange for the child's education.

The earliest reference to Joplin as a musician is in 1891, when he was with the Texarkana Minstrels. In 1893 he performed in **Chicago** during the World's Fair and around 1894 settled in Sedalia, Missouri, where he worked as a pianist, singer, and cornetist and attended George R. Smith College. With his vocal quartet, he traveled as far east as Syracuse, New York, probably in 1895. He composed several conventional songs and marches in the mid-1890s and in 1899 published "Maple Leaf Rag," which memorialized a black social club in Sedalia. This became the most famous and influential piano rag of the era.

With eight music publications to his name, he and his new wife Belle moved to **St. Louis** in 1901, where he worked primarily as a composer and a teacher, performing only occasionally. In 1903 he formed a troupe to perform his opera *A Guest of Honor*, which scholars think depicted black leader **Booker T. Washington**'s dinner with President Theodore Roosevelt in the White House. This event polarized the nation, with those opposed to Roosevelt's gesture claiming that it unacceptably put a black man on a level of social equality with whites. The opera troupe set off in August 1903 to perform in the **Midwestern states**, but a theft of the box-office receipts early in the tour ended it prematurely. The opera was unpublished and is lost.

In Arkansas in 1904, Joplin married for the second time. His wife, Freddie Alexander, eighteen years his junior, died of pneumonia ten weeks later in Sedalia. He indirectly memorializes her, also, in his opera *Treemonisha*.

In 1907, Joplin moved to **New York City**, where he remained for the rest of his life. Around 1913 he married Lottie Stokes. He continued composing piano rags and other short works, but devoted most of his energies to unsuccessful efforts to stage his opera *Treemonisha*. He achieved performances of excerpts, but never saw a full theatrical production. The opera tells the story of Treemonisha, a young woman who lives in a small black community in a dense forest in Arkansas, not far from Texarkana. By virtue of her education, she realizes that her townspeople's problems stem from their ignorance and adherence to superstition. She remedies the situation in part by driving out the conjurors who prey upon the people. The townspeople come to recognize the validity of her view and make her their leader, following her to a brighter future.

Joplin, while using the opera to promote his beliefs in the benefits of education and to celebrate both his mother and his deceased second wife, Freddie, drew upon his childhood experiences and roots in Texas and Arkansas. The opera includes dances and musical types, such as quartet singing by field hands, that he would have known from childhood.

Joplin died on April 1, 1917, at the age of forty-nine. He left fifty-two piano pieces (forty-two are rags), twelve songs, one instructional piece, and one opera. Several larger works—a vaudeville, possibly a symphony and a piano concerto—a few songs, and other rags were never published and are lost. Joplin's music was mostly forgotten after his death, except for his "Maple Leaf Rag," which was absorbed into the **jazz** repertory. Aside from a few aficionados who explored and performed his music from the 1940s through the 1960s, Joplin remained mostly unknown, but in the 1970s his music burst upon the public in a spectacular revival. He was performed by both popular and classical artists, recordings reached the top rungs of the charts, his piano pieces graced the sound track of an award-winning movie, and his opera *Treemonisha* was finally performed, eventually reaching Broadway. He was awarded a special Pulitzer Prize in 1976, and a U.S. postage stamp with his image was issued in 1983. *See also* Europe, James Reese; Handy, W. C. (William Christopher).

Further Reading

Berlin, Edward A. *King of Ragtime: Scott Joplin and His Era*. New York: Oxford University Press, 1994.

Curtis, Susan. *Dancing to a Black Man's Tune: A Life of Scott Joplin*. Columbia: University of Missouri Press, 1994.

Edward A. Berlin

K

Kansas City, Missouri

The Kansas City metropolitan area has a distinctive history of black migration in the nineteenth and twentieth centuries. The allegiance of Missouri to the South during the Civil War, the large number of slaves who lived in the Kansas City, Missouri, area during and after the Civil War, and the development of community leadership in the late nineteenth century emerging from the migration of eastern Protestant families were the salient factors that shaped black migration patterns in the Kansas City area. Because Missouri (statehood in 1821) was a southern slave state and Kansas (statehood in 1861) was a free state, the overall migration patterns for the Kansas City metropolitan area cannot be encompassed in one analysis. This entry focuses mainly on Kansas City, Missouri, and its surrounding suburbs.

Nineteenth-Century Background

Although Kansas City, Missouri, was incorporated in 1838, it did not begin its growth until after the Civil War. The increase of the white population from 4,418 in 1860 to 163,752 by 1900 (see Table 3) illustrates the tremendously rapid growth of this river city, especially between 1870 and 1890 (an increase of 100,000). The growth of the black population between 1860 and 1880, from 190 to 8,143, reflects the emancipation after the end of the Civil War. In 1860 several counties surrounding Kansas City had large slave populations. Clay County alone (most of which has now been annexed by Kansas City) had more than 5,000 slaves in 1860. Thus the growth of the urban black population in Kansas City was due to migration not from the rural South but from the countryside of Missouri. However, several counties in western Missouri, near Kansas City came under Commanding General Thomas Ewing's Order Number Eleven near the end of the war. This order, intended to rid the rural

TABLE 3: Population Growth, Kansas City, Missouri, 1870–2000

Year	Total Pop.	Black Pop.	%Black Pop.
1860	4,418	190	4
1870	32,260	3,764	12
1880	55,785	8,143	15
1890	132,716	13,700	10
1900	163,752	17,567	11
1910	248,381	23,566	10
1920	324,410	30,719	10
1930	399,746	38,574	10
1940	399,178	41,574	10
1950	456,622	55,682	12
1960	475,539	83,130	17
1970	507,330	112,120	22
1980	448,159	122,699	27
1990	435,146	128,768	29
2000	441,545	137,879	31

SOURCE: U.S. Bureau of Census, Census of Population, 1870–2000.

areas surrounding Kansas City of Confederate sympathizers, required all residents outside the larger cities in the area to move to those cities (such as Kansas City, Harrisonville, Independence) or leave the area altogether. Union troops harvested everything of value from those properties and then burned all of them down. Undoubtedly this wholesale burning of plantations and homes influenced many families, including black families, to flee Missouri for the free state of Kansas, reducing the number of local blacks and whites actually migrating into the city. It also influenced the growth of black and white persons in these Missouri cities.

Twentieth-Century Migration Patterns

By 1900, 55 percent of the blacks in Missouri lived in cities, most of whom came from rural areas within the state. Despite Missouri's history as a slave state, Kansas City, as well as small towns on its periphery, had very little residential segregation, according to data analyzed by sociologist Kevin Gotham and historian Sherry Schirmer (2002). These data are consistent with a national study of black residential segregation conducted in 1993 by Douglas Massey and Nancy Denton, who analyzed data from all American cities from the nineteenth century to 1990. They concluded that American cities were racially integrated in 1900 but became more residentially segregated in the nine ensuing decades. This development substantially accounts for a decline in black income and quality of life in present-day urban America.

In the first third of the twentieth century Kansas City's population continued to grow. It increased by 144 percent between 1900 and 1930 (from

163,752 in 1900 to 399,746 in 1930). During this same period the black population grew by 120 percent (from 17,567 to 38,579; see Table 3). This growth occurred during the first major migration of blacks from the South to the urban Northeast and Midwest. The black migration from the South was eclipsed by the waves of foreign immigrants who rushed to America and were stopped only by federal immigration legislation in the 1920s. The largest wave of southern black migration to Kansas City occurred during World War II when the black population grew 25 percent, from 41,724 to 55,682.

Population from 1950 to 1970 in most American cities grew rapidly, including expansion into surrounding suburbs. Kansas City, however, experienced limited growth between 1950 and 1970. Despite the annexation of surrounding land (from 62.02 square miles in 1947 to 316.33 square miles by 1963), the city's total population grew by only 11 percent. On the other hand, the black population of Kansas City grew by 101 percent during these years, foreshadowing the patterns of black population growth in the last third of the twentieth century. Much of this discrepancy between black and white population changes in Kansas City is attributable to the exodus of white families to the surrounding suburbs.

Black Migration Patterns since 1970

The last three decades of the twentieth century witnessed the largest growth of blacks in Kansas City, while the total population of the city declined from 507,330 to 441,545 (a 13 percent decrease). This pattern is well known to urban demographers: **white flight** to the suburbs occurred as African Americans continued to migrate into cities from southern rural areas and small towns. Historian Roger Wilkins, in his 1990 documentary *Throwaway People*, identified two great migrations of the black population in America. The first involved the migration of blacks from the rural South to northern and western cities from World War I to the early 1960s; the second saw the migration of middle-class blacks from the city's core to its suburbs in the 1970s and 1980s. Census data from the 1990s show a continuation of this trend. Gotham highlights this through a comparison of demographic changes between 1990 and 2000 for the Kansas City Metropolitan Statistical Area (MSA), which includes Kansas City, Missouri, Kansas City, Kansas, and the suburbs on both sides of the state line. Although the total population of the Kansas City MSA grew during the 1990s from 1.583 million to 1.776 million, the majority of the gain was due to the increase in minority growth (black, Hispanic, and Asian). The total population of the central city increased by only 30,000, and when the loss of the white population during this period (32,000) is taken into account, the entire growth of the central city (62,000) is accounted for by the in-migration of minorities, of which blacks account for 29 percent and Hispanics account for 56 percent of the increase. This trend also reveals the rapid growth of Hispanics in the Kansas City area. Suburban growth increased from 896,000 in 1990 to 1.059 million in 2000. Of this total growth 90.5 percent was white, 3.67 percent was black, and 4.72 percent was Hispanic and Asian. A look at the black population in the Kansas City, Missouri, suburbs since 1940 indicates that no suburb has had more than 2 percent blacks except Grandview, which jumped from 3 percent in 1980 to 17 percent in 1990 and to 34 percent in 2000.

Hypersegregation of Kansas City and Its Meaning

Within Kansas City the development of **hypersegregation** began in the early 1900s and became more pronounced with each decade over the course of the twentieth century. Because we lack census tract data for the earlier decades, we cannot do a comparative analysis of the degree of increasing residential segregation until 1970; by comparing 1980 with 2000 we can measure the continuing increase in residential segregation. For the Kansas City MSA the exposure index (white to black) went from 4.5 percent to 6.5 percent, for the central city it went from 9 percent to 13.8 percent, and for the suburbs it went from 1.4 percent to 3.2 percent. Indices of exposure to other groups range from 0 to 100, where a larger value means that the average group member lives in a tract with a higher percentage of persons from another group. On this and other measures of segregation Kansas City ranks twenty-fourth in residential segregation of all American cities.

Although Kansas City lay in a southern slave state until emancipation, its social structure never resembled that of a typical southern city, but rather that of a New England city where community elites overtly eschewed racism yet practiced it in subtle ways that were hard to spot and difficult to prosecute in a court of law. Gotham identifies three major factors underlying hypersegregation in Kansas City. First, the real estate industry, led by J. C. Nichols, promoted the belief that quality neighborhoods, a safe environment, and "respectable" residents would protect property values. Second, the federal government, through the policies of the Federal Housing Administration, favored the rapid production of all-white communities in the post–World War II era. Third, the Kansas City School District Board of Education pursued a policy of gerrymandering school boundaries that continued to exclude blacks as that population grew and spilled into previously all-white neighborhoods. Schirmer explains segregation as the result of a set of attitudes shaped by local publications in the early twentieth century and nurtured later by Nichols and other real estate developers in their efforts to sell homes in areas that would patronize Nichols's shopping center (begun in 1922) in the city. According to Schirmer, three publications describing **housing** conditions and race in Kansas City in 1913 highlighted that neighborhoods that had a high proportion of blacks also had higher **crime** rates and the most squalid housing. Gotham also cites these reports and their influence on intensifying segregation. Both Gotham and Schirmer identify the importance of successful efforts by local **banks**, realtors, developers, and investors to privatize the housing industry and keep government out of housing policy. The dismantling of the Kansas City Housing Department in 2004 was largely the result of undue pressure from the business community.

Several patterns emerge that help us understand the distinctiveness of Kansas City's development and its relation to black migration. The large number of slave plantations in the Kansas City area contributed to the growth of its black population and was a major source of in-migration until 1900. Residential segregation was virtually absent from 1880 to 1910. Every neighborhood in the city had more than 10 percent black households. Residential segregation increased throughout the twentieth century and can be linked to a combination of factors: Attitudes developed early in the century that linked blacks to crime and uncivil lifestyles that led to decline in the quality of life in neighborhoods and thus to declining property values. Migration patterns of blacks have shifted from rural to urban (1880–1940) to interurban migration (1950–present). The shift to interurban migration presents more complex and constraining factors as a result of the privatization of the housing industry with its subtle patterns of racism. The future growth of the city, made successful by an increase in the overall quality of life, remains unclear. *See also* Black Suburbanization; St. Louis, Missouri; Urban Crisis of the 1960s.

Further Reading

Gotham, Kevin. *Race, Real Estate, and Uneven Development: The Kansas City Experience, 1900–2000.* Albany: State University of New York Press, 2002.

Greene, Lorenzo J., Gary R. Kremer, and Antonio F. Holland. *Missouri's Black Heritage.* Columbia: University of Missouri Press, 1993.

Lewis Mumford Center on Comparative Urban and Regional Research. www.albany.edu/mumford/census.

Martin, Asa. *Our Negro Population: A Sociological Study of the Negroes of Kansas City, Missouri.* 1913. Reprint, New York: Negro Universities Press, 1969.

Massey, Douglas S., and Nancy A. Denton. *American Apartheid: Segregation and the Making of the Underclass.* Cambridge, MA: Harvard University Press, 1993.

Schirmer, Sherry Lamb. *A City Divided: The Racial Landscape of Kansas City, 1900–1960.* Columbia: University of Missouri Press, 2002.

Wilkins, Roger. *Throwaway People.* PBS Video, Frontline Series. Washington, DC, 1990.

Worley, William S. *J. C. Nichols and the Shaping of Kansas City: Innovation in Planned Residential Communities.* Columbia: University of Missouri Press, 1990.

Philip G. Olson

Kerner Commission *See* National Advisory Commission on Civil Disorders (Kerner Commission)

King, Martin Luther, Jr. (1929–1968)

Martin Luther King, Jr., was the most prominent leader of the Southern Christian Leadership Conference (SCLC) **civil rights movement** of the 1950s and 1960s. After the monumental 1963 March on Washington, King helped mobilize a new wave of civil rights and antipoverty activism in northern cities, taking part in movements in **Chicago, Illinois**, and **Cleveland, Ohio**. Through his own migration to Chicago and his efforts to link the southern and northern freedom movements, King developed radical demands for economic redistribution and black political power. In addition, King's experiences with entrenched white political power, whites' racist opposition to residential integration, and the difficulty of life for African Americans in northern and western cities caused him to conclude that migration was not a viable means to economic and political improvement; integration was a necessary but long-term goal; and the freedom struggle needed to concentrate on improving life in the segregated black communities across the country. In his speeches, books, and articles of the late 1950s and 1960s, King drew attention to the freedom struggle's national and international scope and to the ways in which class-based inequality reinforced and sustained racism. For example, in his December 1965 article in the *Chicago Defender*, "The Myth of the Promised Land," King thanked African Americans in northern and western cities for their support of the southern civil rights movement, pointed to the flaws of the migration's promised lands, and argued that African Americans needed to expand the movement beyond battles against segregated public accommodations into a struggle for open jobs, **housing**, and schools.

King's efforts to extend the movement to the North were integrally tied to the history of African American migration in at least three ways. First, King argued that the economic and social conditions, especially de facto segregation in housing and schools, in northern and western cities illustrated how the migration's promises of racial progress had become a cruel hoax. Second, King increasingly articulated the methods and goals of the freedom struggle in terms of a national battle over class and racial inequality. Finally, the fact that there had been a long history of migration and community building well before King attempted to bring the civil rights movement to the North meant that many northern politicians and civil rights leaders received him as a well-meaning but not necessarily welcome outsider.

The key turning point in King's perspective on the regional differences in racism and freedom struggles was his famous trip to **Los Angeles** during the Watts riot of 1965. King's close collaborator, activist Bayard Rustin, recognized the Watts trip as a formative moment in King's understanding of the **urban crisis** and the class dimensions of racial inequality. In the wake of his Watts visit, King began to strategize about how to connect the ongoing southern movement to struggles to improve life in northern and western cities. During 1965 King visited Chicago, Cleveland, **Philadelphia**, and **Washington, D.C.**, where he urged President Lyndon B. Johnson to confront directly de facto segregation in northern schools and neighborhoods and provide jobs and housing for urban black communities. King also contended that white supremacist terrorism in the South caused the ongoing migration to northern and western cities, and he predicted that this would create further suffering in already overburdened urban black communities.

In 1965, when King discussed the potential move into Chicago with fellow SCLC staff members, he was warned that southern activists might not appreciate the complexity of running a campaign in the North. Potential difficulties included the less visible forms of racism outside the South, resistance on the part of existing civic associations like the Coordinating Council of Community Organizations (CCCO) and black politicians like Harlem's **Adam Clayton Powell, Jr.**, to "outsiders" like King and the SCLC, tensions between "race leaders" and the "masses" of African Americans, and the difficulty of identifying concrete issues around which to mobilize against discrimination in the North. From 1965 to 1968 King found these obstacles to bringing the civil rights movement to the North to be very real as he participated in the Chicago Freedom Movement (CFM) and voter registration drives in Cleveland.

On January 26, 1966, King and his family moved into a tenement at 1550 South Hamlin Avenue in Chicago's Lawndale neighborhood to take a leadership position in the CFM, a coalition of the SCLC, based in **Atlanta, Georgia**, and the Chicago-based CCCO. Although he lived in Chicago for only six months and spent much of his time outside of Lawndale, King's move to the city—along with his encounters with the **Black Power** movement and white liberals' ambivalence toward structural economic change—substantially transformed his perspectives on the African American freedom movement and the implications of migration to overcrowded cities.

While King participated in the ground-level struggles over housing, jobs, and **electoral politics** in Chicago and Cleveland, he also grappled with the intellectual attempts to understand the origins of, and solutions for, the "problems" of urban life. In works such as *Stride toward Freedom* (1958) and *Why We Can't Wait* (1963), King asserted that African Americans in the South were isolated and economically subordinated according to color, while in the North, he began to think, migration to centers of political and economic inequality created a distinct "culture of poverty" in majority-black slums. King's analysis drew on his left-liberal contemporaries, people such as Oscar Lewis and Michael Harrington who argued that structural economic inequalities created a self-perpetuating cycle of **unemployment**, poverty, substandard education, and "broken" families that kept African Americans locked in **ghettos**. African Americans, especially the "new poor" Harrington described, were ostensibly the migrants from the rural South without the cultural and economic capital to succeed in modern American cities.

Until the end of 1966 King continued to stress the effects of the culture of poverty, but his encounter with widespread institutional racism in Chicago compelled him to focus less on the perceived pathologies of ghetto life than on the political and economic structures that perpetuated racial inequality. During the summer of 1966 King sought to assist **community organizing** efforts in Chicago while helping mobilize **open housing** marches, tenants' strikes, boycotts of large retail establishments in black communities, and voter registration drives. King was frustrated by the opposition he encountered from Chicago mayor Richard Daley and by the fact that the CFM was unable to accomplish its rather vague original goals of "abolishing slums" and creating open housing. In the wake of at best ambiguous results of mobilizing and organizing in Chicago and Cleveland, King began to organize an interracial **Poor People's Campaign**. On April 4, 1968, in the midst of this effort, he was assassinated in **Memphis, Tennessee**. The Poor People's Campaign grew out of King's disillusionment with postmigration cities. The campaign did not begin until after King's assassination and suffered from his absence, but it represented King's and the SCLC's attempt to synthesize the struggles for civil rights and economic rights through a combined effort of community organizing and group mobilization on a national scale. *See also* Desegregation; Urban Renewal; War on Poverty; Welfare State; Primary Document 43.

Further Reading

Anderson, Alan B., and George W. Pickering. *Confronting the Color Line: The Broken Promise of the Civil Rights Movement in Chicago.* Athens: University of Georgia Press, 1986.

Branch, Taylor. *Parting the Waters: America in the King Years, 1954-63*. New York: Simon and Schuster, 1988.

———. *Pillar of Fire: America in the King Years, 1963-65*. New York: Simon and Schuster, 1999.

Garrow, David J. *Bearing the Cross: Martin Luther King, Jr., and the Southern Christian Leadership Conference*. New York: Vintage Books, 1988.

Jackson, Thomas F. "Recasting the Dream: Martin Luther King, Jr., African American Political Thought, and the Third Reconstruction, 1955-1968." Ph.D. diss., Stanford University, 1994.

King, Martin Luther, Jr. "Myth of the Promised Land." *Chicago Defender*, December 18-24, 1965, 10.

———. *Stride toward Freedom: The Montgomery Story*. New York: Harper and Row, 1958.

———. *Why We Can't Wait*. New York: Harper and Row, 1963.

Jeffrey Helgeson

King, Riley "B. B." (1925–)

In 1948 the young guitarist Riley King moved from a cotton plantation in the **Mississippi Delta** to **Memphis, Tennessee**, a busy river town with a thriving **blues** scene. Memphis attracted King because it was the metropolis of the Delta hinterland, and his musician cousin, Bukka White, had moved there previously. In moving to Memphis, King walked a common path with many other African Americans leaving the countryside and moving to the commercial and industrial cities of the South. This intrasouthern migration from field to factory is often overshadowed by the more dramatic move by millions of southern African Americans to **Chicago**, **Los Angeles**, and other distant cities; however, those who remained in the southern towns would become quite influential, initiating the **civil rights movement** in the mid-1950s.

B. B. King's career reflected the gains of the civil rights movement just as his work helped further the racial reconciliation of the American people. He grew up among poor sharecroppers on the Henderson cotton plantation near Greenwood, Mississippi. Bukka White gave him a guitar when he was nine years old, and King became a noted musician in church and in nearby Delta towns. King was not miserable as a sharecropper, but he wanted better wages and sought a wider audience for his music. After World War II White secured for him a steel-welding job in Memphis.

King's career took off in 1948 through a brief association with Rice Miller (Sonny Boy Williamson II), who offered King a quick radio spot on KWEM in West Memphis, Arkansas. The KWEM appearance led to a weekly spot on WDIA (the "Mother-Station of the Negroes") and a national endorsement for Lucky Strike cigarettes. At WDIA King became "Blues Boy" or B. B. He adopted a glamorous image of flashy clothes and cars. Unlike **Huddie "Leadbelly" Ledbetter** and other musicians who maintained a "country" stage persona, King shed any semblance of his cotton-farming days in the Delta. Record executive Jules Bihari was impressed with King and arranged a recording session at Sun Records, home to Elvis Presley, Johnny Cash, and Jerry Lee Lewis. "Three o'Clock Blues" emerged as King's first hit in 1953, and he left Memphis to tour.

Developed in the musical crucible of Memphis, King's sound grew out of the chromatic styles of his idol, T-Bone Walker, and the early Delta guitar innovator Lonnie Johnson. King avoided the harsh electric sound of contemporaries such as **Muddy Waters**, instead emitting a sweeter blues sound that was influenced by **swing** musicians such as Benny Goodman. King accompanied himself with a big band dominated by brass, as did Walker, and his guitar solos acquired Johnson's harmony and sophistication. King refashioned blues music as a big-time act that was flashy yet soulful and could broadcast well in person, over radio, and on television. The year that the Supreme Court issued its *Brown v. Board of Education* decision, King was grossing $480,000. After 1953 King stayed on the charts with hits such as "Sweet Sixteen," "Ten Long Years," and a Tampa Red cover, "Sweet Little Angel." These successes made King a role model to the younger generation of African American blues musicians in the 1950s, but in the following decade King found increased popularity among white audiences on both sides of the Atlantic.

During the 1960s King toured on the revival circuit of **jazz** clubs and festivals in the United States, Canada, and Europe. Like that of many Mississippi-born blues artists, King's popularity among mainstream American audiences rose after British musicians such as the Rolling Stones and Eric Clapton began to credit the Mississippi bluesmen on their albums and in interviews. Even though some revival fans favored the grittier tones of Muddy Waters or the late **Robert Johnson**, King produced a Grammy winner in 1969 with "The Thrill Is Gone."

King's popularity remained high for the rest of the twentieth century, and he became known from Carnegie Hall to Moscow as the "ambassador of the blues." He maintains his own clubs in Memphis and other cities and helped establish the Delta Blues Museum in Clarksdale, Mississippi. King continues to tour, spending over half of each year on the road, and in that regard, his career remains a living testament to the opportunities afforded by migration. *See also* Black Appeal Radio; Hopkins, "Lightnin' " Sam; Recording Industry.

Further Reading

King, Riley "B. B." *B. B. King: Greatest Hits.* MCA 11746. 1998. Audio CD.
King, Riley "B. B.," and David Ritz. *Blues All around Me: The Autobiography of B. B. King.* New York: Avon Books, 1996.

R. A. Lawson

KKK *See* Ku Klux Klan (KKK)

Ku Klux Klan (KKK)

It is surprisingly difficult to draw a direct connection between the Ku Klux Klan (KKK) and the Great Black Migration on the basis of the secondary literature and published primary sources now available. Scholars and ordinary citizens have assumed a link between the two movements for good reasons, but it has rarely been documented, even at the peak of Klan power in the 1920s and even in oral histories, the sources most likely to yield information about

Klan activity as a motive for migration. More research is needed to understand the precise relationship, but the way the Klan likely affected the largest number of migrants was as a symbol that condensed all that was wrong with the **Jim Crow** South in a single phrase with human form. To mention the Klan was not only to refer to specific acts of terror but also to signal with a potent shorthand what led many African Americans to embrace the risks of seeking better lives elsewhere: the denial of opportunity, the purposeful humiliation, the crushing of achievement, and the officially condoned violence that devalued black life and personhood.

The Klan could serve as such a symbol because it evoked painful memories and stirred powerful emotions. In the Reconstruction era the first Ku Klux Klan did more than any other force to undermine the nation's first experiment in interracial democracy, to rob freed persons of citizenship rights in all but name, and to inflict a new form of white supremacy compatible with nominally free labor. Thereafter, each successive incarnation of the KKK from 1915 to the present has recruited on the basis of racialist ideology and vigilante practice, even where its members could not carry out acts of terror with impunity, as they could in the Jim Crow South. Other aspects of the Klan's program and activities varied over time and in different settings; these remained constant.

It was not the first but the second and subsequent Klan movements that coincided with the Great Migration. When it was revived in **Atlanta** during World War I, the new organization advertised its commitment to keeping African Americans subordinate by recruiting at showings of the 1915 film *The Birth of a Nation*, the racist epic that demonized enfranchised African Americans and glorified the Reconstruction Klan. In the 1920s the movement pledged to preserve white supremacy, a cause that seemed urgent to some whites because of new civil rights activism on the part of black war veterans and **National Association for the Advancement of Colored People** chapters across the South. Black demands for full citizenship also spurred a split among whites, evident in the Commission on Interracial Cooperation, an organization established in 1919 by diverse groups of people dedicated to ameliorating racial conflict and violence in the South in the wake of World War I. Its racial liberalism, timid though it was, proved deeply unnerving to the Klan. In the 1920s Klan leaders constructed a new kind of reactionary populist politics that yoked white supremacy to "100 percent Americanism," anti-Semitism, anti-Catholicism, anti-Communism, hostility to immigrants, antipathy to liberals, support for "old-time religion," and militant defense of Victorian gender roles and sexual values. In the context of the era's pervasive challenges to old hierarchies, this wide-ranging platform enabled the Klan to become a national movement. It enrolled more members proportionate to population in the northern states of Indiana and Oregon than in many parts of the former Confederacy. It was also a mass movement in the 1920s, with at least 2 million dues-paying members over the decade, the majority in urban areas.

Yet it was in the South that Klan members found it easiest to practice the vigilantism that distinguished their movement from the white mainstream and contributed to the black exodus. Klan night riders there gained legitimacy from regional traditions of "white-capping" and widely accepted everyday brutality against blacks by employers and police. Klan insiders organized a few **lynchings** in the early 1920s and participated in others. Their far more typical vigilante activity, however, was threatening notes or cross burnings, followed by floggings and beatings, which over the years claimed thousands upon thousands of black victims and many whites as well. Sometimes they also destroyed symbols of black achievement and communal solidarity such as schools, businesses, and churches. Because black disfranchisement guaranteed all-white juries, southern Klansmen could get away with practices most of their northern counterparts could not. The very legitimacy of these practices among white leaders in the South meant that only a fraction of the attacks were documented, so historians will never have exact numbers or information.

Reasons for the night-riding raids varied: often Klan participants aimed to intimidate civil rights activists or workers seeking better conditions, sometimes to punish alleged lawbreakers such as bootleggers, and sometimes to drive blacks out of their communities, often successful blacks especially. When Klan threats and vigilantism led to mass black flight from afflicted areas, in a few cases it divided whites. Employers in some communities, for example, organized public meetings to protest the expulsion of their labor forces and call for law and order. Yet these organizations rarely defended black rights per se and appeared to win little trust. Not surprisingly, African Americans only began to return to the South in significant numbers in the 1980s when the first successful prosecutions of Klan terrorism—as in the landmark 1987 verdict in *Beulah Mae Donald v. United Klans*—signaled the long-awaited return of interracial democracy. *See also* Great Migration, White Opposition to.

Further Reading

Chalmers, David. *Hooded Americanism: The History of the Ku Klux Klan.* 3rd ed. Durham, NC: Duke University Press, 1987.

Evans, Hiram Wesley. "The Klan's Fight for Americanism." *North American Review* 223 (1926): 33–63.

Jackson, Kenneth T. *The Ku Klux Klan in the City, 1915–1930.* New York: Oxford University Press, 1970.

MacLean, Nancy. *Behind the Mask of Chivalry: The Making of the Second Ku Klux Klan.* New York: Oxford University Press, 1994.

Nancy MacLean

L

Labor Agents

When African Americans began leaving the South in significant numbers during World War I, southern whites quickly attributed the exodus to the sinister work of labor agents who recruited southern blacks for employment in northern industries. During the war years labor recruiting became one of the conventional explanations of the causes of the Great Migration. Despite the volume of contemporary commentary about labor agents, most historians agree that they played only a secondary role in stimulating black migration.

Certainly labor agents were active in the South during these years. The start of World War I cut off immigration from Europe, and labor recruiters for northern industrialists circulated throughout the South, seeking to enlist blacks to come work in the North. **Railroads** were among the first and most active recruiters, enlisting thousands of southern blacks to work as section hands on railroad construction crews. One railroad in Pennsylvania reportedly hired some 5,000 southern blacks in the second half of 1916 alone, although the company had difficulty retaining them because many of the new recruits found better work in other war industries once they arrived in the North. Agents tried to induce blacks with offers of free train fare and promises of a life in the North free of discrimination and inequality. According to an investigator for the **Division of Negro Economics**, African Americans willing to move north could secure free transportation "for the asking" in the autumn of 1916. Agents generally worked in towns and cities, not in the countryside, and they did so quietly. According to one account, effective agents would walk among a group of blacks in a southern town and whisper, "Anybody want to go to Chicago, see me." When southern whites questioned them about the comings and goings of recruiters, blacks reportedly maintained a "strange silence."

Such dramatic tales of clandestine agents operating in their midst confirmed for southern whites that labor agents were to blame for the mass exodus of black workers. In response, southern authorities took a two-pronged approach. One tactic was to warn blacks of the unsuspected dangers that awaited them in the North. Southern industrialists and planters coordinated with newspaper editors to run stories exposing the unscrupulous behavior of labor agents who told fanciful tales of the bounty of the North, luring masses of blacks who ended up making a journey that they soon regretted. Southern authorities also passed punitive legislation against the labor recruiters. Many states and localities required labor agents to register for expensive licenses, some of which were so costly as to be prohibitive. Other antienticement statutes simply made it a crime, punishable with a fine and a prison sentence, for any outsider to recruit workers. Municipalities energized their police to enforce the laws.

By attributing the Great Migration to the active work of outsiders, southern whites dismissed any claims that blacks left the South of their own accord. Exaggerating the role that labor agents played allowed southern whites to sustain the fiction that the South remained governed by harmonious race relations that were only disturbed by outside agitators such as labor recruiters. To admit that blacks actively pursued economic opportunities outside the region would be tantamount to recognizing the economic and political inequalities of **Jim Crow**. Antienticement legislation, then, never really addressed the root causes of black migration, and its repressive nature only fanned black discontent, adding to blacks' desire to leave for the North.

Historians have long recognized the importance of initiative and self-determination among black southerners in orchestrating their own migration. As historian James R. Grossman has elegantly remarked, labor agents operated in the South "less as 'causes' of migration than as facilitators." Recruiters were one source among many by which African Americans learned of opportunities in the North. Migrants learned about the North from letters from family members, heard stories from fellow congregants at church, and read accounts of life in the North in the **black press**. Migration became a social movement of sorts, sustained as much by rumor and gossip as by the impersonal forces of labor markets. Once that movement was under way, northern industrialists no longer needed to send labor agents south. Blacks were coming north of their own free will. *See also* Chain Migration; Demographic Patterns of the Great Black Migration (1915–1940); Great Migration, Causes of; Great Migration, White Opposition to; Railroads; Railroads, Black Employment on; Primary Documents 34, 42.

Further Reading

Arnesen, Eric. *Black Protest and the Great Migration: A Brief History with Documents*. Boston: Bedford/St. Martin's, 2003.

———. *Brotherhoods of Color: Black Railroad Workers and the Struggle for Equality*. Cambridge, MA: Harvard University Press, 2001.

Gottlieb, Peter. *Making Their Own Way: Southern Blacks' Migration to Pittsburgh, 1916–1930*. Urbana: University of Illinois Press, 1987.

Grossman, James R. *Land of Hope: Chicago, Black Southerners, and the Great Migration*. Chicago: University of Chicago Press, 1989.

Scott, Emmett J. *Negro Migration during the War*. 1920. Reprint, New York: Arno Press, 1969.

U.S. Department of Labor. Division of Negro Economics. *Negro Migration in 1916–17*. 1919. Reprint, New York: Negro Universities Press, 1969.

Steven A. Reich

Larsen, Nella (1891–1964)

Novelist Nella Larsen's protagonists are **women** on the move. Affluent and cosmopolitan, well read and stylish, they struggle to define themselves in a world that confines women and blacks to their "place." These characters resist stereotypical definitions. Similarly, Larsen chafed against the limitations of the roles she was assigned. After pursuing careers as a **nurse** and a librarian, she emerged as a writer. At the height of the **Harlem Renaissance** she published two highly regarded novels, *Quicksand* (1928) and *Passing* (1929).

Born in 1891 in **Chicago** to a white mother and a black father, Larsen was herself a widely traveled woman. She studied at Fisk University in Tennessee, traveled to Copenhagen to live with maternal relatives, worked at **Tuskegee Normal and Industrial Institute** in Alabama, and then moved to **New York City**, where with her husband Elmer Imes, a black physicist, she became prominent on the Harlem social scene. Before *Quicksand* she published two stories under a pseudonym and submitted an article titled "Scandinavian Games" to *The Brownies' Book*, the children's magazine edited by **W.E.B. DuBois** and **Jessie Redmon Fauset**.

Quicksand maps a fictional journey that follows a similar trajectory, but the protagonist Helga Crane ends up without a career or a husband. Keenly aware of her difference, she refuses to conform to the soul-numbing routines of Naxos, a school modeled on Tuskegee. In Chicago she becomes an assistant to a "race woman," who advises her to suppress her white heritage. In New York she joins the circle of sophisticated **New Negroes**, who host literary salons and frequent nightclubs; they pay lip service to race pride but prefer white artists and European culture. Helga then travels to Denmark, where she is treated as an exotic primitive who is always on display. Back in Harlem she finds that as a middle-class African American, she is trapped in the role of lady. Impulsively she marries an illiterate preacher and follows him to rural Alabama, where poverty and pregnancies mire her in the quicksand of the title. The novel paints an unrelievedly bleak portrait of black southern life.

Set in Chicago and New York, *Passing* depicts two childhood friends, both light skinned enough to pass for white. Clare, a janitor's daughter, moves into the white world, while Irene finds security by marrying a black **physician**. Neither escapes the pressures of race, gender, and class. If Clare, who is married to a wealthy bigot, risks being exposed as a Negro, Irene risks being suffocated by the boring and trivial pursuits of black bourgeois life. While the ending of the novel is abrupt and melodramatic, *Passing* raises crucial issues concerning the performance and definition of identity. Though seeming to welcome a more expansive view of racial identity, the Harlem Renaissance, as it is depicted in the novel, trapped black women in roles that were determined in response to familiar racial and gender stereotypes.

After publishing a short story, "Sanctuary," that elicited charges of plagiarism, Larsen withdrew from the public eye. She and her husband divorced, and she resumed her career as a nurse, living quietly in New York until her death in 1964. *See also* Literature, the Great Migration in; Passing.

Further Reading

Davis, Thadious. *Nella Larsen, Novelist of the Harlem Renaissance*. Baton Rouge: Louisiana State University Press, 1994.

Larsen, Nella. *Quicksand and Passing*. Edited with an introduction by Deborah E. McDowell. New Brunswick, NJ: Rutgers University Press, 1986.

McLendon, Jacquelyn Y. *The Politics of Color in the Fiction of Jessie Fauset and Nella Larsen*. Charlottesville: University Press of Virginia, 1995.

Wall, Cheryl A. *Women of the Harlem Renaissance*. Bloomington: Indiana University Press, 1995.

Cheryl A. Wall

Las Vegas, Nevada

The African American community in the City of Lights, Las Vegas, Nevada, developed from the in-migration of southern blacks in the mid-twentieth century. The migratory history of African Americans to Las Vegas in the twentieth century was a means to an end, a way for blacks to escape the harsh realities of racism and disfranchisement in the South. Black migrants to Las Vegas came in a quest for equality of opportunity and better social and economic conditions, thus sharing the same motivations, aspirations, and expectations with black migrants to other cities in the West and North. Therefore, the lives of hundreds of black participants in the Great Black Migration from the American South to Las Vegas, Nevada, were consistent with the sweeping historical and migratory trends in the United States.

Blacks were part of the fledgling Las Vegas community at the turn of the twentieth century, contributing in large measure to the development of the flourishing city. The first African Americans in the area lived in labor camps, and later they were included in the maintenance crews for the new railroad being constructed at the intersection of Main and Fremont streets in the early 1900s. John I. Williams, a white surveyor, platted the land in 1904 that became the site of the Westside, or the black community. Although the black population in Las Vegas in the 1930s remained fairly small—143 out of a population of 5,165 in 1930—white settlers in Las Vegas became cautiously concerned. The attitudes of whites at that time were not necessarily discriminatory or demeaning toward blacks, but neither did they fight to ensure racial harmony. Therefore, to protect their rights, particularly in hiring practices, African Americans formed the Colored Citizens Labor and Protective Association (CCLPA) of Las Vegas on May 5, 1931. In September of that same year the CCLPA had 247 members, revealing a substantial increase in the black population of Las Vegas at that time.

But only with the building of the Hoover Dam, beginning in 1930, did the black and white populations grow significantly apart. A mass migration of unemployed workers, including African Americans, flocked to the Las Vegas region in 1930 in the hope of securing work building the Hoover Dam. Although some African Americans worked on the Hoover Dam and Basic Magnesium Plant projects that essentially made modern Las Vegas, many were denied work. Even when the federal government mandated that **construction** companies hire more blacks, they hired only a few and granted them employment in the toughest, most degrading jobs. Black workers on the dam could not live in Ragtown either, the shantytown on the floor of Black Canyon where white workers and their families resided. Consequently, black workers settled in Las Vegas and daily commuted the thirty miles to the dam construction site.

In the city white employers began segregating their development projects and banning blacks from their various businesses. Redlining also enabled white Las Vegans to force African Americans into segregated neighborhoods, such as the Westside and an area called Carver Park in Henderson, Nevada, near the Basic Magnesium Plant. Whites justified these practices at that time by claiming that there was not enough space downtown for the rapidly growing black population. Since Carver Park was later abandoned by African Americans because the place did not provide for a social life for blacks, many moved to the Westside or the old McWilliams Townsite west of the railroad tracks in Las Vegas.

Whites, especially from the South, who also migrated to Las Vegas, brought with them their racist norms, ideals, and attitudes. When the new hotels and casinos were built and later run by mainly eastern and midwestern mobsters, they professed a need to cater only to a clientele that included customers from segregated areas. This discriminatory notion gave white Las Vegans all the justification they needed to refuse to serve African Americans who wanted to patronize their establishments, or to hire them for anything other than the most menial positions. Persistent job competition between blacks and whites metamorphosed the city into a place closely akin to the racist South. In fact, Las Vegas soon earned a reputation as the "Mississippi of the West" because of the discrimination against African Americans, especially in the early 1930s. Nonetheless, African Americans continued to move to Las Vegas.

Black newcomers from the South had trouble finding adequate living accommodations. Early on, the Westside did not have paved streets, city lights, proper sanitation, or a sufficient sewer system. African American migrants to Las Vegas built houses or ragged shacks with almost any building materials that could be bought or found. But many of these places were without air conditioning, and living conditions could be brutal in the hot desert sun. Moreover, the thriving black population of Las Vegas during the 1940s was forced to move to the Westside for other insidious reasons. For example, blacks were evicted from the Las Vegas Strip because the city refused to give them business licenses to operate downtown. Black business owners could only secure licenses if they agreed to move to the derelict streets of West Las Vegas. The Westside, therefore, became the center of the black community of Las Vegas.

Black patrons at the craps table at the El Morocco on Las Vegas's West Side. Courtesy of Clarence Ray Collection, University of Nevada, Las Vegas Library.

Blatant discrimination was also particularly evident when blacks and whites wanted to commingle together. Integration of the newly arrived black refugees from the South, however, did not sit well with the city fathers. For example, white owners of bars refused to cater to black servicemen and other black patrons, so they could only be entertained by black clubs and businesses on the Westside. The New Town and Tavern, Cotton Club, Brown Derby, El Morocco, and Ebony clubs became hotbeds for late-night entertainment when performers such as Harry Belafonte, Sarah Vaughan, and others appeared at many of these black nightspots after their shows and performances on the Strip. For these reasons, many believed that the famous Moulin Rouge, the first integrated casino and hotel of Las Vegas, was built for the explicit purpose of catering to both a black and white clientele in 1955.

Segregation, of course, had the unintended effect of driving the black community of Las Vegas closer together socially, economically, politically, and physically. In the late 1940s and 1950s Jackson Street in the Westside became the black equivalent of downtown or the Las Vegas Strip. Perhaps this was due partly to comfort, proximity, and familiarity. While some African Americans lived outside the traditional black neighborhood in the late 1960s and early 1970s, most resided in the Westside.

Although some blacks managed to purchase property outside the Westside during the 1960s, local white **banks** continued to discriminate against African Americans, especially when it came to extending home mortgage loans. Before the 1980s African Americans could not buy property in the greater city of Las Vegas or even outside the Westside because of both de jure and de facto segregation. West Las Vegas still continues to have the highest concentration of African Americans, which approaches almost 70 percent of the black population in the city.

In the final analysis, blacks in the past migrated to Las Vegas to seek a better quality of life, but because of segregation in the city and a relatively low standard of living for many African Americans, even with appreciable service jobs, black migrants did not prosper in the gaming capital of the world. A schism developed in Las Vegas between low-income African Americans and the professional or educated classes of blacks. They lived separate and apart from one another, with no real connections, interaction, or communication, eroding to a degree the racial unity among black migrants to the City of Light earlier in the century. *See also* Employment Discrimination; Housing and Living Conditions; Phoenix, Arizona; Western States, Black Migration to; Primary Document 3.

Further Reading

Bracey, Earnest N. "The Moulin Rouge Mystique: Blacks and Equal Rights in Las Vegas." *Nevada Historical Society Quarterly* 39, no. 4 (Winter 1996): 272–88.

Coray, Michael. "African-Americans in Nevada." *Nevada Historical Society Quarterly* 35, no. 4 (Winter 1992): 239–57.

Fitzgerald, Roosevelt. "Blacks and the Boulder Dam Project." *Nevada Historical Society Quarterly* 24 (1981): 255–60.

———. "The Demographic Impact of Basic Magnesium Corporation on Southern Nevada." *Nevada Public Affairs Review*, no. 2 (1987).

———. "The Evolution of a Black Community in Las Vegas, 1905–1940." *Nevada Public Affairs Review*, no. 2 (1987).

Moehring, Eugene P. *Resort City in the Sunbelt: Las Vegas, 1930–1970*. Reno: University of Nevada Press, 1989.

White, Claytee. "'Eight Dollars a Day and Working in the Shade': An Oral History of African American Migrant Women in the Las Vegas Gaming Industry." In *African American Women Confront the West, 1600–2000*, edited by Quintard Taylor and Shirley Ann Wilson Moore, 276–92. Norman: University of Oklahoma Press, 2003.

Earnest N. Bracey

Lawrence, Jacob (1917–2000)

Painter Jacob Lawrence turned to his own community in Harlem for the inspiration for his famed sixty-panel *Migration Series*. He created the series, which portrays the World War I–era migration of southern blacks to the urban, industrial North, in 1941 at the age of twenty-three. The Harlem apartments that surrounded him provided images of the worn tenements. These were the homes of African American immigrants who had migrated north, just as his parents had, in hopes of a better life. His panels, done in a flat, synthetic cubist style with bold primary colors, rely on symbols to show the dramatic action and movement of the migrants and the exodus of black labor and their families. He reveals only the essentials of the migrants' lives.

As a boy growing up in **New York City**, Lawrence was familiar with the basic movements of the history of art, having frequented the Metropolitan Museum of Art in his early teens. The African American artists **Augusta Savage** and Charles Alston served as mentors to Lawrence. Lawrence had not personally migrated north, but his parents had, and he grew up in Harlem from age thirteen, listening to the stories from family and friends and fellow artists of the struggles of moving north and starting over.

Lawrence received support to do the series from the Julius Rosenwald Fund, which granted him a fellowship to create the *Migration Series*. The sixty panels, which are painted on slate, were based on careful research conducted by Lawrence at the 135th Street Branch of the New York Public

Library (now the Schomburg Center for Research in Black Culture), where he worked daily and consulted the writings of historians and sociologists to capture the essence of the migration. **Alain Locke**, one of the premier writers and critics of the **Harlem Renaissance**, wrote a letter in support of the project. Locke had written in *The New Negro* of the importance of the artist to express the experiences of the black community because of the artists' redemptive power. Lawrence's series fit in perfectly with this vision.

The panels are stark and striking in their message. They bear the mark of Lawrence's research, showing that he was familiar with much of the most dominant writings about black migration of the time, including **Carter Woodson**'s *A Century of Negro Migration* (1918) and the work of prominent sociologists. But even more, Lawrence based his work on his own Harlem community and on the work of the dynamic writers of the time who chronicled the migration, including **James Weldon Johnson** and Rudolph Fisher. He did not romanticize the migrants' plight, nor did he blame them for the problems they would encounter, as many sociologists of the time did. Lawrence's work told the tale of the struggle of the black community in this massive migration. The panels reveal the pain of the decision to move north, the fear of departure, and the terrorism migrants risked to leave. His stark rendering of a **lynching**, represented by a branch piercing the composition that contains a lone rope hanging over a downtrodden figure sitting on a rock below, is typical of Lawrence's portrait of the South as a barren wasteland to escape. It is both a statement of why migration was necessary and how migrants were terrorized in the South before departure. Lawrence was clearly aware of the impact of Japanese woodblock prints on the artists who preceded him, including the postimpressionists, with a dramatic diagonal and the partial cropped view of the tree branch.

The *Migration Series* also served the critical function of spiritually empowering the black community, connecting the group with a collective memory and group identity. Not only do the panels express the economic and social reasons for migration, they also celebrate the strength of the black community as migrants took their lives into their own hands and refused to succumb to terrorism and poor living, working, and health conditions. With little differentiation between sexes, no distinctions of skin color in the human figures in the panels, Lawrence centers the story of migration on the life of ordinary folks like his parents. He uses his stark, flat style and radically simplified composition to show overcrowding, imprisonment, terror, and barren communities. But Lawrence's vision is uplifting. He brings the viewer firsthand into the migration; he himself, after all, was the child of migrants. He invites his viewers to be part of the crowd waiting for the train north, to see the beauty and the sorrow, to become part of his collective identity on an emotional and personal level. *See also* Chicago School of Sociology (CSS); Frazier, E. Franklin; Johnson, Charles Spurgeon; Johnson, William Henry; Schomburg, Arthur Alfonso; Visual Arts, the Great Migration in.

Further Reading

Powell, Richard J. *Jacob Lawrence*. New York: Rizzoli International Publications, 1992.

Turner, Elizabeth Hutton, ed. *Jacob Lawrence: The Migration Series*. Washington, DC: Rappahannock Press, 1993.

Amy Kirschke

Lawyers *See* Attorneys

"Leadbelly" *See* Ledbetter, Huddie "Leadbelly"

Ledbetter, Huddie "Leadbelly" (1885–1949)

As one of the twentieth century's most influential African American folk-singers, Huddie Ledbetter reflects in his life's journey the movement of many blacks from the rural South to urban areas and to the North. "Leadbelly" (as he was best known) grew up in the Deep South but moved to **New York City** in 1935 in search of a larger and more racially diverse audience for his music. Through live performances, radio broadcasts, and sound recordings he helped introduce a new (largely white and urban) audience to such important genres as **blues** and gospel music, as well as the late nineteenth-century old-time country dance tunes he performed as a child.

He was born Huddie William Ledbetter on Jeter Plantation in Mooringsport, Louisiana, in 1885 to parents who farmed or sharecropped near the border with Texas. Taught to play accordion and the rudiments of guitar by his uncle Terrell Ledbetter, he soon employed his talents at local "sukey-jump" parties. He left home around 1903 to became by turns an itinerant musician and a farm laborer working between **Dallas** and Shreveport. During this peripatetic period Ledbetter married his first wife "Lethe" Henderson in 1908 and about four years later met and spent about eight months playing with the legendary blues singer Blind Lemon Jefferson and acquired the first of his signature twelve-string guitars.

Huddie's initial brush with the law occurred in 1915, when he was jailed for assault in Harrison County, Texas. He spent much of the next nineteen years incarcerated for a variety of crimes, ranging from simple assault to "assaulting to kill." In a curious turn of events, "Leadbelly" (as he was now known) was granted a full pardon in 1925 by Texas governor Pat Neff, who heard him perform at the Sugarland Prison, located near Houston.

While he was imprisoned in Louisiana's notorious Angola Penitentiary in the early 1930s, Huddie Ledbetter's life changed forever when he met John Lomax and his son Alan, who were collecting African American folk songs for the Library of Congress in the summer of 1933. Lomax recorded Leadbelly and returned the next summer with improved equipment. This time Leadbelly reworked his pardon song, addressing it to Louisiana governor O. K. Allen, as well as recording what would become his trademark song, "Goodnight Irene."

Hopeful of finding a new audience and wishing to escape from the racist South after his release from prison in August 1934, Leadbelly proved a sensation upon his arrival in New York City on December 31, 1934. Newspapers that printed lurid descriptions of his convict past helped spread his fame. John

Lomax quickly negotiated a contract with Macmillan to write *Negro Folk Songs as Sung by Lead Belly* (1936) and persuaded the March of Time's newsreel to film *Huddie*. Leadbelly sent to Louisiana for Martha Promise, whom he had taken up with after being released from Angola, and married her in Wilton on January 21, 1935.

In addition to recording further for the Library of Congress, John Lomax also arranged a recording contract with the American Record Company (now CBS/Sony). The records sold poorly, underscoring the fact that his "down-home" rural blues had lost favor with black record buyers. Progressive, white urban intellectuals, however, found Huddie Ledbetter fascinating, and for the rest of his life he recorded for and entertained virtually all-white audiences.

The Ledbetters survived largely on musical jobs and welfare. Always ready to adapt to his environment, Leadbelly added "topical" and "protest" songs about segregation and natural disasters to his repertoire. These musical and social impulses led him to keep company with "urban folk" musicians such as Woody Guthrie, Sonny Terry, Brownie McGhee, Pete Seeger, the Golden Gate Quartet, and Burl Ives. In addition to performing, Leadbelly eventually recorded dozens of selections for Capitol, RCA, Musicraft, and Asch/Folkways. While he was in Paris late in 1948, persistent muscle problems led to a diagnosis of Lou Gehrig's disease—amyotrophic lateral sclerosis. Some six months later he succumbed to the disorder, on December 6, 1949. Ironically, one year later his trademark song "Goodnight Irene," which he had learned from his uncle Bob Ledbetter, became a nationwide number one hit for the Weavers. *See also* Crime and Criminals; Dance Halls and Nightclubs; Hopkins, "Lightnin' " Sam; Johnson, Robert; Recording Industry.

Further Reading

Lomax, John, and Alan Lomax, eds. and trans. *Negro Folk Songs as Sung by Lead Belly*. New York: Macmillan Co., 1936.

Wolfe, Charles, and Kip Lornell. *The Life and Legend of Leadbelly*. New York: HarperCollins, 1992; New York: Da Capo Press, 1999.

Kip Lornell

Literature, the Great Migration in

The twentieth century witnessed the birth of a number of important African American art forms. The migration narrative is among the most significant. Variously called migration narratives or Great Migration novels, these works attempt to document and explore the massive dislocation of black people and the impact of migration on individual psyches as well as American cities. Migration narratives follow the movement of a protagonist, or a major character who greatly influences the protagonist, from the South to urban centers in the North, Midwest, and West. Throughout the century the form underwent a number of significant changes, most of which were directly related to the historical and political moment of its emergence.

As with the slave narrative that preceded it, the migration narrative developed its own set of tropes and narrative conventions. It usually portrays (1) an event that propels the action northward (at times this moment has happened before the action with which the narrative opens, (2) the initial confrontation with the urban landscape, (3) the migrant's attempt to navigate that landscape and the construction of himself or herself as an urban subject, and (4) a consideration of the possibilities and limitations of migration. These moments may occur at any point in the narrative, and not all narratives contain each and every one.

The earliest migration narratives portray the South as an oppressive site that houses the ancestor but that thwarts black possibility through segregation, violence, and the lingering legacy of slavery. In these texts the northern, midwestern, and western cities provide a limited freedom but also enact acts of psychic and physical violence. After World War II narratives focus more on the urban settings and on the diversity and complexity of black urban communities. They tend also to focus more on the interiority of the protagonists. After the **civil rights movement** writers began to reconsider the South as a site of racial redemption, as a birthright, and as a place of possibility for reconstructing family and community. Given the successes of the civil rights movement in the South, the region is seen as a place of possibility; given the seemingly omnipotent forces of power in the North—riots, urban blight, and drug epidemics—that lead to the demise of black communities and families, the possibilities of the North are called into question.

Paul Laurence Dunbar's north *The Sport of the Gods* (1902) inaugurated the genre of the migration narrative in African American letters. Of the novel, critic Lawrence R. Rodgers writes, "Pushing beyond nineteenth-century southern stereotypes, [Dunbar] mapped a new literary terrain in the urban north that set the stage for twentieth-century African American literature's emphasis on urban subject matter" (Rodgers, 39). Published in 1902 during the period that historians have referred to as the **nadir of race relations** in American history, the novel traces the migration of one black family, the Hamiltons. The Hamiltons are sent north after the deception of Frank Oakley, a white man. Oakley, a northerner, is the younger brother of Maurice Oakley, the kind employer of the Hamilton family. After stealing money from his brother, Frank accuses Berry Hamilton of having taken it. Convicted of the crime, Berry is sent to prison, and his family migrates to **New York City**. Culturally unmoored in the North, the Hamilton family begins to lose its bearings. The unfamiliarity of the urban landscape makes it almost impossible for them to navigate it successfully. Although they attempt to re-create aspects of their southern life, they cannot adequately combat the forces of urbanism that overwhelm them. Individual family members succumb to alcohol and abandon the church for the theater stage. *The Sport of the Gods* bears witness to the deterioration of the black family in the urban setting and maintains a sense of longing and nostalgia for the South they were forced to flee.

While the Hamiltons are forced to flee the South because of the duplicity of a white outsider, in the vast majority of migration narratives, **lynching** is most often the single act that propels the action northward. **Jean Toomer**'s *Cane* (1923) is but one example. Although no single figure migrates to the North, the text itself migrates: "Blood Burning Moon," the final story in the southern section, is the story of a lynching. If migration narratives emphasize the violence and racial horror of the South, characters may have nostalgia for the South, or "home," but they rarely have a sense of it as a site to which they may return. Consequently, these texts often create sites within the narrative that invoke the South as a means of helping the migrant survive the transition to urban life. These sites of the "South in the city" include churches and other ritualistic spaces such as restaurants and homes where traditional southern foods are served or even clubs that play southern-style **blues** music. In these sites various rituals are enacted to invoke the spirit of the ancestors as it is embodied in food, music, dance, speech, and other forms. However, the literal South remains a place where black blood has been shed and where the ancestor is buried.

For Dunbar, the transformation into urban subjects is marked by tragedy and loss. During the **Harlem Renaissance** migration takes on far more positive implications. It is the Great Migration that fuels the emergence of the **New Negro**. Not only were some of the principal participants of the Renaissance migrants to New York (**Langston Hughes**, **Nella Larsen**, **Claude McKay**, to name a few), but so were the masses of anonymous figures who inspired the personas and protagonists of their literary endeavors. For one of the Renaissance's major architects, **Alain Locke**, the migrating masses were central to the spirit of modernity that fueled the New Negro movement. Locke wrote, "The migrant masses, shifting from countryside to city, hurdle several generations of experience at a leap. . . . In the very process of being transplanted, the Negro is becoming transformed" (Locke, 631).

Nella Larsen, a critically acclaimed artist of the Renaissance, wrote one of the first migration narratives to focus on a middle-class African American woman, *Quicksand* (1928). For Helga Crane, the protagonist of the novel, the North is a place where she can lose herself in the anonymity of the crowd and flee the stifling conventional society of the black southern elite. However, cities like **Chicago** and New York, while providing her vibrant settings for her own actualization, are also sites where she is constantly read as a sexual subject: for white men she is read as a **prostitute**, but for the black middle class she is seen as a respectable lady. Consequently, while the North seems to offer greater possibility for physical mobility, it continues to maintain confining categories that bind her as much as the South's more physical strictures. By the novel's end Crane does return to the South, the home of a cursed and despised people. It is not a site of immediate racial violence but instead a place where the expected roles of respectable wife and mother lead to her psychic and physical demise. By the novel's end the South is still a place that costs black people their lives.

Rudolph Fisher's short story "The City of Refuge" (1925) is perhaps the quintessential migration narrative of the period. The story of King Solomon Gillis is one that found echoes decades later in Stevie Wonder's musical migration narrative "Living for the City." Gillis leaves North Carolina after shooting a white man, and in so doing, he "probably escaped a lynching." Upon arriving in the city, "Confronted suddenly by daylight, King Solomon Gillis stood dazed and blinking." The sensations and stimulation of the city overwhelm. In Harlem he encounters a diversity of black people, West Indian immigrants as well as black police officers. It all lends a sense of tremendous freedom and possibility, but before long he too is taken in by the temptations of the city, and violence is enacted at the hands of other black men. Eventually the very black officers who so impressed Gillis arrest him.

For Fisher, as for most authors of migration narratives, power in the South is immediate, violent, and identifiable in the form of the racist sheriff or the lynch mob. But in the North it is more invisible, omnipotent, and in less familiar guises. At times it does not even come in the form of human beings, but instead in segregated, substandard living conditions like those inhabited by **Richard Nathaniel Wright**'s Bigger Thomas or **Ann Petry**'s Lutie Johnson. In *12 Million Black Voices* (1941), another migration narrative by Wright, he describes "the kitchenette": "The kitchenette is our prison, our death sentence without a trial, the new form of mob violence that assaults not only the lone individual, but all of us, in its ceaseless attacks" (Wright, 106). While Wright described the South Side of Chicago, Petry focused on Harlem in her novel *The Street* (1946). Her protagonist Lutie Johnson notes, "Streets like the one she lived on were no accident. They were the North's lynch mobs... The method the big cities used to keep Negroes in their place" (Petry, 323). **Housing** is a central issue of concern for those authors of migration narratives who were publishing during and immediately after World War II. These authors tend to focus more on the northern experience of their migrant characters, often relegating the southern past to a time before the opening of their narratives. The "South in the city" is less likely to help their characters survive the urban landscape; instead, they either ignore these sites or the sites themselves act as stifling spaces that keep them from emerging as modern subjects. Lawrence Rodgers has noted that many of the narratives of this period are fugitive narratives that "contrast any display of fondness for southern pastoral nostalgia.... Fugitive migrant novels also undermine the utopian connotations derived from popular images of the North as the biblical land of Canaan" (Rodgers, 98). Both Bigger Thomas and Lutie Johnson become literal fugitives from the law.

By the 1950s, as the efforts of earlier civil rights activists began to take hold and as the movement built momentum, a new take on the migration narrative emerged. **Ralph Ellison**'s *Invisible Man* (1952) , **James Baldwin**'s *Go Tell It on the Mountain* (1953), and Paule Marshall's *Brown Girl, Brownstones* (1959) all focus as much on the interior psychic geographies of their characters as they do on the physical landscape they inhabit. Also, Marshall documents the migration of her protagonist's parents, who come from Barbados in the **Caribbean**. Hers was the first narrative to focus on a community of migrants from the Caribbean who seek to reestablish their homeland in New York. She portrays the young artist who seeks to escape not the poverty of an island nation but instead the stifling conformity of an immigrant community. The same might be said of Baldwin's first novel, whose protagonist is torn between the offerings of the city and the stifling provinciality of his Harlem home. Although Harlem was a place his parents' generation migrated to, it is a place from which the young John Grimes seeks to escape.

After the civil rights movement a new take on migration began to emerge. No author has been more devoted to documenting the experience of migration than has Toni Morrison throughout her oeuvre. The characters of her first novel, *The Bluest Eye* (1970), and her most critically acclaimed, *The Song of*

Solomon (1977), are all migrants. *The Song of Solomon* documents the **return migration** of a young privileged black man who retraces his family's migration pattern to learn their history and their lineage through a distinctly southern (informed by Africa) form. Morrison's other migration narrative, *Jazz*, was published in 1992. Set during the Harlem Renaissance, the novel is the story of Joe and Violet Race and Joe's dead teenage lover, Dorcas. Joe and Violet migrate from Virginia to New York in 1902. *Jazz* documents not only the crisis of dislocation after migration but also the creativity that emerges from that crisis in the form of **jazz** music, a product of migrants.

Migration is perhaps the most dominant theme in twentieth-century African American prose writing, but it also appears in the plays of **August Wilson**, the poetry of Langston Hughes and **Gwendolyn Brooks**, the autobiographies of **Malcolm X** and Maya Angelou, and blues poetry of countless anonymous bards of the blues tradition, as well as the better-known composers and songwriters of jazz and **rhythm and blues**. *See also* Attaway, William; Bonner, Marita; Fauset, Jesse Redmon; Henderson, George Wylie; Himes, Chester; Hurston, Zora Neale; Mosley, Walter; Naylor, Gloria; Thurman, Wallace Henry; Walker, Alice; West, Dorothy.

Further Reading

Bremer, Sidney H. *Urban Intersection: Meetings of Life and Literature in United States Cities*. Urbana: University of Illinois Press, 1992.

Dixon, Melvin. *Ride Out the Wilderness: Geography and Identity in Afro-American Literature*. Urbana: University of Illinois Press, 1987.

Fullbrook, Kate. "Literature of the Great Migration." In *A Companion to the Literature and Culture of the American South*, edited by Richard Gray and Owen Robinson. Malden, MA: Blackwell, 2004.

Griffin, Farah Jasmine. *"Who Set You Flowin'?" The African-American Migration Narrative*. New York: Oxford University Press, 1995.

Locke, Alain. "Enter the New Negro." *Survey Graphic* 6, no. 6 (March 1925): 631–34.

Petry, Ann. *The Street*. Boston: Houghton Mifflin, 1946.

Rodgers, Lawrence R. *Canaan Bound: The African-American Great Migration Novel*. Urbana: University of Illinois Press, 1997.

Stepto, Robert. *From behind the Veil: A Study of Afro-American Narrative*. Urbana: University of Illinois Press, 1979.

Wright, Richard. *12 Million Black Voices*. 1941. Reprint, New York: Thunders Mouth Press, 2002.

Farah Jasmine Griffin

Little, Malcolm *See* Malcolm X

Living Conditions *See* Housing and Living Conditions

Locke, Alain Leroy (1886–1954)

Alain Leroy Locke, professor, philosopher, and the first African American to be awarded a Rhodes Scholarship (1907), credited the Great Black Migration with the emergence of a **New Negro**, one with cultural awareness and self-confidence. He saw the influx of African Americans as an opportunity for artistic growth that was impossible under the repressive system of the South. He used the geographic shift from rural countryside to urban community to help blacks explore their creative energies and to produce works that stirred whites. Because he recognized the talent of these artists and promoted their work, he is known as the architect of the **Harlem Renaissance**.

Alain Locke was born into a well-established **Philadelphia** family on September 13, 1886. Both parents were teachers. Locke entered Harvard in 1907, graduating magna cum laude three years later with a degree in philosophy and English. He was a professor of philosophy at **Howard University** from 1912 until 1953.

When he was asked to edit the March 1925 special black artisans edition of *Survey Graphic*, a national sociology magazine, he saw an opportunity to showcase such talented writers as Countee Cullen, **Langston Hughes, W.E.B. DuBois, James Weldon Johnson**, and **Jean Toomer**. The issue became a landmark in the **Black Arts movement**. Locke expanded his introductory essay and published an anthology, *The New Negro: An Interpretation* (1925), with added works from **Claude McKay, Zora Neale Hurston**, and **Jessie Redmon Fauset**.

Locke believed that blacks had an obligation to prove the race capable of producing great art and literature and that the source of power was in their African roots. They needed to free themselves from stereotyped depictions and portray blacks accurately, as they lived their everyday lives. He said that the old Negro had bought into the false image, sometimes blaming his own lack of success on a system that held him back. The New Negro would forge his own identity and prove his worth.

In the 1930s Locke's involvement in the adult education movement led to his founding of the Association of Negro Folk Education. He was instrumental in the publishing of nine cultural awareness documents, called the Bronze Booklets, that were intended to bring Negro arts and achievements to the attention of the general public. He published philosophical works and wrote and spoke widely on black culture, hoping that knowledge would advance racial harmony.

Locke believed that with the move from "the cotton-field and farm to the heart of the most complex urban civilization" (Locke, "Harlem," 630), Negroes had to be strong, shedding any of the comforts of familiar surroundings, an old-style economy, and an outdated civilization, with the result that the "Old Negro [became] more of a myth than a man" (Locke, "Enter the New Negro," 631). He said that the New Negro must be "seen through other than the dusty spectacles of past controversy," adding that the "day of 'aunties,' 'uncles,' and 'mammies' [was] equally gone. Uncle Tom and Sambo have passed on" (Locke, "Enter the New Negro," 631). Clearly, he saw the Great Black Migration as a psychologically liberating experience for blacks and a key to general African American advance. *See also* New York City; Primary Documents 26, 27.

Further Reading

Harris, Leonard, ed. *The Philosophy of Alain Locke: Harlem Renaissance and Beyond*. Philadelphia: Temple University Press, 1989.

Locke, Alain. "Enter the New Negro." *Survey Graphic* 6, no. 6 (March 1925): 631–34.
———. "Harlem." *Survey Graphic* 6, no. 6 (March 1925): 629–30.
Stewart, Jeffrey C., ed. *The Critical Temper of Alain Locke: A Selection of His Essays on Art and Culture*. New York: Garland Publishing, 1983.

Gay Pitman Zieger

Los Angeles, California

Throughout the twentieth century Los Angeles has been the center of California's African American population. By the dawn of that century its blacks outnumbered those in **San Francisco**, even though the latter had a larger overall population until 1920. Migrants accounted for most of Los Angeles' population growth, attracted by its image and tangible benefits. Southern California had been touted since the late nineteenth century as a land of sunshine and opportunity. To blacks from southern states, especially, this area also seemed the Promised Land of freedom from overt discrimination and oppression. As the terminus of major transcontinental **railroads**, Los Angeles attracted many Pullman porters, whose quarters formed a nucleus for its black community by 1900. The growing economy provided a variety of urban jobs, and the expanding racial community offered employment for its businesses and professionals. By 1920 Los Angeles was home to 15,579 African Americans; by 1940 that number had grown to 63,774, over half of their population in California. Unlike larger northern centers of the Great Migration, movement to Los Angeles continued during the Great Depression.

African Americans initially were scattered among the general population, but by 1920 a distinct **ghetto** had formed along the north blocks of Central Avenue. Racially **restrictive covenants** became widespread after court decisions in the 1910s upheld their legality, confining most blacks to a few blocks east and west of this street. While small communities were formed in a few adjacent cities, most notably Pasadena, relatively few blacks lived outside the city before World War II. This community developed a vibrant society, anchored in churches that served as cultural as well as religious centers. **Women** formed several service organizations, along with a branch of the **National Association of Colored Women**. The Los Angeles Forum was founded in 1903 as a center for discussing civic affairs, and a **National Association for the Advancement of Colored People** (NAACP) branch was set up in 1913. **Marcus Garvey**'s **Universal Negro Improvement Association** established a vigorous presence during the 1920s, though divided into two factions, and a **National Urban League** branch was formed that same decade. The community had several newspapers, of which the most prominent were the *California Eagle* and the *Los Angeles Sentinel*. Discrimination in jobs and public accommodations was common, but its impact was somewhat lessened by the fact that other minorities, especially Mexicans, Japanese, and Chinese, were similarly treated and sometimes given lower status. Although African Americans constituted only a small minority of any political district, they elected an assemblyman from Los Angeles regularly after 1918. Reflecting national trends, it was a Republican, Frederick Roberts, until 1934, and then Democrat Augustus Hawkins, who served as assemblyman and congressman until 1991.

World War II began the greatest migration of African Americans within the United States, and Los Angeles and other California cities were major destinations. Between 1940 and 1950 their population in California grew over 3.7 times. Over 70 percent of this increase was in Los Angeles County, nearly half in the city of Los Angeles. Wartime jobs in **shipyards** and other defense industries were a magnet for disfranchised, segregated blacks who were widely excluded from such jobs in southern plants. This influx continued during the 1950s and 1960s, increasing their population in Los Angeles to 503,606 by 1970. That nearly two-thirds of California's blacks lived in central cities in 1970 attests to the impact of this migration on intensifying the concentration of blacks in a few inner-city ghettos. Some unions and employers resisted hiring blacks for wartime jobs, but protests by organizations such as the Negro Victory Committee and court suits by the NAACP opened an unprecedented number of manu-

The black population of Los Angeles grew rapidly during World War II as defense industries such as Douglas Aircraft hired black workers to meet the demands of wartime industrial production. Courtesy of the Library of Congress.

facturing jobs during the war. Expansion of the automobile and tire industries after the war, coupled with union support and a state fair employment law in 1959, gave blacks access to good-paying jobs into the 1960s.

Housing segregation proved harder to change. Blacks were excluded from nearly all the growing suburban communities until well into the 1960s, so their neighborhoods in Los Angeles became more completely monoracial. This intensified school segregation, which by 1963 became a main focus of such civil rights organizations as the United Civil Rights Committee and the **Congress of Racial Equality**. Court suits resulted in mandates to desegregate Los Angeles area schools by busing, but **white flight** from many districts and popular opposition ended that by 1980. Within the expanding ghetto, two distinct social areas emerged as South Central became increasingly impoverished and the main port of entry for migrants, while the West Side became a haven for middle-class blacks seeking to escape from deteriorating areas. The latter area provided most political leadership, epitomized by Tom Bradley, one of three blacks who cracked their historic exclusion from the Los Angeles City Council in 1963. The 1960s also saw several blacks represent Los Angeles in the state legislature and Congress.

In August 1965 the other part of the black community gained nationwide notice in the Watts riots. The triggering cause was black residents' resentment of the Los Angeles Police Department due to years of harassment, incidents of **police brutality**, and racist attitudes. High **unemployment**, limited transportation and public services, and growing feelings of racial militancy stemming from such groups as the Black Muslims, as well as national events, fanned the flames of resentment. In the wake of this event, many middle-class blacks left the South Central area. Watts also symbolized the fading image of nonsouthern cities as the Promised Land, and by 1970 black internal migration to Los Angeles had slowed to a trickle.

The big migration of blacks in the Los Angeles area after 1970 was out of the central city into the suburbs. Fair housing laws, especially the federal Civil Rights Act of 1968, had ended most tactics of exclusion, although escalating real estate prices kept poorer blacks from buying homes. While cities close to Los Angeles, like Compton and Inglewood, became predominantly black, the movement dispersed among many suburbs, integrating residential areas and schools. Suburban residence gave blacks greater entry to white-collar jobs, and the Los Angeles area became the home of some of the nation's most successful black celebrities, epitomized by basketball star and real estate magnate Earvin "Magic" Johnson. At the same time, the decline of unionized manufacturing industries and the growth of low-wage alternatives accentuated the economic bifurcation of the black community. South Central became a classic example of the "jobless ghetto," in which street gangs, drugs (especially crack cocaine), and **crime** became social norms. Resentment over these conditions was brought out in 1992 by the acquittal of four police officers who beat Rodney King, resulting in an even costlier, multiracial Los Angeles riot. This deterioration of poorer black areas occurred while outwardly their churches and community organizations remained strong. They increased their political power, including Tom Bradley's twenty-year term as mayor and race for governor in 1982 and 1986, and Mervyn Dymally became California's first black lieutenant governor in 1974. But this was also a time when blacks were being replaced in South Central and in some adjacent cities by Latinos, as their population in Los Angeles fell to 415,195 by 2000. By that year they also had declining numbers in the county and the Los Angeles area as a whole. The torch of a great migration to Los Angeles had clearly been passed to immigrants from Mexico, Central America, and Asia. *See also* Asian Immigrants and Asian Americans, Relations with Black Migrants; Asian Immigration, Comparison with the Great Black Migration; Hispanic Migration, Comparison with the Great Black Migration; Western States, Black Migration to; Zoot-Suit Riots (1943); Primary Document 3.

Further Reading

Allen, James P., and Eugene Turner. *The Ethnic Quilt: Population Diversity in Southern California*. Northridge, CA: Center for Geographical Studies, 1997.

Bunch, Lonnie G., III. "A Past Not Necessarily Prologue: The African American in Los Angeles since 1900." In *20th Century Los Angeles*, edited by Norman M. Klein and Martin J. Schiesl. Claremont, CA: Regina Books, 1990.

Cannon, Lou. *Official Negligence: How Rodney King and the Riots Changed Los Angeles and the LAPD*. New York: Times Books, 1997.

"Charlotta Bass and the *California Eagle*." Southern California Library for Social Science Research. www.socallib.org/bass.

Collins, Keith. *Black Los Angeles: The Maturing of the Ghetto, 1940–1950*. Saratoga, CA: Century Twenty-One Publishing, 1980.

de Graaf, Lawrence B. "City of Black Angels: The Evolution of the Los Angeles Ghetto, 1890–1930." *Pacific Historical Review* 39 (August 1970): 323–52.

de Graaf, Lawrence B., Kevin Mulroy, and Quintard Taylor, eds. *Seeking El Dorado: African Americans in California*. Los Angeles: Autry Museum of Western Heritage and University of Washington Press, 2001.

Horne, Gerald. *Fire This Time: The Watts Uprising and the 1960s*. Charlottesville: University Press of Virginia, 1995.

Los Angeles Urban League. Papers. Department of Special Collections. Young Research Library. University of California, Los Angeles.

Sides, Josh. *L.A. City Limits: African American Los Angeles from the Great Depression to the Present*. Berkeley: University of California Press, 2003.

Sonenshein, Raphael. *Politics in Black and White: Race and Power in Los Angeles*. Princeton, NJ: Princeton University Press, 1993.

Waldinger, Roger, and Mehdi Bozorgmehr, eds. *Ethnic Los Angeles*. New York: Russell Sage Foundation, 1996.

Lawrence B. de Graaf

Louis, Joe (1914–1981)

Black American boxer Joe Louis (born Joe Louis Barrow) rose to stardom during the 1930s and 1940s, holding the title of heavyweight champion from 1937 to 1949 and achieving public acclaim across racial lines. Born in 1914 to a family of sharecroppers in Lafayette, Alabama, Louis endured extreme hardship. After Louis's father, Monroe Barrow, was committed to a segregated mental hospital, Louis's mother, Lillie, married neighboring widower Patrick Brooks. As economic conditions worsened in rural Alabama, Brooks eventually left for **Detroit** in 1926 and found work at the Ford Motor Company. Louis's family soon joined him, and although conditions were crowded and Pat Brooks was often unemployed, Detroit was still a great improvement from southern poverty and racism.

Living in the heart of Detroit's black migrant community shaped Louis's early boxing career, providing him with recreational centers and exposing him to more seasoned fighters who recognized great talent in the teenage boy. Although Louis's training was often stalled by his need to support his family, working at industries such as the Ford River Rouge plant, Detroit's black community rallied around the seemingly unbeatable fighter. Under the tutelage of two black businessmen, John Roxborough and Julian Black, and trainer Jack Blackburn, Louis maintained a stellar record as an amateur fighter and entered his first professional boxing match in 1934.

In light of his predecessor, the controversial heavyweight champion **Jack Johnson**, Louis had to alter white opinion regarding the acceptability of black fighters. Johnson's flamboyant lifestyle and relationships with white women tarnished his reputation among both white and black Americans. With this in mind, Louis carefully monitored his personal life and trained rigorously under the strict supervision of his managers.

By 1935 Louis was scheduled to fight famed white boxers, and descriptions of Louis's abilities abounded in the national press. More controversial opponents emerged, such as Italian Primo Carnera in 1935 and, most famously, German Max Schmeling, who defeated Louis in 1936. Although the Schmeling fight led some Americans to doubt Louis's abilities, Louis went on to capture the heavyweight title from Jim Braddock in 1937 and defeated Schmeling in 1938 in the most highly anticipated rematch in boxing history.

Louis's knockout of Max Schmeling amid Hitler's claims of racial and national superiority made his public reception among both white and black Americans incredibly favorable. Louis's celebrity was only heightened when he joined the armed forces in 1942, serving in the Morale Division and participating in approximately 100 boxing exhibition fights in American and European military camps. After the war Louis continued his international exhibition tours, and his professional boxing record remained unscathed. Although Louis announced his retirement in 1949, because of financial necessity he decided to fight heavyweight champion Ezzard Charles in 1950. At the age of thirty-six Louis lost against Charles, and again against Rocky Marciano in 1951—his last fight. Although age affected Louis's agility as a fighter, in later years he was always remembered for his incredible athleticism, as well as his significance in bridging the gap between white and black Americans. After years of serious medical complications Louis died of a heart attack on April 12, 1981. *See also* Sport.

Further Reading

Astor, Gerald. *". . .And a Credit to His Race": The Hard Life and Times of Joseph Louis Barrow*. New York: Saturday Review Press, 1974.

Bak, Richard. *Joe Louis: The Great Black Hope*. Dallas: Taylor Pub., 1996; New York: Da Capo Press, 1998.

Mead, Chris. *Champion Joe Louis: Black Hero in White America*. New York: Scribner, 1985.

Lauren Rebecca Sklaroff

Louisville, Kentucky

Migration has been a central feature of life for African Americans since Louisville was founded in 1778. Cato Watts, an enslaved black, was among the first people of African or European descent to reach the region as part of the George Rogers Clark expedition of 1778. Like Watts, the first African Americans in Louisville were forced migrants. By 1810 African Americans constituted 37 percent of Louisville's total population of 1,337; however, 484 of the 495 African Americans in the River City were slaves. In fact, Louisville was the center of a growing domestic slave trade centered around a series of slave pens located downtown. In 1830 the black population in Louisville remained a slave population; as the city itself grew, so too did the number of slaves. While African Americans declined to 25 percent of Louisville's total population, the majority (2,406 of 2,638) remained slaves.

Yet between 1830 and 1860 the number of free blacks in Louisville increased 726 percent to 1,917. Despite the shadow slavery cast over the lives of African Americans, both slave and free, the city was home to the largest black population in Kentucky. African Americans established independent churches, businesses, and the *Weekly Planet*, an African American newspaper, by 1874. During this era the cornerstone of one of the most vibrant black communities in the nation was laid. In the 1890s the African American population grew 120 percent because of an influx of rural migrants.

By 1900 Louisville's black population of 29,159 was the seventh largest in the nation. The city's reputation for racial harmony within the South combined with economic opportunity, the right to vote, and a burgeoning black community to make Louisville an ideal destination. However, as historian George C. Wright points out. the "polite racism" blacks faced in the city was no less circumscribed than that of the Deep South. Nonetheless, African Americans created one of the most dynamic communities in the South. By 1900 black Louisville supported 66 black churches, 67 fraternal organizations, 12 **women**'s clubs, 3 newspapers, a black **hospital**, numerous **physicians**, **attorneys**, and **schoolteachers**, and more than 1,000 **skilled workers**. As migrants continued to flow into the city during the early twentieth century, many, such as A. E. Meyzeek, William J. Simmons, Reverend C. H. Parrish, and William Stewart, led African Americans' struggles to attain economic, political, and social equality in the city. By 1942 the nearly 50,000 blacks in Louisville created a cultural and economic center concentrated within an area two blocks wide centered on West Walnut Street and extending from Sixth Street to Eighteenth Street. In addition to 654 black businesses, blacks possessed a small black college, a modern high school, two junior high schools, and "colored" branches of the Louisville Free Public Library.

With the onset of World War II many African Americans moved to southern cities such as **Birmingham**, Charleston, Mobile, and Louisville in search of freedom. The lure of employment in defense industries fueled the growth of Louisville's black population from 47,158 to 56,154 between 1940 and 1946. As in the past, African American migrants led campaigns to desegregate higher education, integrate public accommodations, and achieve **open housing**. Between 1940 and 1970 more than 17,000 migrants made their home in the River City, but by 1970 migration declined because of a number of factors. The victories of the **civil rights movement** made black Louisvillians' access to second-rate facilities and ability to vote less significant. **Urban renewal** destroyed the black business district centered on Walnut Street, and African Americans remained concentrated in domestic or service industries as unskilled labor. Similarly, the city lost its reputation for racial harmony in its violent opposition to desegregation, fair **housing**, and equality. In 1968 the issues of fair housing and **police brutality** sparked a riot in the city. Moreover, blacks faced increasing segregation in the wake of their recent civil rights gains. However, as numerous African Americans return to southern cities, African American migration may prove to be as influential in shaping the future of Louisville as it has the past. *See also* Cincinnati, Ohio; Nashville, Tennessee; Return Migration.

Further Reading

Adams, Luther J. "Way Up North in Louisville: African American Migration in Louis-ville, Kentucky, 1930–1970." Ph.D. diss., University of Pennsylvania, 2002.

Tyler, Bruce. *African American Life in Louisville.* Charleston, SC: Arcadia, 1998.

Wright, George C. *A History of Blacks in Kentucky.* Vol. 2, *In Pursuit of Equality, 1890–1980.* Lexington: Kentucky Historical Society, 1992.

———. *Life behind A Veil: Blacks in Louisville, Kentucky, 1865–1930.* Baton Rouge: Louisiana State University Press, 1985.

———. *Racial Violence in Kentucky, 1865–1940: Lynchings, Mob Rule, and "Legal Lynchings."* Baton Rouge: Louisiana State University Press, 1990.

Luther J. Adams

Low Country South Carolina and Georgia

The Great Migration of the twentieth century began in the South Carolina and Georgia Low Country in 1910 when more than 50,000 blacks moved up the eastern seaboard to the cities of the North. Since 1700 African Americans in the Low Country have outnumbered European Americans by large margins, for much of the region's history by more than a three-to-one ratio. Indeed, over 40 percent of African slaves who entered North America entered through the port of Charleston. Initially, these largely West African people labored on the prosperous but isolated coastal rice and indigo plantations of the Low Country. In the rice lands they thrived, doubling their numbers every fifteen years and forming a distinct Afro-English culture and language known as Gullah. With the invention of the cotton gin in 1793, rice planters sold their surplus people to cotton growers, first in the Carolinas and Georgia and in time in Alabama, Mississippi, and Louisiana. In this way Low Country South Carolina and Georgia became the cultural and ancestral homeland for African Americans throughout the South, who carried their Gullah ways with them and colored all aspects of southern life.

After the Civil War and emancipation this westward movement continued until the start of the twentieth century, when the **boll weevil** undercut the South's cotton economy. The agricultural crisis intensified white racism in the South. Southern state governments disfranchised most African American vot-ers and set up an elaborate system of racial apartheid. Extralegally, many southern whites resorted to violence and intimidation, setting off an epidemic of racially motivated **lynching** that plagued the South until World War II.

Facing economic decline and racial violence, in the first two decades of the twentieth century Low Country African Americans turned north, the start of the Great Migration. In 1924 the U.S. Census Bureau estimated that for the first time since 1700, a majority of South Carolinians were white. In 1970, when black Carolinians ceased to flee the state, ending the Great Migration, they made up only 31 percent of the population of South Carolina, or 790,000 people.

Since emancipation migration has characterized the lives of Low Country African Americans. Each decade from 1870 through 1900, nearly 100,000 Af-rican Americans left South Carolina. Still, this migration failed to equal African American Carolinians' natural increase. Almost all moved to other southern states and remained cotton or timber workers. In 1860 the Census Bureau classified 58.6 percent of South Carolinians as African American; in 1900 it so classified 58.4 percent. In 1860, 412,000 blacks lived in South Carolina, and in 1900 that number had grown to 732,000. The 1910 census recorded the first significant change in the state's racial balance since the introduction of slaves in the seventeenth century. Between 1900 and 1910 the percentage of black Carolinians dropped from 58.4 percent to 55.2 percent. Equally significant, the direction of migration had changed. Virtually all migrants from the South Carolina and Georgia Low Country had moved to **Philadelphia**, **Boston**, or **New York City** rather than to more western areas of the South. In 1900 only 2.7 percent of the African Americans who had left the Low Country moved to a northern state. In 1910 the percentage had more than doubled, and most of these had settled in New York City. In 1900 only about 1,000 black Carolinians had settled in New York; in 1910 nearly 7,000 moved to New York. In 1920 the number who migrated to New York nearly doubled to 13,000. In the next decade migration to New York tripled to 41,000, and by 1940 over one-third of the Low Country's black migrants settled in New York.

Despite the cold winters and white racial hostility, black South Carolinians looked northward for relief. In 1914 the opportunities for blacks in the North increased significantly when World War I cut off European immigration and the North's primary supply of cheap labor. American entry into World War I in 1917 expanded the demand for black labor in the North, a trend that continued during the prosperous 1920s. With the onset of the Great Depression in 1930, migration to the North slowed, but with the outbreak of World War II in 1939, the demand for black labor again expanded as tens of thousands of black Georgians and Carolinians fled the South for jobs in the North, especially New York, **Washington, D.C.**, and Pennsylvania. These South Carolina and Georgia Low Country migrants carried their Gullah culture to the cities of the eastern seaboard, especially Harlem. Above 125th Street in Harlem, Low Country Gullah imprinted itself on twentieth-century America in its churches and music. *See also* Primary Document 61.

Further Reading

Bethel, Elizabeth Rauh. *Promiseland: A Century of Life in a Negro Community.* Philadelphia: Temple University Press, 1981.

Devlin, George A. *South Carolina and Black Migration, 1865–1940.* New York: Garland Publishing, 1989.

Dodd, Donald B., and Wynelle S. Dodd, eds. *Historical Statistics of the South, 1790–1970.* Tuscaloosa: University of Alabama Press, 1973.

Kiser, Clyde Vernon. *Sea Island to City: A Study of St. Helanda Islanders in Harlem and Other Urban Centers.* New York: Columbia University Press, 1932.

Newby, I. A. *Black Carolinians: A History of Blacks in South Carolina from 1895 to 1968.* Columbia: University of South Carolina Press, 1973.

"North by South: Charleston to Harlem, the Great Migrations." Kenyon College. http://northbysouth.kenyon.edu/1998/index.htm.

Tindall, George B. *South Carolina Negroes, 1877–1900.* Columbia: University of South Carolina Press, 1952.

William B. Scott and Peter M. Rutkoff

Lynching

Both contemporary observers and scholars have long agreed that lynching and racial violence pushed African Americans to migrate from the South in the early twentieth century. The relative importance of lynching vis-à-vis other causes of the Great Migration and the impact of the black exodus on lynching in the South, however, are topics of debate for historians.

Lynching and Racial Violence in the United States

The oppression of African Americans at the hands of lynch mobs is beyond doubt. Since 1882 counts of specific individuals lynched have been compiled by newspapers, organizations, and institutions such as the *Chicago Tribune*, the **National Association for the Advancement of Colored People**, the Association of Southern Women for the Prevention of Lynching, and the **Tuskegee Normal and Industrial Institute**. Between 1882 and 1968, for example, Tuskegee reported that 4,743 individuals were lynched in the United States. Most of these victims—3,446, to be exact—were black. Most died in the American South, with Mississippi (581), Georgia (531), and Texas (493) leading the way. The data suggest that lynching rose dramatically in the last two decades of the nineteenth century, slowly declined in the first two decades of the twentieth century, and fell off markedly after 1920. Scholars have elucidated a number of problems with these lynching inventories, noting, for example, that the definition of lynching shifted over time and that the compilers of the lynching data probably undercounted lynching victims in remote locations such as the Texas-Mexican border. These problems, however, do not change the general picture of a southern black population terrorized by white mobs.

Indeed, statistics can never convey the climate of fear, resentment, and outrage that racial violence inculcated among southern blacks. Lynching statistics do not include those times when white mobs whipped, castrated, raped, threatened, intimidated, or assaulted their victims but left them alive. Lynching inventories, by and large, also fail to include victims of rioting and other indiscriminate forms of racial violence. Lynching statistics thus fail to encapsulate the complete range of racial violence under which blacks in the South suffered. Lynching was the most public, visible, and brutal form of violence in the late nineteenth- and early twentieth-century South, but it was just one of a number of mechanisms by which the white majority maintained social, economic, and political control of the region's African Americans.

Lynching as a Cause of the Great Migration

Given the extensive nature of racial violence in the American South, it is only logical that escaping this violence would be a major catalyst for African American migration. This conclusion finds support in the contemporary record. In September 1906 the *Voice of the Negro* concluded that blacks were leaving the South because of murder, lynching, and state-supported tyranny. One black migrant wrote to the ***Chicago Defender*** that he made up his mind to leave for the North because he had spent too many years seeing his people lynched for trivial offenses such as stealing a mule or spitting on the sidewalk.

Similar opinions were expressed in the *Crisis*, the *North American Review*, and a host of other publications.

While most testimonials focused on the general lawlessness and conditions existing in the South, specific episodes of lynching and racial violence sometimes provoked blacks to leave. For example, in 1918 a white mob in Estill Springs, Tennessee, forced black residents to look on as they tortured an African American accused of murder. The mob burned the man with hot irons, chained him to a tree, and burned him alive. A crowd of 1,500 saw the grisly murder. In the aftermath of the killing, the local black population abandoned Estill Springs.

Whether or not the mob at Estill Springs intended to drive off the area's African Americans is unclear. There is no doubt that some white mobs intended to do exactly that. In 1908 an organized band of men attacked the black population of Birmingham, Kentucky. They posted notices warning blacks to leave, shot seven men, and whipped five others. Blacks fled, leaving personal effects and farm equipment where they lay. Only six blacks, protected by white employers, remained in the town after the episode. This combination of killing, intimidation, and forced migration was common in the American South, perhaps most infamously illustrated by the 1923 destruction of Rosewood, Florida.

Problems with Lynching as a Cause of the Great Migration

In many ways the evidence for lynching as a primary cause of the Great Migration is impressive. Yet there are also reasons to question just how important racial violence was in the black exodus. One problem with lynching as a cause of the Great Migration centers on the testimonials of the migrants themselves. Consciously and unconsciously, migrants had reasons to emphasize racial violence as the cause of their decision to migrate. Seen as a response to racial violence, the decision to move is an act of resistance and defiance that helps muster the courage necessary to survive the transition to the new place. In other words, historians should be wary of taking the testimonials of black migrants at face value, especially when there are obvious psychological advantages to collapsing the complex reasons for migration into the singular cause of escaping lynching.

There are additional reasons to doubt that lynching can explain the timing of the Great Migration. From the first arrival of Africans in the Americas, racial violence was a constant factor in the lives of blacks living in the South. Something so unvarying cannot account for a change as dramatic as the Great Migration. Furthermore, the variation that did exist in the history of mob violence seems to work against the link between lynching and the Great Migration. Most scholars note that the highest number of recorded lynchings in the American South occurred in the 1890s and that lynching was in clear decline by 1910, just the time when black out-migration began to accelerate. Lynching does not seem to be a particularly good explanation for the timing of the Great Migration.

Although not a cause of the timing of the Great Migration, lynching did play an important role in the spatial geography of the black exodus. Scholars Stewart Tolnay and E. M. Beck, using data drawn from their own inventory of lynching cases in ten southern states, cite statistical evidence that counties experiencing high levels of mob violence were also those counties most likely to experience especially extensive out-migration of African Americans. Thus it was those African Americans most endangered by mob violence who were the most likely to migrate when social and economic changes created new opportunities in the North.

Impact of the Great Migration on Lynching

How much of an impact lynching had on the Great Migration will continue to be debated by academics. An equally important question is determining the impact of the Great Migration on lynching. In the short run, the Great Migration encouraged lynching because white communities attempted to intimidate blacks from migrating. In 1918 mobs murdered sixty African Americans, an increase from thirty-six the previous year. In 1919 lynchers killed seventy-six, a recorded total greater than in any year since 1908. Not until 1923 did this upsurge in lynching abate. When lynching did begin to decline, however, it did so very rapidly. It seems clear that the exodus of so many cheap, unskilled laborers provoked some whites to reconsider the economic impact of lynching and racial violence. Tolnay and Beck suggest that many local white leaders attempted to check black out-migration by reducing violence targeting the African American community. If this is indeed one of the reasons for the decline of lynching after 1920, the perception that the Great Migration was caused by lynching and racial violence was extremely important. When black migrants claimed that they were leaving the South because of its history of racial oppression, perhaps they were making one last attempt to change the region of their birth before leaving it for a very different future in the North. *See also* Elaine, Arkansas, Massacre of 1919; Great Migration, Causes of; Great Migration, White Opposition to; Red Summer of 1919; Primary Document 41.

Further Reading

Brundage, W. Fitzhugh. *Lynching in the New South: Georgia and Virginia, 1880–1930*. Urbana: University of Illinois Press, 1993.

Litwack, Leon F. *Trouble in Mind: Black Southerners in the Age of Jim Crow*. New York: Alfred A. Knopf, 1998.

Tolnay, Stewart E. *A Festival of Violence: An Analysis of Southern Lynchings, 1882–1930*. Urbana: University of Illinois Press, 1995.

Tolnay, Stewart E., and E. M. Beck. "Racial Violence and Black Migration in the American South, 1910–1930." *American Sociological Review* 57 (February 1992): 103–16.

———. "Rethinking the Role of Racial Violence in the Great Migration." In *Black Exodus: The Great Migration from the American South*, edited by Alferdteen Harrison. Jackson: University Press of Mississippi, 1991.

William D. Carrigan